EDUCATIONAL MEDIA AND TECHNOLOGY YEARBOOK

EDUCATIONAL MEDIA AND TECHNOLOGY YEARBOOK

Robert Maribe Branch and Mary Ann Fitzgerald, Editors

2000 VOLUME 25

Published in Cooperation with the
ERIC® Clearinghouse on Information & Technology
and the
Association for Educational Communications
and Technology

2000

Libraries Unlimited, Inc. • Englewood, Colorado

LIBRARIES UNLIMITED, INC.
P.O. Box 6633
Englewood, CO 80155-6633
1-800-237-6124
www.lu.com

Suggested Cataloging:

Educational media and technology yearbook, 2000 volume 25 /
    Robert Maribe Branch and Mary Ann Fitzgerald, editors—
Englewood, Colo.: Libraries Unlimited, 2000.
    p. cm.
    ISBN 1-56308-840-1
    ISSN 8755-2094
    Published in cooperation with the ERIC Clearinghouse on Information
& Technology and the Association for Educational Communications and
Technology.
    1. Educational technology—yearbooks.   2. Instructional materials
centers—yearbooks.   I. ERIC Clearinghouse on Information & Technology.
II. Association for Educational Communications and Technology.
III. Branch, Robert Maribe.   IV. Mary Ann Fitzgerald.
LB 1028.3.E372   2000   370.778

Contents

v

Part Two
TECHNOLOGY CENTERS AND
INSTITUTES FOR LEARNING

Part Three
SCHOOL LIBRARY MEDIA SECTION

Part Four
LEADERSHIP PROFILE

Part Five
ORGANIZATIONS AND ASSOCIATIONS
IN NORTH AMERICA

Part Six
GRADUATE PROGRAMS

Part Seven
MEDIAGRAPHY
Print and Nonprint Resources

Preface

The purpose of the 25th anniversary volume of the *Educational Media and Technology Yearbook* is to reflect on past accomplishments and consider the future as it relates to educational technology and media development. This volume of the *Yearbook* continues to provide information to help media and technology professionals' practice their craft in a changing, expanding field. This volume is based on the precepts that:

- Technology represents tools that act as extensions of the educator.
- Media serve as delivery systems for educational communications.
- Technology is *not* restricted to machines and hardware, but includes techniques and procedures derived from scientific research about ways to promote change in human performance.

The fundamental tenant is that educational media and technology should be used to:

1. achieve authentic learning objectives,
2. situate learning tasks,
3. negotiate the complexities of guided learning,
4. facilitate the construction of knowledge,
5. support skill acquisition, and
6. manage diversity.

Because common applications of educational technology offer regimented, one-way information presentation formats, the concept of educational technology featured in this volume promotes applications that are interactive and adopts principles of guided learning. Principles of guided learning move away from situations that encumber didactic, limiting, passive, singular modes of teaching and move toward designs that facilitate active, multi-functional, inspirational, situated approaches to learning. A macroscopic view of learner-centered instruction reveals that multiple interactions occur during instructional episodes; each situated within a context during a specified period of time (Figure 1).

Emerging philosophies about instruction, education, and theories of learning have re-focused the "classroom" concept to include a broader array of contexts. While classrooms are defined as "a place where classes meet," classrooms are typically shaped by the prevailing societal paradigm and, until recently, classrooms replicated our desire to compartmentalize, consistent with the industrial age. The desire to regiment and control was reflected in classrooms patterned after military models, but classrooms are beginning to reflect a societal shift to an information age.

Classrooms of the information age can be situated at remote sites, accessed at convenient times, and personalized to match the capability of individual learners. While students may still "meet" to study the same subject, the location, time, and pace are now dynamic. Educators should regard a classroom as any *learning space*. While each episode of guided learning is distinctive and separate, each remains part of a larger curricular scheme. Instructional episodes are characterized by several participating entities that are themselves complex: the learner, the content, the media, the teacher, peers, and the context, all interacting within a discrete period of time while moving toward a common goal.

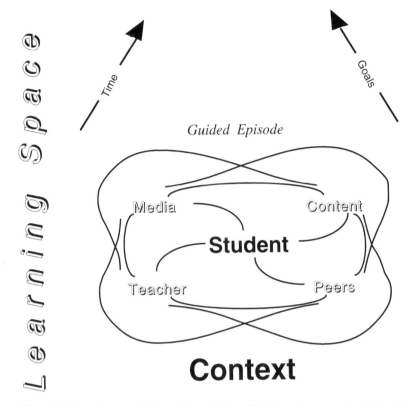

Figure 1. The primary relationships within guided learning space facilitated by technology.

Learner-centered classrooms, wherever they are located, represent an epistemological shift from regarding students as the occupants of learning spaces, to regarding the *actions* of students during guided learning as the prime motivation for the design of instruction. Thus, a clear understanding about the role technology and educational media play in facilitating the interactions of guided learning is important.

The *Educational Media and Technology Yearbook* has become a standard reference in many libraries and professional collections. The intent of this *Yearbook 2000* edition is that readers become more informed about the purposes, activities, programs of study, and accomplishments of the organizations and associations dedicated to the advancement of educational communications and technology. This volume of the *Yearbook* contains sections devoted to Trends and Issues, Technology Centers and Institutes for Learning, School and Library Media, Organizations and Associations in North America, Graduate Programs, and a Mediagraphy (of print and non-print resources). The topics herein allow this volume to remain consistent with most standard references where the contents contain elements that readers expect to find in each new edition.

Robert Maribe Branch

Contributors to
Educational Media and Technology
Yearbook 2000

Douglas Bedient
Virginia Tech University
Instructional Technology
220 War Memorial Hall
Blacksburg, Virginia 24061

Oratile Branch
Acorps
Performance Consultants
118 Robins Nest
Athens, Georgia 30606

Robert Branch, Ed.D., Associate Professor
The University of Georgia
Instructional Technology
604 Aderhold Hall
Athens, Georgia 30602

Edward Caffarella, Ph.D., Professor
University of Northern Colorado
Instructional Technology
5951 26th Street
Greeley, Colorado 80634

Michael Eisenberg, Ph.D., Department
   Head and Professor
University of Washington-Seattle
School of Library and Information Science
328 Old EE Building
P.O. Box 352930
Seattle, Washington 98195-2930

John Emerson, Ph.D., Professor
Middlebury College
Department of Mathematics and Computer
   Science
Middlebury, Vermont 05753

Mary Ann Fitzgerald, Ph.D., Assistant
   Professor
The University of Georgia
Department of Instructional Technology
604 Aderhold Hall
Athens, Georgia 30602

David Fulton, Librarian
Liverpool Public Library
310 Tulip Street
Liverpool, New York 13088

Andrew Gibbons, Ph.D., Professor
Utah State University
Instructional Technology
2830 Old Main Hill
Logan, Utah 84322

Melissa Gross, Ph.D., Assistant Professor
Florida State University
School of Information Studies
101 Shores Building
Tallahassee, Florida 32306

Michael Hannafin, Ph.D., Director and
   Professor
University of Georgia
Learning and Performance Support
   Laboratory
611 Aderhold Hall
Athens, Georgia 30602

Kenneth Hay, Ph.D., Assistant Professor
University of Georgia
Learning and Performance Support Laboratory
611 Aderhold Hall
Athens, Georgia 30602

Thomas Head, Ph.D., Professor
Virginia Tech University
Instructional Technology
220 War Memorial Hall
Blacksburg, Virginia 24061

Janette R. Hill, Ph.D., Assistant Professor
The University of Georgia
Instructional Technology
604 Aderhold Hall
Athens, Georgia 30602

Michael Jacobson, Ph.D., Assistant
  Professor
University of Georgia
Learning and Performance Support Laboratory
611 Aderhold Hall
Athens, Georgia 30602

John Kasokowski, Digital Libraries
  Coordinator
Information Institute of Syracuse
621 Skytop Road, Suite 160
Syracuse, New York 13244-5290

Abby Kasowitz, Project Coordinator
Information Institute of Syracuse
Virtual Reference Desk
621 Skytop Road, Suite 160
Syracuse, New York 13244-5290

James Laffey, Ph.D., Co-Director and Professor
University of Missouri-Columbia
The Center for Technology Innovations in
  Education
111 London Hall
Columbia, Missouri 65211

Bryan Lawrence, Co-Director and Professor
University of Missouri-Columbia
The Center for Technology Innovations in
  Education
111 London Hall
Columbia, Missouri 65211

Carrie A. Lowe, MLS, Administrative Assistant
University of Washington-Seattle
School of Library and Information Science
328 Old EE Building
P.O. Box 352930
Seattle, Washington 98195-2930

Michael Molenda, Ph.D., Professor
Indiana University
Instructional Systems Technology
Education 2234
Bloomington, Indiana 47405

Mike Moore, Ph.D., Professor
Virginia Tech University
Instructional Technology
220 War Memorial Hall
Blacksburg, Virginia 24061

Frederick Mosteller, Ph.D., Professor
  Emeritus
Harvard University
Department of Statistics
Science Center 603,
One Oxford Street
Cambridge, Massachusetts 02138

Dale Musser, Ph.D., Co-Director and
  Professor
University of Missouri-Columbia
The Center for Technology Innovations in
  Education
111 London Hall
Columbia, Missouri 65211

Delia Neuman, Ph.D., Associate Professor
University of Maryland
College of Library and Information Services
4105 Hornbake Library Building
College Park, Maryland 20742-4345

Anton Ninno, Systems Consultant (CAI)
Onondaga-Cortland-Madison BOCES
Central New York Regional Information
  Center
6820 Thompson Road
Syracuse, New York 13221

Eric Plotnick, Managing Associate Director
Information Institute of Syracuse
621 Skytop Road, Suite 160
Syracuse, New York 13244-5290

Carol Simpson, Assistant Professor
University of North Texas
School of Library and Information Science
Denton, Texas 76203

Michael Sullivan, Executive Director
Indiana University
Agency for Instructional Technology
P.O. Box A
Bloomington, Indiana 47402-0120

Stuart Sutton, Ph.D., Associate Professor
University of Washington-Seattle
School of Library and Information Science
328 Old EE Building
P.O. Box 352930
Seattle, Washington 98195-2930

Joann Wasik, Virtual Reference Desk
    Research Consultant
Information Institute of Syracuse
621 Skytop Road, Suite 160
Syracuse, New York 13244-5290

Hans-Erik Wennberg, Ph.D., Professor
Elizabethtown College
Communications Department
One Alpha Drive
Elizabethtown, Pennsylvania 17022-2298

Frank Wilbur, Ph.D., Director
Syracuse University
Project Advance
111 Waverly Place
Syracuse, New York 13244

Part One
Trends and Issues

Introduction

New technological applications are usually preceded by trends. Resources dedicated to media development are usually proportionate to the importance attached to the prevailing issues. While trends do not necessarily predict the future, there is logic in tracing the trends of educational media and technology to determine *indicators* for the future of the field. Soothsaying notwithstanding, this section assesses the status of instructional technology in the United States as we end the twentieth century and identifies the trends that appear to be taking shape as we begin the twenty-first century. Mike Molenda and Michael Sullivan scan the domains in which instructional technology is employed, particularly corporate training and formal education, kindergarten through university, to reveal a diverse and complex picture.

A review of doctoral dissertations in educational media and technology by Ed Caffarella is included in this section to illustrate the diversity of research that has been conducted over the past few decades at the graduate level. The doctoral dissertation is the culmination of any educational technology doctoral program. These programs are offered at institutions across the United States under a wide variety of names such as instructional systems development, educational media, instructional design, and instructional development. Each year an average of about 120 doctoral students graduate from the educational technology programs at universities across the United States. Each of these students completes a dissertation as part of the doctoral program and initial preparation as a researcher in the field. The topics for these dissertations vary widely, with no standard dissertation type, topic, context, or methodology within the field.

John Emerson and Frederick Mostseller point out that the faculties of our schools and colleges currently offer the principal medium for delivering instruction to students. Colleges and universities invest substantial resources and years in faculty development programs. A review of 103 articles and chapters written mostly between 1990 and 1998 reveals the types of programs that have evolved from experiences of earlier decades and that will prepare faculty for a challenging future. Effective programs often provide their client faculty members with "coaches" and "teammates." Most often, these programs are collegial and collaborative, rely on sustained engagement of colleagues, and have an agenda that is specific and focused. These characteristics point toward new development programs that hold promise for instructional improvement. Some of these improvements will rely on wise uses of emerging technologies to enhance the delivery of education by teachers in the twenty-first century.

Stuart Sutton highlights a trend in information access. Enhanced access to educational materials on the Internet for the nation's teachers and students was one of President Clinton's second-term goals. The U.S. Department of Education's National Library of Education (NLE) identified lesson plans and teacher guides as a critical area in which library and information science expertise should be applied. An electronic gateway has been created to improve the organization and accessibility of large collections of educational materials that are already available on various federal, state, university, nonprofit, and commercial Internet sites. The goal of the Gateway to Educational Materials (GEM) project is to achieve this goal through development and deployment of both a metadata element set for describing network-based educational objects and the accompanying technologies and procedures for its use.

1

This section also features Digests created for the ERIC Clearinghouse on Information and Technology at Syracuse University. ERIC Digests are in the public domain and may be freely reproduced and disseminated. The Digests selected for this volume of *EMTY* are:

Tools for Automating Instructional Design *Abby Kasowitz*

The Benefits of Information Technology *John Kosakowski*

E-rate: A Resource Guide for Educators *David Fulton*

Internet Relay Chat *Carol Simpson*

Information Literacy *Eric Plotnick*

Radios in the Classroom: Curriculum Integration and Communication Skills *Anton Ninno*

Building and Maintaining Digital Reference Services *Joann M. Wasik*

Robert Maribe Branch

Issues and Trends in Instructional Technology

Michael Molenda
Indiana University

Michael Sullivan
Agency for Instructional Technology

INTRODUCTION

What we attempt here is an assessment of the status of instructional technology in the United States as we end the twentieth century and a projection of the trends that appear to be taking shape as we begin the twenty-first century. A scan of the arenas in which instructional technology is employed—particularly corporate training and formal education, kindergarten through university—reveals a diverse and complex picture. Different technologies are employed at different rates and in different ways in different settings. Generalizations are possible, but only within the boundaries of particular settings.

In order to provide some consistency across domains, we have organized our findings under a few major issues that impinge on each domain, although these issues play out somewhat differently in each domain. Because each domain has a distinctive structure and distinctive socioeconomic forces at work, we find that different issues predominate and trends move at different rates within these domains.

In the course of surveying the literature, we felt the need to gather additional data, both to get a more current view and to delve more deeply into the practitioner's perspective. Thus, we sponsored three surveys, which are referenced in the paper. We owe a debt of gratitude to the talented and diligent Instructional Systems Technology graduate students from Indiana University (IU) who carried out these studies independently.

We find that trends in instructional technology appear to be driven by underlying forces operating in business and society. In particular, we are struck with the computerization of the economy—the increasing dependence of virtually every segment of the economy on information technology. Other underlying socioeconomic drivers of change are:

- the increasing influence of business on education,

- privatization and corporatization of education, and

- the increasing demand for and options for acquiring continuing education.

From advertising beamed into classrooms via Channel One to shoe contracts for high school coaches, we see a business involvement in education that is historically unprecedented. Businesses view schools as the shaper of future employees . . . and future consumers. "Partnerships" between schools and corporations have blossomed across the country.

Further, education is viewed as a service industry ready to be exploited for financial gain. The merger and acquisition frenzy has struck what was once a "mom-and-pop" business sector. Some of this entrepreneurial drive is coming from the corporate sector, seen in the growth of for-profit institutions such as the University of Phoenix. Some of it is coming from postsecondary schools, who see themselves in a competitive race with the for-profit institutions.

As information technology permeates the workplace, more and more employees need continual upgrading of their computer skills. Further, technological change causes alteration in (and sometimes elimination of) the jobs themselves, precipitating additional sorts of job retraining needs. Some of these continuing education needs are met in the workplace through corporate training. Programs leading to certification or degrees are more likely to be supplied by postsecondary institutions. Public schools are expected to provide entry-level skills in reading, math, computer literacy, and social abilities. Overall, this adds up to an exceptional challenge—and opportunity—for providers of education and training.

The common factor among all these forces is that the players view technology as the most powerful means to achieve their ends. We begin our discussion of these issues with the domain of corporate education, where "the bottom line" is already the primary consideration and where instructional technology is already being transformed. Then we move to higher education, where competition and corporatization are becoming rampant. We end with K–12 education, where instructional technology is just beginning to be affected by the forces of competition and accountability.

CORPORATE TRAINING AND DEVELOPMENT

Issue 1: Use of Technology-Based Media for Delivery of Instruction

Formats. Face-to-face classroom instruction is still the most universally applied format of training, being used in 88 percent of companies (Industry Report 1998, 58). In terms of the percentage of time spent in training, classroom instruction stands at about 70 percent overall. However, at "leading-edge" companies, the percentage is about 60 percent and has been dropping at the rate of about 5 percent per year in recent years (Bassi and Van Buren 1999, 18).

Print materials—manuals and workbooks—are next in popularity, being used at 73 percent of companies, down slightly from previous reports. Some of these materials are used for self-study (at 35 percent of companies represented), and others are used as adjunct materials in classroom-based programs.

Traditional audiovisual media. Videotapes are used at 70 percent of companies; this is a big decrease from a high of 92 percent in 1995. Audiocassettes also have been declining, from 50 percent in 1995 to 39 percent in 1998. The use of slides and overhead transparencies has not been tracked consistently over the years, but these media formats seem to be receding slowly as they are replaced by computer-based display media. The use of games and simulations (noncomputer-based) has declined dramatically, from 63 to 19 percent (Industry Report 1998, 58).

Computer-based media. What has been replacing the traditional delivery systems is instruction delivered via computer. In the early 1990s, this meant delivery via floppy disk or local area network (LAN); more recently, this means delivery via CD-ROM or Internet/intranet. Taken together, these computer-mediated delivery systems account for about 15 percent of all time spent in training, although this figure is higher—closer to 25 percent—at "leading-edge" companies (Bassi and Van Buren 1999, 18). Surveys of future expectations of training directors indicate strongly that they anticipate a rapid growth in the use of intranets for delivery of instruction in the first few years of the new decade, accounting for more than 20 percent of all training time in a typical organization (Bassi and Van Buren 1999, 18).

In some sectors, such as information technology training, the use of Internet/intranet-based training is skyrocketing, doubling every year (Bassi, Cheney, and Lewis 1998, 64).

Issue 2: Constraints on Acceptance and Use of Technology

Level of acceptance. In corporations, the choice of delivery system is controlled at the executive level, not at the level of the individual instructor, so "faculty acceptance" is not an issue. A 1998 national survey of human resources development executives indicates that 70 percent thought that investing in electronic technologies was "very important" (ASTD 1998a). According to training managers interviewed by the Indiana University research team sponsored by the authors, "technology will play a key role in the delivery of training, knowledge, and information to the worker in the future. A few said that it will not replace classroom training, while others thought that it would" (Lauer, Lee, and Plaskoff 1999, 7).

Another reason to expect rapid growth in Internet/intranet use is the simple fact of familiarity. The Internet is fast becoming a feature of everyday home and work life for many; 40 percent of the U.S. adult population had online connections at home by 1999. We know from experience with earlier media that "comfort level" has a good deal to do with people's acceptance of new media as learning channels.

Technical infrastructure and support. Compared to instructional technologists in educational institutions, those in business face fewer challenges in building a technological infrastructure and maintaining it. For the most part, that infrastructure has already been built and is being maintained for other business purposes, and training "piggybacks" onto the existing system—the computer network, teleconferencing network, or the like. However, finding and maintaining the people with requisite technical skills is a problem, according to training managers interviewed by the IU research team:

> Most think that this is a major issue right now facing the training community and a trend that will need to be dealt with in the future—repurposing training skills and increasing technical skills and staff to meet the expanding needs and requests for technology delivered training (Lauer, Lee, and Plaskoff 1999, 8).

Issue 3: Challenges to Existing Instructional Technology Paradigms

Continuing competitive pressures plus rapid advances in information technology have combined to create a business environment in which conventional ways of thinking about the design and delivery of training are under attack. Added to these forces in the late 1990s was the massive adoption of enterprise management software (e.g., SAP) at many large corporations, putting tremendous strain on the training capacities of these companies. Besides requiring the retraining of most employees, enterprise-wide software implementations, as a secondary effect, raised the issue of tying human resource development data into the company's overall information system. The result of these forces is reflected in three challenges to conventional paradigms.

Performance improvement. There is a profound shift taking place in the field of human resources development. The very purpose of the field is changing. "No longer is 'training' the primary deliverable of HRD. Instead, the emphasis has turned to its outcomes, especially performance and, somewhat less so, learning" (ASTD 1998b, 2). In a 1997 survey of HRD practitioners, the shift from training to performance was identified as the most significant trend for the next three years (ibid., 5). Whereas it used to be acceptable to measure the value of the training department in terms of the number of courses offered or the number of employees trained, now it is increasingly expected that HRD demonstrate how its activities actually affect employee performance, and hence profits. This expectation from top management dovetails with practitioners' growing acceptance of the notion that instruction is just one among many types of interventions that affect employee performance. Within the framework of "performance improvement," the design of instruction takes place alongside the design of other interventions, such as electronic performance support systems and incentive systems, and all these are implemented together through a process of change management.

Knowledge management. The knowledge and skills possessed by employees is increasingly characterized as "intellectual capital." As such, it is seen as one of the most valuable assets of an organization. The creation and management of these assets, or knowledge management (KM), is fast becoming the primary source of competitive advantage within a growing number of industries, ranging from auto manufacturing to consulting services (Bassi, Cheney, and Lewis 1998, 52-57). The concept of knowledge management, like performance improvement, is still ill-defined. For an operational definition, one could look at what is actually being done within organizations under the name of KM. These activities include creating an intranet, data warehousing, acquiring decision-support tools, and acquiring groupware for collaboration (ibid., 53). As defined by these examples, it appears that the concept of KM has not yet had a major effect on the conventional activities of training. At this point, turf issues between knowledge management and instructional design are more potential than actual. However, as accessing information and learning are both subsumed under KM, a blurring of the distinction could easily occur. Providing an employee with a computer that gives immediate access to a database of information about manufacturing procedures is not the same as training the employee to understand and follow those procedures. As Jack Gordon editorialized: "The guess in this corner is that people will go right on proving stubbornly unable to master skills by reading about them, any more than they could when the text was on paper" (Gordon 1998, 8).

Object-oriented design. A trend found in the literature, if not yet in practice, is the wide-ranging effort to define "knowledge objects" and use them in instructional design. The goal is to break instructional material into small chunks that can be reused, both to reduce the cost of design through recycling of existing material and to customize lessons to the needs of individual learners. M. David Merrill has developed a well-elaborated theory for object-oriented design (Merrill, 1998). This quest is intimately related to the digitization of instructional materials. As such, it is supported by a number of commercial software producers and information systems managers. Large-scale demonstration and implementation have yet to be performed, but if the concept proves viable it will radically alter instructional design processes, not only in corporate education but also in higher and K–12 education (ASTD 1999).

HIGHER EDUCATION

Issue 1: Use of Technology-Based Media for Delivery of Instruction

Traditional audiovisual media. Although there are no reliable data based on large-scale national surveys of media used in college classrooms, some indications of trends can be gleaned from data gathered by researchers at Indiana University, who surveyed a sample of instructional technology support staff across the United States. First, regarding traditional media, the survey indicates that compared to the mid-1990s, there has been a small but steady decrease in the use of overhead projectors and audiocassettes. Whiteboards are replacing chalkboards, but such display media continue to be a mainstay, as are videocassettes (Anderson, Graham, and Wang-Chavez 1999, 9).

Computer-based media. A 1998 survey (Campus Computing Project 1998, 3) indicates rapid increases in Internet-related uses in college courses, with about one-half of all college courses using E-mail, one-third requiring students to explore Internet resources, and one-fourth offering class materials and resources as web pages. The Indiana research (ibid., 9) confirms a continuation of this trend plus an emerging trend toward the incorporation of online discussion groups into course structure, although the latter is still at the "early adopter" stage. Respondents report, though, that web usage is typically limited to basics such as the posting of course syllabi.

Computer applications other than Internet applications have slower rates of growth. The use of CD-ROM or multimedia courseware is limited to about 15 percent of all college courses (Campus Computing Project 1998, 5). The one non-Internet application that is rapidly becoming ubiquitous is the use of presentation software (PowerPoint being the most frequently mentioned program) for visual displays (Anderson, Graham, and Wang-Chavez 1999, 9).

Distance Education. The most visible trend in technology in higher education is the virtual "land rush" mentality surrounding distance education. Colleges and universities by the hundreds—the IU survey indicates nearly 80 percent of all institutions—are racing to develop distance education programs, fearing that unless they stake out the territory, someone else will. Because geographic boundaries are irrelevant to online learning, higher education institutions are being driven to think in terms of capturing a share of the national—or even global—market.

A good deal of the competitive pressure is coming from proprietary institutions or for-profit subsidiaries of universities. The archetype proprietary institution is the University of Phoenix, a for-profit adult education institution enrolling some 61,000 students at 77 campuses, with some 5,000 students taking courses online. Jones International University in 1999 became the first for-profit Internet-only school to be accredited to grant college degrees. A well-known privatized spinoff of existing universities is the California Virtual University. A new institution devoted fully to distance education is Western Governors University, a consortium involving 18 western states; it offers a website that links students to distance-learning courses and degree programs offered at participating schools. A competing web brokerage consortium has been formed by 14 "Research I" institutions.

It is notable that the current excitement revolves around Internet-based delivery. Only a few years earlier, videoconferencing was all the rage. It is difficult to find hard data tracking the growth of instructional videoconferencing in higher education, but it is safe to say that growth is slow compared with Internet delivery. This conversion experience seems to be based on both cost and convenience. Video requires a great deal of bandwidth, which is expensive, and it is used synchronously, meaning that the sender and receiver have to be on the same schedule. The requirement of synchronous connection simply doesn't square with the realities of how college courses are organized and run, nor with the needs of the growing audience of employed adults.

Some colleges are scrambling to develop their own distance education ventures; others are signing up with companies that provide them with a "virtual university in a box." One of these, eCollege.com, had signed contracts with 150 campuses by mid-1999. All of these ventures are still in their infancy, so it is difficult to predict how they will grow. Early indications are, though, that these ventures are experiencing slower growth than they had expected, suggesting a crowded playing field with tough competition for students. Indeed, many of the entrants (including Western Governors University, California Virtual University, University of Illinois, and Penn State University) subsist on start-up funding from the Alfred P. Sloan Foundation. It remains to be seen whether they prosper as they move from "soft money" support into the marketplace.

Issue 2: Constraints on Acceptance and Use of Technology

Faculty acceptance. The IU survey indicates that acceptance of technology is up among faculty and that the "collective consciousness has been more positive." However, while overall acceptance is rising, among a majority of users usage tends to be limited to basic tools, such as E-mail, word processing, and presentation software (Anderson, Graham, and Wang-Chavez 1999, 12). That is, acceptance is common as long as the usage is consistent with conventional roles. Faculty continue to do what they do, but the tools make the job marginally more efficient or effective.

Technical infrastructure and technical support. Higher education institutions, especially smaller ones, are having a struggle to build and maintain adequate computer infrastructure and then to provide user support to staff. In fact, a 1998 survey of the Consortium of Liberal Arts Colleges (CLAC) indicated that the biggest issue they faced was providing adequate support for campus computing during a time of "increased expectations" by students and faculty (Jaschik 1998, A29). Second on the CLAC issue list was finding and retaining information technology staff. The staffing issue was first on the list of current issues among college information technology managers, representing the large research universities (EDUCAUSE 1998, 1).

Issue 3: Threatened Changes in Faculty Roles

As enrollments increase (especially of working adults) and government financial support declines, demands for greater productivity are becoming louder than ever before. Higher education institutions are searching for ways to get more output for less input. This quest is stated bluntly in an EDUCAUSE report: "Along with the focus on accountability comes pressure to adopt the business model, with greater emphasis on the bottom line" (Twigg and Oblinger 1996). Of course, because personnel costs make up about 80 percent of college budgets, controlling costs means reducing the labor-intensive nature of the conventional teaching-learning process. This means substituting capital for labor—technology for teachers.

Technology tends to be perceived by faculty as a benign force as long as its use fits into the traditional routines of work. However, treating technology use as an add-on cost, which is what it is when used in a supplementary way, does not fit well with a bottom-line mentality. When technology is used in ways that truly reduce costs, it tends to raise conflicts with traditional faculty roles. This issue is characterized well by Sir John Daniel of the Open University. He attributes the success of the Open University and its "mega-university" clones in other countries squarely to "the working practices that underpin the rest of today's modern industrial and service economy: division of labour, specialization, teamwork and project management" (Daniel 1999, 5). This translates into small teams of specialists developing courses that are then delivered to thousands of students via technology and supported by other teams of aides who advise students and grade their work.

These work processes are not only unfamiliar to most faculty, but they also directly contradict the most cherished values of academia. An example of how the systematic design process is viewed through academic lenses is David Noble's description of a process "which includes the detailed study of what professors do, breaking the faculty job down in classic Tayloristic fashion into discrete tasks, and determining what parts can be automated or outsourced" (Noble 1997, 6). The consequence of such a process, according to Noble, is that:

> The administration is now in a position to hire less skilled, and hence cheaper, workers to deliver the technologically prepackaged course. It also allows the administration, which claims ownership of this commodity, to peddle the course elsewhere without the original designer's involvement or even knowledge, much less financial interest. The buyers of this packaged commodity . . . are able thereby to contract out, and hence outsource, the work of their own employees and thus reduce their reliance upon their in-house teaching staff (6).

When technology is applied in this fashion, it poses a serious threat to the academic status quo. At that point, faculty resistance can be expected to rise and, indeed, to evolve from passive to active form.

K–12 EDUCATION

Issue 1: Use of Technology-Based Media for Delivery of Instruction

Traditional audiovisual media. Owing to the shift in popular attention to computer-based media, there has been little research in recent years to track school use of the older technologies. The last Corporation for Public Broadcasting (CPB) survey showed almost universal availability of broadcast and cable television in schools, but the teacher group having the highest percentage of use (science) was well under 50 percent, and most groups were under 10 percent (CPB 1997). In a 1999 IU survey sponsored by the authors, a national sample of school technology coordinators reported that about three-quarters of all classrooms have VCRs and that two-thirds have access to cable or satellite TV. Consistent with the CPB survey, the report indicates that only about one-third of all teachers use cable or satellite systems on a regular basis. The survey also found that about one-half of all classrooms are equipped with whiteboards, replacing chalkboards, and that four of five classrooms are equipped with overhead projectors. The respondents estimated that about one-third of all teachers use the overhead projector daily (Misanchuk, Pyke, and Tuzun 1999, 3).

Computer-based media. There is a near obsession in the K–12 education community with achieving "wired" status. Not only do researchers measure carefully the number of schools with Internet access, but the federal government also supports this access financially through the politically volatile "E-Rate" program administered by the FCC (Federal Communications Commission). And, through a phenomenon known as NetDay, businesses have actively supported access. This is arguably the single most popular issue in education, challenged only by testing and accountability.

More than 90 percent of schools now have some level of access to the Internet (Becker 1999, 2). Fully 51 percent of instructional rooms in public schools are connected (NCES 1999b). The same report notes that 65 percent of schools have dedicated lines for Internet connections. A 1998 report showed that 61 percent of newly constructed schools installed fiber optics/cable lines, and 79 percent established local area networks (MDR 1998, 1). Considering that only 62 percent of these schools built gymnasiums, this would indicate a tremendous commitment to technology!

The presence of communication networks is a necessary factor for Internet access, but the hardware infrastructure is also necessary. The race to purchase computers continues, with the average student-to-computer ratio at 7:1 in public schools and a remarkable 5:1 in Department of Defense schools (U.S. DoDEA 1999). Although there are still numerous foundations and corporations donating used computers to schools, and a tendency on the part of schools to keep computers beyond a normal life expectancy, we believe that progress is being made in terms of an installed base of useful hardware.

Distance Education. Up until about 1997, "distance education" meant the delivery of course materials to schools via satellite or cable broadcasts, or occasionally audio- or videoconferences. Since that time these delivery media have stagnated as computer-based delivery systems have burgeoned. The Star Schools initiatives of the late 1980s have ceased to grow; many have shrunk. A leading contributor to the slowdown has been the age-old bugbear of time schedules. It is difficult to arrange a (synchronous) broadcast schedule that coincides with the schedules of individual teachers in individual schools.

This is a lesson that was learned as long ago as the 1960s with the Midwest Program on Airborne Television Instruction (MPATI), an ambitious multistate project to beam recorded instructional TV programs to schools from a circling airplane. As technically challenging as the project was, it was even more challenging to determine mutually acceptable curricular content to be offered at mutually agreeable times reaching a viable number of schools. This is a lesson that each generation seems to need to learn anew.

Equity in access. A continuing concern in school technology is equity. Schools feel challenged to address the "Cyberghetto" issue of technological discrepancies between Caucasians and minorities, and higher and lower socioeconomic groups (McKissack 1998, 20). While there are small differences found in computer use in school by race and family income, there are dramatic differences in home access to computers. The most recent national data show that 60 percent of Caucasian students used a computer at home, compared with 20 percent of Black and Hispanic students. Likewise, 80 percent of high family income students had home access, compared to 40 percent for middle income and below 20 percent for low income (NCES 1999a, 39).

Issue 2: Constraints on Acceptance and Use of Technology

In-service training. The issue of teacher preparation is certainly related to both the extent of student access and the quality of usage of the Internet. One might assume that the tremendous growth in access to the Internet had been accompanied by a corresponding effort in staff development to prepare teachers for a major movement in instructional practice. In fact, only three of ten teachers reported attending any form of professional development on this topic during the previous 12 months (Becker 1999, 17). In 1994, half of all teachers had had professional development activities in the area of technology (NEGP 1994). If both qtudies are accurate, we can assume that professional development opportunities have actually *declined* in the past five years, even as Internet access has tripled.

The funds available for professional development in technology use have remained fairly constant at about 5 percent of the total technology budget, according to the *Year 2 StaR Report* (CEO Forum 1999, 27). Of course, 5 percent of the 2 percent allocated for technology results in few dollars—$5.65 per student, according to the same source. Because the total amount for each teacher would, therefore, be well under $200, teachers are not likely to be getting extensive training.

Preservice training. A major issue with teacher use is likely to be the cohort of teachers who began teaching prior to the common use of computers. The average teacher is now 44 years old and has 16 years of experience (MDR 1998, 1). With an annual attrition rate of 20 percent, the teaching population will change rapidly, and newer teachers are far more likely to have a high comfort level with technology. They are also increasingly likely to have taken a required course in technology as part of a teacher preparation program, as 25 states now require some form of computer education for licensure (NCATE 1997).

Teacher acceptance. Surveys indicate that 24 percent of teachers have Internet access both at home and in the classroom, and about half of this subgroup of teachers claim to use Internet information weekly or more often (Becker 1999, 4). If this weekly level of usage is assumed to be the basis for determining significant change, we can see that not even 12 percent of all teachers claim to have reached this important level. In fact, the authors' sponsored research indicates that teacher use of computers was overwhelmingly limited to housekeeping tasks such as attendance, record-keeping, word processing, and E-mail (Misanchuk, Pyke, and Tuzun 1999, 3), indicating that even the 12 percent designated as heavy users might well be engaged in activities with only tangential instructional impact.

This finding is quite consistent with research over the past 70 years on teacher acceptance of technology. Technology is welcomed and used by teachers under certain conditions. One is that they are comfortable with the technology by virtue of training or use of media at home. Another is that the technology represents a labor-saving replacement for previous practices. A third condition is that the technological practice or material remain subservient to the teacher; that is, it must not serve as a self-contained instructional system in its own right. An example is the textbook, which has long been welcomed by teachers because it is designed as a resource for students, to be used as directed by the teacher. It doesn't control the educational process; the teacher takes care of that.

Effectiveness claims. The reader might speculate that the apparent lack of enthusiasm for the use of technology is related to a perceived or actual lack of evidence for the effectiveness of technology-based instruction. Certainly there is a history of technology being unable to demonstrate a statistically significant difference in student learning in method A vs. method B research studies. There is even a work, *The No Significant Difference Phenomenon* (Russell 1999), dedicated to documenting the hundreds of research reports that reach the conclusion that no particular technology can, in and of itself, be viewed as causing a significant difference.

The Cognition and Technology Group at Vanderbilt University (Vye 1997) demonstrated that the use of problem-based videodiscs could improve the literacy, math, and science skills of at-risk students. A study in West Virginia (Mann and Shakeshaft 1999) indicates that the use of certain locally produced courseware led to a 4 percent achievement gain in math, reading, and language arts. Weglinsky (1998) documents a positive relationship between academic achievement on the National Assessment of Educational Progress and teacher use of computers for simulations. However, Russell (following the lead of Clark and others) explains this apparent discrepancy in conclusions by pointing out that the mediated treatment consistently outperforms the "conventional" treatment only if and when that treatment incorporates more powerful instructional *methods* than the competing treatment. That is, the method, rather than the medium, accounts for the difference.

However this debate may some day be settled, the outcome is unlikely to make a difference in teacher acceptance of technology. There is little evidence that teachers are persuaded to change their practices by research findings. Indeed, a recent study indicates that only half of all teachers read even one professional journal; and the journals they do read are mostly how-to magazines rather than research reviews (Gough 1999). On the other hand, there is abundant evidence, as Heinich points out, that teachers' media decisions "are based on totally different factors: accessibility of materials, level of supervision required, display requirements, delivery system capability, etc." (Heinich 1984).

Issue 3: Core Vs. Supplemental Use of Technology

Student uses. One school technology coordinator (Quinn 1998) reported on an internal audit of student Internet use that found that the largest percentage of use was for what the author called "electronic recess." This included personal E-mail and unsupervised Web surfing. There are also voluminous reports that at all grade levels, students do use the Internet in class to do research for reports. Regarding computer use in general, although funding for software is reported to be increasing, the software purchased, according to the Indiana survey (Misanchuk, Pyke, and Tuzun 1999, 3) and published sales reports, is primarily tool software (e.g., Microsoft Word and Print Shop) and programs peripheral to the core curriculum (e.g., Math Blaster and Where in the World Is Carmen Sandiego?).

The apparent conclusion, based on data on school spending and student uses of technology, is that technology tends to be employed as a tool and as a supplemental element of instruction rather than to deliver core curriculum content. This is quite consistent with earlier research on the role of media in education. It is particularly understandable in terms of the Internet, which has so far been perceived principally as a resource comparable to a school library, albeit one rife with misinformation and mischief as well as information. Interestingly, this role may yet evolve because there are some websites with planned instruction in K–12 curricular areas, and studies have been done indicating that where units with curricular intent were used as whole units, it was possible to document significant achievement gains (CAST 1999).

CONCLUSIONS

Our findings. An overview of the evidence supports the conventional wisdom that technological tools are increasingly available for use in all sorts of educational settings. A closer look, though, reveals that technology has not yet had a revolutionizing effect, particularly in formal education. Although more teachers and professors use computers to research, prepare, and present their teaching materials—and more students use computers to research, prepare, and present their classwork—the fundamental processes of teaching and learning proceed in the accustomed fashion for the great majority.

Fundamental, qualitative change in the teaching-learning processes appears to be moving faster in corporate education. The discrepancy between the pace of change between formal and nonformal education may be explained by the difference in their mission, and hence in how they are structured.

At the risk of oversimplification, let's look at the essential purposes and power structures of these institutions. The purpose of a company is to stay in business by generating enough revenue to maintain the operation and provide dividends to stockholders. Hence, the mission of corporate education is to equip employees with the knowledge and skills required to produce the goods and services by which the company genepates revenue. Ultimately, training has to meet the test of the bottom line. If the mission can be achieved totally without human instructors, so much the better.

On the other hand, the historical purpose of a college has been to maintain a community of scholars. The faculty *were* the college. The purpose of the educational program was to replenish the community of scholars and to generate enough tuition revenues to maintain the faculty and their ways. There has always been a tension between satisfying the students and maintaining the faculty perquisites, but the balance is skewed toward the faculty. Professors have had success maintaining the teaching-learning process as a craft activity. That is, the curriculum is reinvented and hand delivered in each individual classroom each year.

Public schools have operated essentially in a monopoly environment. Their purpose has officially been to provide the knowledge and skills that society desires to the young, but in practice school bureaucracies have operated to maintain themselves with as little disturbance as possible. Teachers have maintained considerable autonomy because of their numbers and their success at maintaining the teaching-learning process as a craft activity, as in the universities. This leaves the individual teacher in control of the classroom process without regard to efficiency or effectiveness.

The top-level administration is equally uninterested in efficiency and effectiveness because of the monopoly environment.

These differences may go a long way toward explaining the different rates at which technology is embraced and elevated to a central role in these different sectors.

Challenges posed by our findings. Implied in our findings are a number of challenges for instructional technologists.

In all sectors, growth of instructional technology is hampered by a shortage of technical personnel and deficiencies in upgrading the technology skills of existing teaching staff.

In the corporate sector, instructional technologists are facing a struggle for identity. The technologies on which they depend are increasingly subsumed into enterprise-wide information systems. And the instructional function is increasingly subsumed into the larger functions of performance improvement and knowledge management.

In the formal education sectors, the challenges are posed by the increasing corporatization of these institutions. Instructional technologists are going to find themselves having to choose between "labor" or "management." Traditionally, media professionals have allied themselves with teachers, seeing their mission as helping learners learn by helping teachers teach. Increasingly, though, economic pressures are forcing schools and colleges to seek economies of scale (as corporations already have) by *replacing* relatively high-cost faculty with technology and less costly part-time instructional aides. Successful universities have now been created in which the craft model has been broken. It is likely that, as Boettcher (1999, 18) predicts, a new educational sector will emerge, the "career university," focusing on nontraditional degrees, certification, and in-service development. Thriving institutions such as National Technological University and University of Phoenix are the archetypes. Existing major universities can be expected to vie for shares of this sector by spinning off for-profit subsidiaries but keeping them connected in order to support knowledge creation in the "career university" with the research faculty of the traditional university. This new sector is likely to grow up parallel to, rather than as a replacement for, traditional colleges and universities.

The process of corporatization is well under way in higher education; it is only just on the horizon for K–12 education.

REFERENCES

American Society for Training and Development. (1998a). *The 1997 National HRD Executive Survey: Learning Technologies.* Alexandria, VA: ASTD.

American Society for Training and Development. (1998b). *The 1997 National HRD Executive Survey: Trends in HRD.* Alexandria, VA: ASTD.

American Society for Training and Development. (1998c). *The 1997 National HRD Executive Survey: Intellectual Capital.* Alexandria, VA: ASTD.

American Society for Training and Development. (1999). *Issues and Trends Report. Knowledge Objects: Definition, Development Objectives, and Potential Impact.* Alexandria, VA: ASTD.

Anderson, Tiffany, Graham, Charles, and Wang-Chavez, Jenny. (1999). Trends and patterns of technology usage in U.S. institutions of higher education. Typescript. Indiana University–Bloomington Department of Instructional Systems Technology.

Bassi, Laurie, and Van Buren, Mark. (1999). *The 1999 ASTD State of the Industry Report.* Alexandria, VA: American Society for Training and Development.

Bassi, Laurie, Cheney, Scott, and Lewis, Eleesha. (1998, November). Trends in workplace learning: Supply and demand in interesting times. *Training & Development* 51.

Becker, Henry Jay. (1999). *Internet Use by Teachers: Conditions of Professional Use and Teacher-Directed Student Use.* Irvine, CA: Center for Research on Information Technology and Organizations.

Boettcher, Judith V. (June 1999). 21st century teaching and learning patterns; what will we see? *Syllabus* 18–25.

Campus Computing Project. (1998). *The 1998 National Survey of Information Technology in Higher Education.* Claremont, CA: Claremont Graduate University.

Center for Applied Special Technology. (1999). *The Role of Online Communications in Schools: A National Study*. Peabody, MA: CAST.

CEO Forum on Education and Technology. (1999). *Year Two School Technology and Readiness Report.* Washington, DC: CEO Forum.

Corporation for Public Broadcasting. (1997). *Study of School Uses of Television and Video*. Washington, DC: CPB, 1997.

Daniel, John. (1999, April). *Technology Is the Answer: What Was the Question?* Public Address at TechEd99, Ontario CA.

EDUCAUSE. (1998). Current issues for higher education information resources management. *CAUSE/EFFECT* 20(4), 4–7, 62–63.

Gordon, Jack. (1998, October). Editor's notebook. *Training* 35, 8.

Gough, Pauline B. (1999, June). Editor's page: For the record... *Phi Delta Kappan* 80, 722.

Heinich, Robert. (1984). The proper study of instructional technology. *Educational Communications and Technology Journal* 32(2), 83–84.

Industry report 1998. *Training* 35(October 1998), 43–76.

Jaschik, Scott. (1998, October 30). Liberal arts colleges worry about computer support and staffing. *Chronicle of Higher Education*, A29.

Lauer, Mark, Heekap Lee, and Plaskoff, Josh. (1999). Technology I training and education in a corporate setting. Typescript. Indiana University, Bloomington. Department of Instructional Systems Technology.

Mann, Dale, and Shakeshaft, Carol. *Report to West Virginia*. Santa Monica, CA: Milken Exchange on Education Technology, 1999.

Market Data Retrieval. *DataPoints*. Shelton, CT: MDR, 1998.

McKissack, Frederick L. (1998, June). Cyberghetto: Blacks are falling through the Net. *The Progressive*, 20.

Merrill, M. David. Knowledge objects. *CBT Solutions* (March-April 1998): 1–11.

Misanchuk, Melanie, Pyke, J. Garvey, and Tuzun, Hakan. (1999, Spring). Trends and issues in educational media and technology in K–12 public schools in the United States. *Instructional Media*, Newsletter #24, 3–5.

National Center for Education Statistics (1999a). In *The Condition of Education 1999*. Washington, DC: NCES.

National Center for Education Statistics (1999b). *Issue Brief: Internet Access in Public Schools and Classrooms: 1994–98*. Washington, DC: NCES.

National Council for Accreditation of Teacher Education. (1997). *Standards, Procedures, and Policies for the Accreditation of Professional Units.* Washington, DC: NCATE.

National Education Goals Panel. (1994). *National Education Goals*. Washington, DC: NEGP.

Noble, David. (1997). *Digital Diploma Mills: The Automation of Higher Education*. http://www.journet.com

Quinn, Stephen M. (1998, August). Electronic recess: Observations of E-mail and Internet surfing by K–12 students. *T.H.E. Journal* 60.

Russell, Thomas L. (1999). *The No Significant Difference Phenomenon*. Raleigh, NC: North Carolina State University.

Twigg, Carol A., and Oblinger, Diana G. (1996). The virtual university. EDUCAUSE website: http://www.educause.edu/nlii/VU,html

U.S. Department of Defense. (1999, May 26). Education Activity. *Briefing to Advisory Council on Dependents' Education.* Arlington, VA: DoD.

Vye, Nancy J., Goldman, Susan R., Voss, James F., Hmelo, Cindy, and Williams, Susan. (1997). Complex mathematical problem solving by individuals and dyads. *Cognition and Instruction* 15(4), 435–84.

Weglinsky, Harold. *Does It Compute? The Relationship Between Educational Technology and Student Achievement in Mathematics*. Princeton, NJ: Educational Testing Service, 1998.

Doctoral Dissertation Research in Educational Technology
The Themes and Trends from 1977 Through 1998

Edward P. Caffarella
Professor of Educational Technology
University of Northern Colorado
Greeley, CO 80634
caffarel@unco.edu

The doctoral dissertation is the culmination of any educational technology doctoral program. These programs are offered at institutions across the United States under a wide variety of names such as instructional systems development, educational media, instructional design, and instructional development. A complete listing of these institutions with a description of their programs is contained elsewhere in this yearbook. Each year an average of about 120 doctoral students graduate from the educational technology programs at U.S. universities. Each of these students completes a dissertation as part of the doctoral program and initial preparation as a researcher in the field.

The topics for these dissertations vary widely with no standard dissertation type, topic, context, or methodology within the field. As will be shown in this article, there is no single model that is used for dissertations in the field. Some recent dissertation titles demonstrate this diversity.

The development of a systems design model for job performance aids: A qualitative developmental study (Adamski 1998)

The effect of self-regulation on efficacy and problem solving (Armstrong 1998)

An evaluative case report of the group decision manager: A look at the communication and coordination issues facing on-line group facilitation (Bell 1998)

The efficacy of computer screen visual display design and color enhanced text on learning effectiveness when presenting stimulus material for knowledge acquisition to community college students (Buhalis 1998)

Structural overview and learner control in hypermedia instructional programs (Burke 1998)

The field of educational technology has been described as an eclectic one drawing on the expertise from many disciplines and professions. This eclecticism is reflected in the dissertation research of the doctoral students and is indicative of the multiplicity of research concerns for the students and their faculty advisors.

STATEMENT OF PURPOSE

The purpose of this research project was to review the dissertations done in the field of educational technology from 1977 through 1998. During this time more than 2,689 dissertations were completed at 55 U.S. institutions. Approximately 87% of these dissertations were completed at the 25 larger programs. This review reveals student interest and what has been done in doctoral programs over the past two decades. The specific research questions addressed were:

1. What are the major themes over the past 22 years?

2. How have the themes changed over the past 22 years?

3. How have the research methodologies changed over the past 22 years?

4. What trends are evident in the field?

5. What are the emerging trends in dissertation research?

The answers to these questions lead not only to a better understanding of doctoral dissertation research in the field of educational technology, but also to an understanding of the evolving nature of the field as reflected in the research of the students. Robert Heinich (1988) stated that "Dissertations, along with periodic literature, may be the most reliable, if more conservative, index of change in the field" (iv). Dissertation research is a reflection of the field.

METHODOLOGY

The methodology used in this study was a content analysis. The use of content analysis enabled the researcher to identify major constructs within the dissertation research and to classify them. Content analysis, as described by Weber (1990), is a methodology for classifying text into content categories and a set of techniques for text analysis. Content analysis has been used in a number of studies to show trends within a field or body of literature.

Content analysis was used by Ely (1996) in his series of reports on trends in the educational technology field. Insch, Moore, and Murphy (1997) provide further support that content analysis is an appropriate methodology for analyzing written textual materials. Evans (1996) describes recent advances in computer software for supporting content analysis.

The *Doctoral research in instructional design and technology: A directory of dissertations, 1977-1998* (Caffarella 1999) database of dissertations was used in this study. This database is available on the Internet at http://www.edtech.unco.edu/disswww/dissdir.htm. The database directory is divided into five major sections: student listing, Keyword in Context (KWIC) index, institution listing, chairperson listing, and year listing. The student section provides the student's name, graduation year, dissertation title, institution, and chairperson. The KWIC index makes it possible to look up any of the major words in a title. The institution section lists all the dissertations completed at a specific institution. The chairperson section lists all the dissertations directed under the guidance of a particular chairperson. The year index lists all dissertations completed in a particular year.

The data for the directory is supplied directly by the universities in the United States offering graduate programs in instructional design and technology. These programs are offered under a wide variety of titles including educational technology, instructional development, educational media, instructional technology, and instructional systems. The basic list of institutions was taken from the list of doctoral programs in the *Educational Media and Technology Yearbook 1996* (Ely 1996).

This list was checked against the membership list for the Professors of Instructional Design and Technology for the locations of additional programs. The intent was to be as inclusive as possible so that the wide variety of instructional design and technology dissertations would be included in the directory. The decisions to participate and about which dissertations to submit were left to the individual institutions.

The directory currently contains entries for dissertations completed by 2,689 students from 1977 through 1998 at 55 different institutions. As shown in Figure 1, the dissertations are distributed relatively evenly over the years, with an average of approximately 120 completed each year. The numbers shown for 1997 and 1998 are probably underestimates of the actual number of dissertations. Due to the way dissertations are reported, institutions tend to be delayed in forwarding the entries, and there are always additions to the database that are for dissertations completed two to three years earlier.

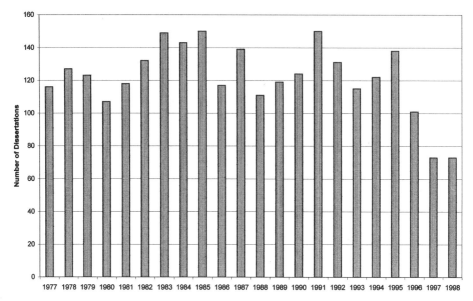

Figure 1. Number of Dissertations Completed for Each Year from 1977 Through 1998.

The dissertation titles were coded using multiple coding points to identify the major themes and constructs within the field. The QSR NUD*IST software was used for coding and analysis. The coding was an evolutionary process of data extraction and reduction to identify major themes and trends within the dissertation research. The initial data reduction identified 61 major constructs within the dissertation research.

Using dissertation titles rather than complete dissertations limits this content analysis. Some dissertation titles provide complete descriptions of the contents of their dissertations, while other titles are vague and abstract. For those dissertations with descriptive titles, content analysis and data extraction can identify major themes and trends. For those with vague titles, content analysis and data reduction do not successfully identify major themes and trends even though they may be present in the dissertation. Therefore the numbers and percentages presented may be an underestimate of the actual.

Ely (1996) did a similar content analysis study of literature sources in the field. His study was limited to 1995 but included journals, dissertations, conference papers, and ERIC documents with the overall purpose of identifying trends forthat year. Among his documents were 37 dissertations from five large doctoral programs completed during 1995. This study builds upon the Ely study by looking at only dissertation research for multiple years.

FINDINGS

Initial analysis of the dissertation data showed a wide variety of topics being investigated by students in educational technology. This is indicative of the eclectic nature of the field and the widely divergent topics included within it. There are no predominate themes or topics for the dissertation research. There are, however, several themes prominent in the data.

Clearly the most popular topic was research on and about computers. Such research took many forms including appropriate uses, software design, individual differences, and the effectiveness of computers as a teaching tool. As shown in Figure 2, the number of studies dealing with computers grew with the introduction of microcomputers. Prior to the introduction of the microcomputer there was some limited dissertation research on the use of mainframe and minicomputers, but most of the doctoral research on computing has taken place since the mid-1980s. The Apple II was introduced during the late 1970s, the IBM PC arrived in the early 1980s, and the Macintosh was released in the mid-1980s. With the introduction of each new platform there was an increase in the number of studies, and for the past 14 years between 15 percent and 25 percent of all dissertations have dealt with computers.

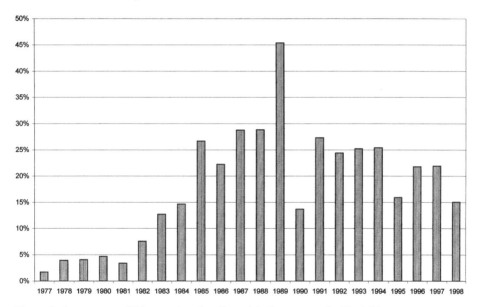

Figure 2. Percentage of Dissertations Dealing with Computers for Each Year.

One theme that was constant throughout the 22-year period was research on instructional development, instructional design, and instructional systems development (see Figure 3). This research amounted to approximately 2 to 5 percent of the dissertations in a given year, for a total of 86 dissertations over the period. This was not an overwhelming number of dissertations but was the most consistent theme of interest over the years. Clearly foundations of the field in instructional design/ development that were important concepts in the late 1970s continue to be major foundations for the field.

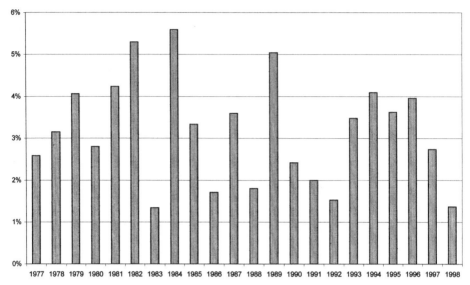

Figure 3. Percentage of Dissertations Dealing with Instructional Development, Instructional Design, or Instructional Systems Development Each Year.

Two other themes seemed to persist throughout the period although both had years of popularity and years with very little research. These themes, shown in Figure 4, are A) simulation and games and B) television and video. The kinds of research done on these topics has varied greatly. Early simulation and game dissertation research was largely related to process and design, while more recent dissertation research has looked at simulations and games within a computer environment. Likewise, the television research has followed the evolution of this technology. Earlier research investigated topics such as broadcast instructional television and cable television. Later research dealt with topics such as distance education and learner perceptions of television images.

As might be expected, at any given point there is research dealing with the newest hardware or software technologies. This research might be characterized with terms such as "trendy" or "hot topics." For example, many studies in the late 1970s dealt with the use of film and video, but more contemporary studies have dealt with computer applications. The growth of research on computing, shown in Figure 1, is one example of this change. The changing nature of the field of educational technology and the tendency of dissertation research to follow the new developments can be seen clearly in Figure 5. During the early years, film research was a major segment of dissertation research. During the middle years, research dealing with videodiscs was popular among doctoral students. In recent years, multimedia and hypermedia have been major topics for research. In the future, with a continuation of this trend, one can expect dissertation research on topics such as virtual reality, DVD, and high definition television.

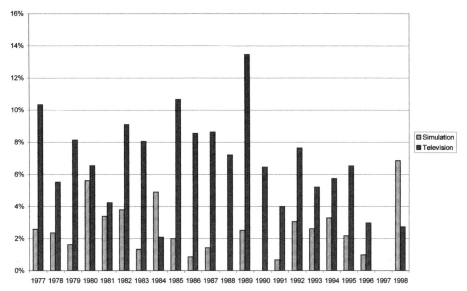

Figure 4. Percentage of Dissertations Dealing with Simulation and Television for Each Year.

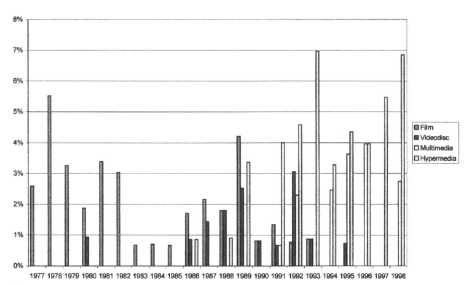

Figure 5. Percentage of Dissertations Dealing with Film, Videodisc, Multimedia, and Hypermedia for Each Year.

The research methodologies used in the dissertations show some interesting trends. The most startling trend is the reduction in the number of comparison studies from 1977 until 1998, as shown in Figure 6. Many of these studies compared one medium against another to determine if one was inherently better than the other. Clark (1983) wrote about the problems with comparison studies and launched a debate that continued into the early 1990s. During the late 1970s, comparison studies represented around 7 percent of all dissertation research. During the late 1980s and early 1990s, the number of comparison studies had dropped to around 5 percent. For the last five years comparison studies have accounted for less than 3 percent of dissertation studies. Over the entire 22-year period there were at least 134 comparison study dissertations, which, as discussed in the limitations, is probably an underestimate of the total number.

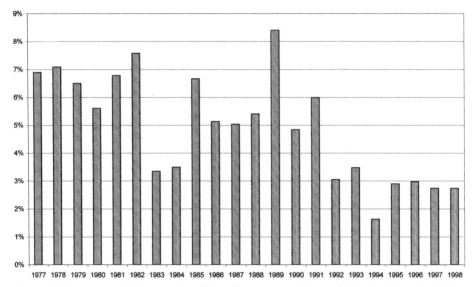

Figure 6. Percentage of Dissertations Using Comparative Research Methodology for Each Year.

Another clear shift in research methodology can be seen in a reduction in the number of experimental studies and an increase in the number of qualitative studies. In the late 1970s, very few qualitative studies were done by students (see Figure 7), and these studies were clearly the exceptions to the norm. Now dissertations with qualitative research designs exceed the number of experimental studies. Again since the determination of the research methodology as derived from the dissertation titles, the percentages reported in Figure 7 are probably underestimates of the actual percentages, but the balance between experimental and qualitative studies will likely continue to show a change.

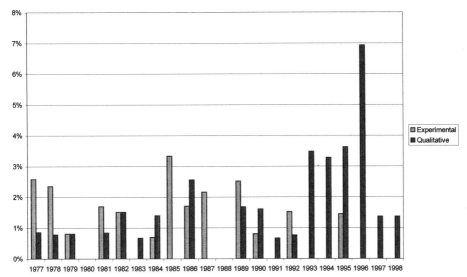

Figure 7. Percentage of Dissertations Using Experimental and Qualitative Research Methodologies for Each Year.

INSTITUTIONS OFFERING DOCTORAL PROGRAMS

There were 55 institutions with doctoral graduates in educational technology during 1977–1999. A complete list of the institutions is available in *Doctoral research in instructional design and technology: A directory of dissertations, 1977-1998* (Caffarella 1999). The number of graduates from each program ranged from a high of 331 to a low of one. The programs with the most doctoral graduates included Indiana University, Boston University, the University of Southern California, Syracuse University, and Florida State University. Figure 8 shows the relative numbers of graduates for the 25 institutions with the largest numbers of graduates. These institutions graduated 2,287 students, while the remaining 30 institutions graduated only 402 students. There is a clear variability in the size of the doctoral programs with many extremely small doctoral programs. Interestingly, only 5 of the 25 are private institutions; the vast majority of large educational technology programs are offered at public institutions. Most of the public institutions are classified as research-level institutions and are among the most prestigious public institutions in each state.

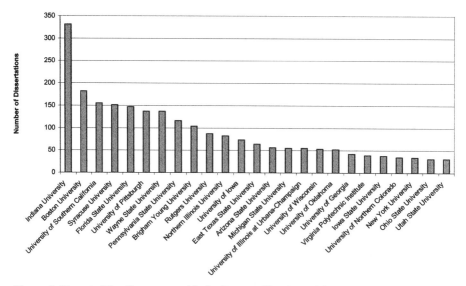

Figure 8. Twenty-Five Programs with the Largest Number of Graduates from 1977 Through 1998.

Figure 9 shows the number of graduates over the past five years for the 25 largest programs. The collection of institutions is essentially the same as the list in Figure 8, but the order of the institutions is somewhat different, with some institutions gaining in the ranking and others moving to the right with declining relative numbers. For the past five years, these 25 institutions graduated 483 students, which is 95 percent of the total graduates. As has been the pattern over the 22-year period, most of the doctoral graduates in the field are coming from a relatively small number of programs.

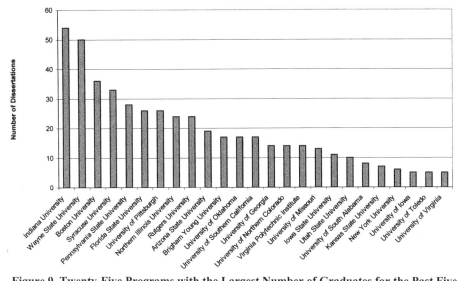

Figure 9. Twenty-Five Programs with the Largest Number of Graduates for the Past Five Years.

CHAIRPERSONS OF DISSERTATIONS

The 25 chairpersons with the largest numbers of doctoral graduates from 1977 through 1998 are shown in Figure 10. As might be expected, the institutions for these chairpersons are a reflection of the larger programs shown in Figure 8. These chairpersons worked with 1,018 students during this period, which represents 37 percent of the total students. A total of 472 chairpersons worked with the doctoral students, but 307 of these worked with three or fewer students. Thirty-seven individuals chaired three dissertations, 65 chaired two dissertations, and 205 chaired only one. Clearly the advisement of large numbers of doctoral students is being done by a relatively small number of educational technology professors.

The cohort of chairpersons with the largest number of graduates over the past five years (see Figure 11) includes a few new individuals. The 27 professors in this group chaired 271 out of 518 dissertations, representing 52 percent of the total. Many of these professors have actively chaired dissertations over the entire 22 years, but there are several new individuals who have assumed these responsibilities. Much of the change in the lists of professors between the entire 22 years (Figure 9) and the last 5 years (Figure 10) can be attributed to the retirement or death of at least eight professors. The list will further change with the retirements of more professors.

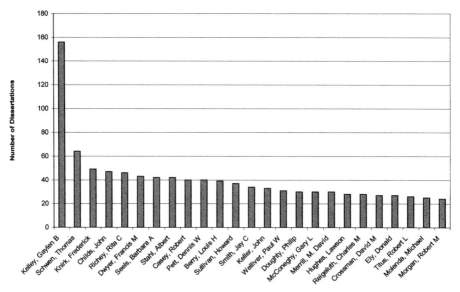

Figure 10. Twenty-Five Chairs with the Largest Number of Graduates from 1977 Through 1998.

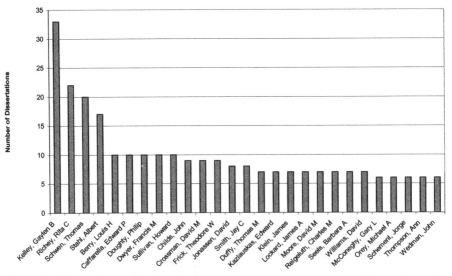

Figure 11. Twenty-Seven Chairs with the Largest Number of Graduates for the Past Five Years.

SUMMARY

The field of educational technology is very varied, as reflected in the research of doctoral students. The students selected a range of topics that have no particular theme or pattern, with their research following the development of new technologies. The field used a variety of research methodologies, with qualitative methodologies having a major role during the past few years. Most of the students graduated from a relatively small number of institutions although there are 55 institutions offering doctoral programs in educational technology. Likewise, a relatively small number of professors chaired most of the doctoral dissertations. Thus, although the field is broadly based and draws upon many disciplines, the doctoral study is highly concentrated with a few institutions and professors.

REFERENCES

Adamski, A. (1998). The development of a systems design model for job performance aids: A qualitative developmental study. Ph.D. diss., Wayne State University.

Armstrong, A. M. (1998). The effect of self-regulation on efficacy and problem solving. Ph.D. diss., University of South Alabama.

Bell, D. M. (1998). An evaluative case report of the group decision manager: A look at the communication and coordination issues facing on-line group facilitation. Ph.D. diss., University of Missouri.

Buhalis, H. (1998). The efficacy of computer screen visual display design and color enhanced text on learning effectiveness when presenting stimulus material for knowledge acquisition to community college students. Ph.D. diss., Wayne State University.

Burke, P. (1998). Structural overview and learner control in hypermedia instructional programs. Ph.D. diss., Arizona State University.

Caffarella, E. P. (1999). Doctoral research in educational technology: A directory of dissertations, 1977–1997. Greeley, CO: University of Northern Colorado. Available http://www.edtech.unco.edu/disswww/dissdir.htm

Clark, R. E. (1983). Reconsidering research on learning from media. *Review of Educational Research 53*(4), 445–59.

Ely, D. P. (1996). *Trends in Educational Technology 1995.* Syracuse, NY: ERIC Clearinghouse on Information and Technology.

Evans, W. (1996). Computer-supported content analysis: Trends, tools, and techniques. *Social Science Computer Review 14*(3).

Heinich, R. (1988). Forward. In E. P. Caffarella and S. G. Sachs, *Doctoral Research in Instructional Design and Technology: A Directory of Dissertations 1977–1986.* Washington, DC: Association for Educational Communications and Technology, iv.

Insch, G. S., Moore, J. E., and Murphy, L. D. (1997). Content analysis in leadership research: Examples, procedures, and suggestions for future use. *Leadership Quarterly 8*(1).

Weber, R. P. (1990). *Basic Content Analysis.* Beverly Hills, CA: Sage.

Development Programs for College Faculty
Preparing for the Twenty-First Century

John D. Emerson
Department of Mathematics and Computer Science,
Middlebury College

Frederick Mosteller
Professor Emeritus,
Department of Statistics,
Harvard University

ABSTRACT

The faculties of our schools and colleges currently offer the principal medium for delivering instruction to students. The nation's colleges and universities invest substantial resources and years in faculty development programs. A review of 103 articles and chapters written mostly between 1990 and 1998 reveals the types of programs that have evolved from experiences of earlier decades and that will prepare faculty for a challenging future. Effective programs often provide their client faculty members with "coaches" and "teammates." Most often, these programs are collegial and collaborative, rely on sustained engagement of colleagues, and have an agenda that is specific and focused. These characteristics point toward new development programs that hold promise for instructional improvement. Some of these improvements will rely on wise uses of emerging technologies to enhance the delivery of education by teachers in the twenty-first century.

INTRODUCTION

The nation's 3,500 colleges and universities employ more than 750,000 faculty members who comprise a most valuable resource for higher education. These faculty members teach about 17 million students each year (Tang and Chamberlain 1997). Their effect extends directly to the nation's schools, which are ultimately staffed by professionals trained at colleges and universities.

Our work (Miech, Nave, and Mosteller 1997; Emerson and Mosteller 1998a and 1998b) in assessing the uses of new computer technologies, especially multimedia programs, for enhancing teaching led us to appreciate that successes for technology depend critically on the effectiveness of faculty members in adapting the technology to their teaching strategies. Effective use of technology for teaching improvement requires faculty members who are willing to both consider new teaching strategies and ask hard questions about how their teaching can be made more effective. Media and technology will increasingly serve the needs of both faculty and students as an integral part of the education enterprise.

This report addresses the effects and benefits of faculty development activities. We summarize and interpret research about these at the college and university level, including community colleges and professional schools. We also review briefly two faculty development initiatives in the public schools. We identify emerging trends in the newer forms of faculty development, and we point to directions that future programs should take as they try to assist faculty in enhancing teaching effectiveness.

One goal of development programs, both in schools and in higher education, is to promote student learning. Some research addresses the effect on the faculty members—their self-reported activities and behavior, their scholarship, and their attitudes about the development programs and about teaching and students. Although the present report reviews some of that research, it directs special attention to research about the effect of programs on instructional improvement. The successes of development programs should be measured using student educational outcomes as well as faculty outcomes; this perspective underlies and motivates the present report.

Our reliance chiefly on work since 1990 heightens the relevance of this report to current programs and to the challenges of the next century. We favor work that is based on empirical findings. Our review is also informed by articles that are reflective, philosophical, or theoretical.

This report traces the evolution and broad transitions in faculty development programs over four decades. It identifies characteristics of the current generation of programs that seem most successful in strengthening the teaching of faculty members. It offers advice about directions for future programs that can improve their effectiveness. Finally, it acknowledges that technology will inevitably play an expanding role in the development needs of faculty early in the twenty-first century.

HISTORICAL NOTES ON COLLEGE FACULTY DEVELOPMENT

Colleges and universities have supported the professional development of their faculty members in various ways over many decades. Support for scholarly work, travel related to research and writing, and sabbaticals were mainstays. Development programs traditionally assumed that competence in one's discipline and active participation in the advancement of a field were likely to help faculty members be more effective in their teaching and in their other roles (Kalivoda, Sorrell, and Simpson 1994, 256). In sum, faculty development in the 1950s and 1960s meant helping faculty *develop expertise in their disciplines.*

Following the rapid expansion of higher education through the 1960s, development programs gave more attention to classroom teaching. Instructional development programs emerged and were accompanied by an increase in related empirical research. In a comprehensive review of research on improving college teaching, Levinson-Rose and Menges (1981) identified three categories of interventions used (and evaluated) to improve college teaching: grants for faculty projects, workshops and seminars, and feedback from student ratings. Levinson-Rose and Menges identified and summarized 71 reports since the mid-1960s providing 97 analyses of variables presumably affected by these interventions. They reported that 78 percent of the comparisons support the intervention being studied (p. 417).

Thus, faculty development had begun to assume different forms by the early 1970s. These forms included new offices of institutional support, increasingly staffed by professionals who focused primarily on the faculty's teaching and on instructional development (Kalivoda, Sorrell, and Simpson 1994, 256). They offered workshops, institutes, seminars, and other forms of training to enhance and update the faculty's subject-matter knowledge, encourage course development, expand the faculty's capacity to use new technologies in research and teaching, and provide training in areas and skills of direct value for classroom teaching. Typically, they offered support from a teaching consultant who gave information, advice, and technical assistance to many faculty members across the disciplines. The new programs placed attention on the individual teacher. In sum, the 1970s *emphasized a faculty member's teaching role and related skills.*

Gaff and Simpson (1994) report that faculty development in the 1980s shifted emphasis from teaching to the curriculum. Colleges and universities attended to curricular challenges that included: coherence in general education; assessing and strengthening academic majors; transforming the curriculum by including education about multicultural issues; and attending to writing across the curriculum, where most departments now include substantial writing instruction in some of their courses (169). The shift in emphasis meant more focus on groups of faculty and on departments (or other academic units). Workshops, seminars, and retreats were vehicles for considering and planning change. Gaff and Simpson also report that the 1980s brought a renewal of faculty development, and that new or redefined centers for development became fully supported within the institutions. In sum, the 1980s were years of expansion for *development emphasizing curricular change.*

Faculty development in the 1990s has a broad focus that incorporates much of what was emphasized in earlier decades. By 1994, about 80 percent of colleges and universities had a separate office or a formal program for supporting teaching development (Crawley 1995b, 83-84). These offices typically provide assistance to individual instructors who want to improve their teaching. They also offer programs to the faculty in the form of workshops or seminars on topics of broad interest: theory of student learning; uses of new technologies in teaching; or themes for college-wide revisions in courses that meet distribution requirements. Development offices may work with departments or other units in support of curricular change. They seek to *incorporate the strengths of each of the three earlier phases of faculty development programs by promoting disciplinary expertise, improved teaching skills, and curriculum development.*

LITERATURE SEARCH AND REVIEW

We used two databases, Educational Resource Information Center (ERIC) and Harvard University Libraries catalog, in systematic computer searches for articles and books that include material on faculty development in higher education. Although the searches targeted the years 1990 through 1998, the references we reviewed led us to useful earlier articles. We also manually searched more than two dozen journals in the fields of education and psychology.

Our initial brief reviews of abstracts and summaries established a collection of material which we photocopied, read, and abstracted using forms we designed for this purpose. We looked for references to other literature of potential value to the project, especially literature likely to contain *empirical* evidence about the outcomes and effects of development programs.

The search ultimately led to 103 articles and chapters; see Table 1. Original empirical studies produced 37 articles. Eleven of these empirical studies (not shown in the table) use measures of student outcomes or data from external assessment. These evaluations tend to have higher credibility because they are not self-reported by the faculty targeted in such development programs. A few of the empirical studies use controlled experiments. Students provide assessments of outcomes in 7 reports; often these take the form of student ratings of their teachers.

TABLE 1. Categories of Articles and Chapters Reviewed.

Category	Count
A. Total number of articles and chapters abstracted	103
book or book chapters	19
ERIC reports	8
published articles	*76*
	103
B. Original empirical research articles	37
data source:	
written surveys, questionnaires	25
interviews	7
experiments and other comparisons	13
major literature review	1
(counts do not total 37 because categories sometimes overlap)	

STRATEGIES FOR IMPROVEMENT:
USE COACHES AND TEAMMATES

Development programs are most effective when they provide faculty members with *coaches or teammates*. This finding identifies a technology for delivering support that can lead to better learning outcomes. Successful faculty development programs usually involve a *collaborative* approach to making changes. This finding is robust. It emerged in the 1970s when research about faculty development often addressed efforts to use student ratings of teaching as feedback for teaching improvement, and it also appears to characterize the wide variety of faculty development programs implemented and studied in the 1980s and 1990s.

From our review of recent empirical research, we have identified three patterns in the findings. Faculty development:

1. Is successful when it is *collegial*;

2. Benefits from making use of *extended intervention*, over a full semester, a year, or more; and

3. Has greater impact when it is *focused and concrete*. Having a specific task to address helps. For example, a consultant may aid a statistics teacher in using computer simulation to help clarify a point of confusion identified in student ratings.

An awareness of these patterns can inform future development programs that will lead to benefits for the next student generation.

Although some writers have identified several dozen different faculty development activities, we review four main program types that address instructional improvement. These types correspond to the areas targeted most often by the research reports appearing in the 1990s and identified in our search:

1. Intervention by professional consultants and facilitators (10 articles);

2. Workshops, seminars, and courses (7 articles);

3. Mentoring programs (16 articles); and

4. Action research, including classroom research (8 articles).

These categories are not comprehensive. For example, they do not explicitly include programs that fund faculty travel. The categories are not disjointed. For example, consultants often use both peer mentoring and workshops for faculty. Nonetheless, four categories seem useful for describing and reflecting upon faculty development initiatives that have evolved to become the programs of the 1990s.

Teaching Consultants and Facilitators

Erickson and Erickson (1979, 672–73) described a typical consulting process in the 1970s as having three stages:

1. *Early-semester analysis of teaching*, in which the consultant gathers information about the instructor's teaching through interviews, classroom observation, videotape, and/or a student questionnaire;

2. *Continuing consultation on strategies for improvement* in which the consultant works with instructors to devise techniques and strategies to help the teachers achieve their teaching goals;

3.   *Late-semester analysis of teaching*, in which the consultant again gathers information about the instructor's teaching in order to assess progress toward the goals and to update the analysis of teaching strengths and areas for improvement.

This process usually involves one-on-one interaction with the trained consultant as the helper and the instructor as the recipient of the consultant's expertise. The interaction sometimes develops around specific technologies—for example, student ratings of teaching and faculty teaching portfolios.

Student Ratings As Tools for Consultants

Consultants often use student ratings of teachers and their courses as a point of departure in their work with college teachers. They help faculty members understand and interpret their ratings, identify the relative strengths and weaknesses of their teaching, and devise and implement specific strategies for teaching improvement. Hoyt and Howard (1978) report modest improvements in student ratings for teachers at Kansas State University who worked voluntarily with an Office of Educational Improvement and Innovation. Their paper also reviews limited efforts to evaluate faculty development programs in the 1970s.

Controlled experiments use ratings from large multisection courses to address research questions about the validity and reliability of student ratings and about their effectiveness in improving teaching. These research programs establish that student ratings are positively associated with student academic achievement, and that instructors can use student ratings to gain modest improvements in their teaching.

When teaching consultants assist teachers in their interpretation of, and responses to, the rating information, the gains for teaching are far more substantial than when no "coach" is involved. The average effect sizes (gains, expressed in standard deviation units) for feedback of student ratings without consultation are about .3, and for feedback with assistance by a consultant are about .64 (Cohen 1980). These average effects summarize the findings of many experiments that used the multisection study design in varied subject areas. Thus, empirical evidence from careful research synthesis supports the use of student ratings by consultants in their efforts to help faculty members improve teaching. Emerson, Mosteller, and Youtz (1999) trace major developments and review some findings of research programs about student ratings of teaching.

Teaching Portfolios As Tools for Consultants

A teaching portfolio is an organized collection of statements, course materials, student work and projects, statistical evidence, peer and student evaluation, and commentary by the teacher that is designed to convey an understanding of a faculty member's teaching. Portfolios are sometimes used in reviews of faculty members for promotion and tenure. Edgerton, Hutchings, and Quinlan (1991) believe that portfolios may also be instrumental in faculty development aimed at instructional improvement. Like student ratings, portfolios can provide raw material that informs the work consultants do with teachers.

Our literature review led to seven articles and chapters, all published since 1985, with a substantial focus on teaching portfolios. One article, by Dorene Ross et al. (1995) at the University of Florida, is an empirical study of 73 award-winning teaching portfolios. This report gives recommendations for assembling effective portfolios; it emphasizes the importance of providing examples of students' work as evidence of their learning and in support of claims made by the faculty member.

Consultants As Collaborators with Faculty

The roles assumed by teaching consultants are determined by each consultant's individual style and by the needs and preferences of the client teacher. Experience gained in the 1970s and 1980s, however, has gradually brought changes in the way a consultant's work is conceptualized. The literature of the 1990s more often uses words like "collaboration" and "partnership" to describe the interaction between a faculty developer and the teacher. Sometimes the consultant focuses on a department or other administrative unit rather than the individual faculty member.

Murray and Holmes (1997) report the results of an institutional case study from the United Kingdom. Systematic interviews with 11 faculty participants in a collaborative staff development program provide detailed data about how partnerships between teachers and staff developers work. The efforts at teaching improvement are more often successful when the partners (developer and teacher) have support and encouragement from other faculty members in the teacher's department.

Wilson (1986) used student ratings aq the basis for a partnership between him (as the collegial consultant) and individual faculty members (as clients) conducted in a private and highly individualized way. Wilson helped faculty members identify teaching strategies that had worked well for other teachers and might aid the faculty member in making improvements. Other studies have described successful programs where the developer becomes a partner with an entire academic department as well as with some of its teachers; see Hativa and Miron (1990) and Hativa (1995) for detailed accounts of work in a physics department at Tel Aviv University. We summarize some aspects of the second of these investigations, in part because we believe it suggests promising directions for future development programs.

Example: A Department-Wide Approach to Instructional Improvement

Hativa (1995) carried out research on faculty development for the improvement of physics teaching during the 1990-1991 and 1991-1992 academic years at Tel Aviv University. Hativa's intervention targeted all physics faculty identified as needing instructional improvement. The treatment focused on a single department, and it used a comprehensive approach to address the department's teaching. The program gained the support of the department chairperson and other influential faculty in the department.

The instructional specialist (Hativa) provided the following consulting services to faculty members who agreed to participate (Hativa 1995, 380):

- Introductory session to discuss the client teacher's identified problems and the methods for solving them;
- Advice on planning the course and the syllabus if the consultation period started at the beginning of the term;
- Observation of several lessons conducted by the instructor throughout the consultation period;
- Discussion based on class observations;
- Continuous student-based feedback on classroom teaching;
- Summative evaluation session at the end of the term.

Hativa used a relatively short questionnaire for obtaining student feedback. The ratings form contained a single global item ("overall teaching performance") and six instructor-attribute items (e.g., "lesson preparation") . For quantitative information, all questionnaires used a five-point Likert scale ranging from 1 (lowest) to 5 (highest).

The assembled ratings information included:

- Mid- and end-of-semester student ratings on a departmental evaluation form of all physics instructors during the two years under study;
- Mid- and end-of-semester ratings on a departmental evaluation form of approximately one-third of the instructors from the year preceding this study;
- End-of-semester ratings taken by the Tel Aviv University Student Association, during the study period and during the three years preceding the study; and

- Retrospective ratings by alumni; first-year graduate physics students rated their teachers from undergraduate years during each of the two years of the study (Hativa 1995, 384).

Hativa used two additional questionnaires: an attitude questionnaire, administered each semester to all physics majors, dealing with general aspects of instruction at the department without reference to a particular instructor; and an attitudes-toward-instruction questionnaire, administered to all instructors in the three departments of the exact-sciences faculty at Tel Aviv University: physics, chemistry, and mathematics (384).

We summarize a few of Hativa's (1995, 391) key findings.

- Other teachers besides those identified as needing improvement interacted with the instructional specialist; some of the better teachers in the department asked for her assistance because they were rated below their own expectations.

- Eleven teachers of the twenty who received some degree of treatment from the consultant showed apparent improvement. For five of these teachers the improvement was substantial, from the low range (below 3.1) to the high range (above 3.9).

- For the department as a whole, there was a minor improvement in faculty ratings from the first year to the second, and a distinct increase in the post study year. (In contrast, for the teaching assistants [TAs] there was a gradual decrease from the first through fourth semesters, and then an increase in the follow-up year, though not to the level of the initial semester.) Hativa concludes that these findings suggest "a noticeable success of the department-wide teaching improvement for the faculty members."

- The global ratings of instruction by all physics majors show ". . . a statistically significant increase from the first year to the second in student satisfaction with (a) instruction in general; (b) instruction provided by the faculty instructors in particular; and (c) faculty attitudes toward students."

- The survey of faculty attitudes about the importance of the quality of teaching in promotion considerations and about the need to improve instruction are significantly more positive than for those of other faculty (in chemistry and mathematics) who did not get special assistance.

Several features contribute to the apparent successes of Hativa's department-wide consulting program. It is *collegial* in at least two ways: as an ally of individual faculty members, Hativa developed personal relationships; and she immersed herself in the department culture, thus encouraging a collaborative approach to instructional improvement. The intervention program is *sustained*: Hativa's formal consultancy extended for two full academic years. Hativa's work with individual faculty members is *focused* on their individual needs, and on issues raised in their own student ratings.

Lessons from Findings About Teaching Consultants

Teaching consultants can serve faculty development effectively by interacting with teachers individually or at the departmental level. Sometimes the consultants need to be *coaches* and assist faculty members in finding strategies for improved instruction. Sometimes they need to be *teammates* and work alongside department members as they strive for improvement. In either situation, sustained intervention wins benefits.

The consultant can aid the client teachers by encouraging focus in their efforts for improvement. For example, both Wilson (1986) and Hativa (1995) helped faculty members choose teaching strategies to address areas of teaching that the teachers identified from student ratings as needing their attention. A *collaborative, sustained, and focused approach* to consulting seems promising. Future research on faculty development programs should address whether this approach leads to measurable gains for student learning.

Workshops, Seminars, and Courses

Terrence Overlock (1994) evaluated the faculty's response to a funded five-year program of faculty development at a technical college in northern Maine. He reports that "university courses" and "seminars or workshops" are the categories of development receiving the highest approval ratings by the participants.

Workshops and courses for faculty members are used frequently, but they have not been evaluated as much as other forms of faculty development (Levinson-Rose and Menges 1981). Most workshops that have been evaluated address TAs rather than experienced college teachers. The emphasis of the workshops is often on changing the attitudes and skills of the developing teachers. In their critical review of research on improving college teaching, Levinson-Rose and Menges (1981) conclude that "most workshops and seminars, even those with specific training goals, are unlikely to produce lasting changes in teacher behavior or lasting impact on students unless participants continue skill practice and receive critical feedback on their efforts" (419).

During the 1980s, seminars and workshops were widely used in support of curriculum changes and related faculty development (Gaff and Simpson 1994, 169-70). We have found few studies that undertook empirical assessment of these programs using data from independent sources; studies more often rely on self-reports of the faculty participants to assess outcomes.

Example: Changing Curricula to Include Teaching About Aging

Neal and White (1996) assess the outcomes of an Oregon program in which faculty participants attended a course about aging and completed an independent project over a one-year period. The course consisted of two parallel independent summer workshops and could be taken for postgraduate credit. Some course components were presented in repeated two-day segments, and others were in week-long blocks. Volunteer consultants made presentations to the teachers, who were health professions faculty at community colleges, colleges, and universities in Oregon. One of the authors organized and coordinated these diverse presentations and assisted the "students" in their networking and information sharing. The research extended over four years, so that each of four faculty cohorts took the year-long program.

Most of the assessment of this program came from the teacher participants themselves. Pretest and posttest measures assessed knowledge gains and changes in aging-related attitudes. Participants completed surveys to report how much geriatric teaching they had done and what clinical changes in their practices they had made as a result of their course participation. Participants also rated their own satisfaction with the various components of the program.

Over four years, 126 teachers (in four cohorts) completed the two workshops. Self-assessment by the participants indicated a high level of satisfaction with the program. The teachers also showed improvement in knowledge of issues for the aging and in their aging-related attitudes. A particular strength of the program was its effect on the participants' knowledge base beyond their own discipline. Between one-third and one-half of the participants expected to revise a course or clinical experience (or to develop new courses or clinical experiences) by incorporating what they had learned about gerontology.

Empirical evaluations of faculty development programs, including those of Neal and White, typically report measurements of changes that result from their development programs. Measurements made on the faculty members often include the teachers' perceptions about the value of their experiences. In general, future research of this type could be strengthened by providing measurements that derive from other, independent sources. For example, a report of changes in teaching from a student whose identity is not known by the teacher could strengthen the findings. We believe that an assessment of the effect of a faculty development technology on subsequent student learning, where possible, is a good measure of success.

Using Student Ratings to Measure the Effect of Workshops

Hativa and Miron (1990) compare two ways of augmenting mid-term feedback of student ratings: a faculty workshop and individual consultation. The workshop consisted of five one-and-a-half-hour weekly sessions that focused on video clips of college teachers in action. Ten faculty members (out of fifty) volunteered to participate in the workshops, but only five of these administered both the preworkshop questionnaire (in week 5, just before the workshop began) and the post-workshop questionnaire (in the last week of the semester). Students in the faculty members' courses completed the questionnaires, and the responses used a scale from 1 to 5.

Although Hativa and Miron found that students rated most specific items higher following the workshops, the rating on the most global item—overall teaching performance—showed only a small, statistically insignificant improvement. But in a separate study during the following semester, two teachers who received intensive consultation designed to help them improve their teaching obtained substantially improved ratings. For one of the teachers the global rating improved from 3.2 to 3.8 on a 5-point scale, and this was statistically significant at the .01 level (Hativa and Miron 1990, 584). Although not presented in the paper, the reported improvements for the other teacher were comparable.

Hativa and Miron (1990, 585) conclude that ratings feedback augmented by faculty workshops can lead to improvement in aspects of teaching that are more technical (e.g., stating the lesson's objectives in the introduction), but that improvement of overall teaching performance requires expert and continuous professional consultation. This finding is consistent with that from research syntheses of studies of ratings feedback; see Emerson, Mosteller, and Youtz (1999, Section 4) for further discussion.

Lessons About Faculty Development That Uses Workshops and Courses

We identify three specific findings about using workshops and courses for college faculty development to support teaching improvement:

1. Faculty members who elect to attend workshops or take courses are likely to report benefits and positive attitudes about these experiences.

2. Workshops and institutes can be developed around other technologies for instructional improvement—for example, feedback of student ratings of teaching.

3. Faculty members may need ratings feedback to be augmented in ways that address the individual needs of their own teaching. For this reason, personal coaches may be more effective than "classroom" instruction in workshops.

Workshops, seminars, and courses for faculty members are likely to be collegial and interactive. Programs that are extended, or that include systematic follow-up, may be more effective. The empirical comparison by Hativa and Miron gives results favoring sustained consultation over workshops; this finding suggests that faculty workshops should be structured in ways that let them address the specific teaching needs of individual faculty members with the help of "coaches." Such programs may be more effective than workshops or courses addressing general topics; these tend to permit some faculty to be passive participants. Future research on faculty development programs at all teaching levels should examine this issue.

Workshops, seminars, and courses which: are *interactive*; involve *sustained engagement* of the faculty; and include a *focus on concrete matters* relevant to the individual faculty member's needs seem likely to give benefits.

Peer Mentoring

Faculty development programs help faculty members at all stages of their academic careers. Robert Boice focuses attention on new faculty members as he documents their experiences over the first few years of their careers. His empirical findings give a bleak picture of overworked young colleagues who, unprepared as teachers, lack confidence and experience teaching as "a surprisingly private experience" about which they receive little guidance from colleagues (Boice 1992, 58). But Boice is optimistic that peer mentoring can bring important benefits to teachers early in their careers.

Arthur Crawley focuses on faculty members who are approaching the ends of their careers. He notes that in 1993, 64 percent of faculty members at all ranks were tenured, and that early in the next century 60 percent of full-time faculty at colleges and universities will be age 50 or older (Crawley 1995b, 71-72). Experts on mentoring believe that peer mentoring is valuable for experienced instructors, including those who serve as mentors.

In her edited volume on mentoring, Marie Wunsch (1994) describes the emergence of faculty mentoring programs in the 1980s as a product of new professional development centers of the 1970s and a strong desire in higher education "to break the barriers to recruitment, retention, tenure and promotion for minority and women faculty" (2). Wunsch identifies nearly 400 articles on mentoring in business and education, published between 1980 and 1990, in the popular press and in academic journals.

Added Value of Mentoring for Teaching Assistants

We found few *controlled empirical studies* that examine the impact of peer mentoring programs on teaching improvement. Linda Williams (1991) reports on one such experiment that compared two groups of TAs, all of whom enrolled in a theory and pedagogy course in English composition. In addition, the TAs in the experimental group met with a teaching consultant who observed their teaching three times, and each TA was assigned to peer mentoring by an experienced TA for a 10-week period. The TAs in the control group only enrolled in the course.

Williams (1991, 585) reports several findings:

- Declines in teaching anxiety were significantly greater for the experimental group;

- Based on posttest means for student ratings, the ratings of teaching effectiveness of the experimental group were significantly higher;

- Student ratings of teaching effectiveness in composition for TAs in the experimental group were significantly higher; and

- There were no statistically significant differences between the two groups in the measured changes in their self-appraisals of their teaching.

Williams concludes that the results "seem to make a strong case for adding consultant observations and peer mentoring to training programs that consist primarily of formal instruction" (596). Williams's optimism stems from the positive outcomes for the treatment group on three different comparisons (among four), derived from the strong research design of a controlled experiment.

Comparing Formal Mentoring with Natural Mentoring

Boyle and Boice (1998) report on the development and assessment of two mentoring programs, one for new faculty and one for new graduate teaching assistants. We review here only the findings from the first program, implemented at a large, public, comprehensive university; we omit the details of their matched-pairs research design.

Boyle and Boice's detailed assessment of faculty mentoring focuses largely on compliance with the program and on the level of involvement in systematic mentoring; it does not focus on long-range benefits. Several findings of this empirical study are particularly instructive (Boyle and Boice 1998, 173–77):

- Systematic mentoring works better than spontaneous natural mentoring;

- It is difficult to maintain natural mentor pairings;

- Mentors learn much about mentoring from each other and thus assume broader roles as coaches and models;

- For new faculty, cross-departmental pairings may work best because they help isolate those being mentored from anxieties about their future reviews for promotion; and

- Group meetings provide participants with a sense of campus involvement, especially around the topic of teaching.

Boyle and Boice conclude:

> Effective mentoring . . . begins with institution-wide programs that coach departments in ways to systematically immerse their newcomers in support programs and provide them with a sense of connectiveness (177).

Teammates As Mentors: Help from Critical Friends

Among many new developments in schools is the National School Reform Faculty sponsored by the Annenberg Institute for School Reform at Brown University. Perhaps the basic goal is to get teachers to examine what, how, and why they are teaching and to discuss such matters with one another. To advance this goal, a number of schools have signed up to form Critical Friends Groups. Schools scattered throughout the United States are participating. Group members are peer faculty mentors, and these mentors are also critics.

At each school two or more teachers decide to participate in a regular discussion of their teaching at least once a month. Each group has a coach who helps members out of ruts. They discuss what they are teaching and how they are doing it; they present a lesson to their colleagues in the group; and they get criticism from the members of the group. One finding reported by Bill Nave from his interviews of the first year's experience is that when teachers have decided to review together actual materials produced by their students, the conversations about teaching seem to become deeper and more appreciative of what is happening in the classroom (Miech, Nave, and Mosteller, 1997). Members of the group begin to produce more new ideas, and the critical process becomes more effective. This idea of regular meetings with deliberate criticism could just as well be used at the college level.

Lessons from Effective Mentoring Programs

Mentors are coaches or teammates (or both). Peer mentoring is, by definition, *collegial* and somewhat *collaborative*. A finding about mentoring by Sands, Parson, and Duane (1991) that teachers consider the Friend factor (friendship, emotional support, and advice) particularly important underscores the benefits from the *highly interactive* nature of mentoring. Mentoring programs that are carefully organized and structured are likely to sustain themselves for a longer period of time. They are also likely to have an articulated purpose and a concrete agenda. Boyle and Boice's finding that systematic, institution-wide mentoring programs seem to be more effective is consistent with the view that *focus* is important for faculty development. The success of mentoring relationships, particularly when the mentoring is made formal (instead of "natural" or ad hoc), likely derives in part from its continuing and *sustained* nature.

Action Research

Action research has emerged in the 1990s as another form of college faculty development. It is a collaborative process that has social change as a primary goal. Action research uses repeated cycles of:

- *planning* strategies for action;
- *implementing* the actions;
- *observing* the outcomes; and
- *reflecting* on what can be learned (Kember and Gow 1992, 298)

Using collaborative research characterized by active participation and democratic decision-making, the team repeats the four steps until the goals are achieved or the project is otherwise terminated.

As practiced by those doing research on college teaching, action research often uses collaboration of a teaching consultant with a group of faculty members in an academic department. The team identifies a specific goal for a course or for the department's instructional program. Webb (1996), Kember and Gow (1992), and Kember and McKay (1996) provide background and further details about action research.

Example: Action Research in Diagnostic Radiography

Jan McKay wanted to bring improvement to programs taught by a department of radiography, and David Kember wanted to use action research to help McKay and her colleagues succeed. Kember and McKay (1996) used repeated cycles of action research to integrate theoretical learning from separate subject areas into students' work in the clinical practice of radiography. This application of action research to college teaching was unusual in that it used a controlled experiment. The experiment addressed the clinical training of second-year students working toward the Professional Diploma in Diagnostic Radiography. The experimental and control groups were "naturally" constituted, and the experimental group (but not the control group) was the target of several steps of action research.

This action research produced changes. The experimental group evaluated the clinical placements they attended over three successive periods of clinical training (Kember and McKay 1996, 540). After attending a period of clinical practice, students were brought together (in groups of 14 in the first cycle, and groups of no more than 8 in the second and third cycles of action research) to discuss relevant journal articles and to consider the significance of theoretical learning in clinical practice. After reflection by the instructors, student discussions of problem-solving situations were added in the third cycle.

The impact of the intervention was measured in several ways. These included preintervention and postintervention measures on a standardized questionnaire about study processes, and preintervention and postintervention academic results. Three open-ended questions were given at the end of the intervention; for example, one question was:

> Think back to the experience of ONE of your general clinical placements and discuss how you feel the equipment you used aided or limited the quality of the examinations taken. In your discussion take patient care, radiation protection/dosage, and film quality into account (Kember and McKay 1996, 541).

One strength of this project is its use of student outcomes for assessment. The investigators compared outcomes for the experimental and control groups. Statistically significant differences favoring the treated group were found between the two groups in the results for the open-ended questions, but not in the other measures. The partial successes of this intervention led to additional and more extensive action research projects in the department over a five-year period. Although the subsequent projects were not controlled experiments, they did lead to a substantially revised curriculum.

Kember and McKay emphasize the value of the action research program for faculty development:

> The approach to faculty development we have described treats quality enhancement of teaching as an academic venture consistent with the manner in which faculty are accustomed to conduct research in their discipline. Faculty are encouraged and empowered to assume responsibility for standards and quality enhancement of their own teaching (1996, 551).

Lessons About Action Research for Faculty Development

Our review of an action research project used to change college teaching reveals several features of this approach to development. Action research:

1. Often involves a *partnership* between specialists in a faculty development office and faculty members in an academic department, and it can benefit from strong leadership in the department and a strong desire for change;

2. Has the potential to make substantial *changes in the attitudes* of participating faculty members toward their teaching and their students;

3. Can be effective for *curricular change* as well as for changes in teaching strategies;

4. Encourages a focus on *student* outcomes; and

5. Invites faculty development for instructional improvement to become a collaborative research project that can lead to *scholarly publication.*

Action research is carried out by *teammates*, and a consultant sometimes serves as a *coach.* By definition, it is a collaborative activity. It uses an iterative process that requires the sustained engagement of its participants over several months or years. It is highly focused—on a specific task or research project and its effect on students. Thus, action research demonstrates that faculty development can be effective when it incorporates *collegiality, sustained engagement,* and *a concrete focus.*

Unifying Threads in Development Programs

This section of our report examines and illustrates four types of faculty development programs. For each type, we examine the roles of *collaboration, sustained engagement*, and a specific and *focused agenda.* For some forms of development, especially peer mentoring and action research, the three qualities are largely inherent in the development activities. For other development programs, especially those using consultants or workshops and courses, the development programs become more effective when they incorporate one or more of the three characteristics. Further research on faculty development should examine whether these features support positive learning outcomes.

MEETING THE CHALLENGES:
AN AGENDA FOR TOMORROW

Colleges and universities are increasingly paying attention to their teaching mission. Donald Kennedy, president emeritus of Stanford University, describes a new reform movement in higher education that is leading to a "balanced respect for teaching, including teaching as scholarship . . ." (Kennedy 1995, 15). Arthur Crawley (1995a) reports "rather dramatic evidence that genuine progress has been made at research universities across the country in honoring teaching excellence through changes in their tenure and promotion systems" (65). Patricia Cranton believes that this increased attention to the quality of teaching has led to renewed attention to faculty growth and development

(Cranton 1994, 726). The time seems ripe for giving still greater attention to faculty development, especially as it relates to student outcomes.

The focus of faculty development programs is shifting in directions that hold promise. There is new emphasis on the importance of support by the faculty peer culture for changes in teaching. The faculty rewards system is under scrutiny; its potential role in instructional improvement is not yet well understood and needs careful investigation. Instructional consultants become professional collaborators with their client teachers in research projects that address teaching improvement.

Evidence-Based Instructional Improvement

In addition to attempting to improve their own teaching, college and university instructors should keep up with new ways of teaching their topics. An important development from the United Kingdom is worthy of attention. In support of evidence-based medicine, the authors of the book *Effective Care in Pregnancy and Childbirth* (Chalmers, Enkin, and Keirse 1989) have decided to extend their research and analysis beyond childbirth and care of the mother to all of medicine through an organization called the Cochrane Collaboration. Cochrane was a physician who early called attention to the value of collecting and analyzing all the clinical trials related to a given medical subject.

Some individuals related to the Cochrane Collaboration, including Iain Chalmers, are now proposing that a similar activity be started in the social sciences, including education. If successful, this movement will produce archives and analyses of topics in teaching both school and college courses. Such topics as class size, cooperative learning, higher standards, and multimedia presentations might be evaluated for their contributions to improved teaching.

In a related field, juvenile justice, Anthony Petrocino (Graduate School of Education, Harvard University) recently over a period of a year collected about 300 controlled experiments from the literature. The British government has shown an interest in encouraging the development, and several U.S. scholars are expected to participate (among them Robert F. Boruch, Mark Lipsey, and Anthony Petrocino).

Improvement in Student Learning As the Primary Goal

Cambridge (1996) reports that attention in faculty development is moving from teaching technique and mechanics toward student learning. However, our literature search found few research reports about faculty development that address the effect of development programs on student achievement. The research to date offers much hope, but only limited empirical evidence, that resources used for faculty development can lead to improved college instruction and better student learning. We believe that research projects that seek to link faculty development programs to student educational outcomes should get the highest priority.

This proposed research agenda will not be easy to carry out. Research designs that can lead to credible links between an intervention with faculty members and subsequent student learning outcomes, while perhaps not difficult to imagine, are likely to be difficult to implement. Practical issues including costs and political considerations impose constraints. Light, Singer, and Willett (1990) give advice for planning and carrying out empirical studies in higher education.

Goals for Future Research

Future empirical studies of faculty development programs at the college level should address the following issues:

- comparisons of two or more approaches to faculty development using as the outcome measured changes in student ratings of teaching or changes in student performance on a common examination;
- the effectiveness of development programs targeting departments or other teaching units;
- the use of peer mentoring or of "critical friends" as a vehicle for improving teaching;

- assistance for faculty members in using technology to enhance their teaching;

- evaluation of uses of technology, including multimedia technology, to enhance the delivery of education to diverse audiences.

An Increasing Role for Technology

The accelerating rate of change fueled by advances in technology and electronic communications challenges the nation's faculty—even a faculty in higher education whose job is to create and disseminate new knowledge and to prepare students for an unknown future. As we enter the twenty-first century, such technologies as computer-driven multimedia, electronic searching of remote databases, large-scale simulation, electronic document exchange for collaboration in writing and revision, searches of the World Wide Web, and even web-based courses are no longer exotic; they are fast becoming routine. Although these technologies may pose opportunities for improving instruction, they also present pitfalls. Our disappointments with the "promising" and costly technologies of past decades taught us that the road from promises to actual gains for education is difficult to navigate.

Faculty members are pressed not only to master the new technologies but also to harness them for teaching students. Faculty development programs must give needed support to faculty members as they face these and other challenges in trying to respond to calls for more effectiveness in, and greater accountability for, their teaching. Specialists in educational media and technology need to work closely with skilled and imaginative educational researchers to identify those paths that can lead to real gains for student learning. We should identify those uses of technology that can enhance the delivery of education to diverse student audiences.

ACKNOWLEDGMENTS

This work was funded by a grant from the Andrew W. Mellon Foundation to the American Academy of Arts and Sciences in support of its program, *Initiatives for Children.* Cleo Youtz gave advice on several drafts, and she typed the manuscript and its revisions. We also benefited from suggestions on earlier drafts by several colleagues: John H. Buehler, Jay Emerson, Edward Miech, Lincoln Moses, Bill Nave, and Marjorie Olson. Robert Branch, editor of this Yearbook, raised several questions that helped broaden the focus of the paper.

REFERENCES

Boice, Robert. (1992). *The New Faculty Member: Supporting and Fostering Professional Development.* San Francisco: Jossey-Bass.

Boyle, Peg, and Boice, Bob. (1998). Systematic mentoring for new faculty teachers and graduate teaching assistants. *Innovative Higher Education* 22, 157–79.

Cambridge, Barbara L. (1996). The paradigm shifts: Examining quality of teaching through assessment of student learning. *Innovative Higher Education* 20, 287–97.

Chalmers, Iain, Enkin, M., and Keirse, M. J. N. C., eds. (1989). *Effective Care in Pregnancy and Childbirth.* New York: Oxford University Press.

Cohen, Peter A. (1980). Effectiveness of student-rating feedback for improving college instruction: A meta-analysis of findings. *Research in Higher Education* 13, 321–41.

Cranton, Patricia. (1994). Self-directed and transformative instructional development. *Journal of Higher Education* 65, 726–44.

Crawley, Arthur L. (1995a). Critical tensions in faculty development: A transformation agenda. *Innovative Higher Education* 20, 65–70.

Crawley, Arthur L. (1995b). Senior faculty renewal at research universities: Implications for academic policy development. *Innovative Higher Education* 20, 71–94.

Edgerton, Russell E., Hutchings, Pat, and Quinlan, Kathleen. (1991). *The Teaching Portfolio: Capturing the Scholarship in Teaching.* Washington, DC: American Association for Higher Education.

Emerson, John D., and Mosteller, Frederick. (1998a). Interactive multimedia for college teaching. Part I: A ten-year review of reviews. In *Educational Media and Technology Yearbook 1998.* Edited by Robert M. Branch and Mary Ann Fitzgerald. Englewood, CO: Libraries Unlimited, 43–58.

Emerson, John D., and Mosteller, Frederick. (1998b). Interactive multimedia for college teaching. Part II: Lessons from research in the sciences. In *Educational Media and Technology Yearbook 1998.* Edited by Robert M. Branch and Mary Ann Fitzgerald. Englewood, CO: Libraries Unlimited, 59–74.

Emerson, John D., Mosteller, Frederick, and Youtz, Cleo. (1999). Students can help improve college teaching: A review and an agenda for the statistics profession. In *Statistics for the 21st century.* Edited by C. R. Rao and G Szekely. To appear.

Erickson, Glenn R., and Erickson, Bette L. (1979). Improving college teaching: An evaluation of a teaching consultation procedure. *Journal of Higher Education* 50, 670–83.

Gaff, Jerry G., and Simpson, Ronald D. (1994). Faculty development in the United States. *Innovative Higher Education* 18, 167–76.

Hativa, Nira. (1995). The department-wide approach to improving faculty instruction in higher education: A qualitative evaluation. *Research in Higher Education* 36, 377–413.

Hativa, Nira, and Miron, Mordecai. (1990). Improving instruction of veteran physics professors. *Research in Higher Education* 31, 573–86.

Hoyt, Donald P., and Howard, George S. (1978). The evaluation of faculty development programs. *Research in Higher Education* 8, 25–38.

Kalivoda, Patricia, Sorrell, Geraldine Rogers, and Simpson, Ronald D. (1994). Nurturing faculty vitality by matching institutional interventions with career-stage needs. *Innovative Higher Education* 18, 256–72.

Kember, David, and Gow, Lyn. (1992). Action research as a form of staff development in higher education. *Higher Education*, 23, 297–310.

Kember, David, and McKay, Jan. (1996). Action research into the quality of student learning. *Journal of Higher Education* 67, 528–54.

Kennedy, Donald. (1995). Another century's end, another revolution for higher education. *Change: The Magazine of Higher Learning* 27, 8–15.

Levinson-Rose, Judith, and Menges, Robert J. (1981). Improving college teaching: A critical review of research, *Review of Educational Research* 51, 403–34.

Light, Richard J., Singer, Judith D., and Willett, John B. (1990). *By Design: Planning Research on Higher Education.* Cambridge, MA: Harvard University Press.

Miech, Edward, Nave, Bill, and Mosteller, Frederick. (1997). On CALL: A review of computer-assisted language learning in U.S. colleges and universities. In *Educational Media and Technmlogy Yearbook 1997.* Edited by Robert M. Branch and Barbara B. Minor. Englewood, CO: Libraries Unlimited, 61–84.

Murray, Rowena, and Holmes, Sheena. (1997). Partnerships in staff development: An institutional case-study. *Studies in Higher Education* 22, 67–81.

Neal, Margaret B., and White, Diana L. (1996). Evaluation of an interdisciplinary faculty development program in geriatrics. *Educational Gerontology* 22, 117–40.

Overlock, Terrence H., Sr. (1994). Assessment of employee perceptions of present and future professional development activities at Northern Maine Technical College: Trends and issues in vocational, technical, and occupational education. Ed.D. dissertation. ERIC ED 373815.

Ross, Dorene D., Bondy, Elizabeth, Hartle, Lynn, Lamme, Linda L., and Webb, Rodman B. (1995). Guidelines for portfolio preparation: Implications from an analysis of teaching portfolios at the University of Florida. *Innovative Higher Education* 20, 45–62.

Sands, Roberta G., Parson, L. Alayne, and Duane, Josann. (1991). Faculty mentoring faculty in a public university. *Journal of Higher Education* 62, 174–93.

Tang, Thomas Li-Ping, and Chamberlain, Mitchell. (1997). Attitudes toward research and teaching: Differences between administrators and faculty members. *Journal of Higher Education* 68, 212–27.

Webb, Graham. (1996). *Understanding Staff Development.* Bristol, PA: Society for Research into Higher Education and Buckingham, England: Open University Press.

Williams, Linda Stallworth. (1991). The effects of a comprehensive teaching assistant training program on teaching anxiety and effectiveness. *Research in Higher Education* 32, 585–98.

Wilson, Robert C. (1986). Improving faculty teaching: Effective use of student evaluations and consultants. *Journal of Higher Education* 57, 196–211.

Wunsch, Marie A., ed. (1994). Mentoring Revisited: Making an Impact on Individuals and Institutions. Number 57, *New Directions for Teaching and Learning*, San Francisco: Jossey-Bass.

Network Information Discovery and Retrieval of Educational Materials
GEM

Stuart A. Sutton
Associate Professor
School of Library and Information Science,
University of Washington-Seattle
Senior Research Scientist, Information Institute of Syracuse

Enhanced access to educational materials on the global Internet for the nation's teachers and students was one of President Clinton's second-term goals. In pursuit of this goal, the U.S. Department of Education's National Library of Education (NLE) identified lesson plans and teacher guides as a critical area in which library and information science expertise should be applied in order to improve the organization and accessibility of large collections of educational materials that are already available on various federal, state, university, nonprofit, and commercial Internet sites. The Department and the NLE charged the ERIC Clearinghouse on Information and Technology at Syracuse University (the Clearinghouse) with the task of spearheading a project to develop an operational framework to provide the nation's teachers with "one-stop/any-stop" access to this vast pool of educational materials. The goal of the Gateway to Educational Materials (GEM) project is to achieve this goal through development and deployment of both a metadata element set for describing network-based educational objects and the accompanying technologies and procedures for its use.

The four major technical tasks addressed by the GEM project in the period of its early development were:

1. To define both a semantically rich metadata element set for the controlled description of educational objects on the Internet and domain-specific controlled vocabularies;

2. To develop a concrete syntax and well-specified practices for its application using the HTML specifications prevalent on the World Wide Web (WWW);

3. To design and implement a set of harvesting tools for retrieving the geographically distributed metadata in order to build a singe access point for teachers and students; and

4. To encourage the independent design of a number of WWW interfaces to the GEM metadata.

In addition to building enabling technologies, the Clearinghouse was charged with developing a consortium-based mechanism for the ongoing governance of GEM both as a metadata standard and as a gateway to resources. At the time of this writing the GEM Gateway provides access to nearly 7,000 network-based educational objects in more than 100 significant collections from around the world and is growing rapidly.

Since its beginning in October 1996, GEM has matured along a number of dimensions. Growing national and international interest in an emerging education object economy (EOE) has driven some of those developments. A second set of drivers has been the rapid development of the technologies shaping the WWW and its use. In the following paragraphs, we describe the work accomplished with GEM and foreshadow directions the project is likely to pursue in the near- and long-term.

THE GEM ELEMENT SET: TODAY

From the outset, GEM developed around emerging standards for networked information discovery and retrieval. The Dublin Core (DC) Element Set became the base referent for the GEM element set. When GEM made this decision, DC was very much in its formative stages. The decision was made due to what then appeared to be DC's growing national and international recognition, acceptance, and support. At the time of this writing, "unqualified" DC is moving toward formal standardization through submission of the first of five Requests for Comments (RFC) to the Internet Engineering Task Force. Subsequent RFCs will consider: conventions for embedding unqualified DC elements in HTML files, principles for "qualifying" DC elements, encoding qualified DC elements in HTML, and encoding qualified DC elements in RDF (Resource Description Framework). NISO and ISO standardization initiatives are also under consideration.

One of the underlying assumptions of the Dublin Core founders was that it would be extensible in two fundamental ways: additional elements could be added to the original 15 in order to meet the needs of particular communities of use, and its elements could be enriched through the use of a broad range of qualifying "schemes" and "subelements"—what are known as the "Canberra Qualifiers" (Weibel, Iannella, and Cathro 1997). The GEM element set is an example of the use of both of these extensions.

A GEM package of 8 elements was added to the 15-element Dublin Core package in order to meet the specific needs of people searching for educational objects. The following two tables contain the complete GEM element set.

TABLE 1. Dublin Core Element Set.

Dublin Core Element	Label	Description
Title	Title	The name given the object by the creator or publisher
Author or Creator	Creator	The person/organization primarily responsible for the intellectual content of the object (author, cinematographer, etc.)
Subjects and Keywords	Subject	The topic or discipline of the educational object
Description	Description	A textual description of the content of the object (e.g., an abstract)
Publisher	Publisher	The entity responsible for making the object available
Other Contributor	Contributor	Secondary contributors to the intellectual content (e.g., editor)
Date	Date	The date the resource was made available in its present form
Resource Type	Type	The category of the object
Format	Format	The data format of the object
Resource Identifier	Identifier	A string or number that uniquely identifies the object (e.g., a URL)
Source	Source	Information about any work from which this object was derived
Language	Language	Language of the intellectual content of the object
Relation	Relation	The relationship of this object to other object
Coverage	Coverage	The spatial and/or temporal characteristics of the object
Rights Management	Rights	A link to copyright and/or use restriction statements

TABLE 2. GEM Element Set Extensions to the Dublin Core.

GEM Element	Label	Description
Audience	Audience	Information that identifies the intended audience of the object
Cataloging Agency	Cataloging	The person/organization responsible for creating the metadata record
Duration	Duration	Time needed to effectively use the object
Essential Resources	Resources	Additional resources essential to the effective use of the object
Educational Level	Grade	Grade, grade span, or educational level of the object's audience
Pedagogy	Pedagogy	Teaching and assessment methods, student instructional groupings, and learning prerequisites
Quality Assessments	Quality	An assessment of the quality of the object
Educational Standards	Standards	State and/or national academic standards mapped to the object

In addition, a number of GEM controlled vocabularies and format schemes were defined. Based on the principles of the Canberra Qualifiers, many of the elements have an array of subelements that modify their semantics (e.g., the Creator element may contain contact information such as telephone numbers and e-mail addresses). The Quality and Standards elements may exist independent of the descriptive metadata for an object, thus permitting third-party agencies with appropriate expertise to handle quality assessments and mapping of resources to state and national academic standards.

CREATING GEM METADATA

While GEM metadata can be created with any text editor, a metadata-generating tool called GEMCat was developed to ease the process of creation by making it possible for the metadata creator to focus solely on content. A freely available Java implementation of the program allows it to operate on any computer platform.

At this time, the storage of GEM metadata is handled in one of two ways. First, where the object being described is an HTML-tagged document, the GEM metadata can be saved as meta tags within the object. Where internal storage of the metadata is either not possible or undesirable, it can be saved as meta tags in a separate HTML document that references the object being described.

Because HTML currently rests at the heart of the WWW, GEM has focused on the evolution of HTML and other significant standards initiatives of the World Wide Web Consortium. From the beginning of the Dublin Core dialog, it has been recognized that only the simplest implementations can be accommodated effectively by HTML 2.0 meta tags (see Weibel, Iannella, and Cathro 1997). Given the HTML 2.0 limitation of relevant meta elements to NAME and CONTENT, there was no other means for dealing with additional information (e.g., Canberra Qualifier "schemes" and "subelements") than through what is called "overloading content" (Weibel, Iannella, and Cathro 1997) of the form: <META NAME="DC.subject" CONTENT="(SCHEME=LCSH) (LANG=en) Computer Cataloging of Network Resources">. The current syntax of GEMCat is based on content overload.

HTML 4.0 comes close to eliminating the content overload problem through the addition of SCHEME and LANG elements. The following GEM metadata example illustrates the same information in the example above in HTML 4.0 meta tags: <META NAME="DC.subject" SCHEME="LCSH" LANG="en" CONTENT="Computer Cataloging of Network Resources">

DISTRIBUTING GEM METADATA

As the Web matures as a publishing environment and generally accepted metadata schemes serving specific subject and practice domains evolve, the existing (and future) general-purpose WWW crawling programs such as AltaVista, Excite, InfoSeek, Lycos and Webcrawler will provide increasingly efficient and effective access to information. In addition to these general retrieval services, a number of services fashioned to meet the needs of specific domains are also emerging (Dempsey 1996). Readily available tools make local "harvesting" of metadata possible, and their extension to multiple websites serving a specific community (such as that served by GEM) have been demonstrated (Beckett and Smith 1996). Based on these models, GEM metadata can be distributed through two mechanisms: through future harvesting by general-purpose web crawlers, and through harvesting of select repositories by means of a GEM harvester. The result of the GEM harvest is the GEM Union Catalog (GUC) that provides access through the GEM Gateway to the collections of a consortium of high integrity repositories.

The rationale for the GUC can be found in the following observation of Lagoze, Lynch, and Daniel in their exploration of issues surrounding the Dublin Core (1996, 6):

> [T]he use of the Dublin Core in a limited context might produce very positive results. For example, assume a set of "high-integrity sites." Administrators at such sites might tag their documents . . . with Dublin Core metadata elements using a set of well-specified practices that include relatively controlled vocabularies and regular syntax. Retrieval effectiveness across these high-integrity sites would probably be significantly better (assuming harvesting and retrieval tools that make use of the metadata) than the unstructured searches available now through Lycos and Alta Vista.

The growing GEM Consortium of more than 100 Internet-based collection holders is just such a set of "high-integrity sites."

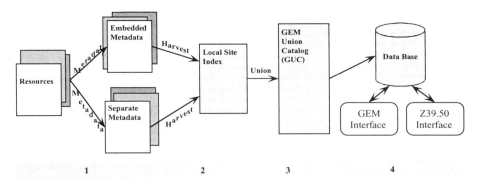

Figure 1. The GEM Architecture.

The technical scope of GEM's four logical processes are noted at the bottom of Figure 1. In process 1, we see the creation of metadata describing WWW-based objects and the storage of that metadata at the collection holder's network-accessible site. Process 2 is the "first-level" harvesting of the metadata from the individual records at the collection holder's site into a single site index for that collection. The third process is the "second-level" harvest of the various local site indexes of GEM metadata to form the single GUC. The final process is the creation of the user interface to the metadata, and, through the metadata, end-user access to the objects themselves.

GEM METADATA: TOMORROW

The private sector is rapidly positioning itself to play major roles in an emerging economy in educational objects on the Internet: the education object economy (EOE). Participants include the publishers of educational resources and the developers of course management (e.g., WebCT, Blackboard, TopClass) and enterprise (e.g., PeopleSoft) systems. Initiatives such as EDUCAUSE's National Learning Infrastructure Initiative (NLII) and the European Union Commission's Alliance of Remote Instructional Authoring and Distribution Networks for Europe (ARIADNE) project signal partnerships among private sector providers of educational resources, major educational institutions, and professional organizations to encourage development of the EOE. As a result, a new emphasis on markets and profit is emerging that will stand beside the culture of cooperation and collaboration that has characterized the domain of educational resources on the Internet in the past. The recent signing into law of the Digital Millennium Copyright Act of 1998 (Pub. L. 105-304) partially paves the way for the full development of the EOE by providing legal protections against both circumventing technical mechanisms protecting copyright interests in digital works and tampering with intellectual property rights information.

In order for the emerging digital publishing and course management/enterprise systems to interoperate, they must be based on some level of metadata standardization. Major national and international efforts are underway to create metadata element sets for cross-domain information discovery and retrieval. The Dublin Core was the first of these efforts. Recently, the ISO/IEC Joint Technical Committee created Sub-Committee 32, Working Group 2 (Metadata), which is responsible for standards that facilitate the specification and management of metadata to enhance interoperability in support of electronic commerce and component-based development.

The creation of education-specific metadata element sets has been the goal of both a number of government-sponsored and private-sector initiatives in the United States. GEM provides a good example of the former, while the EDUCAUSE-sponsored Instructional Management System (IMS) project is an excellent example of the latter. The Learning Object Metadata Group (LOMG) of the National Institute of Standards and Technology is spearheading a project to bring together collaborators, key individuals, and organizations to develop a metadata standard for learning objects. The work of the IEEE P1484.12 Learning Objects Metadata Working Group is closely paralleling that of IMS.

A number of projects abroad have developed metadata schemes to improve WWW access to educational resources. The Education Network Australia (EdNA) has developed an extensive metadata scheme to facilitate access to educational resources throughout Australia. Like GEM, EdNA's element set is rooted in the Dublin Core. The ARIADNE project, sponsored by the European Union Commission and the Swiss Federal Office for Education and Science, is a well-established European metadata effort. ARIADNE, IMS, and IEEE 1484.12 are working to harmonize their efforts in order to achieve a single standard for describing educational objects. As an investment partner in IMS, GEM is part of this standards-making effort.

While these efforts at metadata standardization have been advancing, the World Wide Web Consortium's work on both the Resource Description Framework (RDF) (see Iannella 1997) and Extensible Markup Language (XML) (see Bray, Paoli, and Sperberg-McQueen 1997) point the way toward a potentially rich structural environment for GEM metadata and mark the migration path for GEMCat and the enabling technologies of the GEM Gateway. Already under development, GEMCat 4.0 will generate metadata that will: fully comport with the emerging IEEE

1484.12 standard, be backward compatible with existing GEM metadata, be designed for syntactic bindings in XML/RDF, and be cross-walked to DC and MARC.

CONCLUSION

As the World Wide Web grows exponentially, discovery and retrieval of useful educational materials grows more problematic. The GEM project seeks to meet the needs of educators, students, and parents through development and wide deployment of the GEM standard, an accompanying set of controlled vocabularies, and a well-defined set of practices in their application. In addition, the GEM Union Catalog and its companion Gateway promise enhanced "one-stop/any-stop" access to Internet-based educational materials. The developmental work of the first phase of the project is largely complete. Full-scale application of GEM by Consortium members has begun.

REFERENCES

Beckett, D., and Smith, N. (1996, May). The ACademic DireCtory—AC/DC. *Ariadne.* Internet journal at URL: http://www.ariadne.ac.uk/issue3/acdc/

Bray, T., Paoli, J., and Sperberg-McQueen, C. (1997). Extensible markup language (XML): W3C working draft 07-Aug-97. Internet page at URL: http://www.w3.org/TR/WD-xml-lang

Dempsey, L. (1996, May). Meta detectors. *Ariadne.* Internet journal at URL: http://www.ariadne.ac.uk/issue3/metadata/

Iannella, R. (1997, Aug.). Application of RDF for extensible Dublin Core metadata. Internet page at URL: http://www.dstc.edu.au/RDU/RDF/rdf-dc-app-19970808.html

Lagoze, C., Lynch, C., and Daniel, R. (1996). The Warwick framework: A container architecture for aggregating sets of metadata. TR96-1593. Internet page at URL: http://www.ifla.org/documents/libraries/cataloging/metadata/tr961593.pdf

Weibel, S., Iannella, R., and Cathro, W. (1997, June). The 4th Dublin Core metadata workshop report." *D-Lib Magazine.* Internet journal at URL: http://www.dlib.org/dlib/june97/metadata/06weibel.html.

Tools for Automating Instructional Design

Abby Kasowitz
Project Specialist for KidsConnect
and Virtual Reference Desk
Information Institute of Syracuse

Reprinted from ERIC® Digest, June 1998, EDO-IR-98-01

Instructional design (ID) is the systematic process of planning events to facilitate learning. The ID process encompasses a set of interdependent phases including analysis of learners, contexts and goals; design of objectives, strategies and assessment tools; production of instructional materials; and evaluation of learner performance and overall instructional design effort (Gagne, Briggs, & Wager, 1992).

PURPOSE OF AUTOMATED INSTRUCTIONAL DESIGN TOOLS

Automated instructional design (AID) tools assist instructional designers and others in creating instructional products to improve learning. AID systems aid in the production of courseware (Gros & Spector, 1994), or in the development of computer-based instruction (CBI), although some tools guide users in general decision-making that can apply to a range of instructional products and solutions.

AID tools may eliminate some physical ID tasks such as storyboarding and test generation (Muraida & Spector, 1993). However, the strength of AID tools lies in their ability to guide novices and non-ID professionals through the process of creating effective instruction (Tennyson & Barron, 1995; Chapman, 1995). AID tools are especially useful in situations where instructional design expertise is lacking and subject-matter experts and others are responsible for developing instruction [as seen in military courseware development (Muraida & Spector, 1993)].

TYPES OF AID TOOLS

This Digest focuses on four types of tools that guide users through the ID process: expert systems, advisory systems, information management systems, and electronic performance support systems. Authoring tools are also mentioned as popular mechanisms for supporting the production of computer-based instruction. Some tools contain features representing more than one type of system.

- **Expert Systems:** An expert system contains a domain-specific knowledge-base and performs decision-making and analysis functions for the designer using natural language queries (Schwier & Misanchuk, 1993). Expert systems for instructional design have been developed to provide advice to novice instructional designers (Locatis & Park, 1992) and to facilitate the development process for experienced designers.

ID Expert from the ID2 Research Group (Cline & Merrill, 1995) was created to develop and deliver computer-based instruction more efficiently. *ID Expert* is based on Instructional Transaction Theory, a "second generation" theory of instructional design (Cline & Merrill, 1995; Merrill et al, 1996; Locatis & Park, 1992). According to Instructional Transaction Theory, instruction is based on transactions (sets of interactions) between the system and the learner in order to accomplish a given task. *ID Expert* assists designers in creating transactions by presenting a set of decision-making steps involving instructional components, formatting, resources, etc. *ID Expert* is considered a prototype system and has not yet been released commercially (Merrill, 1997).

The United States Air Force Armstrong Laboratory proposed two AID approaches that use expert system technology to provide expertise to novice instructional designers and subject matter experts in the design, production, and implementation of courseware used in Air Force training (Spector & Song, 1995). *Guided Approach to Instructional Design Advising* (GAIDA) uses tutorials and context-specific advice and examples. *Experimental Advanced Instructional Design Advisor* (XAIDA) uses the Instructional Transaction Theory framework to encapsulate context-specific knowledge. Both of these environments are results of the Advanced Instructional Design Advisor (AIDA) research project (Muraida & Spector, 1993; Spector et al, 1991).

Reactions to Expert Systems: While expert systems for instructional design can teach theory validation and function as authoring tools, they are limited by their inability to support analysis and design tasks (Paquette et al, 1994). ID expert systems attempt to control the instructional design process, a process involving a large number of interrelated elements, and so must rely heavily on the knowledge and experience of the individual practitioner (Duchastel, 1990). Several instructional technologists have proposed systems that more subtly advise the instructional designer, rather than prescribe a set of solutions. Some examples are described below.

- **Advisory Systems:** Duchastel (1990) challenges the expert system model by providing an advisory system model. Instead of controlling the problem-solving process with expert knowledge, advisory systems assist or coach users in accomplishing a given task. A prototype for the advisory system approach is the *Instructional Design Advanced Workbench*, an architecture for a computer-based workbench that supports the cognitive tasks of instructional design without constraining the designer.

- **Information Management Systems:** *Instructional Design Environment* (IDE) from the Institute for Research on Learning (Russell & Pirolli, 1992) is a computer-aided design environment that supports an ID methodology for teaching the use of software in real-life problem-solving contexts. *IDE* helps document design and development options (Locatis & Park, 1992). It is intended for experienced instructional designers (Muraida & Spector, 1993).

- **Electronic Performance Support Systems:** Electronic performance support systems (EPSS) are self-instructional electronic enviponments that provide access to "software, guidance, advice, data, tools, and assessment with minimum support and intervention by others" (Milheim, 1997, 103). EPSS have become popular in the 1990s for business and educational contexts that require "just-in-time" learning and a high level of a particular skill (Milheim, 1997; Leighton, 1996). Some examples of EPSS are listed below.

Building on Duschastel's "workbench," Paquette et al (1994) introduced a performance support system called *AGD* (a French acronym meaning Didactic Engineering Workbench). *AGD* provides procedural instructional design information to guide users in defining the learning system (e.g., analyzing training needs, designing pedagogical structures). *AGD* includes a rules-based advisory component that offers advice regarding specific design decisions made by users (e.g., amount and nature of objectives).

Other performance support systems tools include *Designer's Edge* from Allen Communication (Chapman, 1995) and *Instructional DesignWare* from Langevin Learning Services (Langevin Learning Services). Like *AGD*, these tools support the planning phases of instructional design, but contain a much more general advisory component (e.g., context-specific online help, wizards, and tutorials).

In contrast to *AGD*, *Designer's Edge* and *Instructional DesignWare* lead designers through all tasks involved in instructional design, but place more emphasis on the ultimate production phase. Both tools provide a graphical representation of the instructional systems design model, thus leading to additional support for completing each step of the model. Data entered by users are cross-referenced with all steps to enhance continuity between phases. Usable reports and documents such as evaluation instruments, content outlines, lesson plans, and checklists can be generated by the users.

The primary difference between the two products lies in their intended audiences and purposes. *Designer's Edge* is for both novice and experienced instructional designers planning computer-based instruction. The product includes support for scripts, storyboards and other CBI production needs. Integration with external software applications is also supported (Allen Communication, 1997). *Instructional DesignWare* is intended for course designers and trainers interested in producing either computer-based or classroom training. For this reason, more support is provided for decisions regarding media selection and course and presentation materials (Langevin Learning Services).

AUTHORING TOOLS

Although they do not necessarily support the preliminary planning stages of instructional design, instructional designers use authoring tools in the development phase to produce computer-based instruction (Paquette et al, 1994; Locatis & Park, 1992; Merrill, 1997). Some authoring tools take advantage of the World Wide Web by providing features that integrate Web content into computer-based instruction and deliver instruction over the Web (e.g., WebCT).

According to Merrill (1997), authoring tools simplify the programming process and allow experienced users to create effective and visually-appealing instruction, but require a steep learning curve in order to take full advantage of their features. Current popular authoring tools include Macromedia *Authorware 4.0*, Aim Tech *IconAuthor*, WBT Systems *TopClass*, and Asymetrix *Toolbook*.

SUMMARY

Some AID tools support instructional design by focusing on the cognitive aspects of instructional design (e.g., *ID Expert*, *AGD*, etc.). Some highlight the procedural steps of ID (e.g., *Designer's Edge*, *Instructional DesignWare*). Others support the production phase only (i.e., authoring tools for computer-based instruction).

In general, AID tools that support the planning and evaluation phases of ID are not as widely used by practitioners as tools that focus on the authoring and media production phases (Chapman, 1995). One exception may be *Designer's Edge* which has been cited as one of the most popular CBT authoring tools despite its intended purpose as a pre-authoring system (Kemske, 1997). Regardless of its strength or approach, the value of a particular tool or type of system is measured by how well it can support a particular designer's task (Gros & Spector, 1994).

REFERENCES/SUGGESTED READINGS

Allen Communication. (1997). *Designer's Edge Features*. Allen Communication. Internet WWW page, at URL: <http://www.allencomm.com/software/designer/features.html> (version current at 13 March 1998).

Chapman, B. L. (1995). Accelerating the design process: A tool for instructional designers. *Journal of Interactive Instructional Development, 8*(2), 8–15. (EJ 520 294)

Cline, R. W., and Merrill, M. D. (1995). Automated instructional design via instructional transactions. In Robert D. Tennyson & Ann E. Baron, (Eds.), *Automating instructional design: Computer-based development and delivery tools* (pp. 317–353). New York: Springer-Verlag.

Duchastel, P. C. (1990). Cognitive design for instructional design. *Instructional Science, 19*(6), 437-444. (EJ 423 422)

Gagne, R. M., Briggs, L. J., and Wager, W. W. (1992). *Principles of instructional design*. 4th ed. Fort Worth, TX: Harcourt Brace Jovanovich.

Gros, B., and Spector, J. M. (1994). Evaluating automated instructional design systems: A complex problem. *Educational Technology, 34*(5), 37–46. (EJ 483 719)

Kemske, F. (1997). *The CBT software market.* Internet WWW page, at URL: <http://www-euro.macromedia.com/software/authorware/reviews.html> (version current 13 March 1998).

Langevin Learning Services. *Langevin Instructional DesignWare.* Internet WWW page, at URL: <http://www.langevin.com/designware.shtml> (version current 5 August 1998).

Leighton, C. (1996). *What Is an EPSS?* Internet WWW page, at URL: <http://itech1.coe.uga.edu/EPSS/Whatis.html> (version current at 13 March 1998).

Locatis, C., and Park, O. (1992). Some uneasy inquiries into ID expert systems. *ETR&D, 40*(3), 87–94. (EJ 462 856)

Merrill, M. D., and ID2 Expert Group (1996). Instructional transaction theory: Instructional design based on knowledge objects. *Educational Technology, 36*(3), 30–37. (EJ 524 804)

Merrill, M. D. (1997). Learning-oriented instructional development tools. *Performance Improvement, 36*(3), 51–55. (EJ 544 730)

Milheim, W. (1997). Instructional design issues for electronic performance support systems. *British Journal of Educational Technology, 28*(2), 103–110. (EJ 544 668)

Muraida and Spector (1993). The advanced instructional design advisor. *Instructional Science, 21*(4), 239–253. (EJ 464 301)

Paquette, G., Aubin, C., and Crevier, F. (1994). An intelligent support system for course design. *Educational Technology, 34*(9), 50–57. (EJ 493 315)

Russell, D. M., and Pirolli, P. (1992). *Computer assisted instructional design for computer-based instruction.* Final Report. Working Papers. Berkeley, CA: National Center for Research in Vocational Education. (ED 354 872)

Schwier, R. A., and Misanchuk, E. R. (1993). *Interactive multimedia instruction.* Englewood Cliffs, NJ: Educational Technology Publications.

Spector, J. M., Muraida, D. J., and Marlino, M. R. (1991). *Modeling user interactions with instructional design software.* Paper presented at the Annual Meeting of the American Educational Research Association, Chicago, IL. (ED 332 695)

Spector, J. M., and Song, D. (1995). Automated instructional design advising. In Robert D. Tennyson & Ann E. Baron (Eds.), *Automating instructional design: Computer-based development and delivery tools*, (pp. 377–402). New York: Springer-Verlag.

Tennyson, R. D., and Barron, A. E. (1995). Automating instructional design: An introduction. In Robert D. Tennyson and Ann E. Barron (Eds.), *Automating instructional design: Computer-based development and delivery tools* (pp. 1–10). New York: Springer-Verlag.

The Benefits of Information Technology

John Kosakowski
AskERIC Network Information Specialist

Reprinted from ERIC® Digest, June 1998, EDO-IR-98-94

More than three decades ago, computers and related information technologies were introduced to educators as educational tools. Today, there are computers of various descriptions in nearly all schools in the United States. Teachers, school administrators, government officials, and others faced with the costs involved in technology implementation must constantly evaluate the educational benefits of technology. Is there research or other evidence that indicates computers and advanced telecommunications are worthwhile investments for educators? This Digest summarizes the observed benefits of technology implementation. The importance of evaluating the effects of technology on learning is also addressed.

APPLICATIONS OF TECHNOLOGY TO BASIC SKILLS

Using educational technology for drill and practice of basic skills can be highly effective according to a large body of data and a long history of use (Kulik, 1994). Students usually learn more, and learn more rapidly, in courses that use computer assisted instruction (CAI). This has been shown to be the case across all subject areas, from preschool to higher education, and in both regular and special education classes. Drill and practice is the most common application of CAI in elementary education, the military, and in adult educational settings. Fletcher, et al (1990) reports that in the military, where emphasis is on short and efficient training time, the use of CAI can cut training time by one third. In the military, CAI can also be more cost-effective than additional tutoring, reduced class size, or increased instruction time to attain equivalent educational gains.

APPLICATIONS OF TECHNOLOGY TO ADVANCED SKILLS

The application of educational technologies to instruction has progressed beyond the use of basic drill and practice software, and now includes the use of complex multimedia products and advanced networking technologies. Today, students use multimedia to learn interactively and work on class projects. They use the Internet to do research, engage in projects, and to communicate. The new technologies allow students to have more control over their own learning, to think analytically and critically, and to work collaboratively. This "constructivist" approach is one effort at educational reform made easier by technology, and perhaps even driven by it. Traditional lecture methods are often left behind as students collaborate and teachers facilitate. Students, who often know more about technology than the teacher are able to assist the teacher with the lesson. Since this type of instructional approach, and the technologies involved with it, are recent developments, it is hard to gauge their educational effects. Still, an increasing body of evidence as presented by Bialo and Sivin-Kachala (1996) for example, suggests positive results. The Apple Classrooms of Tomorrow (Dwyer, 1994), a 10-year project where students and teachers were each given two computers, one for school and one for home, illustrates some of the gains made in students' advanced skills. ACOT reports that students:

- Explored and represented information dynamically and in many forms,

- Became socially aware and more confident,

- Communicated effectively about complex processes,
- Became independent learners and self-starters,
- Worked well collaboratively,
- Knew their areas of expertise and shared expertise spontaneously, and
- Used technology routinely and appropriately.

Another effort called the Buddy Project (Indiana's Fourth Grade, 1990) supplied students with home computers and modem access to school. Positive effects included:

- An increase in writing skills,
- Better understanding and broader view of math,
- Ability to teach others, and
- Greater problem solving and critical thinking skills.

EFFECTS OF TECHNOLOGY ON STUDENT ATTITUDES

Numerous studies over the years, summarized by Bialo and Sivin-Kachala (1996), report other benefits enjoyed by students who use technology. These benefits involve attitudes toward self and toward learning. The studies reveal that students feel more successful in school are more motivated to learn and have increased self confidence and self esteem when using CAI. This is particularly true when the technology allows the students to control their own learning. It's also true across a variety of subject areas, and is especially noteworthy when students are in at-risk groups (special education, students from inner-city or rural schools).

ON-LINE TECHNOLOGIES

The Internet and advanced networking technologies are comparative newcomers to the classroom. Efforts such as Net Day and e-rate discounts enacted by the Telecommunications Act (Telecommunications Act, 1996) make it easier for many classrooms around the country to connect to the Internet. Although a large body of research on the effects of the Internet in the classroom does not yet exist, recent studies illustrate some observed positive effects. A study by the Center for Applied Special Technology (1996) shows significantly higher scores on measures of information management, communication, and presentation of ideas for experimental groups with on-line access than for control groups with no access. Also, students in the experimental group reported significantly increased use of computers in four different areas—gathering information, organizing and presenting information, doing multimedia projects, and obtaining help with basic skills.

USE OF TECHNOLOGY BY TEACHERS AND ADMINISTRATORS

Teachers and administrators use computer and information technologies to improve their roles in the educational process. Some examples include:

- Using computer tools to streamline record keeping and administrative tasks, thereby helping to free up time for instruction or professional development,
- Decreasing isolation by using E-mail and the Internet to communicate with colleagues, parents, and the outside world, and
- Increasing professional development activities by taking distance education courses, accessing educational research, and accessing classroom materials such as lesson plans.

FACTORS THAT HELP TECHNOLOGY SUCCEED

Some of the observed benefits associated with educational technology have been reviewed above, but what are the factors that help technology succeed in bringing about these benefits? Glenna & Melmed (1996) and the Technology Counts analysis suggest the following factors observed in successful technology-rich schools:

- **Evidence of a detailed technology plan.** Such a plan should consider funding, installation and integration of equipment, ongoing management of the technology. The plan should also express a clear vision of the goals of the technology integration.

- **Teacher training and continuing education.** Teachers should know how to operate the technology and how to integrate it into the curriculum.

- **Support from administration.** Administrative support can come in the form of funding, or in restructuring schedules and physical space to reflect the new learning environment.

- **Support from the community.** Parents, businesses, and community members can use technology as a springboard to become more involved in the activities of neighborhood schools. All can help with wiring or technical support. Parents can use e-mail to facilitate communication with teachers and administrators. Businesses can use e-mail to help mentor students and help them prepare for the workplace.

- **Support from government.** Adequate funding and appropriate policy making can help to assure that technology is accessible to all schools on an equal basis.

These factors suggest that to succeed, technology, like any educational tool, cannot exist in isolation, but must be made an integral part of the entire instructional process.

EVALUATING THE IMPACT OF TECHNOLOGY

Traditional methods of evaluating the effectiveness of educational technology present a number of problematic issues. Glenna & Melmed (1996) state these succinctly:

- Most available tests do not reliably measure the outcomes being sought. The measures that are reported are usually from traditional multiple-choice tests. New measures need to be developed which would assess the higher-level skills and other effects often affected by technology

- Assessments of the impact of technology are really assessments of the instructional processes enabled by technology, and the outcomes are highly dependent on the quality of the implementation of the entire instructional process. Crucial elements include instructional design, content, and teaching strategies associated with both the software and the classroom environment

- The very dynamic nature of technology makes meaningful evaluation difficult. By the time long-term studies are completed, the technology being evaluated is often outdated.

The U.S. Department of Education and Educational Testing Service (ETS) report that new methods of evaluation that look at technology in context are being investigated. These methods will focus ideally not on the question "Does technology work?" but rather on how it impacts the various components of the educational process.

SUMMARY

Technology has been shown to have positive effects on the instructional process, on basic and advanced skills. Technology is also changing the instructional process itself. To be effective, technology cannot exist in a vacuum, but must become part of the whole educational environment. New measures of evaluation are under development which would help to better define the role of technology in its wider context.

BIBLIOGRAPHY AND FURTHER READING

Bialo, E. R., and Sivin-Kachala, J. (1996). *The effectiveness of technology in schools: A summary of recent research.*Washington, DC: Software Publishers Association.

Birman, B., and others. (January, 1997). *The effectiveness of using technology in K–12 education: A preliminary framework and review*, Washington, DC: American Institutes for Research.

Center for Applied Special Technology. (1996). *The role of online communications in schools: A national study*. Peabody, MA: CAST. Internet WWW page, at URL: <http://www.cast.org/stsstudy.html> (version current at October 1998).

Dwyer, D. (April, 1994). Apple classrooms of tomorrow: What we've learned. *Educational Leadership, 51*(7), 4–10 . (EJ 508 281)

Education week on the web. *Technology counts: Schools and reform in the information age. A special report.* Internet WWW page, at URL: <http://www.edweek.org/sreports/tc/> (version current at April 1998)

Fletcher, J. D., Hawley, D. E., and Piele, P. K. (1990). Costs, effects, and utility of microcomputer assisted instruction in the classroom. *American Educational Research Journal, 27*, 783–806.

Glenna, T. K., and Melmed, A. (1996). *Fostering the use of educational technology: Elements of a national strategy. A Rand Report.* Santa Monica, CA: Rand. Internet WWW page, at URL: <http://www.rand.org/publications/MR/MR682/contents.html> (version current at April 1998).

Indiana's fourth grade project: Model applications of technology. Second Year, 1989–90. (1990). Indiana State Dept. of Education. Indianapolis: Advanced Technology, Inc. (ED 343 550) Internet WWW page, at URL: <http://www.buddynet.net/> (version current at April 1998).

Krendl, K. A., and Clark, G. (Spring, 1994).The impact of computers on learning: Research on in-school and out-of-school settings. *Journal of Computing in Higher Education, 5*(2), 85–112. (EJ 479 669)

Kulik, J. A. (1994). Meta-analytic studies of findings on computer-based instruction. In E. L. Baker and H. F. O'Neil, Jr. (Eds.), *Technology assessment in education and training*. Hillsdale, NJ: Lawrence Erlbaum.

Mann, D., and Shakeshaft, C. (1997). *The impact of technology in the schools of the Mohawk Regional Information Center Area. Technical Report.* Verona, NY:Mohawk Regional Information Center. (ED 405 893)

Poirot, J. L., and Knezek, G. A. (Nov, 1992). Experimental designs for determining the effectiveness of technology in education. *Computing Teacher, 20*(3), 8–9. (EJ 454 689)

Telecommunications Act of 1996. (1996). Congress of the U.S., Washington, DC. (ED 395 583)

Thompson, A. D., Simonson, M. R., and Hargrave, C. P. (1996). *Educational technology: A review of the research.* Second edition. Washington, DC: Association for Educational Communications and Technology.

U.S. Department of Education. (1996). *Getting America's students ready for the 21st century: Meeting the technology literacy challenge*. Washington, DC: U.S. Department of Education. Internet WWW page, at URL: <http://www.ed.gov/Technology/Plan/NatTechPlan/> (version current at April 1998).

U.S. Department of Education. *Using technology to support education reform*. Washington, DC: U.S. Department of Education. Internet WWW page, at URL: <http://www.ed.gov/pubs/EdReformStudies/TechReforms/> (version current at April 1998).

E-rate
A Resource Guide for Educators

David Fulton
AskERIC Network Information Specialist

Reprinted from ERIC® Digest, June 1998, EDO-IR-98-07

On May 7, 1997, the Federal Communications Commission (FCC) adopted a Universal Service Order outlining a plan to guarantee that all eligible schools, libraries, and rural health care providers have affordable connections to the Internet. By making $2.5 billion available annually, this program will provide discounts (commonly known as the E-rate) to eligible organizations on certain telecommunications services. The plan also creates a $400 million fund to lower the prices rural health care providers pay for telecommunications services.

This digest lists resources containing background information, instructions, application forms, help lines and other useful information related to the E-rate. Readers should be aware that the resources and their Internet addresses below, while correct at printing, are subject to change.

WEB SITES

The Schools and Libraries Corporation (SLC)

SLC is the independent not-for-profit corporation established to administer the E-rate. Schools and libraries can file their applications electronically from the SLC Web site. Those who choose to file manually are welcome to mail their applications to Schools and Libraries Corp., P.O. Box 4217, Iowa City, IA 52244-4217. All schools and libraries who file applications for the program will have the technology services they requested posted on the Web site in order to invite competitive bidding from vendors. The Web site operates every day from 5:00 a.m. to midnight Eastern Time and includes FAQ's, a discount matrix, and fund status. In the Service Provider area, vendors can search the posted applications, and users can directly download a report of the highlights of services that were requested on Forms 470 and subsequently posted on the Web site for competitive bidding.

E-mail questions to: <question@slcfund.org> or call 888-203-8100.
http://www.slcfund.org

National Exchange Carrier Association (NECA)

The FCC appointed NECA as temporary administrator of the support mechanisms which will fund the Universal Service programs. This site provides information on Service Provider Identification Numbers (SPIN), consortia, eligible services, rules of priority, pre-existing contracts, disbursement of funds, instructions for completing the online forms and an overview of the E-rate program. The site also links to the Rural Health Care Corporation (RHCC), which administers the rural health care aspects of the E-rate.

http://www.neca.org

FCC SITES

For the latest official government information, FCC orders are available electronically from the FCC Universal Service Home Page.
http://www.fcc.gov/ccb/universal_service/

FCC FAQ

Services and Functionalities Eligible for Discounts.
http://www.fcc.gov/Bureaus/Common_Carrier/Public_Notices/1997/da971374.html#2

FCC LearnNet

The FCC's Informal Education Page dealing with FCC policy and education initiatives. Contains press releases, FCC Orders, recent E-rate public notices, and FAQ's. Use the FCC's fax-on-demand system to obtain a document which contains information similar to that on the LearnNet page. Call 202-418-2830 and follow the directions to request that document #8844 be automatically faxed to the number you provide.
http://www.fcc.gov/learnnet/

DEPARTMENT OF EDUCATION SITES

E-Rate Forms

In addition to the two forms (Form FCC 470 and 471), you will find instructions for completing them and an overview of the Universal Service program. The overview provides information on: kinds of schools and libraries that are eligible, consortia (which are also eligible), calculating the discount, classifying urban and rural locations, eligible services, examples of eligible and ineligible internal connections, rules of priority, pre-existing contracts, what schools and libraries must do before applying, the application process, and Web sites to go to for more information.
http://www.ed.gov/Technology/erateforms/

Nine Steps You Can Take Now to Prepare for the Schools and Libraries Universal Service Program

http://www.ed.gov/Technology/ninestep.html

Questions and Answers on Implementation of the Universal Service Program for Schools and Libraries

http://www.ed.gov/Technology/qanda.html

OTHER E-RATE SITES

National Center for Education Statistics School (NCES) Codes

The E-rate application forms require the district or school NCES (National Center for Educational Statistics) code. This site will help you find those codes.
http://nces.ed.gov/ccdweb/school/school.htm

Consortium for School Networking

CoSN, a non-profit organization, promotes the use of telecommunications in K–12 education to improve learning. This site contains recent SLC Fact Sheets, E-Rate forms, and links to state education departments.

http://www.cosn.org/

The Benton Foundation's Universal Service and Universal Access Virtual Library

The Benton Foundation is a nonprofit, nonpartisan, private foundation which seeks to promote communications in the public interest. The Universal Service and Universal Access Virtual Library includes research, history, policy briefings and bulletins.

http://www.benton.org/Policy/Uniserv/

EdLiNC: Education and Library Networks Coalition

EdLiNC was formed to represent the viewpoint of schools and libraries in FCC proceedings dealing with the implementation of the Telecommunications Act of 1996. The EdLiNC Web site includes the latest updates, free publications, action kits, and links to other Universal Service Sites. One of EdLiNC's projects is the E-Rate Hotline, which includes a toll free number for questions: 1-800-733-6860 (10 a.m.-9 p.m. EST), a Web site <http://www.eratehotline.org> which contains a searchable knowledge base of questions, and an online form to send your questions to an E-rate expert.

http://www.itc.org/edlinc/discounts/

Quality Education Data Information on Universal Service Fund

Quality Education Data (QED) is a research and database company, focused exclusively on education. This site provides information on the application process, eligibility, funding, restrictions and program implementation.

http://www.qeddata.com/usfund.htm

3Com "Everything you always wanted to know about the E-rate, but were afraid to ask."

This workbook, produced in cooperation with the Consortium for School Networking, includes a disk with SLC forms, a list of state education departments, a guide to creating a technology plan, and an example of a technology plan.

http://www.3com.com/erate

"The E-rate and Beyond," A Special Report from T.H.E. (Technological Horizons in Education) Journal

This online journal provides links to breaking news, case histories, technology backgrounders, links to technology plans, and more.

http://www.thejournal.com/features/erate/default.asp

American Library Association Office for Information Technology Policy

This site is directed toward public libraries, and includes links to telecommunication legislation, regulations, policies, and state programs.

http://ala.org/oitp/univserv.html

Mid-continent Regional Educational Laboratory (McREL)

McREL operates several regional centers funded by the U.S. Department of Education that provide research, technical assistance, professional development, evaluation and policy studies, and information services to several state and local education agencies. This extensive site includes news, general information and resources, and state and local initiatives.

http://www.mcrel.org/connect/tech/telecom.html

Merit

Merit is a nonprofit membership organization that provides Internet services and expertise to Michigan's educational community, libraries, governments, communities and businesses. A timeline shows the important dates and deadlines for the universal service program. This site also contains a list of services and facilities that are eligible and ineligible for USF discounts, an SLC Fact Sheet on Discount Calculations, examples and suggestions for calculating the discount as well as updates and K–12 and library resources.

http://www.merit.edu/

On-line Seminar: Universal Service/Network Democracy

This site contains information and activities relating to Information Renaissance's Universal Service/Network Democracy online seminar. The seminar is an attempt to involve local teachers and librarians in the implementation process of the Telecommunications Act of 1996 and, specifically, in the development of rules regarding the Act's new Universal Service provisions for schools and libraries.

http://info-ren.pitt.edu/universal-service/

LISTSERV DISCUSSION GROUPS

FCCsend

A one-way (non-interactive) listserver set up to send you e-mail on the FCC's latest updates and suggestions for preparing your school or library to get the most out of communications technology. To subscribe, address an e-mail message in the following manner:

To: subscribe@info.fcc.gov
   sub FCCsend firstname lastname

FCCshare

An interactive listserver through which you can communicate with other students, teachers, librarians, administrators, and parents who are using or prepaping to use technology. To subscribe, address an e-mail message in the following manner:

To: subscribe@info.fcc.gov
   sub FCCshare firstname lastname

edtech

A one-way (non-interactive) listserver set up to send you the text (via e-mail) of Universal Service-related speeches given by FCC Commissioners. To subscribe, address an e-mail message in the following manner:

To: subscribe@info.fcc.gov
   subscribe edtech firstame lastname

COSNDISC On-Line Discussion Forum

This on-line discussion forum is open to everyone on the Internet. It serves as a meeting place for everyone interested in school networking and helps coordinate policy and projects nationwide.

To subscribe to COSNDISC send e-mail to: listproc@cosn.org

In the body of the message include the single line,

"Subscribe cosndisc, your first name, your last name"

MINWG-share

The Michigan Information Network Working Group (MINWG) mailing list answers questions you may have about the Universal Service Fund. All questions are answered by a panel of representatives in the Michigan education and library community.

To subscribe to the MINWG-share mailing list, address an e-mail message to:

Majordomo@merit.edu. Then write

SUBSCRIBE MINWG-share

in the message.

List Archive:

http://www.merit.edu/mail.archives/html/minwg-share/

Internet Relay Chat

Carol Simpson
Assistant Professor
University of North Texas
School of Library and
Information Sciences
Denton, Texas

Reprinted from ERIC® Digest, January 1999, EDO-IR-99-01

INTRODUCTION

While the World Wide Web receives most of the publicity, another aspect of the Internet also draws considerable attention. IRC, more formally referred to as Internet Relay Chat, provides a means by which one user can type a message in real time to one or more Internet users, and almost instantaneously, the message appears on the monitors of all the other users who are monitoring the transmission. They, in turn, can type messages that all the others may read. These electronic "conversations" run the gamut from general chit-chat to exchanges of highly specific scientific or technical information, to conversations between school children and guest authorities.

WHY USE INTERNET RELAY CHAT?

In the educational arena, individuals from distant places frequently need to discuss plans, projects or theories. Several teachers in different states may wish to collaborate on a workshop that will be presented at a national conference. A group of educators taking a class at a university may wish to "hear" a guest "speaker" via the Internet. Perhaps a class of elementary students wants to discuss a joint project with a partner classroom across the country or even across an ocean. A high school class might wish to arrange a "visit" from a noted author or scientist. IRC can accomplish all of these goals without the problems and expenses associated with conference calls or physical travel.

IRC allows participants to contribute to discussions on an equal basis. Each person types "comments" that the entire group can see. Should the situation require it, the chat environment also allows a user to type private comments, viewable by only one other participant. The IRC environment even allows files to be exchanged. IRC can also provide eyewitness accounts of major world events from revolutions to earthquakes and because most channels are open, students can hear first-hand accounts of newsworthy events.

WHAT IS REQUIRED?

In order to use Internet Relay Chat (IRC), the user must have an Internet connection. The connection can be dial-up or direct. After the Internet connection is in place, a software package allows users to connect to the IRC server's special computers reserved for interactive conversations. The most popular IRC chat software for PCs, *mIRC*, is a shareware program that puts IRC servers and advanced IRC features as close as the click of a mouse. *Pirch* is a newcomer, and has enthusiastic users. Macintosh users usually select *Homer* or *Ircle* as their software program of choice. Any of these programs allow users to log onto IRC servers, join channels, and exchange live conversation. Some of the programs support such advanced features as sound files or color coded text. Another useful feature, supported by some software programs, is URL "catching." This feature will collect and/or automatically display any properly typed URL. This can be especially useful when a user wants to follow a professional discussion or any other seminar-type of chat. All URLs typed can be logged into a database for inspection later.

HOW IS IRC ORGANIZED?

Tens of thousands of people throughout the world may be using IRC at any given time. If all these people were to "talk" simultaneously, chaos would reign. Conversations between two people could be lost among the transmissions of all other people. To sort out the conversations, the Internet Relay Chat world has divided itself into Nets, or groups of chat servers, and each Net is again divided into channels. Choice of a Net will determine which channels will be available, but if the user cannot find a suitable channel, a new channel can be created. While there may be no modem police, IRCops and channel ops (operators) monitor their respective domains very carefully.

NETS

Each Net has its own personality. EfNet, the first IRCNet, and home to channels devoted to high-level computer discussions, is the largest, but it is also slow because of its sheer size. Unfortunately, there are also hundreds of "adult" oriented channels on EfNet and their descriptions are quite public. UnderNet sprang from EfNet. It is smaller, more reliable, and friendlier, though many of the same channels exist on both EdNet and UnderNet. DALnet began as a gamers Net, but has expanded. It offers intrusion protection and registered nicknames. KidsWorld is a Net for those under 18. Adults must register upon entering, and security personnel supervise vigorously. All of these Nets and more are pre-configured in major IRC software packages.

CHANNELS

When a user logs onto an IRC server (using appropriate IRC software), hundreds and maybe thousands of channels will be in operation. Each channel name is preceded by a # sign and each channel was created for the purposes of topical discussion. Typing "/list" will show every public channel on a particular net. Channels can be public or private, and moderated or unmoderated. Establishing a private channel is as simple as typing "/join" followed by an unused channel name starting with #. The channel will cease to exist when the last participant leaves the channel.

OPS

Each channel is controlled by an op(erator). The op is the person who creates the channel. The op has the power to configure the channel as moderated, invitation only, or according to several other parameters. The op can also kick (eject) or ban unruly users from the channel. The op also has the power to bestow op status on other users. In the list of channel members, ops are indicated by the @ sign in front of their names. The op is responsible for maintaining order on the channel and establishing ground rules for participants to follow. Ops realize that once they leave the channel, they lose op status unless someone with op power is left behind to restore the authority of the original op.

NICKS

Users on each channel are known by nicknames, or "nicks." A nickname can be a shortened version of one's own name (Tom_S), or it can be a fantasy name (BlkKnight). IRC programs have a limitation on the length of the nick, so abbreviations or truncations are common.

HOW DO YOU FIND, JOIN, OR CREATE A CHANNEL?

The command "/list" will generate a list of all current channels. To join any one of the channels, type: "/join #channelname", substituting the name of the desired channel (including the # sign) for "#channelname." Those who would like a private channel can create one quite easily. They simply type "/join #channelname", substituting the new channel name (including the # sign) for "#channelname." Private channels are advantageous for educational settings and class-to-class chats since the channel won't show on the channel list and outsiders won't be able to send off-topic messages.

CAN YOU SEND A PRIVATE MESSAGE?

While most IRC messages go to a public area where anyone in the channel can view them, it is possible to send messages to a single person. Each software package has its own method of accomplishing this, but the standard command will always work. To send a private message to user Tom_S, one would type: "/msg Tom_S Are you receiving my message?" A separate window will open for this secondary conversation, and anything typed in the private window will go only to Tom_S. It's possible to maintain multiple private conversations simultaneously, at least to the capacity the human brain has to follow all the conversational threads.

HOW DOES ONE EXIT AN IRC CHAT?

Leaving IRC is as simple as closing the window in which you have been chatting. Good netiquette requires that one announce one's departure.

WHAT ARE THE DISADVANTAGES OF IRC?

IRC, a live activity, has some of the same problems encountered with live radio or live television. Technical problems can cause sessions to be terminated prematurely, equipment or telecommunications failures on the Internet can cause what is known as a "net split" where one group of servers is cut off from another group. Each group will continue to converse within its own servers, but participants registered on a separated portion of the network will not be able to see the conversations of the other half. Of course, IRC participants on the same server will be able to converse no matter what happens to other IRC servers. For classroom projects, teachers would do well to plan in advance which server they will use, and agree to have all classes use the same server to eliminate these problems.

Anyone with an Internet connection can access IRC servers. For educational purposes, this means that anyone in the world can drop in on a classroom chat session. Outside visitors can be simple observers (a.k.a. "lurkers"), but some may be out to cause mischief and mayhem. Savvy Internet users can take over unprotected channels. Teachers creating IRC channels for classroom use must learn how to make a channel private, and how to "kick" or ban unwanted members.

Occasionally, an Internet user will "spam" unprotected channels. "Spam" is an unsolicited message broadcast to many channels at once. The channel op has the ability to configure the channel to reject messages from those outside the channel. Because many spam messages are "adult" in nature, this adjustment would be a wise stance.

WHAT EDUCATIONAL BENEFITS CAN I EXPECT?

IRC allows students and teachers to interact synchronously with live persons. These can be peers, mentors, or guests. Younger students who don't type well might ask an older student, parent, or teacher to type their questions and comments, so that physical limitations do not stand in the way of communication. Classes in remote locations, across town or around the world, can collaborate on joint projects. IRC is more immediate than e-mail exchanges because there is no need to wait a long time to receive a response. IRC also personalizes the Internet, which can sometimes seem cold and robotic. All in all, IRC environments provide an interactive, personal channel through which numerous varieties of communications can occur.

REFERENCES, SUGGESTED READINGS, AND TOPIC RELATED WEB SITES

Harris, S. (1995). *The IRC survival guide*. Reading, MA: Addison-Wesley.

Toyer, K. (1997). *Learn Internet relay chat*. Plano, TX: Wordware Publishing, Inc.

Toyer, K. (1997). *Learn advanced Internet relay chat*. Plano, TX: Wordware Publishing, Inc.

Using the Internet as an Instructional Tool. (1997). Hudson River Center for Program Development, Glenmont, NY. (ED 417 344)
http://www.kidlink.org/IRC/
http://www.irchelp.org/
http://www.wko.com/faq/irc/irc-faq.htm

Information Literacy

Eric Plotnick
Associate Director of the
ERIC Clearinghouse on Information & Technology

Reprinted from ERIC® Digest, February 1999, EDO-IR-99-02

[This Digest is based on "Information Literacy: Essential Skills for the Information Age" by Kathleen L. Spitzer with Michael B. Eisenberg & Carrie A. Lowe. Monograph ordering information is noted at the end of this Digest.]

DEFINITION OF INFORMATION LITERACY

Although alternate definitions for information literacy have been developed by educational institutions, professional organizations and individuals, they are likely to stem from the definition offered in the Final Report of the American Library Association (ALA) Presidential Committee on Information Literacy, "To be information literate, a person must be able to recognize when information is needed and have the ability to locate, evaluate and use effectively the needed information" (1989, p. 1). Since information may be presented in a number of formats, the term *information* applies to more than just the printed word. Other literacies such as visual, media, computer, network, and basic literacies are implicit in information literacy.

THE EVOLUTION OF A CONCEPT

The seminal event in the development of the concept of information literacy was the establishment of the ALA Presidential Committee on Information Literacy whose final report outlined the importance of the concept. The ALA Presidential Committee precipitated the formation of the National Forum on Information Literacy, a coalition of more than 65 national organizations, that seeks to disseminate the concept. The development of information literacy in K–12 education began with the publication of *A Nation at Risk* in 1983. This was soon followed by *Educating Students to Think: The Role of the School Library Media Program* (Hashim, 1986), a concept paper outlining the role of the library and the role of information resources in K–12 education. Kulthau's *Information Skills for an Information Society: A Review of Research* (1987) included library skills and computer skills in the definition of information literacy. The American Association of School Librarians' (AASL) 1988 publication, *Information Power: Guidelines for School Library Media Programs*, and its 1998 publication *Information Power: Building Partnerships for Learning* emphasize the notion that the mission of the school library media program is "to ensure that students and staff are effective users of ideas and information."

INFORMATION LITERACY RESEARCH

Three themes predominate in research on information literacy:

- Information literacy is a process. Information literacy skills must be taught in the context of the overall process.

- To be successful, information literacy skills instruction must be integrated with the curriculum and reinforced both within and outside of the educational setting.
- Information literacy skills are vital to future success.

AN ECONOMIC PERSPECTIVE

The change from an economy based on labor and capital to one based on information requires information literate workers who will know how to interpret information.

- Barner's (1996) study of the new workplace indicates significant changes will take place in the future. Information technology is decentralizing the work force. The work force will be more diverse and the economy will increasingly be more global. The use of temporary workers will increase. These changes will require that workers possess information literacy skills.
- The SCANS (1991) report identifies the skills necessary for the workplace of the future. Rather than report to a hierarchical management structure, workers of the future will be required to actively participate in the management of the company and contribute to its success. The workplace will require workers who possess skills beyond those of reading, writing and arithmetic.

NATIONAL AND STATE STANDARDS

With the passage of the Goals 2000: Educate America Act (1994), subject matter organizations were able to obtain funding to develop standards in their respective subject areas. Information literacy skills are implicit in the National Education Goals and national content standards documents.

- Three of the eight National Education Goals demonstrate the critical nature of information literacy to an information society: Goal 1: School Readiness; Goal 3: Student Achievement and Citizenship; Goal 6: Adult Literacy and Lifelong Learning.
- An analysis of national content standards documents reveals that they all focus on lifelong learning, the ability to think critically, and on the use of new and existing information for problem solving.
- Individual states are creating initiatives to ensure that students attain information literacy skills by the time they graduate from high school. Kentucky (1995), Utah (1996), and California (1994) are but three examples of states that have publications depicting these initiatives.
- National content standards, state standards, and information literacy skills terminology may vary, but all have common components relating to information literacy.

K–12 EDUCATION RESTRUCTURING

Educational reform and restructuring make information literacy skills a necessity as students seek to construct their own knowledge and create their own understandings.

- Educators are selecting various forms of resource-based learning (authentic learning, problem-based learning and work-based learning) to help students focus on the process and to help students learn from the content. Information literacy skills are necessary components of each.

- The process approach to education is requiring new forms of student assessment. Students demonstrate their skills, assess their own learning, and evaluate the processes by which this learning has been achieved by preparing portfolios, learning and research logs, and using rubrics.

INFORMATION LITERACY EFFORTS IN K–12 EDUCATION

Information literacy efforts are underway on individual, local, and regional bases.

- Imaginative Web based information literacy tutorials are being created and integrated with curriculum areas, or being used for staff development purposes.

- Library media programs are fostering information literacy by integrating the presentation of information literacy skills with curriculum at all grade levels.

- Information literacy efforts are not being limited to the library field, but are also being employed by regional educational consortia.

- Parents are encouraging their children to develop information literacy skills at home by contacting KidsConnect, the Internet help and referral service for K–12 students. Parents are also helping students work through the information problem solving process as they assist their children with their homework.

INFORMATION LITERACY IN HIGHER EDUCATION

The inclusion of information competencies as a graduation requirement is the key that will fully integrate information literacy into the curricula of academic institutions.

- Information literacy instruction in higher education can take a variety of forms: stand-alone courses or classes, online tutorials, workbooks, course-related instruction, or course-integrated instruction.

- State-wide university systems and individual colleges and universities are undertaking strategic planning to determine information competencies, to incorporate instruction in information competence throughout the curriculum and to add information competence as a graduation requirement for students.

- Academic library programs are preparing faculty to facilitate their students' mastery of information literacy skills so that the faculty can in turn provide information literacy learning experiences for the students enrolled in their classes.

TECHNOLOGY AND INFORMATION LITERACY

Information Technology is the great enabler. It provides, for those who have access to it, an extension of their powers of perception, comprehension, analysis, thought, concentration, and articulation through a range of activities that include: writing, visual images, mathematics, music, physical movement, sensing the environment, simulation, and communication (Carpenter, 1989, p. 2).

Technology, in all of its various forms, offers users the tools to access, manipulate, transform, evaluate, use, and present information.

- Technology in schools includes computers, televisions, video cameras, video editing equipment, and TV studios.

- Two approaches to technology in K–12 schools are technology as the object of instruction approach, and technology as the tool of instruction approach.

- Schools are starting to incorporate technology skills instruction in the context of information literacy skills.

- Technology is changing the way higher education institutions are offering instruction.

- The use of the Internet is being taught the contexts of subject area curricula and the overall information literacy process.

- There is some empirical indication that students who use technology as a tool may become better at managing information, communicating, and presenting ideas.

CONCLUSION

"In this next century, an 'educated' graduate will no longer be defined as one who has absorbed a certain body of factual information, but as one who knows how to find, evaluate, and apply needed information" (Breivik, 1998, p.2). Our ability to be information literate depends on our willingness to be lifelong learners as we are challenged to master new technologies that will forever alter the landscape of information.

REFERENCES

American Association of School Librarians and Association for Educational Communications and Technology. (1988). *Information power: Guidelines for school library media programs.* Chicago: Author. (ED 315 028)

American Library Association and Association for Educational Communications and Technology. (1998). *Information power: Building partnerships for learning.* Chicago: Author.

American Library Association Presidential Committee on Information Literacy. (1989). *Final report.* Chicago: Author. (ED 315 028)

Barner, R. (1996, March/April). Seven changes that will challenge managers—and workers. *The Futurist, 30*(2), 14–18.

Breivik. P. S., and Senn, J. A. (1998). *Information literacy: Educating children for the 21st century.* (2nd ed.). Washington, DC: National Education Association.

Carpenter, J. P. (1989). *Using the new technologies to create links between schools throughout the world: Colloquy on computerized school links.* (Exeter, Devon, United Kingdom, 17–20 Oct. 1988).

Hashim, E. (1986). Educating students to think: The role of the school library media program, an introduction. In *Information literacy: Learning how to learn.* A collection of articles from *School Library Media Quarterly, (15)*1, 17–18.

Kuhlthau, C. C. (1987). *Information skills for an information society: A review of research.* Syracuse, NY: ERIC Clearinghouse on Information Resources. (ED 297 740)

National Commission of Excellence in Education. (1983). *A Nation at risk: The imperative for educational reform.* Washington, DC: U.S. Government Printing Office. (ED 226 006)

Secretary's Commission on Achieving Necessary Skills. (1991). *What work requires of schools: A SCANS report for America 2000.* Washington, DC: U.S. Government Printing Office. (ED 332 054)

Radios in the Classroom
Curriculum Integration and Communication Skills

Anton Ninno
Systems Consultant
CNY Regional Information Center

Reprinted from ERIC® Digest, March 1999, EDO-IR-99-03

Teachers have explored the use of radio in the classroom almost since radio technology entered into the mainstream of society, yet radio remains a relatively unused mode of instruction. This Digest describes several radio applications and summarizes several radio activities for the classroom.

TEACHING THE HISTORY OF COMMUNICATIONS

Students may begin their study of communications technology by reading about some early devices and their inventors. Radios and telegraphs are part of early communications technology history, and Samuel Morse, Guglielmo Marconi, Lee DeForest, Philo Farnsworth, and David Sarnoff were communications pioneers.

The first popular radios were called crystal radios because they used crystals to receive the broadcast signals. Building a crystal radio, either from a kit or from parts, is an engaging, hands-on science activity. In addition to building the crystal radio, earth science and chemistry teachers might consider making the galena crystals that receive the signals. Many early crystal radio listeners made their own galena crystals before radios were sold in stores. Teachers can also use radio assembly projects to help students learn about electricity, wave energy, the electromagnetic spectrum, the earth's atmosphere, and the sun's effects on the earth's atmosphere. Many popular electronics stores have a full range of reasonably priced, easy to assemble electronics and radio kits.

AM-FM RADIO: HANDS-ON GEOGRAPHY AND LANGUAGE ARTS ACTIVITIES

Depending upon your geographic location, you may hear many AM-FM radio stations from Canada, Mexico, Central America, and the Caribbean. If you are near those regions, you will hear broadcasts by English, French, and Spanish native speakers—a special opportunity for foreign language learners. Some AM-FM stations now maintain Web sites and offer their listeners real-time programming and audio archives. Listening to online audio resources requires computer software such as *RealAudio*, a sound card, and speakers.

Many U.S. AM stations may be heard across the country. Listening to broadcasts from other U.S. locations makes an excellent activity for learning U.S. geography. The term DX means long-distance, so listening to faraway stations is known as "DXing" among radio hobbyists. In the evening, AM radio broadcasts are heard over great distances because atmospheric conditions allow AM radio waves to bounce between the atmosphere and the earth. Students might hear AM broadcasts from several hundred miles away if they listen to AM stations after dark.

INTERNATIONAL SHORTWAVE BROADCASTS: HEARING THE WORLD ON A RADIO

Just as an AM-FM radio is a tool for students learning about local and regional geography, a shortwave radio is a good tool for learning about world geography. Every country in the world has shortwave radio broadcast stations, and most stations have programming in English, as well as their native language. Beginning with 6th-grade social studies curriculum, the study of geography may be enhanced by listening to international shortwave broadcasts. Students will hear news and cultural programming that will enhance the information found in books, encyclopedias, and on the Internet. Topics such as latitude and longitude, time zones, continents, hemispheres, and the tropics may all be highlighted through radio listening activities.

Writing letters to international stations to give listener reports is a long-standing shortwave listening hobby activity. The writing assignment combines listening and language arts skills. Stations usually reply with letters or special postcards, brochures, posters, key chains, and bumper stickers. Teachers may use these items to prepare interesting displays in a classroom learning center.

NOAA NATIONAL WEATHER SERVICE BROADCASTS

Many people listen to a radio to hear weather reports; however, in a classroom it's not always convenient to wait for a radio station's weather report. With a weather radio, you don't have to wait. Weather radios are tuned to the NOAA (National Oceanic and Atmospheric Administration), weather channels that provide broadcasts 24 hours a day. Most NOAA broadcasts range about 50 miles from their main location. Many AM-FM radios, scanner radios, and CB radios include NOAA channels for listeners' convenience and safety. NOAA also coordinates a national program for trained volunteer weather watchers called Skywarn. Teachers may wish to consider Skywarn training for a class weather project or for individual science projects.

SCANNER RADIOS: HEARING THE WORLD OF WORK

A scanner radio will bring the world of work into the classroom. These high-speed scanning receivers monitor government, businesses, and nonprofit organization's frequencies in your local community. Unlike the shortwave radio, a scanner radio receives local FM communications and broadcasts within a range of about 50 miles. Since the conversations you hear on a scanner radio are between people, there is no way to know when they will occur. A scanner radio scans through many frequencies and stops when a transmission signal is detected. The listener will hear many transmissions, and it is important to program the scanner radio to listen to the public service agencies desired. Some occupations that use scanner radios include: police, fire, hospitals, ambulances, aircraft, schools, universities, factories, warehouses, boats, taxis, city buses, delivery trucks, utility companies, TV and radio news crews, the FBI, mall security, hotels, and construction crews.

AMATEUR RADIO: PRACTICING HANDS-ON COMMUNICATION SKILLS

Many students today build their own web pages; however, students in the 1950s and 60s, built stereos and radios with kits from companies like Heathkit. Many students earned amateur radio licenses from the Federal Communications Commission (FCC) and built their own ham radio stations. Today, most ham radio operators buy ready-made radio equipment, and many enthusiasts listen to packet radio (connections between radios and computers) or participate in ham satellite communications. Other ham radio operators communicate with the NASA Space Shuttle and the Mir Space Station via amateur radio. Not long ago, the FCC eased the requirements for the entry-level ham license by eliminating the Morse code requirement. Students and teachers can now become No-Code Technician Class operators by passing two multiple-choice exams. Study guides for these exams include the entire FCC question pool, as well as full explanations for each answer. Kindergarten-age students have earned licenses, however most young hams are in the middle and high school grades.

Many schools across the country and around the world have amateur radio stations. Students can practice speaking, interviewing, listening, and writing skills in an amateur radio school club or classroom activity. Some teachers use the amateur radio as the communications link for school-to-school projects. Real-time radio conversations allow students to practice listening and speaking skills—a valuable experience that is not found with an e-mail connection.

SUMMARY

Radio technology offers a unique way for K–12 teachers to integrate technology into the curriculum. Elementary teachers can help students learn basic electricity and regional geography in entertaining ways using AM radios. Social studies teachers will appreciate shortwave radios as a tool for teaching U.S. and global topics. Science, physics, and earth science teachers can use radios to demonstrate the properties of electricity, wave energy, weather, and the earth's atmosphere. English and language arts teachers will be able to use radios to reinforce listening, writing, and speaking skills. With a shortwave radio, foreign language teachers can provide advanced students with an opportunity to hear the authentic language demonstrated by native speakers. Teachers without Internet connections will find radios an accessible technology for bringing the world to their students.

BIBLIOGRAPHY

Evans, G. (1997, Nov-Dec). Ham radio is Mir magic. *Science Scope, (21)*3, 10,12. (EJ 554 613).

Hollenbeck, M. D. (1997, Nov.). High-frequency learning. *Educational Leadership, (55)*3, 72–74. (EJ 553 843)

Lewis, B., and others. (1996). Successful teaching today. *Learning, (25)*1, 84–85 (EJ 533 410).

Magne, L. (Ed.). (1998). Passport to world band radio 1998 (Serial), (Rev.ed.). International Broadcasting Service. (ISBN 0914941453). http://www.passport.com/

Mustoe, M. (1988). Introduction to shortuave radio in the classroom. *Journal of Geography, (87)*3, 82–87.

Mustoe, M. (1989). Shortwave goes to school: A teachers guide to using shortwave radio in the class room. Lake Geneva, WI: Tiare Press, ISBN 0-936653-17-5.

Ninno, A. (1998, April). Explore the world with a radio. *Technology Connection, (5)*2, 11–13.

Scott, T. (1996). A week with STELAR. *Education in Science, 166*, 28–29. (EJ 523 655).

Smith, P. D. (1977). Shortwave radio and the foreign language classroom. *NALLD Journal, (11)*2, 34–39. (EJ 155 278)

West, K. (1997, March). *Classic radio theatre in contemporary education.* Paper presented at the Annual Joint Meetings of the Popular Culture Association/American Culture Association, San Antonio, TX. (ED 407 693).

WEBSITES

American Radio Relay League (Ham radio)
http://www.arrl.org/ead/teacher/

AskERIC Lesson Plan: Integrated Learning with AM Radio
http://ericir.syr.edu/Virtual/Lessons/Interdisciplinary/INT0093.html

The Complete Shortwave Listener's Handbook, 5th Edition
http://www.rnw.nl/realradio/book_yoder.html
http://www.universal-radio.com/catalog/books/1301.html

Crystal Radio Page
http://freeweb.pdq.net/headstrong/crystal.htm

Grove Enterprises & *Monitoring Times* **magazine**
http://www.grove-ent.com/grove/hmpgmt.html

How Things Work—Radio
http://landau1.phys.virginia.edu/Education/Teaching/HowThingsWork/radio.html
http://ericae.net/db/riecije/ed364216.htm

Morse Code Translator
http://www.soton.ac.uk/~scp93ch/refer/morseform.html

Museum of Broadcast Communications
http://www.neog.com/mbc/

NOAA Weather Homepage
http://www.noaa.gov/

Ontario DX Association
http://www.durhamradio.ca/odxa/

Radio Days—A Sound Bite History
http://www.otr.com/

Radio Netherlands—SWL Resources
http://www.rnw.nl/

Universal Radio Company (shortwave radios and books)
http://www.universal-radio.com/

Building and Maintaining
Digital Reference Services

Joann M. Wasik
*Virtual Reference Desk Research
Consultant and Communications Officer*

Reprinted from ERIC® Digest, March 1999, EDO-IR-99-04

Easily accessible digital information has rapidly become one of the hallmarks of the Internet. Online resources have surged in popularity as more individuals and organizations have connected to the global network. Thousands of organizations have turned to Internet-based information delivery as an effective and cost-efficient alternative to traditional communication methods, and many have expanded their services further by interacting with their users and responding to inquiries via the Internet.

Digital reference services (also known as "AskA services," as in "Ask-an-Expert") provide subject expertise and information referral over the Internet to their users. This Digest provides an overview of the growing digital reference movement and its implications on sponsoring organizations, and examines current practices in the creation and maintenance of such services.

WHAT IS DIGITAL REFERENCE?

Digital reference and AskA services are Internet-based question-and-answer services that connect users with experts in a variety of subject areas. In addition to answering questions, experts may also provide users with referrals to other online and print sources of information. As opposed to traditional expert systems that attempt to capture and model problem-solving tasks in a manner similar to humans, digital reference services use human intermediaries, or experts, to answer questions and provide information to users. The question/answer process in digital reference services is modeled after the methods practiced by reference librarians in traditional library settings. As in a face-to-face interview, experts determine the amount of information appropriate for the user, the applicability of that information, and the level of information required. User queries must occasionally be clarified, and an online reference interview may be conducted to help define the user's information needs.

HISTORY OF DIGITAL REFERENCE

The origins of digital reference can be traced to the library field, where libraries sought to augment traditional services by providing reference assistance in an electronic environment. One of the first services to go online was the Electronic Access to Reference Service (EARS), launched by the University of Maryland Health Services Library in Baltimore in 1984 (Wiese & Borgendale, 1986). Although initial e-mail-based digital reference efforts received little attention from patrons (Still & Campbell, 1993), digital reference services proliferated over time and became increasingly popular, eventually spawning such internationally known services as AskERIC in 1992 and the Internet Public Library in 1995.

During the past several years, digital reference services have become important and effective resources for meeting the information needs of thousands of users, and the number of user requests to these service has continued to increase. In September of 1996, KidsConnect, a question-and-answer, help, and referral service for K–12 students on the Internet, experienced 1000% growth—from 20 questions a week to 200 questions per week (Lankes, 1998). With proper planning, AskA services can effectively manage high volumes of questions and prevent disruptions in service. Services that are launched prematurely, however, may not be prepared for the potential impact a global audience may have on their organizations.

IMPLICATIONS OF DIGITAL REFERENCE

The dynamic nature of the Internet creates an ever-changing information environment and transforms the way information is delivered and accessed. As greater numbers of users connect to the Internet, user expectations for more immediate access to information and knowledge resources steadily rises. While many organizations realize that their best response to shifting user demands is proactive rather than passive service (Cargill, 1992), the online environment can raise important issues for those interested in offering digital reference services.

The creation and maintenance of Internet-based question-and-answer services can be fraught with difficulties. AskA services often struggle with issues such as how to maintain consistent quality of service, which user populations to serve, and how to respond to question overload. The need to secure funding for continued operation also figures prominently in the building and maintaining of digital reference services. Many services devote much time to the pursuit of grants, corporate sponsorship, or non-profit status (Wasik, 1998). Despite such potential problems, organizations offering digital reference services find many rewards. AskA services serve the public good by providing valuable information in a timely fashion, and have the potential to gain international visibility. Parent organizations of many services reap enhanced public relations benefits by having satisfied users and by providing high-quality information. Accessible 24-hours a day and unrestricted by geography, digital reference services are a powerful means for the free exchange of information and the promotion of interactive learning.

A lack of information resources for practitioners of digital reference, however, has allowed many AskA services to go online without a clear understanding of either the process of digital reference itself or how to develop and manage such services effectively. Since many of these services struggle and sometimes fail altogether, methods and standards have been proposed to ensure a consistent level of quality for digital reference and to provide guidance in the introduction of new services. Organizations interested in offering Internet-based information services must understand not only the fundamental tenets of the question-and-answer process, but also how this information is processed and translated into actual service.

HOW DIGITAL REFERENCE SERVICES WORK

Although there are slight variations among services, all digital reference and AskA services function in a similar manner. Human intermediaries evaluate incoming questions via e-mail or Web interface, and then decide on an appropriate course of action. New questions may be checked against an archive of previously answered questions for an appropriate answer, and if no suitable answer is found, passed along to an expert for answering. The expert supplies the necessary information, which may consist of an actual answer (factual information), pointers to additional resources (information referral), or some combination. Responses are sent to the user's e-mail address or posted to a Web site for the user to access at a later date. In some smaller AskA services, the experts themselves may also monitor the incoming questions.

The task of creating and managing Internet-based question-and-answer services is complicated by the ever-changing nature of the Internet. Lankes (1998) examined exemplary K–12 AskA services to determine how such services answered questions, processed information, and operated in a highly complex online environment. Lankes identified five fundamental components that commonly exist in the methods used by digital reference services to answer questions, and which in turn form the basis of a conceptual framework, or "meta-description," of the question/answer process.

Services receive questions electronically (*Question Acquisition*), then route the questions to an appropriate expert according to a set of internal rules. The questions progress to a *Pool of Possible Respondents*, where they are queued according to some criteria, such as user need, date received, etc. In services staffed by multiple experts, some sort of triage may be initially performed to help expedite the answer process, such as selecting the best expert to answer a particular question. The expert composes an answer in compliance with service policy (*Expert Answer Generation*), and replies are sent to the users (*Answer Sent*). The final component of Lankes' meta-description, *Tracking*, identifies popular subjects and trends that may be used to compile statistics or generate archives.

Viewed in its entirety, the meta-description reveals a level of convergence in the volatile online environment. By identifying a set of common methods in the question/answer process, organizations may develop a series of planning documents to assist in the creation and ongoing maintenance of digital reference services.

BUILDING AND MAINTAINING DIGITAL REFERENCE SERVICES

Based on Lankes' meta-description, a six-step process was developed to aid organizations in the creation and operation of digital reference services (Lankes & Kasowitz, 1998). The *AskA Starter Kit* describes each of the six steps in a series of instructional modules. The information presented in the *AskA Starter Kit* is applicable to a wide variety of organizations and audiences including the K–12 education community, government agencies, libraries, and industry. The six stages are briefly outlined as follows:

1. **Informing:** Nascent AskA services conduct preliminary research both into the field of digital reference and into existing services in their area of expertise.

2. **Planning:** AskA services' policies, procedures, and methods must be developed and evaluated to ensure alignment with overall organizational goals.

3. **Training:** The development of a comprehensive training plan, including training materials, activities, and tools, is necessary for the preparation of an effective staff.

4. **Prototyping:** Many digital reference services fail because they are launched prematurely. Services that are first pilot-tested in a controlled environment can identify and correct problems with minimal inconvenience.

5. **Contributing:** Upon launching an AskA service, it is important to institute the development of ongoing publicity and resource development to support the service.

6. **Evaluating:** As with any service, digital reference services benefit from regular evaluations to ensure a quality product and to gather data for continued support from the organization.

The six-step process reveals an overall methodology that many digital reference services do not employ. Due to inadequate planning and perhaps inexperience with Internet-based information delivery systems, many services experience question overloads and are often forced to cease operations as a result. Systematic planning and training such as that outlined in the *AskA Starter Kit* can help digital reference practitioners create robust, high-quality services.

In today's rapidly changing information environment, digital reference and AskA services are important tools that support learning and promote intellectual inquiry. The need for specialized training and information resources for digital reference providers has become increasingly critical as the popularity of such services continues to grow. Without proper planning and without an understanding of digital reference practices, many services will experience significant difficulties. New research and information resources, however, seek to promote standards and practices to ensure high-quality service, and the effective creation and maintenance of exemplary digital reference services.

REFERENCES AND READINGS

AskA Digests. [Online]. Available: http://www.vrd.org/AskA/digests.html [December 28, 1998].

Cargill, J. S. (1992). Electronic reference desk: Reference service in an electronic world. *Library Administration & Management, 6*(2), 82–85. (EJ 444 784)

Lankes, R. D. (1998). *Building and maintaining Internet information services: K–12 digital reference services.* ERIC Clearinghouse on Information and Technology, Syracuse University, Syracuse, NY. (IR-106, ED number pending).

Lankes, R. D., and Kasowitz, A. S. (1998). *The AskA starter kit: How to build and maintain digital reference services.* ERIC Clearinghouse on Information and Technology, Syracuse University, Syracuse, NY. (IR-107, ED number pending).

Lipow, A. G. (1997). Thinking out loud: Who will give reference service in the digital environment? *Reference & User Services Quarterly, 37*(2), 125–129.

Still, J., and Campbell, F. (1993). Librarian in a box: the use of electronic mail for reference. *Reference Services Review, 21*(1), 15–18. (EJ 457 878)

Wasik, J. (1998). AskA services and funding: An overview. [Online]. Available: http://www.vrd.org/AskA/aska_funding.html [January 4, 1999].

Whitwell, S. C. (1997). Internet Public Library: Same metaphors, new service. *American Libraries, 28*(2), 56–59. (EJ 539 658)

Wiese, F. O., and Borgendale, M. (1986). EARS: Electronic access to reference service. *Bulletin of the Medical Library Association, 74*(4), 300–304.

Part Two
Technology Centers and Institutes for Learning

Introduction

This section inaugurates one of two new features for the Yearbook. The editors have endeavored to present several chapters about the goals and accomplishments for research and development centers dedicated to learning, performance support, and technological innovations.

The first chapter focuses on a center that investigates ways technology has transformed social and business enterprises ranging from transportation to communications to manufacturing to banking to medicine and health care. The Learning and Performance Support Laboratory (LPSL) at the University of Georgia is guided by questions like: Will education undergo a transformation analogous to other enterprises? Who will generate the educational ideas, innovations, and inspirations of the third millennium? Which approaches will extend current practices, and which will invent approaches heretofore unknown? What roles will technology assume? These are questions that educational research and development organizations ponder in their daily and long-term efforts and initiatives.

The LPSL conducts research and development designed to advance our knowledge, skills, and practices involving technology in teaching and learning. It was established through a grant written collaboratively by mathematics education and instructional technology faculty members in the University of Georgia's College of Education. The lab was designed to provide a focal point and core capability for collaborative research and development related to educational applications of technology. It was funded initially by a grant from the Georgia Research Alliance, state funds, and private contributions to the university.

The second chapter focuses on the effect of technologies created with the purpose of making it possible to do something that could not be done before or to make the lives of humans easier, more productive, or more enjoyable. The Center for Technology Innovations in Education (CTIE) in the College of Education at the University of Missouri-Columbia builds on these fundamental changes in education by undertaking research and development of innovative learning technology.

In the past several years, according to the research scientists at CTIE, we have witnessed two fundamental changes in our conception of the educational process. First, cognitive psychology is increasingly revealing a picture of learning grounded in active participation, constructed knowledge, and the importance of the situation and context not only for what is learned but also for how it will be able to be used. These new theoretical underpinnings, as well as other forces, argue for learning through problem-solving, authentic projects, and learning communities. The second fundamental change to education comes from advances in technology with a special emphasis on network technologies, in particular the Internet. Dramatic advances in networking and processing capabilities have made possible new tools of mediation, simulation, modeling, and communication. We now have the potential to design teaching and learning experiences that are far less bounded by time, distance, and the limitations of a classroom. Teachers and learners can connect in many different ways offering new opportunities for learning in context, for richer means of communication and sharing, and for new means of performance and self assessment.

Some significant advances have been made in the transforming of teaching and learning with technology, a sampling of which is detailed in this section. The following technology centers and institutes for learning are scheduled to be featured in subsequent volumes of the Yearbook: the Learning Technology Center at Vanderbilt University, the Highly Interactive Computing for Education institute at the University of Michigan, the Center for Innovative Learning Technologies at Stanford University, and the Concord Consortium in Massachusetts.

Robert Maribe Branch

Learning and Performance
Support Laboratory
University of Georgia

Michael Hannafin, Kenneth Hay, Michael Jacobson,
and the faculty and staff of the Learning and
Performance Support Laboratory

Technology has transformed social and business enterprises ranging from transportation to communications, manufacturing, banking, and medicine and health care. Products and services unimaginable at the beginning of the twentieth century now seem commonplace as we begin the twenty-first century. Educators, parents, and children ponder what the new millennium portends. Will education undergo a transformation analogous to other enterprises? Who will generate the educational ideas, innovations, and inspirations of the third millennium? Which approaches will extend current practices, and which will invent approaches heretofore unknown? What roles will technology assume?

These are questions that educational research and development organizations ponder in their daily and long-term efforts and initiatives. Some significant advances have been made in the transforming of teaching and learning with technology, a sampling of which are detailed in this yearbook. In this chapter, we describe some of the visions and initiatives we have undertaken thus far, some that are on our near horizon, and some that we foresee in 10–20 years.

OVERVIEW

The Learning and Performance Support Laboratory (LPSL) conducts research and development designed to advance our knowledge, skills, and practices involving technology in teaching and learning. The LPSL was established through a grant written collaboratively by mathematics education and instructional technology faculty members in the University of Georgia's College of Education. The lab was designed to provide a focal point and core capability for collaborative research and development related to educational applications of technology. It was funded initially by a grant from the Georgia Research Alliance, state funds, and private contributions to the University.

Our approach recognizes current demands, needs, and constraints; indeed, many projects initially emphasize technology approaches that optimize current practices, given existing constraints. However, we also share a commitment to advancing qualitatively different alternatives to existing practices—efforts that advance different goals, establish and test different approaches, feature varied models, and embrace alternative learning and epistemological perspectives. The lab is a vehicle to transform educational practices through disciplined inquiry, balancing near-term issues and priorities with longer-term visions and innovations needed to invent new practices.

The LPSL draws upon the expertise of full-time faculty and research scientists and academic faculty representing diverse departments within and beyond UGA's College of Education. The LPSL also employs a professional support staff as well as a significant number of "soft money" project positions and graduate research assistants through external contracts and grants. In some ways, LPSL projects reflect a diverse range of subject domains, target populations, and technologies; in others, however, they reflect common goals and underlying approaches. In the remainder of this chapter, we describe the themes we believe characterize our underlying approach, identify thematic aspects of our initiatives, summarize representative project efforts, and describe alternative futures and challenges for the instructional technology field.

LAB CULTURE

Three commitments underlie LPSL activities:

1. Theoretically grounded research, both basic and applied, that contributes to our understanding of how learning and performance may be enhanced by technology;

2. Research and development that establishes a leading-edge capability in technology-enhanced learning, performance assessment, and information access at all levels of education, training, and work; and

3. Partnerships and research collaborations with other institutions, businesses, and agencies that establish critical mass of expertise, resources, and perspectives.

The first commitment emphasizes the importance of conceptualizing our work in relevant theoretical frameworks. We see the lab as a resource in synthesizing existing research and theory to better understand the phenomena we study. By sharing the results of our research, we are equally committed to discovering new knowledge and contributing to the research and theory base supporting the educational practices of others.

The second commitment emphasizes the importance of establishing and sustaining the infrastructures—human, technological, facilities, and funding—needed to support, advance, and extend the lab's mission.

Perhaps no commitment is as fundamental to the values of LPSL as the third one, the commitment to collaboration. At its inception, the lab was envisioned as a collaboration incubator; since then, collaboration has become a visible focal point and trademark. Our list of collaborators ranges from departments and colleges within UGA to external labs and universities, corporate foundations, local schools and community groups, and state and federal agencies.

ONGOING INITIATIVES

Faculty, research scientists, postdoctoral fellows, and graduate assistants in the LPSL pursue a range of initiatives and projects. Four themes have emerged related to our technology research and development: cognition and learning, teacher education, school-based reform, and evaluation of effectiveness and impact. Our themes organize interrelated curriculum, teaching and learning methods, telecommunications, schools, and classroom. Individual projects address specific questions, problems, and issues. No single project addresses all, but most address parts of each. In the following sections we describe several representative efforts in each theme, highlighting projects that illustrate values, mission, and commitment to both respond to current challenges and to shape the future of teaching and learning through technology.

Cognition and learning. Projects emphasizing cognition and learning with emerging technologies tend to extend teaching-learning activities substantially beyond what is "typical" in education. Such efforts generally reflect student-centered designs, using technology tools to support activities such as angling from alternative perspectives, manipulating concepts or variables, or becoming immersed in virtual worlds.

One key initiative is advanced by the Learning in/with Virtual Environments (LIVE) team, which applies virtual reality technologies in teaching and learning. The *Virtual Solar System* (VSS) Project (see Figure 1) transforms traditional lecture-based activities into constructionist courses. This project is one of the first Virtual Reality (VR)-based university courses implemented in the United States. Where previously lectures constituted the primary learning activity, students build photorealistic VR scale models of the solar system. Projects are then posted to the Internet, where they can be viewed by others using a readily available plug-in. Students in the course learned more astronomy content in a deeper way; furthermore, they learned inquiry and collaborative skills involved in the science of astronomy.

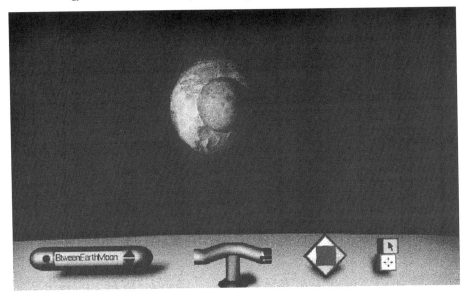

Figure 1. VSS point of reference: looking back toward the Earth.

The *Digital Weather Station* (DWS), shown in Figure 2, is a 3D visualization tool designed to develop understanding of the weather as a three-dimensional system, as well as to develop skills in the scientific process of visualization. It provides an unprecedented opportunity for inquiry-based and problem-based learning activities during which students use the technology to visualize 3D interactive, dynamic visualizations of standard weather parameters. DWS is not a scaled-down tool visualizing fictitious data; rather, it embodies the same tools and data that scientists use in their everyday work. What once required weeks or longer for scientists to program now takes learners a few simple mouse clicks to accomplish. Project collaborators include the Children's Museum of Indianapolis and researchers from Indiana University, University of Illinois, and the University Corporation for Atmospheric Research (UCAR).

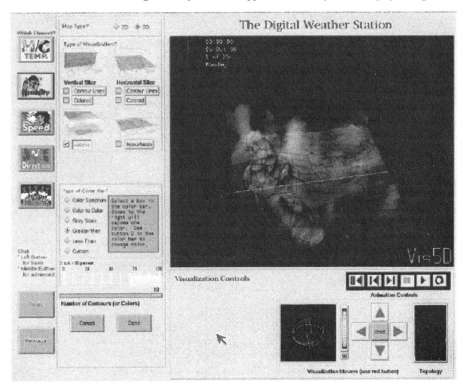

Figure 2. Digital weather station interface.

The *Virtual Gorilla Project* (illustrated in Figure 3), a collaboration among Zoo Atlanta and the Virtual Environments Group at Georgia Institute of Technology, is a head-mounted display (HMD) VR learning environment that facilitates deeper understanding of gorilla behaviors and social interactions. The Virtual Gorilla exhibit enables learners to build and test models to engage animal behavior experientially instead of passively. The technology transforms a learning experience at the Zoo from simply watching to one of creating, exploring and interacting; users learn about habitats and social hierarchies by immersing themselves in a virtual gorilla environment. Through interaction, learners test the appropriateness of their own gorilla models as a participant in a virtual gorilla community.

Figure 3. "Snapshot" of VR Gorilla posturing.

Another initiative focuses on the cognitive challenges of learning scientific knowledge and acquiring the habits of mind demonstrated by experts such as historians, mathematicians, and astrophysicists. The *Knowledge Mediator* (KM) *Project*, shown in Figure 4, explores ways to design and use Web-based hypermedia tools to help students construct deep conceptual understandings of challenging knowledge, change their initial models or preconceptions to reflect more expert-like representations, and apply their knowledge to new problems and issues. KM utilizes cases and problems as resources while scaffolding the learning of abstract concepts and conceptual models. It enables the learner to flexibly interconnect different facets of knowledge related to various cases and abstract concepts and to contrast their views and analyses to those of experts. *Knowledge Mediator* design features and learning activities have demonstrated significant conceptual change as well as improved students' ability to use their knowledge in new ways and situations.

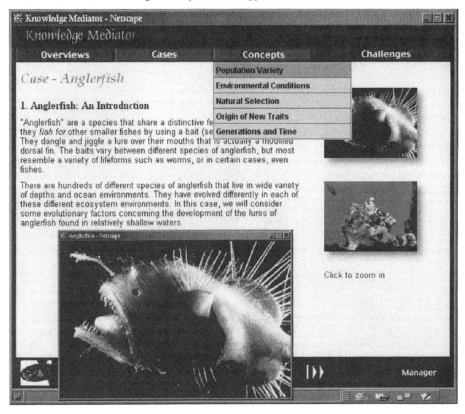

Figure 4. Sample screen from the Evolution Knowledge Mediator.

The study of complexity and complex systems is another thrust within our cognition and learning initiative. During the past century, researchers in a number of areas—including physics, cosmology, nonlinear dynamics, population biology, anthropology, economics, and neuroscience— have challenged the Newtonian view of the universe. Ways of thinking about science in Newtonian metaphors and models have been replaced by perspectives that are biologically inspired, decentralized, probabilistic, and dynamically changing. The implicit "designer" behind the mechanistic universe has been replaced by notions of chaos theory and strange attractors, self-organization, adaptation and selection, and emergent characteristics. This latter way of thinking about science has been characterized by some as complexity, and the phenomena to which these ideas apply as complex systems.

The Cognition, Technology, and Complex System Project, funded by the National Science Foundation, provides information about complex and dynamic systems concepts as well as links to related educational, scientific, and software Internet resources (see Figure 5). We have studied problem-solving about complex systems phenomena (e.g., why do traffic jams form, how did cheetahs evolve to run so fast, weather), documenting distinct differences in the answers given by experts and novices. Students tended to solve problems using beliefs that were reductive (e.g., used stepwise sequences, isolated parts of the system), centralized, predictable, and composed of static structures. Scientists generally solved the problems in a nonreductive manner that viewed the whole as being greater than the parts, described decentralized system interactions, noted randomness, and detailed dynamic processes. This research suggests that many students may need to revise fundamental beliefs about natural and social phenomena in order to understand higher-order concepts and conceptual models related to complexity and complex systems.

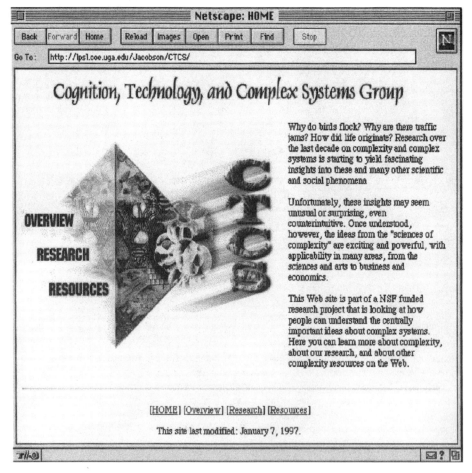

Figure 5. Cognition, Technology, and Complex Systems project home page.

Technology and teacher education. Technology, and its potential in teacher education, has fast become the focus of considerable national interest and concern. Numerous regional (e.g., Southeastern and Islands Regional Technology Consortium's report, *Integration of technology in pre-service teacher education programs*) and national reports (e.g., Educational Testing Service's report, *Does it compute? The relationship between educational technology and student achievement in mathematics*, and the President's Committee of Advisors on Science and Technology [PCAST], *Report to the President on the use of technology to strengthen K–12 education in the United States*) have identified teacher preparation as inadequate to meet the challenges of contemporary children and schools. Most have also suggested that better-prepared teachers are key to educational reform. The LPSL has embarked on teacher education efforts across institution levels (K–12, postsecondary), preparation levels (in-service and pre-service), and subject domains (mathematics, science). These projects examine closely the status of technology in teacher education, globally as well as locally, and emphasize the importance of addressing immediate needs of educators, given the contexts in which they teach.

One such effort, *Foundations for the Future*, is a collaboration among higher education institutions and industry representatives working with key agencies and educators to take advantage of telecommunications technology investments and available expertise to improve K–12 educational practices in Georgia. It involves the LPSL, Georgia Tech Research Institute, Morris Brown Research Institute, and EduLink—a nonprofit agency. Foundations for the Future focuses on transforming K–12 teaching-learning practices across disciplines through tailored professional development. The focus is on problem-based learning using teacher's own classroom teaching-learning environments as the contextual referent for developing technology-enhanced methods. The model employed emphasizes a developmental approach to improvement, where teachers progress from addressing immediate, basic needs through more transformative teaching-learning practices. Foundations for the Future is funded through the generous support of AT&T.

InterMath is another teacher education initiative funded jointly by Georgia's Eisenhower Higher Education Program for Professional Development as well as the Teacher Enhancement program of the National Science Foundation. InterMath is an in-service initiative that focuses on transforming the teaching and learning of mathematics in middle grades by intensive workshops with close-in follow-on support, the creation of a Web-enhanced ongoing support system for participating teachers beyond workshops, and the creation and nurturing of a mathematics transformation-minded teacher community. InterMath links state and local curriculum standards and the standards of the National Council of Teachers of Mathematics (NCTM), and focuses on the transformational nature of technology in the teaching and learning of mathematics.

Technology and school reform. This area has also been the focus of considerable national and international interest. In many ways, school settings define the convergence point of teacher education, curriculum design, and teaching methodology. They represent the "place" wherein education become most evident to the general public—the place where available research, theory, and practice either does or does not affect educational practices. The LPSL's efforts at school reform span K–12 and postsecondary settings where technology can influence the nature and quality of teaching and learning.

The previously mentioned Foundations for the Future project also established a state-of-the-art technology showcase wherein the latest technology applications can be tested and showcased. It supports districts in immediate and long-term technology infrastructure design and planning, provides technical support in the development of grant proposals, and provides on-demand technical support. Several related school-based projects have also been advanced. For example, we established a rural testbed in a nearby county through combined support from Georgia Department of Education and Georgia Center for Advanced Telecommunications Technology. We installed and tested microwave-based WANs and wireless LANs that enabled Internet access and resource sharing throughout the rural school district (*Oglethorpe County Science Initiative*). Using this testbed, we advanced project efforts in middle school science (*Science Connections*) with support from AT&T; a modest grant from Apple Computer enabled us to create a virtual folklore museum reflecting rural values and artifacts (*Wiring the Ties that Bind*).

Evaluation of technology impact. In a sense, evaluation is fundamental to all that we undertake. The LPSL has engaged several projects to advance the techniques and practices in the evaluation of technology effectiveness. In part, this has been in response to the requirements for documented evidence of technology's effects; all projects involve multiple stage evaluation. In no small part, however, this represents a growing need to refine the processes through which "proof" as to effectiveness of technology is alleged.

While the LPSL focuses extensively on research related to technology effectiveness, as educators we are often ill-prepared to address everyday questions of significance to otherq. We have a significant body of research evidence, but we are unable to answer practical questions demanded by different stakeholders. A root cause of this dilemma is the basic difference in priorities of different stakeholders (e.g., policy makers, educators, parents); different constituents ask different questions, each of which has varied methodology and data implications. One initiative, supported by the Educational Technology division of the Southern Regional Education Board, focuses on clarifying the questions and issues relevant to state-level policy makers (e.g., legislators, state and federal departments of education) and identifying the data requirements associated with them. We have also engaged in a two-year evaluation of a comprehensive media and technology effort in a nearby independent school (Media Across the Curriculum), where bottom-line issues of measurable impact on student learning in core disciplines were studied. Yet another initiative focused on the evaluation of armed forces hybrid CD-ROM-Web multimedia instruction. In each of the above efforts, we attempted to both address the basic evaluative questions posed and extend our understanding of varied evaluation methods.

FUTURE CHALLENGES

Fundamentally, we and others who implement technology in teaching and learning require four basic infrastructures: technology, funding, facilities, and people. Of the four, the first two have occupied a great deal of initial attention. Educators have stressed the need for additional financial resources in order to acquire sufficient technology in their institutions. There simply was not sufficient funding to build the technology infrastructure needed to use technology meaningfully. Recently, however, the significance of the latter two infrastructures, facilities and people, have become especially apparent in both schools and R&D laboratories. Whereas we were initially pleased simply to have technology available, the limitations of traditional facility design and availability has hampered our efforts. Increasingly, antiquated floor plans, wiring, and furniture have hampered meaningful technology integration. Simultaneously, the need for better-prepared teachers, administrators, and support personnel has become more acute; the costs associated with maintaining and growing a capability have become more apparent.

For most, the challenges faced by schools and described in reports such as National Academy of Sciences and Engineering's *Reinventing schools: The technology is now* and Georgia State University's Council for School Performance, *Two miles down a ten mile road: Instructional technology and the impact of lottery funding in Georgia*, have been evident for some time. The infrastructure needs of R&D laboratories, however, have often been less obvious to practicing educators. In R&D laboratories, the same infrastructure needs exist. How "cutting-edge" do we need to be? How innovative can we afford to be? How do we select new technologies that will affect innovative learning strategies without buying equipment that requires unreasonable technical support or recurring costs? How will we recruit and retain the intellectual resources needed to advance needed study in significant ways? How will the funding resources be secured to ensure that we remain sufficiently equipped to push rather than seal the envelope? These are significant challenges in organizations that hope to pave the way to new and innovative futures.

Center for Technology Innovation in Education
University of Missouri-Columbia

Dale Musser
James Laffey
Bryan Lawrence

In the past several years we have witnessed two fundamental changes in our conception of the educational process. First, cognitive psychology is increasingly revealing a picture of learning grounded in active participation, constructed knowledge, and the importance of the situation and context not only for what is learned, but for how it will be able to be used. These new theoretical underpinnings, as well as other forces, argue for learning through problem-solving, authentic projects, and learning communities. The second fundamental change to education comes from advances in technology with a special emphasis on network technologies, in particular the Internet. With dramatic advances in networking and processing capabilities, new tools of mediation, simulation, modeling, and communication are possible. We now have the potential to design teaching and learning experiences that are far less bounded by time and distance and less restricted by the limitations of a classroom. Teachers and learners can connect in many different ways offering new opportunities for learning in context, for richer means of communication and sharing, and for new means of performance and self assessment.

The Center for Technology Innovations in Education (CTIE) was formed in the College of Education at the University of Missouri-Columbia to build on these fundamental changes in education by undertaking research and development of innovative learning technology. CTIE was founded by Dr. James Laffey and Dr. Dale Musser in the fall of 1995 and operates by building teams of researchers, software designers and developers, and educators to take on challenging problems of learning and technology development. CTIE has generated more than $3 million in grants and gifts to support projects that involve technology innovation in the College of Education, partner school districts across the State of Missouri, and work with other organizations committed to learning and technology. Project funding has primarily come from the National Science Foundation, the U.S. Department of Education, the SBC (Southwestern Bell Corporation) Foundation, and other corporate sponsors.

CTIE is located in 4,500 square feet of space. A half-million-dollar renovation of the space was completed in 1997, providing a facility that is ideally suited to research and development using technology. The network infrastructure of CTIE supports 10/100 Mbps switched Ethernet to workstations with a 155 Mbps backbone link to the general campus and a 622 Mbps backbone link to the campus research network. Through participation in a grant for connection to the vBNS, CTIE has access to both the traditional Internet as well as Internet 2. Six SGI servers provide Web, E-mail, listserv, database, and other data services with approximately 150 GB of data storage. Oracle serves as the primary database engine for data storage and retrieval. Ten SGI workstations, 15 Macintosh computers, and 35 PC computers serve as workstations for the learning theorists, researchers, interface designers, software developers, and system architects employed in the Center. The software development expertise in CTIE includes C/C++, Java, Perl, and JavaScript for the development of Macintosh, UNIX, Windows, Internet, and Oracle DBMS applications. Software designers, graphic designers, user interface designers, 3D modelers, and application testers round out the technology development teams located in CTIE, which comprise approximately 40 employees, most of whom integrate work at CTIE with advancing their education at MU.

This chapter describes the history and projects of CTIE. The next section provides a brief introduction to our views about the future of technology and education and portrays the role we envision for CTIE in contributing to that future. The chapter concludes with a brief statement of recommendations for technology innovation in education.

HISTORY

The story of CTIE begins in 1993 with enhancement funds from the University Chancellor to the College of Education to improve efforts in educational technology. These funds were principally used to hire Laffey, previously a research scientist at Apple Computer, and Musser, previously a Multimedia Educational Software Product Manager at IBM. Prior to the enhancement, technology use was minimal, and research on technology and learning was nonexistent. Laffey recalls touring the "new" computer lab during his hiring interview and seeing a room of five-year-old IBM PS-2s being used through terminal emulation for reading E-mail. An early payoff of the enhancement hiring was the effort of Musser as he led the development of a high-end multimedia and learning laboratory. Laffey sought and was awarded an NSF planning grant for an investigation of project-based learning. These efforts came together in a project for Oracle to develop a prototype CD-ROM for supporting project-based learning. The Oracle project brought together some of the most talented designers and developers on campus. As the short-term project came to a close, Laffey and Musser discussed ways to keep the team together. On the day Musser posted a sign declaring CTIE, the center was born.

PROJECTS

The next three years saw significant growth and activity primarily in the form of articulating and advancing a research agenda about active, engaged learning through technology innovation. Understanding and enabling such learning is central to all CTIE projects. Projects most often include both a product/demonstration focus and a study of the cognitive, social, and technical aspects of the implementation. Some of the key projects are included in Table 1.

The Future As It Relates to Education and Technology

Technologies are created with the purpose of making it possible to do something that could not be done before or to make the lives of humans easier, more productive, or more enjoyable. Technology aims at improving the condition of humans. In many ways education shares the same aim. We learn so that our lives become better. Core to education and many technological developments is the goal of empowering the individual.

The application of technology to education should improve the method and means of learning of each student. Unfortunately, the organization and methods of teaching in schools have not changed much since the industrial revolution. Individual teachers instruct classes of students. Classes of students march through a series of courses and grades, ready or not, motivated or not, for the next step along the line. Standardized test scores, which do little to promote the success of individuals, drive school reform. This model continues because we know how to do it with the limited human and physical resources allocated to schooling.

Technology, as it has for other enterprises in our society, can be used to provide innovation in education, innovation to focus education on the needs and learning of the individual student. Using technology, the opportunity exists to make learning an individual experience that takes place any time, anywhere, and at any point in a person's life. Technology offers to alter the focus of what is being taught, as well as how it is being taught, to facilitate a student's development at higher cognitive levels. Learning should be interesting, fun, and meaningful and result in active and enthusiastic engagement by students in the learning process.

TABLE 1. Research and development projects of CTIE.

Title	Description
Project MOST (Missouri Supporting Teachers)	An NSF award to improve science and mathematics education by building and studying the implications of an Internet-based support system for secondary teachers and students as they undertake project-based learning and computational science. (Biggerstaff, Laffey, and Nazworthy 1997; Gibney and Laffey 1999; Laffey and Singer 1997; Laffey, Musser, and Tupper 1998a; Tupper and Laffey 1999)
The Mobile Computer Laboratory Program	Provided leadership and technical solutions for the implementation of a new undergraduate teacher education program focused on the innovative use of technology to support teaching and learning. A key feature of this program was providing a laptop computer to every teacher education student entering the College of Education.
Interactive Shared Journal System (ISJS)	An Internet-based software system developed to support the communication and collaboration of students, faculty, and administration by providing a medium in which they could share and record experiences, ideas, and problems and, through collective effort, create solutions. (Laffey and Musser 1996; Laffey, Musser, and Tupper 1998b, 1998c)
Project Whistlestop	A Department of Education Challenge Grant; connects teachers and students with original source material from the Harry S Truman Presidential Library to support learning and inquiry. The project places original resource documents from the Truman Presidential Library online and organizes those documents enabling educators to develop new historical project curriculum and Internet-based instructional education programs. (Kochtanek and Laffey 1998; Kochtanek, Laffey, Tunender, Ervin, and Borwick 1998).
Planet Innovation	Funded by the Department of Education, the project creates Internet-based tools to assist in the planning, implementation, and evaluation of technology programs and curriculum.
IESLP	The Information Environment for School Leadership Preparation is an Internet-based instructional system for preparing leaders of educational organizations. IESLP has created a database model of school communities for problems-based learning.
STI	The Study of the Technology Infrastructure in Teacher Education (STI) project is funded by NSF and studies the effect of a new teacher education program and new technology infrastructure in the MU College of Education. Key questions address technology appropriation for teaching and the socialization of beginning teachers. (Placier, Laffey and Hall 1999).
iExpedition	A research project conducted in partnership with Motorola, Inc., and colleagues at Brigham Young University. The project seeks to develop and understand the use of mediation technologies for supporting distributed learning communities via the Web.
Jefferson School Project	A collaboration between CTIE, Southwestern Bell, and the Jefferson Elementary School in St. Louis, Missouri, to use technology to enrich an elementary school in an impoverished neighborhood. (Laffey, Espinosa, and Musser 1999).
MOTIVE	Missouri Technology Infrastructure for Veterinapy Education (MOTIVE) is creating a model system for technology-enhanced learning in basic biomedical science education, with special focus on group problem solving. (Allen, Germann, and March 1998)
Internet Schools	Internet Schools is a project to re-envision schools based on ubiquitous access to the Internet as well as to develop open-source, innovative technologies to advance toward this vision.

"What do I want to learn today?" That is a question that every student should be able to ask and have the resources and means to pursue. "Too late to learn." Those are words that should never be true. Technology offers the means by which systems and resources can be constructed that allows anyone, anywhere, at any time to pursue learning that is meaningful to them.

Ubiquitous networking and computing provide the means to support the anytime and anywhere notions. A world of people can have access to the tools, resources, and mentors that are needed to support learning. Prior to the existence of an expansive network, distribution was a particularly difficult problem to overcome. Networks provide the means to efficiently distribute the resources for learning. Networks also provide the means for humans to build communities that share knowledge and expertise and that are neither geographically nor temporally bound.

The power of technology in its application to learning yields more than the ability to support learning any time and anywhere. It provides the means to create tools and environments that foster deeper levels of understanding and attainment at higher cognitive levels. It provides the means for students to work to achieve competence rather than a grade. (Working to achieve competence is the same as saying that a student needs to continue to pursue learning a thing until they have an "A." The factory line model requires that we label the product and move on. A competence model requires that a student continue to work until a level of performance is achieved.) Technology-based environments and tools can provide the means for students to receive individualized support and to operate on timelines separate from other students.

Technological environments and tools are not meant to replace physical real-world experiences. They exist to augment and support these experiences. Technology provides scaffolding that helps learners participate in activities in which they are not ready to participate without support.

CTIE engages in research aimed at improving teaching and learning through innovations in technology. These technologies are created with the purpose of supporting people's learning through active and enthusiastic engagement in interesting, fun, and meaningful tasks. Networking, asynchronous learning, performance support, project-based/authentic learning, digital media, and learning communities are themes that run through each project in the Center.

The future of technological innovations in support of learning is aimed at the following areas:

- Developing inexpensive, small, portable, high-performance, wirelessly networked computers that can be provided to every student

- Increasing network bandwidth to support high-quality, real-time delivery of digital media to large numbers of people

- Improving information management techniques to provide intelligent means of organizing and accessing information to meet contextual needs

- Using AI techniques to provide technology-based mentoring, guidance, assessment, and feedback for students

- Improving I/O devices including visual displays, voice input, and voice output

- Improving the interface between humans and computers to make computers more natural for humans to use

- Improving the ability to visualize and model information

- Creating 3D virtual environments to support more realistic simulations

The future of innovations in teaching and learning that is supported by technology is aimed at the following areas:

- facilitated asynchronous learning
- project-based/authentic learning
- developing learning communities
- performance-based assessment

- individualized instruction
- restructuring schools and classrooms

In summary, a connected, mediated, and "smart" technology will have an increasing presence in education. The presence of technology will enable educators to focus on the individual learner rather than on a class of learners and to have learning goals of analysis and communication rather than recall and recognition.

How CTIE Addresses Possible Scenarios of the Future

As we brainstorm about the future, it is hard to imagine any idea we envision as not coming true. This is so because while education and the role of technology in education in the past has been top-down and monolithic, we see the future as diverse, spreading beyond traditional institutions and characterized by empowered learners. So while we expect that in 20 years one will still be able to find many schools with technology in the corner and classroom-based instruction the norm, we also expect that children "of all ages" will find networked experiences, communities, and learning opportunities based on interest and appropriateness. Similarly, we expect that many school communities will find ways to reorganize themselves to focus on the learning of each child, and use teachers and technology to create a connected, mediated, and "smart" learning environment.

Two of the ways that CTIE prepares for this future are to:

1. Create learning technologies that are based on models of learning and performance (e.g., performance support, learning communities, project-based learning), not necessarily models of schooling and teaching; and

2. Work with school-based educators who are engaged in reform.

An example of creating learning technologies based on learning models is the Interactive Shared Journal System. The journal system was created to support a community of learners and to facilitate reflective practice. The journal system was first implemented using Macintosh clients and an SGI server. Subsequent to the creation of a Macintosh client, a client based on DHTML was created that can access services through an Internet browser. The clients and servers communicate over the Internet using TCP/IP connections. Anyone who has access to the Internet can participate. A custom server was created for connecting and maintaining a persistent connection to the journal system. The server provides communication between the client and a multimedia object database.

The journal system is a flexible system for the development and support of learning communities but can be understood as enabling three key processes: access to Internet-based resources, capturing experiences, and sharing experiences. A key technology developed for the journal system has been an approach to creating Internet-shareable documents with rich media (including streaming media) through a simple point-and-click interface. This technology enables the user to easily capture and share richly represented experiences. Through our work on the journal system we are seeing these tools form a basis for new learning communities, and we are learning about shared experiences, the challenges of representation, and new forms of interfaces for enabling representation and engaged learning in Internet spaces.

The Jefferson Elementary School project is an example of CTIE working with school-based educators in a reform effort. Jefferson is an elementary school in an urban area marked by high poverty and low school achievement. Through a unique combination of business and foundation support, the school is being transformed with a vision of how technology can be a lever for building a new type of school and community. From a school in 1998 with a few old standalone computers (Apple IIs and the like), Jefferson has moved to a school in 1999 with a 128K frame relay Internet connection; twisted pair Ethernet (CAT 5); 100 Mbps Ethernet hubs; a fiber, voice, and coax network; one or two Pentium II computers installed into each classroom; and network services that provide all children with E-mail addresses, enterprise calendaring, Usenet News, and roaming NT and Netscape profiles for children and teachers. The year 2000 will see four computers in each classroom, a dial-in server, three ISDN BRI lines for videoconferencing, investigations into a laptop for each student, and networking the housing developments that are homes to the children at Jefferson. Along with this reconstruction of the physical and information space of school, we are working hands-on with teachers and administrators to change the social conditions of the school away from whole-class instruction with incredible amounts of time and energy devoted to law and order. The teachers envision a school devoted to the full development of the emotional, social, and academic potential of each child, but they have not had the strategies and resources to achieve this goal. We are helping them learn, try, and build competency with models of activity and project-based learning that can be implemented with the support of technology.

One of our roles on this project has been to craft a white paper for envisioning how technology could serve the reform goals of this project and contributing to the design and implementation of reform efforts. A second role for CTIE has been to learn with the participants in the school and community about the requirements of this most challenging of problems for our nation—urban school reform—and the potential of technology to offer new solution types and empower individuals in impoverished settings.

CTIE, mostly because of its impatience with the rate of change, not only engages in doing research about aspects of how technology can be used to facilitate and promote learning, but also engages in projects aimed at quickly bringing about change in schools and other learning environments. So much of the knowledge base relating to educational technology is irrelevant to the types of engaged learning in technology-rich environments that are the focus of projects within CTIE. This is frustrating to anyone who desires to see the kinds of changes we envision, but it also means that there is plenty of fertile ground for research and development. CTIE builds teams for projects and puts them in highly resourced environments where the opportunity for innovation is possible. CTIE looks for synergy across projects and uses the results of each project to learn lessons that contribute to our overall knowledge about how best to use technology in support of learning.

Recommendations for the Area of Technology in Education

Thirty years from now we will look back at this era as people in aviation look back at the Wright brothers seeking to get off the ground at Kitty Hawk. We will better appreciate that information technology is a fundamental enabler of human endeavors. Our computational tools will be tightly integrated resources for thought, and our network environments will be the equivalent of having developed spoken and written languages.

To develop an understanding of the best methodologies and tools for effectively supporting learning through the use of technology, we need support for basic learning technology research. The focus of this research needs to be on the "end user." The goal is not on how to better support teaching but how to better support learning.

We must engage in rapid prototyping of new forms of learning support based on ideals of learning systems and what is made possible by new technologies, not what is familiar and comfortable. We must break down the walls of the schools, including universities such as our own, and reach out to learning communities that span the globe.

In order that these goals may be met, collaboration of educational researchers, technology researchers, and educational leaders and practitioners must take place. We must learn how to use the same technologies being developed to support learning to engage a global community of researchers and change agents to bring about the change that will empower a new generation of lifetime learners who embrace learning whenever it is needed.

REFERENCES

Allen, G. K., Germann, P. J., and March, J. Z. (1998, June). MOTIVE: Missouri Technology Infrastructure for Veterinary Education. Paper presented at the 15th Symposium on Veterinary Medical Education, Purdue University.

Biggerstaff, J., Laffey, J., and Nazworthy, J. (1997). Computational science at Lee's Summit high school. In Z. Berge and M. Collins (eds.), *Wired Together: Computer-Mediated Communication in the K–12 Classroom. Volume 2: Case Studies.* Cresskill, NJ: Hampton Press, 107–17.

Gibney, T., and Laffey, J. (1999, April). Technology and project-based learning. Paper presented at Annual Meeting of the American Educational Research Association, Montreal.

Kochtanek, T., and Laffey, J. (1998, May). Project Whistlestop: Design considerations for information retrieval performance in an image database. *Proceedings of the Nineteenth National Online Meeting,* New York.

Kochtanek, T., Laffey, J., Tunender, H., Ervin, J., and Borwick, J. (1998, May). Project Whistlestop: An evaluation of search engines on the web. *Proceedings of the Seventeenth Integrated Online Library Systems Meeting,* New York.

Laffey, J., Espinosa, L., and Musser, D. (1999). Technology and urban elementary school reform. Presented at the AACE World Conference on Educational Multimedia and Hypermedia and on Educational Telecommunications, Seattle, WA.

Laffey, J., and Musser, D. (1996). Building Internet-based electronic performance support for teaching and learning. *Proceedings of AACE World Conference of the Web Society.* San Francisco, CA.

Laffey, J., Musser, D., and Tupper, T. (1998a). A computer-mediated support system for project based learning. *Educational Technology Research and Development* 46(1), 73–86.

Laffey, J., Musser, D., and Tupper, T. (1998b). An Internet-based journal system for enabling a learning community. *Learning Technology Review* 2(Winter), 4–13.

Laffey, J., Musser, D., and Tupper, T. (1998c). An Internet-based journal for professional development. *Proceedings of AACE World Conference of the Society for Information Technology and Teacher Education.* Washington, DC.

Laffey, J., and Singer, J. (1997). Using mapping for cognitive assessment in project based science. *Journal of Interactive Learning Research.* 8(3/4), 363–87.

Placier, P., Laffey, J., and Hall, P. (1999). Study of technology infrastructure for teacher education. Columbia, MO: Center for Technology Innovation in Education.

Tupper, T., and Laffey, J. (1999, April). Understanding student perceptions, effort and learning in a project-based technology rich environment. Paper presented at Annual Meeting of the American Educational Research Association, Montreal.

Part Three
School Library Media Section

Introduction

This section inaugurates a new feature for the Yearbook. The editors have endeavored to present several chapters that relate exclusively to school library media centers and K–12 educational technology. These chapters represent recent research and seminal thinking in these areas. The section should be of practical use to media specialists, and it also should be of interest to those in higher education who are concerned with preparing media specialists and school technology specialists.

The first two chapters engage the essential issue of information literacy, an educational thrust now viewed as the most important student outcome influenced by media centers. *Information Power* (American Association of School Librarians and Association for Educational Communications and Technology 1998) helps define and update the role of the media specialist. Although the central mission of media centers and media specialists has not changed since the 1988 edition, media specialists must constantly weigh priorities as they endeavor to implement the standards in their local settings. Also at question, especially for educators engaged in preparing media specialists, is how school library media fits into the wider field of instructional technology, as well as the alternative field of librarianship. Are we librarians, or are we instructional technologists? Is there a viable means of spanning both disciplines? Michael Eisenberg and Carrie Lowe pursue this question in their chapter, using information technology as the unifying force. Dr. Eisenberg in particular is eminently qualified to discuss this topic due to his years of involvement as a leader in the field.

Delia Neuman's chapter expands upon the principles presented in *Information Power* by addressing the monumental issue of assessment. Now that the standards are in place, how will we know if they are working? How can media specialists and teachers determine if individual students have reached an acceptable level of competency? Dr. Neuman focuses on the Information Literacy Standards themselves, especially the "Sample Assessment Items." Using these elements, she links library media programs to learning and describes how assessment plays an important role in this linkage. Her suggestions for implementing assessments are designed to be collaborative, comprehensive, concrete, and circumspect, and they should help educators improve validity and reliability in their assessments. As writer and member of the 1998 *Information Power* Implementation Committee, Dr. Neuman's chapter represents an extension of the basic concepts presented in this most important of library media publications.

The next two chapters deal directly with aspects of library practice on a specific level. Melissa Gross's chapter describes a phenomenon more or less unique to school library media centers: teacher-imposed questions brought to media centers by students. This chapter explores the differences between questions that students generate from their own personal curiosity and questions that teachers compel them to investigate to satisfy specific educational objectives. Both exercises have value, but the difference between the two embodies a philosophical comparison between student- and teacher-centered instruction. Although she does not suggest that imposed queries are harmful, Dr. Gross describes the implications inherent between these two types of reference situations both for pedagogy and for media service.

The Fitzgerald chapter describes a study exploring the perceptions of adults about specific media formats, and translates these findings into educational implications. The study revealed that sophisticated adults prefer several specific formats in their information search processes, and they make several assumptions about these formats that have interesting implications for critical thinking. Also, because of strong preferences for a limited set of media formats, information found in alternative formats may be neglected. Media specialists often encounter similar behavior in students who avoid periodicals because of their unwieldiness, or who neglect print formats in favor of the Internet. Although this is a subtle problem, the chapter suggests several practices that may help students explore information in varied formats, taking the unique characteristics of each into account.

The final chapter of this section discusses an important aspect of media specialist preparation. Interest in distance learning seems to be increasing although online learning technology can no longer be considered new. Janette Hill's chapter discusses this topic specifically as it applies to library education. Library students and educators have a special interest in this topic because in many areas of the continent it is difficult to obtain school library media certification or MLS degrees. Thus, library education is a fertile area for distance learning development. Dr. Hill describes her experience of teaching two school library media courses completely online via the Web. She relates the accomplishments of this experience, along with its frustrations, and imparts several recommendations for future courses taught in a similar manner. Considering the nationwide rush toward online education (see the Distance Education section of the Mediagraphy within this volume for other examples), reports such as Hill's become more and more important as newcomers to the arena expect to learn from the pioneers.

These five chapters represent the most compelling issues in school library media practice today. The aim of this section is to describe current trends in library media practice and recent research findings. More important, the editors hope that the information printed here will furnish ideas to improve the overall efficacy of school media practice.

Mary Ann Fitzgerald

REFERENCE

American Association of School Librarians and Association for Educational Communications and Technology. (1998). *Information Power: Building Partnerships for Learning*. Chicago: American Library Association.

The Roles and Responsibilities
of Library and Information Professionals
in the Twenty-First Century

Michael Eisenberg and Carrie Lowe
University of Washington

In his address to the 1997 National Education Computing Conference (NECC), Bill Gates directed the audience's attention to the fact that in the past 20 years, computing power has grown a millionfold. Even more amazing, Gates predicts that in the next 20 years, it will happen again. In 20 years, computers will be a million times more powerful than today. Think about this. What might this mean for society? For learning and teaching? Thinking about this means taking a long-term perspective. That's what we hope to do in this paper.

INTRODUCTION

It's a cliché, but nevertheless true to state that the only thing consistent in today's world is change itself. This is certainly true for education on all levels but is particularly true for people working in the field of education who focus on the use of information and technology. Who are these people—those on the cutting edge of applying computer and network technology in learning and teaching situations? The group certainly includes computer teachers—those who teach classes in programming and how to use various computer applications. Also included are the technology specialists who oversee computer labs and computers and networks throughout schools and districts. And, from our perspective, it is also crucial to include those educators directly responsible for providing information resources, services, and skills instruction throughout school—the library media specialists.

Librarians are the original information specialists in society, and library media specialists fill that position in K–12 schools. Their role was clearly and boldly articulated in the 1988 standards for library media programs and reaffirmed in the 1998 standards:

> "The mission of the library media program is to ensure that students and staff are effective users of ideas and information." (*Information Power* 1988, p.1; 1998, p.6)

Today, technology is integral to every aspect of library media work that goes into fulfilling this role:

- Library media programs provide access to information. Computers and networks, including the Internet and World Wide Web, allow libraries to extend access to a vast network of information resources to every corner of the school building and district, and even into the homes of the community.

- Library media programs provide opportunities for students to learn essential information and technology skills. Library media specialists work in partnership with classroom teachers and computer/technology specialists to integrate information and technology skills instruction into classroom curriculum and learning.

Library media specialists also have a special role in seeing that all students have access to technology and information. Technology is everywhere—or at least has the potential to be everywhere. Some speak of a "digital divide" between the technology haves and have-nots in our society. Librarians have traditionally fought against this type of divide—for widespread and open access to books, journals, and other resources. This role is even more crucial today as technology and information extend far beyond computer labs and physical library media centers to classrooms and the home.

Last, library media specialists have a role in helping classroom teachers to first cope with, and later take advantage of, new technological and information capabilities. While technology can be a positive factor, it can also create confusion and uncertainty. For classroom teachers the lines between educator and technologist are increasingly blurred. Classroom teachers are increasingly being asked to integrate technology into their own preparation and delivery as well as to be able to familiarize students with a variety of technologies. Library media specialists can help by consulting with teachers on how technology and information can help to accomplish goals for curriculum and student learning.

In this paper, we will focus on preparing for the workplace of the future. We delve further into the role of the library media specialist in an increasingly complex and technologically challenging world. We begin by looking more closely at technology today and tomorrow while trying to consider the implications of Gates' prediction for growth. We then explain in detail how library media specialists have a unique and vital role to play in education in the twenty-first century. We explore some of the principles that have been the backbone of the library profession for the last hundred years, and think about how they can guide library media for the next hundred years. We conclude with a proposal for bringing library media specialists together with other key educators to provide the necessary critical mass to help schools change.

TECHNOLOGY: TODAY AND TOMORROW

In spite of insufficient funding and lack of systematic planning, technology is rapidly finding its way into schools. The National Center for Education Statistics (1999) reports that in the fall of 1998, 89 percent of public schools were connected to the Internet. This is up from 35 percent in 1994!

Technology is primarily a tool—a tool that extends our abilities. The computer and information technology tools most often found in schools are used for one or more purposes:

- processing
- information
- communication.

We will explore each of these functions and the role that they can play in the context of education.

Processing tools take existing data, information, and ideas and allow the user to format and present them in a number of distinctive ways. For example, today in schools, students routinely use word processing to draft and then finalize their assignments and papers. Many also use HyperStudio, PowerPoint, or other multimedia presentation software to bring together text, images, sound, and even video to create projects and presentations. Increasingly, students are developing their own websites to display and present their work.

Information tools help students to locate and access information. Examples of information tools include library catalogs and print or electronic reference tools (e.g., encyclopedias, atlases, dictionaries, almanacs). Today, the World Wide Web offers an amazing amount of information on most topics. However, while the Web is rich in quantity, it often lacks in quality. Quality requires "adding value" through careful selection, editing, organizing, and presenting information. The full-text periodical databases (e.g., EBSCO, University Microfilms, Electric Library), the online encyclopedias (e.g., Encyclopaedia Britannica, Microsoft Encarta), and the more targeted electronic works (e.g., NewsBank, SIRS, ABC-CLIO) cover almost as wide a range of subjects as the

Web, but the general quality of information included is much higher. More and more school libraries are providing widespread access to these high-quality information tools through their school or district intranets or through the Internet itself. Statewide database licensing or cooperative purchasing agreements are facilitating access to all students, faculty, and staff.

Communications tools create connections between and among people. E-mail has become one of the most common forms of person-to-person contact, and listservs and other forms of mailing lists are just as popular for group communication. Chat and various forms of audio- and videoconferencing provide synchronous (i.e., live) contact. All together, these new capabilities serve to change our perception of distance.

Along with their positive features, communications (and information tools) create special problems for schools—in terms of safety and appropriate use. Many schools have implemented appropriate-use policies and procedures, while others have turned to filtering software to try to control the types of information or people students can access.

All these capabilities are still just the beginning. Remember the Bill Gates quote—although today's computers are a million times more powerful than 20 years ago, in 20 years computers will be a million times more powerful than today! Twenty years ago, in 1979, the Apple II was just coming on the scene. It had an amazing 64 *kilo*bytes of RAM and stored information on a 180K floppy disk. We were able to do some rudimentary word processing and track our budget through Visicalc.

Today, the computer used to write this paper has 128 *mega*bytes of RAM and a 6.2 *giga*byte hard drive. We use a complex word processing program that includes spell and grammar check, flexible "what-you-see-is-what-you-get" display, the ability to include graphics in a document, various printing options (including color), and all kinds of options that customize to our needs and desires. We can also search the World Wide Web, access encyclopedias on CD-ROM, communicate through e-mail, and much more, all for about the same price as that Apple II.

But what kinds of capabilities will we have in 20 years? Certainly, we will have fully connected networks (24 hours a day, 7 days a week), voice-activated commands, and voice recognition for creating documents. But what will we include in our documents beyond sound, video, and graphics? What will a document be like in 20 years? And will we really have computers such as those we have today? Isn't it more likely that every appliance, desk, and even chair will include an embedded computer or network connection that recognizes us as individuals and gives us access to our intelligent computing environment?

Some trends appear clear: we will have more connectivity and technology that is more customized to individuals. Technology will be integrated seamlessly—processing tools will be connected to communications tools will be connected to information tools—with common access mechanisms and interfaces. Technology in 20 years will surely be more assistive, individualized, and moving towards more humanlike interaction. Our personal technological environment will be more intelligent and responsive to our individual needs, able to adapt without prompting or programming. Technology will appear more "intelligent"—just how intelligent, who can say? How intelligent is a technological environment that recognizes individual users, learns and modifies itself to suit an individual's likes and dislikes, and even anticipates what a person will want?

Miniaturization and imbedded technologies are important trends to follow. The computer on our desk is already a reality. What about when it is in our eyeglasses, coat, earring, or even an ear? What capabilities will these provide beyond just allowing us to check our e-mail while we are stuck in traffic?

Clearly, future technology will present a special challenge and opportunity for education. Most education still revolves around a set calendar and schedule, a physical school, and classrooms full of students, with teachers as lecturers, textbooks as the main resources, and tests as the means to evaluate learning. But this no longer needs to be the norm. Technology has finally progressed to the point where students can learn at their own pace. They can interact with other students and teachers remotely from a distance. A range of resources are at students and teachers' fingertips—with flexibility in sequencing, highlighting, organizing, and evaluation.

Implications: So What?

What does all this mean for education, particularly for learning and teaching? Looking at the potential and capabilities for education, it's easy to fall into the trap of saying that "technology is the answer," and attempting to apply technology to every problem and situation.

Looking to technology to solve every problem is tempting. However, if we expect our students to be intelligent and critical users of technology, it is vital that we be skeptical and ask, "So what? What's the point of all this technology? If technology is the answer, then what is the question?"

From a learning and teaching standpoint, there actually are a number of questions that relate to technology:

- What are we trying to accomplish in terms of learning and teaching?

- How can we help our students to be successful in an ever-changing world?

- What are the skills and knowledge related to technology that students need to be successful?

- How can we use technology to meet educational goals and objectives for students?

Library media specialists can help to focus on these questions. As noted, librarians are the original information specialists. In schools, librarians have focused beyond textbooks to consider resources, technologies, and information skills in relation to learning and teaching. We call this *the information perspective*, and it means that library media specialists look at curriculum, assignments, and learning in terms of the information resources, processes, and technologies required for student success.

From early on, library media professionals have tried to teach students that when they have an assignment to complete, they should consider the information resources they need and then use the appropriate access technology to find that resource and information. Years ago, that resource might have been a magazine article or a book, and the technology was a printed magazine index or a card catalog. Today, it's more likely that the resource will be an article in a full-text database or a primary source on a website, and the access technology is an online index or web search engine. The key isn't the technology or the resource—it's the information skills of recognizing the information needed and being able to go out and get that information.

Library media specialists have been pioneers in the area of teaching information skills and integrating technology skills into the information problem-solving process. One of the most popular approaches to integrated information and technology skills, the Big6® approach, was developed by Mike Eisenberg and Bob Berkowitz, both of whom have a background in library and information science (1988). The Big 6® defines six essential stages in the information problem-solving process:

1. Task Definition

2. Information Seeking Strategies

3. Location and Access

4. Use of Information

5. Synthesis

6. Evaluation.

The Big 6® and other models of the information process (such as those by Kuhlthau 1993; Stripling and Pitts 1988; and Pappas and Tepe 1995) define the path that students take to solve information problems. When the focus is on the intellectual endeavor—the problem-solving aspects of learning—technology assumes its rightful place as a tool, a means that is used to get to where we want to be, rather than the answer itself.

Ensuring that students learn essential information skills is at the heart of library media work today. As explained in more detail later in this paper, library media specialists are committed to working in partnership with classroom teachers and others to integrate information and technology skills instruction in curriculum. If library media specialists are successful in their efforts, students will gain these essential skills and leave school as effective users of information and technology.

However, not all library media specialists have been able to completely fulfill this role. There are a number of legitimate reasons for this including understaffing, becoming bogged down in clerical or other nonprofessional duties, and lack of training. But sometimes library media specialists have been unable to clearly define their role or prioritize effectively when faced with limited time, effort, and resources.

In addition, the library and information profession has not done a particularly good job of defining the media specialists' role. Gary Hartzell, former school administrator, prolific author, and professor of education at the University of Nebraska, refers to library media specialists as "invisible" professionals (1997). He argues that in many school districts, library media specialists are routinely excluded from decisions affecting technology, curriculum, and resources at the school and district level. He also points to the widespread trend of cutting library budgets and, in some cases, library media positions to ease school financial problems.

According to Hartzell, the reasons for this are clear. Teachers and administrators are not aware of the valuable contributions that library media specialists can make to the school. In his Fall 1998 keynote address to the Washington Library Media Association, Hartzell pointed out that no course in any major school of education in this country focuses on the use of library and information in learning and teaching. He went on to say that in almost all teacher training programs, there is little mention of the role of the library media program and the library and information professional at all. The library media specialists compound this problem by failing to promote themselves to fellow educators and school administration in communicating the nature and role of library and information work to others.

This does not bode well for the library media field or for education in general. If classroom teachers, administrators, other specialists, parents, and the broader community have limited experience with high-quality library media programs and do not know what to expect from active, cutting-edge library media programs, how can they be expected to value, seek out, or support library media programs? Library media specialists must do a better job of clearly and loudly articulating their role in preparing students for the information and technology rich workplace of the future. In addition, there must be opportunities in pre-and in-service training for educators in all contexts to gain first-hand experience with the value of teaching in partnership with an engaged, high-quality library media program.

Guiding Principles

The core set of beliefs and practices guiding library and information professionals provide the conceptual understandings needed for the future. Although several of theqe principles were developed recently as a result of the influx of technology into schools and the overabundance of information, most of them are as old as the profession of librarianship itself.

Principle One: School Libraries Don't Have Walls

This idea draws from the belief that "library" is not a place; rather, library is everywhere. This belief works on both the micro- and metalevel. Within the school, this means that library media specialists must not be cloistered within the walls of the library and within the constraints of scheduled library time. Instead, teachers and library media specialists must collaborate to give students a valuable learning experience. Library media specialists can assist teachers in recognizing the technology and information problem-solving aspects of a project and assignment; the teacher can then use the librarian's expertise when instructing students in how to approach these sections of the project. With the free flow of information and communication between the classroom and the library media center comes better information skills and richer learning opportunities for all students.

Beyond the classroom setting, the concept of libraries without walls is equally important and will be increasingly so in the future. In order to be effective citizens in the information- and technology-rich society of the future, students will need to make the skills typically associated with "library" a part of their everyday lives. One such skill is information problem-solving. Familiarity with an information problem-solving approach will provide students with a strategy for wading through the deluge of information they will face as a part of modern life. Other library and information literacy skills, such as critical thinking, technology literacy, and comfort with a variety of media formats, will also prove invaluable for students outside of the school setting.

Principle Two: Library and Information Professionals Must Be Flexible

In the opening chapter of *Information Power: Building Partnerships for Learning*, the authors describe the vision of the library media specialist in the information-rich society of the future. This vision presents a portrait of the range of tasks and responsibilities that library and information professionals must undertake in the future to provide students with the learning experiences they will need.

The authors of *Information Power* believe that library media specialists will wear a wide variety of professional hats in the future. These responsibilities can be broken up into four broad categories: teacher, instructional partner, information specialist, and program administrator (1998).

The role of teacher deals with the instructional issues surrounding information literacy and library skills. In this role, library media specialists instruct students on the information problem-solving process and the tools necessary to successfully execute that process. This role makes library media specialists leaders in developing vital curriculum.

The role of instructional partner creates a space for library media specialists as consultants within the school. This role recognizes the library media specialist's expertise in the areas of evaluating resources and teaching students to use information technology skills in context. Library media specialists who embrace the concept of being an instructional partner will have an open-door policy for teachers to approach them for ideas and input on the information and technology aspects of their curriculum.

The role of information specialist makes the library media specialist something of a role model for information literacy skills for students, teachers, and administrators. In this context, library media specialists take the idea of instructing students in information skills one step further, by practicing what they preach. This gives students and other faculty members a chance to see excellent information skills in action, which can be the most effective teaching tool of all.

The role of program administrator envisions a true leadership role for library media specialists. As program administrators, library media specialists will create and implement policies for the appropriate use and acquisition of information technology in the school. In this role, library media specialists also act as advocates for students and for the library media program.

The skills and expertise possessed by the library media specialist will be in high demand in the school of the future. The dynamic roles described by *Information Power* are ones that library media specialists are perfectly suited for, but they will not be handed this role as a birthright. It remains the responsibility of the library media specialist to prove to administrators and faculty that their skills are invaluable, and that they are able to lead schools into the twenty-first century.

Principle Three: Ensure that Students Are Effective Users of Ideas and Information

This principle describes the central vision of *Information Power* (1988). This is also one of the central tenets of the library profession. According to the first *Information Power* standards, this mission is accomplished in three ways:

- By providing intellectual and physical access to materials in all formats;

- By providing instruction to foster competence and stimulate interest in reading, viewing, and using information and ideas; and

- By working with other educators to design learning strategies to meet the needs of individual students.

The significance of this principle lies in the fact that it can be applied just as easily today as it could 10 years ago when it was originally written. It presents the library media specialist as a dynamic, essential member of the school faculty, working to support teachers as they integrate concepts of information literacy into their instruction. It also places library media specialists centrally in the process of acquiring and evaluating information resources, allowing them to model appropriate information literacy skills. This principle has been, and should remain the guiding force for library professionals.

This principle also highlights the most important and enduring role that the library media specialist plays within the school: the provider of information services and skills instruction. It is important that all members of the school community understand that the library media specialist is uniquely qualified and valuable within the school to provide essential information literacy instruction and valuable information services. As underscored by Hartzell (see above), library media specialists must focus on communicating their value to ensure that they survive and thrive in the information society.

Principle Four: Information Is Everywhere, Essential, Central

This principle relates directly to the first principle. Just as school libraries do not have walls, information resources are everywhere, both inside of the library and outside of it. This idea indicates the need for students to master the information literacy skills they will need in everyday life.

The idea that information is everywhere is the basis of the idea of information literacy. Information is a pervasive and essential part of our society, and indeed, our lives. We are, at our essence, processors and users of information. This is not a recent development. Humans have always been dependent on information to help make decisions and guide our actions. Change has come in the sheer volume of information and the complexity of information systems—largely due to advances in information technology and the accelerated rate at which we live out lives.

The American Library Association (1989) defines a person who is information literate as "[someone who is able to] recognize when information is needed and has the ability to locate, evaluate, and effectively use the needed information." Information literacy incorporates several different literacies. Because an information-literate student must be able to comprehend and use information from a variety of formats and layouts, they must possess both Visual and Media Literacy. A great deal of information will be available in the future through computer networks. For this reason, students must possess both Network and Computer literacy (Spitzer, Eisenberg, and Lowe 1998).

Information Power: Lessons and Legacy

Recognizing the pervasive nature of information and the importance of information literacy skills is the key to where educators are and where they are going. It is our responsibility to understand the nature of information and the ways that people use it, so that we can ensure that all individuals have the opportunity to learn the information literacy skills they will need in the future to successfully navigate the landscape of information.

In 1988, the American Library Association published its standards monograph *Information Power*. This publication, along with its significant successor published in 1998, provides a road map to guide educators into the next century. This publication underscores the importance of the role of the library media specialist in producing well-rounded, information-literate students.

The key to equipping students with the skills they will need to succeed in the future lies in information and technology literacy instruction. *Information Power* defines information literacy as "the ability to find and use information" (AASL/AECT 1998, 1). The authors go on to say, "students must become skillful consumers and producers of information in a range of sources and formats to thrive personally and economically in the communication age" (p. 2). To create information-literate students, educators must concentrate on processes (e.g., information problem-solving and critical thinking skills) rather than computer skills.

Information Power does more than offer an inspiring vision of the future of library media specialists in the school. The authors of *Information Power* provide standards for information literacy learning and indicators for each standard. These standards create goals for all educators. The authors name nine standards in three different content areas (1998).

Nine Information Literacy Standards for Student Learning

Information Literacy

Standard 1: The student who is information literate accesses information efficiently and effectively.

Standard 2: The student who is information literate evaluates information critically and competently.

Standard 3: The student who is information literate uses information accurately and creatively.

Independent Learning

Standard 4: The student who is an independent learner is information literate and pursues information related to personal interests.

Standard 5: The student who is an independent learner is information literate and appreciates literature and other creative forms of expression.

Standard 6: The student who is an independent learner is information literate and strives for excellence in information seeking and knowledge generation.

Social Responsibility

Standard 7: The student who contributes positively to the learning community and to society is information literate and recognizes the importance of information to a democratic society.

Standard 8: The student who contributes positively to the learning community and to society is information literate and practices ethical behavior in regard to information and information technology.

Standard 9: The student who contributes positively to the learning community and to society is information literate and participates effectively in groups to pursue and generate information.

These standards extend the reach and scope of information literacy in the K–12 curriculum far more than any effort in the past. The *Information Power* standards paint the portrait of a student who is not simply information literate but also is a good citizen of the information society.

Change and the Library Media Specialist

The 1957 Katherine Hepburn and Spencer Tracy movie *Desk Set* tells the story of several librarians working in the research department of a newspaper. Their jobs are threatened by the arrival of a computer designed to do their work better and faster. This suspicion of technology has not changed in the last 40 years; indeed, many teachers and library media specialists dread the day that they are replaced by computers.

This is far from an irrational fear. For many educators, the introduction to the idea of computers in the classroom came the day machines were wheeled into their classroom and dumped in the corner. This represents a blatant intrusion onto a teacher's turf. It has become commonplace to hear of other workers, such as those in manufacturing, being replaced by computers. What educator hasn't imagined the computers sitting on top of the desk he or she currently occupies, conducting the class?

Can library media specialists, technology teachers, and classroom teachers be replaced by technology? We believe just the opposite. Change is not a death sentence for the members of our profession. In fact, the way that the role of technology in education is changing right now will actually increase opportunity for information literacy educators. As technology becomes more prevalent in learning and teaching, there is even greater need for information, library, and technology work in schools. This is a role that librarians can and must assume to create information-literate students.

The word *disintermediation* is batted around quite a bit in reference to future technologies. Disintermediation is the idea that as technology becomes more advanced, users will no longer require assistance to use it (Gillian 1996). The development of the WWW has told a very different story. We have seen a staggering rise in the use of question and answer services (e.g., AskERIC, the question-and-answer service for education) in the past five years. As the Web becomes larger and more tangled, users need help finding what they want. This is where information and technology specialists step in.

Of course, the roles and responsibilities that members of the school faculty currently assume will change in the future. It will become increasingly important that faculty members and administrators collaborate to ensure the successful integration of technology. One way this can occur is through the formation of an Information and Technology team, composed of technology teachers, library and information professionals, and key administrators. These team members bring together the political muscle, technical savvy, and information literacy expertise to ensure that all students get the information literacy instruction they need.

It is particularly important that library and information professionals recognize the promise of their own future. It is essential that library and information professionals play a leadership role in designing the information literacy curriculum. Librarians are specially trained to see the world through "information-colored" glasses; they recognize that information problems exist everywhere and possess the skills to unravel them. This ability is invaluable in the school of the Information Age.

The future will be a time of immense opportunities for library and information professionals. A hundred years ago, library and information professionals did not exist in schools. Today, they have the opportunity to play a central role in equipping students with the most important skills and knowledge.

The Information and Technology Team

As we mentioned above, the formation of an information and technology team is an important part of creating a learning environment that prepares students for the workplace of the future. This team must work collaboratively to create a true integration of information, library, and instructional technology services, systems, resources, and roles in a unified Information and Technology Team.

The members of the Team can be found within any school: technology teachers, library media specialists, and key administrators. All that needs to be added is commitment, enthusiasm, and teamwork. A unified Information and Technology Team is one where team members work together to provide services and resources to classroom teachers, students, and even parents. Schools with strong, committed Teams invariably see great results in their schools, and not only in terms of what their students are learning. These collaborative programs enjoy excellent funding, the respect of their colleagues, and influence over administrative decisions.

The work of the Information and Technology Team goes beyond creating technology-rich learning environment for students, although this is one of their most important tasks. Great Teams have a close relationship with classroom teachers and administration, and their responsibilities affect every aspect of the school. They provide a technical support system by coordinating tech services and resources and coordinating purchasing decisions. In terms of curriculum, the Team oversees the information and technology literacy program and ensures that it is implemented as part of the classroom curriculum. An active, dynamic Information and Technology Team is an integral part of the school; they are the right arm of overburdened administrators and teachers.

Unfortunately, at this time, we don't see enough of these Teams in schools and districts. Too often we see library media specialists, technology teachers, and administrators working in isolation and fighting for turf and control. At the same time, these educators bemoan their feelings of professional disenfranchisement, their inability to interest colleagues in collaboration, being overwhelmed with work, and worst of all, budget cuts and eliminated positions. Although they all say they are working toward a common goal—preparing students for success in the information age—they are not working together.

It is possible for library media specialists and technology teachers to work together with administrators and other educators. It is not simply possible; it is necessary that they do so in order to become the active players in curriculum and instruction that they must be in the coming decades to ensure the success of students in the Information Age.

The result of a strong, committed Information and Technology Team is an improved educational experience for students. Schools with such a team enjoy full integration of technology and information literacy skills. In this type of environment, students understand the proper role of technology and information in living and working; that they are tools, rather than the answers in and of themselves. This is a worthy goal for any school.

WHERE DO WE GO FROM HERE?

We have outlined some of the important thinking on the role of information technology in the school of the future, and more important, the leadership role that educators must assume to ensure student receive the education they need. The question remains: Where do we go from here? How can we begin to make this vision a reality? There are a few steps that each one of us can take now to create the promising future that we envision for ourselves.

The first step is to learn and absorb. All teachers should read and learn about information literacy. *Information Power* and *Information Literacy: Essential Skills for the Information Age* (Spitzer et al. 1998) are good resources, as are other works cited in the Reference section of this article. Library media specialists in particular need to focus on the teaching and partnership role for information literacy as outlined in *Information Power*.

Teachers also need to become informed about technology. We have explained the profound impact that technology will have on education and schools. Teachers don't have to become information technology experts, but they do have to be informed and aware. The technology sections that appear periodically in newspapers are particularly useful. So is the technology news section on various websites (e.g., Yahoo! Technology News [http://dailynews.yahoo.com/headlines/technology/]). It is crucial for all educators—particularly members of the Information and Technology Team—to stay abreast of what is happening on the technology front. These developments will directly affect every school and classroom.

The second step is to become actively involved in the information and technology program. For library media specialists, this means counteracting Hartzell's invisible librarian syndrome. Library media specialists need to prioritize and focus on the key roles as defined by *Information Power*. Other teachers, administrators, and parents need to become aware of the importance of library media efforts in helping students learn essential skills. Education today demands active, engaged library media programs. *Information Power* states that our mission is "to ensure that students and staff are effective users of ideas and information." It is time that library media specialists explained what this really means and how they can work in partnership throughout the school and community to make it so.

All educators too must take an active role in decision-making and planning. Become involved with your school's technology committee and come to meetings with your own vision of what the school's technology policy should be. Attend PTA meetings and bring up the topic of technology. Organize a school-wide Technology Awareness Week and brainstorm ways to make technology come alive in the classroom with your colleagues. Educators must support the concept of the Information and Technology Team and find ways to bring the necessary people together.

These efforts are not optional. Reflect again on the degree and speed of change that Gates predicts. We cannot ignore or hide from this. As educators, it is our responsibility to prepare our students with the skills and understandings they will need to live in such a world. Clearly, this will require high-quality library and information technology programs meeting students' needs in physical schools or in whatever electronic, networked, virtual learning environment they might find themselves.

REFERENCES

American Association of School Librarians and Association for Educational Communications and Technology. (1988). *Information Power*. Chicago: American Association of School Librarians.

American Association of School Librarians and Association for Educational Communications and Technology. (1998). *Information Power: Building Partnerships for Learning*. Chicago: American Association of School Librarians.

American Library Association Presidential Committee on Information Literacy. (1989). *Final Report*. Chicago: ALAPCIL. (ED 316 074)

Eisenberg, M., and Berkowitz, B. (1988). *Curriculum Initiative: An Agenda and Strategy for Library Media Programs*. Greenwich, CT: Ablex.

Gillian, A. (1996). "Disintermediation: A Disaster or a Discipline?" (ED 411 809)

Hartzell, G. (1997). The invisible school librarian: Why other educators are blind to your value. *School Library Journal* 43(11), 24-29.

Kuhlthau, C. (1993). *Seeking Meaning: A Process Approach to Library and Information Services*. Greenwich, CT: Ablex.

National Center for Education Statistics. (1999). *Issue Brief: Internet Access in Public Schools and Classrooms: 1994–1998*. Available online at: http://nces.ed.gov/pubs99/1999017.html.

Pappas, M., and Tepe, A. (1995). Preparing the information educator for the future. In *School Library Media Annual (SLMA)*, Volume 13. Englewood, CO: Libraries Unlimited, 37–44.

Spitzer, K., Eisenberg, M., and Lowe, C. (1998). *Information Literacy: Essential Skills for the Information Age*. Syracuse, NY: ERIC Clearinghouse on Information and Technology.

Stripling, B., and Pitts, J. (1988). *Brainstorms and Blueprints: Teaching Library Research As a Thinking Process*. Englewood, CO: Libraries Unlimited.

AUTHORS NOTES

Michael Eisenberg is currently director of the School of Library and Information Science of the University of Washington. For many years he worked as professor of information studies at Syracuse University and as director of the Information Institute of Syracuse (including the ERIC Clearinghouse on Information & Technology, AskERIC, KidsConnect, and the Gateway to Educational Materials [GEM]). Mike and his partner Bob Berkowitz created the Big 6® approach to information use. He has worked with thousands of students—pre-K through higher education—as well as people in business, government, and communities to improve their information and technology skills.

Carrie A. Lowe is the Project Representative to the Gateway to Educational Materials (GEM) project, a special project of the Department of Education's National Library of Education and the ERIC Clearinghouse on Information & Technology. Carrie presents frequently to a variety of audiences on the topics of information literacy, information problem-solving, and educational technology. Carrie is a graduate of the University of Wisconsin, Madison, where she earned her bachelor's degree in education. She earned her MLS at Syracuse University's School of Information Studies in 1998. Carrie is a coauthor of the ERIC monograph "Information Literacy: Essential Skills for the Information Age" and is a Column Editor for the bimonthly publication *The Big 6® Newsletter: Teaching Technology & Information Skills.*

Information Power and Assessment
The Other Side of the Standards Coin

Delia Neuman
Associate Professor
College of Library and Information Services, University of Maryland

The publication of *Information Power: Building Partnerships for Learning* (AASL/AECT 1998) marked the beginning of a new era for the school library media field. Yes, this latest set of national guidelines for the profession is only the latest in a series of national standards documents. Yes, like the five "standards" documents that preceded it, it stands on the shoulders of past and current theory, research, and exemplary practice to advance the field in familiar directions. But the real power of this document is that it boosts the field into a significant new direction as well. It includes the first student learning outcomes ever to be published nationally by the school library media field, and these statements make *Information Power* a revolutionary document.

The nine Information Literacy Standards for Student Learning (ILSSL) and their 29 associated indicators are grounded in research in information literacy (Doyle 1992). They have been validated by a national Delphi study (Marcoux 1999) and are endorsed by both the Association for Educational Communications and Technology and the American Association of School Librarians. They are the most important contribution that *Information Power* makes, and the remainder of the document was designed as a blueprint for implementing them. All the discussions of the roles of the library media specialist and all the explanations of the principles that undergird strong library media programs were designed around a single goal: to give building-level library media specialists all the information they need to collaborate with teachers and administrators to use the ILSSL to integrate authentic, information-based learning throughout the curriculum.

THE ILSSL AND STUDENT LEARNING

Revolutionary documents call for change, and *Information Power* is no exception. It summons library media specialists to promote their instructional role as critical in enhancing students' learning, to advertise their role as key resources for the access and delivery of information for learning throughout the school, and to embrace their newly defined role as program administrators and members of the school's management team. Of course, effective library media specialists already meet the substance of these challenges on a daily basis. The goal of *Information Power* is to make that job easier by centering all the library media specialist's roles on the primary goal of any school—student learning. The culmination of years of work—not only by the Vision Committee, which prepared the document, but also by researchers and practitioners throughout the profession who have thought carefully and deeply about the future of library media programs—the document speaks to a field poised to exert strong and effective leadership for learning in the Information Age.

The ILSSL, including their associated indicators, are the library media specialist's primary tool for that job: They provide clear statements that describe the authentic, information-based learning that is the foundation for meaningful learning for the twenty-first century. They are intended to be equally applicable to schools serving all grade levels, working with students of all ability levels, and using either minimal information technology or the full range of technology used in schools today and in the future. They cover a range of behaviors that provide evidence that a student can access, evaluate, and use information for learning, for pursuing nonacademic personal interests, and for working collaboratively to identify and resolve information problems. Most important, they are the basis for the library media specialist's working at the center of the instructional team to integrate information literacy into the curriculum. By linking information concepts and skills to selected standards statements from 14 curriculum areas—areas as diverse as mathematics, physical education, and the visual arts—the ILSSL provide a vehicle for demonstrating the direct relationship of information literacy to students' achievement.

THE CHALLENGE OF IMPLEMENTING THE ILSSL

The ILSSL were designed to be descriptive rather than prescriptive, to set out a range of possibilities rather than to specify narrow behaviors. To make them useful in as many settings as possible, they were crafted under the assumption that individual library media specialists, in collaboration with teachers and other staff, would provide the specific details necessary to integrate them into the curricula of individual schools and districts. But assumptions are meant to be questioned, and there are a number of reasons to question *Information Power's* underlying assumption that library media specialists are ready for the challenge represented by the ILSSL.

First, although the professional literature has advocated an increased instructional role for library media specialists for years, research tells us that neither library media specialists nor teachers and principals have fully accepted that role (see Turner 1993 for a review of this literature). In school climates that are still uncertain about viewing the library media specialist as a teacher or coteacher, integrating student outcomes in information literacy into the various content areas is bound to raise complicated issues.

Second, professional preparation programs for library media specialists have not yet addressed the knowledge, attitudes, and skills required to integrate information literacy into the curriculum in such a specific and detailed way. While the publication of *Information Power* implies a mandate for universities as well as for library media specialists in the field, few if any professional preparation curricula currently include learning experiences—including continuing education offerings—that will enable practitioners to perform the tasks set out by the newest national guidelines.

Third, the idea of standards is itself controversial. The public, the press, educators, and even lawmakers have voiced concerns about the appropriateness, content, and fairness of a variety of national standards documents. When even the U.S. Congress hosts arguments over standards for student learning, library media specialists may themselves question the wisdom of advocating our own field's standards for the students they serve.

All these reasons intersect with a larger and more complex concern that suggests the greatest reason that library media specialists will face significant challenges in using the ILSSL: assessment. Assessment is inherent in the idea of standards. The reason for specifying learning outcomes is to provide statements about what is important for students to learn so that, in turn, instructors can evaluate how well students have achieved those outcomes. Assessment is the intrinsic, unavoidable flip side of the standards coin. And assessment raises a host of complex issues, both philosophical and practical.

Assessment and the School Library Media Specialist:
A New Philosophy

The whole idea of assessing student outcomes in information literacy is a relatively new, untested, and perhaps unwelcome one. As a field, school library media has little or no tradition of evaluating students' work in information gathering and use. While library media specialists may contribute to teachers' evaluations of students' papers and projects by noting that students got an appropriate number of citations from a specified range of sources, they do not typically assess in a formal way—that is, with a grade—either the process that students followed or the quality of the items they found. Many library media specialists, in fact, believe with some passion that students' work in the library media center should NOT be evaluated—that the library media center is the one place in a school where students can learn for learning's sake and that this opportunity should not be taken away from them. Pointing to the fact that today's students are under great pressure to perform well in many areas, these library media specialists worry that the schools' focus on achievement is driving out the focus on learning.

One response to this worry is to note that it is a luxury in most of our schools. Today, a focus on student achievement is a critical component of all our efforts toward educational improvement and school reform. School personnel who cannot demonstrate a contribution to student learning are marginalized or even eliminated. Decisions made under site-based management endorse programs that lead to direct, even measurable, learning while at the same time diminishing efforts that cannot show such a link. As statements of what students are expected to learn to prepare them for life in today's world, standards (and, by implication, their assessment) are key elements in school reform. They are on the agendas of educators and politicians across the country. The ILSSL—our field's statements of what students should learn in relation to information—give library media specialists a voice in the larger school-reform movement. The field cannot afford to forfeit its voice by remaining outside this discussion.

But there is a more positive—and more important—response to the challenges brought by the ILSSL than simply "soldiering on." These statements announce to all that information-based learning is essential for our students and should be the bedrock of contemporary curricula. "[D]eveloping expertise in accessing, evaluating, and using information is in fact the authentic learning that modern education seeks to promote" (*Information Power* 1998, 2). This is not a new idea to library media specialists. Although the term *information literacy* is somewhat new, the field has been aware longer than most of the educational establishment that effective information use is key to successful learning in the twenty-first century. And if we believe that information literacy is essential, why wouldn't we want it to be highlighted as a critical component of the curriculum? As the saying goes, "If it isn't counted, it doesn't count." Why, then, since we know how much it counts, wouldn't we want information literacy to be counted?

Assessment and the School Library Media Specialist: The Practice

Once library media specialists deal with the philosophical demands inherent in the ILSSL and assessment, they must still face a series of practical demands before "doing" assessment successfully. And in some ways it's these practical demands that are likely to create the most pressing concerns. To respond to the call of their profession to adopt and support this new direction for library media programs, library media specialists must learn how to act creatively in yet another "nontraditional" way in their interactions with students and other faculty. They must enlist the support of all their school colleagues to join them in this new focus for their role. And, at the most fundamental level, they must learn how to design and implement assessments that provide valid, reliable evidence of students' achievement. This is a complex and demanding exercise, and the field does not have a long history of addressing it. We are only beginning to develop the concepts and skills that will lead to widespread success in assessing students' mastery of information literacy as it is integrated into the curriculum.

While it's true that instructional design texts like Turner's *Helping Teachers Teach* (1993) and curricular approaches like Eisenberg and Berkowitz's Big6 (1990) have always included an assessment phase in their models, the field's attention to assessment as a general issue begins only with Kuhlthau's *Assessment and the School Library Media Center* (1994). Kuhlthau and her associate editors of the 1993 edition of *School Library Media Annual* identified a need for such attention through preparing that earlier document. A collection of articles culled from that volume and augmented by a few others from the broader educational literature, *Assessment* is a landmark work. It offers an array of theoretical and practical papers dealing with the history, philosophy, and implementation of various assessment strategies, both traditional and alternative. Its inclusion of chapters on assessment as a learning tool—particularly through such alternative models as portfolio assessment and authentic assessment—makes it an important and useful document as the field continues to explore the role of assessment in the school library media program.

Recently, other authors have also provided insights into the intricacies of assessment. Everhart's timely and comprehensive *Evaluating the School Library Media Center* (1998), for example, contains a chapter on the library media specialist's role in the curriculum that offers useful background information on the assessment component of that role, reprints samples of assessment rubrics from a number of sources, and includes a lengthy and helpful list of references. Today, individual states also offer guidelines for developing assessments related specifically to information literacy. Colorado's (1996) are perhaps the most famous, but a number of other states have developed or are developing assessment tools for library media specialists to use.

These documents provide useful contextual information as well as some specific ideas that familiarize the building-level library media specialist with a variety of key issues and practices in assessment. But none of the resources provides a foolproof recipe for designing and implementing valid and reliable assessments that fit the needs of a particular curriculum, teaching staff, and student population. And no outside resource ever will. The core assumption of *Information Power* still holds: Only the individual library media specialist, in collaboration with teachers and other staff, knows enough about a particular school's students and curriculum to craft assessment tools and strategies that can evaluate students' mastery of information literacy as it is integrated into learning experiences within that school.

How Information Power Can Help

It is a daunting task, and *Information Power* includes a tool designed to help individual library media specialists get started with it—the "Levels of Proficiency" provided with each indicator. These sample assessment items were designed to provide suggestions about how to create student evaluations that tap the full range of concepts and skills embodied in the ILSSL. They are a scaffolding of ideas that library media specialists should refine and embellish with their own assessment practices and instruments. Although never subjected to the rigorous processes that professional evaluators use to assure the quality of assessment items, these items offer a starting place and a framework for good evaluation design at the local level. They conform to contemporary assessment practice in important ways, illustrating how to shape assessments that are collaborative, comprehensive, concrete, and circumspect.

Collaborative Assessment

Collaboration is a major theme in *Information Power*; the document relates that idea to the full range of the library media specialist's roles as teacher, instructional partner, information specialist, and program administrator. Collaborative planning and teaching have been staples of good library media programs for years, and collaborative assessment is a natural extension of that approach. At the planning stage, it involves working with teachers to devise assessments that incorporate information literacy concepts and skills; at the teaching stage, it involves ensuring that those concepts and skills are incorporated into teachers' lessons in systematic and meaningful ways; and at the evaluation stage, it involves judging how well students have achieved those concepts and skills within their overall learning. Collaborative evaluation enriches the library media specialist's instructional role by linking it to the total teaching-and-learning process rather than restricting it to its earliest stages.

To illustrate, take Standard 1, Indicator 4, and its associated sample assessment items:

Standard 1: The student who is information literate accesses information efficiently and effectively.

Indicator 4: Identifies a variety of potential sources of information.

Sample assessment items:

Basic: Lists several sources of information and explains the kind of information found in each.

Proficient: Brainstorms a range of sources of information that will meet an information need.

Exemplary: Uses a full range of information resources to meet differing information needs (*Information Power*, 11).

Imagine a fourth-grade unit on the rainforest. The teacher and library media specialist collaborate to plan the unit to culminate in a simple yet substantial evaluation activity: a panel discussion in which groups of student "experts" explain different aspects of the rainforest to the class. To succeed in the content component of this task, students must obviously learn a good deal about the rainforest—the different rainforests around the world, the types of wildlife and vegetation found in each, the lives of indigenous peoples, etc.—and report on it in the panel. To succeed in the information literacy component, they must learn about the information sources that provide that content—atlases, almanacs, fiction and nonfiction materials, CD-ROMs, the Internet, etc.—and tell the class about their use of these resources. To engage in collaborative evaluation, the teacher would judge how well students mastered the content, while the library media specialist would judge how well they mastered tasks like those suggested by the sample assessment items noted above. Did the students name several information sources and describe the kinds of rainforest information found in each? Did their group come up with sources on their own, rather than limiting their information seeking to sources the library media specialist suggested? Did they use the atlas to locate specific rainforests, a book on rainforest life to find information on indigenous peoples, etc.?

Of course, the teacher would have insights about the information sources used, and the library media specialist would have insights about how well students communicated the ideas those sources contain. And, certainly, their assessment could take a different format and focus on different tasks than those suggested here. The key idea, however, is that the insights into student achievement that the teacher and library media specialist reached together would provide a rich understanding of how well students learned both the curricular content and the concepts and skills students had developed to access it. Working together to design and implement collaborative evaluation would ensure that students gained experience in learning to use information literacy skills in the service of content learning.

Comprehensive Assessment

Too often, student learning and its evaluation focus on lower-level skills—regurgitating facts, restating simple concepts, applying formulas without understanding them. The sample assessment items provided in *Information Power* provide suggestions for assessing more advanced stages of students' learning because they reflect all six levels described in Benjamin Bloom et al.'s *A Taxonomy of Educational Objectives: Handbook I. The Cognitive Domain* (1956). The "basic" items reflect Bloom et al.'s knowledge and comprehension levels; the "proficient" items reflect the application and analysis levels; and the "exemplary" items reflect the synthesis and evaluation levels. For each indicator, the three sample items show how students can build from a beginning awareness of that skill to a more complex understanding. Taken together, the 87 sample assessment items in *Information Power* provide guidelines for comprehensively assessing information literacy according to a pattern that has proven successful for more than 40 years.

Once again, a specific standard and indicator along with its sample assessment items illustrate this point:

Standard 2: The student who is information literate evaluates information critically and competently.

Indicator 3: Identifies inaccurate and misleading information.

Sample assessment items:

Basic: Recognizes inaccurate or misleading information in information sources and products.

Proficient: Explains why inaccurate and misleading information can lead to faulty conclusions.

Exemplary: Judges and supports judgments of the degree of inaccuracy, bias, or misleading information in information sources and products (*Information Power*, 15).

Imagine a ninth-grade health class studying over-the-counter medicines that students might take—dietary supplements, weight-loss products, herbal remedies, etc. For the assessment, each student must write a report comparing two magazine or television ads for rival products. Working collaboratively, the teacher and library media specialist have devised criteria for assessing the reports. The teacher's criteria might include statements about the chemical composition, uses, and effects of the products, while the library media specialist's would cover ideas like those suggested in the sample assessment items above: The student identifies inflated statements about weight loss as misleading, explains that someone seeing these statements might conclude that everyone who takes the products can lose large amounts of weight, and gives reasons for judging that one ad is more or less misleading than the other. The student who can identify the inaccuracies in each ad shows basic knowledge of how to evaluate information critically; the student who can explain why the ads are misleading is proficient in applying that knowledge to a specific situation; and the student who can judge which ad is more accurate and give reasons in support of that judgment is exemplary in understanding how to evaluate information in such ads.

In this example, students in the same class might be expected to exhibit the range of understandings sketched here: Some ninth graders might not be able to achieve beyond the "basic" level, for example, while others might be quite "proficient" or even "exemplary." The comprehensive nature of the sample assessment items here and throughout *Information Power* suggests that items can be designed across ability levels for any group of students. Another way to look at this comprehensiveness is to see the items as a framework for designing assessments across grade levels. Even a "typical" third grader, for example, might be able to recognize the most blatant inaccuracies in some ads, while a "typical" twelfth grader might be expected to analyze and evaluate ads from a variety of perspectives. In other words, while the progression from "basic" to "exemplary" doesn't correspond exactly to developmental levels, it does suggest a framework for assessing the full range of information literacy concepts and skills across the curriculum and across student ages, abilities, and grade levels.

Concrete Assessment

Educators need concrete evidence as the basis for stating that learning has occurred, and the sample assessment items suggest student behaviors that provide such evidence: Students define and explain terms, analyze and integrate information, create and evaluate information products. By stating student outcomes in terms of specific, observable behaviors, the sample assessment items provide a model for devising concrete evaluation items at all the levels of Bloom's taxonomy, even the most sophisticated ones. This use of precise, behavior-based terms in the sample assessment items also provides a model for devising evaluations that are valid and reliable—the two chief criteria for designing credible, high-quality assessments.

The terms *valid* and *reliable* have highly specialized meanings when used by the psycho-metricians who create national tests. It's not necessary for library media specialists to know and apply the procedures these experts use to ensure validity and reliability, but it is important that school-based evaluations reflect these criteria. Kemp, Morrison, and Ross (1998) provide clear definitions and a straightforward discussion of the relevant issues. "The key idea [behind validity]," they note, "is that the test assesses what it is supposed to measure" (169), while "Reliability refers to a test's ability to produce consistent results whenever used" (170). In other words, a test of students' mastery of an ILSSL indicator would be valid if it assessed the knowledge and skills that are actually specified in the indicator and reliable if it yielded essentially the same results "if the same learners, without changes in their preparation, were to take the same test or an equal form of the test" (170).

Validity is a key issue for any assessment designer because only a valid assessment provides an accurate picture of student learning. For example, a test of students' mastery of subtraction would not be a valid assessment for a lesson on addition; an attitude survey that focused on an instructor's popularity would not be a valid assessment of that person's skill as a teacher. Similarly, a test of students' mastery of an ILSSL indicator would not be valid if it assessed any learning, no matter how valuable, that exceeded the outcomes defined by that indicator. Building-level teachers and library media specialists—who are rarely concerned about an assessment's usefulness beyond a particular lesson and student group—are far less concerned about reliability than the creators of large-scale standardized tests. But they must always be concerned about the validity of the tests and projects they design to assess student learning.

Again, one of the standards and its associated indicators can provide an example:

Standard 3: The student who is information literate uses information accurately and creatively.

Indicator 3: Applies information in critical thinking and problem-solving.

Sample assessment items:

Basic: Identifies information that meets a particular information need.

Proficient: Uses information from a variety of sources to resolve an information problem or question.

Exemplary: Devises creative approaches to using information to resolve information problems or questions (*Information Power* 1998, 20).

Imagine a twelfth-grade journalism class studying investigative reporting. The students will be evaluated on videotapes of their reports on topics of local interest—an obvious and authentic choice for assessing students' understanding of journalistic principles and techniques. In this case, as in many others, the teacher's and library media specialist's evaluation criteria overlap. Both are concerned about information gathering and use that meets standards of accuracy, fairness, and relevance. In collaboratively designing their assessment rubric, the two instructors build the same criteria into the rubric they'll use to evaluate the videotapes. For example, does the tape focus on information about the topic at hand (e.g., the mayor's proposed tax increase for small businesses) rather than on other topics, no matter how interesting (e.g., the mayor's proposed award for excellence in high school journalism)? Did the student interview several sources with different perspectives on the issue (e.g., businesses that would be affected by the tax) rather than relying on only one (e.g., the mayoral press officer)? Did the student present the information in an interesting way that clearly answered the central questions about the topic (e.g., how much money would be raised by the tax balanced against the loss that might occur if businesses left the city)?

Note that these items address the informational quality of the students' videotapes, not their technical quality. Of course, the teacher and library media specialist could always add technical criteria to the assessment—the use of music, perhaps, or the variety of camera shots and angles included in the tapes. Judging on these technical criteria, however, would not provide valid, concrete evidence of student learning related to the ILSSL indicator—"Applies information in critical thinking and problem solving" (*Information Power*, 20).

For the assessment to be a valid evaluation of students' use of information, it would have to tap directly into the kind of information use the indicator describes. A major threat to validity arises when an assessment substitutes an evaluation of technical quality for an evaluation of information use. Teachers and library media specialists understand fully that an attractive, word-processed report can mask poor research and writing skills; the challenge is to develop the same level of sophistication in judging students' work when it is presented in the compelling formats at our disposal today.

Circumspect Assessment

Derived from Latin roots meaning "to look around," the word *circumspect* suggests a perspective that goes beyond the immediate environment to include a broader view. A circumspect assessment of students' information literacy, then, should reflect a broad understanding of information literacy rather than a narrow, lockstep "testing" of its concepts and skills. This approach is fully consistent with the rich view of information literacy embodied in *Information Power*. All three of the ILSSL's categories assume a circumspect view, and the two "advanced" categories—independent learning and the socially responsible use of information—make it especially clear. These two categories build on the basic components of information literacy—access, evaluation, and use—yet lift it beyond the immediate concerns of day-to-day school learning to highlight the independent, authentic learning students will pursue throughout their lives. The standards and indicators for all three categories were written to encourage a similarly broad view of information literacy, and the sample assessment items for all three categories were written to support the development of wide-ranging, creative assessments that embody that view.

Perhaps one of the best examples of the circumspection of the ILSSL appears in Standard 6, Indicator 2. This standard and its indicators are a unique contribution of the document that "goes beyond" the approach reflected in other fields' standards: None of the standards documents reviewed as part of the development of the ILSSL included "striving for excellence" as a learning outcome. Library media specialists know that revising, improving, and updating one's knowledge are critical to achieving excellence, and the prominence of these ideas in the ILSSL gives the field an important perspective that might otherwise go unrecognized. Not surprisingly, that perspective is also embodied in the sample assessment items:

> Standard 6: The student who is an independent learner is information literate and strives for excellence in information seeking and knowledge generation.

> Indicator 2: Devises strategies for revising, improving, and updating self-generated knowledge.

> Sample assessment items:

>> Basic: Explains basic strategies for revising, improving, and updating work.

>> Proficient: Selects and applies appropriate strategies for revising, improving, and updating work.

>> Exemplary: Recognizes gaps in one's own knowledge and applies appropriate strategies for filling them (*Information Power* 1998, 30).

Imagine any grade level, any curriculum area, and any information task that students might undertake: first graders learning to read, fifth graders learning about timelines, eighth graders learning about the culture of another land, twelfth graders learning about the interplay of politics and economics. Across the curriculum and the student population, every student has to develop and use strategies for the continual improvement of knowledge in these and other domains. Teachers and library media specialists can work collaboratively to design comprehensive, concrete, and circumspect assessments that give evidence of students' mastery of these sophisticated strategies.

Moreover, such assessments can easily take advantage of evaluation formats that themselves go beyond the traditional testing often associated with educational standards. For example, those first graders might make several audiotapes of their reading over the course of the school year and explain how they learned to decode words and gain meaning from context on the way to becoming better readers. The fifth graders might make timelines that begin with simple events, like the dates of the Boston Tea Party and the signing of the Declaration of Independence, and revise and update them by adding the dates of battles they studied in a unit on the Revolutionary War. The eighth graders might create travel brochures about the cities they research, selecting appropriate strategies as they move from draft stage to full production. The twelfth graders might research, plan, and produce a debate they broadcast over the school's closed-circuit television network about the relationship of the Soviet Union's economic conditions to its political collapse—recognizing what they need to know and applying strategies to fill any gaps in their knowledge as a part of the process. In every case, the assessments lend themselves to project-based learning, and the varieties of authentic assessment that are ideally suited to that learning approach. The circumspect view of *Information Power* thus extends to its encouragement of assessments that are linked to authentic learning and to the most advanced notions of contemporary educational theory and practice.

CONCLUSION

Information literacy is, of course, far more than a collection of assessment items. But assessment items that are collaboratively designed, comprehensive in the kinds of learning they tap, concrete in their statement of expected outcomes, and circumspect in their reflection of the richness and complexity of true information literacy can capture many of the key dimensions of information literacy. *Information Power: Building Partnerships for Learning* calls on every library media specialist to develop such assessments, and the sample assessment items included in that document can help. These items offer a model for creating valid and reliable assessment tools and strategies that tap the full range of concepts and skills embodied in the nine Information Literacy Standards for Student Learning and their 29 associated indicators. They point the direction for exploiting the true power of this revolutionary document and for implementing the essential contribution of the library media program to student learning.

Student learning can be inspired or discouraged by assessment. Instructors will always "teach to the test"—the "test," after all, defines what the public and the educational establishment consider important—and assessment devices should be designed not only to test students' achievement but to foster their learning at the highest learning levels. *Information Power* and its sample assessment items are designed to help library media specialists do just that. While no assessment device can ever encompass all the wealth and nuance inherent in information literacy, these sample assessment items offer a framework for library media specialists to devise evaluations that promote learning at the highest levels of Bloom's taxonomy and that reflect the best insights from current educational thought. They can help library media specialists to accomplish *Information Power's* mission "to ensure that students and staff are effective users of ideas and information" (p. 6). They can also help to ensure that library media programs are indeed counted—counted among the most important elements of a vibrant, reform-minded school.

REFERENCES

American Association of School Librarians and Association for Educational Communications and Technology. (1998). *Information Power: Building Partnerships for Learning.* Chicago: ALA Editions.

Bloom, B. S., Englehart, M. D., Furst, E. J., Hill, W. H., and Krathwohl, D. R. (1956). *A Taxonomy of Educational Objectives. Handbook I. The Cognitive Domain.* New York: David McKay.

Colorado Department of Education. (1996). Rubrics for the Assessment of Information Literacy. Denver: Author. ED 401 899.

Doyle, C. S. (1992). *Final Report to the National Forum on Information Literacy*. Syracuse, NY: ERIC Clearinghouse on Information Resources, 1992. ED 351 033.

Eisenberg, M. B., and Berkowitz, R. E. (1990). *Information Problem-Solving: The Big Six Skills Approach to Library and Information Skills Instruction*. Norwood, NJ: Ablex.

Everhart, N. (1998). *Evaluating the School Library Media Center: Analysis Techniques and Research Practices*. Englewood, CO: Libraries Unlimited.

Kemp, J. E., Morrison, G. R., and Ross, S. M. (1998). *Designing Effective Instruction*, 2d ed. Upper Saddle River, NJ: Merrill/Prentice-Hall.

Kuhlthau, C. C., ed. (1994). *Assessment and the School Library Media Center*. Englewood, CO: Libraries Unlimited.

Marcoux, E. L. (1999). Information literacy standards for student learning: A modified Delphi study of their acceptance by the educational community. Ph.D. diss., University of Arizona, Tucson.

Turner, P. (1993). *Helping Teachers Teach*, 2d ed. Englewood, CO: Libraries Unlimited.

Imposed and Self-Generated Queries in the Elementary School Environment

Melissa Gross
University of California, Los Angeles

Recent work on the nature of questions has made explicit what many practitioners have known but may not have fully integrated into their work. There is a difference between questions that are self-generated and those that are imposed. Self-generated questions are internally motivated, springing from the context of an individual's life or in response to their personal interests or life circumstances. For example, a user planning a vacation may seek information about various locales; another user may seek recreational reading material that suits personal reading preferences.

In contrast, imposed queries are questions that, once developed, are passed to someone else (called the agent) to transact in the world. This behavior is very common, and examples can be found in both formal and informal relationships between people. Adult children transact for elderly parents, secretaries retrieve information for employers, and family and patient advocates transact for the critically ill in health care settings.

Research has shown that this behavior occurs in various ethnolinguistic groups (Metoyer-Duran 1993); in certain professional settings (Allen 1979); among immigrant children with non-English-speaking parents (Chu 1995); and between teachers and students, between parents and children, and between children (Gross 1997, 1998, in press). In all these examples, because the person seeking to resolve the question did not think it up, these questions are said to be externally motivated, and in the context of any type of information providing organization they constitute a different set of challenges and require a different set of strategies for successful conclusion.

THE IMPOSED QUERY MODEL

One of the early and most concrete examples given of the imposed query is the school assignment. In terms of the graphic model provided in Figure 1, the life cycle of the imposed query is described as a set of stages in which a question gets passed from one person to another, transacted, and then returned to the person who posed the question to begin with. The person who asks the question is called the *imposer*, and in the school environment is most often the teacher. The person who transacts the question for the imposer is called the *agent* but can be thought of as the student, and in the context of the school library media center, the library media specialist would be in the position of the *intermediary*.

IQ_1, the initiated stage, represents the question as it has been formulated by the imposer for transfer to the agent. At this point the question must be developed enough to be conveyed in language, but the level at which it is formalized will vary. In other words, some questions are better thought out than are others. In some instances, the question may also contain information about possible sources that, if consulted, may contain the needed answer. Questions developed at this level are analogous to teacher questions that include suggestions (or requirements) directing the student to specific reference works or formats.

The transferred stage, IQ_2, is depicted as two overlapping circles to emphasize that at this stage a mutual understanding of the question needs to be developed in the process of conveying the question to the agent. Of course, this mutual understanding is not always optimally achieved. There are many aspects of the relationship between the imposer and agent that can facilitate or impede the successful transfer of the question, as can limitations affecting attention such as illness or lack of sleep.

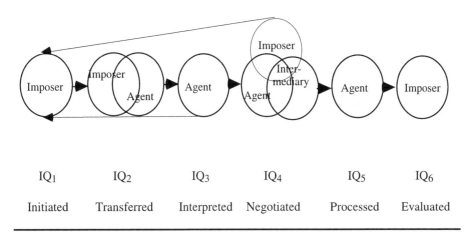

IQ$_1$	IQ$_2$	IQ$_3$	IQ$_4$	IQ$_5$	IQ$_6$
Initiated	Transferred	Interpreted	Negotiated	Processed	Evaluated

Figure 1. The Imposed Query. Source: Gross. (1995).

Source: Gross. (1995).

The limitations inherent in the transfer process are most apparent at stage IQ$_3$, the interpreted stage, which represents the query as the agent has internalized it after interacting with the imposer. Although mutual understanding was attempted, the question may be better or less well understood by the agent than either party realized. Additionally, the arrow that leads back from stage 3 to stage 1 is meant to indicate that the way the agent internalizes the question is also affected by feelings and beliefs the agent has about the imposer. For instance, a student may have preconceived ideas about what the teacher would consider to be a good resource. To the extent that this understanding is correct and relates to the question at hand, this can be an aid to the successful resolution of the query. To the extent that it is misconceived or inappropriate in this instance, it becomes problematic. Feelings and beliefs about the imposer, however, in the affective sense, must also be considered in terms of how they help or hinder the agent in the process of transacting the imposer's question. Finally, stage 3 is important to note because this version of the question is likely to be the one offered to the intermediary (school library media specialist) if the agent seeks assistance.

The overlapping circles in stage IQ_4, the negotiated stage, again are meant to represent the idea that a mutual understanding of the query needs to be achieved between the agent and the intermediary. The imposer is indicated here for the influence he or she has on this process even though she or he is not physically present to oversee it. As in stage 3, an arrow points back to stage 1 indicating that understanding of the query is affected by feelings and beliefs the intermediary has about the imposer in addition to the information received from the agent. For instance, understanding that the question is a school assignment may alter the way the school library media specialist thinks about the question and the types of resources that should be used to answer it. If it turns out that the media specialist happens to know the imposer, the media specialist will also use this knowledge to further understanding of the question and to form an appropriate response to the student. Again, to the extent that these feelings and beliefs are helpful, they can facilitate successful resolution of the question. To the extent that they are not, the question may mutate away from its original intent.

Stage IQ_5, the processed stage, represents the question as it is understood by the agent in light of the entire process the agent has gone through to this point in understanding and transacting the query. It may look different now based on what the agent has learned from the resources consulted. It may be that a better command of the subject or context within which the question is considered will be an aid to formulating an appropriate response. If errors of understanding have been uncovered, mutation of the query may be a necessary and useful part of the response. It is also true that if the query has mutated too far away from the imposer's intent, the agent's answer may not be a viable response to the question.

Stage IQ_6, the evaluated stage, represents the query as it looks to the imposer in light of the response received from the agent. Implicit here is the need for the agent and imposer to again transfer the query in a way that facilitates a mutual understanding of the information that has been accumulated. If all has gone well, the imposer will receive a viable and useful response. It is important to note that while the model appears linear, it can also be viewed as cyclical, depending on the imposer's reaction to the information received. If the answer brings up new questions, the imposer may send the agent out again to retrieve more information. In another scenario, the imposer may choose to pursue a personal question at this point. For instance, the information provided by the agent may serve to empower the imposer to consult with a doctor or lawyer, or to proceed in some other information transaction.

One of the most important points the model makes about the life cycle of imposed queries is that the question is in constant danger of mutating as it is transferred from one person to the next, transacted, and then returned to the imposer. Understanding the forces that threaten to turn it away from the imposer's original intent, dilute the process, or even stop the process completely need to be further understood both from the point of view of library and information science and education.

OVERVIEW OF STUDY

The findings discussed here come from work that seeks to understand imposed queries in the elementary school environment (Gross 1998). Using both quantitative and qualitative methods, this investigation sought to quantify the number of imposed and self-generated queries transacted in the school library media center and to understand when (and to what extent) information seeking in this environment involves the generation of imposed queries, who participates in this process, and how they get involved. This study also looks at how student perceptions of whether an imposed query "belongs" to the student or the teacher (or other imposer) varies based on grade/age level, individual interest, and assignment type. This work was also interested in whether resource choice and use is different for imposed and self-generated questions.

The qualitative portion of this work involved in-depth interviews with key informants and representative subjects at an elementary school. The particular school under study grouped students by levels rather than traditional grade designations, but these levels did correspond to the traditional grade break down as follows: early childhood = preschool (four-year-olds) and K, lower = grades 1 and 2, middle = grades 3 and 4, upper = grades 5 and 6. The key informants included the school library media specialist and two teachers from each grade level except early childhood, where only one teacher volunteered to participate. The representative subjects included four children from each grade level, two females and two males, randomly chosen from the participating teacher's classrooms.

A total of 24 individual interviews were performed. The interviews were audiotaped and guided by general research questions and by information gained in the interviews themselves as issues and themes became apparent. Interview length varied with the maturity of the subjects, ranging from 20 minutes for the four-year-olds to two hours for the adults. Interviews with the older children tended to run about 45 minutes. The following sections discuss some of the findings and issues that resulted from this inquiry.

The Social Construction of Imposition in the Elementary School Environment

As mentioned above, the school assignment has served as a concrete example of what is meant by the term *imposed query*. It is easy to conceptualize the teacher as imposer, the student as agent, and the school library media specialist or the public librarian as intermediary. In the pilot study that this work grew from, this view seemed to imply that because the teacher was the imposer, the questions that teachers transact in the school library media center in service to class assignments are best classified as self-generated queries (Gross 1998). In the current study, the view of the teacher and the teacher's place in the full context of the elementary school environment was greatly enriched, including a deeper understanding of their function in terms of the generation of questions and the roles participants take.

Imposition and Teachers

The teacher is the main imposer in the elementary school environment. But as imposers, teachers have several characteristics that other imposers may not share. For instance, teachers deal mainly with questions that are didactic in nature. In terms of the self-generated/imposed dichotomy, teacher questions do not fit neatly into the self-generated category, as they are not generally developed by the teacher to fill a gap in personal understanding. Most teacher questions developed for classroom use are based on "known" knowledge and serve the dual purposes of providing a learning experience and a medium for student evaluation. It is also not unusual for the teacher to use questions included in textbooks or other materials developed by others in lieu of developing classroom questions themselves.

In understanding teacher-designed questions for classroom use, it is also important to consider what teachers do in terms of the social institution they are part of. In this study the elementary school, as an institution, displays two major features. The first is that the school is an imposing environment made up of several layers of imposition. Yes, the teacher does impose questions on students, but the teacher does this within a broader context of imposition. In terms of the nature of teaching as a profession, this is operationalized by the requirement that teachers respond to formalized curricula, goals, and special emphases that may be defined variously by institutions, organizations, and individuals such as the state, the school district, the principal, and parents.

It is also true that, although teachers operate within an imposed context, they also have a lot of autonomy. For example, the decision as to how a particular curricular framework is actualized is often up to the individual teacher. The questions that they pose to their students were not given to them by the imposing bodies they must ultimately answer to, nor will they return the specific answers they receive from students to anybody for consumption or evaluation. Professional status allows teachers to operate, in a broad sense, as they see fit, and this does leave room for teachers to respond to their own perceptions of student information needs. This is to say that on the basis of student questions, recent neighborhood or news events, or other input, the teacher may determine that students "need" certain information and may seek to fill that gap for them.

There is evidence that many adults significant to various aspects of children's lives routinely determine their information needs for them (Walter 1994). Teachers, however, are subject to evaluation, and this ties them to the structure adopted by the school for student attainment of established grade level competencies. The teacher who does not meet these expectations will have an experience of the imposition inherent in their context in the same way that a child who continuously fails to respond to teacher impositions will be reprimanded.

Nonetheless, teachers don't feel imposed upon and don't relate to what they do as imposition. They see themselves as motivating, inspiring, or exciting students. While some of the teachers interviewed could accept the term in a metaphorical sense, even those who couldn't were able to use the imposed query model to describe what happens with classroom assignments. This finding in part describes a second aspect of the school environment, which is that it is *socially constructed* to ignore, or at least play down, the fact that imposition is taking place.

Imposition and Students

The social construction of the school environment is part of the general social construction of education in our society, and what happens at school is shaped not only by the state, teachers, and administration but also by parents, the experience of friends and siblings, the expectations of the public and private schools that the school feeds into, and general standards and expectations held by the community at large. The way children experience this context can include understanding that they are expected to perform for the teacher who will evaluate them, that attending school is for their own benefit, that securing an education is expected of them, and that at school they represent their family in the public world. The preferred tone at school is one of cooperation and compliance with the goal of eventually bringing the child into full participation in society as an adult citizen. As long as things are going well, there is no advantage to making imposition explicit. Classroom work that generates a sense of ownership in students and a positive relationship between student and teacher facilitates the educative process. Children who balk at the imposition will find it to be more explicit than those who do not, as use of authority, gentle coercion, notes to parents, and other measures are used to gain their participation in the process.

In developmental terms, perceptions of ownership versus imposition in school work vary according to the student's grade/age level, the type of assignment they are working on, and their own personal interest level. Teachers use many devices to help students build a sense of ownership of their work. They do this mainly by including elements that allow the students to make choices or personalize their work in some way and by providing assignments that individual children can respond to at their own developmental level. It is also true, however, that assignments sometimes contain secondary goals that the children are not necessarily aware of. For instance, in the library young children might be encouraged to select books as a personal activity while the teacher has unstated expectations that this activity should encourage reading in the home, generate a love of books, or teach responsibility. When library activities, such as the opportunity to check out materials, are refused, the imposed aspect of the situation, if it exists, may be revealed. For the majority of the younger children, library time is perceived as fun, and they are not conscious that there is any imposition inherent in what they are doing. However, in the interviews teachers related two instances in which young children refused to check out books. In one case the child was forced to charge out materials, whether or not he used them, as an exercise in responsibility. In the other case the child was worked with more slowly, and when she eventually agreed to check out a book, her compliance was treated as an accomplishment.

As these examples suggest, the bottom line of imposition is not always lost on the students, although the teachers' strategies for promoting ownership of the question and the hidden facets of some classwork can cloud the students' sense of imposition, especially for the youngest ones. Older students had little difficulty in recognizing the imposition assignments represented. They understood that the library could be used for their own questions as well as for classwork and could differentiate between the two and sometimes see where they overlapped. However, differentiating between self-generated and imposed queries was not part of the pedagogy at any of the grade levels represented at this school.

Children's Information Seeking

There were several findings from this study that related to the information seeking of children both in the elementary school context as well as in their personal lives. One provocative finding from the pilot study, which was replicated across three schools, was that an almost inverse relationship between age/grade and transaction type (self-generated versus imposed) existed at the pilot site from year-to-year and at two other, similar schools (Gross 1997, 1998, in press). At all three locations the youngest children had zero or very few imposed circulation transactions and a very high number of self-generated transactions. The oldest children, however, not only had a much higher imposed use of library materials, but their self-generated use of library materials was the lowest of all grade levels. While the rise in the number of imposed circulation transactions may seem easy to explain—older children can read better and are developmentally more ready for complex assignments—the coupling of this increase in imposed work with a decline in self-generated library use is compelling. The nature of the work reported here does not allow for causal arguments to be made about any possible relationship between the level of imposition these children deal with and personal use of library materials. What it does is pose many questions for further investigation.

Resource Selection and Use

In terms of differences in resource selection and use, students generally showed a preference for known items. This preference for familiarity appeared to follow a pattern in which the youngest children would often rely on a specific book. This desire for a known item would later broaden to a desire for books by a known author or to a specific genre at the upper level. The preference for familiar works pertained to both imposed and self-generated questions. Familiar works included favorite reference sources that students would try to use for reports if they could.

For classwork, however, teachers often provided the resources themselves either in the classroom library or in specially prepared packets. Particularly in the middle grades, teachers stated that this was done in order to provide for the wide range of reading levels among the students. Teachers felt that they could not count on the availability of materials in libraries to cover this range of reading levels in a specific subject area. Children used more sources and a greater variety of sources in responding to school assignments than they did in satisfying their own information needs. For self-generated needs they most often used materials they already owned or websites they already knew about, or depended on others for information. The children interviewed preferred using their own books to going to the library. Only three students spoke of using the library for self-generated needs, and only two identified themselves as public library users.

Students felt that their teachers preferred paper-based materials to electronic ones, and when asked what their teacher's favorite resource was, children over four years of age routinely answered, "the dictionary." Some children would also add the encyclopedia as a second choice.

It is important to note that the use of electronic resources in the elementary school context must be conceptualized as mainly supporting imposed queries. At all three schools studied, children (and their parents) must sign contracts in which they agree to use these resources only in response to classwork. While it is unlikely that, for instance, Internet use could be completely limited in this way, children's use of electronic resources are highly supervised to eliminate opportunities for self-generated use. When on the Internet, students are expected to be able to justify what they are doing at any given time in terms of an assignment from their teacher.

Student Use of Electronic Resources

The effect of electronic resources on school library media use became a point of interest in this study in the year-to-year analysis of the transaction rates at the pilot school. Imposed transactions dropped and self-generated transactions rose significantly ($P < 0.005$). While this change may have been due to normal fluctuation, or to differences in teacher assignments from year to year, it is also true that at the time the initial data were collected, the school was in the process of providing electronic resources to students for the first time. When data collection was performed one year later, these resources were now firmly in place in all classrooms and in the school library media center.

A second potential effect of computers in this environment was the discovery of a gender difference in boys' and girls' circulation transactions at this school. Boys' imposed transactions fell from 33% of their total transactions in 1996 to 14% in 1997, while girls' imposed queries grew from 17% in 1996 to 25 % in 1997. The chi-square value computed on the hypothesis that the number of imposed transactions would be the same year-to-year for boys and girls was rejected ($P < 0.0005$). While, as noted above, there may be other explanations as to why this happened, it may very well be that what this represents is what has been documented by others as boys' general preference for electronic resources and girls' higher comfort level with libraries and paper-based resources (DeRemer 1989; Fasick 1992). The impact of teacher assignments must also be considered, especially given the high predilection for group and team work at this school. When a variety of resources is required from the group, in the absence of other controls, it may be that the boys respond by using Internet and CD-ROM resources and the girls by searching for books and magazines.

As a counterpoint to this interpretation, the other two schools that participated in this investigation did not show any significant difference in how boys and girls used the school library media center. By coincidence, one of these schools was only two years old and had had the same amount of time to integrate computer resources into the classroom and school library media center as had the pilot school. The thing that stood out about these two schools, when compared with the pilot, was the fact that they provide computer instruction, with a structured and progressive curriculum, as an academic subject at all grade levels. Second, at both of these schools the library media specialists were much more effective at building and maintaining relationships with teachers that included integrating library work with teacher assignments. Another interesting finding was that there was no significant difference in the way girls used their school library media center when a comparison was made across all three schools, and there was no significant difference in boys' use between the two similar schools.

Going to Others for Help

In the interviews with students at the pilot site, the children reported that they were not fond of their library catalog, which was designed for adult users, and relied on knowing the physical location of books as their main strategy for finding materials. They also liked sorting through the books left on tables by previous library users and felt that this was a prime hunting ground for materials. If browsing didn't work, their next strategy was to ask a friend, the library media specialist, or their teacher for help.

The strategy of going to others for help was widely employed and revealed much about how roles are invoked in the imposed query life cycle. While the teacher is the main imposer in this environment, parents and children also functioned as imposers. Parents imposed both on teachers and students in trying to limit or expand their children's reading. Parents also, to the consternation of teachers, often transacted for their children in terms of not only gathering materials but at times also interpreting and completing assignments. This variation of the imposed query, where one agent passes the question to another to transact, is called the *double imposed query* (Gross, 1997). It is common enough behavior that some of the teachers limited the type of assignment they would send home for children to complete. It is interesting to note that none of the children interviewed felt that their parents or caregivers did their work "for" them. It may be that what teachers experience as "doing for, " children experience as helping.

However, this idea of using people as information sources is common in assignments at all levels. The younger the students, the more likely it is that the teacher will ask them to use family or friends as a resource for an assignment. One reason given for this is the limited ability of children to read. With young children this strategy was also used to demonstrate to students that information can be found in a variety of places. Early childhood and lower-level students were encouraged to help each other in information seeking. From early childhood through the middle level there is also an emphasis on group work and working in teams. The classrooms are often physically arranged to facilitate this by sitting groups of children around a table or by arranging tables together.

At the upper level, the emphasis changes. Students not only do fewer team projects but are also expected to take more individual responsibility for their contributions to group work. There are concerns at this level on how children will perform on standardized tests and also on their ability to meet the demands that will be placed on them when they matriculate to middle school. Across all grade/age levels, though, limited reading skills and lack of information seeking instruction were the two biggest stumbling blocks children faced in this environment in gathering information, whether for self-generated or imposed work.

Given the early emphasis on helping peers and using others as sources of information, the fact that certain students were identified by teachers, peers, and the individuals themselves as seeking out the role of information agent makes sense. This behavior was so familiar to teachers that several of them went so far as to classify these children as a type. Teachers identified them as "power brokers," "mother's helpers," and "nurturers" and described them as bright children with some skill-based expertise that was recognized by the group. The contributions of these children went beyond just having the answer to knowing where to look, how to figure out where to look, or having personal access to an information resource, such as extensive collection of baseball cards.

Teachers had a variety of responses to children who especially like being the agent of an imposed query, especially for peers. Some teachers rewarded the behavior, and others punished it. In general, as children matured, peer imposition was less favorably looked upon and even seen as disruptive to the group. Among the children, the recognition of skill-based expertise in their peers was cited as providing motivation to go to a particular student for a particular kind of help. In this respect children reported imposing on each other in school and away from school with classmates, friends, and siblings.

LOOKING TOWARD THE FUTURE

One of the most interesting things about imposed information seeking is that while it is a common behavior, little is known about it in an explicit sense. This behavior is well known to school library media specialists and other information professionals, but the work reported here is part of a recent effort to isolate, describe, and understand imposed queries and what they mean in terms of the provision of information services. In this process, data about self-generated information seeking have been attained, and a rich variety of research questions for both library and information science and education have been revealed.

Some of these have been discussed above, such as the need to ensure that as electronic resources proliferate, certain children are not left out of the loop based on gender or other characteristics. It is also important to better understand the role library instruction plays in determining how students will use, evaluate, and comprehend the information environment as they mature. While this work served to reify many existing understandings about children's information-seeking behavior, it leaves many questions open concerning the developmental, cultural, and theoretical understanding of how children do or should learn to ask and transact questions. The fact that certain children seek out the role of information agent is intriguing and needs to be explored. Who are these children? Do they have experiences, characteristics, and outcomes in common? Should their behavior be reinforced or extinguished? How do they compare to their classmates in school and on standardized tests? How can we improve children's ability to be successful agents of imposed queries?

It will also be useful to better understand how feelings and beliefs that the agent and the intermediary have about the imposer help or hinder the process and to what extent quality of relationship matters.

By separating question type into self-generated versus imposed, it allows practitioners, both teachers and library media specialists, to consider what they do in another light. For instance, one interesting question that came out of the data analysis for this study looks at the potential effects of fixed and flexible scheduling on student use of the school library media center in service to self-generated needs. It may be that the sole employment of flexible scheduling in service to class assignments favors library use for imposed queries, perhaps depriving children of opportunities to satisfy their self-generated information needs. As it is clearly one of the objectives of *Information Power* to produce independent learners who can and will seek "information on aspects of personal interest and well-being," library media specialists may want to further consider what type of scheduling best serves the student's ability to achieve this goal (American Association of School Librarians and the Association for Educational Communications and Technology 1998, 23).

Another critical question in regard to student's self-generated information needs is, what happens when students go to middle school? to high school? to college? This study indicated that by grade six in these three schools, students were using the school library media center more for school assignments than for self-generated needs and that the decline in self-generated use begins around third grade. Work is needed to understand what is happening to the self-generated needs of students as they grow older. How are they satisfying them? Are they satisfying them? Are students faced with increasing imposition as they mature? If so, does this increased imposition affect outcomes such as who becomes a lifelong reader?

There are many other questions about imposed queries that need to be addressed. These include examining other contexts and user groups as well as continuing to look closely at how people go about generating, sharing, transacting, and concluding the imposed query process. The importance of this work is directly related to an enhanced understanding of human information-seeking behaviors and a better comprehension of what information literacy is and means, and how it can best be promoted in children's lives.

SUMMARY

The following summarizes suggestions for future work in this area:

- Investigate ways to ensure that all children are provided with equal training and access to electronic resources.

- Expand comprehension of the role library instruction plays in determining how students will use, evaluate, and understand the information environment as they mature.

- Examine the developmental, cultural, and theoretical aspects of how children do or should learn to ask and transact questions.

- Investigate why some children seek out the role of agent and who these children are, and describe their characteristics and outcomes.

- Search for ways to improve children's ability to successfully negotiate imposed queries.

- Explore how feelings and beliefs that the agent and intermediary have about the imposer help or hinder question negotiation.

- Investigate the effects of fixed and flexible scheduling on student's self-generated information seeking behaviors.

- Understand what happens to the self-generated information needs of middle, high school, and college-age students.

- Investigate other contexts and user groups to improve general understanding of imposed information-seeking behaviors.

REFERENCES

Allen, Thomas J. (1979). *Managing the Flow of Technology: Technology Transfer and the Dissemination of Technical Information Within the Research and Development Organization.* Cambridge, MA: MIT Press.

American Association of School Librarians and the Association for Educational Communications and Technology. (1998). *Information Power: Building Partnerships for Learning.* Chicago: American Library Association.

Chu, Clara M. (1995, June). Immigrant children as mediators and the role of information. In *American Made, Not Born: Working with New American Young Adults Program.* Chicago: Young Adult Library Services Association (YALSA), American Library Association Conference.

DeRemer, M. (1989). The computer gender gap in elementary schools. *Computers in the Schools* 6, 39–49.

Fasick, Adele M. (1992). What research tells us about children's use of information media. *Canadian Library Journal* 49, 51–54.

Gross, Melissa. (In press). Imposed queries in the school library media center: A descriptive study. *Library and Information Science Research.*

Gross, Melissa. (1998). Imposed queries in the school library media center: A descriptive study. *Dissertation Abstracts International*, 59(9), 3261. (University Microfilms, no. 9905536).

Gross, Melissa. (1997). Pilot study on the prevalence of imposed queries in a school library media center. *School Library Media Quarterly* 25, 157–66.

Gross, Melissa. (1995). The imposed query. *RQ* 35, 236–43.

Metoyer-Duran, Cheryl. (1993). *Gatekeepers in Ethnolinguistic Communities.* Norwood, NJ: Ablex.

Walter, Virginia A. (1994). The information needs of children. *Advances in Librarianship* 18, 112–15.

Criticizing Media
The Cognitive Process of Information Evaluation

Mary Ann Fitzgerald
Department of Instructional Technology
University of Georgia

In the modern world, people encounter and process incoming information from print, broadcast, electronic, and spoken sources during a large portion of their waking hours. This flood of information requires scrutiny according to the consumer's purpose for using the information. A small percentage of incoming information messages are likely to be problematic in some way to the interpreting person: they may be difficult to comprehend, deceptive, contradictory to knowledge held in memory, or internally inconsistent. How do people decide which messages need evaluating? How do people evaluate these messages? These questions express the central interesting objects of this chapter. In addition, they express a significant challenge for educators of the twenty-first century, as we grapple with issues of how to prepare the information consumers of the future.

These questions have deep cultural implications. Media producers sift, manipulate, and repackage information for consumer use, and this shaping of the information environment increasingly shapes culture as well. Following a year when respected media vehicles like the *Boston Globe,* the *New Republic,* and CNN carried information later admitted to be false, questions arise about responsibility for information quality. While the media must assume a large portion of the responsibility for credible reporting, consumers need not be passive receivers of information. As information continues to increase in availability, consumers may find it necessary to seize a more active role in promoting information quality through demand. If information consumers are to demand high information quality, they must invest some effort to evaluate the information they encounter.

Evaluation is a critical thinking process that people use in making judgments of quality, truthfulness, and accuracy. Despite its importance in everyday life, evaluation as a process is poorly understood. The purpose of this chapter is to describe the cognitive processes used by well-educated, motivated adults as they make critical judgments of information under naturalistic and conducive conditions.

PERSPECTIVES

Theories about the nature of evaluation arise largely from critical thinking literature and to a lesser degree from cognitive psychology. While any object, idea, or person can be the target of evaluation, this study focuses on the assessment of information in terms of reliability, usability, and quality. This judgment may be based upon the internal characteristics of the information, external criteria (Bloom, Engelhart, Furst, Hill, and Krathwohl 1956), or a combination of the two. An example of external criteria is provided by Taylor's (1986) definition of information quality, which includes a consideration of usefulness, breadth and depth, and objectivity. Bloom et al. consider evaluation to be the most sophisticated of the critical thinking skills.

According to theory from cognitive psychology, metacognition, and critical thinking literature, evaluation is composed of several elements (Bloom et al. 1956; Flavell 1981; Siegel and Carey 1989). The first set of elements consists of characteristics of the individual and of the evaluative situation. These elements include the disposition of the person toward critical thought, prior knowledge the person might have about the problem at hand, and the person's purpose for using the information. A combination of these elements results in a metacognitive message, called the *signal,* to start the evaluation process (Flavell, p. 43). After this initiative event, the person assesses the problem and applies evaluative skills and strategies. This deliberative process results in a decision, which may be a value judgment, a decision to act or not act, or a deferral pending additional information. Once the decision is made, the evaluative episode is complete for the present but may be repeated for related information in the future (Petty and Cacioppo 1986). This listing of evaluation elements results from a synthesis of scattered ideas in the literature. By describing the evaluation process, this chapter aims to present a cohesive understanding of how evaluation occurs and to verify or challenge the elements in this list.

At least two factors complicate the evaluation context. First, some evaluative problems are well-defined, while others are ill-defined. Well-defined problems contain elements and characteristics that allow a reasoned evaluative judgment based solely upon information contained in the problem. Second, ill-defined problems do not contain these elements, and criteria and information external to the problem must be applied (Bloom et al. 1956). Further, ill-defined problems often have no single answer upon which experts would all agree (King and Kitchener 1994). A person confronted with an evaluation problem must at some level decide whether the problem is ill- or well-defined. Another factor complicating evaluation is that people conduct cognitive processes at varying intensities. In typical situations, they exercise skills at a comfortable level of difficulty, called *functional processing* (Fischer 1980). Challenging situations, however, may require people to use skills not within their everyday repertoire. These "optimal" skills are within the individual's capability but require time, focused concentration, deeper processing, and greater effort (Fischer, p. 485). In addition, external supports are often necessary to support optimal processing (Fischer 1980; Vygotsky 1934/1962). There is likely to be a difference between the quality of a person's judgments made at the functional level and those made at the optimal level.

While the psychological and critical thinking literature prescribes a process for evaluative thinking, literature from other domains hints that this process may not always proceed smoothly. Several researchers using deception for various purposes noticed a remarkable passive acceptance of their deceptive information (Belli 1989; Toppino and Brochin 1989; Gilbert, Krull, and Malone 1990; Highhouse and Bottrill 1995). Hoax studies, which trace the origination and naïve acceptance of widely disseminated misinformation, seem to indicate a similar passive acceptance (Bird 1996; Fedler 1989; Tamarkin 1993). Studies of Internet hoaxes suggest that electronic communication may be a ripe context for gullibility also (Aycock and Buchignani 1995; Viehland 1993). Thus, accounts of gullibility appear across several domains under widely varying circumstances.

Literature from several areas may help to explain gullibility, a phenomenon that can be seen as a lack of evaluation. Several factors seem to affect evaluation, including development, epistemology, affect, and prior knowledge. In general, evaluation efficacy is positively correlated with age and education when other factors are held constant (King and Kitchener 1994). Also, epistemologists correlate a relativist philosophy to the likelihood of a person engaging in critical thinking and being open to new evidence (Hofer and Pintrick 1997; Siegel and Carey 1989). Affect and evaluation seem to be inversely related to a mild degree, meaning that people in positive moods tend to be less critical than people in negative moods (Isen, Means, Patrick, and Nowicki 1982). Prior knowledge within the problem domain and of metacognitive strategies is helpful in making evaluative decisions (Alexander, Kulikowich, and Jetton 1994). However, the line where prior knowledge becomes bias is not clearly demarcated. Furthermore, each of these four influences seems to occupy a continuum in terms of effect. None can be said to be strictly positive or negative, but each can have effects varying from extremely negative to neutral to extremely positive.

The cognitive process of evaluation as a holistic entity is poorly understood, although various isolated components have been studied. King and Kitchener described reflective judgment in adults (1994), using problems carefully constructed to minimize the effects of personal motivation and context knowledge. Numerous studies focus on judgment quality under a variety of conditions. Such studies assume a normative standard for judgments (Kahneman 1991), which seems possible when problems are well-defined. Studies of children occasionally compare evaluative skill efficacy, such as inconsistency detection, across age groups. Information search studies (Kuhlthau 1989; McGregor 1994; Pitts 1994) follow the whole process of information search, analysis, and synthesis from beginning to end. These studies, however, either found little or no evaluation occurring (McGregor 1994; Pitts 1994) or did not seek it (Kuhlthau 1989). In sum, evaluation components have been studied as separate constructs. No study discovered to date describes evaluation as a holistic process, nor in the context of an authentic information task.

METHOD

This qualitative collective case study considered evaluation in a realistic setting, incorporating context and influential elements. Well-educated and motivated participants were chosen because past research suggests that these characteristics increase the likelihood of evaluative behavior. Five second-year doctoral students were followed through an information search process involving a topic of personal relevance in late 1997. Methods included collective case study techniques and a phenomenological approach.

Information encountered by these participants primarily included scholarly research publications, usually in the form of peer-reviewed journal articles. Scholarly books and finished dissertations figured heavily in their bibliographies as well. However, due to the naturalistic design of the study, media in other forms came under scrutiny during the information searches of these participants. Popular books, films, mainstream news, the Internet, online databases, and other types of information figured in the hodgepodge of sources considered.

Data sources included interviews, think-aloud protocols, observations, stimulated recalls, retrospective reports, documents, and member checks. Interviews consisted of open-ended questions that allowed participants to describe their thinking about their chosen information sources. Think-aloud sessions revealed more of this thinking and provided an opportunity to observe evaluative processes as they occurred. Participants were observed for six weeks as they examined information sources for the first time, as they reconsidered first impressions, and as they applied this information to personal contexts.

During analysis, data pertaining to evaluation were extracted. These data were first analyzed according to phenomenological principles, building an understanding of each person's processes as isolated cases. Next, categories derived from individual participants were compared across cases. Consistencies and patterns generated hypotheses, which were tested against the data. Surviving hypotheses became conclusions. Finally, conclusions were compared to the theoretical framework. Throughout the process, the qualitative data analysis program *QSR NUD*IST* helped to manage data sources and document analytical developments.

RESULTS AND CONCLUSIONS

One of the most striking results of this study was that participants used evaluation as part of a complex cognitive process. The data support a model of how evaluation fits into a system of thinking about information that prominently includes synthesis and argument, among other processes (see Figure 1). Within this model, the data also support a detailed sequential model of how evaluation operated within these participants (see Figure 2, on page 134). Evaluation occurred as a sequence beginning with a discrete initial event, progressing through three distinct deliberative phases (browsing, functional, and optimal), and ending with a decision in the form of a judgment. Initializations occurred as complex reactions to informational stimuli. Textual characteristics recognized as problems varied widely across participants.

Participants exhibited many evaluative strategies. The nature of strategies differed across the three deliberative phases, and a sequential pattern appeared when optimal incidents were compared across cases. Optimal processing seemed less reactive to information characteristics than functional processing, and time played a greater role during this phase. Judgments occurred through one of three distinct avenues. Evidence indicates that prior knowledge, epistemology, affect, and beliefs all influenced evaluation to varying degrees. In addition, format emerged as an unexpected influence to evaluation, especially regarding the preference or rejection of media types in the early phases of information use.

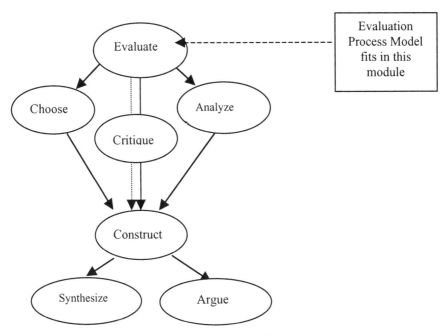

Figure 1. The role of evaluation among other cognitive processes.

The Influence of Media Format

The evidence is strong that format influenced evaluation in these participants. Participants in this study saw various formats as falling into reliable and unreliable categories, and there was a surprising amount of agreement about these classifications (see Table 1). However, participants also varied in the ways they approached different formats. Generally, participants were more likely to trust information found in a format considered reliable and less likely to trust information found in an unreliable one.

TABLE 1. Participants' perceptions of reliable and unreliable information formats.

Reliable		Unreliable	
Format	Pro vs. Con	Format	Pro vs. Con
Scholarly books	5-0	Popular Press books	0-5
Journals	5-0	Magazines	0-5
GALILEO[1]	4-1	Web	0-5
ERIC	4-1		
Split: Dissertations: 1 pro, 1 con, 3 neutral			

---

[1]*GALILEO*—Georgia Library Learning Online—is a state-funded collection of databases widely available within the University system. The system hosts approximately 150 databases, including *ERIC*, *Social Sciences Abstracts*, *Lexis-Nexis' Academic Universe*, *PsycInfo*, and many other powerful academic tools. Several databases include full-text articles.

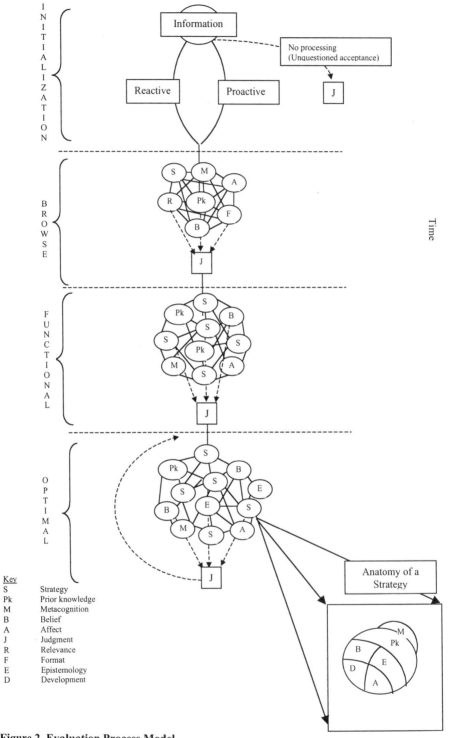

Figure 2. Evaluation Process Model.

Epistemology. There seemed to be a strong relationship between format type and epistemology. Participants often discussed format and the difference between empirical and conceptual literature in close conversational proximity. In the context of a literature review task, participants learned from their instructors to seek empirical studies as a robust form of support. In addition to this learned strategy, all but one participant seemed to consider empirical literature as more valid and useful than conceptual. This acceptance implies an epistemological belief in research as a useful way of knowing. The exception, Natalie, agreed that research was a useful tool. However, her interests focused upon phenomena that do not lend themselves to empirical description.

In addition to avoiding certain formats, participants professed to having favorite formats that differed widely between individuals. For example, Jim preferred dissertations, Ned *GALILEO*, and Natalie books. While their reasons for this favoritism range from practical to philosophical, some were evaluative in nature. In addition to the sensitivity to empiricism discussed above, these reasons included peer review, rigorous editing, and scholarly support. Participants listed lack of support, imprecise language for unsophisticated audiences, and a lack of editing as important evaluative reasons for rejecting the formats in the unreliable category.

Format choices in evaluation initialization. A distrusted format type served as a problem marker in many incidents. In these cases, participants consciously activated their critical mechanisms when they accessed a distrusted format. Each participant listed a clear preference sequence, based in part on ongoing quality decisions and past experience. For example, Ned started with *GALILEO* articles, then print articles, then books, and finally the Web. In this study, people tended to use their favorite formats when information was plentiful and ranged outside their preferences when not. Thus, they attempted to avoid problematical sources from the start. Also, however, they were limiting themselves unnecessarily to favored formats and often ignoring whole categories of other formats.

Participants built format preferences over years, in part for evaluative reasons. They tended to exhaust preferred formats before moving on to less-preferable formats. The influence of format preferences seemed most significant in the initialization phase. Therefore, format influences cannot be ignored in an overall consideration of evaluation.

GALILEO Versus the Web

As stated earlier, participants generally liked *GALILEO* and generally avoided the World Wide Web for scholarly research. All participants except one used *GALILEO* regularly for research purposes. Christina, Gap, and Ned each expressed positive opinions about it, used it heavily, and tended to begin their searches there. They list its positive aspects as follows:

1. Provides access to information containing a high proportion of relevant, scholarly information.

2. Saves time through convenience and efficiency.

3. Contains high-quality abstracts.

Participants tended to use *GALILEO* early in their searches because it enabled them to access high-quality information quickly. This tendency demonstrates that *GALILEO* has made a strong impact in its relatively short period of existence on the search and information processes of these participants. In the cases of two participants, the use of *GALILEO* articles has all but replaced the use of print articles.

Three items appear on the negative side. Natalie avoided *GALILEO* completely because of her strong preference for print. Jim and Ned spoke of missing graphical elements, including photographs of authors and tabular information. Also, one participant mistakenly thought that *GALILEO* articles sometimes omit the bibliography. This participant was aware that *GALILEO* contains journals that do not habitually list references. This minor complaint about missing bibliographies implies a lack of clear differentiation between the types of journals accessed through

GALILEO, and that scholarly and popular journals may seem to blend. Confusion between two important publication types is less of a problem in print because of strong visual differences and advertisements. This misconception corroborates the idea that users may forget that hyperlinking tends to present information in a cognitively undifferentiated sequence (Burbules and Bruce 1995). Further, it implies that this participant temporarily became disoriented enough not to notice straying into nonacademic territory. This incident supports the idea from Reinking (1992) and Gygi (1990) that people sometimes become disoriented in hypertext environments.

In stark contrast, the participants in this study cannot be considered Web enthusiasts. Christina said "I have a certain amount of skepticism about it, I guess because there's a lot of junk out there." Natalie agreed: "Consider the source, you just don't know the sources. It doesn't strike me as gospel at all." These women agreed that while there may be worthy materials there, the amount of high-quality information found in proportion to the amount of time spent is too low. Jim mentioned that web pages tend to be very narrow in range. Ned found the Web useful, but not as useful as *GALILEO*. Further, participants seemed to know little about the many authoritative Web sources available. Instead, they viewed the Web as a single resource indexed haphazardly by search engines.

However, there is evidence that the Web is sneaking into the lives of these people. Jim found two unique items on the Web that added a great deal to his understanding. Also, he had no idea that his favorite author had died until he read a years-old obituary on the Web. Christina commented on the difficulty of finding information about her liberal and cutting-edge topic: "If it's going to be anywhere . . . it's more likely to be on the Web." In fact, there is at least one example for each participant in which the Web seemed useful as an information conduit. They seemed to find it unremarkable to access articles posted on the Web written by authors already considered reputable.

Even three years ago, neither GALILEO nor the Web was available in the form they are today. Yet both have changed the information process behavior of these participants tremendously. As both of these resources evolve, it will be interesting to watch further changes in information search and evaluation behavior.

Altogether, the influence of format preference on these participants seemed substantial. Participants classified formats as reliable or unreliable and used sources in the reliable category as much as possible. These classifications were consistent across participants. This observation raises a question: Do people shut down or decrease evaluative processing when they use a format considered reliable? I found no evidence in this study suggesting that this is so, but I did not seek such evidence. This issue bears further study.

Specific evaluative strategies used by participants while evaluating Web information
Upgrade Web sites that mention research.
Does the site contain all active links?
Consider size of document (both too small and too large are quality liabilities).
Downgrade if overly burdened with graphics.
Does the site offer a quantity of concrete information?
Consider the sponsoring organization. What are their motives?
Apply quality/time ratio. Is the amount of worthwhile information I will likely find here worth the time spent?
Is this information essentially an advertisement? If so, disregard.
Ignore sites or documents that contain illiteracies.
Visit author's Web sites.
Avoid the Internet when plenty of good information can be found in print.

The Popular Press

In terms of commercially published books and magazines as scholarly resources, participants dismissed the popular press altogether because other, more reliable information was readily available to them. They objected to the way that information is digested or "watered down" for a popular audience, causing it to lose much of its value. As scholarly sources, participants felt that their professors would criticize the use of popular press publications. However, participants were able to use this medium in constructive ways for scholarly purposes. Christina and Jim consulted the popular press for trends in their topics and used these trends to help frame their research. Ned often discovered derivative reports in magazines and traced the original research back to its source. He found the secondhand reports more accessible and a valuable indicator, but reserved judgment until he saw the research report itself.

Strategies specific to the popular press
Downgrade spinoffs/derivatives.
Avoid popular press, primarily because authors don't attribute.
Use popular press as a pointer to more rigorous information.
Downgrade if published in the popular press.
Scrutinize anything published in the popular press very closely.

Two interesting themes regarding the effects of media upon individuals emerged from these data. These themes were not expressed by all participants, but their strength is sufficient to merit mention.

Media as experience. Stories have always intrigued people of all ages, and they emerged as a powerful way for people to gain vicarious experience from these data. This theme is important because another finding of the study is that experience is an important way of knowing; investigations of the epistemological assumptions of participants indicated a strong belief in this principle. One way to gain experience is to read the true and imagined stories of other people's experience:

> I think fiction teaches me so much. . . . Books, nonfiction and fiction, popular press, I get five magazines at my house every month. They inform everything that I do. So, so it's like with every theory, I instantly engage it with my life, people I know . . . it's just almost like you . . . do the computer word search, do a keyword search and all these things . . . come to my mind. (Author interview, December 1997)

Three of the five participants indicated a strong affinity for fiction. The emergence and strength of this theme is remarkable given the focus of the study upon scholarly information sources. Despite the current emphasis on fast and useful information promoted by pervasive access to electronic information sources, the importance of stories in the lives of these people remains strong.

Scholarly marginalization through media. All participants in this study understood and accepted that there is a "proper" body of literature suitable for use in academic work. However, the exact titles that can be found on this sanctioned list were a source of confusion and debate. Ned indicated that the best way to find out which publications are acceptable is to ask the professor. Participants indicated that inclusion of a title on this list, and more important, exclusion from it, could be a whimsical matter. Certainly, the list varied from professor to professor, and between academic departments.

Further, participants indicated that there is an element of snobbery involved in this issue. Social pressure exists to read the "proper" journals, a pressure that can be felt reaching into the private life of students:

> To me, I think it says, hey, what we know is better than what you know because what you've been reading is not what we, the authors are reading, what the great minds are reading. . . . You pick up *People*, you're not a great mind. We pick up the *RER*[2]. . . . I guess it's the way I definitely, how I tend to look at how other people behave, when they, the great academe, say THIS is what you need to read because they're great minds. I think it's an unnecessary divider. (Author interview, December 1997)

This sentiment was not expressed in nearly such strong terms by other participants. However, this minority view is an important one that should be pondered. What messages are relayed through the prejudicial selection of media by authority figures? Ultimately, individuals have the right to read any material they desire. Perhaps academic professionals at all levels should examine personal prejudices against media forms and consider how they may be transmitted to students.

EDUCATIONAL SIGNIFICANCE

As the ability to access, evaluate, and apply information increases in importance, educators must understand evaluation in order to design instruction that will prepare students for its effective use. The two primary contributions of this study are a model of the information evaluation process (see Figure 2) and a set of concrete evaluative strategies that can be taught to novice evaluators.

From an instructional designer's point of view, the strategies exhibited by these participants add information that should aid in task analysis (Smith and Ragan 1993). A major shortcoming of the existing literature addressing evaluation is that theorists seldom provide concrete details about how students should go about evaluating information. Yet novices need highly specific instructions. The strategies of these participants often provide these concrete process descriptions.

The results of this study inform educational practice in several ways at almost all levels, beginning in mid-elementary school. The direct route to intervention is to teach the strategies used by the advanced information users in this study to less-advanced information users.

The concern for information literacy seems to be on the rise. Information literacy is a type of literacy that encompasses all types of information, regardless of format. National educational organizations are concerned with this issue as well. New standards for instructional technology and information literacy call for the development of the ability to evaluate information in students (Peck 1998). The value of this study is its clarification of what this evaluation skill entails, including its specific contributions to the understanding of evaluating information in various media formats. This understanding of the evaluation process will assist educators in designing instruction to prepare students for the information of the twenty-first century.

---

[2]The participant did not use RER, but instead the acronym for a highly regarded discipline-specific journal. This title is omitted to protect the identity of the academic department involved in this study.

REFERENCES

Alexander, P. A., Kulikowich, J. M., and Jetton, T. L. (1994). The role of subject-matter knowledge and interest in the processing of linear and nonlinear texts. *Review of Educational Research* 64(2), 201–52.

Aycock, A., and Buchignani, N. (1995). The e-mail murders: Reflections on 'dead' letters. In S. G. Jones (ed.), *Cybersociety*. Thousand Oaks, CA: Sage, 184–231.

Belli, R. F. (1989). Influences of misleading postevent information: Misinformation interference and acceptance. *Journal of Experimental Psychology: General* 118(1), 72–85.

Bird, S. E. (1996). CJ's revenge: Media, folklore, and the cultural construction of AIDS. *Critical Studies in Mass Communication* 13(1), 44–58.

Bloom, B. S., Engelhart, M. D., Furst, E. J., Hill, W. H., and Krathwohl, D. R. (1956). *Taxonomy of Educational Objectives: The Classification of Educational Goals*. New York: David McKay.

Burbules, N. C., and Bruce, B. (1995). This is not a paper. *Educational Researcher* 24(8), 12–18.

Fedler, F. (1989). *Media Hoaxes*. Ames, IA: Iowa State University Press.

Fischer, K. W. (1980). A theory of cognitive development: The control and construction of hierarchies of skills. *Psychological Review* 87(6), 477–531.

Flavell, J. H. (1981). Cognitive monitoring. In W. P. Dickson (ed.), *Children's Oral Communication Skills*. New York: Academic Press, 35–60.

Gilbert, D. T., Krull, D. S., and Malone, P. S. (1990). Unbelieving the unbelievable: Some problems in the rejection of false information. *Journal of Personality and Social Psychology* 59, 601–13.

Gygi, K. (1990). Recognizing the symptoms of hypertext . . . and what to do about it. In B. Laurel (ed.), *The Art of Human-Computer Interface Design*. Reading, MA: Addison-Wesley, 279–87.

Highhouse, S., and Bottrill, K. V. (1995). The influence of social (mis)information on memory for behavior in an employment interview. *Organizational Behavior and Human Decision Processes* 62(2), 220–29.

Hofer, B. K., and Pintrich, P. R. (1997). The development of epistemological theories: Beliefs about knowledge and knowing and their relation to learning. *Review of Educational Research* 67, 88–140.

Isen, A. M., Means, B., Patrick, R., and Nowicki, G. (1982). Some factors influencing decision-making strategy and risk taking. In M. S. Clark and S. T. Fiske (eds.), *Affect and Cognition: The 17th Annual Carnegie Symposium on Cognition*. Hillsdale, NJ: Lawrence Erlbaum, 243–61.

Kahneman, D. (1991). Judgment and decision making: A personal view. *Psychological Science* 2(3), 142–45.

King, P. M., and Kitchener, K. S. (1994). *Developing Reflective Judgment: Understanding and Promoting Intellectual Growth and Critical Thinking in Adolescents and Adults*. San Francisco: Jossey-Bass.

Kuhlthau, C. C. (1989). Information search process: A summary of research and implications for school library media programs. *School Library Media Quarterly* 18(1), 19–25.

McGregor, J. H. (1994). Cognitive processes and the use of information: A qualitative study of higher-order thinking skills used in the research process by students in a gifted program. In C. C. Kuhlthau (ed.), *School Library Media Annual*. Englewood, CO: Libraries Unlimited, 124–33.

Peck, K. L. (1998). Ready . . . fire . . . aim! Toward meaningful technology standards for educators and students. *TechTrends* 43(2), 47–53.

Petty, R. E., and Cacioppo, J. T. (1986). The elaboration likelihood model of persuasion. In L. Berkowitz (ed.), *Advances in Experimental Social Psychology*, vol.19. Orlando, FL: Academic Press, 123–205.

Pitts, J. M. (1994). Personal understandings and mental models of information: A qualitative study of factors associated with the information-seeking and use of adolescents. Ph.D. diss., Florida State University, Tallahassee.

Reinking, D. (1992). Differences between electronic and printed texts: An agenda for research. *Journal of Educational Multimedia and Hypermedia* 1(1), 11–24.

Siegel, M., and Carey, R. F. (1989). *Critical Thinking: A Semiotic Perspective*. Bloomington, IN: ERIC Clearinghouse on Reading and Communication Skills.

Smith, P. L., and Ragan, T. J. (1993). *Instructional Design*. New York: Merrill.

Tamarkin, B. (1993). *Rumor Has It: A Curio of Lies, Hoaxes, and Hearsay*. New York: Prentice Hall.

Taylor, R. S. (1986). *Value-added Processes in Information Systems*. Norwood, NJ: Ablex.

Toppino, T. C., and Brochin, H. A. (1989). Learning from tests: The case of true-false examinations. *Journal of Educational Research* 83(2), 119–24.

Viehland, D. W. (1993). Dear Mr. President: A story of misinformation distribution in cyberspace. *Internet Research* 3(3), 57–60.

Vygotsky, L. S. (1934, 1962). *Thought and Language*. E. Hangman and G. Vaquero, trans. Cambridge, MA: MIT Press.

Web-Based Instruction
Prospects and Challenges

Janette R. Hill
Georgia State University
janette@gsu.edu

ABSTRACT

Web-based instruction (WBI) offers a new and exciting avenue for meeting the needs of learners, particularly the needs of those learners who would not otherwise be able to engage in a formal educational process. WBI enables continued involvement in the learning process in an any-time, anyplace orientation. While the promises of WBI are great, delivery on many of these promises has yet to be realized. One reason for the delay may be the lack of shared experiences for how to create and develop these environments. The purposes of this chapter are to explore the opportunities and possibilities afforded by WBI, and to make recommendations for others involved in the design, development, and implementation of WBI.

WEB-BASED INSTRUCTION: PROSPECTS AND CHALLENGES

The number of websites currently accessible to the everyday Web user is staggering. Millions of web pages have been added to the framework created in 1992, and the number continues to increase at an exponential rate. Recent figures estimate that there are more than two million unique domain names and more than 300 million pages on the Web (Hamilton 1998; Haverkamp and Gauch 1998). The number of websites devoted to educational purposes is also increasing as institutions seek new ways to reach more learners. Despite institutional interest and advocacy, the growth of Web-based instruction (WBI) is bringing mixed messages of educational benefits and learner satisfaction. The literature is filled with compelling cases on the use of WBI (see, for example, Bazillion and Braun 1998; Collis 1997; Diller and Huling 1997; Petersen 1998). There are also several stories relaying the perceived dangers created by WBI (see, for example, Neumann 1998; Noble 1999).

Certainly more research is needed to fully understand the impact of, and potential for, the Web in education. In the interim, WBI continues to grow, offering new and exciting avenues for meeting the needs of learners, particularly the needs of those learners who would not otherwise be able to engage in a formal educational process. WBI also enables continued involvement in the learning process in an anytime, anyplace orientation. This can be particularly appealing to learners who are dispersed across a broad geographic area or want to continue with their formal education and need the convenience WBI can afford.

While WBI does hold a great deal of potential for the delivery of instruction (Khan 1997; Owston 1997), the fulfillment of the opportunities has yet to be fully realized. One reason for the delay may be the lack of shared experiences for how to create and develop these environments. To the credit of those working in this area (see Khan [1997] for an early compilation of chapters written by authors working with WBI), not much time has elapsed since the rapid growth of WBI and the subsequent need for a "best practices" knowledge base. The number of publications related to the Web and instruction is growing (e.g., an ERIC search on "World Wide Web" and "instruction" resulted in 359 hits for articles and documents). However, the necessity of more shared experiences and guidelines for creating and developing WBI exists, and continues to increase as the demand for WBI grows.

The purpose of this chapter is to explore the opportunities and possibilities afforded by WBI. Reasons for the growth of WBI will be considered. Issues related to the design, development, and implementation of WBI will be described within the context of two WBI environments. Suggestions for WBI will be provided. Pending questions for future exploration will be presented.

WBI: OPPORTUNITIES AND POSSIBILITIES

Web-based instruction is making an impact on distance learning unlike any technology that has come before it. Many courses are being offered at a distance via WBI. Subject areas covered in this format range from literature to physics to library reference to business administration. The coverage of grade levels and types of schools also reflects a broad spectrum: children to adults; K–12 to universities to vocational schools. Institutions are devoting considerable resources to take advantage of the opportunities WBI can offer both themselves and their learners.

There are several potential factors motivating institutions to increase implementation efforts for WBI (see Petersen [1998] for other advantages). One motivator may be the perceived ease in moving courses from a face-to-face implementation to a Web-based environment. Corporations involved in assisting institutions with WBI (e.g., RealEducation, WebCT) tout the ability to get an online course uploaded quickly with minimal effort on the part of the instructor (RealEducation 1999; WebCT 1999). Not only does course development appear easy, WBI delivery equipment is low-tech in comparison to other distance technologies (e.g., satellite, videoconferencing). WBI does not require highly sophisticated, dedicated equipment. If an instructor or teacher has access to a word processor and a web server, they can implement a Web-based learning environment. The learners' equipment needs are also minimal, requiring a computer with web access and a web browser.

Another factor that may be increasing the use of the Web for distance delivery of instruction is learner demand. More adults are returning to school to learn new skills needed for their jobs to enhance performance or to move up to a higher position. While the course or degree is important, adults have many other obligations that place demands on their time (see Merriam and Caffarella 1991 for a thorough explanation of adult learner characteristics). Adult learners need ways to meet their educational needs as well as their other responsibilities. WBI enables adults to engage in a course or work toward a degree in an anytime/anyplace orientation, making it easier to add formal learning experiences into already full schedules.

New possibilities for delivering instruction at a distance are yet another factor increasing the use of WBI. Unlike other distance learning implementations that may require the learner to travel to a specific space to engage in class discussions (e.g., a studio) and another space to get course resources (e.g., the library), WBI enables a one-stop shopping model. Course facilitators and learners can go to one space on the Web to access course information, participate in discussion sessions (synchronous and asynchronous), review and submit assignments, and explore various resources. While the different aspects of a course may be stored on multiple web servers, the course websites can be designed so that facilitators and learners only need to visit one location to link out to all necessary materials.

TAKING ON THE CHALLENGE: IMPLEMENTING WBI

Educators at all levels are experiencing increased pressure (internal and external) to provide courses in different ways. I decided to take advantage of the opportunities and possibilities afforded by WBI in designing two courses for distance delivery: one focused on school library media specialists, *Reference and Information Management* (RIM), and the other primarily targeted toward educational technologists, *Distance Education* (DE). These courses were selected for a variety of reasons:

- The courses involved a high level of interaction, something that can be facilitated at a distance using a variety of methods;
- Many learners who were registered to take the courses lived or worked in remote locations from campus; and

• I was interested in continuing research in the area of WBI, discovering ways to best assist learners in obtaining information in an anytime, anyplace orientation.

Course Participants

Both courses were implemented at a university in Colorado where the learner population is dispersed geographically throughout the state and into Wyoming (a geographic region covering more than 100,000 square miles). The learners participating in the courses were adults (ages 25-50) working and living in varied locations throughout Colorado and Wyoming.

In terms of experience with the Web, the learners varied considerably. Some possessed considerable experience, others very little. Only two of the learners (n=26) had engaged in a formal educational experience via the Web. A final characteristic the learners shared was a willingness to try new things and a desire to make the learning process easier for them from a logistic orientation.

Courses Converted to a WBI Format

Reference and Information Management (RIM)

The primary goal of RIM was to assist learners in developing an understanding of the reference process and the activities involved in information management. In developing this understanding, emphasis in the course was placed on the exploration of the various types of materials, databases, and reference services that support K–12 curricula. The learners engaged in several activities (e.g., simulation activities, Reference Collection Plan, philosophy paper); each activity was designed to assist learners in developing an understanding of the reference process, information sources, and evaluation of reference service (see Figures 1-2 for examples of the pages from the websites).

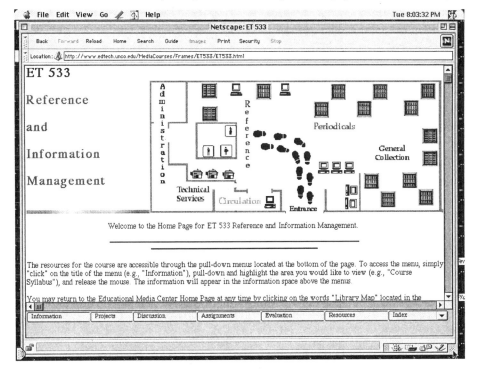

Figure 1. RIM Home Page.

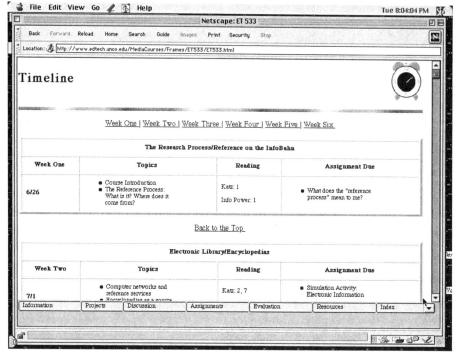

Figure 2. RIM timeline.

Distance Education (DE)

The primary goal of DE was to assist learners in developing an understanding of the fundamental concepts and practices in distance education. In developing this understanding, emphasis was placed on the learners acquiring hands-on experience in the design of distance education learning environments. As in the RIM course, learners participated in several activities (e.g., case studies, critical analysis/position papers, DELE Design Portfolio). Each activity was designed to assist learners in developing a deeper understanding of distance education (see Figures 3-4 for examples of the pages from the websites).

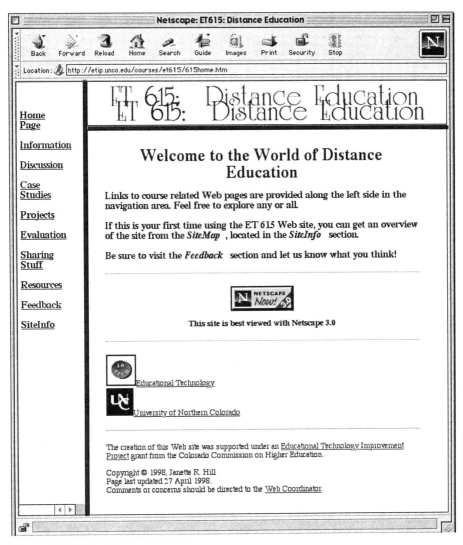

Figure 3. DE Home Page.

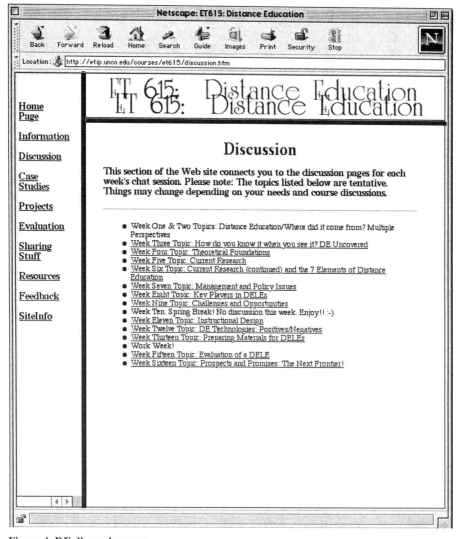

Figure 4. DE discussion area.

IMPLEMENTATION OBSTACLES AND ISSUES

Activities related to the design, development, and implementation of WBI can be divided into three primary activity areas: analysis, design and development, and implementation and ongoing evaluation. In building a context for the reader, obstacles and issues related to the creation and implementation of the two WBI courses will be discussed within these phases.

Phase One: Analysis

Analysis involves investigation of the learner, the learning environment, and establishing course goals (Smith and Ragan 1998). Several activities occurred during analysis for RIM and DE, including identifying a need to offer the courses at a distance, deciding which technologies to use for the learning environment, and deciding which course activities would best lend themselves to WBI (see Hill [1997] for additional elements to consider during analysis).

Prior goals established in earlier implementations of the courses were used during the Web-based delivery of the courses to maintain some consistency between course offerings. This approach is recommended by Gibson and Herrera (1999) as a way to make implementation of WBI smoother. By using preestablished goals, the facilitator can focus on the new delivery method rather than having to focus on delivery method and curriculum development.

Identifying a need to offer the courses at a distance was driven by two factors: my desire to do research in the area of WBI and the learner's desire to experiment with new learning techniques. In RIM, the learners looked at the distance implementation as an opportunity to explore Internet-based environments, an increasingly important technology for library media specialists. DE participants viewed the online offering as a way to learn more about distance education by experiencing it firsthand.

The decisions related to technology use for the WBI environments were largely determined by what the university network structure could support. For example, Web-based videoconferencing was quickly removed as an option; the institution's network infrastructure simply could not handle the demands of the technology. The text-based emphasis on the websites was also driven by the network infrastructure.

The overall goals and objectives of each course (Dick and Carey 1996; Smith and Ragan 1998) guided activities. As interaction and participation were goals in both courses, several telecommunication technologies (e.g., E-mail, listservs, chat, threaded discussion, phone, fax) were used to make sharing ideas and providing feedback as easy as possible.

Phase Two: Design and Development

Design and development involves the creation of plans for a course and then putting those plans into effect by building the course (Shambaugh and Magliaro, 1997). A constructivist approach was used for designing the RIM and DE websites. As stated by Jonassen, Davidson, Collins, Campbell, and Bannan (1995): "Constructivist environments engage learners' knowledge construction through collaborative activities that embed learning in meaningful context and through reflection on what has been learned through conversation with other learners" (p. 13). Several activities in the courses supported using a constructivist approach to distance education (Jonassen et al. 1995), including: deriving solutions to simulations/cases; the completion of reflection papers related to the learner's personal articulation of a particular process; and collaboration and conversation in varied groupings (small, large, individual) and methods (synchronous, asynchronous) in order to reach consensus in meaning making. In essence, the websites became "cognitive tools" to extend and enhance the learners' investigation, creation, and representation of knowledge (Reeves 1999).

Several issues and challenges were encountered during the creation of RIM and DE. These are briefly discussed in the following sections: design/development issues, logistical/management issues, and technological challenges.

Design/Development Issues

Page vs. Site Design. How to best structure the creation of the courses was a major concern for the designers/developers. The question of structure related to designing the site from a page-by-page perspective, or designing on a more global level: site design. The decision was made to follow a more global orientation in creating the sites. Designing from a site level versus at the page level can assist with maintaining cohesion (Waters 1996). Thus, when you view the individual pages, all pages of both sites have a similar layout and design.

Consistency and Style. One of the biggest challenges faced in the design/development of the RIM and DE websites was the consistency and style of the sites. Using a variety of guidelines (see, for example, Lemay 1998; Jones and Farquhar 1997), considerable time and energy was devoted to the design of the sites to ensure a similar look. Given the high levels of interaction in the courses, consistency became important to help learners maintain a sense of orientation.

Cross-Platform Performance. Another design/development issue related to the learners' ability to access the websites regardless of the platform being used. In our context, there were two primary systems used to access the RIM and DE websites: Macintosh and Windows. Several issues arose as we developed the sites, including:

- A need to view the websites on both platforms. We found many scripting anomalies across the two platforms (i.e., what worked in one platform did not work in the other). What we learned was that functionality, style, and cosmetics cannot be assumed to be appropriate across systems, and it is never safe to assume that what you see is what you get!

- A need to view the websites on different size monitors to see what the user will be viewing. This was one of the few ways to truly get the learner's perspective of the sites.

- A need to "code" for downward compatibility. This issue was particularly relevant in the creation of the navigational bar on the bottom of the RIM websites (see Figure 1). The pop-up windows for navigation could be seen on the Mac while there were problems in the Windows environment. This created a need to adjust the pull-up menus to accommodate both platforms. The frames used for the DE course also presented challenges, making it necessary for some learners to update their browser application to view the environment.

Logistical/Management Issues

Dynamic Environment. Things are not stable in a Web environment, often bringing changes that create unanticipated havoc. For example, links we established to other sites would change (e.g., the download site for Netscape Navigator changed the day before we went online with the RIM site). We also found that as we did more development, additional external links would need to be added (e.g., updating resources for topic discussions). While the dynamic characteristics of the Web are what make it such a wonderful resource, they also create significant challenges for site maintenance. We established a systematic method for revisions to make the task more manageable.

Site Access. Where and how learners accessed the websites also became a management issue. Some learners accessed the sites from home or from their places of work; other learners accessed the courses from campus labs. This created many challenges, especially in regard to access speed. Some learners were dialing up via modem while others had direct network access. One solution frequently used is developing two versions of a websites: one text-based and one graphically enhanced. Our limited resources created a need to design and develop for the low-end (modem dial-up) technologies rather than the upper sector (Ethernet connection); thus, the sites are more text-based with minimal graphics.

Technical Assistance. An associated issue was the need for dedicated assistance with the technologies used in the courses. All of the learlers in the RIM course were novices in the use of the Web for formal educational purposes. Many of the learners had never engaged in a distance education environment of any form. This created a need for extensive technical support throughout the course.

Following Willis's (1993) recommendation that technical support be available for all types of distance education implementations, dedicated technical assistance was available in both courses, onsite as well as from a distance. For onsite assistance, the GRA and lab assistants played critical roles, especially in helping learners when they were on campus. The facilitators primarily provided assistance via E-mail or phone. This forethought may have deterred the growth of other logistical/management issues as we were able to assist learners directly at the point of need.

Technological Challenges

Modems and Browsers. The hardware and software used to access the course websites were also a concern during preimplementation of the courses. We beta tested the site using a variety of browsers (e.g., Netscape Navigator, Netscape Communicator, Internet Explorer) and versions, as well as a variety of modems. Given our learners' access environments, we determined that the optimal browser for ease of access was Netscape Navigator 3.0 (or higher) with a 14.4 modem.

Network Stability. The network at the university where the course websites were being served was far less than reliable. It was not unusual for the network to go down, creating access issues for the designers/developers as they worked on the creation of the site. Lack of access also created challenges for the evaluators of the site. No matter how reliable or how well tested, something will go wrong with the technology. Having a contingency plan is important to maintain workflow (Willis 1993). To ensure that data were received, we asked evaluators to send in their online evaluations via regular mail in addition to completing online forms.

Phase Three: Implementation and On-Going Evaluation

Once the courses were underway, refinement and enhancement of the courses remained as ongoing activities. Design decisions were reconsidered; development of the courses continued throughout implementation. Several issues and challenges were encountered during the implementation of RIM and DE. These are briefly discussed in the following sections.

Design/Development Issues

Network Stability. As during design and development, one of the biggest challenges encountered during the implementation of the courses related to the university network. The university servers were continually going down. This affected the learners' access to the websites, as well as their ability to send E-mail and participate in the discussion sessions (synchronous and asynchronous). In order to minimize the stress associated with technological challenges, we talked to the learners about the potential for technological frustrations prior to them going online. We also continuously reassured them not to worry about missed discussions or difficulties retrieving or submitting information. We found these reassurances important for influencing learners' comfort and satisfaction levels.

Web Browsers. Another issue relates to the web browser learners were using to access the sites. While the learners were informed that Netscape Navigator 3.0 was the preferred (and most reliable) browser, it was not always possible for learners to access the sites via Navigator, especially in the RIM course. This created a need to develop two websites for RIM: dynamic and basic. The dynamic version of the RIM websites relied upon JavaScript code to function. The basic version of the websites used basic HTML code. The offering of the two versions enabled easier access for all of the learners.

Content Delivery vs. Data Gathering. Yet another issue related to the learner's understanding of the experimental nature of the course websites. While the courses were being offered for the delivery of content as a part of the Educational Technology program, they were also being developed as research projects. Because the majority of the participants were majoring in educational technology/educational media, we talked about the practice of formative evaluation and revision. By continuously dealing with technical issues that influenced their ability to access and use the site, learners had good lessons in some of the real-world frustrations of instructional design and development for Web-based environments.

Logistical/Management Issues

The Importance of Flexibility and Feedback. Learners were informed at the beginning of classes that prerequisites included flexibility, an open mind, and a sense of humor. They were also encouraged to provide feedback on an ongoing basis. Maintaining constant and open lines of communication can significantly influence the success of a distance education environment (Schrum and Berenfeld 1997). The learners' responses to numerous technical problems, updates, and revisions actually prompted important changes and additions to the Web-based learning environment. For example, the learners complained about the confusing nature of multiple discussions occurring simultaneously in the synchronous chat mode. To minimize the confusion, the chat room for RIM was revised to accommodate 'threads' of conversations. In the DE course, two forms of chat were accommodated: synchronous and asynchronous. Participants were encouraged to choose the mode most easily available to them.

Keeping the Learners Motivated. The situations provided numerous opportunities to discuss sociological aspects of WBI and online information access, including methods for keeping learners motivated in a distance learning environment. One motivating factor we kept stressing when RIM learners balked at using the Web-based environment was that much information in media centers is electronic based these days. Therefore it seemed particularly appropriate to learn about online resources using a Web-based environment. In DE, we stressed the increased use of the Web for instructional purposes and a need for all educational technology professionals to understand the positives and negatives associated with the use of this environment for instruction.

WBI IMPLEMENTATION: A VIEW FROM THE LEARNERS' PERSPECTIVE

Certainly several issues and challenges were overcome in the design and development of the RIM and DE websites. In addition to the suggestions discussed in the previous section, several other suggestions were derived based on formal evaluations of the WBI by learners and other experts, and from my experience in implementing these courses as well as other online environments.

Make Full Use of the Interactive Capabilities of Web-Based Technologies

The ability to draw upon the experience of peers working in the field (i.e., K–12 library media centers) was an important aspect to many of the learners in the courses. The ability to share experiences appeared to be enhanced by the electronic technologies used in the courses to facilitate interaction. As stated by one learner:

> There are some really good and knowledgeable people in this class that have a lot of good ideas and experiences to draw from. A few of the people have spent some time on the job already, and it's interesting to draw on their stories when we talk about the issues.

Take Advantage of the Various Web-Based Tools

The ability to use the tools (e.g., E-mail, listservs, Web) was also reported by several learners as a valuable aspect of the courses. The fact that the courses made use of real-world technologies in real applications was also mentioned as a positive aspect:

- I really liked to see that the new technology is being used.
- I felt that it [the course] gave me an opportunity to learn about the material at hand and learn more about the technology used and how to use it myself.

Given that these learners had a high interest in technology (i.e., the majority were media specialists and educational technologists), they were the perfect audience for exposure to multiple WBI tools. Several of the learners reported have little to no experience with Internet technologies. The fact that they were able to feel more comfortable with the tools was an important accomplishment. As stated by one learner:

> I am learning more about using E-mail every day. . . . I have also been learning how to access and use the [web] site. These have been new concepts for me. I have particularly enjoyed answering the questions using the chat areas.

Provide Guidance in Using the Web-Based (and Other Telecommunication) Technologies Selected for the Course

Many learners expressed frustrations with learning how to use the Web-based environment, reporting that the learning curve with the tools was (perhaps) more than they anticipated. One solution: "More training for those of us who have never used some of the technologies before." As stated by one learner:

> If I were taking this class again, I would like to see more explanation on how to use all of the mechanics of the system. I was a bit confused at the beginning. Possibly a mini-course on how to use the site and the E-mail would be beneficial.

Create a Flexible Environment

Many learners reported that working in a WBI environment "took getting used to." For some learners, working in a Web-based course meant having to overcome personal anxieties associated with electronic communication.

It also is important to note that the facilitators knew they had to be flexible in terms of expectations regarding timelines, learners' performance, and content when the technology impeded "the plan." The modeling was crucial to learners' willingness to participate and take the risks associated with a new learning environment. It becomes important to model the process of flexibility. It is also important to provide one-on-one assistance when seeking solutions to individual learner challenges in WBI. Practice and a friendly reminder can also go a long way toward increasing learner comfort and willingness to continue to participate.

Assist Learners with the Development of Strategies for Working in Online Environments

Several learners reported feeling considerable time pressure in both WBI environments. Many stated that they felt concern regarding completion of the assignments and readings for the courses (e.g., "I'm getting out of the blocks kind of slow, and I need the weekend to get caught up.") . However, some of the comments made about time management related specifically to the websites and interactions within the environments. A learner had the following comment:

> The [website] is a great idea in theory, especially for dazzling friends and family on the wonders of technology, but I haven't really used the chat feature enough to feel comfortable with it. When we began working with it last Tuesday, I really felt the need to push away from the computer and give myself to time to digest the questions and the information before trying to respond. I felt myself being seduced by the power of the moving cursor rather than taking the time to reflect on what I wanted to say.

Take Advantage of the Learning Anytime, Anyplace Capabilities of WBI

The anytime, anyplace convenience of the Web-based learning environment is one of the main benefits of the technology (Reeves 1999). This was also reflected in learner comments in the two WBI courses:

> I loved being able to telecommunicate to class. . . . I had the opportunity to go to some meetings in our district and still attend class! The convenience of the environment has a lot to offer. I would not have been able to meet all my summer obligations without this environment.

Flexibility was also closely associated with convenience for many learners in the Web-based courses. As stated by two learners in the courses:

* I certainly appreciated the flexibility afforded by the [websites]. A couple of times I was off campus accessing the chat discussion while I was still in Longmont getting work done. Having the assignments available anytime, anywhere in computer format [proved] to be a boon on a number of occasions.

* What I liked best about the Web-based learning environment is its ability to be flexible. I enjoyed being able to work on projects at 2:00 a.m. and hand them in immediately.

Create a Safe Environment

One of the responsibilities for those of us involved in distance learning, regardless of the delivery system used, is to prime the expectations of learner participants. In the RIM and DE courses we stressed that WBI is not intended to replicate the traditional face-to-face learning environment. We also talked a great deal about the "experimental" nature of the courses, and how learner feedback would provide a means for improvement and revision, both during the courses and afterward. This emphasis appeared to predispose learners to consider the "oopses" we encountered as learning experiences rather than obstacles hindering their progress.

Many learners reported feeling uneasy about the network—especially in terms of sending and receiving assignments. In general, learners expressed a concern such as the following: "I worried about whether or not my assignments were received." Other comments included:

* . . . I was uneasy about receiving no feedback on the assignments I submitted electronically. I would have appreciated a reply acknowledging that they had been received intact.

For others, the least enjoyable aspect of the courses related to unreliable or lack of access:

* The technology is not reliable. Last Thursday the server was down, and it made me quite nervous. If I had access at another location, it wouldn't have been a problem; however, this was the only place I could complete the projects. When working in this environment, you definitely cannot procrastinate.

Provide a Lot of Feedback

This was the number one suggestion from the learners in the class: more feedback. For some, a simple reply that the assignment had been received was sufficient: "[Set up an] automatic E-mail message indicating that assignment(s) have been received. . . ." Others requested that the feedback be more detailed, but they wanted to receive feedback more frequently and as soon as possible.

LESSONS LEARNED: A SUMMARY OF SUGGESTIONS AND POTENTIAL AREAS OF EXPLORATION FOR WBI

Creating effective and efficient WBI is a challenge (Khan 1997). Luckily, more research is being published to help guide us in this task, including the experiences relayed in this chapter. The next section summarizes the suggestions from the previous sections of the paper to help guide readers in their design, development, and implementation efforts, and it provides recommendations for future research in the area of WBI.

Summary of Suggestions for WBI

- Use an established course during your first WBI experience.
- Analyze your learners' needs to determine if offering courses at a distance is necessary or desirable.
- Understand the strengths and weaknesses of the network you will be using to deliver WBI.
- Let your course goals and objectives determine the activities engaged in during WBI.
- Use a site design approach to maintain consistency and cohesion in your WBI site.
- Make full use of the interactive capabilities of Web-based technologies.
- Take advantage of the various Web-based tools to provide learners with multiple ways to access information and engage in discussion.
- Use the learning anytime, anyplace capabilities of WBI.
- Test your site on multiple platforms and browser applications.
- Produce contingency plans for occasions when the technology does not work.
- Create a flexible environment.
- Know how your learners will be accessing the WBI site and understand how this will influence your decisions (e.g., media, activities) for the site.
- Provide guidance in using the Web-based (and other telecommunication) technologies selected for the course.
- Assist learners with the development of strategies for working in online environments.
- Encourage your learners to use various technologies with which to interact with others in WBI (e.g., E-mail, listservs, chat, phone, fax).
- Create a safe environment.
- Provide a lot of feedback.

Recommendations for Future Exploration

Working with WBI is an exciting area from several perspectives: learner, facilitator, and researcher. While we have made considerable strides since the first web pages were uploaded, we still have many challenges to face and hurdles to overcome.

One area of exploration for WBI relates to the number of participants in a course. We had 12 learners in the RIM course and 13 in the DE course. This appeared to be a comfortable number given the level of interaction in the course and the course timeframe. Several questions impacting class size remain to be explored:

1. How many learners can be enrolled in a WBI environment while effective support and learning guidance is provided?

2. Should there a cap imposed on the number of participants in Web-based courses?

3. Should more than one facilitator be involved in WBI to ensure effective support and engagement with the learners?

The answers to these questions seem imperative if we are to continue to develop meaningful learning environments via the Web.

Another area in need of further investigation relates to hardware/software challenges encountered in the courses. We experienced several challenges in designing and implementing the course websites. However, we do not feel we are unique in our challenges (see Khan [1997] for other case studies related to WBI). It is imperative that we continue investigation of hardware/software issues related to WBI if we are to ensure the long-term viability of this medium for the distance delivery of instruction.

REFERENCES

Bazillion, R. J., and Braun, C. (1998). Teaching on the Web and in the studio classroom. *Syllabus 11*(8), 37–39.

Collis, B. (1997, Fall-Win). Pedagogical reengineering: A pedagogical approach to course enrichment and redesign with the World Wide Web. *Educational Technology Review,* 11–15.

Dick, W., and Carey, L. (1996). *The Systematic Design of Instruction*, 4th ed. Glenview, IL: Scottsman.

Diller, K., and Huling, N. (1997). Distance learning: Opportunities and challenges. *ALKI 13*(3), 10–13.

Gibson, J. W., and Herrera, J. M. (1999). How to go from classroom based to online delivery in eighteen months or less: A case study in online program development. *T.H.E. Journal 26*(6), 57–60.

Hamilton, A. (1998). Annette's Internet speedometer: How fast is it really growing? ZDNet AnchorDesk. Available online: http://www.zdnet.com/anchordesk/story/story_2139.html

Haverkamp, D. S., and Gauch, S. (1998). Intelligent information agents: Review and challenges for distributed information sources. *Journal of the American Society for Information Science 49*(4), 304–11.

Hill, J. R. (1997). Distance learning environments via the World Wide Web. In B. H. Khan (ed.), *Web-Based Instruction*. Englewood Cliffs, NJ: Educational Technology, 75–80.

Jonassen, D., Davidson, M., Collins, M., Campbell, J., and Bannan Haag, B. (1995). Constructivism and computer-mediated communication in distance education. *American Journal of Distance Education 9*(2), 7–26.

Jones, M. G., and Farquhar, J. D. (1997). User interface design for web-based instruction. In B. H. Khan (ed.), *Web-Based Instruction*. Englewood Cliffs, NJ: Educational Technology, 239–44.

Khan, B. H., ed. (1997). *Web-Based Instruction*. Englewood Cliffs, NJ: Educational Technology.

Lemay, L. (1998). *Teach Yourself Web Publishing with HTML 4*. Indianapolis, IN: SAMS.

Merriam, S. B., and Caffarella, R. S. (1991). *Learning in Adulthood: A Comprehensive Guide*. San Francisco: Jossey-Bass.

Neumann, P. G. (1998). Risks of e-education. *Communications of the ACM* 4(10), 136.

Noble, D. F. (1999). Digital diploma mills: The automation of higher education. First Monday. Available online: http://www.firstmonday.dk/issues/issues3_1/noble/

Owston, R. D. (1997). The World Wide Web: A technology to enhance teaching and learning. *Educational Researcher* 26(2), 27–33.

Petersen, R. (1998). The NASA Lewis Research Center's learning technologies project. *T.H.E. Journal* 26(4), 63–66.

RealEducation (1999). RealEducation websites. Available online: http://www.realeducation.com

Reeves, T. C. (1999, March). A model of the effective dimensions of interactive learning on the World Wide Web. Available online: http://itech1.coe.uga.edu/reeves

Schrum, L., and Berenfeld, B. (1997). *Teaching and Learning in the Information Age: A Guide to Educational Telecommunications*. Boston: Allyn and Bacon.

Shambaugh, N., and Magliaro, S. G. (1997). *Mastering the Possibilities: A Process Approach to Instructional Design*. Boston: Allyn and Bacon.

Smith, P. L., and Ragan, T. J. (1998). *Instructional Design*, 2nd ed. Upper Saddle River, NJ: Merrill.

Waters, C. (1996). *Web Concept and Design*. Indianapolis, IN: New Riders.

WebCT (1999). WebCT websites. Available online: http://www.webct.com/webct/

Willis, B. (1993). *Distance Education: A Practical Guide*. Englewood Cliffs, NJ: Educational Technology.

Part Four
Leadership Profile

Introduction

The purpose of this section is to profile individuals who have made significant contributions to the field of educational media and technology. Leaders profiled in the Yearbook have either held prominent offices, written important works, or made significant contributions that have influenced the contemporary vision of the field. Leaders profiled in this part have often been directly responsible for mentoring individuals who themselves became recognized for their contributions. There is no formal survey or popularity contest to determine the persons for whom the profiles are written, but those selected are usually emeritus faculty that remain active in the field or were particularly influential during their association with the profession. The following are the names of those previously profiled in earlier volumes of the Yearbook:

James D. Finn	Charles Francis Schuller
James W. Brown	Harry Alleyn Johnson
Wilbur Schramm	Robert M. Morgan
Robert E. De Kieffer	Paul Saettler
Jean E. Lowrie	Donald P. Ely
Robert Morris	James Okey
William Travers	Constance Dorothea Weinman
Robert Mills Gagné	Castelle (Cass) G. Gentry
Robert Heinich	Thomas F. Gilbert

There are special reasons to feature people of national and international renown, and the editors of the 25th anniversary volume of the *Educational Media and Technology Yearbook* believe that the following are worthy of such distinction:

- Wesley Joseph McJulien
- Stanley A. Huffman
- John C. Belland
- Robert M. Diamond
- Paul Robert Wendt
- Don Carl Smellie

You are welcome to nominate individuals to be featured in this section. Your nomination of someone to be profiled in this section must also be accompanied by the name of the person who will compose the leadership profile. Please direct any comments, questions, or suggestions about the selection process to the Senior Editor.

Robert Maribe Branch

Wesley Joseph McJulien
Leader, Teacher, and Media Pioneer

Hans-Erik Wennberg
Elizabethtown College

Dr. Wesley Joseph McJulien is an instructional technologist who provided leadership to the field throughout his professional career. As his career developed, he built on his abilities as a teacher to become not only a leader of minorities in media but also a leader in the field of educational technology.

Highlights of his career go hand in hand with the development of educational technology, particularly through the changes that have occurred in the most significant professional organization in the field, the Association for Educational Communications and Technology (AECT). As president, he made significant changes, including the educational technologist at the elementary and secondary school level and mentoring minorities in media.

Wes received his B.S. in Health and Physical Education from Southern University in 1957 and immediately began his military service, attending the Southeastern Signal School at Fort Gordon, GA. His training as a radiotelephone operator was perhaps his first introduction to technology. After receiving an honorable discharge, he began his career as a teacher.

Taking advantage of his military experience and interest in technology, Wes became audiovisual coordinator while teaching physical education at Yale Elementary School in Chicago. His practice in educational technology began at the building level.

In 1965, after returning to Southern University in Baton Rouge, LA, he began his long career in higher education, first as a graduate teaching assistant, then as an assistant professor after completing his master's degree. Wes became a graduate fellow at Syracuse in 1969. Working under the able guidance of his advisor, Kenneth Fishell, he completed his Ph.D. in Instructional Technology, in 1971. His dissertation, titled "The Effects of Modes of Presentation and Anxiety Levels in Individual Participant Achievement in an Educational Game," further enhanced his expertise as a teacher and reflected his interest in the humanity of the individual learner.

Wes became a proponent of the systematic process involving the principles and practices of instructional technology. As he states, his focus was on giving "learners and assisting teachers with instructional support skills necessary in the basic techniques of the design and production of instructional materials, operating media for learning and utilizing materials in the teaching learning process." He further used these skills to give the learner content that was more relevant and realistic. He used his dissertation research to include gaming techniques in his scholarly base.

With the completion of his degree, he followed his advisor, Ken Fishell, to the University of Vermont, where he became Director of the Center for Instructional Design and Development and University Media Services. As an assistant professor in the College of Education, he continued to develop his skills as a teacher.

While he became an avid skier, his Cajun roots brought him back to Southern University in Baton Rouge as a professor in the Graduate School of the College of Education. He also took on the position of Director of Continuing Education. This move gave Wes the opportunity to return to his first love, teaching.

Changes in the South were happening slowly, but in 1973 Wes became a member of the Graduate School Faculty in the College of Education at Louisiana State University, where he remained until his retirement as an associate professor in 1997. In 1974, he became a full-time member of the faculty in Instructional Technology. He was a pioneer as one of the first minority faculty hired at previously all-white Louisiana State University. His personality and ability quickly made him a success in the classroom.

While his professional career was progressing, Wes was making significant progress in his rise to leadership in the professional association area. The focus of his activity was the AECT. He became a member of AECT in 1969 while a graduate student at Syracuse University. Quickly realizing the benefits and advantages of association membership, he received the Memorial Scholarship Award in 1971. He also became the first Okoboji Educational Media Leadership Conference Intern in 1972. This opportunity and recognition at Okoboji brought his skills and abilities to the attention of the current leaders in the field of educational technology. Dr. McJulien's AECT career had begun.

Recognized as a leader by the membership at large for his numerous association activities, Wes was elected to the Board of Directors of AECT in 1974. His peers quickly recognized his leadership skills on the AECT Board, and he became a member of the executive committee. During his first term on the Board of Directors, he founded Minorities in Media, an affiliated organization that gave minorities a voice in the governance and direction of the profession. His leadership position gave him the opportunity to question the direction and management of the association. The lessons learned were invaluable in his future leadership roles.

Wes pursued the presidency of AECT for three years before being elected in 1979. His leadership brought about changes in the association management. He founded the Division of School Library Media Specialists. This new division brought school library media specialists into the association as new constituents and showed that Wes recognized the convergence of the library and educational technology fields.

Also during his term on the Board of Directors of AECT, Wes pursued numerous fiscal issues. He served as Chair of the Fiscal Advisory Committee and brought sounder budget management to the national association. His work in the association was recognized when he received the Distinguished Service Award from AECT recognizing his leadership to the association and to minority education in the field of educational technology.

After his service on the Board of Directors of AECT, Wes became an active member of the Educational Communications and Technology Foundation, serving as a trustee. His service continues today as he brings his unique perspective on minority affairs, concerns for the success of AECT, and his strong appreciation for the history of the profession to the ongoing mission of the association.

After the untimely death of his son, Wes started the McJulien Scholarship Award in his memory. The award, administered by Minorities in Media and the ECT Foundation and awarded since 1971, provides a minority student with scholarship aid for graduate study. It is another example of Wes's generosity as he attempts to give something back to the professional that he has served so well.

Throughout his professional career, Wes has been an eloquent spokesperson for the profession and the professional association. He has spoken at professional meetings throughout the country and remains a memorable representative of Educational Technology.

As a faculty member at Louisiana State University, Wes enjoyed working in the classroom and provided educational technology training to graduates and undergraduates in instructional technology. He has left his mark on graduates of the School of Education of LSU.

Wes remains active in educational technology. He continues to serve the ECT Foundation as a trustee and is an active participant in the AECT Past Presidents' Council. In addition, he has been drafted by his wife Demitria, chair of the Social Work Program at Southern University, to work with her in Head Start. Wes is traveling around the country presenting workshops in negotiation, mediation, and conciliation for the staff of Head Start Agencies. His speaking skills and quick wit continue to make him a success.

Dr. Wesley Joseph McJulien, a true leadership pioneer, has established a record as a teacher, scholar, leader, and spokesperson for minorities that has made a substantial contribution to the field of educational technology.

Note: Much of the information in this article came from personal notes and recollections of my longtime friendship with Wes. I want to thank his wife Demitria McJulien for her invaluable assistance in preparing this article.

Stanley A. Huffman, Jr.
Distance Educator

J. Thomas Head
and
David M. Moore
Virginia Tech

Stanley A. Huffman, Jr. made significant contributions to the field of instructional technology throughout his career in the K–12 environment and in higher education. He directed graduate studies, established Learning Resources Centers at two universities, and was a early proponent of electronic distance education. His career was marked by a dedication to service to faculty, students and the profession that was designed to continuously improve the quality of the learning environment through the application of technology.

Stan was a true native of southwest Virginia. He was raised in a small community in Craig County called Huffman, which is about 10 miles east of Newport. He completed his undergraduate degree in General Science at Virginia Tech in 1951. He did his master's work in Educational Psychology at the University of Virginia in 1955 and returned to complete his Ed.D. in Audio-Visual Education in 1958.

After teaching science in the public schools in Martinsville, VA, he went to East Tennessee State University as an assistant professor in Education until 1963, when he and his family moved to Morgantown, WV, where he was Coordinator of Graduate Studies in Audio-Visual Education. From 1966 to 1971 he was Director of Learning Resources at Ohio University. In 1971, he was selected to come to Virginia Tech to create the Learning Resources Center. Dr. Huffman continued as Director until 1987. The Center was established as a service facility to the faculty, and his leadership constantly emphasized this idea to the staff of the Center.

His professional experiences include work as a public school teacher and supervisor in Martinsville, VA, schools and teaching and administrative positions at East Tennessee State University, West Virginia University, and Ohio University. He also had the unique distinction of serving as president of three different state professional media organizations in Tennessee, West Virginia and Virginia. He has served as a consultant to the West Virginia Educational Broadcasting Authority, Tennessee Educational Television Network, American Council on Education, Undergraduate Education Reform Project of the Southern Regional Education Board, and U.S. Army Transportation School. He was a member of the WBRA-TV Advisory Committee in Roanoke. He was on the Board of Directors of AECT and the Public Service Satellite Consortium. He was also a member of the Board of Examiners of the National Council for the Accreditation of Teacher Education and often traveled to other universities to evaluate their programs.

Stan enjoyed working in television and liked to appear on camera. He hosted a number of programs and teleconferences and was involved with Virginia Tech football and basketball when they were broadcast from campus. He has also worked as a consultant or technical advisor on motion pictures and television programs. During 1982, he produced 34 television programs for on-air broadcast. He cowrote the scripts for and appeared in a 20-program series called *Using Media for Learning*, which was broadcast on WBRA-TV in 1982 and on the Learning Channel in 1983. In January 1983, he received the Annual Achievement Award for the television series from the Association of Educational Communications and Technology (AECT) for the most outstanding contribution to the media field in 1982. When he served as the President of the Virginia Educational Media Association, he was recognized by the Association as Media Educator of the Year for 1980. He was on the Board and was President in 1979-1980. He was also extremely active in the AECT, where he was Chairperson for the 1980 and 1987 Convention Program Planning Committees, on the Board of Directors, and part of the Executive Committee.

His publications include the book, *Instructional Media*, and many articles in professional journals, and the "Guide for U.S. Army Representatives to NATO Research and Development Meetings." He was a member of the Advisory Board of the *International Journal of Instructional Media*. Some of his major presentations were made before the American Political Science Association, the International Visual Literacy Association, and the International Conference on University Teaching. He has lectured to many professional groups on copyright law.

During his tenure as Director of the Learning Resource Center at Virginia Tech, Stan provided leadership in development of distance learning strategies. In 1987 he was appointed the Director of Distance Learning at Virginia Tech. In this position he and others throughout the state began the Cooperative Graduate Engineering Program, which offered graduate courses via television throughout the United States. During this time, an MBA program was established in the College of Business that offered courses via satellite. The Office of Distance Learning also scheduled, promoted, developed, and produced teleconferences on varied topics for many departments and organizations.

In his retirement, which began in October 1991, he looked forward to having more time for his hobbies, including collecting antiques, and finishing a book of funeral stories. He died at home in the spring of 1993.

Note: The authors were colleagues of Dr. Huffman at Virginia Tech. They wish to thank Ms. JoAnn Michaels for her assistance.

John C. Belland
A Pioneer in 3D Graphics

Kenneth Hay
University of Georgia

John was born and raised on the south side of Chicago in the Rock Island Station. He often used the train to access the cultural treasures of the big city, setting the foundations for his "aesthetic self." His "logic self" was developed through a love of mathematics. He completed his high school studies by receiving a full scholarship to Northwestern University, where he graduated in 1960 with a BA in mathematics and decided to teach high school mathematics rather than work in computers. In efforts to improve his own teaching, John become interested in audiovisuals in education and enrolled in, and subsequently graduated from, Syracuse University. He worked under the mentorship of Ken Fishell and closely with other leaders of the field like Don Ely and John Tyo.

I remember a story John told us about how he approached his graduate work in instructional technology at Syracuse. He first made a list of all the things he wanted to learn in his graduate education. Next, he surveyed the courses that were offered at Syracuse and checked those items off the list. Then he went off on his own to learn the rest. It was a story that often intrigued me as a graduate student who was hip deep in ideas, theories, and skills that I was attempting to understand, let alone trying to *a priori* plan out before I arrived at OSU. In many ways, John was the prototype learner for what would some day be called learner-centered design.

After a brief stint at North Carolina at Chapel Hill, John was recruited by Edgar Dale to teach at Ohio State University in 1970. As he tells it, he arrived at OSU in the midst of a Vietnam War protest that left a vivid image on the young professor. Even though John was hired to step in for the retiring Dale, who retired the year John arrived, Dale kept an office and secretary at OSU for the next 10 years. In that time he served as a mentor and became a trusted colleague. Dale introduced John to his extensive work in vocabulary and reading and convinced John of the importance of finely crafted conversations. They loved engaging in hours and hours of conversations when "words were used precisely and well." Out of that relationship, Dale asked John to consider developing the next edition of the Dale text *Audiovisual Education*, but John declined. This decision was based on Dale's insistence that the Cone of Experience be dropped and replaced with a new theoretical structure. John believed that this action should not be taken.

Intellectually, I will remember John primarily in two ways: in the areas of learning with 3D graphics and alternative paradigms of instructional design. In the 1970s and 1980s, Ohio State was a hotbed of activity in the area of 3D computer-generated animation. Chuck Csuri, a pioneer in this field, had established the Computer Graphics Research Group (CGRG), and John was a founding faculty member. He persuaded the College of Education to purchase a DEC 11-23+ (then called a microcomputer) to implement educational explorations. This was long before 3D computer games or the likes of the movie *Toy Story*. These were the days when even the most basic 3D image would take hours to generate, and a simple animation would take days. As I sit in front of a machine that can easily create real-time 3D worlds with a direct-manipulation interface, it is hard to picture what 3D animations meant in the 1980s. I remember one of my projects involved making a ball that would bounce back and forth across a net after being hit by imaginary volleyball players. It took me hours and hours of coding in C down in the basement of the CGRG. It was during these days that John began to peer into the hazy future of both the technology of 3D computer-generated animations and its potential for learning.

Building off of Gavriel Solomon's influential book, *The Interaction of Media, Cognition, and Learning*, John and a few graduate students began to explore how 3D imagery could supplant and short-circuit visual cognition of interpreting and connecting 3D houses with 2D floor plans. He and his students transformed a 3D representation of a house into a 2D floor plan, then from 2D back to 3D. The work was truly forward-thinking. Through this work one of John's students won the Young Researcher award from the RTD division of AECT, and another won a national award from the MLA.

The second way I will remember John intellectually is through his work in introducing postmodernism to the field of instructional technology. Together with coeditor Denis Hlynka, John published a volume titled *Paradigms Regained. Paradigms* is a volume that the field is still discussing. It provides words and images for John's internal aesthetic and logic histories, as well as the similar histories of instructional technologies. We are in a field that struggles with the aesthetic history of the educational filmmaker, the literary history of the author, the rational history of programmed instruction, the logical history of the computer programmer, and the philosophical history of those who would claim to be purveyors of knowledge. I believe Belland and Hlynka found a way to talk about the many simultaneous and conflicting selves and history in the pages of *Paradigms*. As John told me when I talked to him during the preparation of this chapter, "In many ways, the acceptance of postmodernism as a state of being makes life very complex, but at the same time makes it more fully explained."

In the final analysis, John was a teacher. The almost 40 doctoral students and many more than 100 masters students whom he advised all appreciated his sharp intellectual yet compassionate demeanor. This combination is one of his strongest qualities. It has been evident in his attempts to always help students fulfill their dreams rather than take predetermined routes. I will always remember him for that.

John is an emeritus faculty at Ohio State and is working with State of Ohio educational leaders to develop and expand distance education opportunities for the K–12 schools of the state. Always the techie and educator, John alternatively works through the challenges of using the "ATM 'cloud' method of connectivity and using the H.323 standard for videocaching" and taking on his biggest challenge: to get the teachers and curriculum specialists to believe that they must engage in serious design work in order to do anything very good.

Note: I am honored to have been a student of John Belland's and delighted to have been asked to write this chapter in honor of his contribution to the field.

Robert M. Diamond
A Thinker in the Ideal Realm

Frank Wilbur
Project Advance
Syracuse University

For more than 40 years, Robert M. Diamond's professional focus has been on the systematic improvement of instruction in higher education. A true leader of educational reform, Bob's foresight in identifying critical issues in higher education places him consistently at the leading edge of change. Through his steadfast challenge of the status quo and continuous speculation about how we can best marshal resources to meet the needs of students, he encourages us to move beyond the constraints of traditional thinking.

Bob's model of instructional design, currently in use in scores of institutions around the world, is one of the most replicated models in higher education today. Through his teaching and his numerous publications, he has profoundly affected generations of graduate students as they launched their careers in the field. His latest book, *Designing and Assessing Courses and Curricula* (Jossey-Bass, 1998) reflects his approach to instructional design. One of the best-known aspects of Bob's instructional design model requires planners to "think in the ideal" before imposing situational constraints. Such thinking about the needs of students and the range of possibilities for course, curricula, and program design has resulted in fresh, effective solutions.

One of the most active members of the American Association for Higher Education (AAHE) since its founding, Bob was cited by AAHE in 1994 for 25 years of Leadership and the Reform of Higher Education. In 1998 Bob was cited as an "Outstanding Citizen of Syracuse University" whose creative energies and innovations contributed to the building of the student-centered research university.

Bob is currently Research Professor and Director of the Institute for Change in Higher Education at Syracuse University, where he was formerly Assistant Vice Chancellor and Director of the Center for Instructional Development. He received his Ph.D. and MA from New York University and his BA from Union College. Bob has held administrative and faculty positions at SUNY Fredonia, the University of Miami, and San Jose State University. A Senior Fulbright Lecturer in India, he has been President of the Division for Instructional Development, Association for Educational Communications and Technology (AECT), and has authored numerous articles and books.

Bob also authored *Serving on Promotion and Tenure Committees: A Faculty Guide* (1994) and *Preparing for Promotion and Tenure Review: A Faculty Guide* (1995), both published by Anker Publishing, and "What It Takes to Lead a Department' in *The Chronicle of Higher Education* (January 1996). Bob coedited a New Directions in Higher Education volume, *Recognizing Faculty Work: Reward Systems for the Year 2000* (Jossey-Bass), and *The Disciplines Speak: Rewarding the Scholarly, Professional & Creative Work of Faculty* (American Association for Higher Education). In 1989, Bob received the Division of Instructional Development AECT Award for outstanding practice in Instructional Development. The Center for Instructional Development was the recipient of the 1996 Theodore M. Hesburgh Award for Faculty Development to Enhance Undergraduate Learning.

Bob was responsible for the initial design of Syracuse University's award-winning high school/college articulation program Project Advance. He was Co-Director of the Syracuse University Focus on Teaching Project and Director of the National Project on Institutional Priorities and Faculty Rewards, funded by the Lilly Endowment with additional support from the Fund for the Improvement of Postsecondary Education, the Pew Charitable Trusts, and the Carnegie Foundation for the Advancement of Teaching.

Through the Institute for Change in Higher Education at Syracuse University, Bob is currently focusing his considerable energies and talents on building the National Academy for Academic Leadership. He also continues to serve as a consultant to colleges and universities throughout the United States and overseas.

Paul Robert Wendt
Programmed Instruction and Visual Literacy Pioneer

David M. (Mike) Moore
Virginia Tech

Douglas Bedient
Southern Illinois University Carbondale

Paul Robert Wendt was a man with a major interest in using technology to teach students how to succeed in higher education by improving their library and information skills. Today, the progress of multimedia technology has permitted us to combine images and sound relatively easily. But Wendt was a man who had these interests long before computers and electronic technology made the advances feasible.

Several highlights of his long career show how Wendt was interested in messages rather than the medium. He came to higher education after serving as a motion picture producer and director and helped form an academic department that combined audiovisual and library science programs. While serving as chairman of Southern Illinois University's (SIU) Department of Instructional Materials in the 1950s and 1960s, he was actively studying programmed instruction that combined print and visual image.

Wendt was challenged with programming and combining images when the technology was crude. In the 1960s, he won grants that permitted him to apply programmed instruction principles to visual and verbal programs to teach library instruction. He was not content to work with linear programs; he was convinced that learning would be better if the program took directions based on learner responses. The *Spindler-Sauppe* projectors that he used were cumbersome and relied on mechanical means for random access. Assistants were required to sequence slides based on learner choices. The slides were glass mounted so that images were protected and safe from deterioration. The response systems were crude and subject to numerous breakdowns.

The research support shops at SIU knew Wendt well because he was calling for innovations in photography, programmed instruction, and computing all at the same time. Here was a researcher who was trying to accomplish with the equivalent of stones and chisels what authoring programs now facilitate for developers. And Wendt was interested in results rather than learning how challenging his requests and demands might be.

Upon graduation from Harvard, Wendt joined the Harvard Film Foundation, which was sponsored by the Carnegie Foundation for Advancement of Teaching. The purpose of the Foundation was to research the effectiveness of educational films in public schools. This was a pioneering effort at educational film production and testing.

Later, Wendt moved to Minnesota, where he joined the St. Paul Public Schools and pursued his doctorate at the University of Minnesota. His doctoral research at Minnesota was innovative. His interests in visual communication and how people see led him to research how students viewed educational motion pictures. He used an eye camera to track subjects' eye movements while viewing films—an early attempt to combine the movie viewing with such a camera. The results of his dissertation were published in *Psychological Monograph* and received national attention both for the methodology and the results and suggestions for future research.

At the University of Minnesota Wendt was research and production director of a motion picture unit. Later he became the unit's manager. During this period he produced several motion pictures for education and for the state and University of Minnesota. He later became the director of the university's Audiovisual Educational Service, one of the first campus audiovisual services to be instigated in the United States. He was also a member of the College of Education and rose from instructor to associate professor. During this period, Wendt completed his master's and doctoral degrees.

Wendt's next move was to California, where he became director of the audiovisual center at San Francisco State. Later he joined the faculty of the University of California's extension division and taught courses there.

In 1955, Dr. Wendt joined the staff of the Audiovisual Services, Southern Illinois University. His responsibilities were to work with faculty of the university and to teach. In 1957, the Department of Instructional Materials was formed by the combining of the Department of Library Science and the courses being taught by Audiovisual Services. This new department was called the Department of Instructional Materials. Wendt became the first permanent chairman of the department and maintained this position for 10 years. During this period the department grew from its original faculty of four to ten members.

The concept of combining the library and audiovisual services into a single agency was a new concept and was the first attempt in the nation to train Instructional Materials Specialists. This concept grew until it became recognized as the way to prepare media specialists.

Though Wendt served as an administrator during much of his professional career, his first love was always research. He made major contributions in two areas: visual literacy and programmed instruction. His continued research in visual literacy as reflected in his early work with the eye camera.

In the 1960s, S. L. Pressey's early work with programmed instruction was rediscovered, and his linear technique of programmed instruction was further developed by B. F. Skinner. Wendt became an early proponent of the new technique of branching programmed instruction and, indeed, became one of the leading figures in branching programming. He was also one of the first researchers to introduce visuals into the branching technique of programmed instruction. He received a federal grant of $100,000 to develop the technique. His major emphasis was in researching library use via programmed audiovisual materials. Over the years his visual research focused around many ideas, from how to measure the related abilities of learning from pictures to the study of students' visual search times and their reactions to pictures.

Wendt will also be remembered as an author. He wrote widely in professional journals. His article in *ETC: A Review of General Semantics* (October 1956), "The Language of Pictures," is a classic and has been widely quoted. It was based on Wendt's work and collaboration with S. I. Hayakawa, the noted linguist and semanticist and was instrumental in the early development of the visual literacy movement that began a few years later. In fact, Wendt was one of the founders on the Annual Conference on Visual Literacy in 1970 (which later became the International Visual Literacy Association). A 1957 pamphlet he authored, "What Research Says to the Teacher: Audiovisual Instruction," was reprinted several times. Another milestone of Wendt's, it pamphlet is an excellent example of his ability to interpret research so that it became usable to the classroom teacher.

Wendt not only was a contributor to research but also a compiler of research. His article in the *Review of Educational Research*, "Audiovisual Materials" (April 1962), is recognized as one of the best compilations of audiovisual research to that time. He added to the reputation of Southern Illinois University as a research institution because he received several research grants during his career there.

Wendt was also active as an educational collaborator and author of Coronet Educational Films. He was one of the first educators to use the innovation of placing keywords on the screen to enhance the learning from the film, which became common practice in elementary education films. His work with Coronet Films enabled him to receive a research grant, where he studied teaching world history with 54 films. In this research project it was shown that with the use of selected educational films, it was possible to teach world history in half the time that it was currently being taught in the schools. Wendt was quick to point out, though, that it would perhaps not be desirable to reduce the teaching of world history to one semester, though with the use of these films world history could come alive for ninth graders.

Dr. Paul Robert Wendt retired from Southern Illinois University in 1973. He moved to Plymouth, MA and was an active author and amateur mountain climber until his death in 1994. He had a truly pioneering and distinguished career as a researcher, educator, author, administrator, and motion picture producer.

Note: Much of the information for this article came from personal notes of, conversations with, and recollections of Dr. Gordon K. Butts (now deceased), Wendt's friend and colleague at Southern Illinois University. The authors were doctoral students of and worked with Paul Wendt at Southern Illinois University, Carbondale from 1968 to 1970.

REFERENCES

Wendt, P. R. (1957). *Audio-Visual Instruction: What the Research Says to the Teacher*. Washington, DC: Department of Classroom Teachers, American Educational Research Association of the National Educational Association.

Don Carl Smellie
Organizer, Motivator, Exemplar, Leader

Andrew S. Gibbons
Utah State University

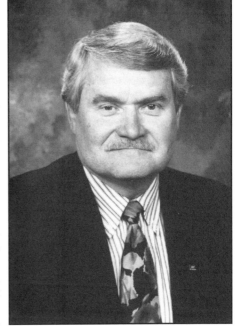

For more than 35 years, Don Carl Smellie has exerted strong leadership in the promotion of new technologies for instruction in education, industry, and government. Rather than pursuing personal ends, Don has consistently chosen to build an influential infrastructure in the form of an academic department from which has emanated a steady stream of ideas, tools, and successful practitioners for more than 32 years. They in turn have amplified the vision and example that they learned from Don. The list of those whom Don Smellie has worked with, motivated, and influenced reads like a "Who's Who" of educational technology.

Don's single greatest achievement has been the founding and nurturing of what is now the Department of Instructional Technology at Utah State University (IT- USU). Over 32 years IT-USU has graduated more than 900 students with master's, specialist, and doctoral degrees. As retiring head of that department, Don has assembled and directed a faculty that shared with him many accomplishments.

In 1967, Don, together with Lester Essig, instituted a School Library Media (SLM) academic program at USU. Its purpose was to teach librarians then-emerging principles of media use and management. This cutting-edge program, which promoted the best technologies of the day, continues bringing to these students—now increasingly central members within the public school faculty—the current technologies: library data systems, Internet and World Wide Web resource access, and computer-based instructional networks. This program is the longest continuously running program of its type in the nation.

Since 1967, Don has led IT-USU to serve in similar manner other groups of educators with specialized technology training needs. He encouraged and supported faculty member Dr. Linda Wolcott in obtaining approval for a Distance Learning Certification program. This program will certify public educators in techniques for development and delivery of distance learning. Over time, this program will prepare the way for increased use of distance learning techniques in both traditional and alternative settings.

In 1994, Don was awarded a $300,000 grant from the Utah Higher Educational Technology Initiative program (HETI) to develop a master's degree program in Educational Technology to be delivered over the Utah's statewide EDNET (two-way video instruction) system. Through this program, educators can obtain a master's degree at home without leaving their classrooms. Ideas learned in EDNET classes can be applied in the classroom immediately. The first cohort of 53 practicing educators graduated from this program in May 1999. A second cohort began classes in September 1999.

The IT department Don founded has been recognized nationally and internationally for its influence and excellence. Larry Lipsitz, publisher at Educational Technology Publications, wrote in December, 1992:

> It is my view, based on covering the total field of educational technology for the past 30 years in our magazine, that the graduate degree programs and overall research and development capabilities at Utah State University in Logan are among the very highest in quality in the world today.

Assistant USU Provost Blythe Ahlstrom wrote in March 1992 regarding a review of IT-USU conducted by the Utah Board of Regents:

> The Board of Regents accepted the recommendation of the university and the Commissioner to judge the Department of Instructional Technology at USU and its programs outstanding and commended for excellence. This is a significant judgment given to a small number of departments in state institutions. Since department reviews were established over a decade ago, this is the fifth commendation of excellence received by a USU department.

A committee of external reviewers commissioned by the Utah Board of Regents reported in April, 1991 that the IT Department:

> has outstanding programs. The department is clearly ranked in the top half dozen similar programs in the country. All of the indications of quality are in place in the department.

Later in the same report, the committee said of Don in particular:

> Without question, the impact that Don Smellie has had on the department has been remarkable. He has moved the department ahead in a very significant fashion. The loyalty and dedication of his faculty is certainly unquestioned. He has been able to extract from them a high level of productivity and at the same time has generated a positive self-image about the Department and where it is headed. Don is seen in a very positive light by the other department heads and also by the Dean of the College of Education. While Don has been the department head for many years, his level of commitment and effectiveness has continued to grow.

The fruits of Don's superb leadership have been felt through a wide range of outcomes:

In the field of technological innovation

- IT-USU obtained one of the first two experimental videodisc machines produced by MCA. (The other went to MIT.) Based on this resource, IT-USU sponsored a Videodisc Innovations Project, headed by Dr. Kent Wood. The project also resulted in the compilation and publication of research and development reports for a special issue (May 1979) of *Educational and Industrial Television*.

- IT-USU held the first National Videodisc/Microcomputer Institute (NVMI), held at Utah State, sponsored by the U.S. Office of Education. The attendees who filled the large ballroom in the Taggart Student Center were many of the early pioneers of computer-based videodisc instruction. Some participants who later contributed important developments to the field recalled the institute as an important beginning point in their own thinking regarding this emerging technology.

- In 1978, Drs. Ron Thorkildsen, Michael DeBloois, and Robert Wooley of IT-USU constructed the first-ever device for computer control of then-new videodisc technology. In a real sense, this accomplishment, which was not performed at a well-funded industrial firm but within an atmosphere of pioneering research, ushered in the age of multimedia. The videodisc controller device was licensed to Colony, a commercial manufacturing firm. It eventually became one of the central products of the Allen Communications Corporation, a worldwide multimedia software and services firm based in Salt Lake City, Utah.

- For more than 10 years, IT-USU has sponsored a Summer Institute, headed by Dr. M. David Merrill and the ID2 Research Team. This annual conference has drawn internationally known speakers and attendees from corporate and academic institutions on the subject of computer-based instruction and the automation of its development processes.

In International Service

- Dr. Steve Soulier of IT-USU was designated by Don to fill a critical role in designing and developing a Lifetime Career Skills Education and Management program for the government of Thailand. Dr. Soulier has designed a framework of technology-based training and assessment that will be applied to more than 50 career skill areas. This multimillion-dollar program will allow Thailand to create and maintain a competitive national workforce.

In Statewide Extension of Educational Services

- IT-USU offered one of the first master's degree programs over the COMNET (slow-scan TV) system statewide.

- A "weekend" program offered for many years allowed students to carpool to campus on Friday afternoons for classes and return home late Saturday.

- A summer-only program for public-school professionals for many years made the master's of education in Instructional Technology available to statewide educators.

- IT-USU currently offers a Multimedia undergraduate minor in a cooperative program with the evening school to help fill the critical need for trained multimedia production workers.

- IT-USU recently joined with three other USU departments (Computer Science, Electrical Engineering, and Business Information Systems Education) in proposing Utah's first interdepartmental degree in Information Technology. This program will meet a critical need created by the continued assimilation by business of the computer technology as part of its business structure.

In Trained Practitioners for Education and Industry

- IT-USU has graduated more than 900 alumni holding master's, specialist, and doctoral degrees who now fill positions worldwide in public and higher education, industry, and government.

- Before graduation, IT-USU students have affected hundreds of Utah and national firms by serving internships.

In the Structure of the University Itself

- A study conducted in 1969 by Don resulted in a major reorganization at Utah State University to create the Merrill Library Learning Resources Program (MLLRP). This change introduced a systematic process for the design, production, procurement, and distribution of media and media systems at USU that is still evident in the position of the Dean of Learning Resources at USU. This important change directed the attention of media experts and library experts toward the learning process and the role of technological tools in that process and institutionalized that perspective.

Representing Utah and Utah State, Don has for decades exerted tremendous personal influence and leadership nationally and internationally within the field of Instructional Technology. He has personally mentored dedicated instructional technologists who have gone on to their own career accomplishments. Among them are Dr. Curt Fawson, the original director of Utah's Educational Technology Initiative (ETI), and Dr. Tish Cavaleri.

In 1998–1999 Don was elected President of the Association for Educational Communications and Technology (AECT), an international association of educators and technologists. During his tenure as president, Don initiated the Student Chapter program of AECT. Today the USU Chapter continues as the first and longest standing in the nation. During his term as president, Don promoted the instructional technology movement in 27 U.S. states and Canada. In 1998 Don was awarded the Lifetime Distinguished Service Award from the AECT, the organization's most prestigious award for outstanding leadership in advancing the theory and practice of educational communications and technology.

In 1972 Don helped found and was elected the first president of the Utah Educational Library Media Association (UELMA), a state professional media association for school library media personnel. Don served in the organization in numerous positions. In 1979 he served as program chairman for the Mountain Plains Media Leadership Symposium (MPMLS), a meeting of regional leaders to plan the implementation of educational technologies.

Don coauthored a textbook with Jerry Kemp, *Planning, Producing, and Using Instructional Technologies* (HarperCollins, 7th edition, 1994). This book, used worldwide as a standard text for pre-service teachers and beginning instructional technologists, has been a major resource in the field and is now also available in Chinese. Don has authored more than 40 published articles and book chapters and given more than 400 speeches nationwide promoting instructional technology. He has served on the editorial boards of three national refereed journals and is a contributing editor for one nonrefereed journal.

Through his accomplishments, Don Smellie has had major influence in directing the course of the Instructional Technology field. His pattern has always been to build others and address them to the important task at hand. He has organized resources, provided opportunities, motivated those who were unsure of their ability to contribute, and provided exemplary leadership. His monument to the future will be the accomplishments of those he pushed ahead.

Part Five
Organizations and Associations in North America

Introduction

Part Five includes annotated entries for associations and organizations headquartered in the United States and Canada whose interests are in some manner significant to the fields of instructional technology and educational media. For the most part, these organizations are associations of professionals in the field or agencies that offer services to the educational media community. Entries are separated into sections for the United States and Canada. The U.S. section begins with a classified list designed to facilitate location of organizations by their specialized interests or services. The Canadian section is small enough not to need such a list.

Information for this section was obtained by direct communication with each organization in early 1999. Several organizations (marked by an asterisk [*]) did not provide updated information, and their entries contain information from the 1999 edition. Several new organizations are listed as well. Readers are encouraged to contact the editors with names of unlisted media-related organizations for investigation and possible inclusion in the 2001 edition.

Figures quoted as dues refer to annual amounts unless stated otherwise.

Oratile Maribe Branch

Section Editor

CLASSIFIED LIST

Adult and Continuing Education

(ALA Round Table) Continuing Library Education Network and Exchange (CLENERT)
Association for Continuing Higher Education (ACHE)
Association for Educational Communications and Technology (AECT)
ERIC Clearinghouse on Adult, Career, and Vocational Education (CE)
National Education Telecommunications Organization & Education Satellite Company (NETO/EDSAT)
National University Continuing Education Association (NUCEA)
Network for Continuing Medical Education (NCME)
PBS Adult Learning Service (ALS)
University Continuing Education Association (UCEA)

Children- and Youth-Related Organizations

Adjunct ERIC Clearinghouse for Child Care (ADJ/CC)
American Montessori Society
Association for Childhood Education International (ACEI)
Association for Library Service to Children (ALSC)
(CEC) Technology and Media Division (TAM)
Children's Television International, Inc.
Close Up Foundation
Computer Learning Foundation
Council for Exceptional Children (CEC)
ERIC Clearinghouse on Disabilities and Gifted Education (EC)
ERIC Clearinghouse on Elementary and Early Childhood Education (PS)
National Association for the Education of Young Children (NAEYC)
National PTA
Young Adult Library Services Association (YALSA)

Communication

Association for Educational Communications and Technology (AECT)
ERIC Clearinghouse on Information & Technology (IR)
ERIC Clearinghouse on Languages and Linguistics (FL)
ERIC Clearinghouse on Reading, English, and Communication Skills (CS)
Health Science Communications Association (HeSCA)
International Association of Business Communicators (IABC)

Lister Hill National Center for Biomedical Communications of the National Library of Medicine
National Communication Association (SCA)
National Council of the Churches of Christ

Computers

(AECT) Division of Interactive Systems and Computers (DISC)
Association for Computers and the Humanities (ACH)
Association for the Advancement of Computing in Education (AACE)
Computer Learning Foundation
Computer-Using Educators, Inc. (CUE)
International Society for Technology in Education (ISTE)
Online Computer Library Center (OCLC)
Society for Computer Simulation (SCS)

Copyright

Association of American Publishers (AAP)
Association of College and Research Libraries (ACRL)
Copyright Clearance Center (CCC)
Hollywood Film Archive
International Copyright Information Center (INCINC)
Library of Congress

Distance Education

Community College Satellite Network (CCSN)
Instructional Telecommunications Council (ITC)
International Society for Technology in Education (ISTE)
International Telecommunications Satellite Organization (INTELSAT)
National Education Telecommunications Organization & EDSAT Institute (NETO/EDSAT)

Education-General

American Society of Educators (ASE)
Association for Childhood Education International (ACEI)
Association for Experiential Education (AEE)
Council for Basic Education
Education Development Center, Inc.
ERIC Clearinghouse for Science, Mathematics, and Environmental Education (SE)
ERIC Clearinghouse for Social Studies/Social Science Education (ERIC/ChESS)

ERIC Clearinghouse on Counseling and Student
Services (CG)
ERIC Clearinghouse on Disabilities and Gifted
Education (EC)
ERIC Clearinghouse on Educational Management
(EA)
ERIC Clearinghouse on Elementary and Early
Childhood Education (PS)
ERIC Clearinghouse on Rural Education and Small
Schools (RC)
ERIC Clearinghouse on Teaching and Teacher
Education (SP)
ERIC Clearinghouse on Urban Education (UD)
Institute for Development of Educational Activities,
Inc. (|I|D|E|A|)
Minorities in Media (MIM)
National Association of State Textbook
Administrators (NASTA)
National Clearinghouse for Bilingual Education
National Council for Accreditation of Teacher
Education (NCATE)
National School Boards Association (NSBA)
Institute for the Transfer of Technology to
Education (ITTE)

Education -Higher
American Association of Community Colleges
(AACC)
American Association of State Colleges and
Universities
Association for Continuing Higher Education (ACHE)
Association for Library and Information Science
Education (ALISE)
Community College Association for Instruction and
Technology (CCAIT)
Consortium of College and University Media
Centers (CCUMC)
ERIC Clearinghouse for Community Colleges (JC)
ERIC Clearinghouse on Higher Education (HE)
Northwest College and University Council for the
Management of Educational Technology
PBS Adult Learning Service
University Continuing Education Association (UCEA)

Equipment
Association for Childhood Education International
(ACEI)
Educational Products Information Exchange (EPIE
Institute)
ERIC Clearinghouse on Assessment and Evaluation
(TM)
ITA
Library and Information Technology Association
(LITA)
National School Supply and Equipment Association
(NSSEA)
Society of Cable Telecommunications Engineers
(SCTE)

ERIC
ACCESS ERIC
Adjunct ERIC Clearinghouse for Art Education
(ADJ/AR)
Adjunct ERIC Clearinghouse for ESL Literacy
Education (ADJ/LE)
Adjunct ERIC Clearinghouse for United States-
Japan Studies (ADJ/JS)
Adjunct ERIC Clearinghouse on Clinical Schools
(ADJ/CL)
Adjunct ERIC Clearinghouse on Consumer
Education (ADJ/CN)
ERIC (Educational Resources Information Center)
ERIC Clearinghouse on Adult, Career, and Voca-
tional Education (CE)
ERIC Clearinghouse on Assessment and Evaluation
(TM)
ERIC Clearinghouse for Community Colleges (JC)
ERIC Clearinghouse on Counseling and Student
Services (CG)
ERIC Clearinghouse on Disabilities and Gifted
Education (EC)
ERIC Clearinghouse on Educational Management
(EA)
ERIC Clearinghouse on Elementary and Early
Childhood Education (PS)
ERIC Clearinghouse on Higher Education (HE)
ERIC Clearinghouse on Information & Technology
(IR)
ERIC Clearinghouse on Languages and Linguistics
(FL)
ERIC Clearinghouse on Reading, English, and
Communication Skills (CS)
ERIC Clearinghouse on Rural Education and Small
Schools (RC)
ERIC Clearinghouse for Science, Mathematics, and
Environmental Education (SE)
ERIC Clearinghouse for Social Studies/Social
Science Education (SO)
ERIC Clearinghouse on Teaching and Teacher
Education (SP)
ERIC Clearinghouse on Urban Education (UD)
ERIC Document Reproduction Service (EDRS)
ERIC Processing and Reference Facility

Film and Video
(AECT) Division of Telecommunications (DOT)
(AECT) Industrial Training and Education Division
(ITED)
Academy of Motion Picture Arts and Sciences
(AMPAS)
Agency for Instructional Technology (AIT)
American Society of Cinematographers
Anthropology Film Center (AFC)
Association for Educational Communications and
Technology (AECT)
Association of Independent Video and Filmmakers/
Foundation for Independent Video and Film
(AIVF/FIVF)

Cable in the Classroom
Central Educational Network (CEN)
Children's Television International, Inc.
Close Up Foundation
Community College Satellite Network
Council on International Non-theatrical Events
(CINE)
Film Advisory Board
Film Arts Foundation (FAF)
Film/Video Arts, Inc.
Great Plains National ITV Library (GPN)
Hollywood Film Archive
International Teleconferencing Association (ITCA)
International Television Association (ITVA)
ITA
National Aeronautics and Space Administration
(NASA)
National Alliance for Media Arts and Culture
(NAMAC)
National Association of Broadcasters (NAB)
National Education Telecommunications Organiza-
tion & Education Satellite Company
(NETO/EDSAT)
National Endowment for the Humanities (NEH)
National Film Board of Canada (NFBC)
National Film Information Service (offered by
AMPAS)
National Information Center for Educational Media
(NICEM)
National ITFS Association (NIA/ITFS)
National Telemedia Council, Inc. (NTC)
The New York Festivals
Pacific Film Archive (PFA)
Public Broadcasting Service (PBS)
PBS Adult Learning Service (ALS)
PBS VIDEO
Society of Cable Telecommunications Engineers
(SCTE)

Games, Toys, Play, Simulation, Puppetry
Puppeteers of America, Inc. (POA)
Society for Computer Simulation (SCS)
USA-Toy Library Association (USA-TLA)

Health-Related Organizations
Health Science Communications Association
(HeSCA)
Lister Hill National Center for Biomedical
Communications
Medical Library Association (MLA)
National Association for Visually Handicapped
(NAVH)
Network for Continuing Medical Education (NCME)

Information Science
Association for Library and Information Science
Education (ALISE)

ERIC Clearinghouse on Information and
Technology (IR)
Freedom of Information Center
International Information Management Congress
(IMC)
Library and Information Technology Association
(LITA)
Lister Hill National Center for Biomedical
Communications
National Commission on Libraries and Information
Science (NCLIS)

Innovation
Institute for Development of Educational Activities,
Inc. (|I|D|E|A|)
Institute for the Future (IFTF)
World Future Society (WFS)

**Instructional Technology, Design, and
Development**
(AECT) Division of Educational Media
Management (DEMM)
(AECT) Division of Instructional Development
(DID)
Agency for Instructional Technology (AIT)
Association for Educational Communications and
Technology (AECT)
Community College Association for Instruction and
Technology (CCAIT)
ERIC Clearinghouse on Information & Technology
(IR)
International Society for Performance and
Instruction (ISPI)
Professors of Instructional Design and Technology
(PIDT)
Society for Applied Learning Technology (SALT)

International Education
Adjunct ERIC Clearinghouse for US-Japan Studies
(ADJ/JS)
(AECT) International Division (INTL)
East-West Center
International Association for Learning Laboratories,
Inc. (IALL)
International Visual Literacy Association, Inc. (IVLA)
National Clearinghouse for Bilingual Education
(NCBE)

Language
ERIC Clearinghouse on Languages and Linguistics
(FL)
ERIC Clearinghouse on Reading, English, and
Communication (CS)
International Association for Learning Laboratories,
Inc. (IALL)
National Clearinghouse for Bilingual Education
(NCBE)

Libraries—Academic, Research
American Library Association (ALA)
Association of College and Research Libraries
(ACRL)
ERIC Clearinghouse on Information & Technology
(IR)

Libraries—Public
American Library Association (ALA)
Association for Library Service to Children (ALSC)
ERIC Clearinghouse on Information & Technology
(IR)
Library Administration and Management
Association (LAMA)
Library and Information Technology Association
(LITA)
Public Library Association (PLA)
Young Adult Library Services Association (YALSA)

Libraries and Media Centers—School
(ALA Round Table) Continuing Library Education
Network and Exchange (CLENERT)
(AECT) Division of School Media Specialists
(DSMS)
American Association of School Librarians (AASL)
American Library Association (ALA)
American Library Trustee Association (ALTA)
Association for Educational Communications and
Technology (AECT)
Association for Library Collections and Technical
Services (ALCTS)
Association for Library Service to Children (ALSC)
Catholic Library Association (CLA)
Consortium of College and University Media Centers
ERIC Clearinghouse on Information & Technology
(IR)
International Association of School Librarianship
(IASL)
Library of Congress
National Alliance for Media Arts and Culture
(NAMAC)
National Association of Regional Media Centers
(NARMC)
National Commission on Libraries and Information
Science (NCLIS)
National Council of Teachers of English (NCTE),
Commission on Media
On-Line Audiovisual Catalogers (OLAC)
Southeastern Regional Media Leadership Council
(SRMLC)

Libraries—Special
American Library Association (ALA)
Association for Library Service to Children (ALSC)
Association of Specialized and Cooperative Library
Agencies (ASCLA)
ERIC Clearinghouse on Information & Technology
(IR)

Medical Library Association (MLA)
Special Libraries Association
Theater Library Association
USA Toy Library Association (USA-TLA)

Media Production
(AECT) Media Design and Production Division
(MDPD)
American Society of Cinematographers (ASC)
Association for Educational Communications and
Technology (AECT)
Association of Independent Video and Filmmakers/
Foundation for Independent Video and Film
(AIVF/FIVF)
Film Arts Foundation (FAF)
International Graphics Arts Education Association
(IGAEA)

Museums and Archives
(AECT) Archives
Association of Systematics Collections
George Eastman House
Hollywood Film Archive
Library of Congress
Museum Computer Network (MCN)
Museum of Modern Art
National Gallery of Art (NGA)
National Public Broadcasting Archives (NPBA)
Pacific Film Archive (PFA)
Smithsonian Institution

Photography
Electronic Camera Repair, C&C Associates
George Eastman House
International Center of Photography (ICP)
National Press Photographers Association, Inc.
(NPPA)
Photographic Society of America (PSA)
Society for Photographic Education (SPE)
Society of Photo Technologists (SPT)

Publishing
Graphic Arts Technical Foundation (GATF)
International Graphics Arts Education Association
(IGAEA)
Magazine Publishers of America (MPA)
National Association of State Textbook
Administrators (NASTA)

Radio
(AECT) Division of Telecommunications (DOT)
American Women in Radio and Television
(AWRT)
Corporation for Public Broadcasting (CPB)
National Endowment for the Humanities (NEH)
National Federation of Community Broadcasters
(NFCB)
National Public Broadcasting Archives (NPBA)

National Religious Broadcasters (NRB)
Western Public Radio (WPR)

Religious Education
Catholic Library Association (CLA)
National Council of the Churches of Christ in the
USA
National Religious Broadcasters (NRB)

Research
(AECT) Research and Theory Division (RTD)
American Educational Research Association
(AERA)
Appalachia Educational Laboratory, Inc. (AEL)
ECT Foundation
Education Development Center, Inc.
ERIC Clearinghouses
HOPE Reports
Mid-continent Regional Educational Laboratory
(McREL)
National Center for Improving Science Education
National Education Knowledge Industry
Association (NEKIA)
National Endowment for the Humanities (NEH)
National Science Foundation (NSF)
The NETWORK
North Central Regional Educational Laboratory
(NCREL)
Northwest Regional Educational Laboratory
(NWREL)
Pacific Regional Educational Laboratory (PREL)
Research for Better Schools, Inc. (RBS)
SouthEastern Regional Vision for Education
(SERVE)
Southwest Educational Development Laboratory
(SEDL)
WestEd

Special Education
American Foundation for the Blind (AFB)
Association for Experiential Education (AEE)
Association of Specialized and Cooperative Library
Agencies (ASCLA)
Council for Exceptional Children (CEC)
ERIC Clearinghouse on Adult, Career, and Voca-
tional Education (CE)
ERIC Clearinghouse on Disabilities and Gifted
Education (EC)
National Association for Visually Handicapped
(NAVH)

National Center to Improve Practice (NCIP)
Recording for the Blind and Dyslexic (RFB&D)

Telecommunications
(AECT) Division of Telecommunications (DOT)
Association for the Advancement of Computing in
Education (AACE)
Association of Independent Video and Filmmakers/
Foundation for Independent Video and Film
(AIVF/FIVF)
Community College Satellite Network (CCSN)
ERIC Clearinghouse on Information & Technology
(IR)
Instructional Telecommunications Council (ITC)
International Telecommunications Satellite
Organization (INTELSAT)
International Teleconferencing Association (ITCA)
Library and Information Technology Association
(LITA)
National Education Telecommunications Organiza-
tion & Education Satellite Company
(NETO/EDSAT)
Research for Better Schools, Inc. (RBS)
Teachers and Writers Collaborative (T&W)

Television
American Women in Radio and Television (AWRT)
Central Educational Network (CEN)
Children's Television International, Inc. (CTI)
Corporation for Public Broadcasting (CPB)
International Television Association (ITVA)
National Cable Television Institute (NCTI)
National Federation of Community Broadcasters
(NFCB)
Society of Cable Telecommunications Engineers
(SCTE)

Training
(AECT) Industrial Training and Education Division
(ITED)
American Management Association (AMA)
American Society for Training and Development
(ASTD)
Association for Educational Communications and
Technology (AECT)
ERIC Clearinghouse on Adult, Career, and Voca-
tional Education (CE)
Federal Educational Technology Association (FETA)
International Society for Performance Improvement
(ISPI)

ALPHABETICAL LIST

All dues are annual fees, unless stated otherwise.

*Academy of Motion Picture Arts and Sciences (AMPAS). 8949 Wilshire Blvd., Beverly Hills, CA 90211-1972. (310)247-3000. Fax (310)859-9351. Website http://www.oscars.org. Bruce Davis, Exec. Dir. An honorary organization composed of outstanding individuals in all phases of motion pictures. Seeks to advance the arts and sciences of motion picture technology and artistry. Presents annual film awards; offers artist-in-residence programs; operates reference library and National Film Information Service. *Membership*: 6,000. *Publications: Annual Index to Motion Picture Credits*; *Academy Players Directory*.

*Agency for Instructional Technology (AIT). Box A, Bloomington, IN 47402-0120. (812)339-2203. Fax (812)333-4218. E-mail ait@ait.net. Website http://www.ait.net. Michael F. Sullivan, Exec. Dir. AIT is a nonprofit educational organization established in 1962 to develop, acquire, and distribute quality technology-based resources, providing leadership to the educational technology policy community. AIT fulfills this mission by being the largest single provider of instructional television programs and is a major player in the development of curriculum products. AIT has established a national model for contextual learning materials. AIT's strength lies in sound instructional design, early and continual involvement of classroom practitioners, formative evaluation, and creative production of video. Web services videodisc, software, and print resources. AIT products have won many national and international awards, including the only Emmy and Peabody awards given to classroom television programs. Since 1970, 37 major curriculum packages have been developed by AIT through a process it pioneered. U.S. state and Canadian provincial agencies have cooperatively funded and widely used these learning resources. Funding for other product development comes from state, provincial, and local departments of education, federal and private institutions, corporations and private sponsors, and AIT's own resources. Currently, AIT offers 130 learning resource products, containing nearly 2,500 separate titles. Programming addresses pre-kindergarten through adult learners covering traditional curricular areas plus career development, early childhood, guidance, mental health, staff development, and vocational education. AIT programs account for 40 percent of the National Instructional Satellite Service (NISS) schedule, which is broadcast to K–12 classrooms across the country. AIT learning resources are used on six continents and teach nearly 34 million students in North America each year via electronic distribution and audio visual use. *Publications: TECHNOS: Quarterly for Education & Technology*, a forum for the discussion of ideas about the use of technology in education with a focus on reform ($28/yr, 4 issues). AIT is also the home of *TECHNOS Press*, publisher of *Final Exam* by Gerald W. Bracey. The website offers an online catalog, compete with program descriptions, ordering information, and direct links to AIT Customer Service.

*American Association of Community Colleges (AACC). One Dupont Cir. NW, Suite 410, Washington, DC 20036-1176. (202)728-0200, ext. 216. Fax (202)833-2467. Website http://www.aacc.nche.edu. David Pierce, Pres. AACC serves the nation's 1,100 community, technical, and junior colleges through advocacy, professional development, publications, and national networking. The annual convention draws more than 2,500 middle and top-level administrators of two-year colleges. Twenty-four councils and 8 commissions address priority areas for community colleges. AACC also operates the Community College Satellite Network, providing teleconferences and other programming and services to colleges. *Membership:* 1,113 institutions, 16 international, 5 foundations, 15 corporations, 157 individuals, and 70 educational associates. *Dues:* vary by category. *Meetings:* Workforce Development Institute (WDI), Jan 27-30, 1999, San Diego. *Publications: Community College Journal* (bi-mo.); *Community College Times* (bi-weekly newspaper); *College Times*; Community College Press (books and monographs).

American Association of School Librarians (AASL). 50 E. Huron St., Chicago, IL 60611. (312)280-4386. (800)545-2433, ext. 4386. Fax (312)664-7459. E-mail aasl@ala.org. Website http://www.ala.org/aasl. Julie A. Walker, Exec. Dir. A division of the American Library Association, AASL is interested in the general improvement and extension of school library media services for children and youth. Activities and projects of the association are divided among 30 committees and 3 sections. *Membership:* 7,820. *Dues:* Membership in ALA (1st yr., $50; 2nd yr., $75; 3rd and subsequent yrs., $100) plus $40. Inactive, student, retired, unemployed, and reduced-salary memberships are available. *Meetings:*National conference every two years; next national conference to be held in 2001. *Publications*: *School Library Media* (electronic research journal, http://www.ala.organization/aasl/SLMR/).

American Association of State Colleges and Universities (AASCU). One Dupont Cir. NW, Suite 700, Washington, DC 20036-1192. (202)293-7070. Fax (202)296-5819. James B. Appleberry, Pres. Membership is open to regionally accredited institutions of higher education (and those in the process of securing accreditation), that offer programs leading to the degree of Bachelor, Master, or Doctor, and that are wholly or partially state-supported and state-controlled. Organized and operated exclusively for educational, scientific, and literary purposes, its particular purposes are to improve higher education within its member institutions through cooperative planning, studies, and research on common educational problems and the development of a more unified program of action among its members; and to provide other needed and worthwhile educational services to the colleges and universities it may represent. *Membership:* 393 institutions (university), 28 systems, and 10 associates. *Dues:* based on current student enrollment at institution. *Publications: MEMO: To the President*; *The Center Associate*; *Office of Federal Program Reports*; *Office of Federal Program Deadlines*. (Catalogs of books and other publications available upon request.)

American Educational Research Association (AERA). 1230 17th St. NW, Washington, DC 20036. (202)223-9485. Fax (202)775-1824. E-mail aera@gmu.edu. Website http://www.asu.edu/aera. William J. Russell, Exec. Dir. AERA is an international professional organization with the primary goal of advancing educational research and its practical application. Its members include educators and administrators; directors of research, testing, or evaluation in federal, state, and local agencies; counselors; evaluators; graduate students; and behavioral scientists. The broad range of disciplines represented includes education, psychology, statistics, sociology, history, economics, philosophy, anthropology, and political science. AERA has over 120 Special Interest Groups including Advanced Technologies for Learning, Computer Applications in Education, Electronic Networking, Information Technology and Library Resources, Instructional Technology, and Text, Technology and Learning Strategies. *Membership:* 23,000. *Dues:* vary by category, ranging from $20 for students to $45 for voting. *Meetings:* 1999 Annual Meeting, April 19-23, Montreal. *Publications: Educational Researcher*; *American Educational Research Journal*; *Journal of Educational Statistics*; *Educational Evaluation and Policy Analysis*; *Review of Research in Education*; *Review of Educational Research.*

American Foundation for the Blind (AFB). 11 Penn Plaza, Suite 300, New York, NY 10001. (212)502-7600, (800)AFB-LINE (232-5463). Fax (212)502-7777. E-mail afbinfo@afb.org. Website http://www.afb.org. Carl R. Augusto, Pres.; Liz Greco, Vice Pres. of Communications. AFB is a leading national resource for people who are blind or visually impaired, the organizations that serve them, and the general public. A nonprofit organization founded in 1921 and recognized as Helen Keller's cause in the United States, AFB's mission is to enable people who are blind or visually impaired to achieve equality of access and opportunity that will ensure freedom of choice in their lives. AFB is headquartered in New York City with offices in Atlanta, Chicago, Dallas, and San Francisco. A governmental relations office in AFB is headquartered in New York City with offices in Atlanta, Chicago, Dallas, San Francisco, and Washington, DC. *Publications: AFB News* (free); *Journal of Visual Impairment & Blindness; AFB Press Catalog of Publications* (free).

American Library Association (ALA). 50 E. Huron St., Chicago, IL 60611. (312)944-6780. Fax (312)440-9374. Website http://www.ala.org. William R. Gordon, Exec. Dir. The ALA is the oldest and largest national library association. Its 58,000 members represent all types of libraries: state, public, school, and academic, as well as special libraries serving persons in government, commerce, the armed services, hospitals, prisons, and other institutions. The ALA is the chief advocate of achievement and maintenance of high-quality library information services through protection of the right to read, educating librarians, improving services, and making information widely accessible. See separate entries for the following affiliated and subordinate organizations: American Association of School Librarians, American Library Trustee Association, Association for Library Collections and Technical Services, Association for Library Service to Children, Association of College and Research Libraries, Association of Specialized and Cooperative Library Agencies, Library Administration and Management Association, Library and Information Technology Association, Public Library Association, Reference and User Services Association, Young Adult Library Services Association, and Continuing Library Education Network and Exchange Round Table. *Membership:* 58,000. *Dues:* Basic dues $50 first year, $100 renewing members. *Meetings:* 1999: Midwinter Meeting Jan 14-19, San Antonio, 2000. Annual Conference, Jun 24-Jul 1, New Orleans, LA. *Publications: American Libraries*; *Booklist*; *Choice*; *Book Links*.

American Library Trustee Association (ALTA). 50 E. Huron St., Chicago, IL 60611. (312)280-2161. Fax (312)280-3257. Website http://www.ala.org. Susan Roman, Exec. Dir. A division of the American Library Association, ALTA is interested in the development of effective library service for people in all types of communities and libraries. Members, as policymakers, are concerned with organizational patterns of service, the development of competent personnel, the provision of adequate financing, the passage of suitable legislation, and the encouragement of citizen support for libraries. *Membership:* 1,710. *Dues:* $50 plus membership in ALA. *Meetings:* Held in conjunction with ALA. *Publications: Trustee Voice* (q. newsletter); professional monographs and pamphlets.

American Management Association International (AMA). 1601 Broadway, New York, NY 10019-7420. (212)586-8100. Fax (212)903-8168. E-mail cust_serv@amanet.org. Website http://www.amanet.org. Barbara M. Barrett, Pres. and CEO. Founded in 1923, AMA provides educational forums worldwide where members and their colleagues learn superior, practical business skills and explore best practices of world-class organizations through interaction with each other and expert faculty practitioners. AMA's publishing program provides tools individuals use to extend learning beyond the classroom in a process of life-long professional growth and development through education. AMA operates management centers and offices in Atlanta, Boston (Watertown), Chicago, Hamilton (NY), Kansas City (Leawood), New York, San Francisco, Saranac Lake (NY), and Washington, DC, and through AMA/International, in Brussels, Tokyo, Shanghai, Islamabad, and Buenos Aires. In addition, it has affiliated centers in Toronto, Mexico City, Sao Paulo, Taipei, Istanbul, Singapore, Jakarta, and Dubai. AMA offers conferences, seminars, and membership briefings where there is an interchange of information, ideas, and experience in a wide variety of management topics. Through its publication division, AMACOM, AMA publishes approximately 70 business-related books per year, as well as numerous surveys and management briefings. Other services offered by AMA include *FYI Video*; *Extension Institute* (self-study programs in both print and audio formats); *AMA Interactive Series* (self-paced learning on CD-ROM); *Operation Enterprise* (young adult program); *AMA On-Site* (videoconferences); the *Information Resource Center* (for AMA members only), a management information and library service; and six bookstores. *Membership:* over 75,000. *Dues:* corporate, $595-1645; growing company, $525-1845; indiv., $165 plus $40 per additional newsletter. *Publications* (periodicals): *Management Review* (membership); *Compensation & Benefits Review; Organizational Dynamics; HR Focus; President; Getting Results . . .; and The Take-Charge Assistant.*

American Montessori Society (AMS). 281 Park Ave. S, New York, NY 10010. (212)358-1250. Fax (212)358-1256. Website http://www.amshq.org. Michael N. Eanes, Natl. Dir. Dedicated to promoting better education for all children through teaching strategies consistent with the Montessori system. Membership is composed of schools in the private and public sectors employing this method, as well as individuals. It serves as a resource center and clearinghouse for information and data on Montessori affiliates, trains teachers in different parts of the country, and conducts a consultation service and accreditation program for school members. *Dues:* teachers, schoolheads,

$40; parents, $30; institutions, from $215 and up. *Meetings:* three regional and one national educational conference per year and four professional development symposia under the auspices of the AMS Teachers' Section. 39th Annual Conference, Apr 21-25, 1999, Cincinnati. *Publications: AMS Montessori LIFE* (q); *Schoolheads* (newsletter); *Montessori in Contemporary American Culture; Authentic American Montessori School; The Montessori School Management Guide;* AMS position papers.

American Society for Training and Development (ASTD). 1640 King St., Box 1443, Alexandria, VA 22313. (703)683-8100. Fax (703)683-8103. E-mail csc@astd.org. Website http://www.astd.org. Curtis E. Plott, Pres. and CEO. Founded in 1944, ASTD is the world's premiere professional association in the field of workplace learning and performance. ASTD's membership includes more than 70,000 people in organizations from every level of the field of workplace performance in more than 100 countries. Its leadership and members work in more than 15,000 multinational corporations, small and medium sized businesses, government agencies, colleges, and universities. ASTD is the leading resource on workplace learning and performance issues, providing information, research, analysis, and practical information derived from its own research, the knowledge and experience of its members, its conferences and publications, and the coalitions and partnerships it has built through research and policy work. *Membership:* 70,000 National and Chapter members. *Dues:* $150. *Meetings:* International Conferences, May 22-27, 1999, Atlanta; May 20-25, 2000, Dallas. Technical Training Conferences, Sep 14-17, 1999, Minneapolis; Sep 19-22, 2000, Indianapolis. *Publications: Training & Development Magazine; Technical Training Magazine; Info-Line; The American Mosaic: An In-depth Report of Diversity on the Future of Diversity at Work; ASTD Directory of Academic Programs in T&D/HRD; Training and Development Handbook; Technical & Skills Training Handbook.* Quarterly publications: *Performance in Practice; National Report on Human Resources; Washington Policy Report.* ASTD also has recognized professional forums, most of which produce newsletters.

*American Society of Cinematographers (ASC). 1782 N. Orange Dr., Hollywood, CA 90028. (213)969-4333. Fax (213)876-4973. Fax (213)882-6391. Victor Kemper, Pres. ASC is an educational, cultural, and professional organization. *Membership:* 336. Membership is by invitation to those who are actively engaged as directors of photography and have demonstrated outstanding ability. Classifications are Active, Active Retired, Associates, and Honorary. *Meetings:* Book Bazaar (Open House); Awards Open House; Annual ASC Awards. *Publications: American Cinematographer Video Manual; Light on Her Face;* and *American Cinematographers Magazine.*

American Society of Educators (ASE). *Media & Methods Magazine.* 1429 Walnut St., Philadelphia, PA 19102. (215)563-6005. Fax (215)587-9706. E-mail michelesok@aol.com. Website http://www.media-methods.com. Michele Sokolof, Publisher & Editorial Dir. ASE services the information needs of K–12 teachers, librarians, media specialists, curriculum directors, and administrators in evaluating the practical applications of today's multimedia and technology resources for teaching and learning purposes. ASE's primary vehicle is to deliver timely information on technology integration in K–12 schools, classrooms and labs is through their bi-monthly magazine. Yearly subscription cost: $33.50.

American Women in Radio and Television (AWRT). 1650 Tyson Blvd., Suite 200, McLean, VA 22102-3915. (703)506-3290. Fax (703)506-3266. Jacci Duncan, Exec. Dir. Organization of professionals in the electronic media, including owners, managers, administrators, and those in creative positions in broadcasting, satellite, cable, advertising, and public relations. AWRT's objectives are to work worldwide to improve the quality of radio and television; to promote the entry, development, and advancement of women in the electronic media and allied fields; to serve as a medium of communication and idea exchange; and to become involved in community concerns. Organized in 1951. *Membership:* 40 chapters. Student memberships available. *Dues:* $125. *Publications: News and Views; Resource Directory; Careers in the Electronic Media; Sexual Harassment,* Mentoring Brochure (pamphlet).

Anthropology Film Center (AFC). 1626 Upper Canyon Rd., Santa Fe, NM 87501-6138. (505) 983-4127. E-mail ziacine@ix.netcom.com, anthrofilm@nets.com, or anthrofilm@archaeologist.com. Website http://www.nets.com/anthrofilm. Carroll Williams, Dir. Offers the Ethnographic/Documentary Film Program, a 30-week full-time course in 16mm film in CD and DVD production and theory. Summer workshops are offered as well. AFC also provides consultation, research facilities, and a specialized library.

Appalachia Educational Laboratory, Inc. (AEL). PO Box 1348, Charleston, WV 25325. (304)347-0400, (800)624-9120. Fax (304)347-0487. E-mail aelinfo@ael.org. Website http://www.ael.org. Terry L. Eidell, Exec. Dir. One of 10 Office of Educational Research and Improvement (OERI) regional educational laboratories designed to help educators and policymakers solve educational problems in their schools. Using the best available information and the experience and expertise of education professionals, AEL seeks to identify solutions to education problems, tests new approaches, furnishes research results, and provides training to teachers and administrators. AEL serves Kentucky, Tennessee, Virginia, and West Virginia.

Association for Childhood Education International (ACEI). 17904 Georgia Ave., Suite 215, Olney, MD 20832. (301)570-2111. Fax (301)570-2212. E-mail ACEIHQ@aol.com. Website http://www.udel.edu/bateman/acei. Anne W. Bauer, Ed. and Dir. of Publications. ACEI publications reflect careful research, broad-based views, and consideration of a wide range of issues affecting children from infancy through early adolescence. Many are media-related in nature. The journal (*Childhood Education*) is essential for teachers, teachers-in-training, teacher educators, day care workers, administrators, and parents. Articles focus on child development and emphasize practical application. Regular departments include book reviews (child and adult); film reviews, pamphlets, software, research, and classroom idea-sparkers. Six issues are published yearly, including a theme issue devoted to critical concerns. *Membership:* 12,000. *Dues:* $45, professional; $26, student; $23, retired; $80, institutional. *Meeting:* 1999 Annual International Conference and Exhibition, Apr 7-11, San Antonio; 2000, Baltimore. *Publications: Childhood Education* (official journal) with *ACEI Exchange* (insert newsletter); *Journal of Research in Childhood Education*; professional division newsletters (*Focus on Infants and Toddlers, Focus on Pre-K and K, Focus on Elementary,* and *Focus on Middle School; Celebrating Family Literacy Through Intergenerational Programming*; *Selecting Educational Equipment for School and Home*; *Developmental Continuity Across Preschool and Primary Grades*; *Implications for Teachers*; *Developmentally Appropriate Middle Level Schools*; *Common Bonds: Antibias Teaching in a Diverse Society*; *Childhood 1892-1992*; *Infants and Toddlers with Special Needs and Their Families* (position paper); and pamphlets.

Association for Computers and the Humanities. Elli Mylonas, Exec. Secretary, Box 1885-C15, Brown University, Providence, RI 02912. E-mail ach@stg.brown.edu. Website http://www.ach.org. The Association for Computers and the Humanities is a forum for humanists who incorporate computing into their teaching and research. *Membership:* 300. *Dues:* $75. *Meetings:* Annual meetings held with the Association for Literary and Linguistic Computing. *Publications: Journal for Computers and the Humanities.*

Association for Continuing Higher Education (ACHE). Continuing Education, Trident Technical College, PO Box 118067, CE-P, Charleston, SC 29423-8067. (803)574-6658. Fax (803)574-6470. E-mail zpbarrineavi@trident.tec.sc.us. Website http://www.charleston.net/organization/ACHE/. Wayne Whelan, Exec. Vice Pres. ACHE is an institution-based organization of colleges, universities, and individuals dedicated to the promotion of lifelong learning and excellence in continuing higher education. ACHE encourages professional networks, research, and exchange of information for its members and advocates continuing higher education as a means of enhancing and improving society. *Membership:* 1,622 individuals in 674 institutions. *Dues:* $60, professional; $240, institutional. *Meetings:* 1999 Annual Meeting, Nov 7-9, Cincinnati. 2000 Oct 14-17, Myrtle Beach, SC. *Publications: Journal of Continuing Higher Education* (3/yr.); *Five Minutes with ACHE* (newsletter, 10/yr.); *Proceedings* (annual).

Association for Educational Communications and Technology (AECT). 1025 Vermont Ave. NW, Suite 820, Washington, DC 20005. (202)347-7834. Fax (202)347-7839. Stanley Zenor, Exec. Dir. AECT is an international professional association concerned with the improvement of learning and instruction through media and technology. It serves as a central clearinghouse and communications center for its members, who include instructional technologists, library media specialists, religious educators, government media personnel, school administrators and specialists, and training media producers. AECT members also work in the armed forces, public libraries, museums, and other information agencies of many different kinds, including those related to the emerging fields of computer technology. Affiliated organizations include the Association for Media and Technology in Education in Canada (AMTEC), Community College Association for Instructional and Technology (CCAIT), Consortium of College and University Media Centers (CCUMC), Federal Educational Technology Association (FETA), Health Sciences Special Interest Group (HESIG), International Association for Learning Laboratories (IALL), International Visual Literacy Association (IVLA), Minorities in Media (MIM), National Association of Regional Media Centers (NARMC), New England Educational Media Association (NEEMA), and the Southeastern Regional Media Leadership Council (SRMLC). Each of these affiliated organizations has their own listing in the *Yearbook*. Two additional organizations, the AECT Archives and the ECT Foundation, are also related to the Association for Educational Communications and Technology and have independent listings. Divisions are listed below. *Membership:* 4,500. *Meetings:* 1999 Annual Convention and InCITE Exposition, Feb 10-14, Houston. *Publications: TechTrends* (6/yr., free with membership; $36 nonmembers); *Report to Members* (6/yr., newsletter); *Educational Technology Research and Development* (q., $40 members; $55 nonmembers); various division publications; several books; videotapes.

Association for Educational Communications and Technology (AECT) Divisions:

(AECT) Division of Educational Media Management (DEMM). 1025 Vermont Ave. NW, Suite 820, Washington, DC 20005-3516. (202)347-7834. Fax (202)347-7839. E-mail aect@aect.org. Website http://www.aect.org/Divisions/aectdiv.html and http://teams.lacoe.edu/demm/demm.html. Nancy McFarlin, Pres. E-mail mcfarlin@ksu.edu. As leaders in the field of educational media, members of DEMM are actively involved in the design, production, and instructional applications of new and emerging multimedia technologies. DEMM members are proactive media managers who provide solutions, share information on common problems, and support the development of model media programs. *Membership:* 438. *Dues:* One division membership included in the basic AECT membership; additional division memberships $10. *Meetings:* DEMM meets in conjunction with the annual AECT National Convention. *Publication: DEMM Perspective* (newsletter, q.).

(AECT) Division of Instructional Development (DID). 1025 Vermont Ave. NW, Suite 820, Washington, DC 20005. (202)347-7834. Rodney Earle, Pres. E-mail rodney-earle@byu.edu. DID is composed of individuals from business, government, and academic settings concerned with the systematic design of instruction and the development of solutions to performance problems. Members' interests include the study, evaluation, and refinement of design processes; the creation of new models of instructional development; the invention and improvement of techniques for managing the development of instruction; the development and application of professional ID competencies; the promotion of academic programs for preparation of ID professionals; and the dissemination of research and development work in ID. *Membership:* 726. *Dues:* One division membership included in the basic AECT membership; additional division memberships $10. *Meetings:* held in conjunction with the annual AECT Convention. *Publications: DID Newsletter*; occasional papers.

(AECT) Division of Interactive Systems and Computers (DISC). 1025 Vermont Ave. NW, Suite 820, Washington, DC 20005. (202)347-7834. E-mail garya@sprynet.com. Website http://www.aect.org/Divisions/disc.html. Gary Addison, Pres. Concerned with the generation, access, organization, storage, and delivery of all forms of information used in the processes of education and training. DISC promotes the networking of its members to facilitate sharing of expertise and interests. *Membership:* 686. *Dues:* One division membership included in the basic AECT membership; additional division memberships $10. *Meetings:* held in conjunction with the annual AECT Convention. *Publication:* Newsletter; listserv at DISC-L@vm.cc.purdue.edu (to subscribe, send the message "subscribe DISC-L firstname lastname").

(AECT) Division of Learning and Performance Environments (DLPE). 1025 Vermont Ave. NW, Suite 820, Washington, DC 20005. (202)347-7834. Website http://dlpe.base.org. Renee Eggers, Pres. E-mail eggersre@emporia.edu. Supports human learning and performance through the use of computer-based technology; design, development, evaluation, assessment, and implementation of learning environments and performance systems for adults. *Dues:* One division membership included in the basic AECT membership; additional division memberships $10. *Meetings:* held in conjunction with the annual AECT Convention.

(AECT) Division of School Media and Technology (DSMT). 1025 Vermont Ave. NW, Suite 820, Washington, DC 20005. (202)347-7834. E-mail freibergs@po.atlantic.county.lib.nj.us. Sherry Freiberg, Pres. DSMS strives to improve instruction and promotes excellence in student learning in the K–12 setting by developing, implementing, and evaluating media programs and by planning and integrating technology in the classroom. *Membership:* 902. *Dues:* One division membership included in the basic AECT membership; additional division memberships $10. *Meetings:* held in conjunction with the annual AECT Convention. *Publication:* Newsletter.

(AECT) Division of Telecommunications (DOT). 1025 Vermont Ave. NW, Suite 820, Washington, DC 20005. (202)347-7834. Steve Mitchell, Pres. E-mail mitchell@wneo.org. DOT represents those members with an interest in a broad range of telecommunications as means of addressing the educational needs of students, the educational community, and the general public. *Membership:* 607. *Dues:* one division membership included in the basic AECT membership; additional division memberships $10. *Meetings:* held in conjunction with annual AECT Convention. *Publication:* newsletter.

(AECT) Industrial Training and Education Division (ITED). 1025 Vermont Ave. NW, Suite 820, Washington, DC 20005. (202)347-7834. Rob Pearson, Pres. E-mail rpearson@ passport.ca. ITED is involved with designing, planning, evaluating, and managing training and performance programs, and promoting appropriate uses of educational techniques and media. *Membership:* 273. *Dues:* one division membership included in the basic AECT membership; additional division memberships $10. *Meetings:* held in conjunction with annual AECT Convention. *Publication: ITED Newsletter.* Back issues of the *Newsletter* are indexed in the ERIC database (ED 409 883).

(AECT) International Division (INTL). 1025 Vermont Ave. NW, Suite 820, Washington, DC 20005. (202)347-7834. Badrul Khan, Pres. E-mail khanb@gwis2.circ.gwu.edu. INTL encourages practice and research in educational communication and distance education for social and economic development across national and cultural lines; promotes international exchange and sharing of information, and enhances relationships among international leaders. *Membership:* 295. *Dues:* one division membership included in the basic AECT membership; additional division memberships $10. *Meetings:* held in conjunction with the annual AECT Convention. *Publication:* Newsletter.

(AECT) Media Design and Production Division (MDPD). 1025 Vermont Ave. NW, Suite 820, Washington, DC 20005. (202)347-7834. Chuck Stoddard, Pres. E-mail chuck@cc.usu.edu. MDPD provides an international network which focuses on enhancing the quality and effectiveness of mediated communication, in all media formats, in educational, governmental, hospital, and corporate settings through the interaction of instructional designers, trainers, researchers, and evaluators with media designers and production team specialists who utilize state-of-the-art production skills. *Membership:* 318. *Dues:* one division membership included in the basic AECT membership; additional division memberships $10. *Meetings:* held in conjunction with annual AECT Convention. *Publication:* Newsletter.

(AECT) Research and Theory Division (RTD). 1025 Vermont Ave. NW, Suite 820, Washington, DC 20005. (202)347-7834. Deborah Lowther, Pres. E-mail lowther.deborah@ coe.memphis.edu. Seeks to improve the design, execution, utilization, and evaluation of educational technology research; to improve the qualifications and effectiveness of personnel engaged in educational technology research; to advise the educational practitioner as to the use of the research results; to improve research design, techniques, evaluation, and dissemination; to promote both applied and theoretical research on the systematic use of educational technology in the improvement of instruction; and to encourage the use of multiple research paradigms in examining issues related to technology in education. *Membership:* 452. *Dues:* one division membership included in the basic AECT membership; additional division memberships $10. *Meetings:* held in conjunction with annual AECT Convention. *Publication:* Newsletter.

(AECT) Systemic Change in Education Division (CHANGE). 1025 Vermont Ave. NW, Suite 820, Washington, DC 20005. (202)347-7834. Mary Herring, Pres. E-mail mch002@alph.morningside.edu. CHANGE advocates fundamental changes in educational settings to improve the quality of education and to enable technology to achieve its potential. *Dues:* one division membership included in the basic AECT membership; additional division memberships $10. *Meetings:* held in conjunction with the annual AECT Convention. *Publication:* Newsletter.

AECT Archives. University of Maryland, Hornbake Library, College Park, MD 20742. E-mail tc65@umail.umd.edu. Website http://www.library.umd.edu/UMCP/NPBA/npba.html. Thomas Connors, Archivist, National Public Broadcasting Archives. (301)405-9255. Fax (301)314-2634. A collection of media, manuscripts, and related materials representing important developments in visual and audiovisual education and in instructional technology. The collection is housed as part of the National Public Broadcasting Archives. Maintained by the University of Maryland in cooperation with AECT. Open to researchers and scholars.

Association for Experiential Education (AEE). 2305 Canyon Blvd., Suite 100, Boulder, CO 80302-5651. (303)440-8844 ext. 10. Fax (303)440-9581. Website http://www.aee.org. Sharon Heinlen, Exec. Dir. AEE is a nonprofit, international, professional organization with roots in adventure education, committed to the development, practice, and evaluation of experiential learning in all settings. AEE's vision is to be a leading international organization for the development and application of experiential education principles and methodologies with the intent to create a just and compassionate world by transforming education and promoting positive social change. *Membership:* more than 2,500 members in over 30 countries including individuals and organizations with affiliations in education, recreation, outdoor adventure programming, mental health, youth service, physical education, management development training, corrections, programming for people with disabilities, and environmental education. *Dues:* $55-$95, indiv. (depending on annual income); $110-$125, family; $200-$500, organizations and corporations. *Meetings:* Annual AEE International Conference, fall. Regional Conferences held in the Northwest, Heartland, Southeast, Mid-South, Mid-Atlantic, Northeast, West, and Rocky Mountains. *Publications: Jobs Clearinghouse* (m.); *The Journal of Experiential Education* (3/yr.); *Experience and the Curriculum; Adventure Education; Adventure Therapy; Therapeutic Applications of Adventure Programming; Manual of Accreditation Standards for Adventure Programs; The Theory of Experiential Education, Third Edition; Experiential Learning in Schools and Higher Education; Ethical Issues in Experiential*

Education, Second Edition; The K.E.Y. (Keep Exploring Yourself) Group: An Experiential Personal Growth Group Manual; Book of Metaphors, Volume II; Women's Voices in Experiential Education; bibliographies, directories of programs, and membership directory. *New publications since last year: Exploring the Boundaries of Adventure Therapy; A Guide to Women's Studies in the Outdoors; Adminstrative Practices of Accredited Adventure Programs; Fundamentals of Experience-Based Training; Wild Adventures: A Guidebook of Activities for Building Connections with Others and the Earth; Truth Zone: An Experimental Approach to Organizational Development.*

Association for Library and Information Science Education (ALISE). Sharon J. Rogers, Exec. Dir. PO Box 7640, Arlington, VA 22207. (703)522-1899. Fax (703)243-4551. E-mail sroger7@ibm.net. Website http://www.alise.org. Seeks to advance education for library and information science and produces annual *Library and Information Science Education Statistical Report.* Open to professional schools offering graduate programs in library and information science; personal memberships open to educators employed in such institutions; other memberships available to interested individuals. *Membership:* 500 individuals, 73 institutions. *Dues:* institutional, sliding scale, $325-600; $200 associate; $125 international; personal, $90 full-time; $50 part-time, $40 student, $50 retired. *Meetings:* 1999, Jan 26-29, Philadelphia; 2000, Jan 11-14, San Antonio; 2001, Jan 9-12, Washington, DC. *Publications: Journal of Education for Library and Information Science; ALISE Directory and Handbook; Library and Information Science Education Statistical Report.*

Association for Library Collections & Technical Services (ALCTS). 50 E. Huron St., Chicago, IL 60611. (312)944-6780. Fax (312)280-5033. E-mail alcts@ala.org. Karen Muller, Exec. Dir; Sheila S. Intner, Pres., July 1998-July 1999. A division of the American Library Association, ALCTS is dedicated to acquisition, identification, cataloging, classification, and preservation of library materials, the development and coordination of the country's library resources, and aspects of selection and evaluation involved in acquiring and developing library materials and resources. Sections include Acquisitions, Cataloging and Classification, Collection Management and Development, Preservation and Reformatting, and Serials. *Membership:* 4,984. *Dues:* $45 plus membership in ALA. *Meetings*: 2000, Chicago, Jul 6-12; 2001, San Francisco, Jun 14-20; 2002, Atlanta, June 13-19; ALA Midwinter Meeting; 2000, San Antonio, Jan 14-19; 2001, Washington, Jan 12-17; 2002, New Orleans, Jan 18-23. *Publications: Library Resources & Technical Services* (q.); *ALCTS Newsletter* (6/yr.); *ALCTS Network News (AN2)*, electronic newsletter issued irregularly.

Association for Library Service to Children (ALSC). 50 E. Huron St., Chicago, IL 60611. (312)280-2163. Fax (312)944-7671. Website: http://www.ala.org/a/sc. E-mail alsc@ala.org. Susan Roman, Exec. Dir. A division of the American Library Association, ALSC is interested in the improvement and extension of library services for children in all types of libraries, evaluation and selection of book and nonbook library materials, and improvement of techniques of library services for children from preschool through the eighth grade or junior high school age. Committee membership open to ALSC members. *Membership:* 3,600. *Dues:* $45 plus membership in ALA. *Meetings:* annual conference and midwinter meeting with ALA National Institutes, next is October 2000 in Baltimore. *Publications: Journal of Youth Services in Libraries* (q.); *ALSC Newsletter* (q.).

Association for the Advancement of Computing in Education (AACE). PO Box 2966, Charlottesville, VA 22902. (804)973-3987. Fax (804)978-7449. E-mail aace@virginia.edu. Website http://www.aace.org. Gary Marks, Exec. Dir.; April Ballard, contact person. AACE is an international, educational, and professional organization dedicated to the advancement of learning and teaching at all levels with information technology. AACE publishes major journals, books, and CD-ROMs on the subject, and organizes major conferences. AACE's membership includes researchers, developers, and practitioners in schools, colleges, and universities; administrators, policy decision-makers, trainers, adult educators, and other specialists in education, industry, and the government with an interest in advancing knowledge and learning with information technology in education. *Membership:* 6,500. *Dues:* basic membership of $75 includes one journal subscription and *Educational Technology Review* subscription. *Meetings:* SITE '99 and M/SET 99, Feb 28-Mar 4, San Antonio. Ed-Media/Ed-Telecom 99, June, New Orleans. Web Net 99, Nov, Hawaii.

SITE 2000, March, Phoenix. *Publications: Educational Technology Review (ED-TECH Review)* (2 or 3 times yearly); *Journal of Computers in Mathematics and Science Teaching (JCMST); Journal of Computing in Childhood Education (JCCE); Journal of Educational Multimedia and Hypermedia (JEMH): Journal of Interactive Learning Research (JILR)* (formerly *Journal of Artificial Intelligence in Education); Journal of Technology and Teacher Education (JTATE); International Journal of Educational Telecommunications (IJET)*. A catalog of books and CD-ROMs is available upon request, or by visiting http://www.aace.organize/conf/pubs.

Association of American Publishers (AAP). 1718 Connecticut Avenue, NW, Washington, DC 20009. (202)232-3335. Fax (202)745-0694. Website http://www.publishers.org. Patricia S. Schroeder, President and CEO (DC); Judith Platt, Director of Communications/Public Affairs (jplatt@publishers.org). The Association of American Publishers is the national trade association of the U.S. book publishing industry. AAP was created in 1970 through the merger of the American Book Publishers Council, a trade publishing group, and the American Textbook Publishers Institute, a group of educational publishers. AAP's approximately 200 members include most of the major commercial book publishers in the United States, as well as smaller and nonprofit publishers, university presses, and scholarly societies. AAP members publish hardcover and paperback books in every field and a range of educational materials for the elementary, secondary, postsecondary, and professional markets. Members of the Association also produce computer software and electronic products and services, such as online databases and CD-ROM. AAP's primary concerns are the protection of intellectual property rights in all media, the defense of free expression and freedom to publish at home and abroad, the management of new technologies, development of education markets and funding for instructional materials, and the development of national and global markets for its' members products.

Association of College and Research Libraries (ACRL). 50 E. Huron St., Chicago, IL 60611-2795. (312)280-3248. Fax (312)280-2520. E-mail ajenkins@ala.org. Website http://www.ala.org/acrl.html. Althea H. Jenkins, Exec. Dir. An affiliate of the American Library Association, ACRL provides leadership for development, promotion, and improvement of academic and research library resources and services to facilitate learning, research, and the scholarly communications process. It provides access to library standards for colleges, universities, and two-year institutions, and publishes statistics on academic libraries. Committees include Academic or Research Librarian of the Year Award, Appointments, Hugh C. Atkinson Memorial Award, Budget and Finance, Colleagues, Committee on the Status of Academic Librarians, Constitution and Bylaws, Copyright, Council of Liaisons, Doctoral Dissertation Fellowship, Government Relations, Intellectual Freedom, International Relations, Samuel Lazerow Fellowship, Media Resources, Membership, Nominations, Orientation, Professional Development, Professional Enhancement, Publications, Racial and Ethnic Diversity, Research, K.G. Saur Award for the Best C&RL Article, Standards and Accreditation, Statistics. The association administers 15 different awards in three categories: Achievement and Distinguished Service Awards, Research Awards/Grants, and Publications. *Membership:* over 10,000. *Dues:* $35 (in addition to ALA membership). *Meetings*: 1999 ACRL National Conference, Apr 8-12, Detroit. *Publications: College & Research Libraries* (6/yr.); *College & Research Libraries News* (11/yr.); *Rare Books and Manuscripts Librarianship* (semi-annual); *CHOICE Magazine: Current Reviews for Academic Libraries* (11/yr.); *CLIP Notes* (current issues are #16,17,20-26). Recent titles include: *Displays and Exhibits in College Libraries; Restructuring Academic Libraries; Documenting Cultural Diversity in the Resurgent American South;* and *CHOICE Reviews in Women's Studies;* and *Proceedings of the 7th ACRL National Conference*. A free list of materials is available. ACRL also sponsors an open discussion listserv, ACRL-FRM@ALA.ORG.

*Association of Independent Video and Filmmakers/Foundation for Independent Video and Film (AIVF/FIVF). 304 Hudson St., 6th Floor, New York, NY 10013. (212)807-1400. Fax (212)463-8519. E-mail info@aivf.org. Website http://www.aivf.org. Elizabeth Peters, Exec. Dir. Michelle Coe, Program & Information Services Dir. AIVF is the national trade association for independent video and filmmakers, representing their needs and goals to industry, government, and the public. Programs include screenings and seminars, insurance for members and groups, and information and referral services. Recent activities include seminars in filmmaking technology, a screening series with mid-career artists, and a monthly forum with industry professionals. AIVF also has advocted for public funding of the arts, public access to new telecommunications systems, and monitoring censorship issues. *Dues:* $45, indiv.; $75, library; $100, nonprofit organization; $150, business/industry; $25, student. *AIVFPublications: The Independent Film and Video Monthly*; *The AIVF Guide to International Film and Video Festivals*; *The AIVF Guide to Film and Video Distributors*; *The Next Step: Distributing Independent Films and Videos*, *The AIVF Self Distribution Toolkit & the AIVF Film & Video Exhibitors Guide.*

Association of Specialized and Cooperative Library Agencies (ASCLA). 50 E. Huron St., Chicago, IL 60611. (800)545-2433, ext. 4398. Fax (312)944-8085. E-mail ascla@ala.org. Website http://www.ala.org/ascla. Cathleen Bourdon, Exec. Dir. An affiliate of the American Library Association, ASCLA represents state library agencies, multitype library cooperatives, independent libraries and libraries serving special clienteles to promote the development of coordinated library services with equal access to information and material for all persons. The activities and programs of the association are carried out by 21 committees, 4 sections, and various discussion groups. *Membership:* 1,300. *Dues:* (in addition to ALA membership) $40, personal; $50, organization; $500, state library agency. *Meetings:* 1999 Conference, Jun 24-Jul 1, New Orleans. 2000, Jul 6-13, Chicago. *Publications: Interface* (q.); *The Americans with Disabilities Act: Its Impact on Libraries*; *Deafness: An Annotated Bibliography and Guide to Basic Materials*; *Library Standards for Adult Correctional Institutions 1992*. Write for free checklist of materials.

Association of Systematics Collections (ASC). 1725 K St. NW, Suite 601, Washington, DC 20006. (202)835-9050. E-mail asc@ascoll.org. Website http://www.ascoll.org. Fosters the care, management, and improvement of biological collections and promotes their utilization. Institutional members include free-standing museums, botanical gardens, college and university museums, and public institutions, including state biological surveys, and agricultural research centers. ASC also represents affiliate societies, keeps members informed about funding and legislative issues, and provides technical consulting about collection care and taxonomy. *Membership:* 79 institutions, 25 societies, 1,200 newsletter subscribers. *Dues:* depend on the size of collections. *Publications: ASC Newsletter* (for members and nonmember subscribers, bi-mo.); *Guidelines for Institutional Policies and Planning in Natural History Collections*; *Access to Genetic Resources*; *Collections of Frozen Tissues*; *Guidelines for Institutional Database Policies.*

Cable in the Classroom. 1900 N. Beauregard St., Suite 108, Alexandria, VA 22311. (703)845-1400. Fax (703)845-1409. E-mail cicofc@aol.com. Website http://www.ciconline.org. Megan Hookey, Managing Dir. Cable in the Classroom is the cable industry's $420 million public service initiative to enrich education. It provides free cable connections to more than 77,000 public and private K–12 schools, reaching more than 82% of all US students with commercial-free, quality educational programming. It also provides curriculum-related support materials for its programming and conducts Teacher Training and Media Literacy workshops throughout the country. *Membership:* Cable in the Classroom is a consortium of more than 8,500 local cable companies and 38 national cable programming networks. *Meetings:* Cable in the Classroom exhibits at 15 major education conferences each year. *Publications: Delivering the Future: Cable and Education Partnerships for the Information Age* (Dr. Bobbi Kamil); *Cable in the Classroom Magazine* (mo.); *Taking Charge of Your TV: A Guide to Critical Viewing for Parents and Children* (booklet, available on request).

Catholic Library Association (CLA). 100 North Street, Suite 224, Pittsfield, MA 01201-5109. (413)443-2CLA. Fax (413)442-2CLA. Jean R. Bostley, SSJ, Exec. Dir. Provides educational programs, services, and publications for Catholic libraries and librarians. *Membership:* approx. 1,000. *Dues:* $45, indiv.; special rates for students and retirees. *Meetings:* Meetings are held in conjunction with the National Catholic Educational Association: 2002 Apr 2-5, Atlantic City; 2003, Apr 22-25, St. Louis; 2001, Apr 17-20, Milwaukee. *Publications: Catholic Library World* (q.); *Catholic Periodical and Literature Index* (q. with annual cumulations).

C&C Associates. 11112 S. Spotted Rd., Cheney, WA 99004. (888) 662-7678 or (509)624-9621. Fax (509) 323-4811 or (509)624-5320. E-mail cc@iea.com. C&C Associates has the only Electronic Camera Repair Home Study course in the world—more than two centuries of educating camera repair technicians. The only college certified camera repair instructor in the world teaches the 18-lesson course. C&C also publishes repair guides for cameras and writes technical repair guides for several manufactures.

Central Educational Network (CEN). 1400 E. Touhy, Suite 260, Des Plaines, IL 60018-3305. (847)390-8700. Fax (847)390-9435. E-mail ceninfo@mcs.net. James A. Fellows, Pres. The Central Educational Network is a not-for-profit, public television membership organization dedicated to leading, supporting, and serving the needs and interests of community, university, and state organizations that are educating and enriching their citizens through public telecommunications services. CEN is associated with the American Telecommunications Group. ATG includes the American Center for Children and Media [Making Children's Television and Media Experiences Better]. The Benton Academy for Public Telecommunications [Continuing Professional Development]. The Center for Education Initiatives [Extending and Improving Educational Opportunities]. Continental Program Marketing [Acquiring and Placing Quality Programming]. Higher Education Telecommunication Consortium [Building on the Distinctive Resources of Colleges and Universities] and the Hartford Gunn Institute [Planning for a Productive and Effective Second Generation of Public Broadcasting]. Membership in the CEN component of ATG is available to public television and telecommunications organizations and agencies.

Children's Television International (CTI)/GLAD Productions, Inc. Planting Field Dr., South Riding, VA 20152. (800)CTI-GLAD (284-4523). Fax (703)327-6470. Ray Gladfelter, Pres. and Dir. of Customer Services. An educational organization that develops, produces, and distributes a wide variety of color television and video programming and related publications as a resource to aid the social, cultural, and intellectual development of children and young adults. Programs cover language arts, science, social studies, history, and art for home, school, and college viewing. *Publications:* teacher guides for instructional series; *The History Game: A Teacher's Guide*; complimentary catalog for educational videos.

Close Up Foundation. 44 Canal Center Plaza, Alexandria, VA 22314. (703)706-3300. Fax (703)706-0000. E-mail alumni@closeup.org. Website http://www.closeup.org. Stephen A. Janger, CEO. A nonprofit, nonpartisan civic education organization promoting informed citizen participation in public policy and community service. Programs reach more than a million participants each year. Close Up brings 25,000 secondary and middle school students and teachers and older Americans each year to Washington for week-long government studies programs, and produces television programs on the C-SPAN cable network for secondary school and home audiences. Meetings are scheduled most weeks during the academic year in Washington, DC, all with a government, history, or current issues focus. *Membership:* 25,000 participants. *Publications: Current Issues*; *The Bill of Rights: A User's Guide*; *Perspectives*; *International Relations*; *The American Economy*; documentary videotapes on domestic and foreign policy issues.

Community College Association for Instruction and Technology (CCAIT). New Mexico Military Institute, 101 W. College Blvd., Roswell, NM, 88201-5173. (505)624-8382. Fax (505)624-8390. E-mail klopfer@ymgi.nmmi.cc.nm.us. Jerry Klopfer, Pres. A national association of community and junior college educators interested in the discovery and dissemination of information relevant to instruction and media technology in the community environment. Facilitates member exchange of data, reports, proceedings, and other information pertinent to instructional technology and the teaching-learning process; sponsors AECT convention sessions, an annual video competition, and social activities. *Membership:* 250. *Dues:* $20. *Meetings:* 1998, AECT National Convention, St. Louis, Feb 18-22. *Publications:* Regular newsletter; irregular topical papers.

(AACC) Community College Satellite Network (CCSN). One Dupont Cir. NW, Suite 410, Washington, DC 20036. (202)728-0200. Fax (202)833-2467. E-mail CCSN@AACC.NCHE.EDU. Website http://www.aacc.nche.edu. Monica W. Pilkey, Dir.

An office of the American Association of Community Colleges (AACC), CCSN provides leadership and facilitates distance education, teleconferencing, and satellite training to the nation's community colleges. CCSN offers satellite training, discounted teleconferences, free program resources, and general informational assistance in telecommunications to the nation's community colleges. CCSN meets with its members at various industry trade shows and is very active in the AACC annual convention held each spring. CCSN produces a directory of community college satellite downlink and videoconference facilities. *Membership:* 150. *Dues:* $400 for AACC members; $800 for non-AACC members. *Publications: Schedule of Programming* (2/yr.; contains listings of live and taped teleconferences for training and staff development); *CCSN Fall & Spring Program Schedule* (listing of live and taped teleconferences for training, community and staff development, business and industry training, and more); *Teleconferencing at US Community Colleges* (directory of contacts for community college satellite downlink facilities and videoconference capabilities). A free catalog is available.

Computer Assisted Language Instruction Consortium (CALICO). 317 Liberal Arts Building, Southwest Texas State University, 601 University Dr., San Marcos, TX 78666. (512)245-2360. Fax (512)245-8298. E-mail execdir@calico.org. Website http://www.calico.org. Robert Fischer, Executive Director. CALICO is devoted to the dissemination of information of the application of technology to language teaching and language learning. *Membership:* 1,000 members from the United States and 20 foreign countries. *Dues:* $50, indiv. *Meetings:* 1999, June, Miami University, Oxford, Ohio. *Publications: CALICO Journal* (q.), *CALICO Monograph Series.*

Computer Learning Foundation. PO Box 60007, Palo Alto, CA 94306-0007. (650)327-3347. Fax (650)327-3349. Website http://www.ComputerLearning.org. Sally Bowman Alden, Exec. Dir. The Computer Learning Foundation is an international nonprofit educational foundation dedicated to the improvement of education and preparation of youth for the workplace through the use of technology. Foundation programs provide parents and educators with the information, resources, and assistance they need to use technology effectively with children. The Computer Learning Foundation is the official host each October of Computer Learning Month, a month-long focus on the important role technology plays in our lives and a major national grass roots educational effort. During Computer Learning Month, the Computer Learning Foundation announces new materials and projects and hosts North American annual competitions for children, adults, community groups, and schools. Thousands of dollars in technology products are awarded to winners and their schools. The Computer Learning Foundation is endorsed by and collaborates with 56 U.S. State Departments and Canadian Ministries of Education and 26 national nonprofit organizations; however, the Foundation is funded by corporate and individual donations. *Publication: Computer Learning;* annual publication.

Computer-Using Educators, Inc. (CUE). 1210 Marina Village Parkway, Suite 100, Alameda, CA 94501. (510)814-6630. Fax (510)814-0195. E-mail cueinc@cue.org. Website http://www.cue.org. Bob Walczak, Exec, Dir. CUE, a California nonprofit corporation, was founded in 1976 by a group of teachers interested in exploring the use of technology to improve learning in their classrooms. The organization has never lost sight of this mission. Today, CUE has an active membership of 11,000 professionals world-wide in schools, community colleges, and universities. CUE's 23 affiliates in California provide members with local year-round support through meetings, grants, events, and mini-conferences. Special Interest Groups (SIGs) support members interested in a variety of special topics. CUE's annual conferences, newsletter, advocacy, Website, and other programs help the technology-using educator connect with other professionals. *Membership:* 11,000 individual, corporate, and institutional members. *Dues:* $30. *Meetings:* 1999 Spring CUE Conference, May 6-8, Palm Springs, CA; Fall CUE Conference, Oct. 28-30, Sacramento. 2000, May 11-13, Palm Springs; Nov 9-11, Sacramento. *Publication: CUE NewsLetter.*

Consortium of College and University Media Centers. 121 Pearson Hall-ITC, Iowa State University, Ames, IA 50011-2203. (515)294-1811. Fax (515)294-8089. E-mail donrieck@iastate.edu; ccumc@ccumc.org. Website www.ccumc.org. Don Rieck, Exec. Dir. CCUMC is a professional group of higher education media personnel whose purpose is to improve education and training through the effective use of educational media. Assists educational and training users in making films, video, and educational media more accessible. Fosters cooperative planning among university media centers. Gathers and disseminates information on improved procedures and new developments in instructional technology and media center management. *Membership:* 400. *Dues:* $175 institutional; $175, corporate; $25, student; $175, associate. *Meetings:* 1999, Oct 21-26, Burlington, VT; 2000, Oct 20-25, Denton, TX. *Media Review* (journal).

*Continuing Library Education Network and Exchange Round Table (CLENERT). 50 E. Huron St., Chicago, IL 60611. (800)545-2433. Website http://www.ala.org. An affiliate of the American Library Association, CLENERT seeks to provide access to quality continuing education opportunities for librarians and information scientists and to create an awareness of the need for such education in helping individuals in the field to respond to societal and technological changes. *Membership:* 350. *Dues:* open to all ALA members; $15, indiv.; $50, organization. *Publications:* *CLENExchange* (q.), available to nonmembers by subscription at $20.

Copyright Clearance Center, Inc. (CCC). 222 Rosewood Dr., Danvers, MA 01923. (978) 750-8400. Fax (978)750-4470. E-mail ihinds@copyright.com. Website http://www.copyright.com/. Joseph S. Alen, President. CCC, the largest licenser of photocopy reproduction rights in the world, was formed in 1978 to facilitate compliance with U.S. copyright law. CCC provides licensing systems involving the reproduction and distribution of copyrighted materials throughout the world. CCC currently manages rights relating to more than 1.75 million works and represents more than 9,600 publishers and hundreds of thousands of authors and other creators, directly or through their representatives. CCC licensed customers in the U.S. number more than 9,000 corporations and subsidiaries (including 90 of the Fortune 100 companies), as well as thousands of government agencies, law firms, document suppliers, libraries, academic institutions, copy shops, and bookstores in the United States. CCC is a member of the International Federation Rights Organizations (IFRRO) and has bilateral agreements with RROs in 11 countries worldwide, under which it repatriates fees for overseas use of U.S. works.

Corporation for Public Broadcasting (CPB). 901 E Street, NW, Washington, DC 20004-2037. (202)879-9600. Fax (202)783-1039. E-mail info@cpb.org. Website http://www.cpb.org. Robert T. Coonrod, Pres. and CEO. A private, nonprofit corporation created by Congress in 1967 to develop noncommercial television, radio, and online services for the American people. CPB created the Public Broadcasting Service (PBS) in 1969 and National Public Radio (NPR) in 1970. CPB distributes grants to more than 1,000 local public television and radio stations that reach virtually every household in the country. The Corporation is the industry's largest single source of funds for national public television and radio program development and production. In addition to quality educational and informational programming, CPB and local public stations make important contributions in the areas of education, training, community service, and application of emerging technologies. *Publications: Annual Report; CPB Public Broadcasting Directory* ($15).

Council for Basic Education. 1319 F St. NW, Suite 900, Washington, DC 20004-1152. (202)347-4171. E-mail info@c-b-e.org. Website http://www.c-b-e.org. Christopher T. Cross, Pres. Maxine P. Frost, Chair of Board of Directors. CBE's mission is to strengthen teaching and learning of the core subjects (mathematics, English, language arts, history, government, geography, the sciences, foreign languages, and the arts) in order to develop the capacity for lifelong learning and foster responsible citizenship. As an independent, critical voice for education reform, CBE champions the philosophy that all children can learn, and that the job of schools is to achieve this goal. CBE advocates this goal by publishing analytical periodicals and administering practical programs as examples to strengthen content in curriculum and teaching. CBE is completing a kit of Standards for Excellence in Education, which includes a CD-ROM, guides for teachers, parents, and principals, and a book of standards in the core subjects. *Membership:* 3,000.

Council for Exceptional Children (CEC). 1920 Association Dr., Reston, VA 20191-1589. (703)620-3660. TTY: (703)264-9446. Fax (703)264-9494. E-mail cec@cec.sped.org. Website http://www.cec.sped.org. Nancy Safer, Exec. Dir. CEC is the largest international professional organization dedicated to improving educational outcomes for individuals with exceptionalities (students with disabilities and the gifted). CEC advocates for appropriate governmental policies, sets professional standards, provides professional development, advocates for newly and historically underserved individuals with exceptionalities, and helps professionals obtain conditions and resources necessary for effective professional practice. Services include professional development opportunities and resources, 17 divisions for specialized information, public policy advocacy and information, conferences, and standards for the preparation and certification of special educators and professional practice. CEC has expanded its professional development activities to include distance learning activities such as satellite broadcasts and internet-based study groups. The CEC annual convention features the most current educational technology as well as adaptive and assistive technology in formats ranging from full-day workshops to hands-on demonstrations. In collaboration with another agency, CEC is involved in a research project that examines teachers' use of technology to promote literacy in children with exceptionalities. *Membership:* teachers, administrators, students, parents, related support service providers. *Publications:* journals and newsletters with information on new research findings, classroom practices that work, and special education publications. (*See also* the ERIC Clearinghouse on Disabilities and Gifted Education.)

(CEC) Technology and Media Division (TAM). Council for Exceptional Children. The Technology and Media Division (TAM) of The Council for Exceptional Children (CEC) encourages the development of new applications, technologies, and media for use as daily living tools by special populations. This information is disseminated through professional meetings, training programs, and publications. TAM members receive four issues annually of the *Journal of Special Education Technology* containing articles on specific technology programs and applications, and five issues of the TAM newsletter, providing news of current research, developments, products, conferences, and special programs information. *Membership:* 1,700. *Dues:* $10 in addition to CEC membership.

Council on International Non-Theatrical Events (CINE). 1001 Connecticut Ave. NW, Suite 625, Washington, DC 20036. (202)785-1136. Fax (202)785-4114. Website http://www.cine.org. Donna Tschiffely, Exec. Dir. Coordinates the selection and placement of US documentary, television, short subject, and didactic films in more than 100 overseas film festivals annually. A Golden Eagle Certificate is awarded to each professional film considered most suitable to represent the US in international competition and to winning films made by adults, amateurs, youths, and university students. Prizes and certificates won at overseas festivals are presented at an annual awards ceremony. CINE receives approximately 1300 entries annually for the competition. Deadlines for receipt of entry forms are Feb 1 and Aug 1. *Meeting:* CINE Showcase and Awards held annually in Washington, DC. *Publications: CINE Annual Yearbook of Film and Video Awards; Worldwide Directory of Film and Video Festivals and Events.*

*East-West Center. 1601 East-West Rd., Honolulu, HI 96848-1601. (808)944-7111. Fax (808)944-7376. E-mail ewcinfo@ewc.hawaii.edu. Website http://www.ewc.hawaii.edu. Dr. Charles E. Morrison, Pres. The U.S. Congress established the East-West Center in 1960 with a mandate to foster mutual understanding and cooperation among the governments and peoples of Asia, the Pacific, and the United States. Officially known as the Center for Cultural and Technical Interchange Between East and West, it is a public, nonprofit institution with an international board of governors. Funding for the center comes from the U.S. government, with additional support provided by private agencies, individuals, and corporations, and several Asian and Pacific governments, private agencies, individuals, and corporations. The center, through research, education, dialog, and outreach, provides a neutral meeting ground where people with a wide range of perspectives exchange views on topics of regional concern. Scholars, government and business leaders, educators, journalists, and other professionals from throughout the region annually work with Center staff to address issues of contemporary significance in such areas as international economics and politics, the environment, population, energy, the media, and Pacific islands development.

Educational Communications. PO Box 351419, Los Angeles, CA 90035. (310)559-9160. Fax (310) 559-9160. E-mail ECNP@aol.com. Website http://home.earthlink.net/~dragonflight/ecoprojects.htm. Nancy Pearlman, CEO. Educational Communications is dedicated to enhancing the quality of life on this planet and provides radio and television programs about the environment. Serves as a clearinghouse on ecological issues. Programming is available on 100 stations in 25 states. *Publications: Compendium Newsletter* (bi-monthly); *Directory of Environmental Organizations.*

ECT Foundation. c/o AECT, 1025 Vermont Ave. NW, Suite 820, Washington, DC 20005. Hans-Erik Wennberg, Pres. The ECT Foundation is a nonprofit organization whose purposes are charitable and educational in nature. Its operation is based on the conviction that improvement of instruction can be accomplished, in part, by the continued investigation and application of new systems for learning and by periodic assessment of current techniques for the communication of information. In addition to awarding scholarships, internships, and fellowships, the foundation develops and conducts leadership training programs for emerging professional leaders. Its operations are closely allied to AECT program goals, and the two organizations operate in close conjunction to each other.

*Education Development Center, Inc. 55 Chapel St., Newton, MA 02158-1060. (617)969-7100. Fax (617)969-5979. Website http://www.edc.org. Janet Whitla, Pres. Seeks to improve education at all levels, in the US and abroad, through curriculum development, institutional development, and services to the school and the community. Produces videocassettes, primarily in connection with curriculum development and teacher training. *Publications: Annual Report.*

Educational Products Information Exchange (EPIE Institute). 103 W. Montauk Hwy., Hampton Bays, NY 11946. (516)728-9100. Fax (516)728-9228. E-mail kowoski@aurora.lionet.edu. Website http://www.epie.org. P. Kenneth Komoski, Exec. Dir. Assesses educational materials and provides consumer information, product descriptions, and citations for virtually all educational software and curriculum-related Websites. All of EPIE's services are available to schools and state agencies as well as parents and individuals. Online access is restricted to states with membership in the States Consortium for Improving Software Selection (SCISS). *Publications: The Educational Software Selector Database (TESS),* available to anyone. All publication material now available on CD-ROM.

Educational Resources Information Center (ERIC). National Library of Education (NLE), Office of Educational Research and Improvement (OERI), 555 New Jersey Ave. NW, Washington, DC 20208-5720. (202)219-2289. Fax (202)219-1817. E-mail eric@inet.ed.gov. Keith Stubbs, Dir. ERIC is a federally funded nationwide information network that provides access to the English-language education literature. The ERIC system consists of clearinghouses, adjunct clearinghouses, and system support components includings ACCESS ERIC, the ERIC Document Reproduction Service (EDRS), and the ERIC Processing and Reference Facility. ERIC actively solicits papers, conference proceedings, literature reviews, and curriculum materials from researchers, practitioners, educational associations and institutions, and federal, state, and local agencies. These materials, along with articles from nearly 800 different journals, are indexed and abstracted for entry into the ERIC database. The ERIC database (the largest education database in the world) now contains more than 850,000 records of documents and journal articles. Users can access the ERIC database online, on CD-ROM, or through print and microfiche indexes. ERIC microfiche collections, which contain the full text of most ERIC documents, are available for public use at more than 1,000 locations worldwide. Reprints of ERIC documents, on microfiche or in paper copy, can also be ordered from EDRS. Copies of journal articles can be found in library periodical collections, through interlibrary loan, or from article reprint services. A list of the ERIC Clearinghouses, together with addresses, telephone numbers, and brief domain descriptions, follows here. *Publications: Resources in Education* (US Government Printing Office); *Current Index to Journals in Education* (Oryx Press).

ACCESS ERIC. Aspen Systems Corp., 2277 Research Blvd., Mailstop 6L, Rockville, MD 20850. 1-800-LET-ERIC [538-3742]. Fax (301)519-6760. E-mail accesseric@accessiceric.org.

ACCESS ERIC coordinates ERIC's outreach and systemwide dissemination activities, develops new ERIC publications, and provides general reference and referral services. Its publications include several reference directories designed to help the public understand and use ERIC as well as provide information about current education-related issues, research, and practice. *Publications: A Pocket Guide to ERIC; All About ERIC; The ERIC Review;* the Parent Brochure series; *Catalog of ERIC Clearinghouse Publications; ERIC Calendar of Education-Related Conferences; ERIC Directory of Education-Related Information Centers; ERIC User's Interchange; Directory of ERIC Resource Collections. Databases:* ERIC Digests Online (EDO); Education-Related Information Centers; ERIC Resource Collections; ERIC Calendar of Education-Related Conferences. The databases are available through the Internet: http://www.accesseric.org.

ERIC Clearinghouse for Community Colleges (JC) (formerly Junior Colleges). University of California at Los Angeles (UCLA), 3051 Moore Hall, PO Box 951521, Los Angeles, CA 90025-1521. (310)825-3931, (800)832-8256. Fax (310)206-8095. E-mail ericcc@ucla.edu. Website http://www.gseis.ucla.edu/ERIC/eric.html. Arthur M. Cohen, Dir. Selects, synthesizes, and distributes reports and other documents about two-year public and private community and junior colleges, technical institutes, and two-year branch university programs, and outcomes of these institutions; linkages between two-year colleges and business, industrial, and community organizations; and articulation between two-year colleges and secondary and four-year postsecondary institutions.

ERIC Clearinghouse for Social Studies/Social Science Education (SO). Indiana University, Social Studies Development Center, 2805 East 10th St., Suite 120, Bloomington, IN 47408-2698. (812)855-3838, (800)266-3815. Fax (812)855-0455. E-mail ericso@indiana.edu. Website http://www.indiana.edu/~ssdc.eric_chess.htm. All levels of social studies and social science education; the contributions of history, geography, and other social science disciplines; applications of theory and research to social science education; education as a social science; comparative education (K–12); content and curriculum materials on social topics such as law-related education, ethnic studies, bias and discrimination, aging, and women's equity. Music and art education are also covered. Includes input from the Adjunct ERIC Clearinghouses for Law-Related Education, for US-Japan Studies, for Service Learning, and for International Civics.

> **Adjunct ERIC Clearinghouse for Art Education**. Indiana University, Social Studies Development Center, 2805 East 10th St., Suite 120, Bloomington, IN 47408-2698. (812)855-3838, (800)266-3815. Fax (812)855-0455. E-mail clarkgil@indiana.edu; zimmerm@ucs.indiana.edu. Enid Zimmerman, Director. Adjunct to the ERIC Clearinghouse on Social Studies/Social Science Education.

> **Adjunct ERIC Clearinghouse for Law-Related Education (ADJ/LR)**. Indiana University, Social Studies Development Center, 2805 East 10th St., Suite 120, Bloomington, IN 47408-2698. (812)855-3838, (800)266-3815. Fax (812)855-0455. E-mail patrick@indiana.edu, tvontz@indiana.edu. Website http://www.indiana.edu/~ssdc/iplre.html. John Patrick and Robert Leming, Co-Directors. Adjunct to the ERIC Clearinghouse on Social Studies/Social Sciences Education.

> **Adjunct ERIC Clearinghouse for United States-Japan Studies (ADJ/JS)**. 2805 E. 10th St., Suite 120, Bloomington, IN 47408-2698. (812)855-3838, (800)266-3815. Fax (812)855-0455. E-mail japan@indiana.edu. Website http://www.indiana.edu/~japan. Marcia Johnson, Assoc. Dir. Provides information on topics concerning Japan and US-Japan relations. Adjunct to the ERIC Clearinghouse for Social Studies/Social Science Education. *Publications: Guide to Teaching Materials on Japan; Teaching About Japan: Lessons and Resources; The Constitution and Individual Rights in Japan: Lessons for Middle and High School Students;*

Internationalizing the US Classroom: Japan as a Model; Tora no Maki II: Lessons for Teaching About Contemporary Japan; The Japan Digest Series (complimentary, concise discussions of various Japan-related topics)*: Fiction About Japan in the Elementary Curriculum; Daily Life in Japanese High Schools; Rice: It's More Than Food in Japan; Ideas for Integrating Japan into the Curriculum; Japanese Education; Japanese-US Economic Relations; Japan's Economy: 21st Century Challenges; Shinbun* (biannual project newsletter).

ERIC Clearinghouse on Adult, Career, and Vocational Education (ERIC/ACVE). The Ohio State University, Center on Education and Training for Employment, 1900 Kenny Rd., Columbus, OH 43210-1090. (614)292-7069, (800)848-4815, ext. 2-7069. Fax (614)292-1260. E-mail ericacve@postbox.acs.ohio-state.edu. Website http://www.ericacve.org. Susan Imel, Dir. Judy Wagner, Assoc. Dir. All levels and settings of adult and continuing, career, and vocational/technical education. Adult education, from basic literacy training through professional skill upgrading. Career awareness, career decision making, career development, career change, and experience-based education. Vocational and technical education, including new subprofessional fields, industrial arts, corrections education, employment and training programs, youth employment, work experience programs, education and business partnerships, entrepreneurship, adult retraining, and vocational rehabilitation for individuals with disabilities. Includes input from the Adjunct ERIC Clearinghouse on Consumer Education.

Adjunct ERIC Clearinghouse for Consumer Education (ADJ/CN). National Institute for Consumer Education, 207 Rackham Bldg., Eastern Michigan University, Ypsilanti, MI 48197-2237. (313)487-2292. Fax (313)487-7153. E-mail nice@emuvax.emich.edu. E-mail NICE@online.emich.edu. Website http://www. emich.edu/public/coe/nice. Rosella Bannister, Dir. Adjunct to the ERIC Clearinghouse on Adult, Career, and Vocational Education.

ERIC Clearinghouse on Assessment and Evaluation (formerly Tests, Measurement, and Evaluation). The University of Maryland, 1129 Shriver Lab, College Park, Maryland 20742-5701 (301)405-7449, (800)464-3742, Fax: (301)405-8134. E-mail ericae@.net. Website http://ericae.net. Lawrence M. Rudner, Dir. Tests and other measurement devices; methodology of measurement and evaluation; application of tests, measurement, or evaluation in educational projects and programs; research design and methodology in the area of assessment and evaluation; and learning theory. Includes input from the Adjunct Test Collection Clearinghouse.

ERIC Clearinghouse on Counseling and Student Services (formerly Counseling and Personnel Services). University of North Carolina at Greensboro, School of Education, 201 Ferguson Building, PO Box 26171, Greensboro, NC 27402-6171. (336)334-4114, (336)334-4116, (800)414-9769. E-mail ericcass@uncg.edu. Website http://www.uncg.edu/ ~ericcas2. Garry R. Walz, Dir. Preparation, practice, and supervision of counselors and therapists at all educational levels and in all settings; theoretical development of counseling and student services; assessment and diagnosis procedures such as testing and interviewing and the analysis and dissemination of the resultant information; outcomes analysis of counseling interventions; groups and case work; nature of pupil, student, and adult characteristics; identification and implementation of strategies which foster student learning and achievement; personnel workers and their relation to career planning, family consultations and student services activities; identification of effective strategies for enhancing parental effectiveness; and continuing preparation of counselors and therapists in the use of new technologies for professional renewal and the implications of such technologies for service provision. *Meeting:* Annual Assessment Conference. *Publications: Career Transitions in Turbulent Times; Exemplary Career Development Programs & Practices; Career Development; Counseling Employment Bound Youth; Internationalizing Career Planning; Saving the*

Native Son; Cultural and Diversity Issues in Counseling; Safe Schools, Safe Students; many others. Call for catalog.

ERIC Clearinghouse on Disabilities and Gifted Education (EC). 1920 Association Dr., Reston, VA 20191-1589. (703)264-9474, (800)328-0272. TTY: (703)264-9449. E-mail ericec@cec.sped.org. Website http://ericec.org. ERIC EC is part of the U.S. Department of Education's information network. ERIC EC collects the professional literature on disabilities and gifted education for inclusion in the ERIC database. ERIC EC also responds to requests for information on disabilities and gifted education, serves as a resource and referral center for the general public, conducts general information searches, and publishes and disseminates free or low-cost materials on disability and gifted education research, programs, and practices.

ERIC Clearinghouse on Educational Management (EA). University of Oregon (Dept. 5207), 1787 Agate St., Eugene, OR 97403-5207. (541)346-5043, (800)438-8841. Fax (541)346-2334. E-mail ppiele@oregon.uoregon.edu. Philip K. Piele, Dir. The governance, leadership, management, and structure of K–12 public and private education organizations; local, state, and federal education law and policy-making; practice and theory of administration; preservice and inservice preparation of administrators; tasks and processes of administration; methods and varieties of organization and organizational change; and the social context of education organizations.

ERIC Clearinghouse on Elementary and Early Childhood Education (PS) and the **National Parent Information Network (NPIN)**. University of Illinois, Children's Research Center, 51 Gerty Dr., Champaign, IL 61820. (217)333-1386, (800)583-4135. Fax (217) 333-3767. E-mail ericeece@uiuc.edu. Website http://ericps.crc.uiuc.edu/ericeece.html. Lilian G. Katz, Dir. E-mail l-katz@uiuc.edu. The physical, cognitive, social, educational, and cultural development of children from birth through early adolescence; prenatal factors; parents, parenting, and family relationships that impinge on education; learning theory research and practice related to the development of young children, including the preparation of teachers for this educational level; interdisciplinary curriculum and mixed-age teaching and learning; educational, social, and cultural programs and services for children; the child in the context of the family and the family in the context of society; theoretical and philosophical issues pertaining to children's development and education. Includes input from the Adjunct ERIC Clearinghouse for Child Care.

> **Adjunct ERIC Clearinghouse for Child Care (ADJ/CC)**. Adjunct ERIC Clearinghouse for Child Care (ADJ/CC). National Child Care Information Center, 301 Maple Ave., Suite 602, Vienna, VA 22180. (703)938-6555, (800)516-2242. Fax (800) 716-2242. E-mail agoldstein@acf.dhhs.gov. Website http://ericps.crc.uiuc.edu/nccic/ nccichome.html. Anne Goldstein, Proj. Dir. Adjunct to the ERIC Clearinghouse on Elementary and Early Childhood Education. Bureau of Administration for Children and Families (ACF), DHHS to complement, enhance and promote child care linkages and to serve as a mechanism for supporting quality, comprehensive services for children and families. NCCIS's activities include dissemination of child care information in response to requests from States, Territories and Tribe, other policy makers, child care organizations, providers, business communities, parents, and the general public; outreach to ACF child care grantees and the boarder child care community; publication of the child care Bulletin and Development and dissemination of other publication on key child care issues; and coordination of National Leadership Forums, which provide an opportunity for experts from across the country to participate in one-day conferences on critical issues affecting children and families. Working closely with ACF Regional offices, the NCCIC also provides technical assistance to states through a network of state technical assistance specialists. Many materials

produced and distributed by NCCIC are available in Spanish. NCCIC is the Adjunct ERIC Clearinghouse for Child Care.

ERIC Clearinghouse on Higher Education (HE). George Washington University, One Dupont Cir. NW, Suite 630, Washington, DC 20036-1183. (202)296-2597, (800)773-3742. Fax (202)452-1844. E-mail eric@eric-he.edu. Website http:/www.eriche.org. Adrianna Kezar, Dir. Topics relating to college and university conditions, problems, programs, and students. Curricular and instructional programs, and institutional research at the college or university level. Federal programs, professional education (medicine, law, etc.), professional continuing education, collegiate computer-assisted learning and management, graduate education, university extension programs, teaching and learning, legal issues and legislation, planning, governance, finance, evaluation, interinstitutional arrangements, management of institutions of higher education, and business or industry educational programs leading to a degree. *Publications: Higher Education Leadership: Analyzing the Gender Gap; The Virtual Campus: Technology and Reform in Higher Education; Early Intervention Programs: Opening the Door to Higher Education; Enriching College with Constructive Controversy; A Culture for Academic Excellence: Implementing the Quality Principles in Higher Education; From Discipline to Development: Rethinking Student Conduct in Higher Education; Proclaiming and Sustaining Excellence: Assessment as a Faculty Role; The Application of Customer Satisfaction Principles to Universities; Saving the Other Two-Thirds: Practices and Strategies for Improving the Retention and Graduation of African American Students in Predominately White Institutions; Enrollment Management: Change for the 21st Century; Faculty Workload: States Perspectives.*

ERIC Clearinghouse on Information & Technology (IR) (formerly Information Resources). Syracuse University, 4-194 Center for Science and Technology, Syracuse, NY 13244-4100. (315)443-3640, (800)464-9107. Fax (315)443-5448. E-mail eric@ericir.syr.edu. AskERIC (question-answering service via Internet) askeric@ericir.syr.edu.R. David Lankes, Dir. Educational technology and library and information science at all levels. Instructional design, development, and evaluation within educational technology, along with the media of educational communication: computers and microcomputers, telecommunications, audio and video recordings, film and other audiovisual materials as they pertain to teaching and learning. The focus is on the operation and management of information services for education-related organizations. Includes all aspects of information technology related to education.

ERIC Clearinghouse on Languages and Linguistics (FL). Center for Applied Linguistics, 4646-403 st., NW, Washington, DC 20016-1859. (202)362-0700, Ext. 200 Fax (202) 362-3740. Fax (202)659-5641. E-mail eric@cal.org. Website http://www.cal.org/ericcll. Joy Peyton, Dir. Dr. Craig Packard, User Services Coordinator, contact person. Languages and language sciences. All aspects of second language instruction and learning in all commonly and uncommonly taught languages, including English as a second language. Bilingualism and bilingual education. Cultural education in the context of second language learning, including intercultural communication, study abroad, and international education exchange. All areas of linguistics, including theoretical and applied linguistics, sociolinguistics, and psycholinguistics. Includes input from the National Clearinghouse for ESL Literacy Education (NCLE).

Adjunct ERIC Clearinghouse for ESL Literacy Education (ADJ/LE). National Clearinghouse for ESL Literacy Education, Center for Applied Linguistics (CAL),4646-403 St., NW, Washington, DC 20016-1859.(202)362-0700, Ext. 200. Fax (202)362-3740. E-mail ncle@cal.org. Website http://www.cal.org/ncle/. Joy Kreeft Peyton, Dir. Adjunct to the ERIC Clearinghouse on Languages and Linguistics. NCLE is the national clearinghouse focusing on the education of adults learning English as a second or additional language. NCLE collects, analyzes, synthesizes, and disseminates information on literacy education for adults and out-of-school youth. NCLE publishes books (available from Delta Systems in McHenry, IL), free ERIC digests and annotated bibliographies on a wide range of topics, and NCLE Notes, a newsletter. *Publication: Literacy and Language Diversity in the United States* by Terrence Wiley (1996), McHenry, IL: Delta Systems.

ERIC Clearinghouse on Reading, English, and Communication (CS) (formerly Reading and Communication Skills). Indiana University, Smith Research Center, Suite 150, 2805 E. 10th St., Bloomington, IN 47408-2698. (812)855-5847, (800)759-4723. Fax (812)855-4220. E-mail ericcs@indiana.edu. Website http://www.indiana.edu/~eric_rec. Carl B. Smith, Dir. Reading, English, and communication (verbal and nonverbal), preschool through college; research and instructional development in reading, writing, speaking, and listening; identification, diagnosis, and remediation of reading problems; speech communication (including forensics), mass communication, interpersonal and small group interaction, interpretation, rhetorical and communication theory, speech sciences, and theater. Preparation of instructional staff and related personnel. All aspects of reading behavior with emphasis on physiology, psychology, sociology, and teaching; instructional materials, curricula, tests and measurement, and methodology at all levels of reading; the role of libraries and other agencies in fostering and guiding reading; diagnostics and remedial reading services in schools and clinical settings. Preparation of reading teachers and specialists. The Website makes available a wealth of information pertaining to the full gamut of language arts topics enumerated above.

ERIC Clearinghouse on Rural Education and Small Schools (RC). Appalachia Educational Laboratory (AEL), 1031 Quarrier St., PO Box 1348, Charleston, WV 25325-1348. (304)347-0465; (800)624-9120. Fax (304)347-0487. E-mail lanhamb@ael.org. Web page http://www.ael.org/erichp.htm. Hobart Harmon, Acting Dir. Economic, cultural, social, or other factors related to educational programs and practices for rural residents; American Indians and Alaska Natives, Mexican Americans, and migrants; educational practices and programs in all small schools; and outdoor education. Check web site to subscribe to print newsletter, or call toll-free.

*ERIC Clearinghouse on Science, Mathematics, and Environmental Education (SE). The Ohio State University, 1929 Kenny Road, Columbus, OH 43210-1080. (614)292-6717, (800)276-0462. Fax (614)292-0263. E-mail ericse@osu.edu. Website http://www.ericse.org. Science, mathematics, and environmental education at all levels, and within these three broad subject areas, the following topics: development of curriculum and instruction materials; teachers and teacher education; learning theory and outcomes (including the impact of parameters such as interest level, intelligence, values, and concept development upon learning in these fields); educational programs; research and evaluative studies; media applications; computer applications.

ERIC Clearinghouse on Teaching and Teacher Education (SP) (formerly Teacher Education). American Association of Colleges for Teacher Education (AACTE), 1307 New York Avenue, NW, Suite 300, Washington, DC 20005. (202)293-2450, (800)822-9229. Fax (202)457-8095. E-mail query@aacte.org. Website http://www.ericsp.org. Mary E. Dilworth, Dir. School personnel at all levels. Teacher recruitment, selection, licensing, certification, training, preservice and inservice preparation, evaluation, retention, and retirement. The theory, philosophy, and practice of teaching. Curricula and general education not specifically covered by other clearinghouses. Organization, administration, finance, and legal issues relating to teacher education programs and institutions. All aspects of health, physical, recreation, and dance education. Includes input from the Adjunct ERIC Clearinghouse on Clinical Schools.

Adjunct ERIC Clearinghouse on Clinical Schools (ADJ/CL). American Association of Colleges for Teacher Education, One Dupont Cir. NW, Suite 610, Washington, DC 20036-1186. (202)293-2450, (800)822-9229. Fax (202)457-8095. E-mail iabdalha@inet.ed.gov. Website http://www.aacte.org/menu2.html. Ismat Abdal-Haqq, Coord. Adjunct to the ERIC Clearinghouse on Teaching and Teacher Education.

ERIC Clearinghouse on Urban Education. Teachers College, Columbia University, Institute for Urban and Minority Education, Main Hall, Rm. 303, Box 40, 525 W. 120th St., New York, NY 10027-6696. (212)678-3433, (800)601-4868. Fax (212)678-4012. E-mail eric-cue@columbia.edu. Website http://eric-web.tc.columbia.edu. Erwin Flaxman, Dir. Programs and practices in public, parochial, and private schools in urban areas and the education of particular ethnic minority children and youth in various settings; the theory and practice of educational equity; urban and minority experiences; and urban and minority social institutions and services.

ERIC Document Reproduction Service (EDRS). 7420 Fullerton Rd., Suite 110, Springfield, VA 22153-2852. (703)440-1400, (800)443-ERIC (3742). Fax (703)440-1408. E-mail service@edrs.com. Website http://edrs.com. Peter M. Dagutis, Dir. Provides subscription services for ERIC document collections in electronic format (from 1996 forward) and on microfiche (from 1966 forward). On-demand delivery of ERIC documents is also available in formats including paper, electronic PDF image, fax, and microfiche. Delivery methods include shipment of hardcopy documents and microfiche, document fax-back, and online delivery. Back collections of ERIC documents, annual subscriptions, cumulative indexes, and other ERIC-related materials are also available. ERIC documents can be ordered by toll-free phone call, fax, mail, or online through the EDRS web site. Document ordering also available from DIALOG and OCLC.

ERIC Processing and Reference Facility. 1100 West Street, 2nd Floor, Laurel, MD 20707-3598. (301)497-4080, (800)799-ERIC (3742). Fax (301)953-0263. E-mail ericfac@inet.ed.gov. Website http://ericfac.piccard.csc.com. Ted Brandhorst, Dir. A central editorial and computer processing agency that coordinates document processing and database building activities for ERIC; performs acquisition, lexicographic, and reference functions; and maintains system-wide quality control standards. The ERIC Facility also prepares *Resources in Education (RIE)*, *ERIC Processing Manual*, *Thesaurus of ERIC Descriptors*, *Identifier Authority List (IAL)*, ERIC Ready References, and other products.

Educational Videos and CD-ROM (originally the PCR Collection). Penn State Media Sales, 118 Wagner Building, University Park, PA 16802. Purchasing info (800)770-2111, (814)863-3102. Fax (814)865-3172. Rental information (800)826-0132. Fax (814)863-2574. Special Services Building, Penn State University, University Park, PA 16802. E-mail mediasales@cde.psu.edu. Website http://www.cde.psu.edu/MediaSales. Sue Oram, Media Sales Coordinator. Makes available to professionals video in the behavioral sciences judged to be useful for university teaching and research. Also distributes training videos to business and industry. A catalog of the videos in the collection is available online. Special topics and individual brochures available. The online catalog now contains videos in the behavioral sciences (psychology, psychiatry, anthropology), animal behavior, sociology, teaching and learning, folklife and agriculture, business, education, biological sciences, and Pennsylvania topics. Videos and CD-ROMs may be submitted for international distribution. Stock footage available also.

Eisenhower National Clearinghouse for Mathematics and Science Education. 1929 Kenny Rd., Columbus, OH 43210-1079. (800)621-5785, (614)292-7784. Fax (614)292-2066. E-mail info@enc.org. Website http://www.enc.org. Dr. Len Simutis, Dir. The Eisenhower National Clearinghouse for Mathematics and Science Education (ENC) is located at The Ohio State University and funded by the US Department of Education's Office of Educational Research and Improvement (OERI). ENC provides K–12 teachers and other educators a central source of information on mathematics and science curriculum materials, particularly those which support education reform. Among ENC's products and services are ENC Online, which is available through a toll-free number and the Internet; 12 demonstration sites located throughout the nation; and a variety of publications, including the *Guidebook of Federal Resources for K–12 Mathematics and Science*, which lists federal resources in mathematics and science education. In 1998 ENC produced CD-ROMs on topics such as equity and professional development including curriculum resources and the ENC Resource Finder, which is the same searchable catalog of curriculum resources and the ENC Online. STET users include K–12 teachers, other educators, policy makers, and parents. *Publications: ENC Update* (newsletter); *ENC Focus* (a magazine on selected topics); *Ideas That Work: Mathematics Professional Development and Ideas That Work: Science Professional Development (two booklets on Professional Development)*; *Guidebook of Federal Resources for K–12 Mathematics and Science* (federal programs in mathematics and science education). ENC Online is available online (http://www.enc.org) or toll-free at (800)362-4448.

Far West Laboratory for Educational Research and Development (FWL). See listing for WestEd.

Federal Communications Commission (FCC). 445-12th St. S.W., Washington, DC 20554. (202)418-0190. Website http://www.fcc.gov. William Kennard, Chairman. The FCC regulates the telecommunication industry in the US.

Federal Educational Technology Association (FETA). FETA Membership, Sara Shick, PO Box 3412, McLean, VA 22103-3412. (703)406-3040. Fax (703)406-4318 (Clear Spring Inc.), E-mail feta@clearspringinc.com. Website http://www.feta.org. Beth Borko, Board Chair. An affiliate of AECT, FETA is dedicated to the improvement of education and training through research, communication, and practice. It encourages and welcomes members from all government agencies, federal, state, and local; from business and industry; and from all educational institutions and organizations. FETA encourages interaction among members to improve the quality of education and training in any arena, but with specific emphasis on government-related applications. *Membership:* 150. *Dues:* $20. *Meetings:* meets in conjunction with AECT InCITE, concurrently with SALT's Washington meeting in August, and periodically throughout the year in Washington, DC. *Publication:* Newsletter (occasional).

Film Arts Foundation (FAF). 346 9th St., 2nd Floor, San Francisco, CA 94103. (415)552-8760. Fax (415)552-0882. E-mail info@filmarts.org. Website http://www.filmarts.org. Innbo Shim, Admin. Dir. Service organization that supports and promotes independent film and video production. Services include low-cost 16mm, Super-8, S-VHS, and AVID equipment rental, resource library, group legal and health plans, monthly magazine, seminars, grants program, annual film and video festival, nonprofit sponsorship, exhibition program, and advocacy and significant discounts on film and video related products and services. *Membership:* 3,300 plus. *Dues:* $45. *Meetings:* Annual Festival. *Publications: Release Print; AEIOU (Alternative Exhibition Information of the Universe); Media Catalog* (over 200 titles of independent media projects completed with FAF's nonprofit fiscal sponsorship).

***Film/Video Arts (F/VA)**. 817 Broadway, 2nd Floor, New York, NY 10003. (212)673-9361. Fax (212)475-3467. Frank Millspaugh, Exec. Dir. Film/Video Arts is the largest nonprofit media arts center in the New York region. Dedicated to the advancement of emerging and established media artists of diverse backgrounds, F/VA is unique in providing a fertile environment where aspiring producers can obtain training, rent equipment, and edit their projects all under one roof. Every year more than 2,500 individuals participate in F/VA's programs. There are more than 50 courses offered each semester, covering topics such as rudimentary technical training in 16mm filmmaking and video production, advanced editing courses in online systems, history, cultural analysis, installation art, fundraising, grant writing, and distribution. F/VA is supported by the New York State Council on the Arts, the National Endowment for the Arts, and numerous foundations and corporations, and is therefore able to offer courses and production services at the lowest possible rates. Artists who got their start at F/VA include Jim Jarmusch, Mira Nair, Leslie Harris, Kevin Smith, and Cheryl Dunye. F/VA takes pride in meeting the needs of a broad range of filmmakers, working on features, documentaries, shorts, experimental pieces, industrials, cable shows, music videos and more by offering affordable services essential to the creation of their work and development of their careers. *Membership:* $40, indiv., $70, organization.

Freedom of Information Center. 127 Neff Annex, University of Missouri, Columbia, MO 65211. (573)882-4856. Fax (573)884-4963. E-mail Kathleen_Edwards@jmail.missouri.edu. Website http://www.missouri.edu/~foiwww. Kathleen Edwards, Manager. The Freedom of Information Center is a research library which maintains files documenting actions by governments, media, and society affecting the movement and content of information. Open 8:00 a.m. to 5:00 p.m., Monday through Friday, except holidays. Located at Missouri's School of Journalism. *Membership:* Research and referral services are available to all. *Publications: Access to Public Information: A Resource Guide to Government in Columbia and Boone County, Missouri.* Updated periodically at Website.

George Eastman House (formerly International Museum of Photography at George Eastman House). 900 East Ave., Rochester, NY 14607. (716)271-3361. Fax (716)271-3970. Website http://www.eastman.org. Anthony Bannon, Dir. World-renowned museum of photography and cinematography established to preserve, collect, and exhibit photographic art and technology, film materials, and related literature, and to serve as a memorial to George Eastman. Services include archives, traveling exhibitions, research library, school of film preservation, center for the conservation of photographic materials, and photographic print service. Educational programs, exhibitions, films, symposia, music events, tours, and internship stipends offered. Eastman's turn-of-the-century mansion and gardens have been restored to their original grandeur. *Dues:* $40, library; $50, family; $40, indiv.; $36, student; $30, senior citizen; $75, Contributor; $125, Sustainer; $250, Patron; $500, Benefactor; $1,000, George Eastman Society. *Membership:* 4,000. *Publications: IMAGE; Microfiche Index to Collections; Newsletter; Annual Report: The George Eastman House and Gardens; Masterpieces of Photography from the George Eastman House Collections;* and exhibition catalogs.

The George Lucas Educational Foundation. PO Box 3494, San Rafael, CA 94912. (415)662-1600. Fax (415)662-1605. E-mail edutopia@glef.org. Website http://glef.org. Dr. Milton Chen, Exec. Dir. The Foundation promotes innovative efforts to improve education, especially those that integrate technology with teaching and learning, so all students will be prepared to learn and live in an increasingly complex world. Projects include a documentary film and resource book, a Website, and bi-annual newsletter, all of which feature compelling education programs from around the country. The target audience is community and opinion leaders, parents, educators, media, corporate executives, and elected officials. The Foundation works to give these stakeholders useful tools to develop, make, and sustain changes in teaching and learning. The George Lucas Educational Foundation is a private operating foundation, not a grantmaking organization. *Publication: EDUTOPIA* (bi-annual newsletter).

Graphic Arts Technical Foundation (GATF). 200 Deer Run Rd., Sewickley, PA 15143-2600. (412)741-6860. Fax (412)741-2311. E-mail info@gatf.org. Website http://www.gatf.org. George Ryan, Pres. GATF is a member-supported, nonprofit, scientific, technical, and educational organization dedicated to the advancement of graphic communications industries worldwide. For 73 years GATF has developed leading-edge technologies and practices for printing, and each year the Foundation develops new products, services, and training programs to meet the evolving needs of the industry. *Membership:* 1,600 corporate members, 520 teachers, 100 students. *Dues:* $40, teachers; $30, students; corporate dues based on percentage of sales (ranges from $350-$4,000). *Meetings:* Annual GATF/PIA Joint Fall Conference. *Publications: Professional Print Buying; Computer-to-Plate: Automating the Printing Industry; Understanding Electronic Communications: Printing in the Information Age; On-Demand Printing: The Revolution in Digital and Customized Printing.*

Great Plains National ITV Library (GPN). PO Box 80669, Lincoln, NE 68501-0669. (402)472-2007, (800)228-4630. Fax (800)306-2330. E-mail gpn@unl.edu. Website http://gpn.unl.edu. Steven Lenzen,, Dir. Produces and distributes educational media, video, laserdiscs, and CD-ROMs, prints and Internet courses. Available for purchase or lease for broadcast use. *Publications: GPN Educational Video Catalogs* by curriculum areas and periodic brochures. Complete listig of GPN's product line is availble via the Internet along with online purchasing. Free previews available.

Health Sciences Communications Association (HeSCA). One Wedgewood Dr., Suite 27, Jewett City, CT 06351-2428. (203)376-5915. Fax (203)376-6621. E-mail HeSCAOne@aol.com. Website http://www.hesca.washington.edu. Ronald Sokolowski, Exec. Dir. An affiliate of AECT, HeSCA is a nonprofit organization dedicated to the sharing of ideas, skills, resources, and techniques to enhance communications and educational technology in the health sciences. It seeks to nurture the professional growth of its members, to serve as a professional focal point for those engaged in health sciences communications, and to convey the concerns, issues, and concepts of health sciences communications to other organizations which influence and are affected by the profession. International in scope and diverse in membership, HeSCA is supported by medical and veterinary schools, hospitals, medical associations, and businesses where media is used to create and disseminate health information. *Membership:* 150. *Dues:* $150, indiv.; $195, institutional ($150 additional institutional dues); $60, retiree; $75, student; $1,000, sustaining. All include subscriptions to the journal and newsletter. *Meetings:* Annual Meetings, May-June. *Publications: Journal of Biocommunications; Feedback* (newsletter); *Patient Education Sourcebook Vol. II.*

Hollywood Film Archive. 8391 Beverly Blvd., #321, Hollywood, CA 90048. (213)933-3345. D. Richard Baer, Dir. Archival organization for information about feature films produced worldwide, from the early silents to the present. *Publications:* comprehensive movie reference works for sale, including *Variety Film Reviews* (1907–1996) and the *American Film Institute Catalogs* (1893–1910, 1911–20, 1921–30, 1931–40, 1941–50, 1961–70), as well as the *Film Superlist* (1894–1939, 1940–1949, 1950–1959) volumes, which provide information both on copyrights and on motion pictures in the public domain, and *Harrison's Reports and Film Reviews* (1919–1962).

HOPE Reports, Inc. 58 Carverdale Dr., Rochester, NY 14618-4004. (716)442-1310. Fax (716)442-1725. E-mail hopereport@aol.com. Thomas W. Hope, Chairman and CEO; Mabeth S. Hope, Vice Pres. Supplies statistics, marketing information, trends, forecasts, and salary and media studies to the visual communications industries through printed reports, custom studies, consulting, and by telephone. Clients and users in the US and abroad include manufacturers, dealers, producers, and media users in business, government, health sciences, religion, education, and community agencies. *Publications: Hope Reports Presentation Media Events Calendar* (annual); *Video Post-Production; Media Market Trends; Educational Media Trends Through the 1990's; LCD Panels and Projectors; Overhead Projection System; Presentation Slides; Producer & Video Post Wages & Salaries; Noncommercial AV Wages & Salaries; Corporate Media Salaries; Digital Photography: Pictures of Tomorrow; Hope Reports Top 100 Contract Producers; Contract Production II; Executive Compensation; Media Production; Outsource or Insource.*

Institute for Development of Educational Activities, Inc. (|I|D|E|A|). 259 Regency Ridge, Dayton, OH 45459. (937)434-6969. Fax (937)434-5203. E-mail IDEADayton@aol.com. Website http://www.idea.org. Dr. Steven R. Thompson, Pres. |I|D|E|A| is an action-oriented research and development organization originating from the Charles F. Kettering Foundation. It was established in 1965 to assist the educational community in bridging the gap that separates research and innovation from actual practice in the schools. Its goal is to design and test new responses to improve education and to create arrangements that support local application. Activities include developing new and improved processes, systems, and materials; training local facilitators to use the change processes; and providing information and services about improved methods and materials. |I|D|E|A| sponsors an annual fellowship program for administrators and conducts seminars for school administrators and teachers.

Institute for the Future (IFTF). 2744 Sand Hill Rd., Menlo Park, CA 94025-7020. (650)854-6322. Fax (650)854-7850. Website http://www.iftf.org. Robert Johansen, Pres. The cross-disciplinary professionals at IFTF have been providing global and domestic businesses and organizations with research-based forecasts and action-oriented tools for strategic decision-making since 1968. IFTF is a nonprofit applied research and consulting firm dedicated to understanding technological, economic, and societal changes and their long-range domestic and global consequences. Its work falls into four main areas: Strategic Planning, Emerging Technologies, Health Care Horizons, and Public Sector Initiatives. IFTF works with clients to think systematically about the future, identify socioeconomic trends and evaluate their long-term implications, identify potential leading-edge markets around the world, understand the global marketplace, track the implications of emerging technologies for business and society, take advantage of expert judgment and data resources, offer an independent view of the big picture, and facilitate strategic planning processes.

Institute for the Transfer of Technology to Education (ITTE) see National School Boards Association.

Instructional Telecommunications Council (ITC). One Dupont Cir., NW, Suite 410, Washington, DC, 20036-1176. (202)293-3110. Fax (202)833-2467. E-mail cdalziel@aacc.nche.edu. Website http://www.sinclair.edu/communit/itc. Christine Dalziel, contact person. ITC represents more than 500 educational institutions from the United States and Canada that are involved in higher educational instructional telecommunications and distance learning. ITC holds annual professional development meetings, tracks national legislation, supports research, and provides members a forum to share expertise and materials. *Membership:* 504. *Dues:* $1,500, Regional Consortia; $525, Institutional; $452, Associate; $550, Corporate; $125, Indiv.. *Meetings:* 1999 Telelearning Conference. *Publications: New Connections: A Guide to Distance Education* (2nd ed); *New Connections: A College President's Guide to Distance Education; Federal Disability Law and Distance Learning; ITC News* (monthly publication/newsletter); ITC Listserv.

International Association for Language Learning Technology (IALL). IALL Business Manager, Malacester College, 1600 Grand Ave., St. Paul, MN 55105-1899. (612)696-6336. E-mail browne@macalstr.edu. Website http://polyglot.lss.wisc.edu/IALL/. Nina Garrett, Pres. Thomas Browne, Bus. Mgr. An affiliate of AECT, IALL is a professional organization working for the improvement of second language learning through technology in learning centers and classrooms. *Members:* 700. *Dues:* $40, regular; $15, student; $40, library; $55 commercial. *Meetings*: Biennial IALL conferences treat the entire range of topics related to technology in language learning as well as management and planning. IALL also sponsors sessions at conferences of organizations with related interests, including AECT. *Publications: IALL Journal of Language Learning Technologies* (3 times annually); materials for labs, teaching, and technology.

International Association of Business Communicators (IABC). One Hallidie Plaza, Suite 600, San Francisco, CA 94102. (415)544-4700. Fax (415)544-4747. E-mail service_centre@iabc.com. Website http://www.iabc.com. Elizabeth Allan, Pres. and CEO. IABC is the worldwide association for the communication and public relations profession. It is founded on the principle that the better an organization communicates with all its audiences, the more successful and effective it will be in meeting its objectives. IABC is dedicated to fostering communication excellence, contributing more effectively to organizations' goals worldwide, and being a model of communication effectiveness. *Membership:* 13,500 plus. *Dues:* $175 in addition to local and regional dues. *Meetings:* 1999, June 20-23, Washington, DC. 2000, June 25-28, Vancouver. *Publication: Communication World.*

International Association of School Librarianship (IASL). Box 34069, Dept. 300, Seattle, WA 98124-1069. (604)925-0266. Fax: (604)925-0566. E-mail iasl@rockland.com. Website http://www.rhi.hi.is/~anne/iasl.html. Dr. Ken Haycock, Executive Dir. Seeks to encourage development of school libraries and library programs throughout the world, to promote professional preparation and continuing education of school librarians, to achieve collaboration among school libraries of the world, to foster relationships between school librarians and other professionals connected with children and youth, and to coordinate activities, conferences and other projects in the field of school librarianship. *Membership:* 900 plus. *Dues:* $50, personal and institution for North America, Western Europe, Japan and Australia; $15 for all other countries. *Meetings:* 1999, Birmingham, AL, November. *Publications: IASL Newsletter* (q.); *School Libraries Worldwide* (semi-annual); *Conference Professionals and Research Papers(annual). Connections: School Library Associations and Contact People Worldwide; Sustaining the Vision: A Collection of Articles and Papers on Research in School Librarianship; School Librarianship: International Issues and Perspectives; Information Rich but Knowledge Poor? Issues for Schools and Libraries Worldwide: Selected Papers from the 26th Annual Conferences of the IASL.*

International Center of Photography (ICP). 1130 Fifth Ave., New York, NY 10128. (212)860-1777. Fax (212)360-6490. ICP Midtown, 1133 Avenue of the Americas, New York, NY 10036. (212)768-4680. Fax (212)768-4688. Website http://www.icp.org. Willis Hartshorn, Dir.; Phyllis Levine, Dir. of Public Information. A comprehensive photographic institution whose exhibitions, publications, collections, and educational programs embrace all aspects of photography from aesthetics to technique; from the 19th century to the present; from master photographers to newly emerging talents; from photojournalism to the avant garde. Changing exhibitions, lectures, seminars, workshops, museum shops, and screening rooms make ICP a complete photographic resource. ICP offers a two-year NYU-ICP Master of Arts Degree in Studio Art with Studies in Photography and one-year certificate programs in Documentary Photography and Photojournalism and General Studies in Photography. *Membership:* 6,500. *Dues:* $50, Indiv.; $60, Double; $125, Supporting Patron; $250, Photography Circle; $500, Silver Card Patron; $1,000, Gold Card Patron; $2,500 Benefactor, corporate memberships available. *Meetings:* ICP Infinity Awards. *Publications: Reflections in a Glass Eye; Images from the Machine Age: Selections from the Daniel Cowin Collection; Library of Photography; A Singular Elegance: The Photographs of Baron Adolph de Meyer; Talking Pictures: People Speak About the Photographs That Speak to Them; ·Encyclopedia of Photography: Master Photographs from PFA Collection; Man Ray in Fashion; Quarterly Program Guide; Quarterly Exhibition Schedule.*

International Council for Educational Media (ICEM). ICEM, Robert LeFranc, ICEM Secretariat, 29 rue d'Ulm, 25230 Oaris, Cedex 05, France. 33-1-46. Fax 33-1-46-35-78-89. Ms. Jackie Hall, General Secretariat, FUS, Grup de Fundacions, Provenca 324,3r -E08037 Barcelona, Spain; 34 3 458 30 04, fax 34 3 458 87 10. E-mail icem-cime@bcn.servicom.es. Website http://www.cndp.fr/icem icem-cime@bcn.servicom.es and http://www.cndp.fr/icem. Richard Cornell, President and US member, University of Central Florida, Education Room 310, Orlando, FL, 32816-0992. (407)823-2053, fax (407)823-5135. E-mail cornell@pegasus.cc.ucf.edu. Website http://pegasus.cc.ucf.edu/~cornell/icem-usa. Deputy Member from the United States: Marina McIsaac, College of Education, Box 870111, Arizona State University,Tempe, AZ 85287-0111, (602)965-4961, fax (602)965-7193. E-mail mmcisaac@asu.edu. The objective of ICEM is to provide a channel for the international exchange of information and experience in the field of educational technology, with particular reference to preschool, primary, and secondary education, technical and vocational training, and teacher and continuing education; to encourage organizations with a professional responsibility for the design, production, promotion, distribution, and use of educational media in member countries; to promote an understanding of the concept of educational technology on the part of both educators and those involved in their training; to contribute to the pool of countries by the sponsorship of practical projects involving international cooperation and co-production; to advise manufacturers of hardware and software on the needs of an information service on developments in educational technology; to provide consultancy for the benefit of member countries; and to cooperate with other international organizations in promoting the concept of educational technology. ICEM has established official relations with UNESCO.

International Graphics Arts Education Association (IGAEA). 200 Deer Run Rd., Sewickley, PA 15143-2328. (412)741-6860. Fax (412)741-2311. Website http://www.igaea.org. 1998-99 Pres. Wanda Murphy, wmurphy184@aol.com, (704)922-8891, fax (704)922-8891. IGAEA is an association of educators in partnership with industry, dedicated to sharing theories, principles, techniques, and processes relating to graphic communications and imaging technology. Teachers network to share and improve teaching and learning opportunities in fields related to graphic arts, imaging technology, graphic design, graphic communications, journalism, photography, and other areas related to the large and rapidly changing fields in the printing, publishing, packaging, and allied industries. *Membership:* approx. 600. *Dues:* $20, regular; $12, associate (retired); $5, student; $10, library; $50-$200, sustaining membership based on number of employees. *Meetings:* 1999, Ferris State University, Big Rapids, MI, Aug 1-6. *Publications: The Communicator; Visual Communications Journal* (annual); *Research and Resources Reports.*

*International Information Management Congress (IMC). 1650 38th St., #205W, Boulder, CO 80301. (303)440-7085. Fax (303)440-7234. Website http://www.iimc.org. John A. Lacy, CEO. IMC's mission is to facilitate the successful adoption of imaging, document management, and workflow technologies. IMC's primary activities include conferences, exhibitions, publications, and membership functions. *Dues:* $85, affiliate (any individual with an interest in the document-based information systems field); $200, associate (any association or society with common goals within the industry); $350-$5100, sustaining (any corporate organization with a common interest in the industry). *Meeting:* Future exhibitions planned for Dubai, UAE, and Singapore (please contact IMC for more information). *Publication: Document World Magazine* (bi-monthly).

International Society for Technology in Education (ISTE) (formerly International Council for Computers in Education [ICCE]). 1787 Agate St., Eugene, OR 97403-1923. (541)346-4414. Fax (541)346-5890. E-mail iste@oregon.uoregon.edu. Website http://www.iste.org. David Moursund, CEO; Maia S. Howes, Exec. Sec. ISTE is the largest nonprofit professional organization dedicated to the improvement of all levels of education through the use of computer-based technology. Technology-using educators from all over the world rely on ISTE for information, inspiration, ideas, and updates on the latest electronic information systems available to the educational community. ISTE is a prominent information center and source of leadership to communicate and collaborate with educational professionals, policy makers, and other organizations worldwide. *Membership:* 12,000 individuals, 75 organizational affiliates, 25 Private Sector Council members. *Dues:* $58, indiv.; $220, all-inclusive (US); $420, Technology Leadership Membership; $1,500– $5,000, Private Sector Council. *Meetings:* Tel-Ed and NECC. *Publications: The Update Newsletter* (7/yr.); *Learning and Leading with Technology* (formerly *The Computing Teacher*) (8/yr.); *The Journal of Research on Computing in Education* (q.); guides to instructional uses of computers at the precollege level and in teacher training, about 80 books, and a range of distance education courses that carry graduate-level credit.

International Society for Performance Improvement (ISPI). 1300 L St. NW, Suite 1250, Washington, DC 20005. (202)408-7969. Fax (202)408-7972. E-mail info@ispi.org. Website http://www.ispi.org. Richard D. Battaglia, Exec. Dir. ISPI is an international association dedicated to increasing productivity in the workplace through the application of performance and instructional technologies. Founded in 1962, its members are located throughout the US, Canada, and 45 other countries. The society offers an awards program recognizing excellence in the field. *Membership:* 5,500. *Dues:* $125, active members; $40, students and retirees. *Meetings:* Annual Conference and Expo, spring; Human Performance Technology Institute (HPTI), late spring and fall. HPTI is an educational institute providing knowledge, skills and resources necessary to make a successful transition from a training department to a human performance improvement organization. Annual Conference & Expo will be held in Cincinnati OH, April 10-14, 2000. *Publications: Performance Improvement Journal* (10/yr.); *Performance Improvement Quarterly*; *News & Notes* (newsletter, 10/yr.); *Annual Membership Directory*; *ISPI Book Program and Catalog.*

International Telecommunications Satellite Organization (INTELSAT). 3400 International Dr. NW, Washington, DC 20008. (202)944-7500. Fax (202)944-7890. Website http://www.intelsat.int. Conng L. Kullman, Dir. Gen. and CEO; Tony A. Trujillo, Dir., Corporate Communications. INTELSAT owns and operates a global communications satellite system providing capacity for voice, video, corporate/private networks, and Internet in more than 200 countries and territories. In addition, the INTELSAT system provides educational and medical programming via satellite for selected participants around the world.

International Teleconferencing Association (ITCA). 100 Four Falls Corporate Center, Suite 105, West Conshohocken, PA 19428. (610)941-2015. Fax (610)941-2015. E-mail staff@itca.org and president@itca.org. Website http://www.itca.org. Henry S. Grove III, Pres.; Eileen Hering, Manager, Member Services; Rosalie DiStasio, Asst. Manager, Member Services. ITCA, an international nonprofit association, is dedicated to the growth and development of teleconferencing as a profession and an industry. ITCA provides programs and services which foster the professional development of its members, champions teleconferencing and related as communications tools, recognizes and promotes broader applications and the development of teleconferencing and related technologies, and serves as the authoritative resource for information and research on teleconferencing and related technologies. *Membership:* ITCA represents over 1,000 teleconferencing professionals throughout the world. ITCA members use teleconferencing services advise customers and vendors, conduct research, teach courses via teleconference, and teach about teleconferencing. They represent such diverse industry segments as health care, aerospace, government, pharmaceutical, education, insurance, finance and banking, telecommunications, and manufacturing. *Dues:* $6,250, Platinum Sustaining; $2,500, Gold Sustaining; $1,250, Sustaining; $625, Organizational; $325, Small Business; $125, Indiv.; and $35, Student. *Meetings:* Spring and Fall MultimediaCom Shows, Spring show in San Jose, Fall show in Boston, August 30th-September 2th. *Publications: Forum* newsletter; *Member Directories; White Paper;Teleconferencing Success Stories.*

ITVA (International Television Association). 6311 N. O'Connor Rd., Suite 230, Irving, TX 75039. (972)869-1112. Fax (972)869-2980. E-mail itvahq@worldnet.att.net. Website http://www.itva.org. Fred M. Wehrli, Exec. Dir. Founded in 1968, ITVA's mission is to advance the video profession, to serve the needs and interests of its members, and to promote the growth and quality of video and related media. Association members are video, multimedia, and film professionals working in or serving the corporate, governmental, institutional, or educational markets. ITVA provides professional development opportunities through local, regional, and national workshops, video festivals, networking, and publications. ITVA welcomes anyone who is interested in professional video and who is seeking to widen horizons either through career development or networking. ITVA offers its members discounts on major medical, production, and liability insurance; hotel, car rental, and long distance telephone discounts; and a MasterCard program. The association is also a member of the Small Business Legislative Council. *Membership:* 9,000; 77 commercial member companies. *Dues:* $150, Indiv.; $425, Organizational; $1,750, Commercial Silver; $750, Commercial Bronze. *Meetings:* Annual International Conference, early summer. *Publications: ITVA News* (6/yr.); *Membership Directory* (annual); *Handbook of Treatments*; *It's a Business First . . . and a Creative Outlet Second*; *Handbook of Forms*; *Copyright Basics for Video Producers; How to Survive Being Laid Off; The Effectiveness of Video in Organizations: An Annotated Bibliography; Management Matters; A Report on the IRS Guidelines Classifying Workers in the Video Industry.*

International Visual Literacy Association, Inc. (IVLA). Gonzaga University, E. 502 Boone AD 25, Spokane, WA 99258-0001. (509)328-4220 ext. 3478, fax (509)324-5812. E-mail bclark@soe.gonzaga.edu. Richard Couch, Pres. Dr. Barbara I. Clark, Exec. Treas. IVLA provides a multidisciplinary forum for the exploration, presentation, and discussion of all aspects of visual learning, thinking, communication, and expression. It also serves as a communication link bonding professionals from many disciplines who are creating and sustaining the study of the nature of visual experiences and literacy. It promotes and evaluates research, programs, and projects intended to increase effective use of visual communication in education, business, the arts, and commerce. IVLA was founded in 1968 to promote the concept of visual literacy and is an affiliate of AECT. *Dues:* $40, regular; $20, student and retired; $45 outside US. *Meeting:* Meets in conjunction with annual AECT Convention. *Publications: Journal of Visual Literacy*; *Readings from Annual Conferences.*

ITA, The International Recording Media Association. 182 Nassau St., Princeton, NJ 08542-7005. (609)279-1700. Fax (609)279-1999. E-mail info@recordingmedia.org. Website http://www.recordingmedia.org. Charles Van Horn, Exec. V.P.; Phil Russo, Dir. of Operations. IRMA is the advocate for the growth and development of all reading media and is the industry forum for the exchange of information regarding global trends and innovations. Members include recording media manufacturers, rights holders to video programs, recording and playback equipment manufacturers, and audio and video replicators. For more than 29 years, the Association has provided vital information and educational services throughout the magnetic and optical recording media industries. By promoting a greater awareness of marketing, merchandising, and technical developments, the association serves all areas of the entertainment, information, and delivery systems industries. *Membership:* 450 corporations. *Dues:* Corporate membership dues based on sales volume. *Meetings:* 30th Annual Conference (IRMA Executive Forum) LaQuita Resort, LaQuita, CA. March 15-19, 2000. Mar 10-14, 1999, Amelia Island, FL; REPLItech North America, Jun 8-10 1999, San Francisco; *Publications: Membership Newsletter*; *Seminar Proceedings*; *1999 International Source Directory.*

Library Administration and Management Association (LAMA). 50 E. Huron St., Chicago, IL 60611. (312)280-5038. Fax (312)280-5033. E-mail lama@ala.org. Website http://www.ala.org/lama. Karen Muller, Exec. Dir.; Thomas L. Wilding, Pres. July 1998-July 1999. Carol L. Anderson, Pres. Elect. A division of the American Library Association, LAMA provides an organizational framework for encouraging the study of administrative theory, improving the practice of administration in libraries, and identifying and fostering administrative skills. Toward these ends, the association is responsible for all elements of general administration that are common to more than one type of library. Sections include: Buildings and Equipment Section (BES); Fundraising & Financial Development Section (FRFDS); Library Organization & Management Section (LOMS); Personnel Administration Section (PAS); Public Relation Section (PRS); Systems & Services Section (SASS); and Statistics Section (SS). *Membership:* 4,996. *Dues:* $45 (in addition to ALA membership); $15, library school students. *Meetings:* 1999 ALA Annual Conference, New Orleans, Jun 24-Jun 30. 2000, Chicago, Jul 6-12. ALA Midwinter Meeting, 1999. 2000, San Antonio, Jan 14-19, 2001, Washington, DC, Jan 12-17. *Publications: Library Administration & Management* (q); *LEADS from LAMA* (electronic newsletter, irregular).

Library and Information Technology Association (LITA). 50 E. Huron St., Chicago, IL 60611. (312)280-4270, (800)545-2433, ext. 4270. Fax (312)280-3257. E-mail lita@ala.org. Website http://www.lita.org. Jacqueline Mundell, Exec. Dir. An affiliate of the American Library Association, LITA is concerned with library automation, the information sciences, and the design, development, and implementation of automated systems in those fields, including systems development, electronic data processing, mechanized information retrieval, operations research, standards development, telecommunications, video communications, networks and collaborative efforts, management techniques, information technology, optical technology, artificial intelligence and expert systems, and other related aspects of audiovisual activities and hardware applications. *Membership:* 5,400. *Dues:* $45 plus membership in ALA; $25, library school students; $35, first year. *Meetings:* National Forum, fall. *Publications: Information Technology and Libraries*; *LITA Newsletter* (electronic only; see Website).

Library of Congress. James Madison Bldg., 101 Independence Ave. SE, Washington, DC 20540. (202)707-5000. Fax (202)707-1389. National Reference Service, (202)707-5522. Website http://www.loc.gov. The Library of Congress is the major source of research and information for the Congress. In its role as the national library, it catalogs and classifies library materials in some 460 languages, distributes the data in both printed and electronic form, and makes its vast collections available through interlibrary loan and on-site to anyone over high school age. The Library is the largest library in the world, with more than 115 million items on 532 miles of bookshelves. The collections include more than 17 million cataloged books, 2 million recordings, 12 million photographs, 4 million maps, and 49 million manuscripts. It contains the world's largest television and film archive, acquiring materials through gift, purchase, and copyright deposit. In 1998, the materials produced by the Library in Braille and recorded formats for persons who are blind or physically challenged were circulated to a readership of 769,000. The collections of the Motion Picture, Broadcasting and Recorded Sound Division include more than 770,000 moving images. The Library's public catalog, as well as other files containing copyright and legislative information, are available over the Internet.

Lister Hill National Center for Biomedical Communications. National Library of Medicine, 8600 Rockville Pike, Bethesda, MD 20894. (301)496-4441. Fax (301)402-0118. Website http://www.nlm.nih.gov. Alexa McCray, Ph.D., Dir. The center conducts research and development programs in three major categories: Computer and Information Science; Biomedical Image and Communications Engineering; and Educational Technology Development. Major efforts of the center include its involvement with the Unified Medical Language System (UMLS) project; research and development in the use of expert systems to embody the factual and procedural knowledge of human experts; research in the use of electronic technologies to distribute biomedical information not represented in text and in the storage and transmission of x-ray images over the Internet; and the development and demonstration of new educational technologies, including the use of microcomputer technology with videodisc-based images, for training health care professionals. A Learning Center for Interactive Technology serves as a focus for displaying new and effective applications of educational technologies to faculties and staff of health sciences, educational institutions and other visitors, and health professions educators are assisted in the use of such technologies through training, demonstrations, and consultations.

Magazine Publishers of America (MPA). 919 Third Ave., 22nd Floor, New York, NY 10022. (212)872-3700. Fax (212)888-4217. E-mail infocenter@magazine.org. Website http://www.magazine.org. Donald D. Kummerfeld, Pres. MPA is the trade association of the consumer magazine industry. MPA promotes the greater and more effective use of magazine advertising, with ad campaigns in the trade press and in member magazines, presentations to advertisers and their ad agencies, and magazine days in cities around the US. MPA runs educational seminars, conducts surveys of its members on a variety of topics, represents the magazine industry in Washington, DC, and maintains an extensive library on magazine publishing. *Membership:* 230 publishers representing more than 1,200 magazines. *Meetings:* 1999 American Magazine Conference, Boca Resort & Country Club, Boca Raton, FL, Oct 28-31; 2000, Southampton Princess, Bermuda, Oct 22-25. *Publications: Newsletter of Consumer Marketing*; *Newsletter of Research*; *Newsletter of International Publishing*; *Magazine*; *Washington Newsletter*.

Medical Library Association (MLA). 6 N. Michigan Ave., Suite 300, Chicago, IL 60602-4805. (312)419-9094. Fax (312)419-9094. E-mail info@mlahq.org. Website http://www.mlanet.org. Rachael K. Anderson, Pres.; Carla J. Funk, Exec. Dir., Kimberly Pierceall, Dir. of Communications. MLA is a professional organization of 5,000 individuals and institutions in the health sciences information field, dedicated to fostering medical and allied scientific libraries, promoting professional excellence and leadership of its members, and exchanging medical literature among its members. *Membership:* 5,000 individual and institutional. *Dues:* $110, regular; $25, students; $75, introductory; $65, affiliate; $2100, life. Institutional dues depend on number of periodical subscriptions. *Meeting:* 1999, Chicago, May 14-20. *Publications: MLA News* (newsletter, 10/yr.); *Bulletin of the Medical Library Association* (q.); *Dockit* series; monographs.

Mid-continent Regional Educational Laboratory (McREL). 2550 S. Parker Rd., Suite 500, Aurora, CO 80014. (303)337-0990. Fax (303)337-3005. E-mail info@mcrel.org. Website http://www.mcrel.org. J. Timothy Waters, Exec. Dir. One of 10 Office of Educational Research and Improvement (OERI) regional educational laboratories designed to help educators and policymakers work toward excellence in education for all students. Using the best available information and the experience and expertise of professionals, McREL seeks to identify solutions to education problems, tries new approaches, furnishes research results, conducts evaluation and policy studies, and provides training to teachers and administrators. McREL serves Colorado, Kansas, Missouri, Nebraska, North Dakota, South Dakota and Wyoming. Its specialty areas are curriculum, learning, and instruction. *Publications: Changing Schools* (q. newsletter); *Noteworthy* (annual monograph on topics of current interest in education reform). Check web site for catalog listing many other publications.

Minorities in Media (MIM). Wayne State University, College of Education, Instructional Technology, Detroit, Michigan 48202. (313)577-5139. Fax (313)577-1693. E-mail GPOWELL@CMS.CC.WAYNE.EDU. Dr. Gary C. Powell, Pres. MIM is a special interest group of AECT that responds to the challenge of preparing students of color for an ever-changing international marketplace and recognizes the unique educational needs of today's diverse learners. It supports the creative development of curricula, instructional strategies, and computer-based instructional materials which promote an acceptance and appreciation of racial and cultural diversity. It promotes the effective use of educational communications and technology in the learning process. MIM seeks to facilitate changes in instructional design and development, traditional pedagogy, and instructional delivery systems by responding to and meeting the significant challenge of educating diverse individuals to take their place in an ever-changing international marketplace. MIM encourages all of AECT's body of members to creatively develop curricula, instructional treatments, instructional strategies, and instructional materials which promote an acceptance and appreciation of racial and cultural diversity. Doing so will make learning for all more effective, relevant, meaningful, motivating, and enjoyable. MIM actively supports the Wes McJulien Minority Scholarship, and selects the winner. *Membership:* contact MIM president. *Dues:* $20, student; $30, non-student. *Publications:* newsletter is forthcoming online. The MIM listserv is a membership benefit.

Museum Computer Network (MCN). 8720 Georgia Ave., Suite 501, Silver Spring, MD 20910. (301)585-4413. Fax (301)495-0810. E-mail mcn@athena.mit.edu; membership office: mdevine@asis.org. Website http://world.std.com/nmcn/index.html. Michele Devine, Admin. Guy Herman, Pres. As a nonprofit professional association, membership in MCN provides access to professionals committed to using computer technology to achieve the cultural aims of museums. Members include novices and experts, museum professionals, and vendors and consultants, working in application areas from collections management to administrative computing. Activities include advisory services and special projects. *Dues:* $300, sponsor; $150, vendor; $150, institution; $60, indiv. *Meeting:* Annual Conference, held in the fall; educational workshops. *Publications: Spectra* (newsletter); *CMI.* Subscription to *Spectra* is available to libraries only for $75 plus $10 surcharge for delivery.

Museum of Modern Art, Circulating Film and Video Library. 11 W. 53rd St., New York, NY 10019. (212)708-9530. Fax (212)708-9531. E-mail circfilm@moma.org. Website http://www.moma.org. William Sloan, Libr. Provides film and video rentals and sales of over 1300 titles covering the history of film from the 1890s to the present. It also incorporates the Circulating Video Library, an important collection of work by leading video artists. The Circulating Library continues to add to its holdings of early silents, contemporary documentaries, animation, avant-garde and independents and to make these available to viewers who otherwise would not have the opportunity to see them. The Circulating Film Library has 16mm prints available for rental, sale, and lease. A few of the 16mm titles are available on videocassette. The classic film collection is not. The video collection is available in all formats for rental and sale. *Publications:* Information on titles may be found in the free *Price List,* available from the Library. *Circulating Film and Video Catalog Vols. 1 and 2,* a major source book on film and history, is available from the Museum's Publications, Sales, and Service Dept. (For mail order, a form is included in the *Price List.*).

National Aeronautics and Space Administration (NASA). NASA Headquarters, Code FE, Washington, DC 20546. (202)358-1110. Fax (202)358-3048. E-mail malcom.phelps@hq.nasa.gov. Website http://www.nasa.gov. Dr. Malcom V. Phelps, Asst. Dir.; Frank C. Owens, Dir., Education Division. From elementary through postgraduate school, NASA's educational programs are designed to capture students' interests in science, mathematics, and technology at an early age; to channel more students into science, engineering, and technology career paths; and to enhance the knowledge, skills, and experiences of teachers and university faculty. NASA's educational programs include NASA Spacelink (an electronic information system); videoconferences (60-minute interactive staff development videoconferences to be delivered to schools via satellite); and NASA Television (informational and educational television programming). Additional information is available from the Education Division at NASA Headquarters and counterpart offices at the nine NASA field centers. Over 200,000 educators make copies of Teacher Resource Center Network materials each year, and thousands of teachers participate in interactive video teleconferencing, use Spacelink, and watch NASA Television. Additional information may be obtained from Spacelink (spacelink.msfc.nasa.gov or http://spacelink.msfc.nasa.gov).

National Alliance for Media Arts and Culture (NAMAC). 346 9th St., San Francisco, CA 94103. (415)431-1391. Fax (415)431-1392. E-mail namac@namac.org. Website http://www.namac.org. Helen DeMichel, National Dir. NAMAC is a nonprofit organization dedicated to increasing public understanding of and support for the field of media arts in the US. Members include media centers, cable access centers, universities, and media artists, as well as other individuals and organizations providing services for production, education, exhibition, distribution, and preservation of video, film, audio, and intermedia. NAMAC's information services are available to the general public, arts and non-arts organizations, businesses, corporations, foundations, government agencies, schools, and universities. *Membership:* 200 organizations, 150 individuals. *Dues:* $50–$250, institutional (depending on annual budget); $50, indiv. *Publications: Media Arts Information Network; The National Media Education Directory.*

National Association for the Education of Young Children (NAEYC). 1509 16th St. NW, Washington, DC 20036-1426. (202)232-8777, (800)424-2460. Fax (202)328-1846. E-mail naeyc@naeyc.org. Website http://www.naeyc.org. Marilyn M. Smith, Exec. Dir.; Pat Spahr, contact person. Dedicated to improving the quality of care and education provided to young children (birth-8 years). *Membership:* over 100,000. *Dues:* $25. *Meeting:* 1999 Annual Conference, Nov 10-13, New Orleans. *Publications: Young Children* (journal); more than 60 books, posters, videos, and brochures.

National Association for Visually Handicapped (NAVH). 22 W. 21st St., 6th Floor, New York, NY 10010. (212)889-3141. Fax (212)727-2931. E-mail staff@navh.org. Website http://www.navn.org. Lorraine H. Marchi, Founder/CEO. Dir.; Eva Cohen, Asst. to CEO. Dir., 3201 Balboa St., San Francisco, CA 94121. (415)221-3201. Serves the partially sighted (not totally blind). Offers informational literature for the layperson and the professional, most in large print. Maintains a loan library of large-print books. Provides counseling and guidance for the visually impaired and their families and the professionals and paraprofessionals who work with them. *Membership:* 12,000. *Dues:* $40 for indiv.; free for those unable to afford membership. *Publications:* Newsletter updated quarterly, distributed free throughout the English-speaking world. *NAVH Update* (q); *Visual Aids and Informational Material Catalog*; *Large Print Loan Library*; informational pamphlets on topics ranging from *Diseases of the Macula* to knitting and crochet instructions.

National Association of Regional Media Centers (NARMC). NARMC, Education Service Center, Region 20, 1314 Hines Ave., San Antonio, TX 78208. (210)270-9256. Fax (210)224-3130. E-mail jtaylor@tenet.edu. Website http://esu3.k12.ne.us/prof/narmc. Larry Vice, Pres.; James H. Taylor, Treasurer. An affiliate of AECT, NARMC is committed to promoting leadership among its membership through networking, advocacy, and support activities that will enhance the equitable access to media, technology, and information services to educational communities. The purpose of NARMC is to foster the exchange of ideas and information among educational communications specialists whose responsibilities relate to the administration of regional media centers and large district media centers. *Membership:* 285 regional centers (institutions), 70 corporations. *Dues:* $55, institutions; $250, corporations. *Meetings:* held annually with AECT/Incite. Regional meetings are held throughout the US annually. *Publications:* Membership newsletter is *'ETIN.* NARMC Press was established in 1996 to provide members with publications related to the field of media and technology. These publications are available for purchase through this publication outlet. Publications are solicited and submitted from the NARMC membership. Current publications include *An Anthology of Internet Acceptable Use Policies* and *Basic MAC/Windows Internet.* In addition, there is the *Annual Membership Report* and the *Biannual Survey Report of Regional Media Centers.*

*National Association of State Textbook Administrators (NASTA). E-mail president@nasta.org. Website http://www.nasta.org. William Lohman, Pres. NASTA's purposes are (1) to foster a spirit of mutual helpfulness in adoption, purchase, and distribution of instructional materials; (2) to arrange for study and review of textbook specifications; (3) to authorize special surveys, tests, and studies; and (4) to initiate action leading to better quality instructional materials. Services provided include a working knowledge of text construction, monitoring lowest prices, sharing adoption information, identifying trouble spots, and discussions in the industry. The members of NASTA meet to discuss the textbook adoption process and to improve the quality of the instructional materials used in the elementary, middle, and high schools. NASTA is not affiliated with any parent organization and has no permanent address. *Membership:* textbook administrators from each of the 23 states that adopt textbooks at the state level. *Dues:* $25, indiv. *Meetings:* conducted with the American Association of Publishers and the Book Manufacturers' Institute.

The National Cable Television Institute (NCTI). 801 W. Mineral Ave., Littleton CO 80120. (303)797-9393. Fax (303)797-9394. E-mail info@ncti.com. Website http://www.ncti.com. Byron Leech, President; Julie Pushefski, Director Student Services. The National Cable Television Institute is the largest independent provider of broadband technology training in the world. More than 120,000 students have graduated from these courses since 1968. NCTI partners with companies by providing self-paced study manuals to be complemented by company hands-on experiences. NCTI admilisters lessons and final examinations and issues the Certificate of Graduation, which is recognized throughout the industry as a symbol of competence and technical achievement.

The National Center for Improving Science Education. 1726 M Street, NW, #704, Washington, DC 20036. (202)467-0652. Fax (202)467-0659. E-mail info@ncise.org. Website www.wested.org. Senta A. Raizen, Dir. A division of WestEd (see separate listing) that works to promote changes in state and local policies and practices in science curriculum, teaching, and assessment through research and development, evaluation, technical assistance, and dissemination. *Publications: Science and Technology Education for the Elementary Years: Frameworks for Curriculum and Instruction; Developing and Supporting Teachers for Elementary School Science Education; Assessment in Elementary School Science Education; Getting Started in Science: A Blueprint Elementary School Science Education; Elementary School Science for the 90s; Building Scientific Literacy: Blueprint for the Middle Years; Science and Technology Education for the Middle Years: Frameworks for Curriculum and Instruction; Assessment in Science Education: The Middle Years; Developing and Supporting Teachers for Science Education in the Middle Years; The High Stakes of High School Science; Future of Science in Elementary Schools: Educating Prospective Teachers; Technology Education in the Classroom: Understanding the Designed World; What College-Bound Students Abroad Are Expected to Know About Biology* (with AFT); *Examining the Examinations: A Comparison of Science and Mathematics Examinations for College-Bound Students in Seven Countries.* Bold Ventures series: *Vol. 1:Patterns of US Innovations in Science and Mathematics Education; Vol. 2: Case Studies of US Innovations in Science Education; Vol. 3: Case Studies of US Innovations in Mathematics.* A publications catalog and project summaries are available on request.

National Center to Improve Practice (NCIP). Education Development Center, Inc., 55 Chapel St., Newton, MA 02158-1060. (617)969-7100 ext. 2387. TTY (617)969-4529. Fax (617)969-3440. E-mail ncip@edc.org. Website http://www.edc.org/FSC/NCIP. Judith Zorfass, Project Dir.; Lucy Lorin, information. NCIP, a project funded by the US Department of Education's Office for Special Education Programs (OSEP), promotes the effective use of technology to enhance educational outcomes for students (preschool to grade 12) with sensory, cognitive, physical, social, and emotional disabilities. NCIP's award-winning Website offers users online discussions (topical discussions and special events) about technology and students with disabilities, an expansive library of resources (text, pictures, and video clips), online workshops, "guided tours" of exemplary classrooms, "spotlights" on new technology, and links to more than 100 sites dealing with technology and/or students with disabilities. NCIP also produces a series of videos, illustrating how students with disabilities use a range of assistive and instructional technologies to improve their learning. *Dues:* Membership and dues are not required. *Meetings:* NCIP presents sessions at various educational conferences around the country. *Publications:* Video Profile Series: *Multimedia and More: Help for Students with Learning Disabilities; Jeff With Expression: Writing in the Word Prediction Software; "Write" Tools for Angie: Technology for Students Who Are Visually Impaired;*

Telling Tales in ASL and English: Reading, Writing and Videotapes; Welcome to My Preschool: Communicating with Technology. Excellent for use in trainings, workshops, and courses, videos may be purchased individually or as a set of five by calling (800)793-5076. A new video to be released this year focuses on standards, curriculum, and assessment in Science.

National Clearinghouse for Bilingual Education (NCBE). The George Washington University, 2011 "I" Street NW, Suite 200, Washington, DC 20006 (202)467-0867. Fax (800)531-9347, (202)467-4283. E-mail askncbe@ncbe.gwu.edu. Website http://www.ncbe.gwu.edu. Dr. Minerva Gorena, Interim Dir. NCBE is funded by the US Department of Education's Office of Bilingual Education and Minority Languages Affairs (OBEMLA) to collect, analyze, synthesize, and disseminate information relating to the education of linguistically and culturally diverse students in the US. NCBE is operated by The George Washington University Graduate School of Education and Human Development, Center for the Study of Language and Education in Washington, DC. Online services include the NCBE web site containing an online library of hundreds of cover-to-cover documents, resources for teachers and administrators, and library of links to related Internet sites; an E-mail-based, bi-weekly news bulletin, *Newsline;* an electronic discussion group, *NCBE Roundtable;* and an E-mail-based question answering service, *AskNCBE. Publications:* short monographs, syntheses, and reports. Request a publications catalog for prices. The catalog and some publications are available at no cost from the NCBE and other web site.

National Commission on Libraries and Information Science (NCLIS). 1110 Vermont Ave. NW, Suite 820, Washington, DC 20005-3552. (202)606-9200. Fax (202)606-9203. E-mail info@nclis.gov. Website http://www.nclis.gov. Robert S. Willard, Acting Exec. Dir. A permanent independent agency of the US government charged with advising the executive and legislative branches on national library and information policies and plans. The Commission reports directly to the President and the Congress on the implementation of national policy; conducts studies, surveys, and analyses of the nation's library and information needs; appraises the inadequacies of current resources and services; promotes research and development activities; conducts hearings and issues publications as appropriate; and develops overall plans for meeting national library and information needs and for the coordination of activities at the federal, state, and local levels. The Commission provides general policy advice to the Institute of Museum and Library Services (IMLS) director relating to library services included in the Library Services and Technology Act (LSTA). *Membership:* 16 commissioners (14 appointed by the president and confirmed by the Senate, the Librarian of Congress, and the Director of the IMLS). *Publication: Annual Report.*

National Communication Association (NCA) (formerly Speech Communication Association), 5105 Backlick Rd., Bldg. E, Annandale, VA 22003. (703)750-0533. Fax (703)914-9471. Website http://www.natcom.org. James L. Gaudino, Exec. Dir. A voluntary society organized to promote study, criticism, research, teaching, and application of principles of communication, particularly of speech communication. *Membership:* 7,000. *Meetings:* 1999 Annual Meeting, Nov 4-7, Chicago. *Publications: Spectra Newsletter* (mo.); *Quarterly Journal of Speech; Communication Monographs; Communication Education; Critical Studies in Mass Communication; Journal of Applied Communication Research; Text and Performance Quarterly; Communication Teacher; Index to Journals in Communication Studies through 1995; National Communication Directory of NCA and the Regional Speech Communication Organizations* (CSSA, ECA, SSCA, WSCA). For additional publications, request brochure.

National Council for Accreditation of Teacher Education (NCATE). 2010 Massachusetts Ave. NW, Suite 500, Washington, DC 20036. (202)466-7496. Fax (202)296-6620. E-mail ncate@ncate.org. Website http://www.ncate.org. Arthur E. Wise, Pres. NCATE is a consortium of professional organizations that establishes standards of quality and accredits professional education units in schools, colleges, and departments of education, and is interested in the self-regulation and improvement of standards in the field of teacher education. *Membership:* Over 500 colleges and universities, over 30 educational organizations. *Publications: Standards, Procedures and Policies for the Accreditation of Professional Education Units; A Guide to College Programs in Teacher Preparation Quality Teaching* (newsletter, 2/yr.).

National Council of Teachers of English (NCTE), Commission on Media. 1111 W. Kenyon Rd., Urbana, IL 61801-1096. (217)328-3870. Fax (217)328-0977. Andrew Garrison, Commission Dir. Rebecca Rickly, Committee Chair. The functions of the Commission are to study emerging technologies and their integration into English and language arts curricula and teacher education programs; to identify the effects of such technologies on teachers, students, and educational settings, with attention to people of color, handicapped, and other students who are not well served in current programs; to explore means of disseminating information about such technologies to the NCTE membership; to serve as liaison between NCTE and other groups interested in computer-based education in English and language arts; and to maintain liaison with the NCTE Commission on Media and other Council groups concerned with instructional technology.

National Council of the Churches of Christ in the USA. Communication Commission, 475 Riverside Dr., New York, NY 10115. (212)870-2574. Fax (212)870-2030. Website http://www.ncccusa.org. Randy Naylor, Dir. Ecumenical arena for cooperative work of Protestant and Orthodox denominations and agencies in broadcasting, film, cable, and print media. Offers advocacy to government and industry structures on media services. Services provided include liaison to network television and radio programming; film sales and rentals; distribution of information about syndicated religious programming; syndication of some programming; cable television and emerging technologies information services; news and information regarding work of the National Council of Churches, related denominations, and agencies. Works closely with other faith groups in the Interfaith Broadcasting Commission. Online communication via Ecunet/NCCLink. *Membership:* 35 denominations. *Publication: EcuLink.*

National Education Knowledge Industry Association (NEKIA) (formerly Council for Educational Development and Research). 1200 19th St., NW, Suite 300, Washington, DC 20036. (202)429-5101. Fax (202)785-3849. Website http://www.nekia.org. C. Todd Jones, Pres. The National Education Knowledge Industry Association (NEKIA) is the only national trade association for organizations dedicated to educational research and development. The mission of NEKIA is to serve the nation's common schools by making cost-effective education innovation and expertise available to all communities. Members of NEKIA include the nations' foremost research and development institutions devoted to using research-based products and services to enhance the quality of education for the common good. NEKIA serves as a national voice for its members, making sure knowledge from research, development, and practical experience is part of the national discussion on education. NEKIA also ensures that educational research and development institutions are able to maintain neutrality and objectivity in reporting findings, and ensures a field-based, decentralized system of setting priorities. *Membership*: 15. *Publications: Checking Up on Early Childhood Care and Education; What We Know About Reading Teaching and Learning; Plugging In: Choosing and Using Educational Technology; Probe: Designing School Facilities for Learning; Education Productivity; Technology Infrastructure in Schools.*

National Education Telecommunications Organization & EDSAT Institute (NETO/EDSAT). 1899 "L" Street NW, Suite 600, Washington, DC 20036. (202)293-4211. Fax (202)293-4210. E-mail neto-edsat@mindspring.com. Website http://www.netoedsat.org. Shelly Weinstein, Pres. and CEO. NETO/EDSAT is a nonprofit organization bringing together US and non-US users and providers of telecommunications to deliver education, instruction, health care, and training in classrooms, colleges, workplaces, health centers, and other distance education centers. NETO/EDSAT facilitates and collaborates with key stakeholders in the education and telecommunications fields. Programs and services include research and education, outreach, seminars and conferences, and newsletters. The NETO/EDSAT mission is to help create an integrated multitechnology infrastructure, a dedicated satellite that links space and existing secondary access roads (telephone and cable) over which teaching and education resources are delivered and shared in a user friendly format with students, teachers, workers, and individuals. NETO/EDSAT seeks to create a modern-day "learning place" for rural, urban, migrant, suburban, disadvantaged, and at-risk students which provides equal and affordable access to and utilization of educational resources. *Membership:* Members includes over 60 US and non-US school districts, colleges, universities, state agencies, public and private educational consortia, libraries, and other distance education providers. *Publications: NETO/EDSAT "UPDATE"* (newsletter, q.); *Analysis of a Proposal for an Education Satellite, EDSAT Institute,* 1991; and *Global Summit on Distance Education Final Report,* Oct, 1996; *International Report of the NETO/EDSAT Working Group on the Education and Health Care Requirements for Global/Regional Dedicated Networks,* June, 1998.

National Endowment for the Humanities (NEH). Division of Public Programs, Media Program, 1100 Pennsylvania Ave., NW, Room 426, Washington, DC 20506. (202)606-8269. E-mail info@neh.gov. Website http://www.neh.gov. Fax (202)606-8557. Jim Vore, Manage of Media/Special Projects. The NEH is an independent federal grant-making agency that supports research, educational, and public programs grounded in the disciplines of the humanities. The Media Program supports film and radio programs in the humanities for public audiences, including children and adults. *Publications: Overview of Endowment Programs; Humanities Projects in Media* (for application forms and guidelines).

National Federation of Community Broadcasters (NFCB). Ft. Mason Center, Bldg. D, San Francisco, CA 94123. (415)771-1160. E-mail nfcb@aol.com. Website http://www.nfcb.org. Lynn Chadwick, Pres. NFCB represents noncommercial, community-based radio stations in public policy development at the national level and provides a wide range of practical services, including technical assistance. *Membership:* 200. *Dues:* range from $150 to $2500 for participant and associate members. *Meetings:* 1999, San Francisco. *Publications: Legal Handbook; Audio Craft; Community Radio News.*

National Film Board of Canada (NFBC). 350 Fifth Ave., Suite 4820, New York, NY 10118. (212)629-8890. Fax (212)629-8502. E-mail j.sirabella@nfb.ca. John Sirabella, US Marketing Mgr./Nontheatrical Rep. Established in 1939, the NFBC's main objective is to produce and distribute high-quality audiovisual materials for educational, cultural, and social purposes.

National Film Information Service (offered by the Margaret Herrick Library of the Academy of Motion Picture Arts and Sciences). Center for Motion Picture Study, 333 So. La Cienega Blvd., Beverly Hills, CA 90211. (310)247-3000. The purpose of this service is to provide information on film. The service is fee-based and all inquiries must be accompanied by a #10 self-addressed stamped envelope. NFIS does not reply to E-mail queries.

National Gallery of Art (NGA). Department of Education Resources: Art Information and Extension Programs, Washington, DC 20565. (202)842-6273. Fax (202)842-6935. Website http://www.hga.gov. Ruth R. Perlin, Head. This department of NGA is responsible for the production and distribution of educational audiovisual programs, including interactive technologies. Materials available (all loaned free to schools, community organizations, and individuals) range from films, videocassettes, and color slide programs to videodiscs and CD-ROMs. A free catalog of programs is available upon request. Two videodiscs on the gallery's collection are available for long-term loan. *Publication: Extension Programs Catalogue.*

National Information Center for Educational Media (NICEM). PO Box 8640, Albuquerque, NM 87198-8640. (505)265-3591, (800)926-8328. Fax (505)256-1080. E-mail nicem@nicem.com. Web page http://www.nicem.com. Roy Morgan, Exec. Dir.; Marjorie M. K. Hlava, Pres., Access Innovations, Inc. The National Information Center for Educational Media maintains an international database of information about educational non-print materials for all age levels and subject areas in all media types. NICEM editors collect, catalog, and index information about media which is provided by producers and distributors. This information is entered into an electronic masterfile. Anyone who is looking for information about educational media materials can search the database by a wide variety of criteria to locate existing and archival materials. Producer and distributor information in each record then leads the searcher to the source of the educational media materials needed. NICEM makes the information from the database available in several forms and through several vendors. CD-ROM editions are available from NICEM, SilverPlatter, and BiblioFile. Online access to the database is available through NICEM, EBSCO, SilverPlatter, The Library Corporation, NICEM also conducts custom searches and prepares custom catalogs. NICEM is used by college and university media centers, public school libraries and media centers, public libraries, corporate training centers, students, media producers and distributors, and researchers. *Membership:* NICEM is a nonmembership organization. There is no charge for submitting information to be entered into the database. Corporate member of AECT, AIME, NAMTC, CCUMC. *Publications; A-V Online on SilverPlatter; NICEM A-V MARC by BiblioFile; NICEM Reference CD-ROM; NICEM MARC CD-ROM; NICEM Producer & CD-ROM.*

National ITFS Association (NIA). 2330 Swan Blvd., Milwaukee, WI 53226. (414)229-5470. Fax (414)229-4777. Website http://www.itfs.org. Patrick Gossman, Chair, Bd. of Dirs.; Don MacCullough, Exec. Dir. Established in 1978, NIA/ITFS is a nonprofit, professional organization of Instructional Television Fixed Service (ITFS) licensees, applicants, and others interested in ITFS broadcasting. The goals of the association are to gather and exchange information about ITFS, to gather data on utilization of ITFS, and to act as a conduit for those seeking ITFS information or assistance. The NIA represents ITFS interests to the FCC, technical consultants, and equipment manufacturers. The association provides its members with a quarterly newsletter and an FCC regulation update as well as information on excess capacity leasing and license and application data. *Meetings:* with AECT and InCITE. *Publications: National ITFS Association Newsletter* (q.); FCC regulation update.

National Parent Teacher Association (PTA). 330 N. Wabash, Suite 2100, Chicago, IL 60611. (312)670-6782. Fax (312)670-6783. Website http://www.pta.com. Ginny Markell, Pres.; Patty Yoxall, Public Relations Dir. Advocates for the education, health, safety, and well-being of children and teens. Provides parenting education and leadership training to PTA volunteers. The National PTA continues to be very active in presenting Family and Television Critical TV Viewing workshops across the country in cooperation with the National Cable Television Association. The workshops teach parents and educators how to evaluate programming so they can make informed decisions about what to allow their children to see. The National PTA in 1997 convinced the television industry to add content information to the TV rating system. *Membership:* 6.8 million. *Dues:* vary by local unit. *Meeting:* National convention, held annually in June in different regions of the country, is open to PTA members; convention information available on the web site. *Publications: Our Children* (magazine); *What's Happening in Washington* (legislative newsletters). In addition, information can be downloaded from the Website. Catalog available.

National Press Photographers Association, Inc. (NPPA). 3200 Croasdaile Dr., Suite 306, Durham, NC 27705. (919)383-7246. Fax (919)383-7261. E-mail nppa@ mindspring.com. Website http://www.nppa.org. Bradley Wilson, Dir. An organization of professional news photographers who participate in and promote photojournalism in publications and through television and film. Sponsors workshops, seminars, and contests; maintains an audiovisual library of subjects of media interest. *Membership:* 9,000. *Dues:* $75, domestic; $105, international; $40, student. *Meetings:* Annual convention and education days. An extensive array of other conferences, seminars, and workshops are held throughout the year. *Publications: News Photographer* (magazine, mo.); *The Best of Photojournalism* (annual book).

National Public Broadcasting Archives (NPBA). Hornbake Library, University of Maryland, College Park, MD 20742. (301)405-9255. Fax (301)314-2634. E-mail tc65@umail.umd.edu. Website http://www.library.umd.edu/UMCP/NPBA/npba.html. Thomas Connors, Archivist. NPBA brings together the archival record of the major entities of noncommercial broadcasting in the US. NPBA's collections include the archives of the Corporation for Public Broadcasting (CPB), the Public Broadcasting Service (PBS), and National Public Radio (NPR). Other organizations represented include the Midwest Program for Airborne Television Instruction (MPATI), the Public Service Satellite Consortium (PSSC), America's Public Television Stations (APTS), Children's Television Workshop (CTW), and the Joint Council for Educational Telecommunications (JCET). NPBA also makes available the personal papers of many individuals who have made significant contributions to public broadcasting, and its reference library contains basic studies of the broadcasting industry, rare pamphlets, and journals on relevant topics. NPBA also collects and maintains a selected audio and video program record of public broadcasting's national production and support centers and of local stations. Oral history tapes and transcripts from the NPR Oral History Project and the Televisionaries Nal History Project are also available at the archives. The archives are open to the public from 9 am to 5 pm, Monday through Friday. Research in NPBA collections should be arranged by prior appointment. For further information, call (301)405-9988.

National Religious Broadcasters (NRB). 7839 Ashton Ave., Manassas, VA 20109. (703)330-7000. Fax (703)330-7100. E-mail ssmith@nrb.organization. Website http://www.nrb.org. E. Brandt Gustavson, Pres. NRB essentially has two goals: (1) to ensure that religious broadcasters have access to the radio and television airwaves, and (2) to encourage broadcasters to observe a high standard of excellence in their programming and station management for the clear presentation of the gospel. Holds national and regional conventions. *Membership:* 1,000 organizational stations, program producers, agencies, and individuals. *Dues:* based on income. *Meetings:*55th Annual NRB Convention and Exhibition, Jan 31-Feb 3, 1998, Washington, DC. *Publications: Religious Broadcasting Magazine* (mo.); *Annual Directory of Religious Media*; *Religious Broadcasting Resources Library Brochure*; *Religious Broadcasting Cassette Catalog.*

National School Boards Association (NSBA) Institute for the Transfer of Technology to Education (ITTE). 1680 Duke St., Alexandria, VA 22314. (800)838-6722. Fax (703)683-7590. E-mail itte@nsba.org. Website http://www.nsba.org/itte. Cheryl S. Williams, Dir. ITTE was created to help advance the wise uses of technology in public education. ITTE renders several services to state school boards associations, sponsors conferences, publishes, and engages in special projects. The Technology Leadership Network, the membership component of ITTE, is designed to engage school districts nationwide in a dialogue about technology in education. This dialog is carried out via newsletters, meetings, special reports, projects, and online communications. The experience of the Network is shared more broadly through the state associations' communications with all school districts. *Membership:* More than 400 school districts in 44 states, Canada, and the United Kingdom. *Dues:* Based upon the school district's student enrollment. *Meetings:* 1999: Technology & Learning Conference, Nov 10-12, Dallas. Oct 28-30: Nov 15-17, Denver. *Publications: Investing in School Technology: Strategies to Meet the Funding Challenge/School Leader's Version; Technology for Students with Disabilities: A Decision Maker's Resource Guide; Leadership and Technology: What School Board Members Need to Know; Plans and Policies for Technology in Education: A Compendium; Telecommunications and Education: Surfing and the Art of Change; Multimedia and Learning: A School Leader's Guide; Electronic School.: Technology Leadership News: Legal Issues & Education Technology: A School Leader's Guide; Models of Success: Case Study of Technology in Schools; Technology & School Design: Creating Spaces for Learning; Leader's Guide to Education Technology; Teacher's and Technology: Staff Development for Tomorrow's Schools; Education Leadership Toolkit: A Desktop Companion* (q.).

National School Supply and Equipment Association (NSSEA). 8300 Colesville Rd., Suite 250, Silver Spring, MD 20910. (301)495-0240. Fax (301)495-3330. E-mail nssea@aol.com. Website http://www.nssea.org. Tim Holt, Pres. A service organization of more than 1,600 manufacturers, distributors, retailers, and independent manufacturers' representatives of school supplies, equipment, and instructional materials. Seeks to maintain open communications between manufacturers and dealers in the school market, and to encourage the development of new ideas and products for educational progress. *Meetings:* 2000, School Equipment Show, Tampa, FL, March 2-4; 2000, Ed Expo '00, Dallas, TX, March 9-11.; Fall Trade Show & Education Conference, Kansas City, MO, Oct 26-28. *Publications: Tidings*; *Annual Membership Directory.*

National Science Foundation (NSF). 4201 Wilson Blvd., Arlington, VA 22230. (703)306-1070. Mary Hanson, Chief, Media Relations and Public Affairs. Linda Boutchyard, Contact Person, E-mail lboutchy@nsf.gov. NSF is an independent federal agency responsible for fundamental research in all fields of science and engineering, with an annual budget of about $3 billion. NSF funds reach all 50 states through grants to more than 2,000 universities and institutions nationwide. NSF receives more than 50,000 requests for funding annually, including at least 30,000 new proposals. Applicants should refer to the NSF Guide to Programs. Scientific material and media reviews are available to help the public learn about NSF-supported programs. NSF news releases and tipsheets are available electronically via *NSFnews*. To subscribe, send an E-mail message to listmanager@nsf.gov; in the body of the message, type "subscribe nsfnews" and then type your name. Also see NSF news products at http://www.nsf.gov/od/lpa/news/start.htm, http://www.eurekalert.org/, and http://www.ari.net/newswise. In addition, NSF has developed a website that offers information about NSF directorates, offices, programs, and publications at http://nsf.gov.

National Telemedia Council Inc. (NTC). 120 E. Wilson St., Madison, WI 53703. (608)257-7712. Fax (608)257-7714. E-mail NTelemedia@aol.com. Website http://danenet.wicip.org/NTC. Rev. Stephen Umhoefer, Interim Pres.; Marieli Rowe, Exec. Dir. The NTC is a national nonprofit professional organization dedicated to promoting media literacy or critical media viewing skills. This is done primarily through work with teachers, parents, and caregivers. NTC activities include publishing *Telemedium: The Journal of Media Literacy,* the Teacher Idea Exchange (T.I.E.), the Jessie McCanse Award for individual contribution to media literacy, assistance to media literacy educators and professionals. *Dues:* $30, basic; $50, contributing; $100, patron. *Publications: Telemedium; The Journal of Media Literacy* (newsletter, q.).

Native American Public Telecommunications (NAPT). 1800 North 33rd St., PO Box 83111, Lincoln, NE 68501-3111. (402)472-3522. Fax (402)472-8675. Website http://nativetelecomn.org. Frank Blythe, Exec. Dir. The mission of NAPT is to inform, educate, and encourage the awareness of tribal histories, cultures, languages, opportunities, and aspirations through the fullest participation of America Indians and Alaska Natives in creating and employing all forms and educational and public telecommunications programs and services, thereby supporting tribal sovereignty. Public Television distribution. Distribute Educational Native American Videos. Public Radio programming and distribution. American Indian Radio on Satellite. Native America Calling. *Publications: The Vision Maker* (newsletter).

*Network for Continuing Medical Education (NCME). One Harmon Plaza, 6th Floor, Secaucus, NJ 07094. (201)867-3550. Produces and distributes videocassettes, CD-ROMs & Web Based Programs to hospitals for physicians' continuing education. Programs are developed for physicians in the practice of General Medicine, Anesthesiology, Emergency Medicine, Gastroenterology, and Surgery. Physicians who view all the programs can earn up to 25 hours of Category 1 (AMA) credit and up to 10 hours of Prescribed (AAFP) credit each year. *Membership:* More than 1,000 hospitals provide NCME programs to their physicians. *Dues:* subscription fees: VHS-$2,160/yr. Sixty-minute videocassettes & CD-ROMs are distributed to hospital subscribers every eighteen days.

The NETWORK, Inc. 136 Fenno Drive, Rowley, MA 01969. (978)948-7764. Fax (978)948-7836. E-mail davidc@network.org. David Crandall, contact person. A nonprofit research and service organization providing training, research and evaluation, technical assistance, and materials for a fee to schools, educational organizations, and private sector firms with educational interests. The NETWORK has been helping professionals manage and learn about change since 1969. A Facilitator's Institute is held at least annually for trainers and staff developers who use the simulations. *Publications: An Action Guide for School Improvement; Making Change for School Improvement: A Simulation Game; Systems Thinking/Systems Changing: A Simulation Game; People, Policies, and Practices: Examining the Chain of School Improvement; Systemic Thinking: Solving Complex Problems; Benchmarking: A Guide for Educators.*

New England Educational Media Association (NEEMA). c/o Jean Keilly, 58 South Mammoth Rd., Manchester, NH 03109. (603)622-9626. Fax (603)424-6229. An affiliate of AECT, NEEMA is a regional professional association dedicated to the improvement of instruction through the effective utilization of school library media services, media, and technology applications. For more than 75 years it has represented school library media professionals through activities and networking efforts to develop and polish the leadership skills, professional representation, and informational awareness of the membership. The Board of Directors consists of Departments of Education as well as professional leaders of the region. An annual conference program and a Leadership Program are offered in conjunction with the various regional state association conferences.

The New York Festivals (formerly the International Film and TV Festival of New York). 780 King St., Chappaqua, NY 10514. (914)238-4481. Fax (914)236-5040. E-mail info@nyfests.com. Website http://www.nyfests.com. Bilha Goldberg, Vice Pres. The New York Festivals sponsors the International Non-Broadcast Awards, which are annual competitive festivals for industrial and educational film and video productions, filmstrips and slide programs, multi-image business theater and interactive multimedia presentations, and television programs. Entry fees begin at $125. First entry deadline is Aug 3 for U.S. entrants and Sep 15 for overseas entrants. The Non-Broadcast competition honors a wide variety of categories including Education Media. As one of the largest competitions in the world, achieving finalist status is a notable credit to any company's awards roster. Winners are announced each year at a gala awards show in New York City and published on the World Wide Web.

North Central Regional Educational Laboratory (NCREL). 1900 Spring Rd., Suite 300, Oak Brook, IL 60523-1480. (630)571-4700, (800)356-2735. Fax (630)571-4716. E-mail info@ncrel.org. Website http://www.ncrel.org/. Jan Bakker, Resource Center Dir. NCREL's work is guided by a focus on comprehensive and systemic school restructuring that is research-based and learner-centered. One of 10 Office of Educational Research and Improvement (OERI) regional educational laboratories, NCREL disseminates information about effective programs, develops educational products, holds conferences, provides technical assistance, and conducts research and evaluation. A special focus is on technology and learning. In addition to conventional print publications, NCREL uses computer networks, videoconferencing via satellite, and video and audio formats to reach its diverse audiences. NCREL's Website includes the acclaimed *Pathways to School Improvement*. NCREL operates the Midwest Consortium for Mathematics and Science Education which works to advance systemic change in mathematics and science education. Persons living in Illinois, Indiana, Iowa, Michigan, Minnesota, Ohio, and Wisconsin are encouraged to call NCREL Resource Center with any education-related questions. NCREL also hosts the North Central Regional Technology in Education Consortium which helps states and local educational agencies successfully integrate advanced technologies into K–12 classrooms, library media centers, and other educational settings. *Publications Learning Point* (q).

Northwest College and University Council for the Management of Educational Technology (NW/MET). c/o WITS, Willamette University, 900 State St., Salem, OR 97301. (503)370-6650. Fax (503)375-5456. E-mail mmorandi@willamette.edu. Listserv NW-MET@willamette.edu. Judi Ross, Pres.; Marti Morandi, Membership Chair. NW/MET was the first regional group representing institutions of higher education in Alberta, Alaska, British Columbia, Idaho, Montana, Oregon, Saskatchewan, and Washington to receive affiliate status in AECT. Membership is restricted to Information Technology managers with campus-wide responsibilities for Information technology services in the membership region. Corresponding membership is available to those who work outside the membership region. Current issues under consideration include managing emerging technologies, reorganization, copyright, and management/administration issues. Organizational goals include identifying the unique status problems of media managers in higher education. *Membership:* approx. 75. *Dues:* $35. *Meetings:* An annual conference and business meeting are held each year, rotating through the region. *Publications:* An annual newsletters and *NW/MET Journal.*

Northwest Regional Educational Laboratory (NWREL). 101 SW Main St., Suite 500, Portland, OR 97204. (503)275-9500. Fax (503)275-0448. E-mail info@nwrel.org. Website http://www.nwrel.org. Dr. Ethel Simon-McWilliams, Exec. Dir. One of 10 Office of Educational Research and Improvement (OERI) regional educational laboratories, NWREL works with schools and communities to improve educational outcomes for children, youth, and adults. NWREL provides leadership, expertise, and services based on the results of research and development. The specialty area of NWREL is school change processes. It serves Alaska, Idaho, Oregon, Montana, and Washington. *Membership:* 817. *Dues:* None. *Publication: Northwest Report* (newsletter).

On-Line Audiovisual Catalogers (OLAC). Formed as an outgrowth of the ALA conference, OLAC seeks to permit members to exchange ideas and information, and to interact with other agencies that influence audiovisual cataloging practices. *Membership:* 700. *Dues:* available for single or multiple years; $10-$27, indiv.; $16-$45, institution. Slight increase expected in 1999. *Meetings:* biannual. *Publication: OLAC Newsletter.*

Online Computer Library Center, Inc. (OCLC). 6565 Frantz Rd., Dublin, OH 43017-3395. (614)764-6000. Fax (614)764-6096. E-mail oclc@oclc.org. Website http://www.oclc.org. Jay Jordan, Pres. and CEO. Nita Dean, Mgr., Public Relations. A nonprofit membership organization that engages in computer library service and research and makes available computer-based processes, products, and services for libraries, other educational organizations, and library users. From its facility in Dublin, Ohio, OCLC operates an international computer network that libraries use to catalog books, order custom-printed catalog cards and machine-readable records for local catalogs, arrange interlibrary loans, and maintain location information on library materials. OCLC also provides online reference products and services for the electronic delivery of information. More than 34,000 libraries contribute to and/or use information in WorldCat (the OCLC Online Union Catalog), OCLC FOREST PRESS, a division of OCLC since 1988, publishes the Dewey Decimal Classification. Reservation Resources, a division of OCLC since 1994, provides preservation reformatting services worldwide. *Publications: OCLC Newsletter* (6/yr.); *OCLC Reference News* (4/yr.); *Annual Report.*

Pacific Film Archive (PFA). University of California, Berkeley Art Museum, 2625 Durant Ave., Berkeley, CA 94720-2250. (510)642-1437 (library); (510)642-1412 (general). Fax (510)642-4889. E-mail pfalibrary@uclink.berkeley.edu. Website http://www.bampfa.berkeley.edu. Edith Kramer, Dir. and Curator of Film; Nancy Goldman, Head, PFA Library and Film Study Center. Sponsors the exhibition, study, and preservation of classic, international, documentary, animated, and avant-garde films. Provides on-site research screenings of films in its collection of over 7,000 titles. Provides access to its collections of books, periodicals, stills, and posters (all materials are noncirculating). Offers BAM/PFA members and University of California, Berkeley affiliates reference and research services to locate film and video distributors, credits, stock footage, etc. Library hours are 1pm-5pm Mon-Thurs. *Membership:* through parent organization, the Berkeley Art Museum. *Dues:* $40 indiv. and nonprofit departments of institutions. *Publication: BAM/PFA Calendar* (6/yr.).

Pacific Resources for Education and Learning (PREL). 828 Fort Street Mall Suite 500, Honolulu, HI 96813-4321. (808)533-6000. Fax (808)533-7599. E-mail askprel@prel.hawaii.edu. Website http://prel.hawaii.edu. John W. Kofel, Exec. Dir. One of ten regional educational laboratories designed to help educators and policymakers solve educational problems in their schools. Using the best available information and the expertise of professionals, PREL furnishes research results, provides training to teachers and administrators, and helps to implement new approaches in education. The PREL Star program, funded by a US Department of Education Star Schools Grant, utilizes telecommunications technology to provide distance learning opportunities to the Pacific region. PREL serves American Samoa, Commonwealth of the Northern Mariana Islands, Federated States of Micronesia, Guam, Hawaii, Republic of the Marshall Islands, and Republic of Palau.

Photographic Society of America (PSA). 3000 United Founders Blvd., Suite 103, Oklahoma City, OK 73112. (405)843-1437. Fax (405)843-1438. E-mail 74521,2414@compuserve.com. Website http://www.psa-photo.org. Jacque Noel, Operations Mgr. A nonprofit organization for the development of the arts and sciences of photography and for the furtherance of public appreciation of photographic skills. Its members, largely advanced amateurs, consist of individuals, camera clubs, and other photographic organizations. Divisions include electronic imaging, color slide, video motion picture, nature, photojournalism, travel, pictorial print, stereo, and techniques. Sponsors national, regional, and local meetings, clinics, and contests. *Membership:* 7,000. *Dues:* $40, North America; $45 elsewhere. *Meetings:* 1999 International Conference of Photography, Aug 30-Sep 4, Toronto, Delta Meadowvale Hotel. *Publication: PSA Journal.*

Professors of Instructional Design and Technology (PIDT). Instructional Technology Dept., 220 War Memorial Hall, Virginia Tech, Blacksburg, VA 24061-0341. (540)231-5587. Fax (540)231-9075. E-mail moorem@VT.EDU. Dr. Mike Moore, contact person. An informal organization designed to encourage and facilitate the exchange of information among members of the instructional design and technology academic and corporate communities. Also serves to promote excellence in academic programs in instructional design and technology and to encourage research and inquiry that will benefit the field while providing leadership in the public and private sectors in its application and practice. *Membership:* 300 faculty employed in higher education institutions whose primary responsibilities are teaching and research in this area, their corporate counterparts, and other persons interested in the goals and activities of the PIDT. *Dues:* none. *Meetings:* Annual Conference; see above E-mail address for information and registration.

*Public Broadcasting Service (PBS). 1320 Braddock Pl., Alexandria, VA 22314. Website http://www.pbs.org. Ervin S. Duggan, CEO and Pres. National distributor of public television programming, obtaining all programs from member stations, independent producers, and sources around the world. PBS services include program acquisition, distribution, and scheduling; development and fundraising support; engineering and technical development; and educational resources and services. Through the PBS National Program Service and PBS uses the power of noncommercial television, the Internet and other media to enrich the lives of all Americans through quality programs and education services that inform and inspire. Subsidiaries of PBS include PBS Adult Learning Service, and PBS Video, which are described below. PBS is owned and operated by local public television organizations through annual membership fees, and governed by a board of directors elected by PBS members for three-year terms.

PBS Adult Learning Service (ALS). 1320 Braddock Pl., Alexandria, VA 22314-1698. (800)257-2578. Fax (703)739-8471. E-mail als@pbs.org. Website http://www.pbs.org/als/college. Will Philipp, Senior Dir. The mission of ALS is to help colleges, universities, and public television stations increase learning opportunities for distance learners; enrich classroom instruction; update faculty; train administrators, management, and staff; and provide other educational services for local communities. A pioneer in the widespread use of video and print packages incorporated into curricula and offered for credit by local colleges, ALS began broadcasting telecourses in 1981. Since that time, over 3 million students have earned college credit through telecourses offered in partnership with more than two-thirds of the nation's colleges and universities. In 1988, ALS established the Adult Learning Satellite Service (ALSS) to provide colleges, universities, and other organizations with a broad range of educational programming via direct satellite. Since 1994, ALS has facilitated the capability for colleges nationwide to offer full two-year degrees at a distance through the popular Going the Distance® project. Over 170 colleges are currently participating in 37 states. In 1998, ALS launched the first teleWEBcourse[SM], *Internet Literacy*, an online credit offering available through the PBS Website. *Membership:* 700-plus colleges, universities, hospitals, and government agencies are now ALSS Associates. Organizations that are not Associates can still acquire ALS programming, but at higher fees. *Dues:* $1,500; multisite and consortia rates are available. *Publications: ALSS Programming Line-Up* (catalog of available programming, 3/yr.); *The Agenda* (news magazine about issues of interest to distance learning and adult learning administrators); *Changing the Face of Higher Education* (an overview of ALS services); *Teaching Telecourses: Opportunities and Options; Ideas for Increasing Telecourse Enrollment; Going the Distance® Handbook* (case studies for offering distance learning degrees).

PBS VIDEO. 1320 Braddock Pl., Alexandria, VA 22314. (703)739-5380; (800)344-3337. Fax (703)739-5269. Jon Cecil, Dir., PBS VIDEO Marketing. Markets and distributes PBS television programs for sale on videocassette or videodisc to colleges, public libraries, schools, governments, and other organizations and institutions. *Publications: PBS VIDEM Catalogs of New and Popular Video (6/yrs): Website:PBS VIDEO Online Catalog at: http://shop2.org/pbsvideo/.*

Public Library Association (PLA). 50 E. Huron St., Chicago, IL 60611. (312)280-5PLA. Fax (312)280-5029. E-mail pla@ala.org. Greta Southard, Exec. Dir. An affiliate of the American Library Association, PLA is concerned with the development, effectiveness, and financial support of public libraries. It speaks for the profession and seeks to enrich the professional competence and opportunities of public librarians. Sections include Adult Lifelong Learning, Community Information, Metropolitan Libraries, Public Library Systems, Small- and Medium-Sized Libraries, Public Policy for Public Libraries, Planning, Measurement and Evaluation, and Marketing of Public Library Services. *Membership:* 8,500. *Dues:* $50, open to all ALA members. *Meetings:* 1999 PLA Spring Symposium, Mar 25-28; 2000 PLA National Conference, Mar 28-Apr 1. "Public Libraries: Vital, Valuable, Virtual." *Publication:Public Libraries* (bi-mo.). Two PLA Committees of particular interest to the Educational Technology field are listed below.

> **Audiovisual Committee** (of the Public Library Association). 50 E.Huron St., Chicago, IL 60611. (312)280-5752. James E. Massey, Chair. Promotes use of audiovisual materials in public libraries.

> **Technology in Public Libraries Committee** (of the Public Library Association). 50 E. Huron St., Chicago, IL 60611. (312)280-5752. William Ptacek, Chair. Collects and disseminates information on technology applications in public libraries.

*Puppeteers of America, Inc. (POA). #5 Cricklewood Path, Pasadena, CA 91107-1002. (818)797-5748. Gayle Schluter, Membership Officer. Website http://www.puppeteers.org. Formed in 1937, POA holds festivals for puppetry across the country, sponsors local guilds, presents awards, sponsors innovative puppetry works, provides consulting, and provides materials through the Audio-Visual Library. *Members:* more than 2,000. *Dues*: $40, regular; $50, couple; $20, junior; $60, family; $30, journal subscription. *Meetings:* National Festival, Aug 1-7, 1999, Seattle. *Publications: The Puppetry Journal* (q).

Recording for the Blind and Dyslexic (RFB&D). 20 Roszel Road, Princeton, NJ 08540. Main phone (609)452-0606. Customer Service (800)221-4792. Fax (609)987-8116. E-mail information@rfbd.org. Website http://www.rfbd.org. Richard Scribner, Pres. RFB&D is a national nonprofit organization that provides educational and professional books in accessible format to people with visual impairments, learning disabilities, or other physical disabilities that prevent them from reading normal printed material. This includes students from kindergarten to graduate school and people who no longer attend school but who use educational books to pursue careers or personal interests. RFB&D's 78,000-volume collection of audio titles is the largest educational resource of its kind in the world. RFB&D provides a wide range of library services as well as "E-Text" books on computer disk, including dictionaries, computer manuals, and other reference books. For an additional fee, a custom recording service is also available to make other publications accessible. Potential individual members must complete an application form, which contains a "disability verification" section. *Membership:* 39,139 individuals, 275 institutions. *Dues:* for qualified individuals, $50 registration, $25 annual. Institutional Memberships also available (contact Customer Service).

Recording Industry Association of America, Inc. (RIAA). 1330 Connecticut Ave. NW #300, Washington DC, 20036; (202)775-0101. Fax (202)775-7253. Website http://www.riaa.com/. Hilary Rosen Pres. and CEO. Founded in 1952, RIAA's mission is to promote the mutual interests of recording companies, as well as the betterment of the industry overall through successful government relations (both federal and state), intellectual property protection, international activities evaluating all aspects of emerging technologies and technology-related issues and promoting an innovative and secure online marketplace. RIAA represents the recording industry, whose members create and/or distribute approximately 90 percent of all legitimate sound recordings produced and sold in the US. RIAA is the official certification agency for gold, platinum, and multi-platinum record awards. *Membership:* over 250 recording companies. *Publications: Annual Report; Fact Book.*

Reference and User Services Association (RUSA). 50 E. Huron St., Chicago, IL 60611. (800)545-2433, ext. 4398. Fax (312)944-8085. Cathleen Bourdon, Exec. Dir. A division of the American Library Association, RUSA is responsible for stimulating and supporting in every type of library the delivery of reference information services to all groups and of general library services and materials to adults. *Membership:* 5,500. *Dues:* $45 plus membership in ALA. *Publications: RUSQ* (q.); *RUSA Update.*

*Research for Better Schools, Inc. (RBS). 444 North Third St., Philadelphia, PA 19123-4107. (215)574-9300. Fax (215)574-0133. Website http://www.rbs.org/. John Connolly, Exec. Dir. RBS is a private, nonprofit corporation which currently operates the Mid-Atlantic Eisenhower Consortium for Mathematics and Science Education, and the Mid-Atlantic Telecommunications Alliance. In its 30 years of service to the education community, RBS has also offered educational technology, development, evaluation, technical assistance, and training services with client funding. RBS also operates an educational publications division.

Smithsonian Institution. 1000 Jefferson Drive SW, Washington, DC 20560. (202)357-2700. Fax (202)786-2515. Website http://www.si.edu. I. Michael Heyman, Sec. An independent trust instrumentality of the US that conducts scientific, cultural, and scholarly research; administers the national collections; and performs other educational public service functions, all supported by Congress, trusts, gifts, and grants. Includes 16 museums, including the National Museum of Natural History, the National Museum of American History, the National Air and Space Museum, and the National Zoological Park. Museums are free and open daily except December 25. The Smithsonian Institution Traveling Exhibition Service (SITES) organizes exhibitions on art, history, and science and circulates them across the country and abroad. *Membership:* Smithsonian Associates. *Dues:* $24-$45. *Publications: Smithsonian*; *Air & Space/Smithsonian*; *The Torch* (staff newsletter, mo.); *Research Reports* (semi-technical, q.); Smithsonian Institution Press Publications, 470 L'Enfant Plaza, Suite 7100, Washington, DC 20560.

Society for Applied Learning Technology (SALT). 50 Culpeper St., Warrenton, VA 20186. (540)347-0055. Fax (540)349-3169. E-mail info@lti.org. Website http://www.salt.org. Raymond G. Fox, Pres. The society is a nonprofit, professional membership organization that was founded in 1972. Membership in the society is oriented to professionals whose work requires knowledge and communication in the field of instructional technology. The society provides members a means to enhance their knowledge and job performance by participation in society-sponsored meetings, subscription to society-sponsored publications, association with other professionals at conferences sponsored by the society, and membership in special interest groups and special society-sponsored initiatives, In addition, the society offers member discounts on society-sponsored journals, conferences, and publications. *Membership:* 1,000. *Dues:* $45. *Meetings:* Orlando Multimedia '99, Kissimmee, FL; Interactive Multimedia '99, Arlington, VA. *Publications: Journal of Educational Technology Systems*; *Journal of Instruction Delivery Systems*; *Journal of Interactive Instruction Development.* Send for list of books.

Society for Computer Simulation (SCS). PO Box 17900, San Diego, CA 92177-7900. (619)277-3888. Fax (619)277-3930. E-mail info@scs.org. Website http://www.scs.org. Bill Gallagher, Exec. Dir. Founded in 1952, SCS is a professional-level technical society devoted to the art and science of modeling and simulation. Its purpose is to advance the understanding, appreciation, and use of all types of computer models for studying the behavior of actual or hypothesized systems of all kinds and to sponsor standards. Additional office in Ghent, Belgium. *Membership:* 1,900. *Dues:* $75 (includes journal subscription). *Meetings:* local, regional, and national technical meetings and conferences, such as the Western Simulation Multiconference Jan 17-21, 1999, San Francisco; Summer and Winter Computer Simulation Conferences, Applied Simulation Technologies Conference, Apr 12-15, 1999, San Diego; and National Educational Computing Conference (NECC). *Publications: Simulation* (mo.); *Simulation* series (q.); *Transactions of SCS* (q.).

Society for Photographic Education (SPE). PO Box 2811, Daytona Beach, FL 32120-2811. (904)255-8131, ext. 3944. Fax (904)255-3044. E-mail SocPhotoEd@aol.com or SPENews@aol.com. Website http://www.spenational.org. James J. Murphy, Exec. Dir. An association of college and university teachers of photography, museum photographic curators, writers, and publishers. Promotes discourse in photography education, culture, and art. *Membership:* 1,700. *Dues:* $55. *Meetings:* 1999, Mar 11-14, Tucson. 2000, Mar 16-19, Cleveland. *Publications: Exposure* (newsletter).

Society of Cable Telecommunications Engineers (SCTE). 140 Philips Rd., Exton, PA 19341-1319. (610)363-6888. Fax (610)363-5898. E-mail info@scte.org. Website http://www.scte.org. John Clark, Pres. SCTE is dedicated to the technical training and further education of members. A nonprofit membership organization for persons engaged in engineering, construction, installation, technical direction, management, or administration of cable television and broadband communications technologies. Also eligible for membership are students in communications, educators, government and regulatory agency employees, and affiliated trade associations. SCTE provides technical training and certification, and is an American National Standards Institute (ANSI)-approved Standards Development Organization for the cable telecommunications industry. *Membership:* 15,500 US and International. *Dues:* $40. *Meetings:* 2000, Conference on Emerging Technologies, Jan.11-13, Anaheim, CA; Cable-Tec Expo, May 25-27, Orlando (hardware exhibits and engineering conference). 2000 Cable-Tec Expo, June 5-8, 2000 Las Vegas (hardware exhibits and engineering conference). *Publication: The Interval;* technical documents, standards, training materials, and videotapes (some available in Spanish).

Society of Photo Technologists (SPT). 11112 S. Spotted Rd., Cheney, WA 99004. (888) 662-7678 or (509)624-9621. Fax (509)323-4811 or (509)624-5320. E-mail ccspt@concentric.net. An organization of photographic equipment repair technicians that improves and maintains communications between manufacturers and independent repair technicians. *Membership:* 1,000. *Dues:* $80-$360. *Publications: SPT Journal; SPT Parts and Services Directory; SPT Newsletter; SPT Manuals—Training and Manufacturer's Tours.*

Southeastern Regional Media Leadership Council (SRMLC). Dr. Vykuntapathi Thota, Director, Virginia State University, PO Box 9198, Petersburg, VA 23806. (804)524-5937. Fax (804)524-5757. An affiliate of AECT, the purpose of the SRMLC is to strengthen the role of the individual state AECT affiliates within the Southeastern region; to seek positive change in the nature and status of instructional technology as it exists within the Southeast; to provide opportunities for the training and development of leadership for both the region and the individual affiliates; and to provide opportunities for the exchange of information and experience among those who attend the annual conference.

SouthEastern Regional Vision for Education (SERVE). SERVE Tallahassee Office, 1203 Governor's Square Blvd., Suite 400, Tallahassee, FL 32301. (800)352-6001, (904)671-6000. Fax (904)671-6020. E-mail bfry@SERVE.org. Mr. Don Holznagel, Exec. Dir. Betty Fry, Contact Person. SERVE is a regional educational research and development laboratory funded by the US Department of Education to help educators, policymakers, and communities improve schools so that all students achieve their full potential. The laboratory offers the following services: field-based models and strategies for comprehensive school improvement; publications on hot topics in education, successful implementation efforts, applied research projects and policy issues; database searches and information search training; a regional bulletin board service that provides educators electronic communication and Internet access; information and assistance for state and local policy development; and services to support the coordination and improvement of assistance for young children and their families. The Eisenhower Mathematics and Science Consortium at SERVE promotes improvement of education in these targeted areas by coordinating regional resources, disseminating exemplary instructional materials, and offering technical assistance for implementation of effective teaching methods and assessment tools. *Meetings:* For dates and topics of conferences and workshops, contact Betty Fry, (800)352-6001. *Publications: Reengineering High Schools for Student Success; Schools for the 21st Century: New Roles for Teachers and Principals* (rev. ed.); *Designing Teacher Evaluation Systems That Promote Professional Growth; Learning by Serving: 2,000*

Ideas for Service-Learning Projects; *Sharing Success: Promising Service-Learning Programs*; *Future Plans* (videotape, discussion guide, and pamphlet); *Future Plans Planning Guides*.

Southwest Educational Development Laboratory (SEDL). 211 East Seventh St., Austin, TX 78701. (512)476-6861. Fax (512)476-2286. E-mail info@sedl.org. Website http://www.sedl.org/. Dr. Wesley A. Hoover, President and CEO; Dr. Joyce Pollard, Dir., Institutional Communications & Policy Services. One of 10 Office of Educational Research and Improvement (OERI) regional educational laboratories designed to help educators and policymakers solve educational problems in their schools. Using the best available information and the experience and expertise of professionals, SEDL seeks to identify solutions to education problems, tries new approaches, furnishes research results, and provides training to teachers and administrators. SEDL serves Arkansas, Louisiana, New Mexico, Oklahoma, and Texas. *Publications: SEDLETTER* for free general distribution and a range of topic-specific publications related to educational change, education policy, mathematics, language arts, science, and disability research.

Special Libraries Association. 1700 Eighteenth St., NW, Washington, DC, 20009-2514. (202)234-4700. Fax (202)265-9317. E-mail sla@sla.org. Website http://www.sla.org. Dr. David R. Bender, Exec. Dir. The Special Libraries Association is an international association representing the interests of nearly 15,000 information professionals in 60 countries. Special Librarians are information and resource experts who collect, analyze, evaluate, package, and disseminate information to facilitate accurate decision-making in corporate, academic, and government settings. The association offers myriad programs and services designed to help its members serve their customers more effectively and succeed in an increasingly challenging environment of information management and technology. These services include career and employment services, and professional development opportunities. *Membership:* 14,500. *Dues:* $105, indiv.; $25, student. *Meetings:* 1999, Jan 21-23, San Francisco; Jun 5-10, Minneapolis. 2000, Jan 20-22, St. Louis; Jun 10-15, Philadelphia; Oct 16-19, Brighton, UK. *Publications: Information Outlook* (monthly glossy magazine that accepts advertising). Special Libraries Association also has an active book publishing program.

Teachers and Writers Collaborative (T&W). 5 Union Square W., New York, NY 10003-3306. (212)691-6590. Toll-free (888)266-5789. Fax (212)675-0171. E-mail info@twc.org. Website http://www.twc.org. Nancy Larson Shapiro, Dir. Sends writers and other artists into New York public schools to work with teachers and students on writing and art projects. Hosts seminars for creative work from across the United States and beyond. Recent projects include the creation of WriteNet, a series of online forums and information for people interested in teaching creative writing. Also, in conjunction with NBC TV, T&W set up a series of residencies around the country focused on teaching creative writing using "classic" literature. See website for updated schedule of events. *Membership:* more than 1,000; for people interested in the teaching of writing. *Dues:* $35, basic personal membership. *Publications: Teachers & Writers* (magazine, 5/yr); *The Story in History; The T&W Handbook of Poetic Forms; Personal Fiction Writing; Luna, Luna, Creative Writing from Spanish and Latino Literature; The Nearness of You: Students and Teachers Writing On-Line.* Request free publications catalog for list of titles.

Theatre Library Association (TLA). 149 W. 45th St., New York, NY 10036. (212)944-3895. Fax (212)944-4139. Website http://www.brown.edu/Facilities/University_Library/beyond/TLA/TLA.html. Maryann Chach, Exec. Sec. Seeks to further the interests of collecting, preserving, and using theater, cinema, and performing arts materials in libraries, museums, and private collections. *Membership:* 500. *Dues:* $30, indiv.; $30, institutional; $20, students and retirees. *Publications: Performing Arts Resources* (membership annual, Vol. 20, Denishawn Collections).

USA Toy Library Association (USA-TLA). 2530 Crawford Ave., Suite 111, Evanston, IL 60201. (847)864-3330. Fax (847)864-3331. E-mail foliog@aol.com. Judith Q. Iacuzzi, Exec. Dir. The mission of the USA-TLA is to provide a networking system answering to all those interested in play and play materials to provide a national resource to toy libraries, family centers, resource and referrals, public libraries, schools, institutions serving families of special need, and other groups and individuals involved with children; to support and expand the number of toy libraries; and to advocate for children and the importance of their play in healthy development. Individuals can find closest toy libraries by sending an E-mail or written inquiry in a self-addressed stamped envelope. *Membership:* 60 institutions, 150 individuals. *Dues:* $165, comprehensive; $55, basic; $15, student. *Meetings:* national meetings in the spring and fall. *Publications: Child's Play* (q. newsletter); *How to Start and Operate a Toy Library*; *Play Is a Child's Work* (videotapes), other books on quality toys and play.

University Continuing Education Association (UCEA). One Dupont Cir. NW, Suite 615, Washington, DC 20036. (202)659-3130. Fax (202)785-0374. E-mail postmaster@nucea.edu. Website http://www.nucea.edu. Tom Kowalik, Pres 1999-2000. Kay J. Kohl, Exec. Dir.; Susan Goewey, Dir. of Pubs; Philp Robinson, Dir. of Govt. Relations & Public Affairs, Joelle Brink, Director of Information Services. UCEA is an association of public and private higher education institutions concerned with making continuing education available to all population segments and to promoting excellence in continuing higher education. Many institutional members offer university and college courses via electronic instruction. *Membership:* 425 institutions, 2,000 professionals. *Dues:* vary according to membership category. *Meetings:* UCEA has an annual national conference and several professional development seminars throughout the year. *Publications:* monthly newsletter; quarterly; occasional papers; scholarly journal, *Continuing Higher Education Review*; *Independent Study Catalog.* With Peterson's, *The Guide to Distance Learning*; *Guide to Certificate Programs at American Colleges and Universities*; UCEA-ACE/Oryx Continuing Higher Education book series; *Lifelong Learning Trends* (a statistical factbook on continuing higher education); organizational issues series; membership directory.

WestEd. 730 Harrison St., San Francisco, CA 94107-1242. (415)565-3000. Fax (415)565-3012. E-mail tross@wested.org. Website http://www.WestEd.org. Glen Harvey, CEO. WestEd is a non-profit research, development, and service agency dedicated to improving education and other opportunities for children, youth, and adults. Drawing on the best from research and practice, WestEd works with practitioners and policymakers to address critical issues in education and other related areas, including early childhood intervention; curriculum, instruction and assessment; the use of technology; career and technical preparation; teacher and administrator professional development; science and mathematics education; and safe schools and communities. WestEd was created in 1995 to unite and enhance the capacity of Far West Laboratory and Southwest Regional Laboratory, two of the nation's original education laboratories. In addition to its work across the nation, WestEd serves as the regional education laboratory for Arizona, California, Nevada, and Utah. A publications catalog is available.

Western Public Radio (WPR). Ft. Mason Center, Bldg. D, San Francisco, CA 94123. (415)771-1160. Fax (415)771-4343. E-mail wprsf@aol.com. Karolyn van Putten, Ph.D., President/CEO; Lynn Chadwick, Vice President/COO. WPR provides analog and digital audio production training, public radio program proposal consultation, and studio facilities for rent. WPR also sponsors a continuing education resource for audio producers, http://www.radiocollege.org.

World Future Society (WFS). 7910 Woodmont Ave., Suite 450, Bethesda, MD 20814. (301)656-8274, fax (301)951-0394. E-mail wfsinfo@wfs.org. Website http://www.wfs.org. Edward Cornish, Pres. Organization of individuals interested in the study of future trends and possibilities. Its purpose is to provide information on trends and scenarios so that individuals and organizations can better plan their future. *Membership*: 30,000. *Dues*: $39, general; $95, professional; call Society for details on all membership levels and benefits. *Meeting*: 1999: Ninth General Assembly, July 29-Aug 1. Washington. 2000: Annual Conference, July 23-25, Houston. *Publications*: *The Futurist: A Journal of Forecasts, Trends and Ideas About the Future; Futures Research Quarterly; Future Survey.* The society's bookstore offers audio- and videotapes, books, and other items.

Young Adult Library Services Association (YALSA). 50 E. Huron St., Chicago, IL 60611. (312)280-4390. Fax (312)664-7459. E-mail yalsa@ala.org. Website http://www.ala.organization/ yalsa. Julie A. Walker, Exec. Dir.; Linda Waddle, Deputy Exec. Dir; Joel Shoemaker, Pres. An affiliate of the American Library Association, YALSA seeks to advocate, promote, and strengthen service to young adults as part of the continuum of total library services, and assumes responsibility within the ALA to evaluate and select books and nonbook media, and to interpret and make recommendations regarding their use with young adults. Committees include Best Books for Young Adults, Popular Paperbacks, Recommended Books for the Reluctant Young Adult Reader, Media Selection and Usage, Publishers' Liaison, and Selected Films for Young Adults. *Membership:* 2,223. *Dues:* $40 (in addition to ALA membership); $15, students. *Publication: Journal of Youth Services in Libraries* (q.).

Canada

This section includes information on nine Canadian organizations whose principal interests lie in the general fields of educational media, instructional technology, and library and information science.

*ACCESS NETWORK. 3720 - 76 Ave., Edmonton, AB T6B 2N9, Canada. (403)440-7777. Fax (403)440-8899. E-mail promo@ccinet.ab.ca. Dr. Ronald Keast, Pres.; John Verburgt, Creative Services Manager. The ACCESS Network (Alberta Educational Communications Corporation) was purchased by Learning and Skills Television of Alberta in 1995. The newly privatized network works with Alberta's educators to provide all Albertans with a progressive and diverse television-based educational and training resource to support their learning and skills development needs using cost-effective methods and innovative techniques, and to introduce a new private sector model for financing and efficient operation of educational television in the province.

Association for Media and Technology in Education in Canada (AMTEC). 3-1750 The Queensway, Suite 1318, Etobicoke, ON M9C 5H5, Canada. (604)323-5627. Fax (604)323-5577. E-mail maepp@langara.bc.ca. Website http://www.amtec.ca. Dr. Geneviev Gallant, Pres.; Dr. Len Proctor, Pres. Elect; Mary Anne Epp, Sec./Treas. AMTEC is Canada's national association for educational media and technology professionals. The organization provides national leadership through annual conferences, publications, workshops, media festivals, and awards. It responds to media and technology issues at the international, national, provincial, and local levels, and maintains linkages with other organizations with similar interests. *Membership:* AMTEC members represent all sectors of the educational media and technology fields. *Dues:* $101.65, Canadian regular; $53.50, student and retiree. *Meeting:* Annual Conferences take place in late May or early June. 1999, Ottawa; 2000, Vancouver. *Publications: Canadian Journal of Educational Communication* (q.); *Media News* (3/yr.); *Membership Directory* (with membership).

*Canadian Broadcasting Corporation (CBC)/Société Radio-Canada (SRC). PO Box 500, Station A, Toronto, Ontario, Canada. Website http://www.cbc.ca. The CBC is a publicly owned corporation established in 1936 by an Act of the Canadian Parliament to provide a national broadcasting service in Canada in the two official languages. CBC services include English and French television networks; English and French AM Mono and FM Stereo radio networks virtually free of commercial advertising; CBC North, which serves Canada's North by providing radio and television programs in English, French, and eight native languages; Newsworld and its French counterpart, Le Réseau de l'information (RDI), 24-hour national satellites to cable English-language and French-language news and information service respectively, both funded entirely by cable subscription and commercial advertising revenues; and Radio Canada International, a shortwave radio service that broadcasts in seven languages and is managed by CBC and financed by External Affairs. The CBC is financed mainly by public funds voted annually by Parliament.

Canadian Education Association/Association canadienne d'éducation (CEA). 252 Bloor St. W., Suite 8-200, Toronto, ON M5S 1V5, Canada. (416)924-7721. Fax (416)924-3188. E-mail cea-ace@acea.ca. Website http://www.acea.ca. Penny Milton, Exec. Dir.; Suzanne Tanguay, Director of Communication Services. The Canadian equivalent of the US National Education Association, CEA has one central objective: to promote the improvement of education. It is the only national, bilingual organization whose function is to inform, assist, and bring together all sectors of the educational community. *Membership:* all 12 provincial and territorial departments of education, the federal government, 400 individuals, 120 organizations, 100 school boards. *Dues:* $120, indiv.; $320, organization; $500, businesses, 10 cents per pupil, school boards. *Meetings:* Annual CEA Convention. *Publications: Promoting Achievement in School: What Works. CEA Handbook; Education Canada* (q.); *CEA Newsletter* (8/yr.); *Education in Canada: An Overview; Class Size, Academic Achievement and Public Policy; Disruptive Behaviour in Today's Classroom; Financing Canadian Education; Secondary Schools in Canada: The National Report of the Exemplary*

Schools Project; Making Sense of the Canadian Charter of Rights and Freedom: A Handbook for Administrators and Teachers; The School Calendar.

Canadian Library Association. 200 Elgin St., Suite 602, Ottawa, ON K2P IL5, Canada. (613) 232-9625. Fax (613)563-9895. E-mail ai075@freenet.carleton.ca. Website http://www.cla.amlibs.ca. Vicki Whitmell, Exec. Dir. The mission of the Canadian Library Association is to provide leadership in the promotion, development, and support of library and information services in Canada for the benefit of Association members, the profession, and Canadian society. In the spirit of this mission, CLA aims to engage the active, creative participation of library staff, trustees, and governing bodies in the development and management of high quality Canadian library service; to assert and support the right of all Canadians to the freedom to read and to free universal access to a wide variety of library materials and services; to promote librarianship and to enlighten all levels of government as to the significant role that libraries play in educating and socializing the Canadian people; and to link libraries, librarians, trustees, and others across the country for the purpose of providing a unified nationwide voice in matters of critical concern. *Membership:* 2,300 individuals, 700 institutions, 100 Associates and Trustees. *Dues:* $50-$300. *Meetings:* 1999 Annual Conference, Jun 18-22, Toronto; 2000, Edmonton, June. *Publication: Feliciter* (membership magazine, 10/yr.).

Canadian Museums Association/Association des musées canadiens (CMA/AMC). 280 Metcalfe St., Suite 400, Ottawa, ON K2P 1R7, Canada. (613)567-0099. Fax (613)233-5438. E-mail info@museums.ca. Website http://www.museums.ca. John G. McAvity, Exec. Dir. The Canadian Museums Association is a nonprofit corporation and registered charity dedicated to advancing public museums and museum works in Canada, promoting the welfare and better administration of museums, and fostering a continuing improvement in the qualifications and practices of museum professionals. *Membership:* 2,000. *Meeting:* CMA Annual Conference, spring. *Publications: Museogramme* (bi-mo. newsletter); *Muse* (q. journal, Canada's only national, bilingual, scholarly magazine devoted to museums, it contains museum-based photography, feature articles, commentary, and practical information); *The Official Directory of Canadian Museums and Related Institutions* (1997-99 edition) lists all museums in Canada plus information on government departments, agencies, and provincial and regional museum associations.

Canadian Publishers' Council (CPC). 250 Merton St., Suite 203, Toronto, ON M4S 1B1, Canada. (416)322-7011. Fax (416)322-6999. Website http://www.pubcouncil.ca. Jacqueline Hushion, Exec. Dir. CPC members publish and distribute an extensive list of Canadian and imported learning materials in a complete range of formats, from traditional textbook and ancillary materials to CDs and interactive video. The primary markets for CPC members are schools, universities and colleges, bookstores, and libraries. CPC also provides exhibits throughout the year and works through a number of subcommittees and groups within the organization to promote effective book publishing. CPC was founded in 1910. *Membership*: 27 companies, educational institutions, or government agencies that publish books as an important facet of their work.

National Film Board of Canada (NFBC). 350 Fifth Ave., Suite 4820, New York, NY 10118. (212)629-8890. Fax (212)629-8502. E-mail gsem78a@prodigy.com. John Sirabella, US Marketing Mgr./Nontheatrical Rep. Established in 1939, the NFBC's main objective is to produce and distribute high-quality audiovisual materials for educational, cultural, and social purposes.

Ontario Film Association, Inc. (also known as the Association for the Advancement of Visual Media/L'association pour l'avancement des médias visuels). 100 Lombard Street 303, Toronto, ON M5C 1M3 Canada (416)363-3388; Fax:1-800-387-1181, E-mail info@accessola.com. Website http://www.accessola.org. Lawrence A. Moore, Executive Director. A membership organization of buyers, and users of media whose objectives are to promote the sharing of ideas and information about visual media through education, publications and advocacy. *Membership*: 112. *Dues*: $120, personal membership; $215, assosiate membership. *Meetings:* OFA Media Showcase, spring.

Part Six
Graduate Programs

Introduction

This directory describes graduate programs in Instructional Technology, Educational Media and Communications, School Library Media, and closely allied programs in the United States. This year's list includes four new programs. One institution indicated that their program had been discontinued, and has been deleted from the listings. Master's, Specialist, and doctoral degrees are combined into one unified list.

Information in this section can be considered current as of early 1998 for most programs. In the majority of cases, department chairs or their representatives responded to a questionnaire mailed or e-mailed to them during November of 1997. Programs for which we received no updated information are indicated by an asterisk (*).

Entries provide as much of the following information as furnished by respondents: (1) name and address of the institution; (2) chairperson or other individual in charge of the program; (3) types of degrees offered and specializations, emphases, or tracks, including information on careers for which candidates are prepared; (4) special features of the degree program; (5) admission requirements; (6) degree requirements; (7) number of full-time and part-time faculty; (8) number of full-time and part-time students; (9) types of financial assistance available; and (10) the number of degrees awarded by type in 1997. All grade-point averages (GPAs), test scores, and degree requirements are minimums unless stated otherwise. The Graduate Record Examination, Miller Analogies Test, National Teacher's Examination, and other standardized tests are referred to by their acronyms. The Test of English as a Foreign Language (TOEFL) appears in many of the *Admission Requirements*, and in most cases this test is required only for international students. Although some entries explicitly state application fees, most do not. Prospective students should assume that most institutions require a completed application, transcripts of all previous collegiate work, and a non-refundable application fee.

Directors of advanced professional programs for instructional technology or media specialists should find this degree program information useful as a means of comparing their own offerings and requirements with those of institutions offering comparable programs. This listing, along with the Classified List, should also assist individuals in locating institutions that best suit their interests and requirements. In addition, a comparison of degree programs across several years may help scholars with historical interests trace trends and issues in the field over time.

Additional information on the programs listed, including admission procedure instructions, may be obtained by contacting individual program coordinators. General or graduate catalogs and specific program information usually are furnished for a minimal charge. In addition, most graduate programs now have e-mail contact addresses and Web sites which provide a wealth of descriptive information.

We are greatly indebted to those individuals who responded to our requests for information. Although the editors expended considerable effort to ensure currency and completeness of the listings, there may be institutions within the United States that now have programs of which we are unaware. Readers are encouraged to furnish new information to the publisher who, in turn, will contact the program for inclusion in the next edition of *EMTY*.

Oratile Maribe Branch
Section Editor

Graduate Programs in
Instructional Technology [IT]

CLASSIFIED LIST

Computer Applications

California State University-San Bernardino [M.A.]

State University of New York at Stony Brook [Master's: Technological Systems Management/Educational Computing]

University of Iowa [M.A.]

Valdosta State University [M.Ed. in IT/Technology Applications]

Computer Education

Appalachian State University [M.A.: Educational Media and Technology/Computers]

Arizona State University, Department of Educational Media and Computers [M.A., Ph.D.: Educational Media and Computers]

Arkansas Tech University [Master's]

Buffalo State College [M.S.: Education/Educational Computing]

California State University-Dominguez Hills [M.A., Certificate: Computer-Based Education]

California State University-Los Angeles [M.A. in Education/Computer Education]

California State University-San Bernardino [Advanced Certificate Program: Educational Computing]

Central Connecticut State University [M.S.: Educational Technology/Computer Technologies]

Concordia University [M.A.: Computer Science Education]

East Carolina University [M.A.: Education/IT Computers]

Eastern Washington University [M.Ed.: Computer Education]

Fairfield University [M.A.: Media/Educational Technology with Computers in Education]

Florida Institute of Technology [Master's, Ph.D.: Computer Education]

Fontbonne College [M.S.]

George Mason University [M.Ed.: Special Education Technology, Computer Science Educator]

Iowa State University [M.S., M.Ed., Ph.D.: Curriculum and IT/Instructional Computing]

Jacksonville University [Master's: Computer Education]

Kansas State University [M.S. in Secondary Education/Educational Computing; Ed.D., Ph.D.: Curriculum and Instruction/Educational Computing]

Kent State University [M.A., M.Ed.: Instructional Computing]

Minot State University [M.Ed., M.S.: Math and Computer Science]

New York Institute of Technology [Specialist Certificate: Computers in Education]

North Carolina State University [M.S., M.Ed.: IT-Computers]

Northern Illinois University [M.S.Ed., Ed.D.: IT/Educational Computing]

Northwest Missouri State University [M.S.: School Computer Studies; M.S.Ed.: Educational Uses of Computers]

Nova Southeastern University [M.S., Ed.S.: Computer Science Education]

Ohio University [M.Ed.: Computer Education and Technology]

Pace University [M.S.E.: Curriculum and Instruction/Computers]

San Diego State University [Master's in Educational Technology/Computers in Education]

San Francisco State University [Master's: Instructional Computing]

San Jose State University [Master's: Computers and Interactive Technologies]

State University College of Arts and Sciences at Potsdam [M.S.Ed.: IT and Media Management/Educational Computing]

State University of New York at Stony Brook [Master's: Technological Systems Management/Educational Computing]

Syracuse University [M.S., Ed.D., Ph.D., Advanced Certificate: Media Production]

Texas A&M University-Commerce [Master's: Learning Technology and Information Systems/Educational Micro Computing]

Texas Tech University [M.Ed.: IT/Educational Computing]

University of Georgia [M.Ed., Ed.S.: Computer-Based Education]

University of Illinois at Urbana-Champaign [M.A., M.S., Ed.M.: Educational Computing; Ph.D.: Education Psychology/Educational Computing]

University of North Texas [M.S.: Computer Education and Instructional Systems]

The University of Oklahoma [Master's: Computer Applications]

University of Toledo [Master's, Ed.S., D.Ed.: Instructional Computing]

University of Washington [Master's, Ed.D., Ph.D.]

Virginia Polytechnic Institute and State University
[M.A., Ed.D., Ph.D.: IT]
Wright State University [M.Ed.: Computer
Education; M.A.: Computer Education]

Distance Education
Fairfield University [M.A.: Media/Educational
Technology with Satellite Communications]
Iowa State University [M.S., M.Ed., Ph.D.:
Curriculum and IT]
New York Institute of Technology [Specialist
certificate]
Nova Southeastern University [M.S., Ed.D.: IT]
San Jose State University [Master's: Telecommuni-
cations & online courses via internet]
Texas A&M University [Ph.D.: EDCI]
Texas Tech University [M.Ed.: IT]
University of Northern Colorado [Ph.D.:
Educational Technology]
Western Illinois University [Master's]

Educational Leadership
Auburn University [Ed.D.]
Barry University [Ph.D.: Educational Technology
Leadership]
George Washington University [M.A.: Education
and Human Development/Educational
Technology Leadership]
United States International University [Master's,
Ed.D.: Technology Leadership for Learning]
University of Colorado at Denver [Ph.D.: Educa-
tional Leadership and Innovation/Curriculum,
Learning, and Technology]
Valdosta State University [M.Ed., Ed.S.: IT/
Technology Leadership]

Human Performance
Boise State University [M.S.: IT and Performance
Technology]
Governors State University [M.A.: Communication
with Human Performance and Technology]
University of Southern California [Ed.D.: Human
Performance Technology]
University of Toledo [Master's, Ed.S., Ed.D.:
Human Resources Development]

Information Studies
Drexel University [M.S., M.S.I.S.]
Emporia State University [Ph.D.: Library and Infor-
mation Management]
Rutgers [M.L.S.: Information Retrieval; Ph.D.:
Communication (Information Systems)]
Simmons College [M.S.: Information Science/
Systems]
Southern Connecticut State University [Sixth Year
Professional Diploma: Library-Information
Studies/IT]

St. Cloud State University [Master's, Ed.S.:
Information Technologies]
Texas A&M-Commerce [Master's: Learning Tech-
nology and Information Systems/Library and
Information Science]
University of Alabama [Ph.D.]
University of Arizona [M.A.: Information
Resources and Library Science]
University of Central Arkansas [M.S.: Information
Science/Media Information Studies]
University of Maryland [Doctorate: Library and
Information Services]
University of Missouri-Columbia [Ph.D.: Informa-
tion and Learning Technologies]
The University of Oklahoma [Dual Master's:
Educational Technology and Library and
Information Systems]
The University of Rhode Island [M.L.I.S.]
University of Washington [Master's, Ed.D., Ph.D.]
Western Oregon State College [MS: Information
Technology]

Innovation
Pennsylvania State University [M.Ed., M.S., Ed.D.,
Ph.D.: Instructional Systems/Emerging
Technologies]
University of Colorado at Denver [Ph.D.: Educa-
tional Leadership and Innovation]
Walden University [M.S., Ph.D.: Educational
Change and Technology Innovation]

Instructional Design and Development
Auburn University [M.Ed., M.S.]
Bloomsburg University [M.S.: IT]
Brigham Young University [M.S., Ph.D.]
Clarion University of Pennsylvania [M.S.:
Communication/Training and Development]
Fairfield University [Certificate of Advanced
Studies: Media/Educational Technology:
Instructional Development]
George Mason University [M.Ed.: IT/Instructional
Design and Development]
Governors State University [M.A.: Communication
with Human Performance and Training/
Instructional Design]
Indiana University [Ph.D., Ed.D.: Instructional
Analysis, Design, and Development]
Iowa State University [M.S., M.Ed., Ph.D.:
Curriculum and IT/Instruction Design]
Ithaca College [M.S.: Corporate Communications]
Lehigh University [Master's]
Michigan State University [M.A.: Educational
Technology and Instructional Design]
North Carolina Central University [M.S.:
Instructional Development/Design]
Northern Illinois University [M.S.Ed., Ed.D.: IT/
Instructional Design]

Pennsylvania State University [M.Ed., M.S., D.Ed., Ph.D.: Instructional Systems/Systems Design]

Purdue University [Master's, Specialist, Ph.D.: Instructional Development]

San Francisco State University [Master's/Training and Designing Development]

San Jose State University [M.S.: Instructional Design and Development]

Southern Illinois University at Carbondale [M.S.: Education/Instructional Design]

State University of New York at Albany [M.Ed., Ph.D.: Curriculum and Instruction/ Instructional Design and Technology]

State University of New York at Stony Brook [Master's: Technological Systems Management/Educational Computing]

Syracuse University [M.S., Ed.D., Ph.D., Advanced Certificate: Instructional Design; Educational Evaluation; Instructional Development]

Towson State University [M.S.: Instructional Development]

University of Cincinnati [M.A., Ed.D.: Curriculum and Instruction/Instructional Design and Technology]

University of Colorado at Denver [Master's, Ph.D.: Instructional Design]

University of Houston at Clear Lake [Instructional Design]

University of Illinois at Urbana-Champaign [M.A., M.S., Ed.M.; Ph.D. in Educational Psychology/Instructional Design]

University of Iowa [M.A., Ph.D.: Training and Human Resources Development]

University of Massachusetts-Boston [M.Ed.]

University of Northern Colorado [Ph.D. in Educational Technology/Instructional Development and Design]

The University of Oklahoma [Master's]

University of Toledo [Master's, Specialist, doctorate: Instructional Development]

University of Washington [Master's, Ed.D., Ph.D.]

Utah State University [M.S., Ed.S.: Instructional Development]

Virginia Polytechnic Institute and State University [Master's, Ed.D., Ph.D.: IT]

Instructional Technology [IT]

Appalachian State University [M.A.: Educational Media and Technology]

Arizona State University, Learning and IT Dept. [M.Ed., Ph.D.]

Azusa Pacific University [M.Ed.]

Barry University [M.S., Ed.S.: Educational Technology]

Bloomsburg University [M.S.: IT]

Boise State University [M.S.]

Boston University [Ed.M., Certificate of Advanced Graduate Study: Educational Media &

Technology; Ed.D.: Curriculum and Teaching/Educational Media and Technology]

California State University-Los Angeles [M.A.: Education/IT]

California State University-San Bernardino [Advanced Certificate in Educational Technology]

Central Connecticut State University [M.S.: Educational Technology]

Clarke College [M.A.: Technology and Education]

East Carolina University [M.A.: Education/IT Computers]

East Tennessee State [M.Ed.]

Eastern Michigan University [M.A.: Educational Psychology/Educational Technology]

Edgewood College [M.A.: Education/IT]

Fairfield University [M,A., Certificate of Advanced Study: Media/Educational Technology]

Fitchburg State College [M.S.: Communications Media/IT]

Florida Institute of Technology [Master's, Ph.D.]

George Mason University [M.Ed., Ph.D.]

George Washington University [M.A.: Education and Human Development/Educational Technology Leadership]

Georgia Southern University [M.Ed., Ed.S.: IT; Ed.D.: Curriculum Studies/IT]

Georgia State University [M.S., Ph.D.]

Harvard University [M.Ed.: Technology in Education]

Indiana State University [Master's, Ed.S.]

Indiana University [M.S., Ed.S., Ed.D., Ph.D.]

Iowa State University [M.S., M.Ed., Ph.D.: Curriculum and IT]

Jacksonville University [Master's: Educational Technology and Integrated Learning]

Johns Hopkins University [M.S. in Educational Technology for Educators]

Kent State University [M.Ed., M.A; Ph.D.: Educational Psychology/IT]

Lehigh University [Master's; Ed.D.: Educational Technology]

Lesley College [M.Ed., Certificate of Advanced Graduate Study: Technology Education; Ph.D.: Education/Technology Education]

Mankato State University [M.S.: Educational Technology]

Michigan State University [M.A.: Educational Technology]

Montclair State College [certification]

New York Institute of Technology [Master's]

New York University [M.A., Certificate of Advanced Study in Education, Ed.D., Ph.D.]

North Carolina Central University [M.A.: Educational Technology]

North Carolina State University [M.Ed., M.S.: IT—Computers; Ph.D.: Curriculum and Instruction/IT]

234   *Graduate Programs*

Northern Illinois University [M.S.Ed., Ed.D.]
Nova Southeastern University [Ed.S., M.S.:
    Educational Technology; M.S., Ed.D.: IT]
Ohio University [M.Ed.: Computer Education and
    Technology]
Purdue University [Master's, Specialist, Ph.D.:
    Educational Technology]
Radford University [M.S.: Education/Educational
    Media/Technology]
Rosemont College [M.Ed.: Technology in Educa-
    tion; Certificate in Professional Study in
    Technology in Education]
San Diego State University [Master's: Educational
    Technology]
Southern Connecticut State University [M.S.]
Southern Illinois University at Carbondale [M.S.:
    Education; Ph.D.: Education/IT]
State University College of Arts and Sciences at
    Potsdam [M.S.: Education/IT]
State University of New York at Albany [M.Ed.,
    Ph.D.: Curriculum and Instruction/
    Instructional Theory, Design, and
    Technology]
State University of West Georgia [M.Ed., Ed.S.]
Texas A&M-Commerce [Master's: Learning
    Technology and Information Systems/
    Educational Media and Technology]
Texas A&M University [M.Ed.: Educational
    Technology; Ph.D.: EDCI/Educational
    Technology; Ph.D.: Educational Psychology
    Foundations/Learning and Technology]
Texas Tech University [M.Ed.; Ed.D.]
United States International University [Ed.D.:
    Technology and Learning]
University of Central Florida [M.A.: IT/
    Instructional Systems, IT/Educational Media;
    doctorate: Curriculum and Instruction/IT]
University of Cincinnati [M.A., Ed.D.: Curriculum
    and Instruction/Instructional Design and
    Technology]
University of Colorado at Denver [Master's, Ph.D.:
    Learning Technologies]
University of Connecticut [Master's, Ph.D.:
    Educational Technology]
University of Georgia [M.Ed., Ed.S., Ph.D.]
University of Hawaii-Manoa [M.Ed.: Educational
    Technology]
University of Louisville [M.Ed.: Occupational
    Education/IT]
University of Maryland [Ph.D.: Library Science
    and Educational Technology/Instructional
    Communication]
University of Massachusetts-Lowell [M.Ed., Ed.D.,
    Certificate of Advanced Graduate Study:
    Educational Technology]
University of Michigan [Master's, Ph.D.: IT]
University of Missouri-Columbia [Master's, Ed.S.,
    Ph.D.]
University of Nebraska at Kearney [M.S.]

University of Nevada [M.S., Ph.D.]
University of Northern Colorado [M.A., Ph.D.:
    Educational Technology]
University of Northern Iowa [M.A.: Educational
    Technology]
The University of Oklahoma [Master's: Educational
    Technology Generalist; Educational Tech-
    nology; Teaching with Technology; dual
    Master's: Educational Technology and
    Library and Information Systems; doctorate:
    Instructional Psychology and Technology]
University of South Alabama [M.S., Ph.D.]
University of South Carolina [Master's]
University of Southern California [M.A., Ed.D.,
    Ph.D.]
University of Tennessee-Knoxville [M.S.:
    Education, Ed.S., Ed.D., Ph.D.]
The University of Texas [Master's, Ph.D.]
University of Toledo [Master's, Specialist,
    doctorate]
University of Virginia [M.Ed., Ed.S., Ed.D., Ph.D.]
University of Washington [Master's, Ed.D., Ph.D.]
University of Wisconsin-Madison [M.S., Ph.D.]
Utah State University [M.S., Ed.S., Ph.D.]
Virginia Polytechnic Institute and State University
    [M.A., Ed.D., Ph.D.: IT]
Virginia State University [M.S., M.Ed.: Educational
    Technology]
Wayne State University [Master's, Ed.D., Ph.D.,
    Ed.S.]
Webster University [Master's]
Western Illinois University [Master's]
Western Washington University [M.Ed.: IT in
    Adult Education; Elementary Education; IT
    in Secondary Education]
Wright State University [Specialist: Curriculum and
    Instruction/Educational Technology; Higher
    Education/Educational Technology]

Integration
Bloomsburg University [M.S.: IT]
George Mason University [M.Ed.: IT/Integration of
    Technology in Schools]
Jacksonville University [Master's: Educational
    Technology and Integrated Learning]
University of Northern Colorado [Ph.D.: Educa-
    tional Technology/Technology Integration]

Management
Bloomsburg University [M.S.: IT]
Central Connecticut State University [M.S.: Educa-
    tional Technology/Media Management]
Drexel University [M.S., M.S.I.S.]
Emporia State University [Ph.D.: Library and
    Information Management]
Fairfield University [Certificate of Advanced
    Studies: Media/Educational Technology
    with Media Management]

Fitchburg State College [M.S.: Communications Media/Management]

Indiana University [Ed.D., Ph.D.: Implementation and Management]

Minot State University [M.S.: Management]

Northern Illinois University [M.S.Ed., Ed.D.: IT/Media Administration]

Rutgers [M.L.S.: Management and Policy Issues]

Simmons College [M.L.S.: History (Archives Management); Doctor of Arts: Administration; Media Management]

State University College of Arts and Science [M.S.: Education/IT and Media Management]

State University of New York at Stony Brook [Master's: Technological Systems Management]

Syracuse University [M.S., Ed.D., Ph.D., Advanced Certificate]

University of Tennessee-Knoxville [Certification: Instructional Media Supervisor]

Virginia Polytechnic Institute and State University [M.A., Ed.D., Ph.D.: IT]

Wright State University [M.Ed.: Media Supervisor; Computer Coordinator]

Media

Appalachian State University [M.A.: Educational Media and Technology/Media Management]

Arizona State University, Department of Educational Media and Computers [M.A., Ph.D.: Educational Media and Computers]

Boston University [Ed.M., Certificate of Advanced Graduate Study: Educational Media and Technology; Ed.D.: Curriculum and Teaching/Educational Media and Technology]

Central Connecticut State University [M.S.: Educational Technology/Materials Production]

Fitchburg State College [M.S.: Communications Media]

Indiana State University [Ph.D.: Curriculum and Instruction/Media Technology]

Indiana University [Ed.D., Ph.D.: Instructional Development and Production]

Jacksonville State University [M.S.: Education/Instructional Media]

Montclair State College [certification]

Radford University [M.S.: Education/Educational Media/Technology]

San Jose State University [Master's.: Media Design and Development/Media Services Management]

Simmons College [Master's: Media Management]

St. Cloud State University [Master's, Ed.S.: Educational Media]

State University College of Arts and Science at Potsdam [M.S.: Education/IT and Media Management]

Syracuse University [M.S., Ed.D., Ph.D., Advanced Certificate: Media Production]

Texas A&M-Commerce [Master's: Learning Technology and Information Systems/Educational Media and Technology]

University of Central Florida [M.Ed.: IT/Educational Media]

University of Iowa [M.A.: Media Design and Production]

University of Nebraska at Kearney [M.S., Ed.S.: Educational Media]

University of Nebraska-Omaha [M.S.: Education/Educational Media; M.A.: Education/Educational Media]

University of South Alabama [M.A., Ed.S.]

University of Tennessee-Knoxville [Ph.D.: Instructional Media and Technology; Ed.D.: Curriculum and Instruction/Instructional Media and Technology]

University of Virginia [M.Ed., Ed.S., Ed.D., Ph.D.: Media Production]

Virginia Polytechnic Institute and State University [M.A., Ed.D., Ph.D.: IT]

Wright State University [M.Ed.: Educational Media; Media Supervision; M.A.: Educational Media]

Multimedia

Bloomsburg University [M.S.: IT]

Brigham Young University [M.S.: Multimedia Production]

Fairfield University [M.A.: Media/Educational Technology with Multimedia]

Ithaca College [M.S.: Corporate Communications]

Jacksonville University [Master's: Educational Technology and Integration Learning]

Johns Hopkins University [Graduate Certificate]

Lehigh University [Master's]

New York Institute of Technology [Specialist Certificate]

San Francisco State University [Master's: Instructional Multimedia Design]

State University of New York at Stony Brook [Master's: Technological Systems Management/Educational Computing]

Syracuse University [M.S., Ed.D., Ph.D., Advanced Certificate: Media Production]

Texas A&M University [M.Ed.: Educational Technology]

University of Northern Colorado [Ph.D.: Educational Technology/Interactive Technology]

University of Virginia [M.Ed., Ed.S., Ed.D., Ph.D.: Interactive Multimedia]

University of Washington [Master's, Ed.D., Ph.D.]

Utah State University [M.S., Ed.S.]

Wayne State University [Master's: Interactive Technologies]

Western Illinois University [Master's: Interactive Technologies]

Research

Brigham Young University [M.S., Ph.D.: Research and Evaluation]
Drexel University [M.S., M.S.I.S.]
Iowa State University [Ph.D.: Educational/ Technology Research]
Syracuse University [M.S., Ed.D., Ph.D., Advanced Certificate: Educational Research and Theory]
University of Washington [Master's, Ed.D., Ph.D.]

School Library Media

Alabama State University [Master's, Ed.S., Ph.D.]
Arkansas Tech University [Master's]
Auburn University [M.ED., Ed.S.]
Bloomsburg University [M.S.]
Boston University [Massachusetts certification]
Bridgewater State College [M.Ed.]
Central Connecticut State University [M.S.: Educational Technology/Librarianship]
Chicago State University [Master's]
East Carolina University [M.L.S., Certificate of Advanced Study]
East Tennessee State [M.Ed.: Instructional Media]
Emporia State University [Ph.D.: Library and Information Management; M.L.S.; School Library certification]
Kent State University
Louisiana State University [M.L.I.S., C.L.I.S. (post-Master's certificate), Louisiana School Library certification]
Mankato State University [M.S.]
Northern Illinois University [M.S.Ed. Instructional Technology with Illinois state certification]
Nova Southeastern University [Ed.S, M.S.: Educational Media]
Radford University [M.S.: Education/Educational Media; licensure]
Rutgers [M.L.S., Ed.S.]
Simmons College [M.L.S.: Education]
Southern Illinois University at Edwardsville [M.S. in Education: Library/Media]
Southwestern Oklahoma State University [M.Ed.: Library/Media Education]
St. Cloud State University [Master's, Ed.S.]
St. John's University [M.L.S.]
State University of West Georgia [M.Ed., Ed.S.: Media]
Towson State University [M.S.]
University of Alabama [Master's, Ed.S.]
University of Central Arkansas [M.S.]
University of Georgia [M.Ed., Ed.S]
University of Maryland [M.L.S.]
University of Montana [Master's, Ed.S.]
University of North Carolina [M.S.]
University of Northern Colorado [M.A.: Educational Media]
University of South Florida [Master's]
University of Toledo

University of Wisconsin-La Crosse [M.S.: Professional Development/Initial Instructional Library Specialist; Instructional Library Media Specialist]
Utah State University [M.S., Ed.S.]
Valdosta State University [M.Ed., Ed.S.: Instructional Technology/Library/Media]
Webster University
Western Maryland College [M.S.]
William Paterson College [M.Ed., Ed.S., Associate]

Special Education

George Mason University [M.Ed.: IT/Assistive/ Special Education Technology; M.Ed.: Special Education Technology; Ph.D.: Special Education Technology]
Johns Hopkins University [M.S. in Special Education/Technology in Special Education]
Minot State University [M.S.: Early Childhood Special Education; Severe Multiple Handicaps; Communication Disorders]
Western Washington University [M.Ed.: IT in Special Education]

Systems

Bloomsburg University [M.S.: IT]
Drexel University [M.S., M.S.I.S.]
Florida State University [M.S., Ed.S., Ph.D.: Instructional Systems]
Pennsylvania State University [M.Ed., M.S., D.Ed.., Ph.D.: Instructional Systems]
Simmons College [Master's: Information Science/Systems]
Southern Illinois University at Edwardsville [M.S.: Education/Instructional Systems Design]
State University of New York at Stony Brook [Master's: Technological Systems Management]
Texas A&M University-Commerce [Master's: Learning Technology and Information Systems]
University of Central Florida [M.A.: IT/ Instructional Systems]
University of Maryland, Baltimore County [Master's: School Instructional Systems]
University of North Texas [M.S.: Computer Education and Instructional Systems]
The University of Oklahoma [Dual Master's: Educational Technology and Library and Information Systems]

Technology Design

Governors State University [M.A.: Design Logistics]
Kansas State University [Ed.D., Ph.D.: Curriculum and Instruction/Educational Computing, Design, and Telecommunications]
United States International University [Master's, Ed.D.: Designing Technology for Learning]

University of Colorado at Denver [Master's, Ph.D.: Design of Learning Technologies]

Telecommunications
Appalachian State University [M.A.: Educational Media and Technology/Telecommunications]
Johns Hopkins University [Graduate Certificate]
Kansas State University [Ed.D., Ph.D.: Curriculum and Instruction/Educational Computing, Design, and Telecommunications]
San Jose State University [Telecommunications and Distance Learning]
Western Illinois University [Masters: Telecommunications]

Training
Clarion University of Pennsylvania [M.S.: Communication/Training and Development]
Pennsylvania State University [M.Ed., M.S., D.Ed.., Ph.D.: Instructional Systems/Corporate Training]

St. Cloud State University [Master's, Ed.S.: Human Resources Development/Training]
Syracuse University [M.S., Ed.D., Ph.D., Advanced Certificate]
University of Maryland, Baltimore County [Master's: Training in Business and Industry]
University of Northern Iowa [M.A.: Communications and Training Technology]
Wayne State University [Master's: Business and Human Services Training]

Video Production
California State University-San Bernardino [M.A.]
Fairfield University [Certificate of Advanced Study: Media/Educational Technology with TV Production]

ALPHABETICAL LIST

Institutions in this section are listed alphabetically by state.

ALABAMA

Alabama State University. P.O. Box 271, Montgomery, AL 36101-0271. (334)229-4462. Fax (334)229-4961. Website http://www.alasu.edu. Dr. Deborah Little, Coord. Instructional Technology and Media. *Specializations:* School media specialist preparation (K-12) only; Master's and Specialist degrees. *Admission Requirements:* Master's: undergraduate degree with teacher certification, two years classroom experience. Specialist: Master's degree in library/media education. *Degree Requirements:* Master's: 33 semester hours with 300 clock-hour internship. Specialist: 33 semester hours in 600-level courses. *Faculty:* 3 full-time, 2 part-time. *Students:* Master's, 27 part-time; Specialist, 6 part-time. *Financial Assistance:* assistantships, student loans, and scholarships. *Degrees Awarded 1997:* Master's, 9; Specialist, 1.

Auburn University. Educational Foundations, Leadership, and Technology, 3402 Haley Center, Auburn, AL 36849-5216. (334)844-4291. Fax (334)844-4292. E-mail bannosh@mail.auburn.edu. Susan H. Bannon, Coord., Educational Media and Technology. *Specializations:* M.Ed. (non-thesis) and Ed.S. for Library Media certification; M.Ed. (non-thesis) for instructional design specialists who want to work in business, industry, and the military. Ed.D. in Educational Leadership with emphasis on curriculum and new instructional technologies. *Features:* All programs emphasize interactive technologies and computers. *Admission Requirements:* all programs: recent GRE test scores, 3 letters of recommendation, Bachelor's degree from accredited institution, teacher certification (for library media program only). *Degree Requirements:* Library Media Master's: 52 qtr. hours. Instructional Design: 48 qtr. hours. Specialist: 48 qtr. hours. Ed.D.: 120 qtr. hours beyond B.S. degree. *Faculty:* 3 full-time, *Students:* 2 full-time, 15 part-time. *Financial Assistance:* graduate assistantships.

Jacksonville State University. Instructional Media Division, Jacksonville, AL 36265. (256)782-5011. E-mail mmerrill@jsucc.jsu.edu. Martha Merrill, Coord., Dept. of Educational Resources. *Specializations:* M.S. in Education with emphasis on Library Media. *Admission Requirements:* Bachelor's degree in Education. *Degree Requirements:* 36-39 semester hours including 24 in library media. *Faculty:* 2 full-time. *Students:* 20 full- and part-time. *Degrees Awarded 1997:* approx. 10.

University of Alabama. School of Library and Information Studies, Box 870252, Tuscaloosa, AL 35487-0252. (205)348-4610. Fax (205)348-3746. E-mail GCOLEMAN@UA1VM.UA.EDU. Website http://www.slism.slis.ua.edu. J. Gordon Coleman, Jr., Chair. Marion Paris, Ph.D. contact person. *Specializations:* M.L.I.S., Ed.S., and Ph.D. degrees in a varied program including school, public, academic, and special libraries. Ph.D. specializations in Historical Studies, Information Studies, Management, and Youth Studies; considerable flexibility in creating individual programs of study. *Admission Requirements:* M.L.I.S., Ed.S.: 3.0 GPA; 50 MAT or 1500 GRE. Doctoral: 3.0 GPA; 60 MAT or 1650 GRE. *Degree Requirements:* Master's: 36 semester hours. Specialist: 33 semester hours. Doctoral: 48 semester hours plus 24 hours dissertation research. *Faculty:* 10 full-time. *Students:* Master's, 55 full-time, 20 part-time; Specialist, 2 full-time; doctoral, 6 full-time, 6 part-time. *Financial Assistance:* assistantships, grants, student loans, scholarships, work assistance, campus work. *Degrees Awarded 1997:* Master's, 69; Ph.D., 1.

University of South Alabama. Department of Behavioral Studies and Educational Technology, College of Education, University Commons 3100, Mobile, AL 36688. (334)380-2861. Fax (334)380-2758. John Lane, Department Chair; Gayle Davidson-Shivers, Program Dir. *Specializations:* M.A. and Ed.S. in Educational Media, M.S. in Instructional Technology, Ph.D. in Instructional Technology. *Features:* The program emphasizes an extensive training sequence in the instructional systems design process, as well as multimedia-based training. *Admissions Requirements:* Master's: undergraduate degree in appropriate academic field; admission to Graduate School; 40 MAT or 800 GRE (any two areas). Ph.D.: Master's degree, transcripts, three recommendations, goal statement, GRE score. *Degree Requirements:* Master's: 3.0 GPA, 61 quarter hours. Ph.D.: 120 quarter hours, dissertation. *Faculty:* 20 full-time in department. *Students:* Master's, 30; Ph.D., 65. *Financial Assistance:* 10 graduate assistantships. *Degrees Awarded 1997:* 10.

ARIZONA

Arizona State University, Dept. of Learning and Instructional Technology. Box 870611, Tempe, AZ 85287-0611. (602)965-3384. Fax (602)965-0300. Website http://seamonkey.ed.asu.edu/ ~gail/programs/lnt.htm. James D. Klein, Prof. (james.klein@asu.edu); Nancy Archer, Admissions Secretary (icnla@asuvm.inre.asu.edu). *Specializations*: M.Ed. and Ph.D. with focus on the design, development, and evaluation of learning systems. *Features*: research and publication prior to candidacy. *Admission Requirements*: M.Ed.: 3.0 undergraduate GPA, 500 GRE (verbal) or 50 MAT, 550 TOEFL. Ph.D.: 3.2 undergraduate GPA, 1200 GRE (V+Q), 600 TOEFL. *Degree Requirements*: M.Ed.: 30 semester hours, internship, comprehensive exam. Ph.D.: 84 semester hours beyond Bachelor's degree, comprehensive exam, research/publication, dissertation. *Faculty*: 6 full-time. *Students*: M.Ed., 15 full-time, 20 part-time; Ph.D., 10 full-time, 10 part-time. *Financial Assistance*: assistantships, tuition waivers, and student loans for qualified applicants. *Degrees Awarded 1997:* M.Ed., 11; Ph.D., 2.

Arizona State University, Dept. of Educational Media and Computers. Box 870111, Tempe, AZ 85287-0111. (602)965-7192. Fax (602)965-7193. E-mail bitter@asu.edu. Dr. Gary G. Bitter, Coord. *Specializations:* M.A. and Ph.D. in Educational Media and Computers. *Features:* A three semester-hour course in Instructional Media Design is offered via CD-ROM or World Wide Web. *Admission Requirements:* M.A.: Bachelor's degree, 550 TOEFL, 500 GRE, 45 MAT. *Degree Requirements:* M.A.: 36 semester hours (24 hours in educational media and computers, 9 hours education, 3 hours outside education); internship; comprehensive exam; practicum; thesis not required. Ph.D.: 93 semester hours (24 hours in educational media and computers, 57 hours in education, 12 hours outside education); thesis; internship; practicum. *Faculty:* 5 full-time, 1 part-time. *Financial Assistance:* assistantships, grants, student loans, and scholarships.

University of Arizona. School of Information Resources and Library Science, 1515 E. First St., Tucson, AZ 85719. (520)621-3565. Fax (520)621-3279. E-mail sirls@u.arizona.edu. Website http://www.sir.arizona.edu. The School of Information Resources and Library Science offers courses focusing on the study of information and its impact as a social phenomenon. The School offers an M.A. degree with a major in Information Resources and Library Science, which is heavily weighted in technology and emphasizes theoretical constructs. Competence and adaptability in managing information and in utilizing advancing technologies are key aims of the curriculum. The program is fully accredited by the American Library Association. The School offers course work that leads toward the Ph.D. degree with a major in Library Science. *Features:* The School offers a virtual education program via the Internet. Between two and three courses are offered per semester. *Admission Requirements:* Very competitive for both degrees. Minimum criteria include: undergraduate GPA of 3.0 or better; competitive GRE scores; two letters of recommendation reflecting the writer's opinion of the applicant's potential as a graduate student; a resume of work and educational experience; written statement of intent. The School receives a large number of applications and accepts the best qualified students. Admission to the doctoral program may require a personal interview and a faculty member must indicate willingness to work with the student. *Degree Requirements:* M.A.: a minimum of 36 units of graduate credit. Students may elect the thesis option replacing 6 units of course work. Ph.D.: at least 48 hours of course work in the major, a substantial number of hours in a minor subject supporting the major, dissertation. The University has a 12-unit residency requirement which may be completed in the summer or in a regular semester. More detailed descriptions of the program are available at the School's Website. *Faculty*: 5 full-time. *Students:* 220 total; M.A.: 51 full-time; Ph.D.: 12 full-time. *Degrees Awarded 1999:* M.A.: 75.

ARKANSAS

Arkansas Tech University. Russellville, AR 72801-2222. (501)968-0434. Fax (501)964-0811. E-mail SECZ@atuvm.atu.edu, czimmer@cswnet.com. Website http://www.atu.edu, http://www.angelfire.com/ar/librarymedia. Connie Zimmer, Asst. Professor of Secondary Education, Coord. *Specializations:* Master's degrees in Education in Instructional Technology with specializations in library media education, computer education, general program of study, and training education. NCATE accredited institution. *Admission Requirements:* GRE, 2.5 undergraduate GPA, Bachelor's degree. *Degree Requirements:* 36 semester hours, B average in major hours, action research project. *Faculty:* 1 full-time, 5 part-time. *Students:* 22 full-time, 57 part-time. *Financial Assistance:* graduate assistantships, grants, student loals. *Degrees Awarded 1997:* 50.

University of Central Arkansas. Educational Media/Library Science, Campus Box 4918, Conway, AR 72035. (501)450-5463. Fax (501)450-5680. E-mail selvinr@mail.uca.edu. Website http://www.coe.uca.edu/aboutaat.htm. Selvin W. Royal, Prof., Chair, Academic Technologies and Educational Leadership. *Specializations:* M.S. in Educational Media/Library Science and Information Science. Tracks: School Library Media, Public Information Agencies, Media Information Studies. *Admission Requirements:* transcripts, GRE scores, 2 letters of recommendation, personal interview, written rationale for entering the profession. *Degree Requirements:* 36 semester hours, optional thesis, practicum (for School Library Media), professional research paper. *Faculty:* 5 full-time, 2 part-time. *Students:* 6 full-time, 42 part-time. *Financial Assistance:* 3 to 4 graduate assistantships each year. *Degrees Awarded 1997:* 28.

CALIFORNIA

Azusa Pacific University. 901 E. Alosta, Azusa, CA, 91702. (626)815-5376, fax (626)815-5416. E-mail arnold@apu.edu. Brian Arnold, contact person. *Specializations:* M.Ed. with emphasis in Technology. *Admission Requirements:* undergraduate degree from accredited institution, 3.0 GPA, ownership of a designated laptop computer and software. *Faculty:* 2 full-time, 16 part-time. *Students:* 180 part-time. *Financial assistance:* student loans. *Degrees Awarded 1997:* 20.

California State University-Dominguez Hills. 1000 E. Victoria St., Carson, CA 90747. (310)243-3524. Fax (310)243-3518. E-mail pdesberg@dhvx20.csudh.edu. Website http://www.csudh.soe.edu. Peter Desberg, Prof., Coord., Computer-Based Education Program. *Specializations*: M.A. and Certificate in Computer-Based Education. *Admission Requirements*: 2.75 GPA. *Degree Requirements*: M.A.: 30 semester hours including project. Certificate: 15 hours. *Faculty*: 2 full-time, 2 part-time. *Students*: 50 full-time, 40 part-time. *Degrees Awarded 1997*: M.A., 20.

California State University-Los Angeles. Division of Educational Foundations and Interdivisional Studies, Charter School of Education, 5151 State University Drive, Los Angeles, CA 90032. (323)343-4330. Fax (323)343-5336. E-mail efis@calstatela.edu. Website http://web.calstatela.edu/academic/found/efis/index.html. Dr. Fernando A. Hernandez, Division Chairperson. *Specializations:* M.A. degree in Education, option in New Media Design and Production;Computer Education and Leadership. *Degree Requirements:* 2.75 GPA in last 90 qtr. units, 45 qtr. units, comprehensive written exam or thesis or project. Must also pass Writing Proficiency Examination (WPE), a California State University-Los Angeles requirement. *Faculty:* 7 full-time. *Degrees Awarded 1998:* 20.

*California State University-San Bernardino. 5500 University Parkway, San Bernardino, CA 92407. (909)880-5600, (909)880-5610. Fax (909)880-7010. E-mail monaghan@wiley.csusb.edu. Website http://soe.csusb.edu/soe/programs/eyec/. Dr. Jim Monaghan, Program Coord. *Specializations:* M.A. with two emphases: Video Production and Computer Applications. These emphases allow students to choose courses related to the design and creation of video products or courses involving lab and network operation of advanced microcomputer applications. The program does not require teaching credential certification. Advanced certificate programs in Educational Computing and Educational Technology are available. *Admission Requirements:* Bachelor's degree, appropriate work experience, 3.0 GPA, completion of introductory computer course and expository writing course. *Degree Requirements:* 48 units including a Master's project (33 units completed in residence); 3.0 GPA; grades of "C" or better in all courses. *Faculty:* 5 full-time, 1 part-time. *Students:* 106. *Financial Assistance:* Contact Office of Graduate Studies. *Degrees Awarded 1996:* 12.

San Diego State University. Educational Technology, San Diego, CA 92182-1182. (619)594-6718. Fax (619)594-6376. E-mail patrick.harrison@sdsu.edu. Website http://edweb.sdsu.edu. Dr. Patrick Harrison, Prof., Chair. *Specialization:* Master's degree in Educational Technology with specializations in Computers in Education, Workforce Education, and Lifelong Learning. The Educational Technology Department participates in a College of Education joint doctoral program with The Claremont Graduate School.*Degree Requirements:* 36 semester hours (including 6 prerequisite hours), 950 GRE (verbal + quantitative). *Faculty:* 8 full-time, 5 part-time. *Students:* 120. *Financial Assistance:* graduate assistantships. *Degrees Awarded 1996:* Master's, 40.

San Francisco State University. College of Education, Department of Instructional Technology, 1600 Holloway Ave., San Francisco, CA 94132. (415)338-1509. Fax (415)338-0510. E-mail michaels@sfsu.edu. Dr. Eugene Michaels, Chair; Mimi Kasner, Office Coord. *Specializations:* Master's degree with emphasis on Instructional Multimedia Design, Training and Designing Development, and Instructional Computing. The school also offers an 18-unit Graduate Certificate in Training Systems Development, which can be incorporated into the Master's degree. *Features:* This program emphasizes the instructional systems approach, cognitivist principles of learning design, practical design experience, and project-based courses. *Admission Requirements:* Bachelor's degree, appropriate work experience, 2.5 GPA, interview with the department chair. *Degree Requirements:* 30 semester hours, field study project, or thesis. *Faculty:* 1 full-time, 16 part-time. *Students:* 250-300. *Financial Assistance:* Contact Office of Financial Aid. *Degrees Awarded 1998:* 50.

San Jose State University. One Washington Square, San Jose, CA 95192-0076 (408)924-3618 (Office), Fax (408)3713. Website: http://www.sjsu.edu.depts/it/Home.html. Dr. Roberta Barba, Program Chair. *Degrees:* Master's degree. *Special Features:* Has six areas of specialization: Instructional Design and Development, Media Design and Development. Media Services and Management, Computers and Interactive Technologies, Telecommunications and Distance Learning, and Teaching and Technology. We offer many courses that can be taken online via the internet. Three certificate programs are offered: Multimedia, training methods for business and industry, and computer concepts and applications. *Admission Requirements:* Baccalaureate degree from approved university, appropriate work experience, minimum GPA of 2.5, and minimum score of 550 on TOEFL(Test of English as a Foreign Language). 36 semester hours (which includes 6 prerequisite hours). *Faculty:* $ full-time, 12 part-time. 10 full-time master's students, 260 part-time. *Financial Assistance:* Assistantships, grants, student loans and scholarships are available. *Degrees Awarded 1998:* 52.

*United States International University. School of Education, 10455 Pomerado Rd., San Diego, CA 92131-1799. (619)635-4715. Fax (619)635-4714. E-mail feifer@sanac.usiu.edu. Richard Feifer, contact person. *Specializations:* Master's in Designing Technology for Learning, Planning Technology for Learning, and Technology Leadership for Learning. Ed.D. in Technology and Learning offers three specializations: Designing Technology for Learning, Planning Technology for Learning, and Technology Leadership for Learning. *Features:* interactive multimedia, cognitive approach to integrating technology and learning. *Admission Requirements:* Master's: English proficiency, interview, 3.0 GPA with 1900 GRE or 2.0 GPA with satisfactory MAT score. *Degree Requirements:* Ed.D.: 88 graduate qtr. units, dissertation. *Faculty:* 2 full-time, 4 part-time. *Students:* Master's, 32 full-time, 12 part-time; doctoral, 6 full-time, 1 part-time. *Financial Assistance:* internships, graduate assistantships, grants, student loans, scholarships. *Degrees Awarded 1996:* Master's, 40; Ed.D., 2.

University of Southern California. 702C W.P.H., School of Education, Los Angeles, CA 90089-0031. (213)740-3288. Fax (213)740-3889. Instructional Technology, Dept. of Educational Psychology and Technology. E-mail kazlausk@mizar.usc.edu. Website http://www.usc.edu/department/itp/; also http://www.usc.edu/department/education/sed.index.htm. Dr. Richard Clark, Prof., Doctoral programs; Dr. Edward J. Kazlauskas, Prof., Program Chair, Master's programs in Instructional Technology. *Specializations:* M.A., Ed.D., Ph.D. to prepare individuals to teach instructional technology; manage educational media and training programs in business, industry, research and development organizations, schools, and higher educational institutions; perform research in instructional technology and media; and deal with computer-driven technology. A new Ed.D. program in Human Performance Technology was implemented in 1996 with satellite programs in Silicon Valley and Orange County. *Features:* special emphasis upon instructional design, systems analysis, and computer-based training. *Admission Requirements:* Bachelor's degree, 1000 GRE. *Degree Requirements:* M.A.: 28 semester hours, thesis optional. Doctoral: 67 units, 20 of which can be transferred from a previous Master's degree. Requirements for degree completion vary according to type of degree and individual interest. Ph.D. requires an outside field in addition to course work in instructional technology and education, more methodology and statistics work, and coursework in an outside field. *Faculty:* 5 full-time, 1 part-time. *Students:* M.A., 5 full-time, 15 part-time; doctoral, 50 full-time, 15 part-time. *Financial Assistance:* part-time, instructional technology-related work available in the Los Angeles area and on campus.

COLORADO

University of Colorado at Denver. School of Education, Campus Box 106, P.O. Box 173364, Denver CO 80217-3364. (303)556-6022. Fax (303)556-4479. E-mail brent.wilson@cudenver.edu. Website http://www.cudenver.edu/public/education/ilt/ILThome.html. Brent Wilson, Program Chair, Information and Learning Technologies, Division of Technology and Special Services. *Specializations*: M.A.; Ph.D. in Educational Leadership and Innovation with emphasis in Curriculum, Learning, and Technology. *Features*: design and use of learning technologies; instructional design. Ph.D. students complete 10 semester hours of doctoral labs (small groups collaborating with faculty on difficult problems of practice). Throughout the program, students complete a product portfolio of research, design, teaching, and applied projects. The program is cross-disciplinary, drawing on expertise in technology, adult learning, systemic change, research methods, reflective practice, and cultural studies. *Admission Requirements*: M.A. and Ph.D.: satisfactory GPA, GRE, writing sample, letters of recommendation, transcripts. *Degree Requirements*: M.A.: 36 semester hours including 19 hours of core course work and portfolio; practicum and additional requirements for state certification in library media; internship required for careers in corporate settings. Ph.D.: 40 semester hours of coursework and labs, plus 30 dissertation hours; portfolio; dissertation. *Faculty*: 5 full-time, 3 part-time. *Students:* M.A., 25 full-time, 120 part-time; Ph.D., 6 full-time, 20 part-time. *Financial Assistance*: assistantships, internships. *Degrees Awarded 1998*: M.A.: 33; Ph.D: 3.

University of Northern Colorado. Division of Educational Psychology, Statistics, and Technology, College of Education, Greeley, CO 80639. (970)351-2368. Fax (970)351-1622. E-mail bauer@edtech.unco.edu. Website http://www.edtech.unco.edu/COE/EDTECH/EDTECH.html. Jeffrey Bauer, Assoc. Prof., Chair, Educational Technology. *Specializations:* M.A. in Educational Technology; M.A. in Educational Media; Ph.D. in Educational Technology with emphases in Distance Education, Instructional Development/Design, Interactive Technology, and Technology Integration. *Features:* Graduates are prepared for careers as instructional technologists, course designers, trainers, instructional developers, media specialists, and human resource managers. *Admission Requirements:* M.A.: Bachelor's degree, 3.0 undergraduate GPA, 1500 GRE. Ph.D.: 3.2 GPA, three letters of recommendation, congruency between applicant's statement of career goals and program goals, 1650 GRE, interview with faculty. *Faculty:* 5 full-time, 2 part-time. *Students:* M.A., 5 full-time, 60 part-time; Ph.D., 12 full-time, 22 part-time. *Financial Assistance:* assistantships, grants, student loans, scholarships. *Degrees Awarded 1997:* M.A., 25; Ph.D., 5.

CONNECTICUT

Central Connecticut State University. 1615 Stanley St., New Britain, CT 06050. (860)832-2130. Fax (860)832-2109. E-mail abedf@ccsu.ctstateu.edu. Website http://www.ccsu.edu. Farough Abed, Coord., Educational Technology Program. *Specializations:* M.S. in Educational Technology. Curriculum emphases include instructional technology, instructional design, message design, and computer technologies. *Features:* The program supports the Center for Innovation in Teaching and Technology to link students with client-based projects. *Admission Requirements:* Bachelor's degree, 2.7 undergraduate GPA. *Degree Requirements:* 33 semester hours, optional thesis or Master's final project (3 credits). *Faculty:* 2 full-time, 4 part-time. *Students:* 45. *Financial Assistance:* graduate assistant position. *Degrees Awarded 1997:* 14.

Fairfield University. N. Benson Road, Fairfield, CT 06430. (203)254-4000. Fax (203)254-4047. E-mail imhefzallah@fair1.fairfield.edu. Dr. Ibrahim M. Hefzallah, Prof., Dir., Educational Technology Department; Dr. Justin Ahnn, Assistant Professor of Educational Technology, E-mail jahnn@fair.fairfield.edu. *Specializations:* M.A. and a certificate of Advanced Studies in Educational Technology in one of four areas of concentrations: Computers-in-Education. Instructional Development, School Media Specialist, and Television Production; customized course of study also available. *Features:* emphasis on theory, practice, and new instructional developments in computers in education, multimedia, and satellite communications. *Admission Requirements:* Bachelor's degree from accredited institution with 2.67 GPA. *Degree Requirements:* 33 credits. *Faculty:* 2 full-time, 8 part-time. *Students:* 4 full-time, 110 part-time. *Financial Assistance:* assistantships, student loans. *Degrees Awarded 1999:* 18.

Southern Connecticut State University. Department of Library Science and Instructional Technology, 501 Crescent St., New Haven, CT 06515. (203)392-5781. Fax (203)392-5780. E-mail libscienceit@scsu.ctstateu.edu. Website http://scsu.ctstateu.edu. Nancy Disbrow, Chair. *Specializations:* M.S. in Instructional Technology; Sixth-Year Professional Diploma Library-Information Studies (student may select area of specialization in Instructional Technology). *Degree Requirements:* for Instructional Technology only, 36 semester hours. For sixth-year degree: 30 credit hours with 6 credit hours of core requirements, 9-15 credit hours in specialization. *Faculty:* 1 full-time. *Students:* 3 full-time and 38 part-time in M.S./IT program. *Financial Assistance:* graduate assistantship (salary $1,800 per semester; assistants pay tuition and a general university fee sufficient to defray cost of student accident insurance). *Degrees Awarded 1997:* M.S., 2.

University of Connecticut. U-64, Storrs, CT 06269-2064. (860)486-0181. Fax (860)486-0180. E-mail sbrown@UConnvm.UConn.edu, or myoung@UConnvm.UConn.edu. Website http://www.ucc.uconn.edu/~wwwepsy/. Scott W. Brown, Chair; Michael Young, contact person. *Specializations:* M.A. and Ph.D. degrees with an emphasis in Educational Technology as a specialization within the Program of Cognition and Instruction, in the Department of Educational Psychology. *Features:* The emphasis in Educational Technology is a unique program at UConn. It is co-sponsored by the Department of Educational Psychology in the School of Education and the Psychology Department in the College of Liberal Arts and Sciences. The emphasis in Educational Technology within the Cognition and Instruction Program seeks to provide students with knowledge of theory and applications regarding the use of advanced technology to enhance learning and thinking. This program provides suggested courses and opportunities for internships and independent study experiences that are directed toward an understanding of both the effects of technology on cognition and instruction, and the enhancement of thinking and learning with technology. Facilities include the UCEML computer lab featuring Mac and IBM networks upgraded for 1998 and a multimedia development center. The School of Education also features a multimedia classroom and auditorium. Faculty research interests include interactive videodisc for anchored instruction and situated learning, telecommunications for cognitive apprenticeship, technology-mediated interactivity for generative learning, and, in cooperation with the National Research Center for Gifted and Talented, research on the use of technology to enhance cooperative learning and the development of gifted performance in all students. *Admission Requirements:* admission to the graduate school at UConn, GRE scores (or other evidence of success at the graduate level). Previous experience in a related area of technology, education, or training is a plus. *Faculty:* The program in Cognition and Instruction has 7 full-time faculty; 3 full-time faculty administer the emphasis in Educational Technology. *Students:* M.A. 4, Ph.D., 18. *Financial Assistance:* graduate assistantships, research fellowships, teaching assistantships, and federal and minority scholarships are available competitively. *Degrees Awarded 1998:* Ph.D., 4 and M.A., 2.

DISTRICT OF COLUMBIA

*George Washington University. School of Education and Human Development, Washington, DC 20052. (202)994-1701. Fax (202)994-2145. Website http://www.gwu.edu/~etl. Dr. William Lynch, Educational Technology Leadership Program. Program is offered through Jones Education Company (JEC). Contact student advisors at (800)777-MIND. *Specialization:* M.A. in Education and Human Development with a major in Educational Technology Leadership. *Features:* 36-hour degree program available via cable television, satellite, Internet, and/or videotape to students across North America and in other locations. The degree is awarded by George Washington University (GWU). Students may work directly with JEC or GWU to enroll. Student advisors at JEC handle inquiries about the program, send out enrollment forms and applications, process book orders, and set up students on an electronic listserv or Web forum. *Admission Requirements:* application fee, transcripts, GRE or MAT scores (50th percentile), two letters of recommendation from academic professionals, computer access, undergraduate degree with 2.75 GPA. *Degree Requirements:* 36 credit hours (including 24 required hours). Required courses include computer application management, media and technology application, software implementation and design, public education policy, and quantitative research methods. *Faculty:* Courses are taught by GWU faculty. *Financial Assistance:* For information, contact the Office of Student Financial Assistance, GWU. Some cable systems that carry JEC offer local scholarships.

FLORIDA

Barry University. Department of Educational Computing and Technology, School of Education, 11300 N.E. Second Ave., Miami Shores, FL 33161. (305)899-3608. Fax (305)899-3718. E-mail jlevine@bu4090.barry.edu. Joel S. Levine, Dir. *Specializations:* M.S. and Ed.S. in Educational Technology, Ph.D. degree in Educational Technology Leadership. *Features:* Majority of the courses (30/36) in M.S. and Ed.S. programs are in the field of Educational Technology. *Admission Requirements:* GRE scores, letters of recommendation, GPA, interview, achievements. *Degree Requirements:* M.S. or Ed. S.: 36 semester credit hours. Ph.D.: 54 credits beyond the Master's including dissertation credits. *Faculty:* 7 full-time, 10 part-time. *Students:* M.S., 8 full-time, 181 part-time; Ed.S., 5 full-time, 44 part-time; Ph.D., 3 full-time, 15 part-time. *Financial Assistance:* assistantships, student loans. *Degrees Awarded 1999:* M.S., 37; Ed.S., 6; Ph.D., 2.

Florida Institute of Technology. Science Education Department, 150 University Blvd., Melbourne, FL 32901-6988. (407)674-8126. Fax (407)674-7598. E-mail fronk@fit.edu. Dr. Robert Fronk, Dept. Head. Website http://www.fit.edu/AcadRes/sci-ed/degree.html#comp-tech-ed. *Specializations*: Master's degree options in Computer Education and Instructional Technology; Ph.D. degree options in Computer Education and Instructional Technology. *Admission Requirements:* 3.0 GPA for regular admission; 2.75 for provisional admission. *Degree Requirements:* Master's: 33 semester hours (15 in computer or and technology education, 9 in education, 9 electives); practicum; no thesis or internship required. Ph.D.: 48 semester hours (12 in computer and technology education, 12 in education, 24 dissertation and research). *Faculty*: 5 full-time. *Students:* 11 full-time, 10 part-time. *Financial Assistance:* graduate student assistantships (full tuition plus stipend) available. *Degrees Awarded 1997:* Master's, 7; Ph.D., 3.

Florida State University. Instructional Systems Program, Department of Educational Research, College of Education, 305 Stone Bldg., Tallahassee, FL 32306. (904)644-4592. Fax (904)644-8776. Website http://www.fsu.edu/~edres/. *Specializations:* M.S., Ed.S, Ph.D. in Instructional Systems with specializations for persons planning to work in academia, business, industry, government, or military. *Features:* Core courses include systems and materials development, development of multimedia, project management, psychological foundations, current trends in instructional design, and research and statistics. Internships are recommended. *Admission Requirements:* M.S.: 3.2 GPA in last two years of undergraduate program, 1000 GRE (verbal plus quantitative), 550 TOEFL (for international applicants). Ph.D.: 1100 GRE (V+Q), 3.5 GPA in last two years; international students, 550 TOEFL. *Degree Requirements:* M.S.: 36 semester hours, 2-4 hour internship, written comprehensive exam. *Faculty:* 5 full-time, 5 part-time. *Students:* M.S., 55; Ph.D., 50. *Financial Assistance:* some graduate research assistantships on faculty grants and contracts, university fellowships. *Degrees Awarded 1997:* M.S.,38; Ph.D., 14 (approximate).

Jacksonville University. Division of Education, 2800 University Boulevard North, Jacksonville, FL 32211. (904)745-7132. Fax (904)745-7159. E-mail mjanz@mail.ju.edu. Dr. Margaret Janz, Interim Dir., School of Education, or Dr. June Main, Coordinator of MAT in Integrated Learning with Educational Technology (jmain@junix.ju.edu). *Specializations:* The Master's in Educational Technology and Integrated Learning is an innovative program designed to guide certified teachers in the use and application of educational technologies in the classroom. It is based on emerging views of how we learn, of our growing understanding of multiple intelligences, and of the many ways to incorporate technology in teaching and learning. Activity-based classes emphasize instructional design for a multimedia environment to reach all students. M.A.T. degrees in Computer Education and in Integrated Learning with Educational Technology. *Features:* The M.A.T. in Computer Education is for teachers who are already certified in an area of education, for those who wish to be certified in Computer Education, kindergarten through community college level. *Degree Requirements:* M.A.T. in Computer Education and in Integrated Learning with Educational Technology: 36 semester hours, including 9-12 hours in core education graduate courses and the rest in computer education with comprehensive exam in last semester of program. Master's in Educational Technology and Integrated Learning: 36 semester hours, including 9 in core graduate education courses, 6 in integrated learning, and the rest in educational technology. Comprehensive exam is to develop a practical group of multimedia applications. *Students:* Computer Education, 8; Integrated Learning with Educational Technology, 20. *Financial Assistance:* student loans and discounts to graduate education students. *Degrees Awarded 1996-97:* Computer Education, 12; Integrated Learning with Educational Technology, 24.

Nova Southeastern University. Fischler Center for the Advancement of Education, 3301 College Ave., Fort Lauderdale, FL 33314. (954)475-7440. (800)986-3223, ext. 8563. Fax (954)262-3905. E-mail simsmich@fcae.nova.edu. Michael Simonson, Program Professor, Instructional Technology and Distance Education. *Specializations:* M.S. and Ed.D in Instructional Technology and distance Education. *Feactures*: Program courses delivered via distance education and face-to-face instruction on weeks-ends and during week-long summer institutes. Emphasis on developing leaders in distance education and instructional technology. Instructional design, systems design, distance education, and media and technology are stressed. Computer-based learning at a distance is emphasized and used as an intergral component of course delivery. Courses geared to the working professional. M.S. Practicum is job-related, as is the practical dissertation. *Admission :* M.S. three letters of recommendation, completed application and transcripts. Ed.D. Three letters of recommendation, completed application, transcripts and completed Masters degree in Instructional Technology or distance Education, or related area. *Degree Requirements:* M.S.: 21 months and 30 semester credits. Ed.D. 3 years and 66 semester credits. *Faculty:* 6 full-time and 20 adjuncts. *Students:* 250 full time. *Degrees awarded 1998:* 40 M.S. and 20 Ed.D.

University of Central Florida. College of Education, ED Room 318, UCF, Orlando, FL 32816-1250. (407)823-2153. Fax (407)823-5622. Websites http://pegasus.cc.ucf.edu/~edmedia and http://pegasus.cc.ucf.edu/~edtech. Richard Cornell, Instructional Systems (cornell@pegasus.cc.ucf.edu); Judy Lee, Educational Media (jlee@pegasus.cc.ucf.edu); Glenda Gunter, Educational Technology (ggunter@pegasus.cc.ucf.edu). *Specializations:* M.A. in Instructional Technology/Instructional Systems; M.Ed. in Instructional Technology/Educational Media; M.A. in Instructional Technology/ Educational Technology. A doctorate in Curriculum and Instruction with an emphasis on Instructional Technology is offered. *Admission Requirements:* interviews for Educational Media and Educational Technology programs. *Degree Requirements:* M.A. in Instructional Technology/Instructional Systems, 39-42 semester hours; M.Ed. in Instructional Technology/Educational Media, 39-45 semester hours; M.A. in Instructional Technology/Educational Technology, 36-45 semester hours. Practicum required in all three programs; thesis, research project, or substitute additional course work. *Faculty:* 4 full-time, 6 part-time. *Students:* Instructional Systems, 70; Educational Media, 35; Educational Technology, 50. Full-time, 120; part-time, 35. *Financial Assistance:* competitive graduate assistantships in department and college, numerous paid internships, limited number of doctoral fellowships. *Degrees Awarded 1997:* 40.

University of South Florida. Instructional Technology Program, Secondary Education Department, College of Education. 4202 Fowler Ave. East, EDU 208B, Tampa, FL 33620. (813)974-1632 (M.Ed.); (813)974-1629 (doctoral). Fax (813)974-3837. E-mail breit@tempest.coedu.usf.edu (M.Ed.), jwhite@typhoon.coedu.usf.edu (doctoral). Website http://www.coedu.usf.edu/institute_tech/. Dr. Frank Breit, master's program, Dr. James A. White, doctoral program. *Specialization:* M.Ed. in Curriculum and Instruction with emphasis in Instructional Technology; Ph.D. in Curriculum and Instruction with emphasis in Instructional Technology. *Features:* Student gain practical experience in the Florida Center for Instructional Technology (FCIT), which provides services to the Department of Education and other grants and contracts, and the Virtual Instructional Team for the Advancement of Learning (VITAL), which provides USF faculty with course development services. The College of Education is one of the largest in the US in terms of enrollment and facilities. As of Fall 1997, a new, technically state-of-the-art building was put into service. *Admission Requirements:* M.Ed.: 3.0 undergraduate GPA, at least half of undergraduate degree earned from accredited institution, and 800 GRE (V+Q), or 2.5 undergraduate GPA in last half of undergraduate degree from accredited institution and 1000 GRE, or a prior graduate degree from an accredited institution and 800 GRE. Applicants must also have a minimum of two years of relevant educational or professional experience as judged by the program faculty. Ph.D.: contact Dr. White for full details; include 3.0 undergraduate GPA in last half of coursework or 3.5 GPA at master's level and 1000 GRE, a master's degree from an accredited institution, three letters of recommendation, and favorable recommendations from program faculty. *Degree Requirements:* M.Ed.: 36-38 semester hours, comprehensive exam. Ph.D.: 77-79 hours, two research tools, two semesters of residency, qualifying examination, and dissertation. *Faculty:* 3 full-time, 2 part-time. *Students:* M.Ed.: 100 full-time, 100 part-time (approx.); Ph.D.: 2 full-time, 14 part-time. *Financial assistance:* assistantships, grants, loans, scholarships, and fellowships. *Degrees Awarded 1997:* M.Ed.: 40, Ph.D., 2.

GEORGIA

Georgia Southern University. College of Education, Statesboro, GA 30460-8131. (912)681-5307. Fax (912)681-5093. Kenneth F. Clark, Assoc. Prof., Dept. of Leadership, Technology, and Human Development. *Specialization:* M.Ed. The school also offers a six-year specialist degree program (Ed.S.), and an Instructional Technology strand is available in the Ed.D. program in Curriculum Studies. *Features:* strong emphasis on technology. *Degree Requirements:* 36 semester hours, including a varying number of hours of media for individual students. *Financial Assistance:* See graduate catalog for general financial aid information. *Faculty:* 4 full-time.

Georgia State University. Middle-Secondary Education and Instructional Technology, University Plaza, Atlanta, GA 30303. (404)651-2510. Fax (404)651-2546. E-mail swharmon@gsu.edu. Website http://www.gsu.edu/~wwwmst/. Dr. Stephen W. Harmon, contact person. *Specializations:* M.S., Ed.S., and Ph.D. in Instructional Technology or Library Media. *Features:* focus on research and practical application of instructional technology in educational and corporate settings. *Admission Requirements:* M.S.: Bachelor's degree, 2.5 undergraduate GPA, 44 MAT or 800 GRE, 550 TOEFL. Ed.S.: Master's degree, teaching certificate, 3.25 graduate GPA, 48 MAT or 900 GRE. Ph.D.: Master's degree, 3.30 graduate GPA, 53 MAT or 500 verbal plus 500 quantitative GRE or 500 analytical GRE. *Degree Requirements:* M.S.: 36 sem, hours, internship, portfolio, comprehensive examination. Ed.S.: 30 sem. hours, internship, and scholarly project. Ph.D.: 66 sem. hours, internship, dissertation. *Faculty:* 6 full-time, 3 part-time. *Students:* 200 M.S., 30 Ph.D. *Financial Assistance:* assistantships, grants, student loans. *Degrees Awarded 1997:* Ph.D., 5; M.S., 30.

State University of West Georgia (formerly West Georgia College). Department of Research, Media, and Technology, 137 Education Annex, Carrollton, GA 30118. (770)836-6558. Fax (770)836-6729. E-mail bmckenzi@westga.edu. Website http://www.westga.edu/soe/rmt/. Dr. Barbara K. McKenzie, Assoc. Prof., Chair. *Specializations:* M.Ed. with specializations in Media and Instructional Technology and add-on certification for students with Master's degrees in other disciplines. The school also offers an Ed.S. program in Media with two options, Media Specialist or Instructional Technology. The program strongly emphasizes technology in the schools. *Admission Requirements:* M.Ed.: 800 GRE, 44 MAT, 550 NTE Core, 2.5 undergraduate GPA. Ed.S.: 900 GRE, 48 MAT, or 575 NTE and 3.25 graduate GPA. *Degree Requirements:* minimum of 60 qtr. hours. *Faculty:* 5 full-time in Media/Technology and 3 in Research; 3 part-time in Media/Technology. *Students:* 6 full-time, 130 part-time. *Financial Assistance:* two graduate assistantships and three graduate research assistantships for the department. *Degrees Awarded 1998:* M.Ed., 20; Ed.S., 20.

University of Georgia. Department of Instructional Technology, College of Education, 604 Aderhold Hall, Athens, GA 30602-7144. (706)542-3810. Fax (706)542-4032. E-mail kgustafs@coe.uga.edu. Website http://itech1.coe.uga.edu. Kent L. Gustafson, Prof. and Chair. *Specializations:* M.Ed. and Ed.S. in Instructional Technology; Ph.D. for leadership positions as specialists in instructional design and development and college faculty. The program offers advanced study for individuals with previous preparation in instructional media and technology, as well as a preparation for personnel in other professional fields requiring a specialty in instructional systems or instructional technology. Representative career fields for graduates include designing new courses, tutorial programs, and instructional materials in the military, industry, medical professional schools, allied health agencies, teacher education, staff development, state and local school systems, higher education, research, and in instructional products development. *Features:* minor areas of study available in a variety of other departments. Personalized programs are planned around a common core of courses and include practica, internships, or clinical experiences. Research activities include special assignments, applied projects, and task forces, as well as thesis and dissertation studies. *Admission Requirements:* all degrees: application to graduate school, satisfactory GRE score, other criteria as outlined in Graduate School Bulletin. *Degree Requirements:* M.Ed.: 36 semester hours with 3.0 GPA, portfolio with oral exam. Ed.S.: 30 semester hours with 3.0 GPA and portfolio exam. Ph.D.: three full years of study beyond the Master's degree, two consecutive semesters full-time residency, comprehensive exam with oral defense, internship, dissertation with oral defense. *Faculty:* 10 full-time, 3 part-time. *Students:* M.Ed and Ed.S., 18 full-time, 53 part-time; Ph.D., 24 full-time, 10 part-time. *Financial Assistance:* graduate assistantships available. *Degrees Awarded 1998:* M.Ed. and Ed.S., 31; Ph.D., 0.

Valdosta State University. College of Education, 1500 N. Patterson St., Valdosta, GA 31698. (912)333-5927. Fax (912)333-7167. E-mail cprice@valdosta.edu. Catherine B. Price, Prof., Head, Dept. of Instructional Technology. *Specializations:* M.Ed. in Instructional Technology with three tracks: Library/Media, Technology Leadership, or Technology Applications; Ed.S. in Instructional Technology; Ed.D. in Curriculum and Instruction. *Features:* The program has a strong emphasis on technology in M.Ed., Ed.S., and Ed.D.; strong emphasis on applied research in Ed.S and Ed.D.

Admission Requirements: M.Ed.: 2.5 GPA, 750 GRE. Ed.S.: Master's in Instructional Technology or related area, 3.0 GPA, 850 GRE. Ed.D.: Master's degree, 3 years of experience, 3.50 GPA, 1000 GRE. *Degree Requirements:* M.Ed.: 33 semester hours. Ed.S.: 27 semester hours. *Faculty:* 7 full-time, 3 part-time. *Students:* 15 full-time, 90 part-time. *Financial Assistance:* graduate assistantships, student loans, scholarships. *Degrees Awarded 1998:* M.Ed., 16; Ed.S., 2 and Ed.D., 14 (new programs).

HAWAII

University of Hawaii-Manoa. Department of Educational Technology, 1776 University Ave., Honolulu, HI 96822. (808) 956-7671. Fax (808) (956-3905. E-mail edtech-dept@hawaii.edu. Website http://www2.hawaii.edu/edtech. Geoffrey Z. Kucera, Prof., Chair. *Specialization:* M.Ed. in Educational Technology. *Degree Requirements:* min. 39 semester hours, including 3 in practicum, 3 in internship; thesis and non-thesis available. *Faculty:* 5 full-time, 2 part-time. *Financial Assistance:* Consideration given to meritorious second-year students for tuition waivers and scholarship applications. *Degrees awarded July 1997 through June 1998*: 9. *Degrees Awarded July 1998 through June 1999*: 9.

IDAHO

Boise State University. IPT, 1910 University Drive, Boise, ID 83725. (208)385-4457, (800)824-7017 ext. 4457. Fax (208)342-7203. E-mail bsu-ipt@micron.net. Website http://www.cot.idbsu.edu/~ipt/. Dr. David Cox, IPT Program Dir.; Jo Ann Fenner, IPT Program Developer and distance program contact person. *Specialization:* M.S. in Instructional & Performance Technology available in a traditional campus setting or via computer conferencing to students located anywhere on the North American continent. The program is fully accredited by the Northwest Association of Schools and Colleges and is the recipient of an NUCEA award for Outstanding Credit Program offered by distance education methods. *Features:* Leading experts in learning styles, evaluation, and leadership principles serve as adjunct faculty in the program via computer and modem from their various remote locations. *Admission Requirements:* undergraduate degree with 3.0 GPA, one-to-two page essay describing why you want to pursue this program and how it will contribute to your personal and professional development, and a resume of personal qualifications and work experience. *Degree Requirements:* 36 semester hours in instructional and performance technology and related course work; project or thesis available for on-campus program and an oral comprehensive exam required for distance program (included in 36 credit hours). *Faculty:* 3 full-time, 7 part-time. *Students:* 140 part-time. *Financial Assistance:* DANTES funding for some military personnel, low-interest loans to eligible students, graduate assistantships for on-campus enrollees. *Degrees Awarded 1997:* 12.

ILLINOIS

Chicago State University. Department of Library Science and Communications Media, Chicago, IL 60628. (312)995-2278, (312)995-2503. Fax (312)995-2473. Janice Bolt, Prof., Chair, Dept. of Library Science and Communications Media. *Specialization:* Master's degree in School Media. Program has been approved by NCATE: AECT/AASL through accreditation of University College of Education; State of Illinois Entitlement Program. *Admission Requirements:* teacher's certification or Bachelor's in Education; any B.A. or B.S. *Degree Requirements:* 36 semester hours; thesis optional.*Faculty:* 2 full-time, 5 part-time. *Students:* 88 part-time. *Financial Assistance:* assistantships, grants, student loans. *Degrees Awarded 1997:* 15.

Concordia University. 7400 Augusta St., River Forest, IL 60305-1499. (708)209-3088. Fax (708)209-3176. E-mail boosmb@crf.cuis.edu. Website http://www.curf.edu. Dr. Manfred Boos, Chair, Mathematics/Computer Science Education Dept. *Specialization:* M.A. in Computer Science Education. *Admission Requirements:* 2.85 GPA (2.25 to 2.85 for provisional status); Bachelor's degree from regionally accredited institution; two letters of recommendation. *Degree Requirements:* 33 semester hours of course work. *Faculty:* 7 full-time, 5 part-time. *Students:* 3 full-time,

18 part-time. *Financial Assistance:* a number of graduate assistantships, Stafford student loans, Supplement Loan for Students. *Degrees Awarded 1998:* 5.

Governors State University. College of Arts and Sciences, University Park, IL 60466. (708)534-4082. Fax (708)534-7895. E-mail m-stelni@govst.edu. Michael Stelnicki, Prof., Human Performance and Training. *Specializations:* M.A. in Communication with HP&T major. *Features:* emphasizes 3 professional areas: Instructional Design, Performance Analysis, and Design Logistics. *Admission Requirements:* undergraduate degree in any field. *Degree Requirements:* 36 credit hours (trimester), all in instructional and performance technology; internship or advanced field project required. Metropolitan Chicago area based. *Faculty:* 2 full-time. *Students:* 32 part-time. *Degrees Awarded 1998:* 8.

Northern Illinois University. Leadership and Educational Policy Studies Department, College of Education, DeKalb, IL 60115-2896. (815)753-0464. Fax (815)753-9371. E-mail LSTOTT@NIU.EDU. Website http://coe.cedu.niu.edu. Dr. Peggy Bailey, Chair, Instructional Technology. *Specializations*: M.S.Ed. in Instructional Technology with concentrations in Instructional Design, Distance Education, Educational Computing, and Media Administration; Ed.D. in Instructional Technology, emphasizing instructional design and development, computer education, media administration, and preparation for careers in business, industry, and higher education. In addition, Illinois state certification in school library media is offered in conjunction with either degree or alone. *Features:* considerable flexibility in course selection, including advanced seminars, numerous practicum and internship opportunities, individual study, and research. Program is highly individualized. More than 60 courses offered by several departments or faculties, including communications, radio/television/film, art, journalism, educational psychology, computer science, and research and evaluation. Facilities include well-equipped computer labs. Students are encouraged to create individualized Web pages. Master's program started in 1968, doctorate in 1970. *Admission Requirements:* M.S.: 2.75 undergraduate GPA, GRE verbal and quantitative scores, two references. Ed.D.: 3.5 M.S. GPA, GRE verbal and quantitative scores (waiver possible), writing sample, three references. *Degree Requirements:* M.S.: 39 hours, including 30 in instructional technology; no thesis. Ed.D.: 63 hours beyond Master's, including 15 hours for dissertation. *Faculty:* 8 full-time, 12 part-time. *Students:* M.S., 135 part-time; Ed.D., 115 part-time. *Financial Assistance:* assistantships available at times in various departments, scholarships, minority assistance. *Degrees Awarded 1997:* M.S., 26; Ed.D., 6.

Southern Illinois University at Carbondale. Department of Curriculum and Instruction, Carbondale, IL 62901-4610. (618)536-2441. Fax (618)453-4244. E-mail sashrock@siu.edu. Website http://www.siu.edu/~currinst/index.html. Sharon Shrock, Coord., Instructional Technology/ Development. *Specializations*: M.S. in Education with specializations in Instructional Development and Instructional Technology; Ph.D. in Education including specialization in Instructional Technology. *Features*: All specializations are oriented to multiple education settings. The ID program emphasizes nonschool (primarily corporate) learning environments. *Admission Requirements*: M.S.: Bachelor's degree, 2.7 undergraduate GPA, transcripts. Ph.D.: Master's degree, 3.25 GPA, MAT or GRE scores, letters of recommendation, transcripts, writing sample. *Degree Requirements:* M.S., 32 credit hours with thesis; 36 credit hours without thesis; Ph.D. , 40 credit hours beyond the master's degree in courses, 24 credit hours for the dissertation. *Faculty:* 5 full-time, 2 part-time. *Students*: M.S., 35 full-time, 45 part-time; Ph.D., 8 full-time, 19 part-time. *Financial Assistance*: some graduate assistantships and scholarships available to qualified students. *Degrees Awarded 1997*: Master's, 16; Ph.D., 4.

Southern Illinois University at Edwardsville. Instructional Technology Program, School of Education, Edwardsville, IL 62026-1125. (618)692-3277. Fax (618)692-3359. E-mail cnelson@siue.edu. Website http://www.siue.edu. Dr. Charles E. Nelson, Dir., Dept. of Educational Leadership. *Specialization:* M.S. in Education with concentrations in (1) Instructional Design and (2) Teaching, Learning, and Technology. *Features:* evening classes only. *Degree Requirements:* 36 semester hours; thesis optional. *Faculty:* 6 part-time. *Students:* 125. *Degrees Awarded 1997:* 30.

University of Illinois at Urbana-Champaign. Department of Educational Psychology, 210 Education Bldg., 1310 S. 6th St., Champaign, IL 61820. (217)333-2245. Fax (217)244-7620. E-mail c-west@uiuc.edu. Charles K. West, Prof., Div. of Learning and Instruction, Dept. of Educational Psychology. *Specializations:* M.A., M.S., and Ed.M. with emphasis in Instructional Design and Educational Computing. Ph.D. in Educational Psychology with emphasis in Instructional Design and Educational Computing. *Features:* Ph.D. program is individually tailored and strongly research-oriented with emphasis on applications of cognitive science to instruction. *Admission Requirements*: excellent academic record, high GRE scores, and strong letters of recommendation. *Degree Requirements:* 8 units for Ed.M., 6 units and thesis for M.A. or M.S. Ph.D.: 8 units coursework, approx. 4 units of research methods courses, minimum 8 hours of written qualifying exams, 8 units Thesis credits. *Faculty:* 8 full-time, 5 part-time. *Students:* 31 full-time, 7 part-time. *Financial Assistance:* scholarships, research assistantships, and teaching assistantships available; fellowships for very highly academically talented; some tuition waivers. *Degrees Awarded 1997:* Ph.D., 5.

Western Illinois University. Instructional Technology and Telecommunications, 37 Harrabin Hall, Macomb, IL 61455. (309)298-1952. Fax (309)298-2978. E-mail mh-hassan@wiu.edu. Website http://www.wiu.edu/users/miitt/. M.H. Hassan, Chair. *Specialization:* Master's degree. *Features:* New program approved by Illinois Board of Higher Education in January 1996 with emphases in Instructional Technology, Telecommunications, Interactive Technologies, and Distance Education. Selected courses delivered via satellite TV and compressed video. *Admission Requirements:* Bachelor's degree 3.0/4.0 GRE score. *Degree Requirements:* 32 semester hours, thesis or applied project, or 35 semester hours with portfolio. *Certificate Program in Instructional Technology Specialization.* Graphic applications, training development, video production. Each track option is made of 5 courses or a total of 15 semester hours. Admission Requirements: Bachelor's degree. Must be completed within three years. *Faculty:* 8 full-time. *Students:* 35 full-time, 150 part-time. *Financial Assistance:* graduate and research assistantships, internships, residence hall assistants, veterans' benefits, loans, and part-time employment.

INDIANA

Indiana State University. Dept. of Curriculum, Instruction, and Media Technology, Terre Haute, IN 47809. (812)237-2937. Fax (812)237-4348. E-mail efthomp@befac.indstate.edu. Dr. James E. Thompson, Program Coord. *Specializations:* Master's degree in Instructional Technology with education focus or with non-education focus; Specialist Degree program in Instructional Technology; Ph.D. in Curriculum, Instruction with specialization in Media Technology. *Degree Requirements:* Master's: 32 semester hours, including 18 in media; thesis optional; Ed.S.: 60 semester hours beyond bachelor's degree; Ph.D., approximately 100 hours beyond bachelor's degree. *Faculty:* 5 full-time. *Students:* 17 full-time, 13 part-time. *Financial Assistance:* 7 assistantships. *Degrees Awarded 1997:* Master's, 2; Ph.D., 1.

*Indiana University. School of Education, W. W. Wright Education Bldg., Rm. 2276, 201 N. Rose Ave., Bloomington, IN 47405-1006. (812)856-8451 (information), (812)856-8239 (admissions). Fax (812)856-8239. Thomas Schwen, Chair, Dept. of Instructional Systems Technology. *Specializations:* M.S. and Ed.S. degrees designed for individuals seeking to be practitioners in the field of Instructional Technology. Offers Ph.D. and Ed.D. degrees with four program focus areas: Foundations; Instructional Analysis, Design, and Development; Instructional Development and Production; and Implementation and Management. *Features:* requires computer skills as a prerequisite and makes technology utilization an integral part of the curriculum; eliminates separation of various media formats; and establishes a series of courses of increasing complexity integrating production and development. The latest in technical capabilities have been incorporated in the new Center for Excellence in Education, including teaching, photographic, computer, and science laboratories, a 14-station multimedia laboratory, and television studios. *Admission Requirements:* M.S.: Bachelor's degree from an accredited institution, 1350 GRE (3 tests required), 2.65 undergraduate GPA. Ed.D and Ph.D.: 1550 GRE (3 tests required), 3.5 graduate GPA. *Degree Requirements:* M.S.: 40 credit hours (including 16 credits in required courses); colloquia; an instructional product or Master's thesis; and 12 credits in outside electives. Ed.D.: 60 hours in addition to previous Master's degree, thesis. Ph.D.: 90 hours, thesis. *Faculty:* 6 full-time, 5 part-time. *Financial Assistance:* assistantships, scholarships. *Degrees Awarded 1996:* M.S., 59; Ed.S., 1; Ed.D., 1; Ph.D.: 5.

Purdue University. School of Education, Department of Curriculum and Instruction, W. Lafayette, IN 47907-1442. (765)494-5669. Fax (765)496-1622. E-mail edtech@soe.purdue.edu. Website http://www.soe.purdue.edu/edci/et/. Dr. James D. Lehman, Prof. of Educational Technology. *Specializations:* Master's degree, Educational Specialist, and Ph.D. in Educational Technology. Master's program started in 1982, Specialist and Ph.D. in 1985. *Admission Requirements:* Master's and Ed.S.: 3.0 GPA, three letters of recommendation, statement of personal goals. Ph.D.: 3.0 GPA, three letters of recommendation, statement of personal goals, 1000 GRE (V+Q). *Degree Requirements:* Master's: 33 semester hours (15 in educational technology, 9 in education, 12 unspecified); thesis optional. Specialist: 60-65 semester hours (15-18 in educational technology, 30-35 in education); thesis, internship, practicum. Ph.D.: 90 semester hours (15-18 in educational technology, 42-45 in education); thesis, internship, practicum. *Faculty:* 6 full-time. *Students:* M.S., 51; Ed.S, 1; Ph.D., 55. *Financial Assistance:* assistantships and fellowships. *Degrees Awarded 1998:* Master's, 10; Ph.D., 3.

IOWA

Clarke College. Graduate Studies, 1550 Clarke Drive, Dubuque, IA 52001. (319)588-6331. Fax (319)588-6789. E-mail RADAMS@KELLER.CLARKE.EDU. Website http://www.clarke.edu. Robert Adams, Clarke College, (319)588-6416. *Specializations:* M.A. in Technology and Education. *Admission Requirements:* 2.5 GPA, GRE (verbal + quantitative) or MAT, $25 application fee, two letters of recommendation. *Degree Requirements:* 25 semester hours in computer courses, 12 hours in education. *Faculty:* 1 full-time, 1-2 part-time. *Students:* 20 part-time. *Financial Assistance:* scholarships, student loans. *Degrees Awarded 1997:* 8.

Iowa State University. College of Education, Ames, IA 50011. (515)294-6840. Fax (515)294-9284. Gary Downs, Professor and Department Head.*Specializations:* M.S., M.Ed., and Ph.D. in Curriculum and Instructional Technology with specializations in Instructional Computing, Ph.D. in Education with emphasis in Instructional Computing, Technology Research. *Features:* practicum experiences related to professional objectives, supervised study and research projects tied to long-term studies within the program, development and implementation of new techniques, teaching strategies, and operational procedures in instructional resources centers and computer labs, program emphasis on technologies for teachers. *Admission Requirements:* M.S. and M.Ed.: three letters, top half of undergraduate class, autobiography. Ph.D.: three letters, top half of undergraduate class, autobiography, GRE scores. *Degree Requirements:* Master's: 30 semester hours, thesis, no internship or practicum. Ph.D.: 78 semester hours, thesis, no internship or practicum. *Faculty:* 4 full-time, 6 part-time. *Students:* Master's, 40 full-time, 40 part-time; Ph.D., 30 full-time, 20 part-time. *Financial Assistance:* 10 assistantships. *Degrees Awarded 1998:* Master's, 2; Ph.D., 2.

University of Iowa. Division of Psychological and Quantitative Foundations, College of Education, Iowa City, IA 52242. (319)335-5519. Fax (319)335-5386. Website http://www.uiowa.edu/~coe2/facstaff/salessi.htm. Stephen Alessi, 361 Lindquist Center, Iowa City, IA 52242. *Specializations:* M.A. and Ph.D. with specializations in Training and Human Resources Development, Computer Applications, and Media Design and Production (MA only). *Features:* flexibility in planning to fit individual needs, backgrounds, and career goals. The program is interdisciplinary, involving courses within divisions of the College of Education, as well as in the schools of Business, Library Science, Radio and Television, Linguistics, and Psychology. *Admission Requirements:* MA: 2.8 undergraduate GPA, 500 GRE (V+Q), personal letter of interest. Ph.D.: Master's degree, 1000 GRE (V+Q), 3.2 GPA on all previous graduate work for regular admission. Conditional admission may be granted. Teaching or relevant experience may be helpful. *Degree Requirements:* MA: 35 semester hours, 3.0 GPA, final project or thesis, comprehensive exam. Ph.D.: 90 semester hours, comprehensive exams, dissertation. *Faculty:* 4 full-time, 3 part-time. *Financial Assistance:* assistantships, grants, student loans, and scholarships.

University of Northern Iowa. Educational Technology Program, Cedar Falls, IA 50614-0606. (319)273-3250. Fax (319)273-5886. E-mail SmaldinoS@UNI.edu. Website www.uni.edu/edtech. Sharon E. Smaldino, contact person. *Specialization:* M.A. in Educational Technology, M.A. in Communications and Training Technology. *Admission Requirements:* Bachelor's degree, 3.0 undergraduate GPA, 500 TOEFL. *Degree Requirements:* 38 semester credits, optional thesis worth 6 credits or alternative research paper of project, comprehensive exam. *Faculty:* 3 full-time, 6 part-time. *Students:* 120. *Financial Assistance:* assistantships, grants, student loans, scholarships, student employment. *Degrees Awarded 1997:* 20.

KANSAS

Emporia State University. School of Library and Information Management, 1200 Commercial, P.O. Box 4025, Emporia, KS 66801. (316)341-5203. Fax (316)341-5233. E-mail vowellfa@ esumail.emporia.edu. Website http://www.emporia.edu/slim/slim.htm. Faye N. Vowell, Dean. *Specializations:* Master's of Library Science (ALA accredited program); School Library Certification program, which includes 27 hours of the M.L.S. program; Ph.D. in Library and Information Management. *Features:* The M.L.S. program is also available in Colorado, Oregon, Utah, and Nebraska. Internet courses are under development. *Admission Requirements:* selective admissions process for M.L.S. and Ph.D. based on a combination of admission criteria, including (but not limited to) GRE or TOEFL score, personal interview, GPA, statement of goals and references. Request admission packet for specific criteria. *Degree Requirements:* M.L.S.: 42 semester hours, comprehensive exam. Ph.D.: total of 83-97 semester hours depending on the number of hours received for an M.L.S. *Faculty:* 12 full-time, 35 part-time. *Students:* M.L.S.: 64 full-time, 305 part-time; Ph.D.: 23 part-time. *Financial Assistance:* assistantships, grants, student loans, scholarships. *Degrees Awarded 1997:* 156.

Kansas State University. Educational Computing, Design, and Telecommunications, 363 Bluemont Hall, Manhattan, KS 66506. (913)532-7686. Fax (913)532-7304. E-mail dmcgrath@coe.educ.ksu.edu. Website http://www2.educ.ksu.edu/Faculty/McGrathD/ECDT/ECDTProg..htm. Dr. Diane McGrath, contact person. *Specializations:* M.S. in Secondary Education with an emphasis in Educational Computing, Design, and Telecommunications; Ph.D. and Ed.D. in Curriculum & Instruction with an emphasis in Educational Computing, Design, and Telecommunications. Master's program started in 1982; doctoral in 1987. *Admissions Requirements:* M.S.: B average in undergraduate work, one programming language, 590 TOEFL. Ed.D. and Ph.D.: B average in undergraduate and graduate work, one programming language, GRE or MAT, three letters of recommendation, experience or course in educational computing. *Degree Requirements:* M.S.: 30 semester hours (minimum of 12 in Educational Computing); thesis, internship, or practicum not required, but all three are possible. Ed.D.: 94 semester hours (minimum of 18 hours in Educational Computing or related area approved by committee, 16 hours dissertation research, 12 hours internship); thesis. Ph.D.: 90 semester hours (minimum of 21 hours in Educational Computing, Design, and Telecommunications or related area approved by committee, 30 hours for dissertation research); thesis; internship or practicum not required but available. *Faculty:* 2 full-time, 1 part-time. *Students:* M.S., 10 full-time, 27 part-time; doctoral, 16 full-time, 14 part-time. *Financial Assistance:* currently four assistantships directly associated with the program; other assistantships sometimes available in other departments depending on skills and funds available. *Degrees Awarded 1997:* M.S., 7.

KENTUCKY

University of Louisville. School of Education, Louisville, KY 40292. (502)852-0609. Fax (502)852-4563. E-mail cparkins@louisville.edu. Website http://www.louisville.edu/edu. Carolyn Rude-Parkins, Dir., Education Resource & Technology Center. *Specialization:* M.Ed. in Early Childhood, Middle School, Secondary Education, Training and Development with Instructional Technology focus. *Features:* technology courses appropriate for business or school audiences. Program is based on ISTE standards as well as ASTD standards. *Admission Requirements:* 2.75 GPA, 800 GRE, 2 letters of recommendation, application fee. *Degree Requirements:* 30 semester hours, thesis optional. *Faculty:* 2 full-time, 3 part-time. *Students:* 4 full-time, 30 part-time. *Financial Assistance:* graduate assistantships. *Degrees Awarded 1997:* 10.

LOUISIANA

Louisiana State University. School of Library and Information Science, Baton Rouge, LA 70803.(225)388-3158. Fax (225)388-4581, Website http://adam.slis.lsu.edu. Bert R. Boyce, Dean, Prof., School of Library and Information Science. *Specializations:* M.L.I.S., C.L.I.S. (post-Master's certificate), Louisiana School Library Certification. An advanced certificate program is available. *Degree Requirements:* M.L.I.S.: 40 hours, comprehensive exam, one semester full-time residence, completion of degree program in five years. *Faculty:* 10 full-time. *Students:* 84 full-time, 86 part-time. *Financial Assistance:* A large number of graduate assistantships are available to qualified students. *Degrees Awarded 1997:* 91.

MARYLAND

The Johns Hopkins University. Graduate Division of Education, Technology for Educators Program, Columbia Gateway Park, 6740 Alexander Bell Dr., Columbia, MD 21046. (410)309-9537. Fax (410)290-0467. Website http://www.jhu.edu. Dr. Jacqueline A. Nunn, Department Chair; Dr. Linda Tsantis, Program Coordinator (tsantis@jhu.edu). *Specialization:* The Department of Technology for Education offers programs leading to the M.S. degree in Education, the M.S. in Special Education, and three specialized advanced Graduate Certificates: Technology for Multimedia and Internet-Based Instruction; Teaching with Technology for School to Career Transition; and Assistive Technology for Communication and Social Interaction. *Features:* focuses on training educators to become decision makers and leaders in the use of technology, with competencies in the design, development, and application of emerging technologies for teaching and learning. Incorporates basic elements that take into account the needs of adult learners, the constantly changing nature of technology, and the need for schools and universities to work together for schoolwide change. The Center for Technology in Education is a partnership project linking research and teaching of the University with the leadership and policy direction of the Maryland State Department of Education. The Center is directed by Dr. Nunn (2500 E. Northern Parkway, Baltimore, MD 21214-1113, 254-8466, jnunn@jhuniz.hcf.jhu.edu). *Admission Requirements:* Bachelor's degree with strong background in teaching, curriculum and instruction, special education, or a related service field. *Degree Requirements:* M.S. in Education, Technology for Educators: 36 semester hours (including 9 credits technical courses, 18 credits instructional courses, 9 credits research and school improvement courses). M.S. in Special Education, Technology in Special Education: 36 semester hours (including 9 credits technical courses, 15 credits instructional courses, 12 credits research and school improvement courses). *Faculty:* 2 full-time, 30 part-time. *Students:* 201 part-time. *Financial Assistance:* grants, student loans, scholarships. *Degrees Awarded 1997:* 38.

Towson State University. College of Education, Hawkins Hall, Rm. 103B, Towson, MD 21252. (410)830-6268. Fax (410)830-2733. E-mail wiser@toe.towson.edu. Website http://www.towson.edu/~coe/istc.html. Dr. David R. Wiser, Assistant Professor. Dept.: Reading, Special Education, & Instructional Development, School Library Media and Education Technology. Prof., General Education Dept. *Specializations:* M.S. degrees in Instructional Development and School Library Media. *Admission Requirements:* Bachelor's degree from accredited institution with 3.0 GPA. (Conditional admission granted for many applicants with a GPA over 2.75). *Prerequisites:* For School Library Media & Education Technology specializations include teacher certification or completion of specific coursework. *Degree Requirements:* 36 graduate semester hours without thesis. *Faculty:* 7 full-time, 5 adjunct. *Students:* 150. *Financial Assistance:* graduate assistantships, work study, scholarships. *Awarded 1998:* 18.

University of Maryland. College of Library and Information Services, 4105 Hornbake Library Bldg., South Wing, College Park, MD 20742-4345. (301)405-2038. Fax (301)314-9145. Ann Prentice, Dean and Program Chair. *Specializations:* Master's of Library Science, including specialization in School Library Media; doctorate in Library and Information Services including specialization in Educational Technology/Instructional Communication. *Features:* Program is broadly conceived and interdisciplinary in nature, using the resources of the entire campus. The student and the advisor design a program of study and research to fit the student's background, interests, and professional objectives. Students prepare for careers in teaching and research in information science and librarianship and elect concentrations including Educational Technology and Instructional Communication. *Admission Requirements:* doctoral: Bachelor's degree (the majority of doctoral students enter with Master's degrees in Library Science, Educational Technology, or other relevant disciplines), GRE general tests, three letters of recommendation, statement of purpose. Interviews required when feasible for doctoral applicants. *Degree Requirements:* M.L.S.: 36 semester hours; thesis optional. *Faculty:* 15 full-time, 8 part-time. *Students:* Master's, 106 full-time, 149 part-time; doctoral, 5 full-time, 11 part-time. *Financial Assistance:* assistantships, grants, student loans, scholarships, fellowships.

University of Maryland, Baltimore County (UMBC). Department of Education, 1000 Hilltop Cir., Baltimore, MD 21250. (410)455-2310. Fax (410)455-3986. E-mail gist@umbc.edu. Website http://www.research.umbc.edu/~eholly/ceduc/isd/. Dr. William R. Johnson, Dir., Graduate Programs in Education. *Specializations:* M.A. degrees in School Instructional Systems, Post-Baccalaureate Teacher Certification, Training in Business and Industry. *Admissions Requirements:* 3.0 undergraduate GPA, GRE scores. *Degree Requirements:* 36 semester hours (including 18 in systems development for each program); internship. *Faculty:* 18 full-time, 25 part-time. *Students:* 59 full-time, 254 part-time. *Financial Assistance:* assistantships, scholarships. *Degrees Awarded 1997:* 68.

Western Maryland College. Department of Education, Main St., Westminster, MD 21157. (410)857-2507. Fax (410)857-2515. E-mail rkerby@wmdc.edu. Dr. Ramona N.Kerby, Coord., School Library Media Program, Dept. of Education. *Specializations*: M.S. in School Library Media. *Degree Requirements*: 33 credit hours (including 19 in media and 6 in education), comprehensive exam. *Faculty*: 1 full-time, 7 part-time. *Students*: 140, most part-time.

MASSACHUSETTS

Boston University. School of Education, 605 Commonwealth Ave., Boston, MA 02215-1605. (617)353-3181. Fax (617)353-3924. E-mail whittier@bu.edu. Website http://web.bu.edu/EDUCATION. David B. Whittier, Asst. Professor and Coord., Program in Educational Media and Technology. *Specializations*: Ed.M., CAGS (Certificate of Advanced Graduate Study) in Educational Media and Technology; Ed.D. in Curriculum and Teaching, Specializing in Educational Media and Technology; preparation for Massachusetts public school certificates as Library Media Specialist and Instructional Technologist. *Features:* The Master's Program prepares graduates for professional careers as educators, instructional designers, developers of educational materials, and managers of the human and technology-based resources necessary to support education and training with technology. Graduates are employed in settings such as K-12 schools, higher education, industry, medicine, government, and publishing. Students come to the program from many different backgrounds and with a wide range of professional goals. The doctoral program sets the study of Educational Media & Technology within the context of education and educational research in general, and curriculum and teaching in particular. In addition to advanced work in the field of Educational Media and Technology, students examine and conduct research and study the history of educational thought and practice relating to teaching and learning. Graduates make careers in education as professors and researchers, technology directors and managers, and as developers of technology-based materials and systems. Graduates also make careers in medicine, government, business, and industry as instructional designers, program developers, project managers, and training directors. Graduates who work in both educational and non-educational organizations are often responsible for managing the human and technological resources required to create learning experiences that include the development and delivery of technology-based materials and distance education.: *Admission Requirements*: Ed.M.: good recommendations, solid graduate test scores, 2.7 undergraduate GPA, GRE or MAT must be completed within past five years. CAGs: Ed.M., good recommendations, solid graduate test scores, 2.7 undergraduate GPA, GRE or MAT must be completed within past five years. Ed.D.: 3 letters of recommendation, 50 MAT or GRE scores, transcripts, writing samples, statement of goals and qualifications, analytical essay, 2.7 GPA. *Degree Requirements:* Ed.M.: 36 credit hours (including 22 hours from required core curriculum, 14 from electives). CAGs: 32 credits beyond Ed.M., one of which must be a curriculum and teaching course and a mini-comprehensive exam. Ed.D.: 60 credit hours of courses in Educational Media and Technology, curriculum and teaching, and educational thought and practice with comprehensive exams; course work and apprenticeship in research; 60 credit hours; dissertation. *Faculty*: 1 full-time, 1 half-time, 10 part-time. *Students*: 2 full-time, 12 part-time. *Financial Assistance*: U.S. Government sponsored work study, assistantships, grants, student loans, scholarships. *Degrees Awarded 1997*: Ed.M., 11; Ed.D., 1.

Bridgewater State College. Library Media Program, Hart Hall, Rm. 219, Bridgewater, MA 02325. (508)697-1320. Fax (508)697-1771. E-mail fzilonis@bridgew.edu. Website http://www.bridgew.edu. Mary Frances Zilonis, Coord., Library Media Program. *Specialization:* M.Ed. in Library Media Studies. *Features:* This program heavily emphasizes teaching and technology. *Degree Requirements:* 39 semester hours; comprehensive exam. *Faculty:* 2 full-time, 6 part-time. *Students:* 58 in degree program, 30 non-degree. *Financial Assistance:* Graduate assistantships, graduate internships. *Degrees Awarded 1997:* 5.

Fitchburg State College. Division of Graduate and Continuing Education, 160 Pearl St., Fitchburg, MA 01420. (978)665-3181. Fax (978)665-3658. E-mail dgce@fsc.edu. Website http://www.fsc.edu. Dr. Lee DeNike, Chair. *Specialization:* M.S. in Communications Media with specializations in Management, Technical and Professional Writing, Instructional Technology, and Library Media. *Features:* Collaborating with professionals working in the field both for organizations and as independent producers, Fitchburg offers a unique M.S. program. The objective of the Master of Science in Communications/Media Degree Programs is to develop in candidates the knowledge and skills for the effective implementation of communication within business, industry, government, not-for-profit agencies, health services, and education. *Admission Requirements:* MAT or GRE scores, official transcript(s) of a baccalaureate degree, two or more years of experience in communications or media, department interview and portfolio presentation, three letters of recommendation. *Degree Requirements:* 36 semester credit hours. *Faculty:* 1 full-time, 7 part-time. *Students:* 84 part-time. *Financial assistance:* assistantships, student loans, scholarships. *Degrees Awarded 1998:* 40.

Harvard University. Appian Way, Cambridge, MA 02138. (617)495-3541. Fax (617)495-3626. E-mail Admit@hugse2.harvard.edu. Website http://GSEWeb.harvard.edu/TIEHome.html. David Perkins, Interim Dir. of Technology in Education Program. *Specialization*: M.Ed. in Technology in Education; an advanced certificate program is available. *Admission Requirements*: Bachelor's degree, MAT or GRE scores, 600 TOEFL, 3 recommendations. Students interested in print information about the TIE Program should E-mail a request to the address above. *Degree Requirements*: 32 semester credits. *Faculty*: 1 full-time, 9 part-time. *Students*: approx. 50: 39 full-time, 11 part-time. *Financial Assistance*: within the school's policy. *Degrees Awarded 1997*: 50.

Lesley College. 29 Everett St., Cambridge, MA 02138-2790. (617)349-8419. Fax (617)349-8169. E-mail nroberts@mail.lesley.edu. Website http://www.lesley.edu/soe/tech-in-ed/techined.html. Dr. Nancy Roberts, Prof. of Education. *Specializations:* M.Ed. in Technology Education; C.A.G.S. (Certificate of Advanced Graduate Study) in Technology Education; Ph.D. in Education with a Technology Education major. *Features:* M.Ed. program is offered off-campus at 65 sites in 16 states; contact Professional Outreach Associates [(800)843-4808] for information. The degree is also offered completely online. Contact Maureen Yoder, myoder@mail.lesley.edu, or (617)348-8421 for information. *Degree Requirements:* M.Ed.: 33 semester hours in technology, integrative final project in lieu of thesis, no internship or practicum. C.A.G.S.: 36 semester hours.

Ph.D. requirements available on request. *Faculty:* 9 full-time, 122 part-time on the Master's and C.A.G.S. levels. *Students:* 1200 part-time. *Degrees Awarded 1997:* 575.

Simmons College. Graduate School of Library and Information Science, 300 The Fenway, Boston, MA 02115-5898. (617)521-2800. Fax (617)521-3192. E-mail jbaughman@simmons.edu. Website http://www.simmons.edu/gslis/. Dr. James C. Baughman, Prof. *Specializations:* M.S. Dual degrees: M.L.S./M.A. in Education (for School Library Media Specialists); M.L.S./M.A. in History (Archives Management Program). A Doctor of Arts in Administration is also offered. *Features:* The program prepares individuals for a variety of careers, media technology emphasis being only one. There are special programs for School Library Media Specialist and Archives Management with strengths in Information Science/Systems, Media Management. *Admission Requirements:* B.A. or B.S. degree with 3.0 GPA, statement, three letters of reference. *Degree Requirements:* 36 semester hours. *Faculty:* 14 full-time. *Students:* 75 full-time, 415 part-time. *Financial Assistance:* assistantships, grants, student loans, scholarships. *Degrees Awarded 1997:* Master's, 185.

University of Massachusetts-Boston. Graduate College of Education, 100 Morrissey Blvd., Boston, MA 02125. (617)287-5980. Fax (617)287-7664. E-mail babcock@umbsky.cc.umb.edu. Website http://www.umb.edu. Donald D. Babcock, Graduate Program Dir. *Specialization:* M.Ed. in Instructional Design. *Admission Requirements:* MAT or previous Master's degree, goal statement, three letters of recommendation, resume, interview. *Degree Requirements:* 36 semester hours, thesis or project. *Faculty:* 1 full-time, 9 part-time. *Students:* 8 full-time, 102 part-time. *Financial Assistance:* graduate assistantships providing tuition plus stipend. *Degrees Awarded 1997:* 24.

University of Massachusetts-Lowell. College of Education, One University Ave., Lowell, MA 01854-2881. (508)934-4621. Fax (508)934-3005. E-mail John_Lebaron@uml.edu. Website http://www.uml.edu/College/Education/. John LeBaron, Faculty Chair. *Specializations:* M.Ed and Ed.D. Educational Technology may be pursued in the context of any degree program area. The Certificate of Advanced Graduate Study (CAGS), equivalent to 30 credits beyond a M.Ed., is also offered. *Admission Requirements:* Bachelor's degree in cognate area, GRE or MAT scores, statement of purpose, three recommendations. *Degree Requirements:* M.Ed.: 30 credits beyond Bachelor's. Ed.D.: 60 credits beyond Master's. *Faculty:* 1 full-time for technology courses. *Students:* 454. *Financial Assistance:* assistantships, student loans, limited scholarships. *Degrees Awarded 1997:* M.Ed., 120; Ed.D., 14; CAGS, 5.

MICHIGAN

Eastern Michigan University. 234 Boone Hall, Ypsilanti, MI 48197. (734)487-3260. Fax (734)484-6471. Anne Bednar, Prof., Coord., Dept. of Teacher Education. *Specialization:* M.A. in Educational Psychology with concentration in Educational Technology. *Admission Requirements:* Bachelor's degree, 2.75 undergraduate GPA or MAT score, 500 TOEFL. *Degree Requirements:* 30 semester hours, optional thesis worth 6 credits. *Faculty:* 3 full-time. *Students:* 15. *Financial Assistance:* graduate assistantship. *Degrees Awarded 1997:* 12.

Michigan State University. College of Education, 431 Erickson, East Lansing, MI 48824. (517)355-6684. Fax (517)353-6393. E-mail yelons@pilot.msu.edu. Dr. Stephen Yelon. *Specialization:* M.A. in Educational Technology and Instructional Design. *Admission Requirements:* Bachelor's degree, 800 TOEFL, recommendations, goal statement. *Degree Requirements:* 30 semester hours, certification exam, field experience. *Faculty:* 5 full-time. *Students:* approx. 45. *Financial Assistance:* some assistantships for highly qualified students. *Degrees Awarded 1997:* approx. 12.

University of Michigan. Department of Educational Studies, 610 East University, Ann Arbor MI 48109-1259. (313)763-4668. Fax (313)763-4663. E-mail carl.berger@umich.edu. Website http://www.soe.umich.edu. Carl F. Berger, Chair. *Specializations:* M.Ed.; Ph.D. in Instructional Technology with concentrations in Science, Math, or Literacy. *Features:* Programs are individually designed. *Admission Requirements:* GRE, B.A. for M.Ed., Master's for Ph.D. *Degree Requirements:* M.Ed.: 30 hours beyond B.A. Ph.D.: 60 hours beyond B.A. or 30 hours beyond Master's plus comprehensive exams and dissertation. *Faculty:* 3 full-time, 6 part-time. *Students:* 35 full-time, 7 part-time. *Financial Assistance:* assistantships, grants, student loans, scholarships, internships. *Degrees Awarded 1997:* M.Ed., 15; Ph.D., 3.

Wayne State University. Wayne State University. 381 Education, Detroit, MI 48202. (313)577-1728. Fax (313)577-1693. Website http://www.coe.wayne.edu/InstructionalTechnology. E-mail rrichey@coe.wayne.edu. Rita C. Richey, Prof., Program Coord., Instructional Technology Programs, Div. of Administrative and Organizational Studies, College of Education. *Specializations*: M.Ed. degrees in Performance Improvement and Training, K-12 Educational Technology, and Interactive Technologies. Ed.D. and Ph.D. programs to prepare individuals for leadership in business, industry, health care, and the K-12 school setting as instructional design and development specialists; media or learning resources managers or consultants; specialists in instructional video; and computer-assisted instruction and multimedia specialists. The school also offers a six-year specialist degree program in Instructional Technology. *Features*: Guided experiences in instructional design and development activities in business and industry are available. *Admission Requirements*: Ph.D.: Master's degree, 3.5 GPA, GRE, MAT, strong professional recommendations, interview. *Degree Requirements*: M.Ed.: 36 semester hours, including required project; internship recommended. *Faculty*: 6 full-time, 5 part-time. *Students*: M.Ed., 525; doctoral, 95, most part-time. *Financial Assistance*: student loans, scholarships, and paid internships. *Degrees Awarded 1997-1998:* M.Ed., 57; doctoral, 16.

MINNESOTA

Mankato State University. MSU Box 20, P.O. Box 8400, Mankato, MN 56001-8400. (507)389-1965. Fax (507)389-5751. E-mail pengelly@mankato.msus.edu. Website http://lme.mankato.msus.edu. Frank R. Birmingham Ph.D., Dept. of Library Media Education. *Specialization:* M.S. in Educational Technology with three tracks. *Admission Requirements:* Bachelor's degree, 2.75/4.0 for last 2 years of undergraduate work. *Degree Requirements:* 32 semester hour credits, comprehensive exam. *Faculty:* 4 full-time. *Degrees Awarded 1997:* 12.

St. Cloud State University. College of Education, St. Cloud, MN 56301-4498. (612)255-2022. Fax (612)255-4778. E-mail jberling@tigger.stcloud.msus.edu. John G. Berling, Prof., Dir., Center for Information Media. *Specializations:* Master's degrees in Information Technologies, Educational Media, and Human Resources Development/Training. A Specialist degree is also offered. *Admission Requirements:* acceptance to Graduate School, written preliminary examination, interview. *Degree Requirements:* Master's: 51 qtr. hours with thesis; 54 qtr. hours, Plan B; 57 qtr. hours, portfolio; 200-hour practicum is required for media generalist licensure. Course work applies to Educational Media Master's program. *Faculty:* 7 full-time. *Students:* 15 full-time, 150 part-time. *Financial Assistance:* assistantships, scholarships. *Degrees Awarded 1997:* Master's, 12.

Walden University. 155 5th Avenue South, Minneapolis, MN 55401. (800)444-6795. E-mail www@waldenu.edu or info@waldenu.edu. Websites http://www.waldenu.edu; http://www.waldenu.edu/ecti/ecti.html. Dr. Gwen Hillesheim, Chair. *Specializations:* M.S. in Educational Change and Technology Innovation. Ph.D. in Education in Learning and Teaching with specialization in Educational Technology. In 1998 a specialization in Distance Learning will be added. In addition, there is a generalist Ph.D. in Education in which students may choose and design their own areas of specialization. *Features:* delivered primarily on-line. *Admission Requirements:* accredited Bachelor's.

Ph.D.: accredited Master's, goal statement, letters of recommendation. *Degree Requirements:* Master's: 45 credit curriculum, 2 brief residencies, Master's project. *Faculty:* 18 part-time. *Students:* 50 full-time, 53 part-time in Master's program. *Financial Assistance:* student loans, 3 fellowships with annual review. *Degrees Awarded 1997:* 4 (program instituted in 1996).

MISSOURI

Fontbonne College. 6800 Wydown Blvd., St. Louis, MO 63105. (314)889-1497. Fax (314)889-1451. E-mail mabkemei@fontbonne.edu. Dr. Mary K. Abkemeier, Chair. *Specialization:* M.S. in Computer Education. *Features:* small classes and course work immediately applicable to the classroom. *Admission Requirements:* 2.5 undergraduate GPA, 3 letters of recommendation. *Degree Requirements:* 33 semester hours, 3.0 GPA. *Faculty:* 2 full-time, 12 part-time. *Students:* 4 fulltime, 90 part-time. *Financial Assistance:* grants. *Degrees Awarded 1998:* 32.

Northwest Missouri State University. Department of Computer Science/Information Systems, 800 University Ave., Maryville MO 64468. (660)562-1600. E-mail pheeler@mail.nwmissouri.edu. Website http://www.nwmissouri.edu/~csis. Dr. Phillip Heeler, Chairperson. *Specializations:* M.S. in School Computer Studies; M.S.Ed. in Educational Uses of Computers. *Features:* These degrees are designed for computer educators at the elementary, middle school, high school, and junior college level. *Admission Requirements:* 3.0 undergraduate GPA, 700 GRE (V+Q). *Degree Requirements:* 32 semester hours of graduate courses in computer science and/or educational computing courses. *Faculty:* 12 full-time, 4 part-time. *Students:* 5 full-time, 20 part-time. *Financial Assistance:* assistantships, grants, student loans, and scholarships. *Degrees Awarded 1998:* 10.

University of Missouri-Columbia. College of Education. 217 Townsend Hall, Columbia, MO 65211. (573)882-4546. Fax (573)884-4944. Jim Laffey, Assoc. Prof. (cilaffey@showme.missouri.edu). Website:http:www.coe.missouri.edu/sisInformation Science and Learning Technologies Program, School of Information Science & Learning Technologies. *Specializations*: Master's degree program prepares professionals to design, develop, and implement technology in educational settings. Ph.D. in Information Science & Learning Technologies prepares professionals to understand and influence learning, information organization and retrieval, and performance in diverse learning environments, especially through the design, development, and use of interactive technologies. An Education Specialist degree program is also available. *Features*: Master's program is competency-based. Graduates leave with the ability to plan, implement, and evaluate educational technology innovations, and to design, develop, and evaluate technology-based learning and performance support products. Ph.D. program includes a major in Information Science and Learning Technologies with research tools, and R&D apprenticeship experiences. In addition to the competency-based objectives of the Master's program, doctoral graduates will be able to conduct systematic research which contributes to the knowledge base of learning, information organization and retrieval, performance, and technology. *Admission Requirements*: Master's: Bachelor's degree, GRE score. Ph.D.: 3.2 graduate GPA, 1500 GRE, letter of recommendation, statement of purpose. *Faculty*: Master's, 8 full-time, 10 part-time; Ph.D., 13 full-time, 18 part-time, plus selected faculty in related fields. *Students*: Master's, 18 full-time, 52 part-time; Ph.D., 13 full-time, 12 part-time. *Financial Assistance*: Master's: assistantships, grants, student loans, scholarships. Ph.D.: graduate assistantships with tuition waivers; numerous academic scholarships ranging from $200 to $18,000. *Degrees Awarded 1998*: Master's, 7 Ph.D., 5.

Webster University. Instructional Technology, St. Louis, MO 63119. (314)968-7490. Fax (314)968-7118. E-mail steinmpe@websteruniv.edu. Website http://www.websteruniv.edu. Paul Steinmann, Assoc. Dean and Dir., Graduate Studies and Instructional Technology. *Specialization:* Master's degree (M.A.T.); State Certification in Media Technology is a program option. *Admission Requirements:* Bachelor's degree with 2.5 GPA. *Degree Requirements:* 33 semester hours (including 24 in media); internship required. *Faculty:* 5. *Students:* 7 full-time, 28 part-time. *Financial Assistance:* partial scholarships, minority scholarships, government loans, and limited state aid. *Degrees Awarded 1997:* 6.

MONTANA

University of Montana. School of Education, Missoula, MT 59812. (406)243-5785. Fax (406)243-4908. E-mail cjlott@selway.umt.edu. Dr. Carolyn Lott, Assoc. Prof. of Library/Media. *Specializations:* M.Ed. and Specialist degrees; K-12 School Library Media specialization with School Library Media Certification endorsement.*Admission Requirements:* (both degrees): GRE, letters of recommendation, 2.5 GPA. *Degree Requirements:* M.Ed.: 37 semester credit hours (18 overlap with library media endorsement). Specialist: 28 semester hours (18 overlap). *Faculty:* 2 full-time. *Students:* 5 full-time, 20 part-time. *Financial Assistance:* assistantships; contact the University of Montana Financial Aid Office. *Degrees Awarded 1998:* 5.

NEBRASKA

University of Nebraska at Kearney. Kearney, NE 68849-1260. (308)865-8833. Fax (308)865-8097. E-mail fredrickson@unk.edu. Dr. Scott Fredrickson, Dir. of Instructional Technology. Website http://www.unk.edu/departments/pte. *Specializations:* M.S. in Instructional Technoloey, M.S. in Educational Media, Specialist in Educational Media. *Admission Requirements:* M.S. and Specialist: GRE, acceptance into graduate school, approval of Instructional Technology Committee. *Degree Requirements:* M.S.: 36 credit hours, Master's comprehensive exam or field study. Specialist: 39 credit hours, field study. *Faculty:* 5 full-time, 10 part-time. *Students:* 62 full-time. *Financial Assistance:* assistantships, grants, student loans. *Degrees Awarded 1997:* M.S., 12; Ed.S., 0.

University of Nebraska-Omaha. Department of Teacher Education, College of Education, Kayser Hall 208D, Omaha, NE 68182. (402)5543790. Fax (402)554-3491. E-mail langan@unomaha.edu. John langan, Teacher Education. *Specializations:* M.S. in Education, M.A. in Education, both with Educational Media concentration. *Degree Requirements:* 36 semester hours (including 24 in media), practicum; thesis optional. *Faculty:* 2 full-time, 4 part-time. *Students:* 10 full-time, 62 part-time. *Financial Assistance:* Contact Financial Aid Office. *Degrees awarded 1997:* 45.

NEVADA

University of Nevada. Counseling and Educational Psychology Dept., College of Education, Reno, NV 89557. (702)784-6327. Fax (702)784-1990. E-mail ljohnson@unr.edu. Website http://www.unr.edu/unr/colleges/educ/cep/cepindex.html. Dr. LaMont Johnson, Program Coord., Information Technology in Education. Marlowe Smaby, Dept. Chair. *Specializations:* M.S. and Ph.D. *Admission Requirements:* Bachelor's degree, 2.75 undergraduate GPA, 750 GRE (V+Q). *Degree Requirements:* 36 semester credits, optional thesis worth 6 credits, comprehensive exam. *Faculty:* 2 full-time, 1 part-time. *Students:* M.S., 15; Ph.D., 10. *Degrees Awarded 1997:* M.S., 4; Ph.D., 1.

NEW JERSEY

Montclair State University. Department of Reading and Educational Media, Upper Montclair, NJ 07043. (973)655-7040. Fax (973)655-5310. Website http://www.monclair.edu. Robert R. Ruezinsky, Dir. of Academic Technology. *Specializations:* No degree program exists. Two certification programs, A.M.S. and E.M.S, exist on the graduate level. *Certification Requirements:* 18-21 semester hours of media and technology are required for the A.M.S. program and 30-33 hours for the E.M.S. program. *Faculty:* 7 part-time. *Students:* 32 part-time.

Rutgers-The State University of New Jersey. Ph.D. Program in Communication, Information, and Library Studies, The Graduate School, New Brunswick, NJ 08901-1071. (732)932-7447. Fax (732)932-6916. Dr. Lea P. Stewart, Director. Master's Program, Dept. of Library and Information Studies, School of Communication, Information and Library Studies. (732)932-9717. Fax (732)932-2644. Dr.Carol Kuhlthau, Chair. *Specializations:* M.L.S. degree with specializations in Information Retrieval, Technical and Automated Services, Reference, School Media Services, Youth Services, Management and Policy Issues, and Generalist Studies. Ph.D. programs in

Communication; Media Studies; Information Systems, Structures, and Users; Information and Communication Policy and Technology; and Library and Information Services. The school also offers a six-year specialist certificate program. *Features:* Ph.D. Program provides doctoral-level course work for students seeking theoretical and research skills for scholarly and professional leadership in the information and communication fields. A course on multimedia structure, organization, access, and production is offered. *Admission Requirements:* Ph.D.: Master's degree in Information Studies, Communication, Library Science, or related field; 3.0 undergraduate GPA; GRE scores; TOEFL (for applicants whose native language is not English). *Degree Requirements:* M.L.S.: 36 semester hours, in which the hours for media vary for individual students; practicum of 150 hours. *Faculty:* M.L.S., 15 full-time, 12 adjunct; Ph.D., 43. *Students:* M.L.S., 97 full-time, 199 part-time; Ph.D., 104. *Financial Assistance:* M.L.S.: scholarships, fellowships, and graduate assistantships. Ph.D.: assistantships. *Degrees Awarded 1998:* Master's, 169; Ph.D., 8.

William Paterson University. College of Education, 300 Pompton Rd., Wayne, NJ 07470. (973)720-2140. Fax (973)720-2585. Website http://pwcweb.wilpaterson.edu/wpcpages/library/default.htp. Dr. Amy G. Job, Librarian, Assoc. Prof., Coord., Program in Library/Media, Curriculum and Instruction Dept. *Specializations:* M.Ed. for Educational Media Specialist, Associate Media Specialist, Ed.S. *Admission Requirements:* teaching certificate, 2.75 GPA, MAT or GRE scores, 1 year teaching experience. Ed.S.: certificate, 2.75 GPA. *Degree Requirements:* M.Ed.: 33 semester hours, including research projects and practicum. Ed.S.: 18 sem. hours. *Faculty:* 6 full-time, 2 part-time. *Students:* 30 part-time. *Financial Assistance:* limited. *Degrees Awarded 1998:* M.Ed., 4; Ed.S., 2.

NEW YORK

Buffalo State College. 1300 Elmwood Ave., Buffalo, NY 14222-1095. (716)878-4923. Fax (716)878-6677. E-mail nowakoaj@buffalostate.edu. Dr. Anthony J. Nowakowski, Program Coord. *Specializations:* M.S. in Education in Educational Computing. *Admission Requirements:* Bachelor's degree from accredited institution, 3.0 GPA in last 60 hours, 3 letters of recommendation. *Degree Requirements:* 33 semester hours (15 hours in computers, 12-15 hours in education, 3-6 electives); thesis or project (see:www.buffalostate.edu/edc). *Faculty:* 5 part-time. *Students:* 3 full-time, 98 part-time. *Degrees Awarded 1997:* 16.

Fordham University. Rose Hill Campus, 441 E. Fordham Rd., Bronx, NY. 10458. (718)817-4860. Fax (718)817-4868. E-mail pcom@murray.fordham.edu. Website http://www.fordham.edu. Robin Andersen, Department Chair, James Capo, Director of Graduate Studies. *Specializations:* M.A. in Public Communications. *Features:* Internship or thesis option; full-time students can complete program in 12 months. *Admission Requirements:* 3.0 undergraduate GPA. *Degree Requirements:* 10 courses plus internship or thesis. *Faculty:* 8 full-time, 2 part-time. *Students* 8 full-time, 22 part-time. *Financial Assistance:* assistantships, student loans, scholarships. *Degrees Awarded 1997:* 12.

Ithaca College. School of Communications, Ithaca, NY 14850. (607)274-1025. Fax (607)274-1664. E-mail Herndon@Ithaca.edu. Website http://www.ithaca.edu/rhp/corpcomm/corpcomm1/. Sandra L. Herndon, Prof., Chair, Graduate Communications; Roy H. Park, School of Communications. *Specialization:* M.S. in Communications. Students in this program find employment in such areas as instructional design, multimedia, public relations and marketing, and employee communication. The program can be tailored to individual career goals. *Admission Requirements:* 3.0 GPA, TOEFL 550 (where applicable). *Degree Requirements:* 36 semester hours, seminar. *Faculty:* 8 full-time. *Students:* approx. 25 full-time, 10 part-time. *Financial Assistance:* graduate assistantships. *Degrees Awarded 1998:* 18.

New York Institute of Technology. Dept. of Instructional Technology, Tower House, Old Westbury, NY 11568. (516)686-7777. Fax (516)686-7655. E-mail dplumer460@aol.com. Website http://www.nyit.edu. Davenport Plumer, Chair, Depts. of Instructional Technology and Elementary Education - pre. Service & in-service. *Specializations:* M.S. in Instructional Technology;

M.S. in Elementary Education; Specialist Certificates in Computers in Education, Distance Learning, and Multimedia (not degrees, but are earned after the first 18 credits of the Master's degree). *Features:* computer integration in virtually all courses; online courses; evening, weekend, and summer courses. *Admission Requirements:* Bachelor's degree from accredited college with 3.0 cumulative average. *Degree Requirements:* 36 credits with 3.0 GPA for M.S., 18 credits with 3.0 GPA for certificates. *Faculty:* 11 full-time, 42 part-time. *Students:* 112 full-time, 720 part-time. *Financial Assistance:* graduate assistantships, institutional and alumni scholarships, student loans. *Degrees Awarded 1998:* M.S., 51; Specialist, 41.

New York University. Educational Communication and Technology Program, School of Education, 239 Greene St., Suite 300, New York, NY 10003. (212)998-5520. Fax (212)995-4041. Website http://www.nyu.edu. Francine Shuchat Shaw, Assoc. Prof., Dir.; Donald T. Payne, Assoc. Prof., Doctoral Advisor. *Specializations:* M.A., Ed.D., and Ph.D. in Education for the preparation of individuals to perform as instructional media designers, developers, producers, and researchers in education, business and industry, health and medicine, community services, government, museums, and other cultural institutions; and to teach in educational communications and instructional technology programs in higher education, including instructional television, microcomputers, multimedia, and telecommunications. The school also offers a post-M.A. 30-point Certificate of Advanced Study in Education. *Features:* emphasizes theoretical foundations, especially a cognitive perspective of learning and instruction, and their implications for designing media-based learning environments. All efforts focus on multimedia, instructional television, and telecommunications; participation in special research and production projects and field internships. *Admission Requirements:* M.A.: 3.0 undergraduate GPA, responses to essay questions, interview related to academic and professional goals. Ph.D.: 3.0 GPA, 1000 GRE, responses to essay questions, interview related to academic or professional preparation and career goals. For international students, 600 TOEFL and TWE. *Degree Requirements:* M.A.: 36 semester hours including specialization, elective courses, thesis, English Essay Examination. Ph.D.: 57 semester hours including specialization, foundations, research, content seminar, and elective course work; candidacy papers; dissertation; English Essay Examination. *Faculty:* 2 full-time, 10 part-time. *Students:* M.A.: 40 full-time, 35 part-time. Ph.D.: 14 full-time, 20 part-time. *Financial Assistance:* graduate and research assistantships, student loans, scholarships, and work assistance programs. *Degrees Awarded 1997:* M.A., 12; Ph.D., 2.

Pace University. Westchester Dept, School of Education, Bedford Road, Pleasantville, NY 10570. (914)773-3829, (914)773-3979. Fax (914)773-3521. Website http://www.pace.edu. E-mail keyes@pacevm.dac.pace.edu. Dr. Carol Keyes, Chair. *Specialization:* M.S.E. in Curriculum and Instruction with a concentration in Computers. Computer courses are related to evaluating program packages, instructional applications of computer technology in educational software, and the Internet, multimedia in the classroom, and cognitive processing with computers. *Admission Requirements:* GPA 3.0, interview. *Degree Requirements:* 33-34 semester hours (15 in computers, 18 in educational administration). *Faculty:* 8 full-time, 50 part-time. *Students:* 60-70 part-time. *Financial Assistance:* assistantships, scholarships.

St. John's University. Division of Library and Information Science, 8000 Utopia Parkway, Jamaica, NY 11439. (718)990-6200. Fax (718)990-2071. E-mail libis@stjohns.edu. Website http://www.stjohns.edu/gsas/dlis/. James Benson, Dir. *Specializations:* M.L.S. with specialization in School Media. The school also offers a 24-credit Advanced Certificate program. *Admission Requirements:* 3.0 GPA, 2 letters of reference, statement of professional goals. *Degree Requirements:* 36 semester hours, comprehensive exam, practicum. *Faculty:* 7 full-time, 12 part-time. *Students:* 19 full-time, 78 part-time. *Financial Assistance:* 8 assistantships. *Degrees Awarded 1997:* Master's, 48.

State University College of Arts and Science at Potsdam. School of Education, 116 Satterlee Hall, Potsdam, NY 13676. (315)267-2535. Fax (315)267-4895. E-mail mlynarhc@potsdam.edu, Dr. Charles Mlynarczyk, Chair,Teacher Education. *Specializations*: M.S. in Education in Instructional Technology and Media Management with concentrations in General K-12, Educational

Communications Specialist, and Training and Development. *Degree Requirements*: 33 semester hours, including internship or practicum; culminating project required. *Faculty*: 3 full-time, 2 part-time. *Students:* 26 full-time, 45 part-time. *Financial Assistance*: student loans, student assistantships. *Degrees Awarded 1998:* 41.

State University of New York at Albany. School of Education, 1400 Washington Ave., Albany, NY 12222. (518)442-5032. Fax (518)442-5008. E-mail swan@cnsunix.albany.edu. Karen Swan (ED114A), contact person. *Specialization:* M.Ed. and Ph.D. in Curriculum and Instruction with specializations in Instructional Theory, Design, and Technology. Med offered entirely online over the www. *Admission Requirements:* Bachelor's degree, GPA close to 3.0; transcript, three letters of recommendation. Students desiring New York State permanent teaching certification should possess preliminary certification. *Degree Requirements:* M.Ed.: 30 semester hours with 15-18 credits in specialization. Ph.D.: 78 semester hours, internship, portfolio certification, thesis. *Faculty:* 13 full-time, 7 part-time. *Students:* 100 full-time, 350 part-time. *Financial Assistance:* fellowships, assistantships, grant, student loans, minority fellowships. *Degrees Awarded 1997:* M.Ed., 165; Ph.D., 7.

State University of New York at Stony Brook. Technology & Society, College of Engineering & Applied Sciences, SUNY at Stony Brook, Stony Brook, NY 11794-2250. (516)632-8763. (516)632-7809. E-mail dferguson@dts.tns.sunysb.edu. Website: http://www.ceas.sunysb.edu/DTS/. Prof. David L. Ferguson, Contact Person. *Specializations:* Master's Degree in Technological Systems Management with concentration in Educational Computing. *Features:* emphasis on courseware design, multimedia and modeling, applications, and problem-solving. *Admission Requirements:* bachelor's degree in engineering, natural sciences, social sciences, mathematics, or closely related area; 3.0 undergraduate GPA; experience with computer applications or computer applications or use of computers in teaching. *Degree Requirements:* 30 semester credits, including two general technology core courses, 5 required educational computing courses, and 3 eligible electives. *Faculty:* 5 full-time, 3 part-time. *Students*: 10 full-time, 15 part-time. *Financial Assistance:* assistantships, grants, student loans. *Degrees Awarded 1997:* 5.

Syracuse University. Instructional Design, Development, and Evaluation Program, School of Education, 330 Huntington Hall, Syracuse, NY 13244-2340. (315)443-3703. Fax (315)443-9218. E-mail lltucker@sued.syr.edu. Website http://www.idde.syr.edu. Philip L. Doughty, Prof., Chair. *Specializations:* M.S., Ed.D., and Ph.D. degree programs for Instructional Design of programs and materials, Educational Evaluation, Human Issues in Instructional Development, Media Production (including computers and multimedia), and Educational Research and Theory (learning theory, application of theory, and educational media research). Graduates are prepared to serve as curriculum developers, instructional developers, program and product evaluators, researchers, resource center administrators, communications coordinators, trainers in human resource development, and higher education instructors. The school also offers an advanced certificate program. *Features:* field work and internships, special topics and special issues seminar, student- and faculty-initiated minicourses, seminars and guest lecturers, faculty-student formulation of department policies, and multiple international perspectives. *Admission Requirements:* M.S.: undergraduate transcripts, recommendations, personal statement, interview recommended; TOEFL for international applicants; GRE recommended. Doctoral: Relevant Master's degree from accredited institution, GRE (3 tests required) scores, recommendations, personal statement, TOEFL for international applicants; interview recommended. *Degree Requirements:* M.S.: 36 semester hours, comprehensive exam and portfolio required. *Faculty:* 2 full-time, 4 part-time. *Students:* M.S., 22 full-time, 23 part-time; doctoral, 25 full-time, 30 part-time. *Financial Assistance:* fellowships, scholarships, and graduate assistantships entailing either research or administrative duties in instructional technology. *Degrees Awarded 1998:* M.S., 8; doctorate, 7.

NORTH CAROLINA

Appalachian State University. Department of Leadership and Educational Studies, Boone, NC 28608. (704)262-2243. Fax (704)262-2128. E-mail Webbbh@appstate.edu. Website http://www.ced.appstate.edu/ltl.html. John H. Tashner, Prof., Coord. *Specialization:* M.A. in Educational Media and Technology with three areas of concentration: Computers, Telecommunications, and Media Production. *Features:* IMPACT NC (business, university, and public school) partnership offers unusual opportunities. *Degree Requirements:* 36 semester hours (including 15 in Computer Education), internship; thesis optional. *Faculty:* 2 full-time, 1 part-time. *Students:* 10 full-time, 60 part-time. *Financial Assistance:* assistantships, grants, student loans. *Degrees Awarded 1997:* 15.

East Carolina University. Department of Library Studies and Educational Technology, Greenville, NC 27858-4353. (919)328-6621. Fax (919)328-4368. E-mail kesterd@mail.ecu.edu. Website eastnet.educ.ecu.edu/schofed/lset. Dr. Diane D. Kester, Assoc. Prof., Chair. *Specializations:* Master of Library Science; Certificate of Advanced Study (Library Science); Master of Arts in Education (Instructional Technology Computers). *Features:* M.L.S. graduates are eligible for North Carolina School Media Coord. certification; C.A.S. graduates are eligible for North Carolina School Media Supervisor certification; M.A.Ed. graduates are eligible for North Carolina Instructional Technology-Computers certification. *Admission Requirements:* Master's: Bachelor's degree; C.A.S.: M.L.S. or equivalent degree. *Degree Requirements:* M.L.S.: 38 semester hours; M.A.Ed.: 36 semester hours; C.A.S.: 30 semester hours. *Faculty:* 9 full-time. *Students:* 7 full-time, 150 part-time. *Financial Assistance:* assistantships. *Degrees Awarded 1997:* M.L.S., 21; M.A.Ed., 19; C.A.S., 3.

North Carolina Central University. School of Education, 1801 Fayetteville St., Durham, NC 27707. (919)560-6692. Fax (919)560-5279. Dr. James N. Colt, Assoc. Prof., Coordinator., Graduate Program in Educational Technology. Specialization: M.A. with special emphasis on Instructional Development/Design. *Features*: Graduates are prepared to implement and utilize a variety of technologies applicable to many professional ventures, including institutions of higher education (college resource centers), business, industry, and professional schools such as medicine, law, dentistry, and nursing. *Admission Requirements*: undergraduate degree, GRE. *Degree Requirements*: 33 semester hours (including thesis). *Faculty*: 2 full-time, 2 part-time. *Students*: 19 full-time, 18 part-time. *Financial Assistance*: assistantships, grants, student loans. *Degrees Awarded 1998:* 15.

North Carolina State University. Department of Curriculum and Instruction, P.O. Box 7801, Raleigh, NC 27695-7801. (919)515-1779. Fax (919)515-6978. E-mail esvasu@unity.ncsu.edu. Dr. Ellen Vasu, Assoc. Prof. *Specializations:* M.Ed. and M.S. in Instructional Technology-Computers (program track within one Master's in Curriculum and Instruction). Ph.D. in Curriculum and Instruction with focus on Instructional Technology as well as other areas. *Admission Requirements:* Master's: undergraduate degree from an accredited institution, 3.0 GPA in major or in latest graduate degree program; transcripts; GRE or MAT scores; 3 references; goal statement, interview (see http://www2.ncsu.edu/ncsu/cep/ci/it/mitmain.html). Ph.D.: undergraduate degree from accredited institution, 3.0 GPA in major or latest graduate program; transcripts; recent GRE scores, writing sample, interview, three references, vita, goal statement (see http://www2.acs.ncsu.edu/grad/admision.htm). *Degree Requirements:* Master's: 36 semester hours, practicum, thesis optional; Ph.D.: 60 hours beyond Master's (minimum 33 in Curriculum and Instruction core, 27 in Research); other information available upon request. *Faculty:* 2 full-time. *Students:* Master's, 32 part-time; Ph.D., 6 part-time. *Degrees Awarded 1997:* Master's, 1; Ph.D., 2.

University of North Carolina. School of Information and Library Science (CB#3360), Chapel Hill, NC 27599. (919)962-8062, 962-8366. Fax (919)962-8071. E-mail daniel@ils.unc.edu. Website http://www.ils.unc.edu/. Evelyn H. Daniel, Prof., Coord., School Media Program. *Specialization:* Master of Science Degree in Library Science (M.S.L.S.) with specialization in school library media work. *Features:* rigorous academic program plus teaching practicum requirement; excellent placement record. *Admission Requirements:* competitive admission based on all three GRE components, undergraduate GPA, letters of recommendation, and student statement of career interest. *Degree Requirements:* 48 semester hours, comprehensive exam, Master's paper. *Faculty:* 18 full-time, 10 part-time. *Students:* 30 full-time, 20 part-time. *Financial Assistance:* grants, assistantships, student loans. *Degrees Awarded 1997* (School Media Certification): 30.

NORTH DAKOTA

Minot State University. 500 University Ave. W., Minot, ND 58707. (701)858-3250. Fax (701)839-6933. Dr. Jack L. Rasmussen, Dean of the Graduate School. *Specializations:* M.S. in Elementary Education (including work in educational computing); M.S. in Special Education with Specialization in Severe Multiple-Handicaps, Early Childhood Special Education, Education of the Deaf, and Learning Disabilities; M.S. in Communication Disorders, Specializations in Audiology and Speech Language Pathology. *Features:* All programs include involvement in computer applications appropriate to the area of study, including assistive technologies for persons with disabilities. Computer laboratories are available for student use in the library and various departments. Some courses are offered through the Interactive Video Network, which connects all universities in North Dakota. All programs have a rural focus and are designed to offer a multitude of practical experiences. *Admission Requirements:* $25 fee, three letters of recommendation, 300-word autobiography, transcripts, GRE in Communication Disorders or GMAT for M.S. in Management. *Degree Requirements:* 30 semester hours (hours in computers, education, and outside education vary according to program); written comprehensive exams; oral exams; thesis or project. *Faculty:* 10 full-time. *Students:* 61 full-time, 63 part-time. *Financial Assistance:* loans, assistantships, scholarships. *Degrees Awarded 1997:* M.S.: Elementary Education, 15; S.P.Ed., Severe Multiple Handicaps, 4; S.P.Ed. Early Childhood Special Education, 4; Communication Disorders, 35; S.P.Ed. Learning Disabilities, 13.

OHIO

*Kent State University. 405 White Hall, Kent, OH 44242. (330)672-2294. Fax (330)672-2512. E-mail tchandler@emerald.edu.kent.edu. Website http://amethyst.educ.kent./edu/itec/. Dr. Theodore Chandler, Coord., Instructional Technology Program. *Specializations:* M.Ed. or M.A. in Instructional Technology, Instructional Computing, and Library/Media Specialist; Ph.D. in Educational Psychology with emphasis in Instructional Technology. *Features:* Programs are planned individually to prepare students for careers in elementary, secondary, or higher education, business, industry, government agencies, or health facilities. Students may take advantage of independent research, individual study, practica, and internships. *Admission Requirements:* Master's: Bachelor's degree with 2.75 undergraduate GPA. *Degree Requirements:* Master's: 34 semester hours; thesis required for M.A. *Faculty:* 5 full-time, 7 part-time. *Students:* 39.*Financial Assistance:* 6 graduate assistantships, John Mitchell and Marie McMahan Awards, 4 teaching fellowships. *Degrees Awarded 1996:* Master's: 14.

Ohio University. School of Curriculum and Instruction, 248 McCracken Hall, Athens, OH 45701-2979. (740)593-9826. Fax (740)593-0177. Sandra Turner, Chair. *Specialization:* M.Ed. in Computer Education and Technology. Ph.D. in Curriculum and Instruction with emphasis in Technology also available; call for details. *Admission Requirements:* Bachelor's degree, 2.5 undergraduate GPA, 35 MAT, 420 GRE (verbal), 400 GRE (quantitative), 550 TOEFL, three letters of recommendation. *Degree Requirements:* 54 qtr. credits, optional thesis worth 2-10 credits or alternative seminar and paper. Students may earn two graduate degrees simultaneously in education and in any other field. *Faculty:* 2 full-time, 1 part-time. *Students:* M.Ed.: 60. *Financial Assistance:* assistantships. *Degrees to Awarded 1998:* 25.

*University of Cincinnati. College of Education, 401 Teachers College, ML002, Cincinnati, OH 45221-0002. (513)556-3577. Fax (513)556-2483. Website http://uc.edu/. Randall Nichols and Janet Bohren, Div. of Teacher Education. *Specialization:* M.A. or Ed.D. in Curriculum and Instruction with an emphasis on Instructional Design and Technology; Educational Technology degree programs for current professional, technical, critical, and personal knowledge. *Admission Requirements:* Bachelor's degree from accredited institution, 2.8 undergraduate GPA; conditional admission for candidates not meeting first two criteria possible. *Degree Requirements:* 54 qtr. hours, written exam, thesis or research project. *Faculty:* 3 full-time. *Students:* 20 full-time. *Financial Assistance:* scholarships, assistantships, grants. *Degrees Awarded 1996:* M.A., 12.

University of Toledo. Area of Education, 2801 West Bancroft, Toledo, OH 43606. (419)530-6176. Fax (419)530-7719. E-mail APATTER@UTNET.UTOLEDO.EDU. Website http://carver.carver.utoledo. Dr. Lester J. Elsie, Dir. *Specializations:* Master's (M.Ed. and M.S.Ed.), Ed.S, doctorate (Ed.D., Ph.D.) degrees in Instructional Development, Library/Media Education, Instructional Computing, and Human Resources Development. *Admission Requirements:* Master's: 3.0 undergraduate GPA, GRE, recommendations; Ed.S.: Master's Degree, GRE, recommendations; doctorate: Master's degree, GRE, TOEFL, recommendations, entrance writing sample, and interview. *Degree Requirements:* Master's: 36 semester hours, Master's project; Ed.S.: 32 semester hours, internship; doctorate: 84 semester hours, dissertation. *Faculty:* 5 full-time, 1 part-time. *Students:* Master's, 10 full-time, 72 part-time; Ed.S., 2 full-time, 21 part-time; doctoral, 9 full-time, 56 part-time. *Financial Assistance:* assistantships, student loans, scholarships, work assistance program. *Degrees Awarded 1997:* Master's, 26; Ed.S., 3; doctoral, 3.

Wright State University. College of Education and Human Services, Dept. of Educational Leadership, 228 Millett Hall, Dayton, OH 45435. (937)775-2509 or (937)775-2182. Fax (937)775-4485. Website http://www.ed.wright.edu. Dr. Bonnie K. Mathies, Asst. Dean Communication and Technology. E-mail bonnie.mathies@wright.edu. *Specializations:* M.Ed. in or for Media Supervisor or Computer Coord.; M.A. in Educational Media or Computer Education; Specialist degree in Curriculum and Instruction with a focus on Educational Technology; Specialist degree in Higher Education with a focus on Educational Technology. *Admission Requirements:* completed application with nonrefundable application fee, Bachelor's degree from accredited institution, official transcripts, 2.7 overall GPA for regular status (conditional acceptance possible), statement of purpose, satisfactory scores on MAT or GRE. *Degree Requirements:* M.Ed. requires a comprehensive exam that includes a portfolio with videotaped presentation to the faculty. M.A. requires a 6-hour thesis. *Faculty:* 2 full-time, 12 part-time, including other university full-time faculty and staff. *Students:* approx. 3 full-time, approx. 200 part-time. *Financial Assistance:* 3 graduate assistantships in the College's Educational Resource Center; plus graduate fellowship for full-time students available limited number of small graduate scholarships. *Degree Awarded 1998:* 11.

OKLAHOMA

Southwestern Oklahoma State University. School of Education, 100 Campus Drive, Weatherford, OK 73096. (405)774-3140. Fax (405)774-7043. E-mail mossg@swosu.edu. Website http://www.swosu.edu. Gregory Moss, Asst. Prof., Chair, Dept of School Service Programs. *Specialization:* M.Ed. in Library/Media Education. *Admission Requirements:* 2.5 GPA, GRE or GMAT scores, letter of recommendation, GPA x 150 + GRE = 1100. *Degree Requirements:* 32 semester hours (including 24 in library media). *Faculty:* 1 full-time, 4 part-time. *Students:* 17 part-time. *Degrees Awarded 1997:* 11.

*The University of Oklahoma. Instructional Psychology and Technology, Department of Educational Psychology, 321 Collings Hall, Norman, OK 73019. (405)325-2882. Fax (405)325-6655. E-mail psmith@ou.edu. Website http://www.uoknor.edu/education/iptwww/. Dr. Patricia L. Smith, Chair. *Specializations:* Master's degree with emphases in Educational Technology Generalist, Educational Technology, Computer Application, Instructional Design, Teaching with Technology; Dual Master's Educational Technology and Library and Information Systems. Doctoral degree in Instructional Psychology and Technology. *Features:* strong interweaving of principles of instructional psychology with design and development of Instructional Technology. Application of IP&T in K-12, vocational education, higher education, business and industry, and governmental agencies. *Admission Requirements:* Master's: acceptance by IPT program and Graduate College based on minimum 3.00 GPA for last 60 hours of undergraduate work or last 12 hours of graduate work; written statement that indicates goals and interests compatible with program goals. Doctoral: 3.0 in last 60 hours undergraduate, 3.25 GPA, GRE scores, written statement of background and goals. *Degree Requirements:* Master's: approx. 39 hours course work (specific number of hours dependent upon Emphasis) with 3.0 GPA; successful completion of thesis or comprehensive exam. Doctorate: see program description from institution or http://www.ou.education.iptwww. *Faculty:* 10 full-time. *Students:* Master's, 10 full-time, 200 part-time; doctoral, 10 full-time, 50 part-time. *Financial Assistance:* assistantships, grants, student loans, scholarships. *Degrees Awarded 1996:* Master's, 35; doctoral, 4.

OREGON

*Western Oregon State College. 345 N. Monmouth Ave., Monmouth, OR 97361. (503)838-8471. Fax (503)838-8228. E-mail engler@fsa.wosc.osshe.edu. Dr. Randall Engle, Chair. *Specialization:* M.S. in Information Technology. *Features:* offers advanced courses in library management, instructional development, multimedia, and computer technology. Additional course offerings in distance delivery of instruction and computer-interactive video instruction. *Admission Requirements:* 3.0 GPA, GRE or MAT. *Degree Requirements:* 45 qtr. hours; thesis optional. *Faculty:* 3 full-time, 6 part-time. *Students:* 6 full-time, 131 part-time. *Financial Assistance:* assistantships, grants, student loans, scholarship, work assistance. *Degrees Awarded 1996:* 12.

PENNSYLVANIA

Bloomsburg University. Institute for Interactive Technologies, 1210 McCormick Bldg., Blooms-burg, PA 17815. (717)389-4506. Fax (717)389-4943. E-mail tphillip@bloomu.edu. Website http://iit.bloomu.edu. Dr. Timothy L. Phillips, contact person. *Specialization:* M.S. in Instructional Technology with emphasis on preparing for careers as interactive media specialists. The program is closely associated with the Institute for Interactive Technologies. *Features:* instructional design, authoring languages and systems, media integration, managing multimedia projects. *Admission Requirements:* Bachelor's degree. *Degree Requirements:* 33 semester credits (27 credits + 6 credit thesis, or 30 credits + three credit internship). *Faculty:* 4 full-time. *Students:* 53 full-time, 50 part-time. *Financial Assistance:* assistantships, grants, student loans. *Degrees Awarded 1997:* 50.

Clarion University of Pennsylvania. Becker Hall, Clarion, PA 16214. (814)226-2245. Fax (814)226-2186. Carmen S. Felicetti, Chair, Dept. of Communications. *Specialization:* M.S. in Communication with specialization in Training and Development. The curriculum is process and application oriented with basic courses in television and computer applications, Internet, Web, and html authoring. Major projects are team and client oriented with an emphasis on multimedia presentations. *Admission Requirements:* Bachelor's degree; 2.75 undergraduate GPA, MAT score. *Degree Requirements:* 36 semester credits (including 27 specific to Training and Development) with 3.0 GPA, optional thesis worth 6 credits. *Faculty:* 9 full-time. *Financial Assistance:* ten 1/4 time or five 20-hour graduate assistantships. *Degrees awarded 1997:* 5.

Drexel University. College of Information Science and Technology, Philadelphia, PA 19104. (215)895-2474. Fax (215)895-2494. Richard H. Lytle, Prof. and Dean. Website http://www.cis.drexel.edu. *Specializations:* M.S. in Library and Information Science; M.S.I.S. in Information Systems. *Admission Requirements:* GRE scores; applicants with a minimum 3.2 GPA in last half of undergraduate credits may be eligible for admission without GRE scores. *Degree Requirements:* 60 credits. *Faculty:* 16 full-time, 47 adjunct. *Students:* M.S., 29 full-time, 174 part-time; M.S.I.S., 23 full-time, 275 part-time. *Degrees Awarded 1997:* M.S., 69; M.S.I.S, 57.

Lehigh University. College of Education, Bethlehem, PA 18015. (610)758-3231. Fax (610)758-6223. E-mail WMC0@LEHIGH.EDU. Website http://www.lehigh.edu. Leroy Tuscher, Coord., Educational Technology Program. *Specializations*: M.S. degree with emphasis on design and development of interactive multimedia (both standalone and on the Web) for teaching and learning; Ed.D. in Educational Technology. *Admission Requirements*: M.S.: competitive; 2.75 undergraduate GPA or 3.0 graduate GPA, GRE recommended, transcripts, at least 2 letters of recommendation, statement of personal and professional goals, application fee. Ed.D.: 3.5 graduate GPA, GRE required. Deadlines are Jul 15 for fall admission, Dec 1 for spring admission, Apr 30 for summer admission. *Degree Requirements*: M.S.: 33 semester hours (including 8 in media); thesis option. Ed.D.: 48 hours past the Master's plus dissertation. *Faculty*: 3 full-time, 2 part-time. *Students:* M.S.: 13 full-time, 34 part-time; Ed.D.: 6 full-time, 32 part-time. *Financial Assistance*: university graduate and research assistantships, graduate student support as participants in R&D projects, employment opportunities in local businesses and schools doing design and development. *Degrees Awarded 1997:* M.S., 16; Ed.D., 3.

Pennsylvania State University. 314 Keller Bldg., University Park, PA 16802. (814)865-0473. Fax (814)865-0128. E-mail bgrabowski@psu.edu. B. Grabowski, Prof. in Charge. *Specializations:* M.Ed., M.S., D.Ed, and Ph.D. in Instructional Systems. Current teaching emphases are on Corporate Training, Interactive Learning Technologies, and Educational Systems Design. Research interests include multimedia, visual learning, educational reform, emerging technologies, and constructivist learning. *Features:* A common thread throughout all programs is that candidates have basic competencies in the understanding of human learning; instructional design, development, and evaluation; and research procedures. Practical experience is available in mediated independent learning, research, instructional development, computer-based education, and dissemination projects. *Admission Requirements:* D.Ed., Ph.D.: GRE, TOEFL, transcript, three letters of recommendation, writing sample, vita or resume, and letter of application detailing rationale for interest in the degree. *Degree Requirements:* M.Ed.: 33 semester hours; M.S.: 36 hours, including either a thesis or project paper; doctoral: candidacy exam, courses, residency, comprehensives, dissertation. *Faculty:* 10 full-time, 5 affiliate and 1 adjunct. *Students:* Master's, approx. 46; doctoral, 103. *Financial Assistance:* assistantships, graduate fellowships, student aid loans, internships; assistantships on grants, contracts, and projects. *Degrees Awarded 1998:* master's, 43; doctoral, 6.

Rosemont College. Graduate Studies in Education, 1400 Montgomery Ave., Rosemont, PA 19010-1699. (610)526-2982; (800)531-9431 outside 610 area code. Fax (610)526-2964. E-mail roscolgrad@rosemont.edu. Website http://techined.rosemont.edu/CSTE/info.html. Dr. Richard Donagher, Dir. *Specializations:* M.Ed. in Technology in Education, Certificate in Professional Study in Technology in Education. *Admission Requirements:* GRE or MAT scores. *Degree Requirements:* Completion of 12 units (36 credits) and comprehensive exam. *Faculty:* 7 full-time, 10 part-time. *Students:* 110 full- and part-time. *Financial Assistance:* graduate student grants, assistantships, Federal Stafford Loan Program. *Degrees Awarded 1997:* 13.

RHODE ISLAND

The University of Rhode Island. Graduate School of Library and Information Studies, Rodman Hall, Kingston, RI 02881-0815. (401)874-2947. Fax (401)874-4964. Website http://www.uri.edu/artsci/lsc. W. Michael Novener, Assoc. Prof. and Dir. *Specializations:* M.L.I.S. degree with specialties in Archives, Law, Health Sciences, Rare Books, and Youth Services Librarianship. *Degree Requirements:* 42 semester-credit program offered in Rhode Island and regionally in Boston and Amherst, MA, and Durham, NH. *Faculty:* 7 full-time, 24 part-time. *Students:* 48 full-time, 196 part-time. *Financial Assistance:* graduate assistantships, some scholarship aid, student loans. *Degrees Awarded 1997:* 73.

SOUTH CAROLINA

University of South Carolina. Educational Psychology Department, Columbia, SC 29208. (803)777-6609. Dr. Margaret Gredler, Prof., Chair. *Specialization*: Master's degree. *Degree Requirements*: 33 semester hours, including instructional theory, computer design, and integrated media. *Faculty*: 3. *Students*: 10.

TENNESSEE

East Tennessee State University. College of Education, Dept. of Curriculum and Instruction., Box 70684, Johnson City, TN 37614-0684. (423)439-4186. Fax (423)439-8362. *Specializations:* M.Ed. in Instructional Media (Library), M.Ed. in Instructional Technology. *Admission Requirements:* Bachelor's degree from accredited institution, transcripts, personal essay; in some cases, GRE and/or interview. *Degree Requirements:* 39 semester hours, including 18 hours in instructional technology. *Faculty:* 2 full-time, 4 part-time. *Students:* 9 full-time, 40 part-time. *Financial Assistance:* Scholarships, assistantships, aid for disabled. *Degrees Awarded 1997:* 12.

*University of Tennessee-Knoxville. College of Education, Education in the Sciences, Mathematics, Research, and Technology Unit, 319 Claxton Addition, Knoxville, TN 37996-3400. (423)974-4222 or (423)974-3103. Dr. Al Grant, Coord., Instructional Media and Technology Program. *Specializations:* M.S. in Ed., Ed.S., and Ed.D. under Education in Sciences, Mathematics, Research, and Technology; Ed.D. in Curriculum and Instruction, concentration in Instructional Media and Technology; Ph.D. under the College of Education, concentration in Instructional Media and Technology. *Features:* course work in media management, advanced software production, utilization, research, theory, psychology, instructional computing, television, and instructional development. Course work will also meet the requirements for state certification as Instructional Materials Supervisor in the public schools of Tennessee. *Admission Requirements:* Send for Graduate Catalog, The University of Tennessee. *Degree Requirements:* M.S.: 33 semester hours; thesis optional. *Faculty:* 1 full-time, with additional assistance from Ed SMRT Unit, College of Ed. and university faculty. *Students:* M.S., 2 part-time; Ed.S., 2 part-time.

TEXAS

Texas A&M University. Educational Technology Program, Dept. of Curriculum & Instruction, College of Education, College Station, TX 77843. (409)845-7276. Fax (409)845-9663. E-mail zellner@tamu.edu. Website http://educ.coe.tamu.edu/~edtc/edtc/prog/edtcintro.html. Ronald D. Zellner, Assoc. Prof., Coord. *Specializations*: M.Ed. in Educational Technology; EDCI Ph.D. program with specializations in Educational Technology and in Distance Education; Ph.D. in Educational Psychology Foundations: Learning & Technology. The purpose of the Educational Technology Program is to prepare educators with the competencies required to improve the quality and effectiveness of instructional programs at all levels. A major emphasis is placed on multimedia instructional materials development and techniques for effective distance education and communication. Teacher preparation with a focus on field-based instruction and school to university collaboration is also a major component. The program goal is to prepare graduates with a wide range of skills to work as professionals and leaders in a variety of settings, including education, business, industry, and the military. *Features*: Program facilities include laboratories for teaching, resource development, and production. Computer, video, and multimedia development are supported in a number of facilities. The college and university also maintain facilities for distance education materials development and fully equipped classrooms for course delivery to nearby collaborative school districts and sites throughout the state. *Admission Requirements*: M.Ed.: Bachelor's degree, 800 GRE, 550 TOEFL; Ph.D.: 3.0 GPA, 800 GRE. *Degree Requirements*: M.Ed.: 39 semester credits, oral exam; Ph.D.: course work varies with student goals. *Faculty*: 4 full-time. *Students*: M.Ed., 25 full-time, 15 part-time; Ph.D., 2 full-time, 6 part-time. *Financial Assistance*: several graduate and teaching assistantships. *Degrees Awarded 1997*: M.Ed., 18.

Texas A&M University-Commerce. Department of Secondary and Higher Education, East Texas Station, Commerce, TX 75429-3011. (903)886-5607. Fax (903)886-5603. E-mail bob_mundayb@tamu-commerce.edu. Dr. Robert Munday, Prof., Head. Specialization: M.S. or M.Ed. degree in Learning Technology and Information Systems with emphases on Educational Computing, Educational Media and Technology, and Library and Information Science. *Admission Requirements*: 700 GRE (combined*)*. *Degree Requirements*: 36 hours (Educational Computing): 30 hours in Educational Technology. M.S. (Educational Media and Technology): 21 hours in Educational Technology. M.S. (Library and Information Science): 15 hours in Library/Information Science, 12 hours in Educational Technology. *Faculty*: 3 full-time, 5 part-time. *Students*: 30 full-time, 150 part-time. *Financial Assistance:* graduate assistantships in teaching and research, scholarships, federal aid program.

Texas Tech University. College of Education, Box 41071, TTU, Lubbock, TX 79409. (806)742-1997, ext. 299. Fax (806)742-2179. Website http://www.educ.ttu.edu. Dr. Robert Price, Dir., Instructional Technology. Specializations: M.Ed. in Instructional Technology (Educational Computing and Distance Education emphasis); Ed.D. in Instructional Technology. *Features:* Program is NCATE accredited and follows ISTE and AECT guidelines. *Admission Requirements*: holistic evaluation based on GRE scores, GPA, student goals and writing samples. *Degree Requirements:* M.Ed.: 39 hours (24 hours in educational technology, 15 hours in education or outside education); practicum. Ed.D.: 87 hours (45 hours in educational technology, 18 hours in education, 15 hours in resource area or minor); practicum. *Faculty:* 5 full-time. *Students:* M.Ed., 10 full-time, 20 part-time; Ed.D., 15 full-time, 15 part-time. *Financial Assistance:* teaching and research assistantships available ($8,500 for 9 months); small scholarships. *Degrees Awarded 1998:* Ed.D., 5; M.Ed., 6.

University of North Texas. College of Education, Box 311337, Denton, TX 76203-1337. (940)565-2057. Fax (940)565-2185. Website http://www.cecs.unt.edu. Dr. Terry Holcomb, Program Coord., Computer Education and Cognitive Systems. Dr. Jon Young, Chair, Dept. of Technology and Cognition. *Specializations:* M.S. in Computer Education and Instructional Systems. *Admission Requirements:* 1000 GRE (400 verbal and 400 quantitative minimums). *Degree Requirements:* 36 semester hours (including 27 in Instructional Technology and Computer Education), comprehensive exam. *Faculty:* 7 full-time, 1 part-time. *Students:* 90+ 500 service/ minor students, approx. half full-time. *Degrees Awarded 1997:* 30.

The University of Texas. College of Education, Austin, TX 78712. (512)471-5211. Fax (512)471-4607. Website http://www.edb.utexas./coe/depts/ci/c&i.html. Paul Resta, Professor, Department of Curriculum and Instruction, College of Education, The University of Texas, Austin, Texas 78753. E-mail resta@mail.utexas.edu. *Specializations*: Master's degree (MA and MEd). Ph.D. program emphasizes research, design, and development of instructional systems and communications technology. *Features*: The program is interdisciplinary in nature, although certain competencies are required of all students. Programs of study and dissertation research are based on individual needs and career goals. Learning resources include a model Learning Technology Center, computer labs and classrooms, a television studio, and interactive multimedia lab. Many courses are offered cooperatively by other departments, including Radio-TV Film, Computer Science, and Educational Psychology. *Admission Requirements*: both degrees: 3.5 GPA, 1150 GRE. *Degree Requirements*: Master's: 30-36 semester hours depending on selection of program (21 in Instructional Technology plus research course); thesis option. A 6-hour minor is required outside the department. Ph.D.: written comprehensive and specialization exam with oral defense, dissertation with oral defense. *Facul*ty: 3 full-time, 4 part-time. *Students*: approx. 45 Master's, 55 doctoral. *Financial Assistance*: Assistantships may be available to develop instructional materials, teach undergraduate computer tools, and assist with research projects. There are also some paid internships. *Degrees Awarded 1997*: Master's, 13; doctorate, 9.

UTAH

Brigham Young University. Department of Instructional Psychology and Technology, 201 MCKB, BYU, Provo, UT 84602. (801)378-5097. Fax (801)378-8672. E-mail paul_merrill@byu.edu. Website http://www.byu.edu/acd1/ed/InSci/InSci.html. Paul F. Merrill, Prof., Chair. *Specializations:* M.S. degrees in Instructional Design, Research and Evaluation, and Multimedia Production. Ph.D. degrees in Instructional Design, and Research and Evaluation. *Features:* Course offerings include principles of learning, instructional design, assessing learning outcomes, evaluation in education, empirical inquiry in education, project management, quantitative reasoning, microcomputer materials production, multimedia production, naturalistic inquiry, and more. Students participate in internships and projects related to development, evaluation, measurement, and research. *Admission Requirements:* both degrees: transcript, 3 letters of recommendation, letter of intent, GRE scores. Apply by Feb 1. Students agree to live by the BYU Honor Code as a condition for admission. *Degree Requirements:* Master's: 38 semester hours, including prerequisite (3 hours), core courses (14 hours), specialization (12 hours), internship (3 hours), thesis or project (6 hours) with oral defense. Ph.D.: 94 semester hours beyond the Bachelor's degree, including: prerequisite and skill requirements (21 hours), core course (16 hours), specialization (18 hours), internship (12 hours), projects (9 hours), and dissertation (18 hours). The dissertation must be orally defended. Also, at least two consecutive 6-hour semesters must be completed in residence. *Faculty:* 9 full-time, 2 half-time. *Students:* Master's, 25 full-time, 2 part-time; Ph.D., 47 full-time, 3 part-time. *Financial Assistance:* internships, tuition scholarships, loans, and travel to present papers. *Degrees Awarded 1997:* Master's, 7; Ph.D., 3.

Utah State University. Department of Instructional Technology, College of Education, Logan, UT 84322-2830. (435)797-2694. Fax (435)797-2693. E-mail dsmellie@cc.usu.edu. Website http://www.coe.usu:edu/it/. Dr. Don C. Smellie, Prof., Chair. *Specializations:* M.S. and Ed.S. with concentrations in the areas of Instructional Development, Multimedia, Educational Technology, and Information Technology/School Library Media Administration. Ph.D. in Instructional Technology is offered for individuals seeking to become professionally involved in instructional development in corporate education, public schools, community colleges, and universities. Teaching and research in higher education is another career avenue for graduates of the program. *Features:* M.S. and Ed.S. programs in Information Technology/School Library Media Administration and Educational Technology are also delivered via an electronic distance education system. The doctoral program is built on a strong Master's and Specialist's program in Instructional Technology. All doctoral students complete a core with the remainder of the course selection individualized, based upon career goals. *Admission Requirements:* M.S. and Ed.S.: 3.0 GPA, a verbal and quantitative score at the 40th percentile on the GRE or 43 MAT, three written recommendations. Ph.D.: Master's degree in Instructional Technology, 3.0 GPA, verbal and quantitative score at the 40th percentile on the GRE, three written recommendations. *Degree Requirements:* M.S.: 39 sem. hours; thesis or project option. Ed.S.: 30 sem. hours if M.S. is in the field, 40 hours if not. Ph.D.: 62 total hours, dissertation, 3-sem. residency, and comprehensive examination. *Faculty:* 9 full-time, 7 part-time. *Students:* M.S., 70 full-time, 85 part-time; Ed.S., 6 full-time, 9 part-time; Ph.D., 15 full-time, 14 part-time. *Financial Assistance:* approx. 18 to 26 assistantships (apply by April 1). *Degrees Awarded 1997:* M.S., 42; Ed.S., 3; Ph.D., 3.

VIRGINIA

George Mason University. Instructional Technology Programs, Mail Stop 4B3, 4400 University Dr., Fairfax, VA 22030-4444. (703)993-2051. Fax (703)993-2013. E-mail mbehrman@wpgate.gmu.edu. Website http://gse.gmu.edu/programs/it/index.htm. Dr. Michael Behrmann, Coord. of Instructional Technology Academic Programs. *Specializations:* M.Ed. in Curriculum and Instruction with tracks in Instructional Design and Development, Integration of Technology in Schools, and Assistive/Special Education Technology; M.Ed. in Special Education; Ph.D. with specialization in Instructional Technology or Special Education Technology. Certificate Programs (12-15cr) in: Integration of Technology in Schools; Multimedia Development; Assistive Technology. *Features:* Master's program started in 1983 and doctoral in 1984. Integration of Technology in Schools is a cohort program in which students are admitted in the Spring semester only. ID & D full-time immersion admits students in summer. All other tracks admit throughout the year. *Admission Requirements:* teaching or training experience, introductory programming course or equivalent; introductory course in educational technology or equivalent. *Degree Requirements:* M.Ed. in Curriculum and Instruction: 36 hours; practicum, internship, or project. M.Ed. in Special Education: 36-42 hours. Ph.D.: 56-62 hours beyond Master's degree for either specialization. Certificate programs: 12-15 hours. *Faculty:* 6 full-time, 5 part-time. *Students:* M.Ed. in Curriculum and Instruction: 5 part-time, 125 part-time. M.Ed. in Special Education: 10 full-time, 8 part-time. Ph.D.: 19 part-time, 10 full time. ITS certificate, 250; MM Certificate, 30; At Certificate, 45. *Financial Assistance:* Assistantships and tuition waivers available for full-time graduate students. *Degrees Awarded 1997:* M.Ed. in Curriculum and Instruction, 17; M.Ed. in Special Education Technology, 6.

Radford University. Educational Studies Department, College of Education and Human Development, P.O. Box 6959, Radford, VA 24142. (540)831-5302. Fax (540)831-5059. E-mail ljwilson@runet.edu. Website http://www.radford.edu. Dr. Linda J. Wilson. *Specialization*: M.S. in Education with Educational Media/Technology emphasis. *Features*: School Library Media Specialist licensure. *Admission Requirements*: Bachelor's degree, 2.7 undergraduate GPA. *Degree Requirements*: 33 semester hours, practicum; thesis optional. *Faculty:* 2 full-time, 3 part-time. *Students*: 2 full-time, 23 part-time. *Financial Assistance*: assistantships, grants, student loans, scholarships. *Degrees Awarded 1998:* 6.

University of Virginia. Department of Leadership, Foundations, and Policy, Curry School of Education, Ruffner Hall, Charlottesville, VA 22903. (804)924-7471. Fax (804)924-0747. E-mail jbbunch@virginia.edu. Website http://curry.edschool.virginia.edu/curry/dept/edlf/instrtech/. John B. Bunch, Assoc. Prof., Coord., Instructional Technology Program, Dept. of Leadership, Foundations and Policy Studies. *Specializations:* M.Ed., Ed.S., Ed.D, and Ph.D. degrees with focal areas in Media Production, Interactive Multimedia, and K-12 Educational Technologies. *Admission Requirements:* undergraduate degree from accredited institution in any field, undergraduate GPA 3.0,1000 GRE (V+Q), 600 TOEFL. Admission application deadline is March 1st of each year for the fall semester for both Master's and doctoral degrees. *Degree Requirements:* M.Ed.: 36 semester hours, comprehensive examination. Ed.S.: 60 semester hours beyond undergraduate degree. Ed.D.: 54 semester hours, dissetation, at least one conference presentation or juried publication, comprehensive examination, residency; Ph.D.: same as Ed.S. with the addition of 18 semester hours. For specific degree requirements, see Website, write to the address above, or refer to the UVA *Graduate Record. Faculty:* 4 full-time, 1 part-time. *Students:* M.Ed. 24; Ed.D, 3; Ph.D., 15. *Financial Assistance:* Some graduate assistantships and scholarships are available on a competitive basis. *Degrees Awarded 1996:* Master's, 4; doctorate, 2.

Virginia Polytechnic Institute and State University (Virginia Tech). College of Human Resources and Education, 220 War Memorial Hall, Blacksburg, VA 24061-0341. (540)231-5587. Fax (540)231-9075. E-mail moorem@vt.edu. Website http://www.chre.vt.edu/Admin/IT/. David M. (Mike) Moore, Program Area Leader, Instructional Technology, Dept. of Teaching and Learning. *Specializations*: M.A., Ed.D., and Ph.D. in Instructional Technology. Preparation for education, higher education, faculty development, business, and industry. *Features*: Areas of emphasis are Instructional Design, Educational Computing, Evaluation, and Media Management and Development. Facilities include two computer labs (70 IBM and Macintosh computers), plus interactive video, speech synthesis, telecommunication labs, distance education classroom, and computer graphics production areas. *Admission Requirements*: Ed.D. and Ph.D.: 3.3 GPA from Master's degree, GRE scores, interview, writing samples, three letters of recommendation, transcripts. MA.: 3.0 GPA Undergraduate. *Degree Requirements*: Ph.D.: 96 hrs above B.S., 2 year residency, 12 hrs. research classes, 30 hrs. dissertation; Ed.D.: 90 hrs. above B.S., 1 year residency, 12 hrs. research classes; MA.: 30 hrs. above B.S. *Faculty*: 7 full-time, 5 part-time. *Students*: 35 full-time and 10 part-time at the doctoral level. 10 full-time and 15 part-time at the masters level. *Financial Assistance*: 10 assistantships, limited tuition scholarships. *Degrees Awarded 1998*: doctoral, 6; masters, 3.

Virginia State University. School of Liberal Arts & Education, Petersburg, VA 23806. (804)524-6886. Vykuntapathi Thota, Chair, Dept. of Education. *Specializations:* M.S., M.Ed. in Educational Technology. *Features:* Video Conferencing Center and PLATO Laboratory, internship in ABC and NBC channels. *Degree Requirements:* 30 semester hours plus thesis for M.S.; 33 semester hours plus project for M.Ed.; comprehensive exam. *Faculty:* 1 full-time, 2 part-time. *Students:* 8 full-time, 50 part-time. *Financial Assistance:* scholarships through the School of Graduate Studies.

WASHINGTON

Eastern Washington University. Department of Computer Science, Cheney, WA 99004-2431. (509)359-7093. Fax (509)359-2215. E-mail LKieffer@ewu.edu. Dr. Linda M. Kieffer, Assoc. Prof. of Computer Science. *Specializations:* M.Ed. in Computer and Technology Supported Education; M.S. in Computer Education (Interdisciplinary). Master's program started in 1983. *Features:* Many projects involve the use of high-level authoring systems to develop educational products, technology driven curriculum, and Web projects. *Admission Requirements:* 3.0 GPA for last 90 qtr. credits. *Degree Requirements:* M.S.: 52 qtr. hours (30 hours in computers, 15 hours outside education; the hours do not total to 52 because of freedom to choose where Methods of Research is taken, where 12 credits of supporting courses are taken, and where additional electives are taken); research project with formal report. M.Ed.: 52 qtr. hours (28 hours in computer education, 16 hours in education, 8 hours outside education). *Faculty:* 3 full-time. *Students:* approx. 35. *Financial Assistance:* some research and teaching fellowships. *Degrees Awarded 1997:* 3.

University of Washington. College of Education, 115 Miller Hall, Box 353600 Seattle, WA 98195-3600. (206)543-1847. Fax (206)543-8439. E-mail stkerr@u.washington.edu. Website http://www.educ.washington.edu/COE/c-and-i/c_and_i_med_ed_tech.htm. Stephen T. Kerr, Prof. of Education. *Specializations:* M.Ed., Ed.D, and Ph.D. for individuals in business, industry, higher education, public schools, and organizations concerned with education or communication (broadly defined). *Features:* emphasis on instructional design as a process of making decisions about the shape of instruction; additional focus on research and development in such areas as message design (especially graphics and diagrams); electronic information systems; interactive instruction via videodisc, multimedia, and computers. *Admission Requirements:* M.Ed.: goal statement (2-3pp.), writing sample, 1000 GRE (verbal plus quantitative), undergraduate GPA indicating potential to successfully accomplish graduate work. Doctoral: GRE scores, letters of reference, transcripts, personal statement, Master's degree or equivalent in field appropriate to the specialization with 3.5 GPA, two years of successful professional experience and/or experience related to program goals. *Degree Requirements:* M.Ed.: 45 qtr. hours (including 24 in media); thesis or project optional. Ed.D.: see www.educ.washington.edu/COE/admissions/DoctorOfEducationProgram.htm. Ph.D.: see www.educ.washington.edu/COE/admissions/DoctorOfPhilosophyDegree.htm. *Faculty:* 2 full-time, 3 part-time. *Students:* 12 full-time, 32 part-time; 26 M.Ed., 18 doctoral. *Financial Assistance:* assistantships awarded competitively and on basis of program needs; other assistantships available depending on grant activity in any given year. *Degrees Awarded 1997:* M.Ed., 10; doctorate, 4.

Western Washington University. Woodring College of Education, Instructional Technology, MS 9087, Bellingham, WA 98225-9087. (360)650-3387. Fax (360)650-6526. E-mail Les.Blackwell@ wwu.edu. Website http://www.wce.wwu.edu/depts/IT/. Dr. Les Blackwell, Prof., Deparment Chair. *Specializations:* M.Ed. with emphasis in Instructional Technology in Adult Education, Special Education, Elementary Education, and Secondary Education. *Admission Requirements:* 3.0 GPA in last 45 qtr. credit hours, GRE or MAT scores, 3 letters of recommendation, and, in some cases, 3 years of teaching experience. *Degree Requirements:* 48-52 qtr. hours (24-28 hours in instructional technology; 24 hours in education-related courses, thesis required; internship and practicum possible). *Faculty:* 6 full-time, 8 part-time. *Students:* 5 full-time, 10 part-time. *Financial Assistance:* assistantships, student loans, scholarships. *Master's Degrees Awarded 1998:* 4.

WISCONSIN

Edgewood College. Department of Education, 855 Woodrow St., Madison, WI 53711-1997. (608)257-4861, ext. 2293. Fax (608)259-6727. E-mail schmied@edgewood.edu. Website http://www.edgewood.edu. Dr. Joseph E. Schmiedicke, Chair, Dept. of Education. *Specializations:* M.A. in Education with emphasis on Instructional Technology. Master's program started in 1987. *Features:* classes conducted in laboratory setting with emphasis on applications and software. *Admission Requirements:* 2.75 GPA. *Degree Requirements:* 36 semester hours. *Faculty:* 2 full-time, 3 part-time. *Students:* 5 full-time, 135 part-time. *Financial Assistance:* grants, student loans. *Degrees Awarded 1997:* 12.

University of Wisconsin-La Crosse. Educational Media Program, Rm. 235C, Morris Hall, La Crosse, WI 54601. (608)785-8121. Fax (608)785-8128. E-mail Phill.rm@mail.uwlax.edu. Dr. Russell Phillips, Dir. *Specializations:* M.S. in Professional Development with specializations in Initial Instructional Library Specialist, License 901; Instructional Library Media Specialist, License 902 (39 credits). *Degree Requirements:* 30 semester hours, including 15 in media; no thesis. *Faculty:* 2 full-time, 4 part-time. *Students:* 21. *Financial Assistance:* guaranteed student loans, graduate assistantships.

University of Wisconsin-Madison. Dept. of Curriculum and Instruction, School of Education, 225 N. Mills St., Madison, WI 53706. (608)263-4672. Fax (608)263-9992. E-mail adevaney@ facstaff.wisc.edu. Ann De Vaney, Prof. *Specializations:* M.S. degree and State Instructional Technology License; Ph.D. programs to prepare college and university faculty. *Features:* The program is coordinated with media operations of the university. Traditional instructional technology courses are processed through a social, cultural, and historical frame of reference. Current curriculum emphasizes communication and cognitive theories, critical cultural studies, and theories of textual analysis and instructional development. Course offered in the evening. *Admission Requirements:* Master's and Ph.D.: previous experience in Instructional Technology preferred, previous teaching experience, 3.0 GPA on last 60 undergraduate credits, acceptable scores on GRE, 3.0 GPA on all graduate work. *Degree Requirements:* M.S.: 24 credits plus thesis and exam; Ph.D.: 3 years of residency beyond the Bachelor's (Master's degree counts for one year; one year must be full-time), major, minor, and research requirements, preliminary exam, dissertation, and oral exam. *Faculty:* 3 full-time, 1 part-time. *Students:* M.S., 33; Ph.D., 21. Most master's candidates are part-time; half of Ph.D. students are full-time. *Financial Assistance:* several stipends of approx. $1000 per month for 20 hours of work per week; other media jobs are also available. *Degrees Awarded 1997:* M.S., 16; Ph.D., 3.

Part Seven
Mediagraphy

Print and Nonprint Resources

Introduction

CONTENTS

This resource lists media-related journals, books, ERIC documents, journal articles, and nonprint media resources of interest to practitioners, researchers, students, and others concerned with educational technology and educational media. The primary goal of this section is to list current publications in the field. The majority of materials cited here were published in 1998 or early 1999. Media-related journals include those listed in past issues of *EMTY* and new entries in the field.

It is not the intention of the authors for this chapter to serve as a specific resource location tool, although it may be used for that purpose in the absence of database access. Rather, readers may peruse the categories of interest in this chapter to gain an idea of recent developments within the field. For archival purposes, this chapter serves as a snapshot of the field in 1998. Readers must bear in mind that technological developments occur well in advance of publication, and should take that fact into consideration when judging the timeliness of resources listed in this chapter.

SELECTION

Items were selected for the Mediagraphy in several ways. The ERIC (Educational Resources Information Center) Database was the source for most ERIC document and journal article citations. Others were reviewed directly by the editors. Items were chosen for this list when they met one or more of the following criteria: reputable publisher, broad circulation, coverage by indexing services, peer review, and coverage of a gap in the literature. The Editors chose items on subjects that seem to reflect the Instructional Technology field as it is today. Due to the increasing tendency for media producers to package their products in more that one format and for single titles to contain mixed media, titles are no longer separated by media type. The editors make no claims as to the comprehensiveness of this list. It is, instead, intended to be representative.

OBTAINING RESOURCES

Media-Related Periodicals and Books. Publisher, price, and ordering/subscription address are listed wherever available.

ERIC Documents. ERIC documents can be read and often copied from their microfiche form at any library holding an ERIC microfiche collection. The identification number beginning with ED (for example, ED 332 677) locates the document in the collection. Copies of most ERIC documents can also be ordered from the ERIC Document Reproduction Service. Prices charged depend upon format chosen (microfiche or paper copy), length of the document, and method of shipping. Online orders, fax orders, and expedited delivery are available.

To find the closest library with an ERIC microfiche collection, contact:

ACCESS ERIC
1600 Research Blvd.
Rockville, MD 20850-3172
1-800-LET-ERIC (538-3742)
E-mail: acceric@inet.ed.gov

To order ERIC documents, contact:

ERIC Document Reproduction Service (EDRS)
7420 Fullerton Rd., Suite 110
Springfield, VA 22153-2852
1-800-443-ERIC (443-3742), 703-440-1400
fax: 703-440-1408
E-mail: service@edrs.com

Journal Articles. Photocopies of journal articles can be obtained in one of the following ways: (1) from a library subscribing to the title; (2) through interlibrary loan; (3) through the purchase of a back issue from the journal publisher; or (4) from an article reprint service such as UMI.

UMI Information Store
500 Sansome St., Suite 400
San Francisco, CA 94111
1-800-248-0360 (toll-free in U.S. and Canada)
(415) 433-5500 (outside U.S. and Canada)
E-mail: orders@infostore.com

Journal articles can also be obtained through the Institute for Scientific Information (ISI).

ISI Document Solution
P.O. Box 7649
Philadelphia, PA 19104-3389
(215)386-4399
Fax (215)222-0840 or (215)386-4343
E-mail: ids@isinet.com

ARRANGEMENT

Mediagraphy entries are classified according to major subject emphasis under the following headings:

- Artificial Intelligence, Robotics, and Electronic Performance Support Systems
- Computer-Assisted Instruction
- Distance Education
- Educational Research
- Educational Technology
- Information Science and Technology
- Innovation
- Instructional Design and Training
- Interactive Multimedia
- Libraries and Media Centers
- Media Technologies
- Professional Development
- Simulation, Gaming, and Virtual Reality
- Special Education and Disabilities
- Telecommunications and Networking

Mediagraphy

ARTIFICIAL INTELLIGENCE, ROBOTICS, AND ELECTRONIC PERFORMANCE SUPPORT SYSTEMS

Arkin, R. C. (1998). **Behavior-based robotics (intelligent robots and autonomous agents).** [Book, 447p., $50]. MIT Press, 292 Main Street, Cambridge, MA 02142-1399, (617)253-5249, books@mit.edu, www-mitpress.mit.edu. Surveys the robotics field, providing an appropriate text for graduate students with no prior background. Presents theory and applications of robotics.

Dennett, D. C. (1998). **Brainchildren: Essays on designing minds.** [Book, 424p., $20]. MIT Press, 292 Main Street, Cambridge, MA 02142-1399, (617)253-5249, books@mit.edu, www-mitpress.mit.edu. Combines a number of Dennett's essays about cognitive psychology, artificial intelligence, philosophy of mind, and cognitive ethology.

Fuller, J. L. (1998). **Robotics: Introduction, programming, and projects** (2nd ed.). [Book, 560p., $90]. Prentice Hall, www.prenhall.com. Comprehensive undergraduate-level text, presenting basic techniques, themes, and applications of robotics.

Hoffman, A. G. (1998). **Paradigms of artificial intelligence: A methodological and computational analysis.** [Book, 310p., $49.95]. Springer-Verlag, 800-SPRINGER, orders@springer-ny.com, www.springer-ny.com. Introduces the competing paradigms of the symbolicism versus the connectionism in artificial intelligence and cognitive science research, and suggests objectives for future research.

Hogan, J. P. (1998). **Mind matters: Exploring the world of artificial intelligence.** [Book, 381p., $25]. Del Rey Books, 201 East 50th Street New York 10022, delrey@randomhouse.com, www.crescentbooks.com/delrey/. Provides overview of the history of intelligent machines up to the present, and raises issues about their future development.

International Journal of Robotics Research. Sage Science, (805)499-0721. [Bi-mo., $112 indiv. (foreign $128), $485 inst. (foreign $252), $50 students and retired (foreign $72)]. Interdisciplinary approach to the study of robotics for researchers, scientists, and students.

Keramus, J. (1999). **Robot technology fundamentals.** [Book, 448p., $61.95]. Delmar Publishers, (800)865-5840, www.delmar.com. Addresses practical issues and latest developments, written in layperson terminology.

Knowledge-Based Systems. Elsevier Science Inc., P.O. Box 882, Madison Square Station, New York, NY 10159-0882. [Q., $641]. Interdisciplinary applications-oriented journal on fifth-generation computing, expert systems, and knowledge-based methods in system design.

Luger, G. F., & Stubblefield, W. A. (1998). **Artificial intelligence: Structures and strategies for complex problem-solving** (3rd ed.). [Book, 868p., $59.95]. Addison-Wesley. Discusses logic, rule, and object, and agent-based architectures; contains examples in LISP and PROLOG.

Minds and Machines. Kluwer Academic Publishers, Box 358, Accord Station, Hingham, MA 02018-0358. [Q., $333.50, American inst.]. Discusses issues concerning machines and mentality, artificial intelligence, epistemology, simulation, and modeling.

Moravec, H. (1998). **Robot: Mere machine to transcendent mind.** [Book, 224p., $25]. Oxford. Summarizes contemporary status of robotic technology, and projects a development plan for future research.

Nilsson, N. J. (1998). **Artificial intelligence: A new synthesis.** [Book, 536p., $59.95]. Morgan Kaufmann, (800)745-7323, mkp@mkp.com, www.mkp.com. Describes the application of the intelligent agent through several domains: neural networks, genetic programming, computer vision, heuristic search, knowledge representation and reasoning, Bayes networks, planning, and language understanding.

Rasmus, D. W. (1998). **Rethinking smart objects: Building artificial intelligence with objects.** [Book, 300p., $39.95]. Cambridge University Press, 110 Midland Avenue, Port Chester, NY 10573, (800)872-7423, orders@cup.org, www.cup.org. Explains the integration of object technology and knowledge software development.

Sabelli, N. H., & Kelly, A. E. (1998). The NSF learning and intelligent systems research initiative: Implications for educational research and practice. **Educational Technology, 38** (2), 42–46. The goal of the National Science Foundation (NSF) Learning and Intelligent Systems (LIS) program is to focus research attention on the learning aspects of cognition, neuroscience, information technologies, and related disciplines. Goal-oriented descriptions of the three Collaborative Research on Learning Technology Centers funded under LIS are provided. Selected LIS research topics of interest to classroom instruction are discussed.

Sandler, B. Z. (1999). **Robotics: Designing the mechanisms for automated machinery** (2nd ed.). [Book]. Academic Press, ap@acad.com, www.apnet.com. Describes the design process for building machines. Includes plans for using *Mathematica* as a design tool.

Thornton, C., & DuBoulay, B. (1998). **Artificial intelligence: Strategies, applications, and models through SEARCH.** [Book, 400p., $55]. Fitzroy Dearborn. Describes 11 modeling techniques, including a low-level and high-level implementation for each.

Wagman, M. (1999). **The human mind according to artificial intelligence: Theory, research and implications.** [Book, $59]. Greenwood, 88 Post Road West, Westport CT 06881, (203) 226-3571, www.auburnhouse.com/praeger.htm. Discusses and evaluates the strengths and weaknesses of artificial intelligence in several application domains. Also assesses its roles as a collaborative partner, a competitive foe, and a theoretical model.

Weiss, G. (1999). **Multiagent systems: A modern approach to distributed artifical intelligence.** [Book, 643p., $60]. MIT Press, 292 Main Street, Cambridge, MA 02142-1399, (617) 253-5249, books@mit.edu, www-mitpress.mit.edu. Covers basic and advanced topics regarding multiagent systems and contemporary distributed artificial intelligence; suitable as textbook.

COMPUTER-ASSISTED INSTRUCTION

Abramovich, S. (1998). Manipulative and numerical spreadsheet templates for the study of discrete structures. **International Journal of Mathematical Education in Science and Technology, 29** (2), 233–252. Argues that basic components of discrete mathematics can be introduced to students through gradual elaboration of experiences with iconic spreadsheet-based simulations of concrete materials. Suggests that the study of homogeneous and heterogeneous patterns of manipulative spreadsheet templates allows for appreciation of the development of knowledge about discrete structures. Offers a vision of mathematics as a human activity.

Apple Library Users Group Newsletter. Kluwer Academic Publishers Group, P.O. Box 358, Accord Station, Hingham, MA 02018-0358. [4/yr., free]. For people interested in using Apple and Macintosh computers in libraries and information centers. Encompasses philosophical aspects of computer science.

Barksdale, K., Steffee, J., & Harman, S. (1998). **Math with computers.** [Book, 228p., $22.95]. ISTE, (800)336-5191, fax (541)302-3778, www.iste.org. Strengthens foundational, computational, and statistical skills through the use of spreadsheets.

Barksdale, K., & Steffee, J. (1998). **Writing with computers.** [Book, 295p., $22.95]. ISTE, (800) 336-5191, fax (541)302-3778, www.iste.org. Integrates writing with computer instruction for the purpose of improving writing and simultaneously strengthening computer literacy skills.

Buchanan, L. (1998). Three portable options: AlphaSmart, DreamWriter, Apple eMate. **MultiMedia Schools, 5** (1), 36–38, 40, 42–43. Examines which of three portable computers—AlphaSmart, DreamWriter, and Apple eMate—is the best choice for the classroom. The DreamWriter was selected as having the best combination of price and functionality, while the eMate is the choice if money is no object or the extra functionality is needed; the AlphaSmart has the benefit of a proven track record.

BYTE. Box 550, Hightstown, NJ 08520-9886. [Mo., $29.95; $34.95 Canada and Mexico; $50 elsewhere]. Current articles on microcomputers provide technical information as well as information on applications and products for business and professional users.

CALICO Journal. Computer Assisted Language and Instruction Consortium, 317 Liberal Arts Building, Southwest Texas State University, 601 University Dr., San Marcos, TX 78666, execdir@calico.org. [Q.; $50/$40 indiv., $65 inst., $140/$130 corporations]. Provides information on the applications of technology in teaching and learning languages.

Callender, J. T., & Jackson, R. (1998). Wheels, cranks, and cams: An animated spreadsheet-based mathematical model of a four-stroke engine. **International Journal of Mathematical Education in Science and Technology, 29** (2), 187–194. Analyzes the mathematics of rotational and translational motion and how one can influence the other in the context of cams and cranks. Describes how the individual components can be brought together to simulate a four-stroke engine and how the engine animates again using the same simple macro.

Catchings, M. H., & MacGregor, K. (1998). Stoking creative fires: Young authors use software for writing and illustrating. **Learning and Leading with Technology, 25** (6), 20–24. Investigating the effects of computer paint programs, the authors observed two groups of first and fourth graders—one using crayons and word processors, the other using a paint program and word processors. Discusses student collaboration, visual literacy, creativity, advantages and disadvantages, and paint programs in the classroom. A table compares features of 13 paint programs.

Caudill, G. (1998). Matching teaching and learning styles. **Technology Connection, 4** (8), 11, 24–25. Outlines three basic learning modalities—auditory, visual, and tactile—and notes that technology can help incorporate multiple modalities within each lesson, to meet the needs of most students. Discusses the importance in multiple modality teaching of effectively assessing students. Presents visual, auditory, and tactile activity suggestions.

Center for Electronic Studying, University of Oregon. (1998). **Concept-mapping companion.** [Book and 2 Mac disks, 125p., $29.95]. ISTE, (800)336-5191, fax (541)302-3778, www.iste.org. Explores electronic concept mapping, a graphic-based tool for developing visual thinking, organizing information, and encouraging higher-level thinking skills.

Children's Software Review. Active Learning Associates, Inc., 44 Main St., Flemington, NJ 08822, www.childrenssoftware.com. [6/yr., $29]. Provides reviews and other information about software to help parents and educators more effectively use computers with children.

Computer Book Review. 735 Ekekela Place, Honolulu, HI 96817. [6/yr., $30]. Provides critical reviews of books on computers and computer-related subjects.

Computers and Composition. Ablex Publishing Corp., 55 Old Post Road - No. 2, P.O. Box 5297, Greenwich, CT 06831-0504, (203)661-7602, fax (203)661-0792. [3/yr., $40 indiv., $79.50 inst.]. International journal for teachers of writing focuses on the use of computers in writing instruction and related research and dialogue.

Computers and Education. Elsevier Science Regional Sales Offices, Customer Support Department, 655 Avenue of the Americas, New York 10010. [8/yr., $945]. Presents technical papers covering a broad range of subjects for users of analog, digital, and hybrid computers in all aspects of higher education.

Computers and the Humanities. Kluwer Academic Publishers Group, P.O. Box 358, Accord Station, Hingham, MA 02018-0358. [Bi-mo., $310.50 US inst.]. Contains papers on computer-aided studies, applications, automation, and computer-assisted instruction.

Computers in Human Behavior. Pergamon Press, 660 White Plains Rd., Tarrytown, NY 10591-5153. [Q., $638]. Addresses the psychological impact of computer use on individuals, groups, and society.

Computers in the Schools. Haworth Press, 10 Alice St., Binghamton, NY 13904-1580, (800)HAWORTH, fax (800)895-0582, getinfo@haworth.com, www.haworth.com. [Q., $40 indiv., $85 inst., $250 libraries]. Features articles that combine theory and practical applications of small computers in schools for educators and school administrators.

Dr. Dobb's Journal. Miller Freeman Inc., 600 Harrison St., San Francisco, CA 94107. [Mo., $34.95 US, $45 Mexico and Canada, $70 elsewhere]. Articles on the latest in operating systems, programming languages, algorithms, hardware design and architecture, data structures, and tele-communications; in-depth hardware and software reviews.

Education Technology News. Business Publishers, Inc., 951 Pershing Dr., Silver Spring, MD 20910-4464. [Bi-w., $286]. For teachers and those interested in educational uses of computers in the classroom. Features articles on applications and educational software.

Electronic Learning. Scholastic Inc., 555 Broadway, New York, NY 10012, (212)505-4900. [6/yr., $23.95; single copy, $4]. Features articles on applications and advances of technology in education for K–12 and college educators and administrators.

Forcier, R. C. (1999). **The computer as an educational tool: Productivity and problem-solving** (2nd ed.). [Book, 383p., $52]. Prentice Hall Merrill, www.merrilleducation.com. Examines the computer's role in education and problem-solving and as a cognitive tool. Integrates theory and current issues.

Ginsberg, R., & McCormick, V. (1998). Computer use in effective schools. **Journal of Staff Development**, **19**, 22–25. Reports the results of a large study of K–12 computer use in K–12 schools. Findings include a common perception among teachers that hardware presents the greatest challenge to technology integration.

Greenberg, R., Raphael, J., Keller, J. L., & Tobias, S. (1998). Teaching high school science using image processing: A case study of implementation of computer technology. **Journal of Research in Science Teaching, 35** (3), 297–327. Outlines an in-depth case study of teachers' use of image processing in biology, earth science, and physics classes in one high school science department. Explores issues surrounding technology implementation.

Home Office Computing. Box 51344, Boulder, CO 80321-1344. [Mo., $19.97, foreign $27.97]. For professionals who use computers and conduct business at home.

InfoWorld. InfoWorld Publishing, 155 Bovet Rd., Suite 800, San Mateo, CA 94402, (650) 572-7341. [W., $155]. News and reviews of PC hardware, software, peripherals, and networking.

Jankowski, L. (1998). Educational computing: Why use a computer for writing? **Learning and Leading with Technology, 25** (6), 30–33. Discusses using word processing programs with beginning writers, including story illustration and keyboarding. An approach to student writing with computers is outlined, highlighting planning, goals definition, and teacher and student aims. Sample student assignments and a sample writing task card are provided.

Johnson, J. M. (1998). **1998 Educational software preview guide.** [Book, 135p., $17.95]. ISTE, (800)336-5191, fax (541)302-3778, www.iste.org. Fifteenth edition of this title lists more than 800 titles of favorably reviewed software for K–12 use. Provides specifications for each title; developed by the Educational Software Preview guide Consortium.

Jonassen, D. H., Carr, C., & Yueh, H. P. (1998). Computers as mindtools for engaging learners in critical thinking. **TechTrends, 43** (2), 24–32. Mindtools are computer applications that, when used by learners to represent what they know, engage them in critical thinking. This article discusses computers as semantic organization (databases and semantic networking), dynamic modeling (spreadsheets, expert systems, systems modeling, microworlds), information interpretation, knowledge construction, hypermedia, and conversation tools and presents rationales for using technology as Mindtools.

Journal of Computer Assisted Learning. Blackwell Scientific Ltd., Journal Subscriptions, journals.cs@blacksci.co.uk, www.blackwell-science.com. [Q., $307 inst.]. Articles and research on the use of computer-assisted learning.

Journal of Educational Computing Research. Baywood Publishing Co., 26 Austin Ave., P.O. Box 337, Amityville, NY 11701. [8/yr. (2 vols., 4 each); $98 indiv. (per vol.), $209 inst. (per vol.)]. Presents original research papers, critical analyses, reports on research in progress, design and development studies, article reviews, and grant award listings.

Journal of Research on Computing in Education. ISTE, University of Oregon, 1787 Agate St., Eugene, OR 97403-1923. (800)336-5191, cust_svc@ccmail.uoregon.edu. [Q., $78 nonmembers, $32.10 Canada, $88 intl., $98 intl. air]. Contains articles reporting on the latest research findings related to classroom and administrative uses of technology, including system and project evaluations.

Kahn, J. (1998). **Ideas and strategies for the one-computer classroom.** ISTE, (800)336-5191, fax (541)302-3778, www.iste.org. [Book, 120p., $24.95]. Provides field-tested ideas for using a single computer in the classroom. Addresses classroom management, record-keeping, technical issues, hardware selection, and software selection.

Kaplowitz, J., & Contini, J. (1998). Computer-assisted instruction: Is it an option for bibliographic instruction in large undergraduate survey classes? **College & Research Libraries, 59** (1), 19–27. Summative evaluation of library instruction at UCLA found no difference between undergraduate biology students in a lecture group and those in a computer-assisted instruction (CAI) group and prompted the elimination of the lecture method. This article discusses the conceptual framework for the CAI and includes the follow-up survey results.

Laffey, J., Tupper, T., Wedman, J., & Musser, D. (1998). A computer-mediated support system for project-based learning. **Educational Technology Research and Development, 46** (1), 73–86. Describes a computer-mediated learning-support system designed as a suite of integrated, Internet-based client-server tools to provide: (1) intelligent support both for the processes of doing a project and for learning from doing a project, and (2) a shared dynamic knowledge base for working and learning in a community supporting project-based education.

Lazarick, L. (1998). Managing the computer invasion. **Community College Journal, 68** (5), 26–29. Explains how to use technology to enhance learning and teaching in the community college, and how to provide adequate user support for computer systems. Describes the technology plan implemented at Howard Community College.

Learning and Leading with Technology: Serving Teachers in the Classroom. ISTE, University of Oregon, 1787 Agate St., Eugene, OR 97403-1923. (800)336-5191, iste@oregon.uoregon.edu. [8/yr., $65 nonmembers, Canada $79.55, intl. $75, intl. air $95]. Focuses on the use of technology, coordination, and leadership; written by educators for educators. Appropriate for classroom teachers, lab teachers, technology coordinators, and teacher educators.

Littleton, K., & Light, P. (1998). **Learning with computers: Analysing productive interactions.** [Book, 224p., $25.99]. Routledge, (800)634-7064, cserve@routledge-ny.com, www.routledge-ny.com. Provides chapters authored by researchers of collaborative learning through technology. Includes experimental studies of process and product, naturalistic studies, and a discussion of collaborative contexts.

Liu, X., MacMillan, R., & Timmons, V. (1998). Integration of computers into the curriculum: How teachers may hinder students' use of computers. **McGill Journal of Education, 33** (1), 51–69. Reports the results of an extensive case study of a single rural high school, with special attention to whether teachers hinder the integration of technology into curriculum

Logo Exchange. ISTE, University of Oregon, 1787 Agate St., Eugene, OR 97403-1923. (800)336-5191, cust_svc@ccmail.uoregon.edu. [Q., $34, $47.08 Canada, $44 intl., $51 intl. air]. Brings ideas from Logo educators throughout the world, with current information on Logo research, resources, and methods.

MacWorld. MacWorld Communications, Box 54529, Boulder, CO 80322-4529. [Mo., $39.97]. Describes hardware, software, tutorials, and applications for users of the Macintosh microcomputer.

McDermott, I. E. (1998). Solitaire confinement: The impact of the physical environment on computer training. **Computers in Libraries, 18** (1), 22, 24–27. Institutions spend millions of dollars on computer training rooms yet give little thought to lighting, temperature, ambient noise, furniture arrangement, and other physical factors that affect learning. This article examines some problems and suggests remedies: changing furniture, controlling monitors, and redesigning rooms. Lists selected computer-training hardware and software suppliers and products.

McKay, M. D. (1998). Scheduling THE computer. **Technology Connection, 5** (1), 17–18. Focuses on how to schedule the use of a single computer so that all students are represented and given equal access. Suggests that a computer management team be selected from within the class; discusses the teacher's role and student role definition and responsibility assignments.

Microcomputer Abstracts. Information Today, 143 Old Marlton Pike, Medford, NJ 08055, (800) 300-9868. [4/yr., $199 US; $208 Canada/Mexico; $214 elsewhere]. Abstracts literature on the use of microcomputers in business, education, and the home, covering over 175 publications.

Monahan, S. (1998). Synthesizing that social studies unit: Do it with a database! **Technology Connection, 4** (8), 12–13. Describes two elementary social studies projects where a ClarisWorks database was used to teach database vocabulary and to teach students to develop and design a curriculum-related database.

Novodvorsky, I. (1998). Derivatives projects. **Mathematics Teacher, 91** (4), 298–299. Offers information on a project to improve students' understanding of derivatives. Students use the software package "Cactusplot," which allows them to calculate the slope at various points, and "Graphical Analysis III" software to graph the data and modify the graphs if necessary.

O'Callaghan, B. R. (1998). Computer-intensive algebra and students' conceptual knowledge of functions. **Journal for Research in Mathematics Education, 29** (1), 21–40. Describes a research project that examined the effects of the Computer-Intensive Algebra (CIA) and traditional algebra curricula on students' (N=802) understanding of the function concept. Results indicate that CIA students achieved a better understanding of functions and were better at the components of modeling, interpreting, and translating. Concludes that the CIA students showed significant improvements in their attitudes towards mathematics.

Pagon, D. (1998). Performing operations with matrices on spreadsheets. **Mathematics Teacher, 91** (4), 338–341. Describes how different operations on matrices can be modeled with simple spreadsheets. Presents three activities on this topic.

PC Magazine: The Independent Guide to IBM-Standard Personal Computing. Ziff-Davis Publishing Co., Box 54093, Boulder, CO 80322. [Bi-w., $49.97]. Comparative reviews of computer hardware and general business software programs.

PC Week. Ziff-Davis Publishing Co., 1 Park Ave., New York, 10016. [W., $195, Canada and Mexico $250, free to qualified personnel]. Provides current information on the IBM PC, including hardware, software, industry news, business strategies, and reviews of hardware and software.

PC World. PC World Communications, Inc., Box 55029, Boulder, CO 80322-5029. [Mo., $29.90 US, $53.39 Canada, $49.90 Mexico, $75.90 elsewhere]. Presents articles on applications and columns containing news, systems information, product announcements, and hardware updates.

Read, K. L. Q., & Shihab, L. H. (1998). Two-way ANOVA problems with simple numbers. **International Journal of Mathematical Education in Science and Technology, 29** (2), 261–269. Describes how to construct simple numerical examples in two-way ANOVAs, specifically randomized blocks, balanced two-way layouts, and Latin squares. Indicates that working through simple numerical problems is helpful to students meeting a technique for the first time and should be followed by computer-based analysis of larger, real datasets when the basic mechanics of the method are understood.

Shoemaker, A. L. (1998). Using the Macintosh as an oscilloscope in psychology courses. **Teaching of Psychology, 25** (1), 59–60. Examines the Digital Oscilloscope program that allows most Macintosh computers to dynamically display the waveform of any sound recorded by a microphone. Describes how the program can be used to illustrate the concept of timbre as well as reinforcing concepts of frequency, amplitude, and wavelength.

Social Science Computer Review. Sage Publications Inc., 2455 Teller Rd., Thousand Oaks, CA 91320, order@sagepub.com, www.sagepub.com. [Q., $180 inst.]. Features include software reviews, new product announcements, and tutorials for beginners.

Software Digest (formerly Software Digest Ratings Report). National Software Testing Laboratories Inc., Plymouth Corporate Center, Box 1000, Plymouth Meeting, PA 19462. [Mo., $450]. For IBM personal computer users. Each issue reports the ratings for one category of IBM PC software, based on multiple-user tests.

Software Magazine. Sentry Publishing Co., Inc., 1 Research Dr., Suite 400B, Westborough, MA 01581-3907. [Mo., $65 US, $75 Canada, $125 elsewhere, free to qualified personnel]. Provides information on software and industry developments for business and professional users, and announces new software packages.

Walker, V. K. (1998). A powerful solution: PowerBooks for all. **MultiMedia Schools, 5** (2), 38–41. Integrating computers into teachers' work can be achieved with laptops. This article describes how the Southwest Allen County (Fort Wayne, Indiana) Schools provided laptops for teachers, administrators, and students and increased teacher use of technology, improved student access to computers, and gave students a tool for research in the field. Includes sample teacher and administrator technology skills.

Whitaker, T., & Hays, C. (1998). Parent-student computer clubs: Teaming with technology. **Schools in the Middle, 7** (3), 15–16. Suggests that parent-student computer clubs are an effective use of technology to bring parents into the middle school and promote family time. Describes how sixth through eighth graders and their parents attend monthly evening meetings in which they are introduced to computers, word processing, databases, spreadsheets, graphics, multimedia applications, and the Internet. Presents suggestions for developing a similar program.

DISTANCE EDUCATION

American Journal of Distance Education. American Center for the Study of Distance Education, Pennsylvania State University, 110 Rackley Building, University Park, PA 16802-3202, www.cde.psu.edu/ACSDE/. [3/yr.; $35 indiv. ($41 Canada and Mexico, $50 elsewhere); $65 inst. (Canada and Mexico $71, $80 elsewhere)]. Created to disseminate information and act as a forum for criticism and debate about research in and practice of distance education in the Americas. Focuses on the role of print, electronic, and telecommunications media and multimedia systems in the delivery of education and training in universities and colleges, business and industry, the military, and in the public schools.

Andrews, T., & Klease, G. (1998). Challenges of multisite videoconferencing: The development of an alternative teaching/learning model. **Australian Journal of Educational Technology,14** (2), 88–97. Discusses the use of group teaching as a method for enhancing videoconference-based classes.

Bear, J., & Bear, M. (1998). **College degrees by mail and modem, 1999.** [Book, 216p., $12.95]. Ten Speed Press, Box 7123, Berkeley, CA 94707, (800)841-2665, fax (510)559-1629. Provides a tool for discriminating between authentic and less reputable educational services offered at a distance.

Bennett, P. G. (1998). The heart of distance learning: A student's perspective. **International Journal of Lifelong Education, 17** (1), 51–60. The challenge of distance learning is to create purposeful working relationships through distance communication systems. Distance learning systems that overemphasize educational technology, materialism, and modularized approaches to learning run counter to individual processes of growth and change.

Blumenstyk, G. (1998). Western Governors U. takes shape as a new model for higher education. **Chronicle of Higher Education, 44** (22), A21–A24. Backers of Western Governors University hope it will revolutionize the ways colleges compete for students, professors teach, and education is measured, and believe the virtual university can help contain the costs of educating growing numbers of students in the 16 participating states. However, the administration faces challenges in areas of accreditation, faculty, eligibility for student aid, and curriculum.

Chute, A., Thompson, M., & Hancock, B. (1998). **The McGraw-Hill handbook of distance learning.** [Book, 300p., $39.95]. McGraw-Hill, (800)2MCGRAW or (800)262-4729, customer.service@mcgraw-hill.com, www.pbg.mcgraw-hill.com. Provides basic instruction for conducting distance learning programs (both videoconferencing and online modules) in business settings.

Clayden, J. (1998). Overcoming the tyranny of distance. **Library Mosaics, 9** (1), 11. Edith Cowan University (Perth, Western Australia) has introduced a Bachelor of Science degree in Library Technology, a three-year distance education program with no residency requirement and the first Australian degree for library technicians. This article describes the program and its use of the World Wide Web for flexible course delivery, e-mail, and virtual campus.

Connick, G. P. (1998). **The distance learner's guide.** [Book, 225p., $20]. Prentice Hall, www.prenhall.com. Provides a comprehensive set of tools for the prospective distance learner, including definitions and advice for overcoming personal barriers.

Distance Education. University College of Southern Queensland Publications, Darling Heights, Toowoomba, Queensland 4350, Australia. [Semi-ann., $67]. Papers on the history, politics, and administration of distance education.

Distance Education Report. Magna Publications, Inc., 2718 Dryden Dr., Madison, WI 53704. [Mo., $299]. Digests periodical, Internet, and conference information into monthly reports.

Eastmond, D., & Granger, D. (1998). Using Type II computer network technology to reach distance students. **Distance Education Report, 2** (3), 1–3, 8. This article, in a series on computer technology and distance education, focuses on "Type II Technology," courses using textbooks and course guides for primary delivery, but enhancing them with computer conferencing as the main vehicle of instructional communication. Discusses technology proficiency, maximizing learning in conferencing environments, sequencing and pacing course modules, and activities and assignments.

Educational Satellite Long Guarantee Program Act, and distance learning: hearing before the US Senate. (1998). [Book, 157p., $35]. Diane Publishing. Discusses important distance learning legislation, with statements from Committee members and corporate stakeholders.

Feyten, C. M., & Nutta, J. (1999). **Virtual instruction: Issues and insights from an international perspective.** [Book, 300p., $45]. Libraries Unlimited, (800)237-6124, lu-books@lu.com, www.lu.com. Includes essays about the theoretical issues raised by recent developments in distance, online, and virtual learning.

Filho, W. F., & Tahir, F. (1998). **Distance education and environmental education.** [Book, 180p., $34.95]. Peter Lang. Provides a situated look at distance learning within a specific discipline, using case studies.

Guerrero, L. K., & Miller, T. A. (1998). Associations between nonverbal behaviors and initial impressions of instructor competence and course content in videotaped distance education courses. **Communication Education, 47** (1), 30–42. Finds that instructors who are viewed as expressive, warm, and involved are most likely to be judged (by students viewing instructional videotapes used in distance education courses) as highly competent and that, when instructors are expressive, warm, involved, and articulate, their course content is likely to be judged favorably, especially if they are not overly composed and fluent.

Hardy, D. W. (1998). University of Texas launches UT TeleCampus initiative. **Distance Education Report, 2** (1), 1,3. Highlights the important features of the University of Texas (UT) Tele-Campus Master Plan, designed to support distance delivery of academic programs from all 15 UT component institutions. Discusses the student-centered learning approach; faculty issues; and the use of videoconferencing and the World Wide Web.

Harris, J. (1998). **Virtual architecture: Designing and directing curriculum-based telecomputing.** [Book, 180p., $19.95]. ISTE, (800)336-5191, fax (541)302-3778, www.iste.org. Asserts that integrating computer-mediated technology into the classroom is worthwhile as long as it helps accomplish innovative and sound educational goals. Presents an adaptable framework for enacting such a program.

Harrison, N. (1998). **How to design self-directed and distance learning programs: A guide to instructional design for creators of Web-based training, computer-based training, and self-study materials.** [Book, 310p., $39.95]. McGraw-Hill, (800)2MCGRAW or (800)262-4729, customer.service@mcgraw-hill.com, www.pbg.mcgraw-hill.com. Provides detailed instructions for the complete process of designing any type of Web-based instruction.

Hazemi, R. (1998). **Digital university: Reinventing the academy (computer supported cooperative work).** [Book, 384p., $59.95]. Springer-Verlag, 800-SPRINGER, orders@springer-ny.com, www.springer-ny.com. Discusses the use of groupware for collaboration and distance learning.

Herring, M., & Smaldino, S. (1998). **Planning for interactive distance education.** [Book, 108p., $30]. AECT, www. aect.org. Designed to enhance distance education practice through presentation of innovative applications.

Johnson, J. E., Hill, M., & Lankford, W. (1998). Teaching computer skills via distance learning. **Business Education Forum, 52** (3), 39–42. Presents strategies for teaching computer skills at a distance. Explains the operation of the Georgia Statewide Academic and Medical System interactive distance learning network and describes nine sample class activities.

Journal of Distance Education. Canadian Association for Distance Education, Secretariat, One Stewart St., Suite 205, Ottawa, ON K1N 6H7, Canada. (Text in English and French.) [2/yr., $40, add $5 outside Canada]. Aims to promote and encourage scholarly work of empirical and theoretical nature relating to distance education in Canada and throughout the world.

Lippert, R. M., Plank, O., Camberato, J., & Chastain, J. (1998). Regional extension in-service training via the Internet. **Journal of Extension, 36** (1). In South Carolina, Georgia, and Alabama, 32 extension agents used in-service training materials on the World Wide Web and engaged in discussions via a listserv. Post-program responses from 16 were strongly favorable of this type of training for certain topics.

Liu, D., Walter, L. J., & Brooks, D. W. (1998). Delivering a chemistry course over the Internet. **Journal of Chemical Education, 75** (1), 123–25. Access to professional development opportunities for in-service high school chemistry teachers remains a problem. In an effort to increase teacher access, a new cross-listed course was created at the University of Nebraska and offered via the Internet. Describes this course and its results.

Macdonald, J., & Mason, R. (1998). Information handling skills and resource-based learning in an open university course. **Open Learning, 13** (1), 38–42. Discusses the results of an interview survey of 21 students enrolled in an Open University (Great Britain) course with a resource-based structure. The study examined use of CD-ROM materials, use of computer-mediated-communication as an information source, use of the Internet, and attitudes toward resource-based learning.

Murphy, T. H., & Terry, H. R. (1998). Faculty needs associated with agricultural distance education. **Journal of Agricultural Education, 39** (1), 17–27. Agricultural education college faculty (256 of 314) felt they lacked competence and confidence in using distance education technologies. They believed the technology would enhance their teaching and technology use would change how they teach in future.

Open Learning. Pitman Professional, Subscriptions Dept., P.O. Box 77, Harlow, Essex CM19 5BQ, England. [3/yr., £68 UK, £73 Europe, $78 elsewhere]. Academic, scholarly publication on aspects of open and distance learning anywhere in the world. Includes issues for debate and research notes.

Open Praxis. International Council for Distance Education, National Extension College, 18 Brooklands Ave., Cambridge CB2 2HN, England. [2/yr., $70 indiv., $55 libraries]. Reports on activities and programs of the ICDE.

Peterson's staff. (1998). **Peterson's guide to distance learning programs** (3rd ed.). [Book, 636p., $26.95]. Petersons Guides, www.petersons.com. Describes more than 1,000 programs from more than 900 accredited institutions.

Phillips, V., & Yager, C. (1999). **The best distance learning graduate schools 1999: Earning your degree without leaving home.** [Book, 336p., $16]. Princeton Review, www.review.com/index.cfm. Provides comprehensive information about 170 graduate distance learning programs.

Risser, J. (1998). Telemedicine: The up side, and. . . . **Distance Education Report, 2** (2), 1–3. Explores universities involved with training in telemedicine and medical care provided through technology (International Telemedicine Center Inc. www.int-telemedicine.comuniv.html). Discusses the market for telemedicine, companies and university medical centers involved in its development, costs and savings to health care system, barriers to the practice of telemedicine, and future developments such as government-funded Internet2.

Sandelands, E. (1998). Creating an online library to support a virtual learning community. **Internet Research, 8** (1), 75–80. International Management Centres (IMC), an independent business school, and Anbar Electronic Intelligence (AEI), a database publisher, have created a virtual library for IMC's virtual business school. Topics discussed include action learning; IMC's partnership with AEI; the virtual university model; designing virtual library resources; and benefits of the online action learning library.

Shoemaker, C. (1998). **Leadership in continuing and distance education in higher education.** [Book, 288p., $36.50]. Allyn & Bacon, (800)666-9433, www.abacon.com/contact/. Reviews innovative distance learning programs in the context of continuing education programming.

Slattery, J. M. (1998). Developing a Web-assisted class: An interview with Mark Mitchell. **Teaching of Psychology, 25** (2), 152–155. Presents an interview with an associate professor of psychology who has written extensively on the use of the World Wide Web in the classroom. Discusses various options and functions of the Web from the very simple to the more complex. Discusses student reactions for and against these innovations.

Spitzer, D. R. (1998). Rediscovering the social context of distance learning. **Educational Technology, 38** (2), 52–56. Argues that the tendency to focus on the technical aspects of distance learning contributes to the infrequency of distance learning methods usage in education and training. Discusses the technical and human dimensions of distance learning, resistance to change, user perspective, and inertia and entropy. Outlines ten human dimension principles fundamental to successful distance learning systems design.

Spooner, F., Jordan, L., Algozzine, B., & Spooner, M. (1999). Student ratings of instruction in distance learning and on-campus classes. **Journal of Educational Research, 92**, 132–140. Evaluates implementations of distance learning technology in two situations, both involving students with physical disabilities. Includes a summary of relevant studies and a set of implementation guidelines.

Stadtlander, L. M. (1998). Virtual instruction: Teaching an online graduate seminar. **Teaching of Psychology, 25** (2), 146–148. Provides some cursory guidance on the mechanics of establishing and instructing in a virtual classroom. Briefly discusses the history and central issues of distance education, describes how to teach an online virtual seminar, and offers recommendations for future courses. Discusses such issues as instructor availability, directing discussions, student evaluations, and student performance.

Usip, E. E., & Bee, R. H. (1998). A discriminant analysis of students' perceptions of Web-based learning. **Social Science Computer Review, 16** (1), 16–29. Users and nonusers of Web-based instruction (WBI) in an undergraduate statistics classes at Youngstown State University were surveyed. Users concluded that distance learning via the Web was a good method of obtaining general information and a useful tool in improving their academic performance. Nonusers thought the university should provide financial assistance for going online and that WBI should not be required for graduation.

Vassileva, J., & Deters, R. (1998). Dynamic courseware generation on the WWW. **British Journal of Educational Technology, 29** (1), 5–14. The Dynamic Courseware Generator (DCG), which runs on a Web server, was developed for the authoring of adaptive computer-assisted learning courses. It generates an individual course according to the learner's goals and previous knowledge, and dynamically adapts the course according to the learner's success in knowledge acquisition. The tool may be used also for collaborative authoring-learning.

Westera, W., & Sloep, P. B. (1998). The virtual company: Toward a self-directed, competence-based learning environment in distance education. **Educational Technology, 38** (1), 32–37. Discusses the concept of a Virtual Company—a collaborative, distributed learning environment built on the notions of competence-based, constructivist, open learning, and distance education. It features an authentic role-playing game that is strongly modeled upon the functional structures of real-life companies. Outlines the set-up of a Virtual Company in the Netherlands, focusing on the underlying educational principles.

Willis, W. (1998). Effective distance education planning: lessons learned. **Educational Technology, 38** (1), 57–59. Presents guidelines for effective distance education planning that confront the issues of planning, organization, technology, and faculty development academic policies. Concludes that understanding the unique characteristics and constraints of any particular program or target audience is the first step in selecting appropriate distance education practices.

EDUCATIONAL RESEARCH

American Educational Research Journal. American Educational Research Association, 1230 17th St., NW, Washington, DC 20036-3078. [Q., $41 indiv., $56 inst.]. Reports original research, both empirical and theoretical, and brief synopses of research.

Current Index to Journals in Education (CIJE). Oryx Press, 4041 N. Central at Indian School Rd., Phoenix, AZ 85012-3397, [Mo., $245 ($280 outside North America); semi-ann. cumulations $250 ($285 foreign); combination $475]. A guide to articles published in some 830 education and education-related journals. Includes complete bibliographic information, annotations, and indexes. Semiannual cumulations available. Contents are produced by the ERIC (Educational Resources Information Center) system, Office of Educational Research and Improvement, and the US Department of Education.

Education Index. H. W. Wilson, 950 University Ave., Bronx, NY 10452. [Mo., except July and August; $1,295 for CD-ROM, including accumulations]. Author-subject index to educational publications in the English language. Cumulated quarterly and annually.

Educational Research. Routledge, 11 Fetter Ln., London EC4P 4EE, England. [3/yr., £30 indiv. ($62 US and Canada)]. Reports on current educational research, evaluation, and applications.

Educational Researcher. American Educational Research Association, 1230 17th St., NW, Washington, DC 20036-3078. [9/yr., $44 indiv., $61 inst.]. Contains news and features of general significance in educational research.

Research in Science & Technological Education. Carfax Publishing Co., 875–81 Massachusetts Ave., Cambridge, MA 02139, (800)354-1420, www.carfax.co.uk/rst.ad.htm. [2/yr., $134 indiv., $432 inst.]. Publication of original research in the science and technological fields. Includes articles on psychological, sociological, economic, and organizational aspects of technological education.

Resources in Education (RIE). Superintendent of Documents, US Government Printing Office, P.O. Box 371954, Pittsburgh, PA 15250-7954. [Mo., $77 US, $96.25 elsewhere]. Announcement of research reports and other documents in education, including abstracts and indexes by subject, author, and institution. Contents produced by the ERIC (Educational Resources Information Center) system, Office of Educational Research and Improvement, and the US Department of Education.

EDUCATIONAL TECHNOLOGY

Albrecht, B., & Firedrake, G. (1998). The hands-on and far-out physics team: It starts out walking. **Learning and Leading with Technology, 25** (6), 36–40. The Hands-On and Far-Out Physics project is part of the Center for Technology, Environment, and Communication (C-TEC), a project-based learning community at Piner High School in Santa Rosa (California). This article introduces the project team, discusses member activities, presents a walking-speed experiment, and describes a Mars Colony course offered at Sonoma State University.

Appropriate Technology. Intermediate Technology Publications, Ltd., 103–105 Southampton Row, London, WC1B 4HH, England, journals.edit@itpubs.org.uk. [Q., $28 indiv., $37 inst.]. Articles on less technologically advanced, but more environmentally sustainable, solutions to problems in developing countries.

Armijo, E. J., McKee, C. M., Stowitschek, J. J., & Smith, A. J. (1998). User-friendly technology to guide a case management team: The computer-assisted risk accountability system. **Preventing School Failure, 42** (2), 66–72. Describes a computer-based adaptation of a case management model, Computer-Assisted Risk Accountability System (CARAS), which provides an on-site desktop evaluation tool for school-based case management teams to manage their cases efficiently. Discusses the user-friendliness of the CARAS software; how school programs benefit from CARAS; and CARAS components, including intake, assessment, service planning, and agency referrals.

Barker, B. O., & Hall, R. F. (1998). Planning for technology implementation in rural schools. **Rural Educator, 19** (3), 1–6. Outlines steps and considerations in planning a technology infrastructure for a rural school: the need for a long-term plan; the elements of a well-articulated plan; questions to consider in assessing needs and interests in selected technologies; staff development; software and equipment selection; and funding issues. Lists resources on technology planning.

Battista, M. T., & Borrow, C. V. A. (1998). Using spreadsheets to promote algebraic thinking. **Teaching Children Mathematics, 4** (8), 470–478. States that thinking about numerical procedures starts in the elementary grades and continues in successive grades until students can eventually express and reflect on the procedures using algebraic symbolism. Outlines how such thinking can progress to algebraic reasoning. Illustrates how computers can be used to promote this progression through the use of spreadsheets.

Behnke, R. R., & Sawyer, C. R. (1998). New wave computer technology and the administration of speech communication performance courses. **Journal of the Association for Communication Administration, 27** (1), 1–6. Contends that the development of a new wave of computers, some characterized by small size and portability and others noted for powerful capabilities to record and edit electronically stored motion pictures, suggests a wide range of applications of these new technologies to the teaching and administration of performance-based communication courses. Lists eight Internet addresses of speech communication courses.

Bete, T. (1998). Technology. **School Planning and Management, 37** (1), 58–61. Presents the predictions of nine technology experts regarding the future of technology in U.S. schools. Predictions include technology's hold on classroom instruction, its power to eliminate the gap between students with and without disabilities, electronic media replacing physical school libraries, the replacement of textbooks by digital media, and the advent of the virtual school replacing the physical location.

Blaschke, C. L. (1998). Evolution of a federal policy on educational technology. **Educational Technology, 38** (2), 36–41. Discusses the educational technology policy and funding of the United States Department of Education from the 1960s to the present, including two current programs: the Technology Literacy Challenge Fund and telecommunications educational rate (E-rate) discounts. Future technology initiatives and critical factors impacting the future and are considered.

Boone, W. J., & Gabel, D. L. (1998). Effectiveness of a model teacher preparation program for the elementary level. **Journal of Science Teacher Education, 9** (1), 63–84. Reports on the Quality University Elementary Science Teaching (QUEST) program. Focuses on changes in how teachers enable student conceptual understanding of science, how students modify their views of scientific inquiry during instruction, and how teachers value the use of technology in science instruction.

British Journal of Educational Technology. National Council for Educational Technology, Millburn Hill Rd., Science Park, Coventry CV4 7JJ, England. [3/yr., £82 inst. U.K., £95 overseas airmail; personal subscriptions £32 U.K., £42 overseas]. Published by the National Council for Educational Technology, this journal includes articles on education and training, especially theory, applications, and development of educational technology and communications.

Bromley, H., & Apple, M. W. (1998). **Education/Technology/Power: Educational computing as a social practice.** [Book, 256p., $19.95]. State University of New York Press, (518)472-5000, info@sunypress.edu, www.sunypress.edu. Presents a critical perspective regarding the use of technology in schools through a series of essays.

CÆLL Journal. ISTE, University of Oregon, 1787 Agate St., Eugene, OR 97403-1923, (800)336-5191, cust_svc@ccmail.uoregon.edu. [Q., $35; $48.15 Canada; $45 intl., $51 intl. air]. Focuses on current issues facing computer-using language teachers; covers trends, products, applications, research, and program evaluation.

California Instructional Technology Clearinghouse. (1998). **Guidelines for the evaluation of instructional technology resources.** [Book, 44p., $14.95]. ISTE, (800)336-5191, fax (541)302-3778, www.iste.org. Provides rubrics for the evaluation of instructional technology resources on the criteria of curriculum content, instructional design, and learner attributes. Formats include software, distance learning resources, online learning experiences, presentation tools, reference materials, and productivity tools.

Canadian Journal of Educational Communication. Association for Media and Technology in Education in Canada, AMTEC-CJEC Subscription, 3–1750 The Queensway, Suite 1318, Etobicoke, ON, M9C 5H5, Canada. [3/yr., $80.25 Canada, $101.65 foreign]. Articles, research reports, and literature reviews on all areas of educational communication and technology.

Clark, F. T. (1998). Integrating technology into the classroom: A teacher's perspective. **TechTrends, 43** (2), 45–46. The iNtegrating Technology for inQuiry (NTeQ) model teaches students to use computers to solve problems, as adults do in the workplace and home. This article presents a third grade teacher's experience using the NTeQ model for a thematic unit in which student entrepreneurs developed and marketed a new pizza requiring no refrigeration or cooking.

Cockrell, K., Cockrell, D., & Harris, E. L. (1998). Generational variability in the understanding and use of technology. **Alberta Journal of Educational Research, 44** (1), 111–114. A study of 91 college students aged 20–27, representing the mid-range of the Generation X cohort, examined their technological attitudes, knowledge, and usage in comparison to those of the Baby Boom cohort. Generational differences in technology learning experiences, information-seeking behaviors, and comfort with technology and technological change are discussed.

Crafton, J. A. (1998). From pipe dream to reality: Creating a technology-rich school environment. **School Business Affairs, 64** (2), 28–31. Methuen Public Schools, Massachusetts, has become a wired school system with computers in every classroom, Internet access, and state-of-the-art mixed media. Five citizens who work in the technology industry formed a steering committee to drive the project. A long-term partnership with a private vendor, Lucent Technologies, addresses the multimedia needs over the next decade.

Dede, C. (1998). Casting a wider net: Investing in "distributed learning." **MultiMedia Schools, 5** (2), 10, 12, 14. Information technology is a cost-effective investment in public schools only with innovations in pedagogy, curriculum, assessment, and school organization. This article examines the impracticality of equipping every student with high performance computing and communication and proposes a "distributed learning" model, orchestrating educational activities among classrooms, workplaces, homes, and community settings.

Dede, C., Ed. (1998). **Learning with technology: ASCD Yearbook 1998.** [Book, 226p., $18.95]. Association for Supervision and Curriculum Development, Alexandria, VA, (800)933-2723, www.ascd.org. Presents a series of model implementations, including CoVis, Union City Online, and the Schools for Thought Project.

Educational Technology. Educational Technology Publications, Inc., 700 Palisade Ave., Englewood Cliffs, NJ 07632-0564, (800)952-BOOK. [Bi-mo., $119 US, $139 elsewhere]. Covers telecommunications, computer-aided instruction, information retrieval, educational television, and electronic media in the classroom.

Educational Technology Abstracts. Carfax Publishing Co., 875–81 Massachusetts Ave., Cambridge, MA 02139. [6/yr., $218 indiv., $582 inst.]. An international publication of abstracts of recently published material in the field of educational and training technology.

Education Technology News. Business Publishers, Inc. 951 Pershing Drive, Silver Spring, MD 20910-9973, (800)274-6737, fax (301)589-8493, bpinews@bpinews.com, www.bpinews.com. [Bi-weekly, $270 per 25 issues]. Newsletter containing news, product reviews, funding sources, useful Internet sites, and case studies for technology coordinators, administrators, and teachers.

Educational Technology Research and Development. AECT, www.aect.org. [Q., $55 US, $63 foreign]. Focuses on research, instructional development, and applied theory in the field of educational technology; peer-reviewed.

Electronic School. NSBA Distribution Center, P.O. Box 161, Annapolis Jct., MD 20701-0161, (800)706-6722, Fax (301)604-0158, www.nsba.org/itte. [Q., $5 per issue]. Provides resource for all school personnel covering school technology trends, staff development, funding, telecommunications, and restructuring.

Farmer, L. S. J. (1998). Training for techies: A schoolwise commitment. **Technology Connection, 5** (1), 14–16. Outlines the Technical Aide (TA) internship program in the Tamalpais Union High School District (Larkspur, California) where students skilled in computer use facilitate technology use within the school. A TA program can provide needed personnel and service in the library as well as highlight library staff competence in technology. Presents tips for implementing such a program.

Fetterman, D. (1998). Learning with and about technology: A middle school nature area. **Meridian, 1** (1), 1–7. Discussion of learning with technology as well as about technology focuses on a case study of a middle school nature area that uses technology to extend accessibility of environmental data. Highlights include the design of web pages to describe the nature area; file sharing software; and the use of videoconferencing.

French, F. G. (1998). The divisibility of x(n)-y(n) by x-y: A constructive example. **Mathematics Teacher, 91** (4), 342–345. Provides an activity to investigate and construct an inductive proof. Claims that this particular example helps students better understand the nature of inductive reasoning and inductive proofs because the expression can be investigated by spreadsheets or calculators, hypothesized, tested, and modeled, both physically and pictorially, to at least three dimensions.

Fries, B., & Monahan, B. (1998). School district technology planning in an era of rapid change. **Educational Technology, 38** (1), 60–62. Advocates a new form of long-range educational technology planning and presents as an example the North Rockland (Garnerville, New York) Central School District Technology Planning Grid. Describes infrastructure and hardware, and discusses team planning, staff development, and resources.

Goldman-Segall, R. (1998). Gender and digital media in the context of a middle school science project. **Meridian, 1** (1), 1–12. Reports on a two-year ethnographic study focusing on gender, science education, and the introduction of networked digital media for learning in middle schools. Describes how learners become active participants, exploring gender attitudes.

Green, K., & Jenkins, R. (1998). IT financial planning 101: Developing an institutional strategy for financing technology. **Business Officer, 31** (9), 32–37. A three-step plan for colleges and universities to use in financing technology is presented: (1) establishing an effective asset management program; (2) developing a life-cycle budget process that annualizes total technology costs into streams of longer-term perpetuities; (3) identifying and matching funding sources to meet total annual costs. Administrators are also urged to learn about market and demand trends.

Griffin, R. A., & Griffin, A. D. (1998). Texas school districts plan for hi-tech. **School Business Affairs, 64** (2), 14–18. A program titled the "Superintendents' Institute" organized by the Harris County Department of Education (Texas), Rice University, and Compaq Computer Corporation provides a forum for public school leaders to discuss leadership and major decision-making in integrating technology into all school levels.

Hamilton, W. A. (1998). To lease or not to lease. **School Administrator, 55** (4), 30–32. Thanks to previous bond issues, the Walled Lake (Michigan) Schools had a well-defined technology plan featuring staff development, student performance benchmarks, and rooms of outdated computers. After three bond issues failed, the district adopted leasing as an alternative. Their present three-year contract supplies 154 used computers and a maintenance contract for $237,172—less than the computer maintenance budget.

Hanor, J. H. (1998). Concepts and strategies learned from girls' interactions with computers. **Theory into Practice, 37** (1), 64–71. Data from observations, focus interviews, symbolic representation interviews, and student art provide an aesthetic framework for studying young girls' interactions with computers and examining what may be unique about those experiences. Their experiences provide insight into girls' ways of knowing and engagement with technology. The paper discusses how the educational community can help enhance girls' experiences.

Heinich, R., Molenda, M., Russell, J. D., & Smaldino, S. E. (1999). **Instructional media and technologies for learning (6th ed.).** [Book, 428p., $44.25]. Prentice Hall, www.prenhall.com. Updates classic practitioner's guide to instructional media and technology.

Helfgott, M., & Simonsen, L. M. (1998). Using technology (instead of calculus) to derive the law of reflection for parabolic mirrors from Fermat's Principle of Least Time. **Mathematics and Computer Education, 32** (1), 62–73. Presents an activity to investigate physico-mathematical concepts and provide mathematics arguments that are very close to a proof with the advent and availability of powerful technology. Demonstrates without using calculus how the law of reflection for parabolas is derived from Fermat's principle of least time.

Heller, N. (1998). **Technology connections for grades 3–5: Research projects and activities.** [Book, 210p., $24]. Libraries Unlimited, (800)237-6124, lu-books@lu.com, www.lu.com. Promotes information literacy, technology skills, problem-solving, and collaborative teaching approaches.

Hemmer, J. (1998). Melissa's year in sixth grade: A technology integration vignette. **Learning & Leading with Technology, 25** (5), 11–14. Demonstrates how technology can be integrated into the middle school curriculum, replacing exploratory computer classes.

Higher Education Technology News. Business Publishers, Inc., 8737 Colesville Rd., Suite 1100, Silver Spring, MD 20910-3928, www.bpinews.com. [25/yr., $297 in North America, add $16 elsewhere]. Presents short news items concerning higher education and technology in a newsletter format.

Holden, L. S., & Holden, L. K. (1998). Tacoma shuffle. **Mathematics Teacher, 91** (3), 212–216. Presents activities on problem-solving, mathematical induction, proof by induction, and use of the phrase "without loss of generality." Provides a computer application illustrating recursive and iterative functions using C language.

HomePC. CMP Media Inc., (800)829-0119, hpc-order@palmcoastd.com, www.homepcmag.com. [Monthly; $21.97]. Consumer computer magazine that reviews selected children's software each month.

Ingram, T. (1998). Solving the technology support dilemma: The solution is students. **Technology Connection, 5** (1), 11–13. Describes the Computer Support Program (CSP) at Monett (Missouri) Schools where high school students operating from a "control room" assist students and teachers throughout the district in their use of technology. Benefits include increased teacher self-reliance and increased self-esteem in CSP students, and CSP student-created Internet scavenger hunts for nearly every grade level and subject area.

Innovations in Education and Training International (formerly *Educational and Training Technology International*). Kogan Page, FREEPOST 1, 120 Pentonville Road, London N1 9JN. [Q., £61, $102 US]. The international journal of the Association for Educational and Training Technology emphasizes developing trends in and the efficient use of educational technology. It is now extending its interest to include the field of staff and educational development.

International Journal of Technology and Design Education. Kluwer Academic Publishers, Order Dept., P.O. Box 358, Accor Station, Hingham, MA 02018-0358, (617)871-6600, fax (617)871-6528, kluwer@wkap.com. [3/yr., $154]. Publishes research reports and scholarly writing about aspects of technology and design education.

ISTE Accreditation & Standards Committee. (1998). **Curriculum guidelines for accreditation of educational computing and technology programs: A folio preparation manual** (3rd ed.). [Book, 55p., $20]. ISTE, (800)336-5191, fax (541)302-3778, www.iste.org. Provides tools for applying NCATE standards for technology-related teaching credentials. Guides teacher preparation institutions through the development or updating of programs.

Johnson, D. (1998). The less simple answer to evaluating technology's impact. **School Administrator, 55** (4), 12–14, 16–18. Recognizing educational technology's four major uses helps assess its value. Technology can improve administrative effectiveness through efficient communication, planning, and record keeping; provide learners with cost-effective access to current, accurate, and extensive information resources; provide teachers with enabling tools and resources; and facilitate student engagement in higher-order problem-solving.

Johnson, R. R. (1998). **User-centered technology: A rhetorical theory for computers and other mundane artifacts.** [Book, 195p., $19.95]. State University of New York Press, (518)472-5000, info@sunypress.edu, www.sunypress.edu. Discusses how a more user-centered approach to software design might improve academic communication, ethics, and curricula.

Jonassen, D. H., Peck, K. L., & Wilson, B. G. (1999). **Learning with technology: A constructivist perspective.** [Book, 234p.]. Columbus, OH: Merrill/Prentice Hall, www.merrilleducation.com. Pursues constructivist learning theory through technology, capitalizing on the themes of meaning making, exploration, visualization, constructing reality, community, critical thinking, and immersion.

Journal of Instruction Delivery Systems. Learning Technology Institute, 50 Culpeper St., Warrenton, VA 22186. [Q., $60 US, $75 elsewhere]. Devoted to the issues and applications of technology to enhance productivity in education, training, and job performance.

Journal of Science Education and Technology. Plenum Publishing Corporation, 233 Spring St., New York, NY 10013-1578, (212)620-8495, (800)221-9369, info@plenum.com, www.plenum.com. [Q., $59 individual, $195 institution]. Publishes studies aimed at improving science education at all levels in the US.

Kamp, S. (1998). How does "fair use" apply to software being used in schools? **Technology Connection, 5** (1), 19. Discusses the Copyright Act, four factors that courts must consider in determining permission by the "fair use" doctrine, and the educational exemption for using copyrighted software. Suggests that the best strategy in determining fair use is to contact the publisher, as well as requesting guidelines from the U.S. Copyright Office.

Kearsley, G. (1998). Educational technology: A critique. **Educational Technology, 38** (2), 47–51. Argues that the amount of attention and resources devoted to the use of technology in education and training distracts from important problems and issues that need to be addressed for effective teaching and learning. Discusses instructional television, computer-based instruction, adaptive technology, distance learning, teacher education, and the flawed logic of educational technology.

Kellner, D. (1998). Multiple literacies and critical pedagogy in a multicultural society. **Educational Theory, 48** (1), 103–122. Multiple literacies are needed to meet the challenges of today's new technologies and multicultural society. Media literacy is necessary because media culture strongly influences people's worldview. Education must foster various literacies to empower students and to make education relevant to society. Critical pedagogy can promote multicultural education and sensitivity to cultural differences.

Lamb, A. (1999). **Building treehouses for learning: Technology in today's classroom.** 2nd ed. [Book, 613p., $34.95]. ISTE, (800)336-5191, fax (541)302-3778, www.iste.org. Discusses the design and development of effective informational and instructional materials and techniques for managing a technology-rich K–12 classroom; for beginning teachers.

Lamb, A. (1998). **The magic carpet ride: Integrating technology into the K–12 classroom**, 2nd ed. [Book, 207p., $23.95]. ISTE, (800)336-5191, fax (541)302-3778, www.iste.org. Instructs the experienced K–12 teacher in creating active learning environments, selecting educational software, integrating learning resources, and developing multimedia projects.

Lowther, D. L., & Morrison, G. R. (1998). The NTeQ model: A framework for technology integration. **TechTrends, 43** (2), 33–38. The "iNtegrating Technology for inQuiry" (NTeQ) model provides a framework for creating an environment for students to use computers as tools to build a strong educational background while solving meaningful problems. This article outlines the NTeQ philosophy, describes the design process for lesson plans, and discusses professional development and implementation of the NTeQ model.

Maiden, J. A., & Zepeda, S. J. (1998). Dealing with obsolescence. **School Business Affairs, 64** (2), 32–35. Emerging technology changes to obsolete technology in a short time. Formal policies need to be adopted as technology becomes a more fundamental element of school administrative and instructional programs. A survey of 17 unified school districts in 2 Midwestern states revealed that only 2 districts had a formal written obsolescence policy.

Manouchehri, A., Enderson, M. C., & Pugnucco, L. A. (1998). Exploring geometry with technology. **Mathematics Teaching in the Middle School, 3** (6), 436–442. Addresses some concerns about teaching and learning geometry by describing how The Geometer's Sketchpad software program allows for the implementation of many of the recommendations from the National Council of Teachers of Mathematics (NCTM) in the mathematics classroom. Explains the types of activities that can be used with the software and students' reactions to technology-based geometry instruction.

Marshall, J. (1998). The arts and technology: An oxymoron? Don't bet your palette on it. **Technology Connection, 4** (2), 8–9, 47. The use of technology is integral to learning at the Minnesota State Arts High School (Golden Valley, Minnesota), an arts-integrated school where students focus on dance, literary arts, media arts, music, theater, and visual arts. This article discusses technology use in the arts curriculum and in the learning resource center.

McGehee, J. J. (1998). Interactive technology and classic geometry problems. **Mathematics Teacher, 91** (3), 204–208. Argues that interactive geometry computer software connects visual justification and empirical thinking to higher levels of geometric thinking with logical justification in formal proof. Presents classic geometry activities using The Geometer's Sketchpad interactive software.

McGonigle, D., & Mastrian, K. (1998). Learning along the way: Cyberspacial quests. **Nursing Outlook, 46** (2), 81–86. Describes the use of scavenger hunts on the World Wide Web as a research tool promoting active participation, idea exchange, and critical thinking skills in nursing education.

McKenzie, J. (1998). Technology's webs. **School Administrator, 55** (4), 6–10. After 2 decades of effort and investment, new technologies remain tangential in most American classrooms. To integrate technology, schools must clarify learning goals, identify classroom opportunities, provide funding and equipment, stress robust staff development, combine rich information with powerful tools, match rigorous program assessment to learning goals and student outcomes, and combine these elements.

Milshtein, A. (1998). STAC-ed in their favor. **School Planning and Management, 37** (3), 29–30, 34–35, 37. Describes the Superintendent's Technology Advisory Committee (STAC), which was created by 43 district superintendents in San Diego County, California. STAC pools resources to promote and provide equity, assuring access to new technology for all students in San Diego County. STAC's accomplishments and lessons learned are listed.

Moersch, C. (1998). Enhancing students' thinking skills: Exploring model technology-integration sites. **Learning and Leading with Technology, 25** (6), 50–53. Examines ways to integrate technology into social studies, science, mathematics, and language arts. Describes model elementary and middle-school classrooms in which technology is used to investigate the concept of property, study soil porosity and the water cycle, run a student store, and promote environmental activism.

Monteith, M. (1998). **IT for learning enhancement.** [Book, 192p., $65]. Swets & Zeitlinger, P.O. Box 613, Royersford, PA 19468, (800)447-9387, fax (610)524-5366, www.swets.org/sps/books/bhome.html#Education. Lists ways through which educational technology can assist learning, and how instruction can improve through reflective research. Highlights the connection between home and school, discussing implications of pervasive technology within students' homes.

Murphy, P. J. (1998). Everyone finishes FIRST. **TECHNOS, 7** (1), 27–30. Describes Dean Kamen's FIRST foundation (For Inspiration and Recognition of Science and Technology) and its sporting competition that offers high school students hands-on acquaintance with robots of their own creation; its goal is to inspire students to pursue future studies in science and technology by showing them that learning in this area can be fun, exciting, and important.

Norton, R. (1998). Corporate largesse or glad hand? **TECHNOS, 7** (1), 14–16. Gives a background on early educational sponsorship programs initiated by corporations. Discusses skepticism by consumers; Channel One and direct advertising to students; the need for schools to manage relationships with corporations providing technology; and the necessity of corporate support for the future of technology in schools.

Ohler, J. (1998). The promise of MIDI technology: A reflection on musical intelligence. **Learning and Leading with Technology, 25** (6), 6–15. Describes MIDI (Musical Instrument Digital Interface) technology and music education; provides information on conducting a MIDI workshop for all ages; and offers guidelines for creating a MIDI workstation for the classroom. Hardware and software vendor contact information is provided.

Peck, K. L. (1998). Ready . . . fire . . . aim! Toward meaningful technology standards for educators and students. **TechTrends, 43** (2), 47–53. Educators will face a public backlash against educational technology unless they clearly state what K–12 students are to gain from it, ensure teachers are prepared to use it, and document the results. This article discusses the development of a document describing required technology competencies for students and educators, focusing on national and international projects.

Peto, E. L., Onishi, E. O., & Irish, B. K. (1998). **Tech team: Student technology assistants in the elementary and middle school.** [Book, 105p., $34.95]. Linworth, (800)786-5017, fax (614)436-9490, linworth.com. Outlines the management and organization of a technology support program using student aides, including rationale, initiation, and implementation strategies.

Reiser, R. A., & Butzin, S. M. (1998). Project TEAMS: Integrating technology into middle school instruction. **TechTrends, 43** (2), 39–44. The Technology Enhancing Achievement in Middle School (TEAMS) model is an instructional approach in which technology plays an integral part in the curriculum. This article describes why TEAMS was developed, how instructional units are organized, key elements of the model, and first-year results. Includes a sample sixth grade interdisciplinary station rotation chart.

Sabella, R. A. (1998). Practical technology applications for peer helper programs and training. **Peer Facilitator Quarterly, 15** (2), 4–13. Presents four computer applications that can complement the work of peer helper trainers and peer helpers themselves. The applications include multimedia presentations, databases, desktop publishing, and the Internet. The article describes each application and also discusses the use of electronic mail, KeyPals, listservs, and the World Wide Web to enhance peer helper training.

Schmidt, W. D., & Rieck, D. A. (1999). **Managing media services: Theory and practice** (2nd ed). [Book, 475p., $45]. Libraries Unlimited, (800)237-6124, lu-books@lu.com, www.lu.com. Covers all aspects of the media management role, from supervision and budgeting to public relations and evaluation. Includes descriptions of such tasks as acquisition, circulation, collection development and maintenance, and facility design.

Schwartz, J. E., & Beichner, R. J. (1998). **Essentials of educational technology.** [Book, 256p., $26.25]. Allyn & Bacon, (800)666-9433, www.abacon.com/contact/. Addresses curricular integration of technology, encouraging practitioners to think expansively about wide-ranging possibilities offered by educational technology. Also discusses possible negative effects with suggestions for how to avoid them.

Sharpe, T., & Hawkins, A. (1998). Technology and the information age: A cautionary tale for higher education. **Quest, 50** (1), 19–32. Examines the use of technology in physical education within higher education. Lessons for and against using technology to advance the disciplines are presented as an examination of what constitutes appropriate technological practice. A path-analysis model is provided to promote technology as a facilitator of professional practice rather than an end in itself.

Shneiderman, B., Borkowski, E. Y., Alavi, M., & Norman, K. (1998). Emergent Patterns of Teaching/Learning in Electronic Classrooms. **Educational Technology Research and Development, 46** (4), 23–42. Studies faculty use of three teaching/learning "theaters" at the University of Maryland, College Park.

Science Communication (formerly **Knowledge: Creation, Diffusion, Utilization**). Sage Publications, Inc., 2455 Teller Rd., Thousand Oaks, CA 91320. [Q., $189 inst.]. An international, interdisciplinary journal examining the nature of expertise and the translation of knowledge into practice and policy.

SIGTC Connections. ISTE, University of Oregon, 1787 Agate St., Eugene, OR 97403-1923. (800)336-5191, cust_svc@ccmail.uoregon.edu. [Q., $29, $41.73 Canada; $39 intl., $42 intl. air]. Provides forum to identify problems and solutions, and to share information on issues facing technology coordinators.

Stone, D. M. (1998). Teaming with opportunity. **Science Teacher, 65** (4), 51–53. Discusses the merits of the National Science Teachers Association (NSTA) Toshiba ExploraVision competition, one of the world's largest international science competitions. Gives teams of three to four students the opportunity to use imagination and other skills to create a vision of technology in the future.

Tan, S. B. (1998). Making one-computer teaching fun. **Learning & Leading with Technology, 25** (5), 6–10. Demonstrates how a single computer can serve in the classroom by projecting instructional materials, recording information, accessing the Internet, and conducting quizzes.

Technology and Learning. Peter Li Education Group, P.O. Box 49727, Dayton, OH 45449-0727. [8/yr., $24, $32 foreign]. Publishes features, reviews, news, and announcements of educational activities and opportunities in programming, software development, and hardware configurations.

Technology Leadership News. NSBA Distribution Center, P.O. Box 161, Annapolis Jct., MD 20701-0161, (800)706-6722, Fax (301)604-0158, www.nsba.org/itte. [9/yr., $75]. Official newsletter of the National School Boards Association Institute for the Transfer of Technology to Education. Updates issues, trends, products, programs, applications, district profiles, case studies, government initiatives, funding, and videoconferences in layperson's terms.

TECHNOS. Agency for Instructional Technology, Box A, 1111 W. 17th St., Bloomington, IN 47402-0120. [Q., $28 indiv., $24 libr., $32 foreign]. A forum for discussion of ideas about the use of technology in education, with a focus on reform.

TechTrends. AECT, www. aect.org. [6/yr., $40 US, $44 elsewhere, $6 single copy]. Targeted at leaders in education and training; features authoritative, practical articles about technology and its integration into the learning environment.

Tetreault, D. R. (1998). How technology affects student achievement. **School Business Affairs, 64** (2), 9–13. Technology is a tool that can support good teaching and well-managed schools. To assure taxpayers and parents that investments in educational technology are worthwhile, schools can emphasize access, focus on teaching, link it to reform, encourage research, and plan for the future. Lists websites for finding information about the effectiveness of technology in the schools.

T.H.E. Journal (Technological Horizons in Education). T.H.E., 150 El Camino Real, Suite 112, Tustin, CA 92680-3670. [11/yr., $29 US, $95 elsewhere]. For educators of all levels. Focuses on a specific topic for each issue, as well as technological innovations as they apply to education.

Traubitz, N. (1998). A semester of action research: Reinventing my English teaching through technology. **English Journal, 87** (1), 73–77. Investigates whether technology supports curriculum content, how to get technology into average-level English classes, and what strategies using technology would appeal to students. Discusses reassessing teaching strategies, formulating a question and collecting data, initial survey results, implementing strategies, student response, difficulties implementing technology, and the final student survey.

Viau, E. A. (1998). Color me a writer: Teaching students to think critically. **Learning & Leading with Technology, 25** (5), 17–20. Discusses how teachers can use color coding and a color printer to teach students to analyze texts for argumentation, emotion, and persuasion.

Woods, C. B. (1998). Using a function generator to produce auditory and visual demonstrations. **Teaching of Psychology, 25** (2), 135–136. Identifies a function generator as an instrument that produces time-varying electrical signals of frequency, wavelength, and amplitude. Sending these signals to a speaker or a light-emitting diode can demonstrate how specific characteristics of auditory or visual stimuli relate to perceptual experiences. Provides specific instructions for using this in classroom demonstrations.

Yee, D. L. (1998). Chalk, chips, and children. **Educational Leadership, 55** (7), 57–59. In 1989, Swift Current Division in Saskatchewan, Canada, initiated the Chalk, Chips, and Children technology project. The project was funded by various corporate partners and developed by a broadly constituted advisory committee. The principal's role changed drastically as he reexamined leadership competencies and faculty developed their own technology integration ideas via in-school sabbaticals and miniconferences.

Young, J. R. (1998). Requiring theses in digital form: The first year at Virginia Tech. **Chronicle of Higher Education, 44** (23), A29–A31. Virginia Polytechnic Institute and State University is aggressively pursuing a plan to change the presentation and dissemination of student research by requiring students to submit theses and dissertations in digital form and creating a database on the World Wide Web that provides free, instantaneous access to graduate students' research. Some feel this approach is not appropriate for student work.

INFORMATION SCIENCE AND TECHNOLOGY

Bachman, J. A., & Panzarine, S. (1998). Enabling student nurses to use the information superhighway. **Journal of Nursing Education, 37** (4), 155–161. Twenty nursing graduate students in an Internet-based course were compared with 23 who did not take the course. The former were more likely to be connected to nursing networks, to have used Internet-based health information in practice, to have used computer skills for other classes, and to have understood the relevance of telemedicine.

Becker, H. J. (1998). Running to catch a moving train: Schools and information technologies. **Theory into Practice, 37** (1), 20–30. Utilizing national data about the presence and use of educational computers, the paper explains that computer-based applications still play only modest roles in education. Schools face insufficient quantities of any one technology to make efficient use in classroom-based teaching, and they invest little in supporting teachers' efforts to learn to apply technology in education.

Bollentin, W. R. (1998). Can information technology improve education? Measuring voices, attitudes and perceptions. **Educom Review, 33** (1), 50–52, 42. The Educom Medal honors individuals who have demonstrated that information technology improves undergraduate education. This article presents the viewpoints of the 1997 winners, examining fear of and resistance to technology in higher education, rigidity of the university system as an obstacle to bottom-up change, success of Web-based tutorials, and expansion of traditional classroom walls.

Bucher, K. T. (1998). **Information technology for schools** (2nd ed.). [Book, 400p., $39.95]. Linworth, (800)786-5017, fax (614)436-9490, linworth.com. Describes purchasing new technologies, hardware, software, networking, management, troubleshooting, and introducing students and staff to technology. Includes updates on videoconferencing, media retrieval systems, and Internet applications.

Byrne, D. J. (1998). **MARC manual: Understanding and using MARC records** (2nd ed.). [Book, 263p., $37.50]. Libraries Unlimited, (800)237-6124, lu-books@lu.com, www.lu.com. Provides beginning instruction about MARC records, including format integration and updated MARC codes.

Canadian Journal of Information and Library Science/Revue canadienne des sciences de l'information et de bibliothèconomie. CAIS, University of Toronto Press, Journals Dept., 5201 Dufferin St., Downsview, ON M3H 5T8, Canada. [Q., nonmembers $95, $110 inst.]. Published by the Canadian Association for Information Science to contribute to the advancement of library and information science in Canada.

CD-ROM Databases. Worldwide Videotex, Box 3273, Boynton Beach, FL 33424-3273. [Mo., $150 US, $190 elsewhere]. Descriptive listing of all databases being marketed on CD-ROM with vendor and system information.

CD-ROM Professional. Online, Inc., 462 Danbury Rd., Wilton, CT 06897. [Bi-mo., $55, indiv. and school libraries; $98, inst., $148 foreign]. Assists publishers, librarians, and other information professionals in the selection, evaluation, purchase, and operation of CD-ROM systems and titles.

Cheek, J., Gilham, D., & Mills, P. (1998). Using clinical databases in tertiary nurse education: An innovative application of computer technology. **Nurse Education Today, 18** (2), 153–157. A hospital database was used for problem-solving activities in nursing education to enhance theory-practice integration and transition of entry nurses. Faculty faced a challenge in integrating the critically reflective curriculum with the highly prescriptive database.

Data Sources. Ziff-Davis Publishing Co., One Park Ave., New York, NY 10016. [2/yr., $440]. Comprehensive guide to the information-processing industry. Covers equipment, software, services, and systems, and includes profiles of 10,000 companies.

Database. Online, Inc. 462 Danbury Rd., Wilton, CT 06897. [Bi-mo., $110 online]. Features articles on topics of interest to online database users; includes database search aids.

Datamation. Cahners Publishing Co., 8773 S. Ridgeline Blvd., Highlands Ranch, CO 80126. [24/yr.; $75; $110 Canada, Mexico; $195 Japan, Australia, New Zealand; $165 elsewhere (free to qualified personnel)]. Covers semi-technical news and views on hardware, software, and data-bases, for data- and information-processing professionals.

Eiblum, P., & Ardito, S. C. (1998). Royalty fees part I: The Copyright Clearance Center and publishers. **Online, 22** (2), 83–86. Discussion of copyrights, royalty fees, and intellectual property focuses on the Copyright Clearance Center and publishers. Topics include results of a survey of library and information science journal publishers; how users verify royalty fees; how publishers determine fees; royalty fee reporting; and terms and conditions imposed on electronic works.

Ferguson, B. (1998). **MARC/AACR2/Authory control tagging** (a Blitz Cataloging Workbook). [Book, 175p., $18.50]. Libraries Unlimited, (800)237-6124, lu-books@lu.com, www.lu.com. Addresses construction of MARC authority records and bibliographic records as well as the detection and correction of cataloging errors. Intended to supplement a standard cataloging text.

Ferguson, B. (1998). **Subject analysis** (a Blitz Cataloging Workbook). [Book, 135p., $17.50]. Libraries Unlimited, (800)237-6124, lu-books@lu.com, www.lu.com. Provides basic instruction for cataloging, including AACR2 rules, LCSH and Sears subject headings, and LC and Dewey classification. Intended to supplement a standard cataloging text.

Ferguson, B. (1999). **Cataloging nonprint materials** (a Blitz Cataloging Workbook). [Book, 160p., $18]. Libraries Unlimited, (800)237-6124, lu-books@lu.com, www.lu.com. Provides basic instruction for cataloging nonprint materials, as a supplement to primary cataloging texts.

Gale Directory of Databases (in 2 vols: Vol. 1, **Online Databases**; Vol 2, **CD-ROM, Diskette, Magnetic Tape Batch Access, and Handheld Database Products**). Gale Research Inc., 835 Penobscot Building, Detroit, MI 48226. [Annual plus semi-annual update $280; Vol. 1, $199; Vol. 2, $119]. Contains information on database selection and database descriptions, including producers and their addresses.

Glossbrenner, A., & Glossbrenner, E. (1998). **Search engines for the World Wide Web: Visual quickstart guide.** [Book, 228p., $16.95]. ISTE, (800)336-5191, fax (541)302-3778, www.iste.org. Provides detailed information about individual search engines to inform subject-specific choices.

Gould, C. (1998). **Searching smart on the World Wide Web.** Library Solutions Press, 5000 Windplay Dr., Suite 4, El Dorado Hills, CA 95762, (916)939-2018, sales@library-solutions.com, www.library-solutions.com. [Book, 90p., $40]. Provides a series of exercises that takes the reader through web searching, search tools, and analysis of results.

Information Processing and Management. Pergamon Journals, Inc., 660 White Plains Rd., Tarrytown, NY 10591-5153. [Bi-mo., $152 indiv. whose inst. subscribes, $811 inst.]. International journal covering data processing, database building, and retrieval.

Information Retrieval and Library Automation. Lomond Publications, Inc., Box 88, Mt. Airy, MD 21771. [Mo., $66 US, foreign $79.50]. News, articles, and announcements on new techniques, equipment, and software in information services.

Information Services & Use. I.O.S. Press, Box 10558, Burke, VA 22009-0558. [4/yr., $254]. An international journal for those in the information management field. Includes online and offline systems, library automation, micrographics, videotex, and telecommunications.

The Information Society. Taylor and Francis, 47 Runway Road, Suite G, Levittown, PA 19057, tisj@indiana.edu. [Q., $140; $168 with online edition]. Provides a forum for discussion of the world of information, including transborder data flow, regulatory issues, and the impact of the information industry.

Information Technology and Libraries. American Library Association, ALA Editions, 50 East Huron St., Chicago, IL 60611-2795, (800)545-2433, fax (312)836-9958. [Q., $50 US, $55 Canada, Mexico; $60 elsewhere]. Articles on library automation, communication technology, cable systems, computerized information processing, and video technologies.

Information Today. Information Today, 143 Old Marlton Pike, Medford, NJ 08055, (800)300-9868. [11/yr., $49.95; Canada and Mexico, $63; outside North America, $68]. Newspaper for users and producers of electronic information services. Articles and news about the industry, calendar of events, and product information.

Journal of Database Management. Idea Group Publishing, 4811 Jonestown Rd., Suite 230, Harrisburg, PA 17109-1751. [Q., $65 indiv., $110 inst.]. Provides state-of-the-art research to those who design, develop, and administer DBMS-based information systems.

Journal of Documentation. Mercury International, 365 Blair Road, Avenel, NJ 07001. [5/yr.; £124 ($155) members , £148 ($252) nonmembers]. Describes how technical, scientific, and other specialized knowledge is recorded, organized, and disseminated.

Jukes, I., Dosaj, A., & The NetSavvy Group. (1998). **NetSavvy: Information literacy for the communication age.** ISTE, (800)336-5191, fax (541)302-3778, www.iste.org. [Book, 80p., $20]. Provides a guide for teaching students to use new information technologies, addressing information overload.

Kelly, M. S. (1998). **Uncle Sam's net of knowledge guide for schools.** [Book, 196p., $39.95]. Neal-Schuman, fax (800)584-2414, orders@neal-schuman.com, www.neal-schuman.com. Facilitates the use of online government information for use in school settings.

Knowledge Quest. American Library Association, www.ala.org/aasl. [5/yr. $40 nonmembers].The official journal of the American Association of School Librarians. Publishes a variety of articles addressing a wide range of library media center practice, along with AASL association news.

Lankes, R. D., & Kasowitz, A. S. (1998). **The AskA starter kit: How to build and maintain digital reference services.** [Book, 232p., $20]. ERIC Clearinghouse on Information & Technology, (800)464-9107, ericir.syr.edu/ithome. Presents a model for developing and managing an inquiry-based information service on the Internet.

Lankes, R. D. (1998). **K–12 digital reference services.** [Book, 231p., $20]. ERIC Clearinghouse on Information & Technology, (800)464-9107, ericir.syr.edu/ithome. Presents the foundations of digital reference, outlines how K–12 digital reference services build and maintain services in the changing Internet environment, and uses qualitative methods to look for similarities among several exemplary services.

Lee, O. (1998). Information technology applications in the centralized educational system: Ten years of Korean experience. **Educational Technology Research and Development, 46** (1), 91–98. Discusses government plans and implementation of a centralized educational technology system in Korean schools. Investigates the current situation in the field; hardware and software distribution; teacher readiness and training; Internet applications and multimedia; government role; and reengineering the system.

Library & Information Science Research. Ablex Publishing Corp., 100 Prospect Student., Stamford, CT 06901. [Q., $75 indiv., $195 instn.]. Reports library-related research to practicing librarians, emphasizing planning and application.

MacAdam, B., Folger, K. M., & Look, H. (1998). Creating knowledge facilities for knowledge work in the academic library. **Library Hi Tech, 16** (1), 91–99. Describes the creation of the Knowledge Navigation Center (KNC) in the Graduate Library at University of Michigan. The planning group identified five main specialty areas: GIS; imaging and multimedia; text; distance learning-interactive technologies; and Internet tools.

Mercado, M. I. (1998). Information technology monopolies: Implications for library managers. **Bottom Line, 11** (1), 4–9. Explores library-related implications of the U.S. Department of Justice's investigations into the operations of Microsoft and Intel and suggests that developing a broader understanding of information technology marketing is crucial to the short- and long-term future of libraries.

Microcomputers for Information Management. Ablex Publishing Corp., 55 Old Post Road, No. 2, P.O. Box 5297, Greenwich, CT 06831-0504, (203)661-7602, fax (203)661-0792. [Q., $45 indiv., $135 instn]. Addresses information networking issues for libraries.

Milbury, P. (1998). Daily news on the Internet: Finding and effectively using free online news sources (Full text daily news archives with search engines). **Technology Connection, 5** (1), 28–30. Free online news sources are plentiful, but their useful access is problematic. The Chico High School (California) library's collection of Full Text Daily News Archives with Search Engines offers many advantages in a number of curriculum areas. Accessible from school and home, it provides an opportunity for teachers and librarians to collaborate to develop information literacy skills.

Moursand, D. (1999). **Project-based learning using information technology.** ISTE, (800)336-5191, fax (541)302-3778, www.iste.org. [Book, 160p., $24.95]. Offers a methodological approach to implementing technology-assisted project-based learning projects. Designed for inservice and preservice teachers.

Online and CD-ROM Review. Information Today, 143 Old Marlton Pike, Medford, NJ 08055, (800)300-9868. [Bi-mo., $130, Canada and Mexico, $140]. An international journal of online information systems featuring articles on using and managing online and optical information systems, training and educating online users, developing search aids, creating and marketing databases, policy affecting the continued development of systems and networks, and the development of new professional standards.

Pappas, M. L., Geitget, G. A., & Jefferson, C. A. (1999). **Searching electronic resources** (2nd ed.). [Book, 105p., $34.95]. Linworth, (800)786-5017, fax (614)436-9490, linworth.com. Provides a revised information search process model, including a four-step search process. Includes individual search strategy forms for popular CD-ROMS and online databases.

Resource Sharing and Information Networks. Haworth Press, 10 Alice St., Binghamton, NY 13904-1580, (800)HAWORTH, fax (800)895-0582, getinfo@haworth.com, www.haworth.com. [2/yr., $42 indiv., $160 inst. and libraries]. A forum for ideas on the basic theoretical and practical problems faced by planners, practitioners, and users of network services.

Rosenberg, D. (1998). IT and university libraries in Africa. **Internet Research, 8** (1), 5–13. Reviews 19 university libraries in 12 African countries, comparing the benefits and drawbacks of information technology (IT), concluding that IT will not reduce the need for books and journals and that IT's biggest potential is in increasing intra-Africa communication and providing links to the outside world.

Stielow, F. (1999). **Creating a virtual library: A how-to-do-it manual.** [Book, 200p., $55]. Neal-Schuman, fax (800)584-2414, orders@neal-schuman.com, www.neal-schuman.com. Guides the creation and maintenance of single-interface, web-based catalogs; written by MCI's Cybrarian of the Year.

Streibel, M. J. (1998). Information technology and physicality in community, place, and presence. **Theory into Practice, 37** (1), 31–37. Raises several questions about information technology. After arguing for the importance of physical place and presence in how people construct meaning, form personal biographies and public histories, and develop living communities, the article contrasts this with the consequences of the abstractions of place and presence in virtual, online communities.

Timmermann, S. (1998). The role of information technology in older adult learning. **New Directions for Adult and continuing Education, 77**, 61–71. Identifies the number and characteristics of older adults using computers and barriers to their computer learning. Describes model programs such as SeniorNet and outlines future trends and issues in computer use.

Walker, G., & Janes, J. (1999). **Online retrieval: A dialogue of theory and practice**, 2nd ed. [Book, 370p., $45]. Libraries Unlimited, (800)237-6124, lu-books@lu.com, www.lu.com. Designed for beginning searchers at all levels. Includes a description of the Dialog and Lexis-Nexis databases.

Web Feet. Rock Hill Press, 14 Rock Hill Road, Bala Cynwyd, PA 19004, fax (610)667-2291, www.rockhillpress.com. [12/yr., $66.50]. Indexes Web sites for general interest, classroom use, and research; reviews Web sites for quality, curricular relevance, timeliness, and interest.

INNOVATION

Barnes, S. B., Perkinson, H. J., & Talbott, S. L. (1998). Culture and risk: Does the future compute? A symposium. **New Jersey Journal of Communication, 6** (1), 1–20. Presents a symposium on the impact of computers on culture. Argues that the computer has mathematized culture and that widespread risk aversion has been generated everywhere. Finds that the ways in which communication technologies are used in social contexts is a topic of concern to communication scholars.

Bromley, H., & Apple, M. W. (1998). **Education/Technology/Power: Educational computing as a social practice.** [Book, 263p., $19.95]. State University of New York Press, (518)472-5000, info@sunypress.edu, www.sunypress.edu. Addresses educational practices involving technology from a critical perspective.

Damarin, S. K. (1998). Technology and multicultural education: The question of convergence. **Theory into Practice, 37** (1), 11–19. Examines the potential for convergence of technology and multicultural education, identifying strategies for and barriers to developing common ground. The paper explains differences and oppositions, examines parallels in the pedagogical work of the two groups, and discusses whether parallel beliefs and pedagogies might support collaborative, simultaneous efforts toward the achievement of both agendas.

De Vaney, A. (1998). Can and need educational technology become a postmodern enterprise? **Theory into Practice, 37** (1), 72–80. Explores the field of educational technology as a modern project that has capitalized classrooms, highlighting efforts to reclaim the field for student interests; discussing how formation of the field has constrained its practice, especially around race, gender, and power; examining the commodification of students and construction of subjectivity; and asking whether postmodern scholarship can lessen the constraints.

Farmer, L. S. J. (1998). Empowering young women through technology. **Technology Connection, 4** (9), 18–21. Libraries are the logical place to model gender-equitable practices, broadening the scope of technology and equipping young people with skills to succeed in a diverse and changing environment. This article discusses gender attitudes about technology, library, and teaching issues related to technology and gender. Argues that separate Internet training for girls can be beneficial.

Gorry, G. A. (1998). Technology's place in teaching and learning. **School Business Affairs, 64** (2), 4–8. In education, the inclination to use new technology for old purposes is strong. Teachers and administrators need to think about the interplay of technology and teaching and to imagine new ways to use technology.

Kershaw, A., & Safford, S. (1998). From order to chaos: The impact of educational telecommunications on post-secondary education. **Higher Education, 35** (3), 285–298. Convergence of digital communications technology is changing the nature of relationships between postsecondary institutions, students, and private sector. The current predictable, ordered world of interinstitutional relationships is being replaced by one of perpetual change. Contemporary relationships can be modeled using central place theory, but chaos theory must be consulted to understand how institutions operate in a complex, fluctuating environment.

Lowther, D. L., Bassoppo-Moyo, T., & Morrison, G. R. (1998). Moving from computer literate to technologically competent: The next educational reform. **Computers in Human Behavior, 14** (1), 93–109. Proposes that educators must go beyond computer literacy to achieve technological competence if successful integration of technology into the classroom is to occur. An educator who is technologically competent understands the relationship between basic computer functions and student learning, and uses this understanding to design, facilitate, and manage a student-centered multidimensional learning environment.

Mason, R. (1998). **Globalising education: Trends and applications.** [Book, 184p., $24.99]. Routledge, (800)634-7064, cserve@routledge-ny.com, www.routledge-ny.com. Analyzes how technologies have altered and influenced the delivery and reception of education. Emphasizes actual and potential impact of the World Wide Web.

Means, B. (1998). Melding authentic science, technology, and inquiry-based teaching: Experiences of the GLOBE Program. **Journal of Science Education and Technology, 7** (1), 97–105. Reports findings from the evaluation of the Global Learning and Observations to Benefit the Environment (GLOBE) Program. Examines issues concerning student-scientist partnerships such as benefits of the program to students and scientists, enhancement of authentic science in schools through technology, and the relationship between this program and other reform efforts.

Pagnucci, G. S. (1998). Crossing borders and talking tech: Educational challenges. **Theory into Practice, 37** (1), 46–53. In developing a college English course on reading and writing in the Information Age that would make use of the Internet and cyberspace-based science fiction, a professor encountered considerable resistance from colleagues who did not understand the language and concepts being used and who worried about crossing the boundaries into other disciplines.

Singarella, T. (1998). The evolution of modern technology and its societal impact on biocommunications in academe. **Journal of Biocommunication (25)**, 1 (2–11). Comments on how communications technology has evolved over the last century, resulting in the digital revolution. Discusses the relationship between information technology and societal factors that affect higher education and health care.

Thompson, T. H. (1998). Three futures of the electronic university. **Educom Review, 33** (2), 34–40. Presents and evaluates three possible futures of traditional universities in the face of the onslaught of budget-cutters and technophiles: (1) ultimate-digital-McLuhanism; (2) modest digital infusion; and (3) stalled revolution. It is concluded that—however refined and elegant the technological tools become—they must subordinate themselves to the ends for which the university was created.

INSTRUCTIONAL DESIGN AND DEVELOPMENT

Barab, S. A., Hay, K. E., & Duffy, T. M. (1998). Grounded constructions and how technology can help. **TechTrends, 43** (2), 15–23. Educators are adopting learner-centered instruction in which students, facilitated by technology, collaborate with peers and engage in problem-solving and inquiry. This article discusses ways to use technology in authentic learner inquiry as an information resource, content contextualizer, communication tool, construction kit, and visualization manipulation tool.

Carlson, R. D. (1998–99). Portfolio assessment of instructional technology. **Journal of Educational Technology Systems, 27** (1), 81–92. Analyzes the current trend toward authentic assessment methods, including portfolios. Describes the results of two case studies.

Considine, D. M., & Haley, G. E. (1999). **Visual messages: Integrating imagery into instruction** (2nd ed.). [Book, 410p., $38]. Libraries Unlimited, (800)237-6124, lu-books@lu.com, www.lu.com. Promotes bridging the curriculum of the classroom to home learning. Defines visual literacy and traces the history of the media literacy movement. Focuses on helping students think critically about the way the media uses images to influence attitudes and behavior.

Educational Technology and Society. Online journal of International Forum of Educational Technology & Society and the IEEE Learning Technology Task Force; available at ifets.gmd.de/periodical/. Publishes academic articles on the issues affecting the developers of educational systems and educators who implement and manage such systems, discussing the perspectives of both communities and their relation to each other.

Ertmer, P. A., & Quinn, J. (1998). **The ID casebook: Case studies in instructional design.** [Book, 150p., $15]. Prentice Hall Merrill, www.merrilleducation.com. Features 24 contributed cases describing authentic instructional design situations.

Evaluation Practice. Jai Press, 55 Old Post Road, No. 2, P.O. Box 1678, Greenwich CT, 06836-1678. [Tri-annual, $80 indiv., $180 instn]. Interdisciplinary journal aimed at helping evaluators improve practice in their disciplines, develop skills, and foster dialog.

Greening, T. (1998). Building the constructivist toolbox: An exploration of cognitive technologies. **Educational Technology, 38** (2), 23–35. Examines the role of educational technology from a constructivist perspective. Discusses the subset of computer-based technologies, especially the Internet, that are changing the way interactivity is defined, and examines how these technologies interface with constructivist approaches to pedagogy. Explores the place of constructivism as a pedagogical testing ground for establishing the value of such technological offerings.

Harrison, N. (1998). **How to design self-directed and distance learning programs: A guide to instructional design for creators of Web-based training, computer-based training, and self-study materials.** [Book, 310p., $39.95]. McGraw-Hill, (800)2MCGRAW or (800)262-4729, customer.service@mcgraw-hill.com, www.pbg.mcgraw-hill.com. Provides detailed instructions for the complete process of designing any type of Web-based instruction.

Human-Computer Interaction. Lawrence Erlbaum Associates, 365 Broadway, Hillsdale, NJ 07642. [Q., $39 indiv. US and Canada, $69 elsewhere, $230 inst., $260 elsewhere]. A journal of theoretical, empirical, and methodological issues of user science and of system design.

Instructional Science. Kluwer Academic Publishers, Order Dept., P.O. Box 358, Accor Station, Hingham, MA 02018-0358, (617)871-6600, fax (617)871-6528, kluwer@wkap.com. [Bi-mo., $345 inst.]. Promotes a deeper understanding of the nature, theory, and practice of the instructional process and the learning resulting from this process.

Journal of Educational Technology Systems. Baywood Publishing Co., 26 Austin Ave., Box 337, Amityville, NY 11701. [Q., $146]. In-depth articles on completed and ongoing research in all phases of educational technology and its application and future within the teaching profession; enhancing instruction and facilitation of learning in the typical classroom; design and implementation of telecommunication networks and web sites; contributions of librarians to Web-based teaching.

Journal of Interactive Instruction Development. Learning Technology Institute, Society for Applied Learning Technology, 50 Culpeper St., Warrenton, VA 22186. [Q., $60 indiv., $75 inst.; add $18 postage outside North America]. A showcase of successful programs that will heighten awareness of innovative, creative, and effective approaches to courseware development for interactive technology.

Journal of Technical Writing and Communication. Baywood Publishing Co., 26 Austin Ave., Box 337, Amityville, NY 11701. [Q., $143 inst.]. Essays on oral and written communication, for purposes ranging from pure research to needs of business and industry.

Journal of Visual Literacy. International Visual Literacy Association, c/o John C. Belland, 122 Ramseyer Hall, 29 West Woodruff Ave., Ohio State University, Columbus, OH 43210. [Semiann., $18; $26, foreign]. Interdisciplinary forum on all aspects of visual/verbal languaging.

Milano, M., & Ullius, D. (1998). **Designing powerful training: The sequential-iterative model.** [Book, 304p., $49.95]. Jossey-Bass, (800)956-7739, fax (800)605-2665, webperson@jbp.com, www.jbp.com. Based on extensive experience with adult learners, this book outlines the SIM instructional training design model.

Performance and Instruction. International Society for Performance Improvement, 1300 L St. NW, Suite 1250, Washington, DC 20005. [10/yr., $69]. Journal of ISPI; promotes performance science and technology. Contains articles, research, and case studies relating to improving human performance.

Performance Improvement Quarterly. International Society for Performance Improvement, 1300 L St. NW, Suite 1250, Washington, DC 20005. [Q., $50]. Presents the cutting edge in research and theory in performance technology.

Seels, B., & Glasgow, Z. (1998). **Making instructional design decisions.** [Book, 342p., $65]. AECT, www. aect.org. Updates **Exercises in Instructional Design** with an increased emphasis on instructional design as a decision-making process.

Training. Lakewood Publications, Inc., 50 S. Ninth, Minneapolis, MN 55402. [Mo., $78 US, $88 Canada, $99 elsewhere]. Covers all aspects of training, management, and organizational development, motivation, and performance improvement.

Young, A. C., Reiser, R. A., & Dick, W. (1998). Do superior teachers employ systematic instructional planning procedures? A descriptive study. **Educational Technology Research and Development, 46** (2), 65–78. Reports results of a qualitative study of the instructional design methods of superior teachers. Found that few of these teachers employ a formal planning model for four reasons centering around objective identification.

INTERACTIVE MULTIMEDIA

Beltcheva, O., Ponta, D., & Da Bormida, G. (1998). An authoring and learning kit for digital electronics. **British Journal of Educational Technology, 29** (1), 15–24. Presents a multimedia component kit for digital electronics authoring and learning. Components available on the Internet facilitate sharing and reuse of educational software and provide authoring support. Emphasizes the implementation of a number of components based on simulation and animation that provide a high level of interactivity and allow some presentation difficulties to be overcome.

CD-ROM World. PC World Communication Inc., 501 Second St., Suite 600, San Francisco, CA 94107. [10/yr., $29]. Articles and reviews for CD-ROM users.

Dillon, A., & Gabbard, R. (1998). Hypermedia as an educational technology: A review of the quantitative research literature on learner comprehension, control, and style. **Review of Educational Research, 68** (3), 322–349. Sifts through the voluminous amount of hypermedia research and singles out 30 relevant articles, isolating important factors for instructional design.

Goldman, J. (1998). Multimedia for research and technology: The Oyez Oyez Oyez and the History and Politics Out Loud projects. **Social Science Computer Review, 16** (1), 30–39. Describes the creation of web-based multipurpose multimedia databases concerned with the Supreme Court and other historically and politically significant institutions, events, and actors. Addresses four evaluation questions on whether the database will help less-skilled students, help bright students and scholars improve their understanding and theories, and be used by faculty and students.

Handler, M. G., & Dana, A. S. (1998). **Hypermedia as a student tool: A guide for teachers** (2nd ed.). [Book, 345p., $30]. Libraries Unlimited, (800)237-6124, lu-books@lu.com, www.lu.com. Demonstrates a variety of hypermedia programs, provides instructional strategies, and describes hypermedia learning environments conducive to collaboration.

Hilgendorf, T. R. (1998). CD-ROM technology for developing college-level skills. **Journal of Adolescent and Adult Literacy, 41** (6), 475–476. Describes how CD-ROM technology and a subscription to a weekly news magazine were integrated into the curriculum of a community college developmental reading and writing course. Discusses how this system (1) adapts to the mix of ages, ability level, interests, and cultural experiences of students; (2) facilitates assignments on reading and writing strategies; and (3) engages developmental students in research processes.

Ivers, K. S., & Barron, A. E. (1997). **Multimedia projects in education: Designing, producing, and assessing.** [Book, 201p., $25]. Libraries Unlimited, (800)237-6124, lu-books@lu.com, www.lu.com. Describes the use of multimedia projects as learning tools, including planning, classroom management, computer scheduling, and assessment.

Journal of Educational Multimedia and Hypermedia. Association for the Advancement of Computing in Education, Box 2966, Charlottesville, VA 22902-2966, aace@virginia.edu. [Q., $65 indiv., $75 foreign; $93 inst., $103 foreign]. A multidisciplinary information source presenting research about and applications for multimedia and hypermedia tools.

Journal of Hypermedia and Multimedia Studies. ISTE, University of Oregon, 1787 Agate St., Eugene, OR 97403-1923. (800)336-5191, cust_svc@ccmail.uoregon.edu. [Q., $29; $41.73, Canada; $39 intl., $42 intl. air]. Features articles on projects, lesson plans, and theoretical issues, as well as reviews of products, software, and books.

Journal of Interactive Learning Research. Association for Advancement of Computing in Education, Box 2966, Charlottesville, VA 22902-2966, aace@virginia.edu, www.aace.org. [Q.; $75 indiv. (foreign, $85), $105 inst. ($113 foreign)]. International journal publishes articles on how intelligent computer technologies can be used in education to enhance learning and teaching. Reports on research and developments, integration, and applications of artificial intelligence in education.

Kenny, R. (2000). **Media literacy through TV and multimedia production: A mediated course book.** Libraries Unlimited, (800)237-6124, lu-books@lu.com, www.lu.com. [Book, 150p., $18]. Presents an alternative approach to teaching television production to high school students. Includes thematic mapping, media and visual literacy, broadcast history, video production skills, and multimedia animation.

Kesten, M. (1998). Multimedia distribution: A view from the supply side. **Computers in Libraries, 18** (3), 66–69. Describes how multimedia products start as ideas and go through the stages of design, production, manufacturing, and marketing. Highlights include corporate consolidation, market distribution in 1997, encyclopedias and the growing Internet trend, direct marketers and sales, CD-ROM and DVD (digital video disc), costs, and future directions.

Mattson, M. (1998). Multimedia math: Fractions are just a fraction of what is available. **Technology Connection, 5** (1), 24–25, 30. Describes recent offerings in math software for fractions lessons that provide instruction and interactivity not previously available in electronic formats. Compares three products, including selection criteria for multimedia supplemental materials. A table provides specific information on the products, including grade level, format, system requirement, price, and features.

Powers, P. (1998). One path to using multimedia in chemistry courses. **Journal of College Science Teaching, 27** (5), 317–318. Describes the development and implementation of computer-based multimedia techniques in organic chemistry courses. Provides technical details and some examples of student perspectives on the use of this technology.

Smith, I., & Yoder, S. (1998). **On the Web or off: Hypermedia design basics**. [Book, 151p., $18.95]. ISTE, (800)336-5191, fax (541)302-3778, www.iste.org. From the Instant Success Series. Presents clear instructions and basic guidelines for designing media, supplemented by a discussion of design elements added by hypermedia.

LIBRARIES AND MEDIA CENTERS

American Association of School Librarians & Association for Educational Communications and Technology. (1998). **Information power: Building partnerships for learning.** AECT, www.aect.org. [Book, 205p., $35]. Presents new standards for school library media programs; also inaugurates a set of information literacy standards.

Baule, S. M. (1999). **Facilities planning for your school library media center.** [Book, 100p., $36.95]. Linworth, (800)786-5017, fax (614)436-9490, linworth.com. Updates facilities planning to include new technological requirements. Emphasizes flexibility, planning, expandability, and security.

Benson, A. C. (1998). **Securing library PCs and data: A handbook with menuing, anti-virus, and other protective software.** [Book and CD-ROM, 252p., $125]. Neal-Schuman Publishers, 100 Varick St., New York, NY, 10013-1506, (212)925-8650, fax (800)584-2414, orders@neal-schuman.com. Discusses Windows security problems for library application. Topics include blocking unauthorized access, viruses, hacking, theft, usage policies, backup procedures, disaster recovery, and hard drive maintenance.

Bielefield, A., & Cheeseman, L. (1999). **Interpreting and negotiating licensing agreements: A guidebook for the library, research, and teaching professions.** [Book, 150p., $55]. Neal-Schuman, fax (800)584-2414, orders@neal-schuman.com, www.neal-schuman.com. Presents in nonlegal language information about copyright licenses, including useful wording for licenses, model clauses, and a glossary.

Book Report. Linworth Publishing, 480 E. Wilson Bridge Rd., Suite L., Worthington, OH 43085-2372, (800)786-5017, fax (614)436-9490, orders@linworth.com, linworth.com. [5/school yr., $44 US, $9 single copy]. Journal for junior and senior high school librarians provides articles, tips, and ideas for day-to-day school library management, as well as reviews of audiovisuals and software, all written by school librarians.

Breivik, P. S., & Senn, J. A. (1998). **Information literacy: Educating children for the 21st century** (2nd ed.). NEA, 1201 16th St., NW, Washington, DC 20036, (202)833-4000. Updates the original seminal work.

Bua, J., & Jackson, N. (1998). One day in the life of Western High School. **MultiMedia Schools, 5** (2), 22–26. Library media staff at Western High School (Fort Lauderdale, Florida) established a library media center without walls and an information hub without limits. This article describes the planning, funding, wiring, equipping, programming, managing, and benefits of the $624,500 network.

Clyde, L. A. (1999). **Managing infotech in school library media centers.** [Book, 275p., $32.50]. Libraries Unlimited, (800)237-6124, lu-books@lu.com, www.lu.com. Presents a method for developing information technology plans and managing technology within the framework of the learning mission of the individual school. Offers an overview of many educational technologies, with recommendations.

Collection Building. M.C.B. University Press Ltd., 60–62 Toller Ln., Bradford, W. Yorks. BD8 9BY, England, www.mcb.co.uk. [Q., $89]. Focuses on all aspects of collection building, ranging from microcomputers to business collections to popular topics and censorship.

Computers in Libraries. Information Today, 143 Old Marlton Pike, Medford, NJ 08055, (800)300-9868. [10/yr., $89.95 US, $41.95 indiv./K–12; $99.95 Canada, Mexico, $59.95 outside North America]. Covers practical applications of microcomputers to library situations and recent news items.

Corson-Finnerty, A., & Blanchard, L. (1998). **Fundraising and friend-raising on the Web.** [Book, 152p., $45]. American Library Association, ALA Editions, 50 East Huron St., Chicago, IL 60611-2795; (800)545-2433; fax (312)836-9958. Presents innovative ideas for web-based fundraising strategies for libraries and other nonprofit organizations.

Del Vecchio, S. (1999). **CD-ROM reference materials for children and young adults: A critical guide for school and public libraries.** [Book, 275p., $35]. Libraries Unlimited, (800)237-6124, lu-books@lu.com, www.lu.com. Reviews digital reference materials (including some Internet sources), using standard selection criteria.

Doiron, R., & Davies, J. (1998). **Partners in learning: Students, teachers, and the school library.** [Book, 182p., $28]. Libraries Unlimited, (800)237-6124, lu-books@lu.com, www.lu.com. Focuses on teaching information literacy through collaboration between library media specialists and classroom teachers and curricular integration. Provides practical advice, project ideas, and ways to incorporate reading programs for elementary school contexts.

Donham, J. (1998). **Enhancing teaching and learning: A leadership guide for school library media specialists.** [Book, 274p., $45]. Neal-Schuman, fax (800)584-2414, orders@neal-schuman.com, www.neal-schuman.com. Discusses how to balance the dual demands of helping to shape curriculum and providing services for patron needs.

Eisenberg, M. (1998). More on sports and the Big6. **Big6 Newsletter, 1** (3), 6. Presents strategies for relating the Big6 information problem-solving process to sports to gain students' attention, sustain it, and make instruction relevant to their interests. Lectures by coaches, computer-based sports games, sports information sources, the use of technology in sports, and judging sports events are discussed.

The Electronic Library. Information Today, 143 Old Marlton Pike, Medford, NJ 08055, (800)300-9868. [Bi-mo, $127 US; $137 Canada/Mexico]. International journal for minicomputer, microcomputer, and software applications in libraries; independently assesses current and forthcoming information technologies.

Everhart, N. (1998). **Evaluating the school library media center: Analysis techniques and research practices.** [Book, 262p., $32.50]. Libraries Unlimited, (800)237-6124, lu-books@lu.com, www.lu.com. Describes how to conduct research, collect statistics, and evaluate media programs through practical guidelines and tools. Includes assessment of information literacy skills through rubrics.

Farmer, L. S., & Fowler, W. (1999). **More than information: The role of the library media center in the multimedia classroom.** [Book, 150p., $34.95]. Linworth, (800)786-5017, fax (614)436-9490, linworth.com. Uses multimedia as a focus to discuss the media specialists' role in the shift toward using technology in education. Covers several multimedia-related issues, including assessment, authorship, resources and projects, modernized classrooms, and broadening the learning community.

Flowers, H. F. (1998). **Public relations for school library media programs: 500 ways to influence people and win friends for your school library media center.** [Book, 159p., $35]. Neal-Schuman, fax (800)584-2414, orders@neal-schuman.com, www.neal-schuman.com. Provides strategies for developing and implementing a public relations plan. Organized by stakeholder groups (students, faculty, principals, support staff, district administrators, boards of education, parents, community, and legislators).

Garlock, K. L., & Piontek, S. (1998). **Designing Web interfaces to library services and resources.** [Book, 112p., $32]. ALA Editions, (800)545-2433, www.ala.org/editions. Describes current interface design principles for Web-based library resources.

Government Information Quarterly. JAI Press, 55 Old Post Rd., No. 2, P.O. Box 1678, Greenwich, CT 06836-1678. [Q., $80 indiv., $100 foreign; $205 inst., $225 foreign]. International journal of resources, services, policies, and practices.

Haycock, K. (1999). **Foundations for effective school library media programs.** [Book, 331p., $54]. Libraries Unlimited, (800)237-6124, lu-books@lu.com, www.lu.com. Identifies current trends and thinking about library media specialists as change agents and their roles in school improvement, curriculum design, collaboration with teachers, and building information literacy. Reprinted from recent issues of *Emergency Librarian.*

Heller, N. (1998). **Technology connections for grades 3–5: Research projects and activities.** [Book, 210p., $24]. Libraries Unlimited, (800)237-6124, lu-books@lu.com, www.lu.com. Present practical projects connecting information literacy, technology skills, and the elementary curriculum through collaboration between teachers and media specialists.

Houghton, J. M., & Houghton, R. S. (1999). **Decision points: Boolean logic for computer users and beginning online researchers.** [Book, 155p., $20]. Libraries Unlimited, (800)237-6124, lu-books@lu.com, www.lu.com. For educators working with grades 5–12; suggests strategies to help students retrieve information, build information literacy, and make considered decisions.

Iannuzzi, P., Mangrum, C. T., & Strichart, S. S. (1999). **Teaching information literacy skills.** [Book and disk, $24.95]. Prentice Hall, www.prenhall.com. Describes information literacy instruction and provides computerized applications.

Information Outlook (formerly Special Libraries). Special Libraries Association, 1700 18th St., NW, Washington, DC 20009-2508. [Q., $65 nonmembers (foreign $75), $10 single copy]. Discusses administration, organization, and operations. Includes reports on research, technology, and professional standards.

Information Services and Use. Elsevier Science Publishers, Box 10558, Burke, VA 22009-0558. [4/yr., $254]. Contains data on international developments in information management and its applications. Articles cover online systems, library automation, word processing, micrographics, videotex, and telecommunications.

Iowa City Community School District. (1998). **Developing an information literacy program K–12.** [Book and CD-ROM, 306p., $75]. Neal-Schuman, fax (800)584-2414, orders@neal-schuman.com, www.neal-schuman.com. Developed by the 1997 National Library Media Program of the Year Award winner, this manual provides a description of a complete information literacy program. Includes suggestions for almost 100 student products, an information literacy model, a curriculum design, and model lesson plans.

Journal of Academic Librarianship. JAI Press, Inc., 55 Old Post Rd., No. 2, Box 1678, Greenwich, CT 06836-1678. [Bi-mo., $60 indiv., $80 foreign; $160 inst., $185 foreign inst.]. Results of significant research, issues and problems facing academic libraries, book reviews, and innovations in academic libraries.

Journal of Government Information (formerly **Government Publications Review**). Elsevier Science Ltd., Journals Division, 660 White Plains Rd., Tarrytown, NY 10591-5153. [Bi-mo., £251, $472 US]. An international journal covering production, distribution, bibliographic control, accessibility, and use of government information in all formats and at all levels.

Journal of Librarianship and Information Science. Worldwide Subscription Service Ltd., Unit 4, Gibbs Reed Farm, Ticehurst, E. Sussex TN5 7HE, England. [Q., $155]. Deals with all aspects of library and information work in the United Kingdom and reviews literature from international sources.

Journal of Library Administration. Haworth Press, 10 Alice St., Binghamton, NY 13904-1580, (800)-HAWORTH, fax (800)895-0582, getinfo@haworth.com, www.haworth.com. [Q., $40 indiv., $115 inst.] Provides information on all aspects of effective library management, with emphasis on practical applications.

Kelly, M. S. (1998). **Uncle Sam's net of knowledge guide for schools.** [Book, 196p., $39.95]. Neal-Schuman, fax (800)584-2414, orders@neal-schuman.com, www.neal-schuman.com. Facilitates the use of online government information for use in school settings.

Langhorne, M. J. (1998). **Developing an information literacy program K–12: A How-to-do-it Manual and CD-ROM package.** [Book & CD-ROM, 300p., $75]. Neal-Schuman, fax (800)584-2414, orders@neal-schuman.com, www.neal-schuman.com. Provides an implementation plan for an effective information literacy program; CD-ROM contains reproducible forms.

Latrobe, K. H. (1998). **The emerging school library media center: Historic issues and perspectives.** [Book, 288p., $42]. Libraries Unlimited, (800)237-6124, lu-books@lu.com, www.lu.com. Relates the history of the school library movement to times of rapid change through personal and objective perspectives. Discusses how the mission of school library media centers has been shaped by professional organizations, standards, accrediting associations, and higher education.

Library and Information Science Research. Ablex Publishing Corp., 100 Prospect Student., Stamford, CT 06901. [Q., $75 indiv., $195 inst.]. Research articles, dissertation reviews, and book reviews on issues concerning information resources management.

Library Hi Tech. Pierian Press, Box 1808, Ann Arbor, MI 48106, (800)678-2435. [Q., $45 indiv., $75 inst.]. Concentrates on reporting on the selection, installation, maintenance, and integration of systems and hardware.

Library Journal. Box 59690, Boulder, CO 80322-9690, (800)677-6694, fax (800)604-7455. [22/yr., $94.50 US, $116 Canada, $159 elsewhere]. A professional periodical for librarians, with current issues and news, professional reading, a lengthy book review section, and classified advertisements.

Library Quarterly. University of Chicago Press, 5720 S. Woodlawn Ave., Chicago, IL 60637. [Q., $35 indiv., $67 inst.]. Scholarly articles of interest to librarians.

Library Resources and Technical Services. Association for Library Collections and Technical Services, 50 E. Huron St., Chicago, IL 60611-2795. [Q., $55 nonmembers]. Scholarly papers on bibliographic access and control, preservation, conservation, and reproduction of library materials.

Library Software Review. Sage Publications, Inc., 2455 Teller Rd., Thousand Oaks, CA 91320. [Q., $75 indiv., $190 US inst.; foreign add $8]. Emphasizes practical aspects of library computing for libraries of all types, including reviews of automated systems ranging from large-scale mainframe-based systems to microcomputer-based systems, and both library-specific and general-purpose software used in libraries.

Library Trends. University of Illinois Press, Journals Dept., 1325 S. Oak St., Champaign, IL 61820. [Q., $50 indiv.; $75 inst.; add $7 elsewhere]. Each issue is concerned with one aspect of library and information science, analyzing current thought and practice and examining ideas that hold the greatest potential for the field.

LISA: Library and Information Science Abstracts. Bowker-Saur Ltd., Maypole House, Maypole Rd., E. Grinsted, W. Sussex, RH19 1HH, England. [Mo., $785 US, £380 elsewhere]. More than 500 abstracts per issue from more than 500 periodicals, reports, books, and conference proceedings.

Mendrinos, R. B. (1999). **Building information literacy using technology: A practical guide for schools and libraries.** [Book, 250p., $32]. Libraries Unlimited, (800)237-6124, lu-books@lu.com, www.lu.com. Connects the infusion of technology into curricula with information literacy, emphasizing information technology; promotes constructivist techniques and critical thinking.

Microcomputers for Information Management. Ablex Publishing, 355 Chestnut St., Norwood, NJ 07648. [Q., $40 indiv., $120 inst.]. Focuses on new developments with microcomputer technology in libraries and in information science in the US and abroad.

Murray, L. K. (1998). **Basic Internet for busy librarians: A quick course for catching up.** [Book, 152p., $26]. ALA Editions, (800)545-2433, www.ala.org/editions. Provides basic instruction in telecommunications for late adopters.

Naumer, J. N., & Thurman, G. B. (1998). **The works for library and media center management.** [Book, 200p., Windows disk, $32.50]. Libraries Unlimited, (800)237-6124, lu-books@lu.com, www.lu.com. Demonstrates how media specialists can use integrated software packages to analyze and meet management needs. Disk contains templates. [See Thurman & Naumer for similar book in Macintosh version.]

Prostano, E. T., & Prostano, J. S. (1999). **The school library media center** (5th ed.). [Book, 170p., $35]. Libraries Unlimited, (800)237-6124, lu-books@lu.com, www.lu.com. Focusing on the operation of school library media centers as systems, this newest edition integrates trends and developments of the past decade. Issues include the impact of global forces and school districts, programming and goals, guidance and consultation, and curriculum development and improvement.

Prince, R. M., & Barron, D. D. (1998). Computer-based reading programs and rewards: Some misleading intentions and possible side effects. **School Library Media Activities Monthly, 14** (8), 48–50. While there may be positive benefits to computerized reading programs and awards, there may be greater negative consequences to their use. Studies suggest that use of the widely known Accelerated Reader Program alone cannot create better lifelong learners. Educators need to examine practices that have worked well in the past and work hard to establish sound principles that will produce able learners and readers.

The Public-Access Computer Systems Review. An electronic journal published on an irregular basis by the University Libraries, University of Houston, Houston, TX 77204-2091, LThompson@uh.edu. Free to libraries. Contains articles about all types of computer systems that libraries make available to their patrons and technologies to implement these systems.

Public Libraries. Public Library Association, American Library Association, ALA Editions, 50 East Huron St., Chicago, IL 60611-2795; (800)545-2433; fax (312)836-9958. [Bi-mo., $50 US nonmembers, $60 elsewhere, $10 single copy]. News and articles of interest to public librarians.

Public Library Quarterly. Haworth Press, 10 Alice St., Binghamton, NY 13904-1580, (800)-HAWORTH, fax (800)895-0582, getinfo@haworth.com, www.haworth.com. [Q., $40 indiv., $140 inst.]. Addresses the major administrative challenges and opportunities that face the nation's public libraries.

Rankin, V. (1999). **The thoughtful researcher: Teaching the research process to middle school students.** [Book, 211p., $27]. Libraries Unlimited, (800)237-6124, lu-books@lu.com, www.lu.com. Guides the research of middle schoolers, focusing on thinking skills, critical thinking, and quality outcomes; includes time management and visual information displays as helpful tools.

Reference Librarian. Haworth Press, 10 Alice St., Binghamton, NY 13904-1580, (800)-HAWORTH, fax (800)895-0582, getinfo@haworth.com, www.haworth.com. [2/yr.; $60 indiv., $160 inst.]. Each issue focuses on a topic of current concern, interest, or practical value to reference librarians.

RQ. Reference and Adult Services Association, American Library Association, ALA Editions, 50 East Huron St., Chicago, IL 60611-2795; (800)545-2433; fax (312)836-9958. [Q., $50 nonmembers, $55 nonmembers Canada/Mexico, $60 elsewhere, $15 single copy]. Disseminates information of interest to reference librarians, bibliographers, adult services librarians, those in collection development and selection, and others interested in public services; double-blind refereed.

Safford, B. R. (1998). **Guide to reference materials for school library media centers (5th ed.).** [Book, 353p., $45]. Libraries Unlimited, (800)237-6124, lu-books@lu.com, www.lu.com. Identifies the best, most affordable, and most appropriate reference materials for school library collections. Organized by topics within broad subject categories; covers many new and varied types of reference sources.

School Library Journal. Box 57559, Boulder, CO 80322-7559, (800)456-9409, fax (800)824-4746. [Mo., $79.50 US, $105 Canada, $125 elsewhere]. For school and youth service librarians. Reviews about 4,000 children's books and 1,000 educational media titles annually.

School Library Media Activities Monthly. LMS Associates LLC, 17 E. Henrietta St., Baltimore, MD 21230-3190. [10/yr., $49 US, $54 elsewhere]. A vehicle for distributing ideas for teaching library media skills and for the development and implementation of library media skills programs.

School Library Media Research. American Association of School Librarians, American Library Association. [Available online, www.ala.org/aasl/SLMR/index.html]. For library media specialists, district supervisors, and others concerned with the selection and purchase of print and nonprint media and with the development of programs and services for preschool through high school libraries.

Spitzer, K., & Eisenberg, M. B. (1998). **Information literacy: Essential skills for the Information Age.** [Book, 150p., $18]. ERIC Clearinghouse on Information & Technology, (800)464-9107, ericir.syr.edu/ithome. Traces the history and development of the term "information literacy," examines the economic necessity of being information literate, and explores related research. Examines recent revisions in national subject matter standards that imply a recognition of the process skills included in information literacy.

Sutter, L., & Sutter, H. (1999). **Where to go and what to do: Pathfinder and research approaches for the elementary age child.** [Book, 125p., $36.95]. Linworth, (800)786-5017, fax (614)436-9490, linworth.com. Groups sets of materials in a variety of media formats together for in-depth research on a broad collection of subjects, applying the pathfinder approach. Includes information about specific research process models, library skills, websites, and children's magazines.

Teacher Librarian. Box 34069, Dept. 284, Seattle, WA 98124-1069, TL@rockland.com. [Bi-mo. except July-August, $49]. " The journal for school library professionals;" previously known as *Emergency Librarian.* Articles, review columns, and critical analyses of management and programming issues for children's and young adult librarians.

Thomas, N. P. (1999). **Information literacy and information skills instruction: Applying research to practice in the school library media center.** [Book, 182p., $30]. Libraries Unlimited, (800)237-6124, lu-books@lu.com, www.lu.com. Synthesizes material from research, scholarly writings, and prescriptive literature into a review on information skills instruction with a meta-analysis of research in bibliographic instruction, literacy skills, instruction, and learning styles. Designed for use in information skills instruction classes for school media specialists.

Thompson, H. M., & Henley, S. A. (1999). **Fostering information literacy: Connecting national standards, GOALS 2000, and the SCANS report.** [Book, 265p., $37.50]. Libraries Unlimited, (800)237-6124, lu-books@lu.com, www.lu.com. Presents a plan for the strategic implementation of information literacy in all K–12 levels. Sketches the relationships between the Information Literacy Standards for Student Learning (AASL/AECT) and national subject area curriculum standards.

Thurman, G. B., & Naumer, J. N. (1998). **The works for library and media center management.** [Book, 200p., Macintosh disk, $33]. Libraries Unlimited, (800)237-6124, lu-books@lu.com, www.lu.com. Demonstrates how media specialists can use integrated software packages to analyze and meet management needs. Disk contains templates. [See Naumer & Thurman for similar book in Dos/Windows version.]

The Unabashed Librarian. Box 2631, New York, NY 10116. [Q., $40 US, $48 elsewhere]. Down-to-earth library items: procedures, forms, programs, cataloging, booklists, software reviews.

Van Vliet, L. W. (1999). **Media skills for middle schools: Strategies for library media specialists and teachers.** [Book, 231p., $28]. Libraries Unlimited, (800)237-6124, lu-books@lu.com, www.lu.com. Provides lesson plans for teaching information and computer skills as an integral part of the middle school curriculum. Emphasizes the role shared by media specialists teachers, and administrators in connecting students to electronic information sources.

Voice of Youth Advocates. Scarecrow Press, 52 Liberty St., Box 4167, Metuchen, NJ 08840. [Bi-mo., $38.50 US, $43.50 elsewhere]. Contains articles, bibliographies, and media reviews of materials for or about adolescents.

Wadham, T. (1999). **Programming with Latino children's material: A how-to-do-it manual for librarians.** [Book, 225p., $39.95]. Neal-Schuman, fax (800)584-2414, orders@neal-schuman.com, www.neal-schuman.com. Provides background about Latino culture and literature; describes useful media center materials.

Wasman, A. M. (1998). **New steps to service: Common-sense advice for the school library media specialist.** [Book, 184p., $18]. ALA Editions, (800)545-2433, www.ala.org/editions. Updated version of classic concise guide to media center administration.

Wilson Library Bulletin. H. W. Wilson Co., 950 University Ave., Bronx, NY 10452. [Available online www.hwwilson.com/default.html; also available in microform from UMI, PMC]. Significant articles on librarianship, news, and reviews of films, books, and professional literature.

Woolls, B. (1999). **The school library media manager** (2nd ed.) [Book, 340p., $38.50]. Libraries Unlimited, (800)237-6124, lu-books@lu.com, www.lu.com. Places the school library media program in the context of recent changes in guidelines and technology. Provides overview of the profession, covering available education programs, guidelines for selecting a position, and all aspects of media center management.

Wynar, B. S., ed. (1999). **Recommended reference books for small and medium-sized libraries and media centers 1999.** [Book, 305p., $55]. Libraries Unlimited, (800)237-6124, lu-books@lu.com, www.lu.com. Selects more than 500 books from the same publisher's *American Reference Books Annual* as most appropriate and valuable for smaller collections. Provides titles by subject, citations for other reviews, designations of suitable library type, and comparisons between similar titles.

MEDIA TECHNOLOGIES

A-V ONLINE. Knight-Ridder Information (formerly Dialog), 2440 El Camino Real, Mountain View, CA 94040. (DIALOG File 46; customer@corp.dialog.com.) Updated quarterly, this NICEM database provides information on nonprint media covering all levels of education and instruction. Nonprint formats covered are 16mm films, videos, audiocassettes, CD-ROMs, software, laserdiscs, filmstrips, slides, transparencies, motion cartridges, kits, models, and realia. Entries date from 1964 to the present, with over 425,000 records.

AV Market Place 1999: The complete business directory of audio, audio visual, computer systems, film, video, programming, with industry yellow pages. (1999). [Book, $195]. R. R. Bowker, 121 Chanlon Road, New Providence, NJ 07974, (888)269-5372, info@bowker.com, www.bowker.com. Comprehensive directory of vendors, manufacturers, producers, distributors, services, media techniques, and applications.

Baines, L. A. (1998). From tripod to cosmos: A new metaphor for the language arts. **English Journal, 87** (2), 24–35. Argues that the contemporary language arts curriculum encompasses eight areas: literature, language, composition, speech and drama, critical thinking, technology, media literacy, and interdisciplinary studies. Offers a rationale for "cosmos" as a new metaphor for the language arts. Discusses the content of each of the eight curricular areas and provides a glimpse at some relevant texts and research.

Broadcasting and Cable. Box 6399, Torrence, CA 90504, www.broadcastingcable.com. [W., $129 US, $169 Canada, $199 elsewhere, $350 foreign air, $7.95 single copy]. All-inclusive newsweekly for radio, television, cable, and allied business.

CableVision. Chilton Co./ABC Publishing Group, Box 10727, Riverton, NJ 08076-0727, www.cvmag.com. [Semi-monthly; $59 US surface, $89 US air, $165 elsewhere]. A newsmagazine for the cable television industry. Covers programming, marketing, advertising, business, and other topics.

Communication Abstracts. Sage Publications, Inc., 2455 Teller Rd., Thousand Oaks, CA 91320. [Bi-mo., $498 inst.]. Abstracts communication-related articles, reports, and books. Cumulated annually.

Communication Booknotes. C.H. Sterling, 4507 Airlie Way, Annandale VA 22003, (202)994-6211, Cbooknotes@aol.com, members.aol.com/Cbooknotes/index.html. [Bi-mo., $45 indiv., $95 inst., $80 foreign air, $130 foreign air inst.]. Newsletter that reviews books and periodicals about mass media, telecommunications, and information policy for academic, research, and library readership.

Communications News. Nelson Publishing Co., 2504 N. Tamiami Trail, Nokomis, FL 34275. [Mo.]. Up-to-date information from around the world regarding voice, video, and data communications.

Document and Image Automation (formerly **Optical Information Systems Magazine**). Meckler Publishing Corp., 11 Ferry Lane W., Westport, CT 06880-5808. [Bi-mo., $125]. Features articles on the applications of videodisc, optical disc, and teletext systems; future implications; system and software compatibilities; and cost comparisons. Also tracks videodisc projects and covers world news.

Document and Image Automation Update (formerly **Optical Information Systems Update**). Meckler Publishing Corp., 11 Ferry Lane W., Westport, CT 06880-5808. [12/yr., $297]. News and facts about technology, software, courseware developments, calendar, conference reports, and job listings.

Educational Media International. Routeledge, 11 New Fetter Lane, London EC49.4EE, UK. [Q., $128 US, $44 single copy]. The official journal of the International Council for Educational Media.

Ekhaml, L. (1998). Seven common mistakes found in student-produced video productions. **School Library Media Activities Monthly, 14** (8), 39–41. Outlines seven common mistakes in student-produced videos; suggests ways to avoid them. Mistakes include too much open screen space; unnatural, abrupt transitions between camera shots; odd juxtapositions of performers with background objects; endless talk without shot changes; no space between the subject's head and top of the video screen; overuse of zoom shots; and text or graphic titles that are not within the essential area.

Federal Communications Commission Reports. Superintendent of Documents, Government Printing Office, Box 371954, Pittsburgh, PA 15250-7954. [Irreg., price varies]. Decisions, public notices, and other documents pertaining to FCC activities.

Historical Journal of Film, Radio, and Television. Carfax Publishing Limited in association with the International Association for Media and History, 875–81 Massachusetts Ave., Cambridge, MA 02139. [Q., $150 N. America, $428 inst.]. Articles by international experts in the field, news and notices, and book reviews concerning the impact of mass communications on political and social history of the 20th century.

International Journal of Instructional Media. Westwood Press, Inc., 116E 16th Street, New York 10003. [Q., $135 per vol., $30 single issue]. Focuses on quality research; ongoing programs in instructional media for education, distance learning, computer technology, instructional media and technology, telecommunications, interactive video, management, media research and evaluation, and utilization.

Journal of Broadcasting and Electronic Media. Broadcast Education Association, 1771 N St., NW, Washington, DC 20036-2891. [Q., $40 US, $25 student, $50 elsewhere]. Includes articles, book reviews, research reports, and analyses. Provides a forum for research relating to telecommunications and related fields.

Journal of Educational Media (formerly Journal of Educational Television). Carfax Publishing Co., 875–81 Massachusetts Ave., Cambridge, MA 02139. [3/yr., $148 indiv., $438 inst.]. This journal of the Educational Television Association serves as an international forum for discussions and reports on developments in the field of television and related media in teaching, learning, and training.

Journal of Educational Media and Library Sciences (formerly Journal of Educational Media). Carfax Publishing Co., 875–81 Massachusetts Ave., Cambridge, MA 02139. [3/yr., $30 indiv., $360 inst.]. Forum for discussion of issues concerning educational television and related media.

Journal of Popular Film and Television. Heldref Publications, 1319 Eighteenth St., NW, Washington, DC 20036-1802. (800)365-9753. [Q., $34 indiv., $66 inst., $9 single copy]. Articles on film and television, book reviews, and theory. Dedicated to popular film and television in the broadest sense. Concentrates on commercial cinema and television, film and television theory or criticism, filmographies, and bibliographies. Edited at the College of Arts and Sciences of Northern Michigan University and the Department of Popular Culture, Bowling Green State University.

Media International. Reed Business Information, Publisher. Oakfield House, Perrymount Rd., W. Sussex RH16 3DH, UK. [Mo., £42 Europe, £76 elsewhere]. Contains features on the major media developments and regional news reports from the international media scene and global intelligence on media and advertising.

Multimedia Monitor (formerly **Multimedia and Videodisc Monitor**). Phillips Business Information, Inc., 1201 Seven Locks Rd., Potomac, MD 20854, (301)424-3338, fax (301)309-3847, pbi@phillips.com. [Mo., $395 indiv., $425 foreign]. Describes current events in the worldwide interactive multimedia marketplace and in training and development, including regulatory and legal issues.

Multimedia Schools. Information Today, 143 Old Marlton Pike, Medford, NJ 08055, (800)300-9868. [5/yr., $39.50 US; $41.75 Canada/Mexico, $60 elsewhere]. Reviews new titles, evaluates hardware and software, offers technical advice and troubleshooting tips, and profiles high-tech installations.

NICEM (National Information Center for Educational Media) EZ. NICEM, P.O. Box 8640, Albuquerque, NM 87198-8640. (505)265-3591, (800)926-8328, fax (505)256-1080, nicem@nicem.com. A custom search service to help those without access to the existing NICEM products. Taps the resources of this specialized database. Fees are $50 per hour search time plus $.20 for each unit identified.

NICEM (National Information Center for Educational Media) NlightN. Contact NlightN, The Library Corp, 1807 Michael Faraday Ct., Reston, VA 20190. (800)654-4486, fax (703)904-8238, help@nlightn.com, www.nlightn.com. [Subscription service]. NlightN, an Internet online service, widens the accessibility of information in the NICEM database to users of the Internet. The NICEM database of 425,000 records, updated quarterly, provides information on non-print media for all levels of education and instruction in all academic areas.

Porter, S. (1998). The fine art of using a laserdisc in the art classroom. **Technology Connection, 4** (9), 14–16, 47. Laserdiscs are an efficient and flexible medium for art presentations in schools. This article discusses laserdiscs, also called videodiscs; distinguishes between constant linear velocity (CLV) and constant angular velocity (CAV), which allows more flexible access; describes the use of bar coding for access; and lists selected visual art laserdiscs, producers, distributors, format, and price.

Schmidt, W. D., & Rieck, D. A. (1999). **Managing media services: Theory and practice,** 2nd ed. [Book, 530p., $45]. Libraries Unlimited, (800)237-6124, lu-books@lu.com, www.lu.com. Covers all aspects of the media manager's role: supervision, budgeting, public relations, evaluation, and management. Intended for graduate-level media management classes, also includes a section on managing innovations.

Technology Connection. Linworth Publishing, 480 E. Wilson Bridge Rd., Suite L., Worthington, OH 43085-2372, (800)786-5017, fax (614)436-9490, orders@linworth.com, linworth.com. [9/yr., $43 US, $7 single copy]. A forum for K–12 educators who use technology as an educational resource, this journal includes information on what works and what does not, new product reviews, tips and pointers, and emerging technology.

Telematics and Informatics. Elsevier Science Regional Sales Office, Customer Support Department, P.O. Box 945, New York, NY 10159-0945. (888)4ES-INFO, usinfo-f@elsevier.com. [Q., £395]. Publishes research and review articles in applied telecommunications and information sciences in business, industry, government and educational establishments. Focuses on important current technologies including microelectronics, computer graphics, speech synthesis and voice recognition, database management, data encryption, satellite television, artificial intelligence, and the ongoing computer revolution. Contributors and readers include professionals in business and industry, as well as in government and academia, who need to keep abreast of current technologies and their diverse applications.

Treadway, G., & Stein, B. (1998). **Finding and using educational videos: A how-to-do-it manual.** [Book, 373p., $35]. Neal-Schuman, fax (800)584-2414, orders@neal-schuman.com, www.neal-schuman.com. Guides selection of videos for elementary and middle school; includes video bibliography referenced by topics.

Video Systems. Intertec Publishing Corp., 9800 Metcalf, Overland Park, KS 66212-2215. [Mo., $45, free to qualified professionals]. For video professionals. Contains state-of-the-art audio and video technology reports. Official publication of the International Television Association.

Videography. Miller Freeman, PSN Publications, 2 Park Ave., 18th floor, New York, NY 10016. [Mo., $30]. For the video professional; covers techniques, applications, equipment, technology, and video art.

PROFESSIONAL DEVELOPMENT

Alexander, L., & Newsom, R. (1998). Internet listservs: A follow-up to faculty development at two-year colleges. **Community College Review, 25** (4), 61–74. Analyzes the use of a listserv after a teleconference as part of a faculty development activity. Indicates that 62% of participants in the listserv actively contributed to discussions, 82% reported that using the listserv enhanced the teleconference, and 44% reported that the listserv facilitated changes in the way they completed their work.

Anderson, M. A. (1998). Ongoing staff development: Sideways, bubbly, and chaotic! **MultiMedia Schools, 5** (1), 16–19. Describes the successful, grass-roots approach to staff development at Winona Middle School in Winona, Minnesota. Discusses categories of learners from early adapters to technophobes, staff training models, technical support, networking, policy plans, funding, and new challenges.

Anglin, G. J. (1999). **Critical issues in instructional technology.** [Book, 275p., $47]. Libraries Unlimited, (800)237-6124, lu-books@lu.com, www.lu.com. Addresses critical issues in the field, including communications; learning and instructional technology; instructional technology in schools, higher education, and industry; research, theory, and instructional design.

Atkins, S. L. (1998). Windows of opportunity: Preservice teachers' perceptions of technology-based alternatives to field experiences. **Journal of Computers in Mathematics and Science Teaching, 17** (1), 95–105. Investigates pre-service teachers' perceptions of the impact of nonfield experiences in shaping their vision of mathematics teaching. Describes a study in which pre-service teachers were engaged in a number of technology-based activities and asked to complete questionnaires prior to and after the activities. Teachers associated the lack of a required field experience with a lack of opportunity.

Ayers, S. V. (1998). Collective bargaining as an instrument of change. **School Business Affairs, 64** (2), 19–22. The Hilton Central School District, New York, used the collective bargaining process to create a financial incentive that would motivate teachers to achieve a baseline level of technological competency. Describes the negotiated agreement, results obtained during the initial year of implementation, and future plans.

Cuban, L. (1998). High-tech schools and low-tech teaching: A commentary. **Journal of Computing in Teacher Education, 14** (2), 6–7. Both college faculty and public school teachers make limited, unimaginative use of new technologies, despite having equipment available. This is partially the result of teachers' attitudes toward computers in the classroom, conflicting beliefs about the purposes of schools, and teachers' feelings about rapidly changing technology. To increase technology use, values conflicts must be resolved.

Emmans, C. C. (1998). Turning teachers on to the Net. **TECHNOS, 7** (1), 31–32. Pre-service programs often lack resources, time, and faculty expertise to instruct teachers in new technology. At Central Washington University in Ellensburg, faculty volunteers overcame these deficits by using the Internet to present technology in small doses. After just one year, Internet activities were incorporated into almost every pre-service course.

Georgi, D., & Crowe, J. (1998). Digital portfolios: A confluence of portfolio assessment and technology. **Teacher Education Quarterly, 25** (1), 73–84. Summarizes two trends in teacher education: using performance-based portfolios for assessment, instruction, and professional development and transforming computers from complicated instruments to universally available tools that facilitate tasks involving knowledge access and processing. The article explores connections between the two trends and poses possibilities for teacher educators as they plan for the future.

ISTE Accreditation and Standards Committee. (1998). **Curriculum guidelines for accreditation of educational computing and technology programs: A folio preparation manual** (3rd ed.). [Book, 55p., $20]. ISTE, (800)336-5191, fax (541)302-3778, www.iste.org. Updates NCATE-approved guidelines for technology teacher preparation programs.

Johnson, D. (1998). Rubrics for restructuring. **Technology Connection, 4** (8), 17–19. Presents advanced rubrics to help schools measure the effectiveness of their teacher training efforts and to guide teachers on their own learning paths. Highlights include instructional software use, information literacy skills, modification of instructional delivery, assessment of student performance, individualization of the educational program, professional growth and communication, and research and evaluation of technology use.

Johnson, D. (1999). **The indispensable teacher's guide to computer skills.** [Book, 119p., $39.95]. Linworth, (800)786-5017, fax (614)436-9490, linworth.com. Provides practical guidelines for teachers, librarians, and technology coordinators for conducting staff development. Contains rubrics for specific computer competencies appropriate for teachers.

Journal of Technology and Teacher Education. Association for the Advancement of Computing in Education (AACE), P.O. Box 2966, Charlottesville, VA 22902, AACE@virginia.edu, www.aace.org. [Q., $65 indiv. US, $93 US inst., $20 single copy]. Serves as an international forum to report research and applications of technology in preservice, inservice, and graduate teacher education.

Journal of Computing in Teacher Education. ISTE, University of Oregon, 1787 Agate St., Eugene, OR 97403-1923, (800)336-5191, cust_svc@ccmail.uoregon.edu. [Q., $29, $41.73 Canada, $39 intl., $42 intl. air]. Contains refereed articles on preservice and inservice training, research in computer education and certification issues, and reviews of training materials and texts.

McKinney, M. (1998). Preservice teachers' electronic portfolios: Integrating technology, self-assessment, and reflection. **Teacher Education Quarterly, 25** (1), 85–103. Investigated the evolution of electronic portfolios by pre-service elementary teachers, examining how they constructed and thought about electronic self-assessment portfolios. Data from portfolios, interviews, and surveys indicated that creating portfolios allowed participants to be reflective because of how the portfolio development process built-in the nature of reflection. Students found the experience positive and useful.

Oppong, N. K., & Russell, A. (1998). Using combinations of software to enhance pre-service teachers' critical thinking skills. **Mathematics and Computer Education, 32** (1), 37–43. Uses the study of quadratic equations to illustrate the use of combinations of software to enhance critical thinking in pre-service mathematics teachers. Concludes that the use of multiple software enriches students' learning experiences and improves their critical thinking skills.

Overbaugh, R. C. (1998). The effects of three different foci in graduate introductory computer courses on educators' stages of concern. **Journal of Computing in Teacher Education, 14** (2), 15–23. Compared beginning educational computer user's beliefs about classroom computing before and after completing one of three types of introductory computer courses. Stages of Concern survey data indicated that each course had the desired effect on teachers' attitudes. All three groups became aware of educational computing and were not concerned with how to integrate technology.

Salomon, G. (1998). Technology's promises and dangers in a psychological and educational context. **Theory into Practice, 37** (1), 4–10. Explores two pedagogical aspects of the reciprocal relationship between the human psyche and current technology, describing how that interaction expands and constrains pedagogy and ultimately teacher education. The paper discusses novel understandings of learning (constructivism and social aspects of learning), novel technological affordances, psychology and technology together (proximal and distal effects), and implications for teacher education.

Saye, J. W. (1998). Technology in the classroom: The role of dispositions in teacher gatekeeping. **Journal of Curriculum and Supervision, 13** (3), 210–234. Summarizes a study using in-depth interviews and observations to explore 10 secondary teachers' perceptions of educational technology and its role in their classrooms. Study data suggested that acceptance of educational technology may not imply a radical shift in educational practices. Although some teachers embraced technology's potential for alternative schooling approaches, others adapted it to bolster traditional, teacher-centered instruction.

Schulz, C. D. (1998). Too many cooks do not spoil the broth: Staffing schools for successful implementation of technology. **Technology Connection, 5** (1), 8–10. Argues the need for school districts to provide a number of academically prepared employees to help teachers implement digital technology or to encourage use of technological resources. Presents options for large and small school districts; discusses employee communication and job responsibilities. Describes a program in Washington state where nine Educational Service Districts were created to help educators improve instruction.

Sharp, V. F. (1998). **Computer education for teachers** (3rd ed.). [Book, $55]. McGraw-Hill, (800)2MCGRAW or (800)262-4729, customer.service@mcgraw-hill.com, www.pbg.mcgraw-hill.com. Provides basic computing information for teachers, including applications, using computers in instruction, activities, title recommendations, vendor lists, and online resources.

Spitulnik, M. W., & Krajcik, J. (1998). Technological tools to support inquiry in a science methods course. **Journal of Computers in Mathematics and Science Teaching, 17** (1), 63–74. Discusses how to promote scientific and technological literacy within a science methods course. Describes the rationale for the design of the course, structure of the course, prospective students, types of technological tools, integration of those tools into the course with examples of student-constructed artifacts, and challenges experienced throughout the course.

Sprague, D., Kopfman, K., & Dorsey, S. L. (1998). Faculty development in the integration of technology in teacher education courses. **Journal of Computing in Teacher Education, 14** (2), 24–28. Describes implementation of a mentoring program to improve university faculty members' technology skills. Students in a graduate instructional technology course were paired with faculty according to students' computer skills and faculty members' needs. Surveys and student journals indicated that the program benefited both groups, as students learned to mentor and faculty learned about technology.

Van Gorp, M. J. (1998). Computer-mediated communication in preservice teacher education: Surveying research, identifying problems, and considering needs. **Journal of Computing in Teacher Education, 14** (2), 8–14. Examines computer-mediated communication (CMC) in pre-service teacher education, documenting emerging problems and arising needs. After describing CMC and categorizing its utilization in pre-service teacher education, the paper calls for creation of new CMC technologies that nurture pre-service teachers' learning and discusses a web-based classroom management tool that is a potential support tool.

Whitenack, J. M., Knipping, N., Novinger, S., Coutts, L., & Reys, B. (1998). Using technology to foster teachers' reflections about children's arithmetical thinking. **Teaching Children Mathematics, 4** (8), 484–87. Presents information on a project to promote young students' mathematical thinking in which teachers attempt to explore ways to foster students' mathematical development by watching a CD-ROM containing student interviews. Discusses the role that technology might play as a catalyst for teachers to reflect upon their teaching experiences against the backdrop of students' arithmetical problem-solving.

Wittenburg, D. K., & McBride, R. E. (1998). Enhancing the student-teaching experience through the Internet. **Journal of Physical Education, Recreation and Dance, 69** (3), 17–20. Describes how Texas A&M University uses the Internet in pre-service teacher education, explaining how to construct a basic interactive website, taking the concept of E-mail communication a step further to include use of the Internet to enhance student teaching supervision, and examining ways of trouble-shooting common problems that may arise when using the Internet.

Woolley, G. (1998). Connecting technology and learning. **Educational Leadership, 55** (5), 62–65. Teacher training programs must go beyond "how-to" workshops to facilitate understanding about technology's relationship to learning. An International School of Bangkok training program transforms teachers into learners immersed in technology-rich environments. The process involves seven phases: getting ready, learning about technology, hands-on learning, reflecting on experiences, applying technology to instructional design, planning, and forging collegial connections.

Zbiek, R. M. (1998). Prospective teachers' use of computing tools to develop and validate functions as mathematical models. **Journal for Research in Mathematics Education, 29** (2), 184–201. Explores the strategies used by prospective secondary mathematics teachers (N=13) to develop and validate functions as mathematical models of real-world situations. Uses a grounded hypothesis on strategy selection. Concludes that strategy choice was influenced by task characteristics and interactions with other student modelers.

SIMULATION, GAMING, AND VIRTUAL REALITY

Aspects of Educational and Training Technology Series. Kogan Page Ltd., 120 Pentonville Rd., London N1 9JN, England. [Annual, £35]. Covers the proceedings of the annual conference of the Association of Educational and Training Technology.

Benno, M. (1998). Virtual reality. **Gifted Child Today Magazine, 21** (1), 12–14. First examines how virtual reality affects the world today (such as training people for hazardous occupations) and then looks at how gifted students can use technology to create their own virtual worlds. Applications of such software packages as QuickTime Virtual Reality are described.

De Jong, T., & van Joolingen, W. R. (1998). Scientific discovery learning with computer simulations of conceptual domains. **Review of Educational Research, 68** (2), 179–201. Identifies skills necessary for successful scientific discovery learning; analyzes this learning method and provides recommendations for its application.

Eidson, S., & Simmons, P. E. (1998). Microcomputer simulation graphic and alphanumeric modes: Examining students' process skills and conceptual understanding. **Journal of Computers in Mathematics and Science Teaching, 17** (1), 21–61. Examines the relationship of microcomputer simulation graphics and alphanumeric modes of data presentation to ninth-grade biology students' science process skills and conceptual understanding of selected science topics (N=64). Concludes that use of microcomputers and appropriate software can result in significant learning and understanding of genetics concepts and enhance students' abilities to use specific process skills in problem-solving.

Kelly, P. (1998). Transfer of learning from a computer simulation as compared to a laboratory activity. **Journal of Educational Technology Systems, 26** (4), 345–351. Discusses the implications of using computer-based simulations to replace laboratory experiences in higher education, including issues of fidelity and transfer.

Keppell, M., & Macpherson, C. (1998). Virtual reality: What is the state of play in education? **Australian Journal of Educational Technology, 14** (1), 60–74. [olt-bta.hrdc-drhc.gc.ca/info/eljoue.html]. Provides an overview of VR use in education as of 1997.

Khoo, G. S., & Koh, T. S. (1998). Using visualization and simulation tools in tertiary science education. **Journal of Computers in Mathematics and Science Teaching, 17** (1), 5–20. Describes a study conducted in undergraduate science classes in Singapore using computer modeling and simulation. Reports that the use of computer models and simulations proved to be valuable in explaining many aspects of science. Students reported that three-dimensional images helped them in their understanding.

Lehaney, B., Kogetsidis, H., Platt, A., & Clarke, S. (1998). Windows-based simulation software as an aid to learning. **Journal of European Industrial Training, 22** (1), 12–17. Demonstrates how principles of simulation help students develop working models or prototypes. Explains how computer software enables this process for learners with only basic computer knowledge.

McLellan, H. (1998). Virtual events: A cyberspace resource for educators. **Educational Technology, 38** (2), 57–61. Discusses how virtual events can be used to enhance education. Topics include balancing virtual and real encounters; finding the best mix of communication options; and finding patterns of interaction that support reflective cognition, knowledge amplification, community-building, learning, and global understanding. GLOBENET 1997, an international conference that took place in Warsaw, Poland and in cyberspace, is described.

Pappo, H. A. (1998). **Simulations for skills training: Design and development.** [Book, 208p., $42.95]. Educational Technology Publications, Inc., 700 Palisade Ave., Englewood Cliffs, NJ 07632-0564, (800)952-BOOK. Provides basic instruction for modeling complex constructs, from analysis to organizing the training system.

Rieber, L. P., Luke, N., & Smith, J. (1998). Constructivism at work through play. **Meridian, 1** (1), 1–9. Describes KID DESIGNER, a project that emphasizes play as a lifelong learning process by teaching elementary school students how to design their own educational computer games that embed content from subjects studied in the classroom. Topics include constructivism; cooperative learning; project-based activities; prior learning; group dynamics; and empowerment.

Simulation and Gaming. Sage Publications, Inc., 2455 Teller Rd., Thousand Oaks, CA 91320. [Q., $64 indiv., $244 inst., $18 single issue]. An international journal of theory, design, and research focusing on issues in simulation, gaming, modeling, role-play, and experiential learning.

SPECIAL EDUCATION AND DISABILITIES

Bigler, E. D., Lajiness-O'Neill, R., & Howes, N. L. (1998). Technology in the assessment of learning disability. **Journal of Learning Disabilities, 31** (1), 67–82. Reviews recent neuroradiologic and brain imaging techniques in the assessment of learning disability. Technologies reviewed include computerized tomography; magnetic resonance imaging; electrophysiological and metabolic imaging; computerized electroencepholographic studies of evoked potentials, event-related potentials, spectral analysis, and topographic brain mapping; positron emission tomography; and single photon emission computerized tomography.

Bryant, D. P., & Bryant, B. R. (1998). Using assistive technology adaptations to include students with learning disabilities in cooperative learning activities. **Journal of Learning Disabilities, 31** (1), 41–54. Discusses a process for integrating technology adaptations for students with learning disabilities into cooperative-learning activities in terms of three components: (1) selecting adaptations, (2) monitoring use of adaptations during cooperative-learning activities, and (3) evaluating the adaptations' effectiveness. Barriers to and support systems for technology integration and effective instructional practices are also addressed.

Bryant, D. P., Erin, J., Lock, R., Resta, P. E., & Allan, J. M. (1998). Infusing a teacher preparation program in learning disabilities with assistive technology. **Journal of Learning Disabilities, 31** (1), 55–66. Offers curriculum design steps and describes barriers to and solutions for infusing learning disability teacher preparation programs with assistive technology (AT), because AT devices and services have major implications for individuals with learning disabilities regarding life span issues, environmental and curricular accessibility, and compensatory strategies.

Bryant, B. R., & Seay, P. C. (1998). The technology-related assistance to individuals with disabilities act: Relevance to individuals with learning disabilities and their advocates. **Journal of Learning Disabilities, 31** (1), 4–15. Discusses implications of the Technology-Related Assistance to Individuals with Disabilities Act (1988, 1994) for people with learning disabilities. It discusses the rationale for the act; its provisions and goals; and systems change and advocacy activities of state projects concerning policy analysis, funding, interagency collaboration, consumer empowerment, outreach to rural and underrepresented populations, and protection and advocacy.

Burgstahler, S., Comden, D., & Fraser, B. (1998). **Universal access: Electronic resources in libraries.** [Binder/video package, $75]. ALA Editions, (800)545-2433, www.ala.org/editions. Provides advice for training library staff about issues, needs, and concerns of people with disabilities in accessing electronic resources.

James, M. L., & Meske, M. W. (1998). Using technology to assist disabled students in their quest for success. **Business Education Forum, 52** (4), 45–46. The use of assistive technology that increases the functional capabilities of persons with disabilities is specified in the Americans with Disabilities Act of 1990 and the Technology-Related Assistance for Individuals with Disabilities Act of 1988. Business educators should help students with disabilities learn to use these technologies to enhance their employability.

Lewis, R. B. (1998). Assistive technology and learning disabilities: Today's realities and tomorrow's promises. **Journal of Learning Disabilities, 31** (1), 16–26, 54. Surveys the current status of assistive technology for individuals with learning disabilities and considers future promises and potential problems. A model is presented for conceptualizing assistive technology in terms of the types of barriers it helps to surmount. Efficacy research is reviewed for word processing, computer-based instruction, interactive videodisc interventions in math, and daily living aids.

Mates, B. T. (1999). **Adaptive technology for the Internet: Making electronic resources accessible.** [Book, 224p., $36]. ALA Editions, (800)545-2433, www.ala.org/editions. Provides advice for purchasing and managing adaptive technologies such as screen readers, Braille screens, voice recognition systems, hearing assistance devices, and HTML coding for accessibility for library settings.

Raskind, M. H., & Higgins, E. L. (1998). Assistive technology for postsecondary students with learning disabilities: An overview. **Journal of Learning Disabilities, 31** (1), 27–40. Reviews assistive technology as it relates to postsecondary students with learning disabilities by (1) tracing its development, (2) identifying models of assistive technology service delivery and specific services, (3) describing specific assistive technologies, and (4) reviewing research on the effectiveness of assistive technology with postsecondary students.

Spooner, F., Jordan, L., Algozzine, B., & Spooner, M. (1999). Student ratings of instruction in distance learning and on-campus classes. **Journal of Educational Research, 92**, 132–140. Evaluates implementations of distance learning technology in two situations, both involving students with physical disabilities. Includes a summary of relevant studies and a set of implementation guidelines.

Wassmuth, B. L. (1998). Using a digital camera to teach physically challenged students. **Journalism and Mass Communication Educator, 52** (4), 80–85. Describes how an innovative application of new technology, in a Graphics of Journalism course, not only accommodated a physically challenged student but empowered her to participate in the learning process and allowed her to discover and develop talents and skills that may lead to career opportunities not previously imagined.

Wehmeyer, M. L. (1998). National survey of the use of assistive technology by adults with mental retardation. **Mental Retardation, 36** (1), 44–51. A national survey (N=1,218) examining use of assistive technology by people with mental retardation found that, in four of five areas (mobility, hearing and vision, communication, home adaptation, environmental control), the percentage of individuals who used assistive devices was under 10%, although many more individuals would likely benefit from such devices.

TELECOMMUNICATIONS AND NETWORKING

Agarwal, R., & Day, A. E. (1998). The impact of the Internet on economic education. **Journal of Economic Education, 29** (2), 99–110. Presents the results of a class experiment that documented the significance of use of the Internet on learning and retention of economic concepts. The results offer evidence of the positive effects of Internet use on both academic performance and students' attitudes toward economics.

Atamian, R., & DeMoville, W. (1998). Office hours—none: An e-mail experiment. **College Teaching, 46** (1), 31–35. In a college accounting course, two faculty members experimented with a new approach to office hours, with no communication between students and teachers other than classroom dialog, through electronic mail and other methods of data transmission. This included distribution of course syllabus, reading lists, study materials, and exams, and submission of all student work, including exams and course projects.

Barron, A. E., & Ivers, K. S. (1998). **The Internet and instruction: Activities and ideas** (2nd ed.). [Book, 244p., $28.50]. Libraries Unlimited, (800)237-6124, lu-books@lu.com, www.lu.com. Provides relevant, feasible, and practical activities that encourage students to explore the Internet and engage in interdisciplinary learning.

Baumbach, D. (1998). Helping teachers teach: Integrating the Internet into the classroom. **Multi-Media Schools, 5** (1), 26–28. Describes how media specialists can lead staff development and help teachers integrate the Internet into instruction. Discusses benefits of the Internet as a professional development tool; research skill development, information policies, and legal and ethical issues; and information sources and models for student involvement in curriculum integration.

Berger, P. (1998). **Internet for active learners: Curriculum-based strategies for K–12.** [Book, 206p., $35]. ALA Editions, (800)545-2433, www.ala.org/editions. Part of the ICONnect Publication Series. Includes curricular integration of technology, and evaluation of web resources. Includes selected websites specializing in curricular integration and active learning.

Bigham, V. S., & Bigham, G. D. (1998). **The Prentice Hall directory of online education resources.** [Book, 416p., $34.95]. Prentice Hall, www.prenhall.com. Eliminates online searching time by providing teachers with a subject-oriented guide to recommended websites.

Bludnicki, M. (1998). Understanding telecommunications. **Reading Improvement, 35** (1), 2–10. Introduces the major concepts in telecommunications technologies that are used in distance education.

Burge, E. J., & Roberts, J. M. (1998). **Classrooms with a difference: Facilitating learning on the Information Highway** (2nd ed.). [Book, 142p., $34.95]. McGraw-Hill, (800)2MCGRAW or (800)262-4729, customer.service@mcgraw-hill.com, www.pbg.mcgraw-hill.com. Describes the integration of information technology into the curriculum from three perspectives: learning environment, design models, and technological applications.

Buzzeo, T., & Kurtz, J. (1999). **Terrific connections with authors, illustrators, and storytellers: Real space and virtual links.** [Book, 215p., $26.50]. Libraries Unlimited, (800)237-6124, lu-books@lu.com, www.lu.com. Describes a method for creating encounters between students and authors using telecommunications.

Canadian Journal of Educational Communication. Association for Media and Technology in Education in Canada, 3–1750 The Queensway, Suite 1318, Etobicoke, ON M9C 5H5, Canada. [3/yr., $75]. Concerned with all aspects of educational systems and technology.

Carlitz, R. D., & Zinga, M. (1998). Extending common knowledge. **Internet Research, 8** (1), 59–69. Common Knowledge: Pittsburgh (CK-P) is a school networking project that develops network connectivity and curricular applications in the Pittsburgh Public Schools. This article describes CK-P's network architecture; products developed, including a virtual classroom for German-language instruction, online physics instruction, online research, and a poetry forum; and future challenges.

Ciardulli, L. (1998). Increasing student interaction in the distance learning classroom (or any other classroom). **Technology Connection, 4** (8), 8–10. Presents ideas for increasing the level of student interaction in "tele-teaching" (distance learning) courses. Highlights include icebreakers, daily activities for review or class preparation, student-centered activities to replace lectures, and hand-outs incorporating interactive learning.

Classroom Connect. Classroom Connect, 1866 Colonial Village Lane, P.O Box 10488, Lancaster, PA 17605-0488, (800)638-1639, fax (717)393-1507, connect@classroom.net. [9/yr., $39]. Provides pointers to sources of lesson plans for K–12 educators as well as descriptions of new Web sites, addresses for online "keypals," Internet basics for new users, classroom management tips for using the Internet, and online global projects. Each issue offers Internet adventures for every grade and subject.

Collins, M. (1998). The use of email and electronic bulletin boards in college-level biology. **Journal of Computers in Mathematics and Science Teaching, 17** (1), 75–94. Presents a study using an electronic bulletin board as the software platform for students in a large second-year college biology course to improve communications among students and between students and the instructor. Reports that the bulletin board was successful in fostering interaction between students as well as improving student-instructor interaction.

Computer Communications. Elsevier Science, Inc., P.O. Box 882, Madison Square Station, New York, NY 10159-0882. [14/yr., $1,136]. Focuses on networking and distributed computing techniques, communications hardware and software, and standardization.

Cooper, G., & Cooper, G. (1999). **More virtual field trips.** [Book, 146p., $25.50]. Libraries Unlimited, (800)237-6124, lu-books@lu.com, www.lu.com. Organized by subject area; provides "trips" and topics reflecting current curricular requirements and goals.

Data Communications. Box 473, Hightstown, NJ 08520. [Mo., $160]. Provides users with news and analysis of changing technology for the networking of computers.

Donlan, L. (1998). Visions of online projects dance in my head. **MultiMedia Schools, 5** (1), 20–22, 24–25. Illustrates benefits of online class projects and describes different types of projects, including collaborations, data collection or exchange, mentoring projects, vicarious adventures, and one-time-only events. Discusses where to find such projects and selection criteria, designing projects, and signs of success.

Ebenezer, J. V., & Lau, E. (1998). **Science on the Internet: A resource for K–12 teachers.** [Book, 128p., $14]. Prentice Hall, www.prenhall.com. Describes and lists hundreds of high-quality science sites for K–12 applications, in addition to providing Internet basics.

EDUCOM Review. EDUCOM, 1112 Sixteenth St., NW, Suite 600, Washington, DC 20036-4823, (800)254-4770, offer@educom.edu. [Bi-mo., $18 US, $24 Canada, $43 elsewhere]. Features articles on current issues and applications of computing and communications technology in higher education. Reports of EDUCOM consortium activities.

EMMS (Electronic Mail & Micro Systems). Telecommunications Reports, 1333 H Street NW, 11th Floor-W., Washington, DC 20005. [Semi-mo., $657 US, $816 elsewhere]. Covers technology, user, product, and legislative trends in graphic, record, and microcomputer applications.

Farmer, L. S. J. (1998). Networking for remote benefits. **Technology Connection, 4** (8), 22–24. Describes local networking approaches that encourage student interaction and better information access for the school community, while maintaining security measures. Discusses computer-supported collaborative work, simultaneous online discussion, educator support and curriculum development, courses on the Internet, and implementation.

Farmer, L. S. J. (1998). Printing on the LAN: Positives and pratfalls. **Technology Connection, 5** (1), 26–27, 47. Presents insights of what does and doesn't work in school library local area network (LAN) printing in terms of five "myths": (1) "You need a network to share a printer"; (2) "Printing is much faster on a network"; (3) "All printers are created equal"; (4) "If one is good, two are better"; and (5) "I'll never learn."

Frazier, D., Kurshan, B., & Armstrong, S. (1998). **The Internet for kids.** [Book, 353p., $19.99]. ISTE, (800)336-5191, fax (541)302-3778, www.iste.org. Provides a comprehensive guide to the Internet written for children.

Glavac, M. (1998). **The busy educator's guide to the World Wide Web.** [Book, 178p., $14.95]. ISTE, (800)336-5191, fax (541)302-3778, www.iste.org. Provides an overview of leading educational sites for teachers, parents, and children. Includes eight ongoing telecommunications projects, searching tips, expert sites, and educational search engines.

Gregory, V. L., Stauffer, M. H., & Keene, T. W. (1999). **Multicultural resources on the Internet.** [Book, 366p., $28]. Libraries Unlimited, (800)237-6124, lu-books@lu.com, www.lu.com. Gathers and organizes information about Internet sources addressing multicultural issues; selected for permanence and quality.

Harris, J. (1998). **Virtual architecture: Designing and directing curriculum-based telecomputing.** [Book, 146p., $24.95]. ISTE, (800)336-5191, fax (541)302-3778, www.iste.org. Proposes that integrating computer-mediated technology into the classroom is beneficial if new skills and activities are afforded, and provides strategies for doing so.

Hayes, C., & Holmevik, J. R. (1998). **High wired: On the design, use, and theory of educational MOOs.** [Book, 300p., $44.50]. University of Michigan Press, (734)764-4388, fax (800)876-1922, www.press.umich.edu/. Describes the use of interactive Internet sites for educational purposes; includes access to a specially created MOO.

Heide, A., & Stilborne, L. (1999). **The teacher's complete and easy guide to the Internet.** [Book, 368p., $29.95]. Teachers College Press. (800)575-6566, P.O. Box 20, Williston, VT 05495-0020. Shares Internet experiences of teachers and their classes, and provides a directory of resources.

Hixson, S., & Schrock, K. (1998). **Beginner's handbook: Developing Web pages for school and classroom.** [Book, 256p., $19.95]. ISTE, (800)336-5191, fax (541)302-3778, www.iste.org. Provides a rationale for using web page design as instructional projects, and describes a procedure.

Hollenbeck, J. (1998). Democracy and computer conferencing. **Theory into Practice, 37** (1), 38–45. Discusses virtual online communities, probing claims about the Internet as a place for fostering democracy. The paper examines the democratic nature of computer conferencing in classrooms, focusing on a study of graduate students' online interactions. Results indicated that students were able to master the medium and act as responsible, equal partners in education.

Insinnia, E., & Skarecki, E. C. (1998). **Educators take charge: Teaching in the Internet revolution.** [Book, 160p., $25.95]. ISTE, (800)336-5191, fax (541)302-3778, www.iste.org. Explores issues and opportunities likely to be encountered as teachers introduce telecommunications into the classroom: student mentoring, team teaching, Internet literacy, censorship, reformation of practice due to technology, and staff development.

International Journal of Educational Telecommunications. Association for the Advancement of Computing in Education, P.O. Box 2966, Charlottesville, VA 22901, (804)973-3987, fax (804)978-7449, AACE@virginia.edu, www.aace.org. [Q., $75 indiv., $95 inst., $20 single copy]. Reports on current theory, research, development, and practice of telecommunications in education at all levels.

The Internet and Higher Education. Jai Press Inc., 55 Old Post Road, No. 2, P.O. Box 1678, Greenwich CT, 06836-1678, order@jaipress.com. [Q., $50 indiv., $175 inst.]. Designed to reach faculty, staff, and administrators responsible for enhancing instructional practices and productivity via the use of information technology and the Internet in their institutions.

Internet Reference Services Quarterly. Haworth Press, 10 Alice St., Binghamton, NY 13904-1580, (800)-HAWORTH, fax (800)895-0582, getinfo@haworth.com, www.haworth.com. [Q., $36 indiv., $48 institutions, $48 libraries]. Describes innovative information practice, technologies, and practice. For librarians of all kinds.

Internet Research (previously Electronic Networking: Research, Applications, and Policy). MCB University Press Ltd., 60–62 Toller Ln., Bradford, W. Yorks. BD8 9BY, England. [Q., $499 US, $619 elsewhere]. A cross-disciplinary journal presenting research findings related to electronic networks, analyses of policy issues related to networking, and descriptions of current and potential applications of electronic networking for communication, computation, and provision of information services.

Internet World. Mecklermedia Corporation. Orders for North and South America, Internet World, P.O. Box 713, Mt. Morris, IL 61054; elsewhere, Mecklermedia Ltd., Artillery House, Artillery Row, London SW1P 1RT, UK. [M., $29 U.S]. Analyzes development with National Research and Education Network, Internet, electronic networking, publishing, and scholarly communication, as well as other network issues of interest to a wide range of network users.

Jones, D. (1998). **Exploring the Internet using critical thinking skills: A self-paced workbook for learning to effectively use the Internet and evaluate online information.** [Book, 94p., $35]. Neal-Schuman, fax (800)584-2414, orders@neal-schuman.com, www.neal-schuman.com. Provides instruction for finding and using Internet information at the high school and undergraduate level.

Joseph, L. C. (1998). Blue chip mathematics sites. **MultiMedia Schools, 5** (1), 44–47. Highlights websites of math and science resources for the classroom. Discusses mathematics curriculum standards, competitions, projects, and activities for primary, elementary, and upper grades.

Journal of Online Learning. ISTE, University of Oregon, 1787 Agate St., Eugene, OR 97403-1923, (800)336-5191, cust_svc@ccmail.uoregon.edu. [Q., $29, $41.73 Canada, $39 intl., $42 intl. air]. Reports activities in the areas of communications, projects, research, publications, international connections, and training.

Kaldhusdal, T., Wood, S., & Truesdale, J. (1998). Virtualville votes: An interdisciplinary project. **MultiMedia Schools, 5** (1), 30–35. Describes a project where fourth- and fifth-grade students in the Wales School District (Wisconsin) simulated a political campaign as part of their social studies curriculum, using HyperStudio, ClarisWorks, and the Internet. Also discusses fund-raising activities and how the unit came about.

Knupfer, N. N. (1998). Gender diVisions across technology advertisements and the WWW: Implications for educational equity. **Theory into Practice, 37** (1), 54–63. Examines images and patterns of gender stereotypes within mediated and electronic advertisements that reach students online or when viewing computer software and educational television, and questions decisions made in the construction of these images. The paper explains the importance of teachers, parents, and the community working together to promote gender equity in online advertising.

Kouki, R., & Wright, D. (1999). **Telelearning via the Internet.** [Book, 200p., $45.95]. IGP Books, (800)345-4332; fax (717)533-8661, www.idea-group.com. Discusses online learning from an organizational and managerial perspective. Topics include copyright, security, accreditation, and cost effectiveness, as well as planning and design.

Kyker, K. (1998). **Wading the World Wide Web: Internet activities for beginners.** [Book, 170p., $18]. Libraries Unlimited, (800)237-6124, lu-books@lu.com, www.lu.com. Offers reproducible classroom activities design to reinforce curriculum content, emphasizing informational and educational aspects of the Web.

Lamb, A. (1998). **Spinnin' the Web: Designing and developing Web projects.** [Book, 301p., $26.95]. ISTE, (800)336-5191, fax (541)302-3778, www.iste.org. Provides guidelines for planning, implementing, and evaluating K–12 web-based projects, including practical considerations and ideas.

Lamb, A., Smith, N., & Johnson, L. (1998). **Surfin' the Internet: Practical ideas from A to Z** (2nd ed.). [Book, 324p., $26.95]. ISTE, (800)336-5191, fax (541)302-3778, www.iste.org. Presents complete unit and lesson plans for interdisciplinary thematic curriculum applications.

Leshin, C. B. (1998). **Internet adventures: Integrating the Internet into the curriculum, version 2.0.** [Book, $29.95, 314p.] AECT, 1025 Vermont Ave., NW, Suite 820, Washington, DC 20005-3547, fax (202)347-7839, www. aect.org. Instructs educators about the use of search engines, directories, and Internet collections leading to valuable classroom resources. Includes evaluation of Internet sources for validity and several interdisciplinary instructional units.

Leshin, C. B. (1998). **Internet for educators.** [Video, 120min., $59.95]. AECT, 1025 Vermont Ave., NW, Suite 820, Washington, DC 20005-3547, fax (202)347-7839, www. aect.org. Companion resource for **Internet adventures: Integrating the Internet into the curriculum** (see above).

Li, H. (1998). Information-technology-based tools for reengineering construction engineering education. **Computer Applications in Engineering Education, 6** (1), 15–21. Reviews three learning models (objectivist, collaborative, and constructivist) and information technologies that can be used to support the effective application of these learning models in construction engineering education. The effectiveness of an information technology is analyzed through the appropriateness of the technology in supporting a particular learning model.

Link-Up. Information Today, 143 Old Marlton Pike, Medford, NJ 08055, (800)300-9868. [Bi-mo., $29.95 US, $36 Canada/Mexico; $54 elsewhere]. Newsmagazine for individuals interested in small computer communications; covers hardware, software, communications services, and search methods.

Littman, M. K. (1998). Cable model technology implementation: Challenges and prospects. **Journal of Online Learning, 9** (2), 5–11. Describes cable modem technology. Examples of cable field trials carried out in collaboration with educational user communities are presented, and cable technical capabilities, advantages, and constraints are considered.

McLellan, H. (1998). The Internet as a virtual learning community. **Journal of Computing in Higher Education, 9** (2), 92–112. Describes one Internet-based model for implementing university classes that uses listservs, electronic mail, and the World Wide Web. Compares Internet and conventional classes; looks at the potential of both asynchronous and synchronous virtual learning experiences and activities. Argues that an Internet-based virtual learning community, with its dynamic interactions between students and teachers, is a powerful approach to distance education.

Milheim, W. D., & Harvey, D. M. (1998). Design and development of a World Wide Web resource site. **Educational Technology, 38** (1), 53–36. Focuses on the design, development, and maintenance of web-based resource sites developed for specific target audiences. The case study described is a site developed to support web-based instruction in both corporate and educational settings; however, the principles are also applicable for web resource sites developed for many other content areas.

Miller, E. B. (1999). **The Internet resource directory for K–12 teachers and librarians, 1999/2000 edition.** [Book, 438p., $27.50]. Libraries Unlimited, (800)237-6124, lu-books@lu.com, www.lu.com. Offers access to current and accurate information about the Internet. Contains resource sections on curricular standards, professional associations, early childhood, special education, and curricular themes.

Miller, S. (1998). **Searching the World Wide Web: An introductory curriculum for using search engines.** [Book, 55p., $12.95]. ISTE, (800)336-5191, fax (541)302-3778, www.iste.org. Presents a sequenced, time-efficient approach to skills and concepts for web navigation and searching. Includes adaptations for individual students, small groups, and entire classes, as well as exceptional students.

Minkel, W. (1998). **Delivering Web reference services to young people.** [Book, 136p., $32]. ALA Editions, (800)545-2433, www.ala.org/editions. Assists librarians and media specialists who serve youth ages 8–18 in finding resources on the Web. Targeted at all levels of telecommunications skill.

Morton, J. G., & Cohn, A. L. (1998). **Kids on the 'Net: Conducting Internet research in K–5 classrooms.** [Book, 96p., $9.95]. Heinemann, 361 Hanover St., Portsmouth, NH 03801-3912, (800)793-2154, www.heinemann.com. Tells the story of one teacher and her class who used the Internet for a research project, along with tips and practical information.

Newcomb, A. F., Berkebile, N. M., Parker, S. W., & Newman, J. E. (1998). Student projects embracing new computer technologies: Opportunities for student scholarship on the World Wide Web. **Teaching of Psychology, 25** (1), 52–58. Explores implementation of electronic term papers (ETP), objectives of these assignments, educational benefits of the ETP, an exemplar ETP, grading of ETPs, copyright issues, and student evaluations of the approach. Includes a schematic diagram of a sample electronic term paper and a list of web resources for developing ETPs.

Online. Online, Inc., 462 Danbury Rd., Wilton, CT 06897, www.onlineinc.com/onlinemag/. [6/yr., $110]. For online information system users. Articles cover a variety of online applications for general and business use.

Online-Offline. Rock Hill Press, 14 Rock Hill Road, Bala Cynwyd, PA 19004, (888)ROCK HILL, fax (610)667-2291, www.rockhillpress.com. [9/yr., $66.50]. Examines classroom resources, linking curricular themes with Web sites and other media.

Reese, J. (1999). **Internet books for educators, parents, and children.** [Book, 299p., $32.50]. Libraries Unlimited, (800)237-6124, lu-books@lu.com, www.lu.com. Lists and annotates recommended books about the Internet, covering more than 250 English-language materials published since 1995.

Rose, R. (1998). Detour on the I-way. **Training, 35** (1), 70–72, 74, 76, 78. Examines the recent past of network certification; concludes that web-based training works best under the guidance of a trainer with personal investment in the learners.

Schneider, A. (1998). Sociology: The Internet as an extended classroom. **Social Science Computer Review, 16** (1), 53–57. The implementation of an electronic syllabus on the World Wide Web is described. Web pages serve as administrative tools, as powerful research instruments, and as a tool skill to prepare students for their careers. The empirical example of an electronic syllabus is used to illuminate potentials, problems, and the acceptance of the Internet as an extended sociology classroom by students.

Seguin, A. (1998). Using the Internet in continuing education. **Catalyst, 27** (1), 15–18. Describes the Internet as a useful tool for communication between instructors and students via electronic mail and as a research engine using the World Wide Web. Delineates its potential use in education as a means of information delivery and access to sophisticated programs and as an additional link to the community.

Sharp, V. F., Levine, M. G., & Sharp, R. M. (1998). **The best Web sites for teachers** (2nd ed.). [Book, 352p., $29.95]. ISTE, (800)336-5191, fax (541)302-3778, www.iste.org. Lists recommended websites for educational purposes, categorized by curriculum area.

Skomars, N. (1998). **Educating with the Internet: Using net resources at home and at school.** [Book & CD-ROM, 350p., $29.95]. Charles River Media, 403 VFW Dr., P.O. Box 417, Rockland, MA 02370, (800)382-8505, chrivmedia@aol.com, www.charlesriver.com. Presents instructions at the novice level for using the Internet as a teaching tool. Enclosed CD-ROM includes a copy of a monitoring program that randomly samples computer activity and provides copies of downloaded graphics.

Smethers, J. S. (1998). Cyberspace in the curricula: New legal and ethical issues. **Journalism and Mass Communication Educator, 52** (4), 15–23. Finds that most journalism and mass communication programs integrate legal and ethical issues surrounding cyberspace and interactive media into existing courses, especially into ethics and communication law courses, but also into introductory survey courses, communication technology, and reporting classes. Details reasons why some programs do not currently deal with these issues, and notes topics included in cyberspace legal-ethics instruction.

Smith, L. D., & Satterwhite, R. R. (1999). **Debunking the Web: Evaluating Internet resources.** [Book, 120p., $25]. Libraries Unlimited, (800)237-6124, lu-books@lu.com, www.lu.com. Presents criteria for evaluating electronic resources, focusing on the Web. Provides examples and exercises; targets secondary level teachers, media specialists, and administrators.

Stroh, B. (1998). Intranet before Internet: Let's talk to our neighbors before perfecting our global conversation. **Contemporary Education, 69** (2), 103–106. A district-wide intranet offers school districts the potential for communication, efficiency, and organizational growth. This paper explains the difference between intranets and the Internet, discusses how an intranet can help schools, and notes potential problems when working with it. The paper recommends learning to communicate and collaborate locally before moving on to global networking.

Telecommunications. (North American Edition.) Horizon House Publications, Inc., 685 Canton St., Norwood, MA 02062. [Mo., $75 US, $135 elsewhere, free to qualified individuals]. Feature articles and news for the field of telecommunications.

T.I.E. News (Telecommunications in Education). ISTE, 1787 Agate St., Eugene, OR 97403-1923. [Q., $20 members, $29 nonmembers, $39 foreign]. Contains articles on all aspects of educational telecommunications.

Vallance, M. (1998). The design and use of an Internet resource for business English learners. **ELT Journal, 52** (1), 38–42. Details the design of a hypertext decision-making activity located on the Internet for Business English students wishing to review techniques and vocabulary for conducting business meetings (World Wide Web address is given). Provides statistical data on students using the activity worldwide, and makes recommendations for further development of Internet resources for language learners.

Index

(AACC) Community College Satellite Network
(CCSN), 190–91
AASL. *See* American Association of School
Librarians (AASL)
Abramovich, S., 277
"The ACademic DireCtory-AC/DC," 46
Academy of Motion Picture Arts and Sciences
(AMPAS), 179
"Accelerating the design process: A tool for instruc-
tional designers," 49, 50
ACCESS Network, 228
"Action research as a form of staff development in
higher education," 37
"Action research into the quality of student learning,"
37–38
Adamski, A., 14
*Adaptive technology for the Internet: Making elec-
tronic resources accessible,* 319
"The advanced instructional design advisor," 49, 50
AECT. *See* Association for Educational Communi-
cations and Technology (AECT)
Agarwal, R., 319
Agency for Instructional Technology (AIT), 179
ALA. *See* American Library Association (ALA)
Alabama
graduate programs in instructional technology,
238–39
Alavi, M., 294
Albrecht, B., 287
Alexander, L., 314
Alexander, P. A., 131
Algozzine, B., 286, 319
Allan, J. M., 318
Allen Communication, 51
Allen, G. K., 91
Allen, Thomas J., 120
American Association of Community Colleges
(AACC), 179
American Association of School Librarians
(AASL), 180
Information Power, 96, 98, 103–4, 107
*Information Power: Building partnerships for
learning,* 66, 96, 103, 105, 107, 110,
111, 112, 113–14, 115, 116–17,
118, 128, 305
*Information Power: Guidelines for school library
media programs,* 66
American Association of State Colleges and Uni-
versities (AASCU), 180

American Educational Research Association
(AERA), 180
American Educational Research Journal, 286
American Foundation for the Blind (AFB), 180
American Journal of Distance Education, 282
American Library Association (ALA), 66, 180–81
American Library Association Presidential Com-
mittee on Information Literacy. *Final
Report,* 66, 104
American Library Trustee Association (ALTA), 181
American Management Association International
(AMA), 181
American Montessori Society (AMS), 181–82
American Society for Training and Development
(ASTD), 182
*Issues and Trends Report. Knowledge Objects:
Definition, Development Objectives,
and Potential Impact,* 6
*The 1997 National HRD Executive Survey:
Learning Technologies,* 4
*The 1997 National HRD Executive Survey:
Trends in HRD,* 5
American Society of Cinematographers (ASC), 182
American Women in Radio and Television (AWRT),
182
Anderson, M. A., 314
Anderson, T., 6, 7
Andrews, T., 282
Anglin, G. J., 314
"Annette's Internet speedometer: How fast is it
really growing?," 141
Anthropology Film Center (AFC), 183
Appalachia Educational Laboratory, Inc. (AEL), 183
"Apple classrooms of tomorrow: What we've
learned," 53
Apple Library Users Group Newsletter, 277
Apple, M. W., 288, 300
"Application of RDF for extensible Dublin Core
metadata," 44–45
Appropriate Technology, 287
Ardito, S. C., 297
Arizona
graduate programs in instructional technology,
239–40
Arkansas
graduate programs in instructional technology,
240
Arkin, R. C., 276
Armijo, E. J., 287
Armstrong, A. M., 14